LIFE AND DEATH IN THE MAGIC CITY

LIFE & DEATH IN THE MAGIC CITY

Jay M. Glass

Media Mint Publishing
Birmingham, Alabama, USA

Print EDITION, 1st Printing 2020

This is not a work of fiction. All characters and incidents portrayed in this book were real except where indicated. Life And Death In The Magic City Copyright @ 2019 by Jay M. Glass. All rights reserved. No part of this book may be used or reproduced in any manner whatsoever without written permission except in the case of brief quotations embodied in critical articles or reviews.

For Information:
Media Mint Publishers,
2021 Brae Trail,
Hoover, Al 35242
www.mediamint.net

Library of Congress Cataloging-in-Publication Data
Jay M. Glass
Life & Death in The Magic City

ISBN: 978-0-9969446-3-2

Book design by Boris Datnow

Cover design by Sean Glass

Printed in the United States of America

For Barbara Ann

Who will never have to ask again
"Are we there yet?"

*"The past is a foreign country:
they do things differently there."*

—-L.P. Hartley

Table of Contents

Preface —————————————— 9

Prologue ————————————— 11

1. The Coroner ———————————— 18
2. Statistics ————————————— 30
3. Passion ————————————— 52
4. Race ——————————————— 75
5. Mines —————————————— 96
6. Prison —————————————— 109
7. Work —————————————— 128
8. Homicide ————————————— 144
9. Police —————————————— 204
10. Capital Punishment ——————— 317
11. Honor —————————————— 339
12. Suicide ————————————— 365
13. Vice ——————————————— 378
14. Disease and Medicine —————— 415
15. Women ————————————— 435
16. Children ————————————— 447
17. Elements ————————————— 469
18. Vehicles ————————————— 486
19. Animals ————————————— 527
20. War ——————————————— 542

21. Weapons	550
22. Forensics	562
23. Unknown	595
24. Atlas Obscura	599
Epilogue	615
Notes	617
Copyright Acknowledgements	625
About The Author	626

PREFACE

Much has been written regarding the history of Jefferson County during the first half of the 20th century. To my knowledge, however, there has been no attempt to provide an understanding of life during this period through a review and analysis of deaths based on the coroner's files, newspaper accounts and statistical and other related records which had been compiled during that period. My purpose is to present an overview, as well as to provide more detailed examinations of selected cases, which depict the daily realities of life, death and human relations in Jefferson County during that dynamic era in history.

Material for this book was compiled over a period of many years. My determination to assemble it into a cohesive final product was driven by my desire to avoid the fate of the non-fictional character depicted by Joseph Mitchell in his story titled "Joe Gould's Secret."[1]

This book includes portions of a number of transposed verbatim official record entries. These include the actual, uncorrected content to include misspellings and grammatical errors contained in the original documents. This foreknowledge precludes the repetitive use of the Latin term for "thus it was originally written," abbreviated as "sic," to indicate these errors. Interview records and newspaper accounts have been edited to reduce their length by not including statements or material which were considered to be redundant or which did not directly relate to the matter presented.

There is only one fictionalized entry which is clearly indicated. My personal opinions and interpretations are identified as such, as are comments and material from other authors and reference sources. Certain terminology included within some of the original documents might be offensive to some readers and may not be considered "politically correct." This material is not fabrication, but is drawn from factual, referenced historical records and newspaper accounts which include commonly used and socially acceptable terminology of those times. It would have been disingenuous for me to alter, redact or otherwise censor such material which reflects for better, or usually for worse, the tenor of society's accepted values and mores of that era, not only in the South, but across America.

In specific regard to Birmingham in the 21st century, Mark Kelly noted that:

> "History is Truth, and the truth sets us free.
> Except that in Birmingham, the truth has continued to hold us captive. Rather than embrace the truth of what makes us what we are, we spend our time trying to escape it—and marginalizing those who take it upon themselves to remind us of it.
> We go to great lengths to deny it, and even greater ones to avoid learning anything from it."[2]

The term "Magic City" in the title of this book is employed as a metaphor for the entirety of Jefferson County and not just for the city of Birmingham. A number of incidents which are presented occurred in Bessemer---"The Marvel City," as well as in the adjacent, then bustling West Jefferson County area commonly known as the "Cut-Off." The period which is covered extends from the late 1890s to a point just prior to the start of the World War II.

The use of selected Blues music verses, which I believe serve as relevant introductions to subject matter contained in certain chapters, is predicated on the statement that: "The Blues are about the most elemental stuff in our lives---love, sex, betrayal---and our deepest longings."[3]

Similar, and even more extensive historical information, can be found within the coroner's records of most cities in this country and every jurisdiction has its own tales to tell. However, this is a partial story of this particular town, the "Magic City," in the early 20th century as portrayed through documented incidents and certain statistics. Although much of the material in these pages is about death, the actual subject is life.

Jay M. Glass
Helena, Alabama

PROLOGUE

*"We need our witnesses and archivists to say
we lived, we died, we made this difference.
Where death means nothing, life is meaningless.
We try to reassemble their lives from the stingy details
and the exercise teaches us something about how
to live. Is it kindness or wisdom, honor or self-interest?
We remember because we want to be remembered."*[1]

—Thomas Lynch

Records

The unmistakable musty odor of mildew pervades the entire second floor of the Jefferson County Courthouse Annex building. It emanates from this dumping ground for thousands of old paper files and docket books dating back to the first decade of the 20th century. They have been generated by various governmental agencies which were required to document essential matters such as tax payments received, jail food expenses, the details of deaths coming under the jurisdiction of the coroner, as well as other matters of civic import. It is the scent of history and, as far as the coroner's records are concerned, past memories of lives, deaths and endings. Of physical and mental suffering. Of justifiable and non-justifiable homicide. Of natural deaths and of infanticide. Of lives unfulfilled and, as succinctly stated by Luc Sante, "...the traces of innumerable human beings lost to history once and for all, without monuments or descendants or living memory, just a name somewhere in an official record consulted rarely if at all."[2] There is a ghostly presence here. Or at least written representations of persons physically long gone. Absent are the memories of those who knew them in different ways and extent. Some are perhaps vaguely remembered by those still living who knew, loved or hated them. Here are the records generated by the legal system's investigating and judicial agents regarding each person's demise. Some records contain detailed information, but many are sparse.

Such records can be found in varying degrees of condition and organization within courthouses throughout this country. In some jurisdictions they may have been lost to fire or other forms of destruction or disposal over the years. Until a reorganization in the mid 1980's, coroner's records relating to the Birmingham Division of Jefferson County were fairly well preserved, although disorganized and partially missing. A separate collection of better maintained records dating back to 1907 were located at the Bessemer Division courthouse.

The Annex building contained office space until the construction of the Criminal Justice Center. It was then relegated to the storage of old records which had previously been kept within an unused jail cellblock in the courthouse. These records could not be legally destroyed unless they were preserved in some other format. There was no desire or perceived need to microfilm them, nor were the manpower or funds available to accomplish such a large task. It was usually only the coroner's office which would receive an occasional request for a copy of an old file. Prior to its destruction, only the Barber's Commission maintained an office on the ground floor of the Annex. This building is now gone--replaced by a parking lot. As is the old Jefferson County courthouse which was located at 3rd Avenue and 21st Street North, the courtyard of which was the site of judicial hangings which were conducted in the individual counties until 1926. At that time, the method of execution was changed to electrocution and became a state function which was conducted at one prison location.

Summer. There are no windows to open on the second floor of the Annex building. The stifling heat, humidity and lack of circulating air will become unbearable and will lead to a sense of being smothered within 15 minutes. Total silence. Poor lighting by the few scattered low wattage bulbs which are still working requires the use of a flashlight in order to try to find a particular file located in a box in a dark corner. Maybe I'll get lucky today and the file will be found in an intact box with the folders maintained in perfect numerical order. Find the right box and I could quickly locate the record I am looking for. However, it seems that the higher the humidity, the more likely it is that I will have to search through the other partially collapsed boxes. These had apparently been quickly launched into the corners of the room, likely by overheated laborers who had transferred the heavy containers up the stairs to this location many years ago, possibly during a hot summer day like today. Those file folders now lie strewn in disorder on the floor. There are thousands of death records dating back to the 1920's. I have to find the one I am looking for quickly! I always seem to underestimate the heat and the time required to search for a file and before long I am covered in perspiration. I have delayed this particular search due to the intense heat, but I have received another call from the relative requesting the file for whatever genealogical research purposes they may have or just to satisfy their curiosity about the details surrounding the death of some relative many years ago. Such knowledge may have been intentionally withheld by other, older relatives who may be well aware of what happened but prefer this information be forgotten. Or perhaps they have taken their knowledge to the grave due to the perceived embarrassment associated with a suicide or murder of an individual by a relative. Unanswered questions which may, or may not, be resolved by examination of the recovered file. These are public records; copies of which are available upon request and at no charge.

To those without some academic or personal interest, these records are merely peculiar reminders of the passing of mostly forgotten individuals whose deaths may have affected their relatives, and possibly society at the time of their demise, but with the passage of many years have faded into obscurity. After awhile, it is as if these people had never existed at all.

Over the years I had received many requests to search for these documents from individuals who were seeking information relating to the death of a relative. Most often, this led to the disappointing provision of the minimal data usually contained in these files and docket books. However, on a few rare occasions I experienced the thrill of finding and revealing some long hidden gem of meaningful or crucial information. Material which provided a missing piece of a puzzle. Data which had not been uncovered, or which was not found anywhere else, despite extensive searches of old microfilmed newspapers and other genealogical resources by those persons seeking answers. On other occasions, the recovered information would only add some new, tantalizing detail to the previously known history about a particular person's death.

Finding Joe

On rare occasions, the information recovered from these old records could change people's lives. Such was the case of Joe "Collier". As reported in The Birmingham Post-Herald in the early 1990's with the headline "Coroner helps a family find its identity," writer Steve Joynt noted the following: "Jack Collier wandered through Elmwood Cemetery many times over the years, scanning tombstones for a glimpse of his father's name. He did not remember his father, Joe Collier, because Joe was gunned down in 1916 when Jack was only 17 months old.

He and his 19 year old mother were not welcome at the funeral, because it was her father who shot her husband. Ostracized by both families, she was left to raise her son alone. And growing up, when he asked questions about his father, "I was told it wasn't any of my concern," said Jack Collier, now 79. All he was ever told was that his father was buried at Elmwood. He had all but given up any hope of visiting his father's grave when his daughter, Margaret Fields, took up the search.

After 10 years of rummaging through documents, dealing with surly records keepers and attending reunions of families named Collier, she finally found the one fact that opened the door to her past. Joe Collier's last name was, in fact, Calia. "I didn't know who I was until I was 52 years old," Mrs. Fields said. "It was the happiest day of my life, when I saw it there on the page,"

The page she saw was filled with handwritten entries by the Jefferson County coroner in 1916. And at entry No. 5,098 was written "Joe Calia," born "Italy," died "Adger, Ala" at age "35" on 1916 Nov. 5," cause--"gun shot wound." "If it weren't for our records, she never would have found him," said Jay Glass, Jefferson County's Chief Deputy Coroner. "And besides, she had the wrong last name. That's what kept her from finding anything."

Mrs. Fields said she had written Glass and called him, telling him of her search. Then one day, he called her and said he found something "that might be of some interest to me. He brought out this big dusty old book and pointed out the name. You can't imagine the feeling that went through me. I just cried right there." Glass said he was looking for Joe Collier when he saw the "Calia" entry. "It sounded pretty close to Collier and the circumstances were the same. I figured that had to be it."

From the coroner's office Mrs. Fields ran out to get a copy of her grandfather's death certificate. Now armed with the correct name, the search that had been fruitless so many times before, turned up the document in 12 minutes. Next she went to the Elmwood office and asked them to check their upkeep records for the grave of a Joe Calia. They had no such listing. "I said, well, do you have a box of records from 1916? And they pointed me to it. After about 20 minutes, at the bottom of the stack, I found it."

The documents showed that Giuseppe Calia was buried in an unmarked grave on Lot 56, division 3. "I guess with the murder and all of the bad feelings, his family just didn't want anybody to know where he was buried," Mrs. Fields said. Elmwood placed a temporary marker at the grave that day, and Mrs. Fields went out to purchase a tombstone. And then she went back to Adger to get her father. "I've never seen such a beautiful peaceful look on the face of my daddy as I saw that day," she said.

Since then, Mrs. Fields has been able to find out even more about her grandfather and, she feels, herself. On Sept. 20, 1909, Giuseppe Calia, his mother and his two brothers arrived at the Port of New Orleans from Italy. They made their way to Alabama to start their new lives. Less than six years later, Calia married Lena Hardyman. Five months later, Jack Lester Collier was born. About 17 months later, Calia and his wife and son were visiting her family at the home of her father, Bob Hardyman, in Adger. Hardyman had been charged with killing a man three years earlier and generally was not known to be a nice person.

Something happened that Sunday afternoon, though. Collier said he was told Calia was shot with a shotgun after Hardyman was stabbed by another son-in-law, but thought Calia had done it. "From what I could find out, he claimed the shotgun fired by accident. He was indicted and it remained in court for two years, but then the prosecutor dropped the charges."

Looking at the documents she was able to find, its easy to see what Mrs. Fields was up against. A newspaper article about Calia's slaying gave his last name as Colie. His marriage license was made out to a Joe Collier, and even Calia himself signed it "Callia." "I figure that he didn't speak English very well," Mrs. Fields said. "I keep picturing this little Italian man saying his last name: 'Ca-lee-uh' and people writing down Collier. He finally just accepted it." As for her father, "he said he's glad to know where he came from and glad to see his father's grave every couple of weeks."

The earliest available records are contained only in coroner docket books. There were no individual case files found for these early years. There is a typewritten list of individuals serving as coroner in Jefferson County which begins in 1908. On that document there is an entry indicating that at the time this list was compiled, apparently sometime in the 1940's, that the "First record now in Coroner's Office dated August, 1902." This would indicate that at least docket books, if not individual case files, were being maintained at that time to record information about deaths investigated by the coroner. Those early records have since been lost, perhaps to flooding, decay or disposal.

The pages contained in the existing docket books are relatively well preserved due to the use of heavy leather and board bindings. Each one contains alphabetical index pages in the back where entries based on the last name of the deceased individuals were entered in consecutive order of occurrence, therefore necessitating a search of an entire page in order to find the name of a particular person and which, in turn, would yield the page number of the entry. Many of the short, sometimes rather cryptic docket book entries are frustrating due to their sparse content, while others go into greater detail. It appears that these latter cases must have been those that caught the attention of authorities and the public for various reasons, as the public and the news media are currently drawn to those incidents of a more salacious nature.

When reviewing the numerous docket book entries made over the years, there is an eerie feeling when one comes across original records relating to historical events. These often include lists of witnesses whose local family names would be recognized today. These notations tell of turbulent times. Incidents such as the murder of the Catholic priest Father James Coyle in 1921 and the pages listing the deaths of the children killed in the 16th Street Baptist Church bombing are among those which cause one to pause and reflect on these historical matters. These simple emotionless written notes stand as moot evidence of the great and widespread public reactions and far reaching ramifications which were associated with these incidents.

Many of the docket entries leave much to the imagination in regard to the outcome of the death investigations which they initially describe. It is difficult, if not impossible, to research the microfilmed newspaper records of the day in order to determine what the outcome of a particular case might have been. Was there a trial? If so, was the defendant found innocent or guilty? If guilty, what was the punishment handed down? On very rare occasions, a later entry of such a particular outcome is found on the original docket entry page. The difficulty in locating additional information about a case within newspaper files lies in the inability to determine when such later actions may have occurred, as there is no index listing multiple entries or articles regarding a specific named individual, something which is currently possible with computerized data retrieval systems.

The documentary history is incomplete. There are several lost docket books from this period as well as some missing boxes of case files from the 1920's and 30's. These files may have been transferred at some time to microfilm. I had seen a collection of these films stored at the courthouse along with records from other county agencies. Years later when I attempted to retrieve them they could not be found.

Entries in the coroner docket books can tell stories of their own. Some of Coroner B.L. Brasher's early entries after he first assumed the job in December, 1908, reveal poor handwriting and numerous misspellings. There is then an abrupt change to entries where the writing is in beautifully rendered script and there are no spelling errors. These were not uncommon skills for those individuals who had received a formal education within the public schools of the time, where the practice of exacting penmanship and correct spelling were strictly enforced. This change in the writing and grammatical qualities in Brasher's docket books suggests secretarial assistance. One secretary has been identified as Mrs. Edwina Whiteside who worked for many years as an assistant within the coroner's office starting with Brasher. Interestingly, Whiteside was appointed as "Acting Coroner" on several occasions over a 30 year period during temporary absences of the elected and appointed coroners. As noted in a 1946 article in The Birmingham News, she thereby had the "distinction of serving as one of the very few women coroners in the United States but says she still shudders at the thought of having to get up in the middle of the night and journeying to a funeral parlor, where she once used a coffin for a desk while she took notes from a physician."[3]

Luc Sante, in his book "Evidence,"[4] presents a mainly photographic record depicting death scenes which were produced by New York City Police Department photographers. These pictures were taken during the early 20th century and were fortuitously recovered by city archivists just prior to their planned destruction. Many other similar photographs had already been destroyed by the police department by dumping them into the East River along with mugshots and other historical records due to their age and the perceived lack of storage space. In Sante's presentation, although there are a number of photographs there was little detailed accompanying information other than dates and locations listed on the back of the pictures. Sante attempted to speculate and draw possible conclusions about the circumstances of the incidents depicted based only on the sparse data and the pictures themselves.

In the case of Jefferson County records the situation is the opposite. Here there are varying degrees of written documentation, but there are no pictures included in these old files. Photographs would not routinely appear in the case files until the late 1940's. In regard to death investigation during this era, and especially in the poor post civil war deep South, there was probably little concern for, or understanding of even the rudimentary forensic science techniques which were available or known of at that time. Funds were likely limited or unavailable for the purchase of cameras, film and the cost of processing. There really was no need for photographic documentation anyway, for as will be shown throughout this book, such niceties were not required when it could be said that the cause and manner of any particular death were what the coroner said they were. There would rarely be any legal requirement or need for second guessing. Case closed!

CHAPTER 1

THE CORONER

*"I went down to the St. James Infirmary,
Saw my baby there,
Stretched out on a long, white table,
So sweet, so cold, so bare."*

---*St. James Infirmary Blues*

Coroner Docket Entry: December 29, 1908:
I, B.L. Brasher, Coroner of Jefferson County, certify that I held a preliminary investigation on the body of W.D. Paris with the following result: That he died from acute alcoholism.
Remarks: Did not make any charges for this case as it was my predicesser and my first investigation. On the 29th Dec 1908 was appointed by B.B. Comer to fill his unexpired term which was from 29 Dec. 1908 to Jan. 18, 1909.

Origins

The Coroner system of death investigation in the United States can be traced back to England where it was first developed as an important position in the 12th century. The Coroner was selected to represent the King, especially in regard to investigating the discovery of treasure and crimes punishable by fines. C.B. Ransone, Jr., in his 1957 seminal work, "The Office of Coroner in Alabama," noted that "Under early English law the possessions of persons who committed suicide or who were convicted of a felony were forfeited to the Crown", as were "an animal or some inanimate object which caused the death."[1] The term Coroner appears to be a corruption of the early title of "Crowner" which in turn was derived from the term "Corona", or crown. Although the individual serving as coroner had the duty to investigate deaths occurring within his jurisdiction, the creation of this office originally had the primary purpose of insuring that any money due to the King actually reached him and was not diverted to the local "Shire Reeves" or Sheriffs, who up to this point had been the King's representatives in the counties, and as "the Sheriffs were a corrupt, rapacious lot, and the Coroner was most unpopular with them at first, as he was a check on their greed."[2] The medieval coroner was at first, "really a fiscal officer, whose investigation of sudden deaths was only a sideline."[3] As time passed and the English civil and judicial systems developed, the coroner's duty as a revenue collection agent began to decline and he turned his attention primarily to death investigation.

United States

The office of the Coroner was brought to this country in the early 1600's along with other "common law" entities by English colonists. It is ironic that this transferred system was radically improved upon in England in the late 19th century when the requirement for the involvement of physicians in death investigations became mandatory. Ransone noted that "The office of Coroner in Alabama, as well as the majority of the country in the early 20th century was so similar that an 18th century occupant of the office would have no trouble assuming the duties of his more modern counterpart in most counties in America."[4] Reform in this country, with the implementation of the modern medical examiner system within larger cities and some states would have to wait for many years.

Alabama

There is no reference to the office of Coroner in the Alabama Constitution. The Code of Alabama establishes the legal basis of this entity. It originally provides for a coroner in each county who was to be elected for a four year term. The Code itself does not prescribe any specific qualifications for the holder of this office. In the early years, the only qualifications required of a candidate for this, as well as other county political offices, was that the nominee not be a convicted felon and that he was a resident of the particular county. Coroners were most often lay people. The low fees paid for investigations, travel and issuing subpoenas were often their only compensation. It was usually the local undertaker who filled this position as he had to deal with deaths occurring in the community in any event. It was also felt that these individuals, exposed as they were to death on a regular basis, would possess some degree of expertise in determining the cause and manner of deaths that they investigated. Sadly, as time progressed this belief would be shown to be erroneous in many instances, especially as it related to child death investigations. This would lead to important changes only much later in the century. Except when there was obvious violence, there were few coroners who had the requisite training and experience which would allow them to recognize and properly interpret the more complex or subtle medical-legal issues that they might be confronted with.

If required, a coroner could call upon local citizens to act as a "jury" in order to assist him in determining the cause and manner of death in a particular case. In addition, this inquest process could lead to a recommendation to pursue further legal action on the part of the District Attorney or Grand Jury. The employment of such inquests fell into disuse in most Alabama counties by the 1930's. Also rare was the performance of autopsies by local physicians who typically had little, if any, training in forensic pathology.

Also notable is that the coroner was to act as sheriff should that office become vacant and he was the only official who could serve legal papers on the sheriff.

Jefferson County

The place on the ballot form for the office of Coroner was usually listed last. If there had been an office of "Dog Catcher," it would probably have ranked higher on the ticket. The possibility that charity or political favoritism may have been involved in choosing a candidate for this office is suggested by records indicating various physical disabilities suffered by several of the incumbents. Were these injuries suffered in wartime? Or perhaps in one of the many mines or factories? These were matters which were not typically fit for discussion in the news media of the time, although an occasional odd reference can be found. Those selected to be placed on the ballot were likely picked by the powerful men who decided such issues and which was based on various factors to include political favoritism.

ALTHOUGH ARMLESS THE CORONER IS A PUGILIST
The Birmingham Age-Herald, January 29, 1905

"Although Coroner W.D. Paris had the misfortune many years ago to lose both of his arms at the elbow, that does not prevent him from protecting the rights of himself or others whom he thinks have been wronged. This was demonstrated Thursday afternoon when Jefferson county's coroner put two young men to rout, for abusing a negro woman who Mr. Paris knows to be helpless and harmless. Before conquering one of the men the Coroner was compelled to "punch" one of them under the chin with the remaining portion of his right arm.

"No, I am not a prize fighter and do not care to get that reputation," said the Coroner, "but when I went to my home near Idlewild, I was informed that two young white men who live in the community had been abusing an old negro woman who I have known for years. While talking to the old woman the two young men re-appeared. While I was admonishing them, one said that he had wanted a fight out of me for three years. He cursed me and I let go my right arm striking him under the chin. He fell over in the bushes and I made for the other, who left immediately. The one I struck scrambled out of the bushes and joined his companion who was doing the rabbit act. I have seen nothing more of them. You will notice my right arm is rather bruised but I do not mind that."

CORONER WILL LOSE TWO INCHES OF LEG
Russum Will Undergo Operation
Because Of Old Injuries

The Birmingham News, December 8, 1927

"Coroner J.D. Russum will undergo an operation at the Baptist Hospital by which he will lose two more inches from his right leg. A number of years ago Coroner Russum lost both feet in a train wreck, necessitating his wearing artificial feet on both legs.

During his term of office, Coroner Russum has been called upon to make many difficult and diplomatic investigations into deaths by violence occurring in the county. Scarcely a day or night passes that he is not called, frequently to distant parts of the territory he serves. Until recently he has driven and walked with ease despite of the handicap of having no feet."

Holders of the Office of Coroner

Untitled notes on file regarding the Jefferson County Coroner's Office history:
---First record now in Coroner's Office dated Aug, 1902.
---Before Paris was Dusenberry.
---W.D. Paris--Without hands, Died December, 1908. (Note: Paris had been Coroner since 1900).
—B.L. Brasher--Minus one hand and one foot. Already elected as Coroner was appointed by B.B. Comer, Governor, to fill unexpired term of W.D.Paris, Dec. 29, 1908 to Jan. 18, 1909. His regular term of office began Jan. 1909. Brasher in 1912 did not run for reelection but ran for Board of Revenue.
—Charles L. Spain (minus one foot) served from Jan. 19, 1913--1917.
---John R. T. Rives and Dr. C.C. Wiley served from Jan. 19, 1917 to March, 1917.
---Dr. Geo. A. Hogan became Coroner March, 1917. (Bill passed whereby Coroner had to be a doctor). Hogan served until September, 1920.

---J.D. Russum (both legs off) served as Acting Asst. Coroner from Sept. 1920 until his regular term of office began January, 1921. Served until May 31, 1931.
---George C. Moore, served as Asst. Coroner from Sept. 1920 to Feb. 1921.
---Office of Jefferson County Coroner abolished by Act of the Legislature, May 27, 1931.
---G.M. Evans, appointed by County Commission, June 1, 1931 called "Agent, County Commission, as Coroner" until his death Oct. 8, 1944.
---During Evans illness, the Secretary Reporter Mrs. Edwina W. Whiteside was appointed by the County Commission to serve as "Acting Coroner until (after Mr. Evan's death) a new Coroner was appointed.
---Joe. L. Hilderbrand was appointed Coroner Oct. 18, 1944.
---T. J. McCollum has been the deputy at Bessemer since June 1, 1931.
---J. O. Butler, Asst. Coroner June 1, 1951.
---J.O. Butler, Coroner 1959 to 1977.

In addition to his numerous publicized indignant complaints, to be discussed in detail in the next chapter, regarding the perceived high rates of homicides in Jefferson County, Coroner Charles L. Spain also spoke out about the lack of adequate compensation and assistance for the job he was called upon to perform in the most populous county in the state.

SPAIN, DISGUSTED AT LOW PAY AND HEAVY EXPENSES MAY QUIT
Paying $150 Per Month for Privilege of Acting as Coroner,
He Says "I Have No Moral or Financial Support
Says He Has Ten Investigations of Unlawful Deaths to Make--
Much Sympathy Manifested for the Coroner

The Birmingham Age-Herald, August 27, 1913

"According to Coroner Charles L. Spain, accidents and murders are so frequent lately that he has no time to look after all of them. The coroner asserts that he is about 10 unlawful deaths behind and does not know when he will catch up, as automobile speeders and gunmen are again decreasing the population of Jefferson county.

Yesterday Coroner Spain rendered a verdict that the drowning of Victor Lawson in West Lake, Bessemer, was an accident, but did not investigate the killing of Nathan Lowenstein yesterday afternoon as he had to go to Bessemer to investigate a killing. "So much work and so little pay," said Coroner Spain, disgustedly, "has about worn out my patience and I think it is about time to quit before I go into bankruptcy. In the time that I have held the coroner's position deaths that needed investigation have occurred at an average of three or four a day in all parts of the county, and for this I am paid $100 a month, but must pay my own office and traveling expenses, which so far have never amounted to less than $250 a month. There is so much work that I must have a clerk to tabulate the records and this expense also comes out of my pocket. I find in reviewing my work that I am paying the state of Alabama about $150 a month for the privilege of acting as coroner of Jefferson county. And this very great honor of being coroner means that I must be awake at all hours of the night and be gone for days at a time in woods, swamps and in the slums of Birmingham digging out the facts of sordid murders which occur daily with monotonous regularity. In truth, I feel that it is time for me to go home and rest and get acquainted with my family again. It seems to me that the people of Jefferson county do not desire a coroner, for one who does his work well is very unpleasant to some people. After making a strenuous attempt to serve the public as coroner since last January in a way that left no stone unturned to discover all the facts concerning any killing, I find that I have no moral or financial support to my work and the net result of my efforts has been to make plenty of enemies, who are mostly in jail, and a depleted purse."

Around the courthouse sympathy was expressed for Coroner Spain because of the law that was passed at the last legislature that forbids the board of revenue to pay the coroner more than $100 per month and no expenses. This law, according to members of the sheriff's office and other courthouse officials, works well in the small counties where the office of the coroner is unimportant, but in Jefferson county the office of the coroner is of the greatest importance, as great in fact as the coroner's office in any county in the United States. It is urged on behalf of Coroner Spain that more atrocious murders occur within the limits of Jefferson county and in greater number than any section of the country and it is felt that the coroner should be allowed a good salary, several deputy coroners and office assistants to conduct his work that justice might have something like an equal chance with persons who kill others wantonly in Jefferson county.

Many called on Coroner Spain yesterday and urged him to reconsider and not resign, stating that some effort would be made to arouse the people of the county to the injustice that was being done to him. There was much conjecture as to who would be the successor of Coroner Spain as there has been so much publicity about the inadequate pay and the vast amount of work attached to the office that it was felt that the board of revenue would have a lot of trouble finding a competent man to succeed Coroner Spain.

In the time that Coroner Spain has held his office his investigations have been the result of clearing many killings and placing behind bars the guilty persons. If he resigns it will cue much regret with a great many of the substantial citizens of Birmingham who have felt that in Coroner Spain there was at least one public servant who was always on the job."

The legislative limitations placed on compensation for all county coroners in Alabama at the time of Spain's election to that office were most likely in response to excessive abuse of the fee system for investigations made, subpoenas issued and miles traveled for each investigation by many of the office holders. Apparently, adequate adjustments in compensation and added assistance to Spain were made as he remained to serve out the rest of his term as coroner. However, his continued complaints regarding financial issues, coupled with widely publicized arguments with Birmingham city officials regarding the number of homicides committed in Jefferson County, would lead to Spain not seeking reelection in 1917 whether he wanted to or not. It is believed that due to his public and controversial claims and complaints, some of which were proven to be substantially in error, led to retributive legislation being forced into passage by local political entities that he had embarrassed prior to the 1917 election. Such law, which only applied to Jefferson County, would require the coroner to be a physician, thereby disqualifying any layman from holding that office.

There are various legislative Acts in existence which include special rules and regulations which relate to specific counties, either by name or on a population basis. Various legal changes were made over the years in an attempt to improve the system of death investigation. As noted, this process started with the implementation of legislation in 1917 which required that the Coroner of Jefferson County must be a medical doctor. This rule was apparently ignored or the law changed after Dr. Hogan left office in 1920. After that there would not be another physician to hold the office until 1977.

Another major change occurred in May, 1931, when population based legislation directed specifically to Jefferson County abolished the elected office of Coroner and placed the legal responsibility for this agency in the hands of the elected members of the County Commission. Although this change was protested as being unconstitutional by the elected incumbent at the time, it was upheld and the Commission assumed responsibility and appointed a non-elected county employee, G.M. "Gip" Evans to act as their agent to perform the duties of the coroner on a daily basis. This immediately led to the discontinuation of the existing fee for service system, as well as providing for the appointment of an individual who would hopefully possess a modicum of experience necessary for the performance of adequate death investigations. Although with more detailed guidelines administered by a Medical Examiner's Commission in 1977, this primary legal power of the Jefferson County Coroner continues to be vested in the members of the County Commission to this day.

Over the years, these various modifications appear to have been attempts to gradually upgrade the system of death investigation in Jefferson County. Despite extensive research, there is little documented information to indicate the specific underlying rationale for implementing these changes, as in that era it was apparently not acceptable to air "dirty laundry" within the public media which was then mainly limited to the daily newspapers. However, it is believed that repetitive instances of favoritism, misuse of the fee system and outright incompetence over the years fueled the desire to upgrade the existing system.

Although the use of formal inquests had been discontinued in Jefferson County in the 1920's, the role of the coroner remained an important and powerful factor in death investigations, especially as it related to the process which allowed this official to render "quasi-judicial" rulings in regard to whether or not a particular homicidal act should be considered "justifiable" or not. These determinations were apparently acceptable to the citizenry on most occasions with their assent likely being based on the perception that the holder of this office was an independent agent who would conduct unbiased investigations. It was widely believed that he would reach a fair and just decision as to the manner of each death. On occasion, however, human nature with its biases would be expressed even in a public forum.

COMMENDS RIDDANCE NOTORIOUS BURGLAR BY SUNDAY SHOOTING
Coroner Offers To Present To C.E. Hopkins Bullet Causing Death

The Birmingham Age-Herald, June 19, 1923

"I haven't a medal to give you, but I will give you the steel-jacket bullet that did the job, in order that you may remember the time when you rid Birmingham of one of its worst negro burglars."

With these words, Coroner J.D. Russum acquitted C.E. Hopkins of any charges in connection with the shooting and killing of "Rabbit" Coleman, notorious Birmingham negro, Sunday night at 11:30 o'clock, when he attempted to enter the home at 2417 Fifth avenue, north, in which Hopkins was a boarder.

At the coroner's hearing Hopkins testified that on several instances he had seen Coleman lurking around the back yard of the home and had ordered the negro away. He stated that as he started into the bath room late Sunday night he saw the negro half way into the house, climbing through the window. Immediately upon being seen, the negro began to run. Hopkins stated that he shouted to the negro to stop, but that he kept on running. Hopkins then fired twice into the air in an effort to scare him, and this failing, shot the negro in the left side, killing him instantly. Hopkins is an auto mechanic and used a .45 caliber pistol in the shooting. Coroner Russum pronounced a verdict of justifiable homicide and congratulated Hopkins upon the riddance of one of the most notorious negro burglars known to the Birmingham police."

The coroner's "rulings" would also be fully supported and condoned on the part of law enforcement officials and especially the District Attorney who had to run for reelection while the Coroner, after 1931, did not. This allowed the DA to disassociate himself from those high profile incidents which might affect his political future if he had to make an unpopular decision in a particular case. It would also allow him to say something to the effect that this was the Coroner's legal authority and opinion. This "buffer" system would continue until 1977 when the newly appointed physician medical examiner in charge refused to continue the practice of making quasi-judicial "rulings," stating that he was a doctor and not a police officer or judge. This refusal was met with great dismay by the District Attorney who would now be forced to assume a more responsible and direct role, along with the Grand Jury if necessary, in making such legal decisions on a regular basis.

The Bessemer Cut-Off

As a peculiar political entity, the "Cut-Off" was established in the early part of the 20th century with a separate courthouse being built within the City of Bessemer in 1915. In the 21st century the rationale for, and the politics behind its formation, had mainly been forgotten. This currently comparatively quiet part of Jefferson County belies its past history as an industrial and mining powerhouse. If you travel west on Alabama Highway 150, as you enter the City of Bessemer you can look off to your right and see the remnants of the heavy industrialization from that time. Reminiscent of the ancient Roman aqueducts, there are thick concrete overpasses which supported the train trestles over which railroad cars travelled, taking coal from the mines in West Jefferson County to the foundries. There were underpasses for local traffic but the overlying tracks and supports have long been removed due to deterioration and fear of collapse. One which is still intact bears the date "1907," as does the old library built with the help of Carnegie funds. The Roman ruins may be better preserved, however, they did not have to support railroad cars laden with millions of tons of coal which passed over these trestles for many years. Facing the street in the park to your left you cannot miss seeing the World War I German artillery gun which was brought back to be prominently displayed as a "war trophy." Its presence speaks to the role played by local industry in supplying materiel destined for the "War To End All Wars."

The rapidly burgeoning population in the Bessemer area in the early 20th century and the associated political clout that accompanied it were major factors which led to the passage of the local law which would provide for "separate but equal" standing in ways that still persist today. Such matters include, in addition to a courthouse, a dedicated county jail facility, a separately elected District Attorney and the requirement that the Jefferson County Commission physically meet within the cut-off on a periodic basis. Other reasons for the demand for duplication of governmental services early in the century may have been due to the distance from civil and other governing functions which were located in Birmingham and the limitations of transportation and the roadway system during that time period.

In regard to the coroner, the requirement for maintaining a separate substation with a permanently assigned deputy coroner was not modified until 1978, shortly after the first Medical Examiner system was established. Change was accomplished only with difficulty as politicians, other officials and citizens in the cut-off loudly protested the planned consolidation with closure of the Bessemer office. In addition to the increasing population in the eastern portion of the county, there was just not enough of a caseload in the cut-off to support the full time presence of an investigator. Additionally, with the completion of the interstate highway segment through the western area the argument that response time to Bessemer would be diminished could not be sustained. This was shown by a statistical analysis which proved that it actually took longer to respond to some calls in the far northern and eastern reaches of the county from downtown Birmingham than it did to respond even to locations on the Warrior River in extreme western Jefferson County. Following a review of this study by the County Commission, the closure of the Bessemer Division office was allowed to proceed quietly and without much publicity.

Upon consolidation of records from the Bessemer Division with those of the main office, a number of case files were found to contain evidence envelopes which held various items and personal effects collected many years in the past from deceased individuals and which had never been claimed by their next of kin or used as evidence in some legal hearing. This detritus acted as "time capsules" of a sort and included oxidized expended bullets, a few old coins or a piece of cheap jewelry. One envelope contained a murder weapon in the form of an ice pick. This item, which was in common use prior to modern refrigeration, revealed its age by the worn advertising imprint on the handle which showed a three digit telephone number for an ice company in Mississippi. There were a few traces of old dried blood still present on the handle and metal shaft.

Jurisdiction

In the early 20th century there were certain complex jurisdictional issues regarding the investigation of deaths by the coroner. Then, as now, Birmingham was the center for advanced medical treatment of illnesses as well as trauma. Individuals from surrounding areas, some quite distant, were transported to medical facilities in Jefferson County to include the Hillman and St. Vincent's hospitals in Birmingham, as well as to the Tennessee Coal and Iron Hospital in west Jefferson County. It has been said that a popular pastime and a form of entertainment on hot and humid Friday and Saturday evenings was to sit outside the entrance to Hillman Hospital and to watch as the numerous victims of violence were brought in for treatment, many times by hearses owned by funeral homes which doubled as ambulances.

Along with deceased victims who had sustained their injuries within the confines of Jefferson County, there came those who had been hurt in surrounding counties and who died after their arrival at a hospital in Jefferson County. Assumption of jurisdiction and investigation of these cases was typically declined by the coroner on a practical basis. This was due to the fact that he felt he had no legal right to investigate the circumstances surrounding such incidents which had occurred in a county outside of the one to which he had been elected to serve. Additionally, there would be no fees payable for such unauthorized investigations. Other factors included the possibility of having to testify in court proceedings in another county at a later date and which could require lengthy travel, as this was not a minor consideration in that era.

Docket Entry:
Date: October 29, 1917
Deceased: Charlie C. Fleming, White.
Defendant: J.M. Knight, White.
Address: St. Vincent's Hospital
Cause Of Death: Pistol shot wound of abdomen.
Remarks: Shot in Mississippi. Copy to Coroner, Aberdeen, Miss.

Docket Entry:
Date: May 27, 1918
Deceased: Joe Pope, Col.
Cause Of Death: From traumatize, caused by being run over by loaded cars of rocks. Accidental.
Remarks: This happened in St. Clair County and the body passed through Birmingham.

CHAPTER 2

STATISTICS

*"There are three kinds of lies:
lies, damned lies, and statistics."*

---Mark Twain

The misinterpretation and misuse of statistics to bolster weak or outright fabricated arguments has been a constant during the course of modern history. Mark Twain and other observers knew that statistics could be manipulated with differing results and interpretations for the same issue and from the same data. However, when correctly compiled and presented, especially in clear graphic form, the results could be likened to a photograph which can be "worth a thousand words"---as long as it can be assured that their depiction has not been modified for ulterior motives. When properly collected, honestly analyzed and interpreted, statistical products can be quite helpful in explaining and supporting particular arguments or points of view. The review of data comprised only of numbers can be mind numbing to all but professional statisticians. Such products can be improved by translating them into more visually acceptable forms such as pie charts and other graphic representations.

One of the most striking examples of the graphic visual portrayal of multiple interrelated statistical data points over space and time, and yet on a flat one dimensional plane, is the classic work of Charles Joseph Minard. In 1861 this French engineer portrayed the devastating losses and fate of Napoleon's army in Russia during the campaign of 1812. This graphic "tells a rich, coherent story with its multivariate data. Six variables are plotted: the (diminishing) size of the army, its location, direction of the army's movement and temperature on various dates during the retreat from Moscow."[1]

While attempting to keep the use of numbers simple and to a minimum, the presentation of certain statistics is essential to gaining a greater understanding of the demographics, as well as the dynamics, of violent death in Jefferson County during the early 20th century. Just as importantly, it will allow for the depiction of homicide rates on a per capita basis during that time, along with a comparison of rates during the reportedly worst period for homicides within the City of Birmingham during the entire 20th century. This situation occurred during the early 1990's and the pertinent statistics provide some surprising results.

Statistical Methodology

The modern methods of the collection and analysis of homicide rates within Jefferson County have typically utilized statistics related only to the City of Birmingham as based on FBI data collection standards. These yearly compilations are based on rates within individual cities across the country. Since statistics have been compiled, it has always been true that the greatest number of homicides in Jefferson County have taken place within the Birmingham city limits. However, it would be erroneous to try to compare modern rates to those from the early 20th century based only on data relating to the number of homicides occurring within the currently existing city limits. In order to obtain a more valid comparison, it is necessary to compare and analyze homicide rates from these periods within Jefferson County as a whole for several reasons. First, the area encompassing the city limits of Birmingham was much smaller in the early 20th century than it has been since mid century. Many of today's residents are unaware that a number of areas which seem to have "always" been considered as part of Birmingham only became annexed into the city during that time. Secondly, the demographics of the region have changed with time. For example, the distribution of the population within the City of Birmingham and the heavily industrialized and mining areas of Bessemer and west Jefferson County have seen radical change over the years.

The statistical methods applied are different from those in current use by most police departments. As a matter of practice, homicides which are adjudicated at some point as having been considered "justifiable" or "excusable" are not included in a city's submission of data to the FBI for compilation. The numbers of deaths that are tabulated here, both from early 20th century coroner's records, as well as from modern times, include all homicides, whether considered "justifiable" or not.

Some of the included statistical analyses, other than the compilation of raw numbers, are depicted on a "per capita" basis. This is a Latin term that translates to "by head", and basically means "average per person" and is used in many population studies, descriptions and other statistical comparisons. In the case of relating the number of murders that occur within a certain designated population group, e.g., a city, such an analysis will technically yield a statistical numerical chance that an individual will become a victim of homicide in a specific jurisdiction or population group. In actuality, there are numerous other social factors which may come into play in the "real world" outside of the pure numbers that would put a particular individual at increased risk. Obviously, those individuals that are poor, drug abusers, homeless, mentally ill or otherwise impaired or disenfranchised from mainstream society will, as a subgroup, experience a much greater chance of meeting a violent demise than those persons who have the advantage of living in a safer environment.

In relation to per capita statistics as opposed to raw numbers, it is interesting to note that large cities, for example New York and Chicago, have never been included in the yearly FBI list of top ten cities for homicides. It is the use of per capita statistics that leads to many smaller cities being continuously placed on this recurring list of shame, mainly based on the relatively high number of homicides occurring within their constantly diminishing inner city populations. In contrast, the larger cities have never even been closely challenged by any of the routinely listed top ten cities in regard to the pure number of homicides committed. Their large populations of millions of persons preclude them from ever competing with the smaller included cities on a "per capita" basis.

"A Hell Hole"

That is what the nationally famous evangelist Sam Jones called Birmingham during a revival meeting in the city in the 1890's.[2] He noted that "Saloons, dance halls and brothels thrived. Murder, gambling, drunkenness, and prostitution characterized the city's national reputation more than its fine steel."[3]

During these early years the city was known as "Bad Birmingham" and "the murder capital of the World."[4] Birmingham was a "wild west" town in more ways than our supposedly "true" Western frontier of cowboys, Indians and gunslingers ever was despite the popular portrayal in books and movies, both then and now. "The town was for all intents and purposes a frontier society..with the population drawn by jobs in the booming steel industry and which included waves of immigrants from the countryside and abroad. Russians and Poles, Italians, Greeks were all pouring in bringing with them their different languages and customs, a recipe for conflict. Underlying this was a brutally repressed, disenfranchised Black population."[5]

According to Edward L. Ayers:

> "Studies of the American West and Midwest challenge the stereotype of rampant violence on these frontiers of the United States. The violence that did erupt in Western cattle towns and on the open range may well have been Southern violence transplanted. Bloodshed was the product of a culture frontiersmen brought with them, not something they found waiting in the wilderness. In other English colonies such as Canada and Australia frontier challenges similar to those in the United States did not breed notoriously high levels of violence among the settlers."6

During this era it was not unusual for social and other issues of public import to be discussed and presented in a vigorous fashion. In addition to being employed by many politicians and religious preachers of the day, this style of discourse also found its way into the courtroom where loud questioning of witnesses and bombastic presentations to juries regarding issues to be adjudicated were routinely employed by attorneys and were, indeed, expected and accepted by the public. A similar approach to presenting information extended to the popular news media of the day which was mainly the province of the two daily newspapers---The Birmingham Age Herald and The Birmingham News. As will be seen in the many examples of reporting during that era which are reproduced verbatim throughout this book, the accepted style of writing during this era differs markedly from today. In addition to the racially charged invective routinely incorporated into news stories at that time, the public was spared no gory detail about an incident and suicides were publicly and almost gleefully reported on a daily basis. As the journalist Peggy Noonan noted, "There were no politically correct limits placed on their ability to describe a scene." These daily newspapers were supplemented by various weekly and irregularly issued publications, typically addressing specific matters of note by religious organizations, anti-saloon and other special interest groups.

With today's modern means of instantaneous news delivery through the internet, personal electronic devices and television, it may be hard to appreciate the major and powerful role played by the daily newspapers in delivering information about world and local affairs to the literate population of the early 20th century. One must take into consideration that there were no other forms of media at that time which were available to compete with the newspapers, as the development of radio as a means of news delivery would not become popularized on a wide public basis until the mid 1920's.

Before then, the newspapers were the "only game in town" in regard to what information would be disseminated and what, if any, bias would be applied.

Over the years, the diminishing role of the print media from its lofty position to a shell of its former self as it attempts to compete electronically can be likened to the bygone days of the system of railroads in light of the modern development of air and motorized ground movement of people and of the transportation of food and other vital material. However, many timely issues of great importance were presented and discussed in the print media in, for example, 1913. The insurrections in Mexico and the political instability in Europe on the eve of world war were matters of national interest which received front page treatment on a daily basis. Subjects of local significance were routinely presented in the newspapers and some of those which garnered much public interest were related to rates of crime and cases of violence which for years had been perceived to be out of control and worsening in the "Magic City."

Within two months of assuming the elected office of Coroner, Charles L. Spain was quoted at length in a newspaper article regarding his opinions about crime and murder in Jefferson County and for the first time indicated that there were 306 homicides in the county for the year 1912, a statement which would soon be hotly contested.

PISTOL "TOTING" IS RESPONSIBLE FOR MANY HOMICIDES IN COUNTY, SAYS SPAIN
"In Nine Cases Out of Ten I Have Investigated Killing Resulted From Pistol Wound
31 Unlawful Deaths During First
Three Months Of The Year
Of the 31, All But Two Were Negroes
Law Providing Severe Penalty for Carrying Concealed Weapons Needed, Thinks the County Coroner

The Birmingham Age-Herald, March 30, 1913

"In the investigation of all the unlawful homicides of the first three months of this year I was unable to find that liquor or intoxication entered as a factor or as an agent to any of the numerous killings," said Coroner C.L. Spain.

To what does Mr. Spain attribute the appalling number of homicides in Jefferson county? That 'pistol toting' is at the bottom of the majority of the homicides is the opinion of Coroner Spain, for he states: "In nine cases out of 10 unlawful homicides that I have investigated, the killing resulted from gun shot wounds invariably fired from a pistol. The evils of pistol toting cannot be underestimated for it is the chief agency to crime and murder in Jefferson county.

Of the 115 violent deaths investigated since January 1, by the coroner's office, 50 of them came during March, being in all parts of the county and keeping Coroner Spain extremely busy. This month has also the largest record so far this year for unlawful homicides, the past week being a record breaker with six since last Sunday afternoon. Unless there is a great increase in the killing in the next nine months the record of 306 unlawful homicides in Jefferson county for 1912 is not likely to be surpassed.

SPAIN IS PESSIMISTIC

In further commenting on the homicide figures for the first three months of the year Coroner C.L. Spain said: "In my opinion conditions are growing worse instead of better, as far as crime is concerned in Jefferson county. The figures for the first three months of this year may not show so many killings in proportion to last year's record breaking number, but it does not alter the fact that as long as convicts are employed in the mines about this district and released to prey upon the community when their terms are up that crime conditions will steadily grow worse; the next three months may double the number of unlawful homicides registered in the past 90 days. There should be legislation passed to prevent the carrying of concealed arms. Any man caught with a pistol should not be fined, but sentenced to a term in jail and no appeal should be allowed. It is entirely due to the general prevalence of white and colored people to carrying pistols that the number of unlawful homicides in Alabama overtop those of every other state in the union. 'Pistol toting' should be stopped and until the people of Jefferson county awake to the fact they might as well reconcile themselves to hear and read of killings as a daily occurrence.

Deaths Not Reported

It is also a fact that the corporations in this county do not take the office of the coroner seriously, for they hardly ever take the trouble to notify me of any fatality in their mines or works. For instance, the explosion of Indio Mines early in the week has not yet been officially reported to me, the only information I got of this mine disaster being from the newspapers. The same may be said of a man that got killed in Bessie mines two or three days ago. I've read in the papers of the fatality, but the managers of Bessie mines have not notified me of any fatality in their mines. I am going to get after these corporations and show them that they are not above the law and must report to me any fatality that happens on their premises."

It has been suggested that the board of revenue could well afford to put an automobile at Mr. Spain's disposal, so that he could investigate quickly every violent death. At the present time it is not infrequent that dead bodies must lie for hours and sometimes days wherever they happened to be before Coroner Spain can pass on them and order their removal."

Spain's indication that some companies and mines were not reporting cases may be a reason why records of some cases were not found in docket books or in newspaper accounts during my research. The lack of coroner's records for the late nineteenth and early part of the twentieth centuries makes it impossible to verify the high number of prisoner deaths in the mines which occurred during that time period as reported by Douglas Blackmon, who obtained the figures from state convict death logs.

Political and public interest regarding the high rate of homicides occurring within Jefferson County, and especially within the City of Birmingham, reached the boiling point on December 1, 1913 when a bold headline article was published in the Birmingham Age-Herald which brought out startling personal and professional opinions about crime, violence and the number of homicides in the opinion of Coroner Spain. His statements were believed to be both incorrect as well as inflammatory by other powerful political actors and a series of rebuttals by one of these officials, City Commissioner and Judge A.O. Lane in response to the coroner became headline news over a period of several weeks with associated articles being printed in both major papers. Although the discourse is somewhat lengthy, it is felt that a verbatim reproduction of some of the content of these articles provides valuable insight into the issues of crime, violence and homicide as perceived by government agents and the public at that time. It also serves as a "time capsule" of those earlier days with its use of a different style of "flowery" English language not typically used today.

Coroner to Probe Falilia Murder
The Shooting And Killing Of Falilia Remains
One Of The Murder Mysteries
Of Greater Birmingham In The Last 11 Months
Estimates There Have Been 300 Murders
In The County So Far This Year

But With Very Few Arrests And Convictions
Says Indifference Is Cause of Local Crime
The Birmingham Age Herald, December 1, 1913

"Murder in Birmingham is such a common occurrence, said Coroner Charles L. Spain, that the assassination of this Italian grocer in Pratt City a few nights ago has attracted little attention. There has been so far this year in Jefferson County approximately 300 and some odd murders. Not only your unlawful homicides but the cold blooded variety of murder. Now I would like to ask just how many murderers have been tried and convicted so far this year? How many murderers have been taken to the gallows? How many murderers are now in jail? From these statistics in my office this is not an abnormal year for murders as last year and the year before the number of homicides was practically the same. A the rate of 300 or more murders per year for the last four years as the report of my predecessor in the office showed, if only 50 percent had been convicted there should have been at least 150 murderers sent to the gallows every year. Just think of it a moment if 150 murderers have been hanged so far this year whether it would have had a retarding effect on the tendency in Birmingham to take human life on every possible occasion. But as long as Negroes and white people know for a certainty that through legal technicalities they can make a little bond and escape trial for months and even years and after a trial and conviction through the appeals can get more delay until all the witnesses die or disappear, and in the end the state nolle prosses the charges, murders will continue in Birmingham; they will not only continue but they will increase in number. We encourage outlawry by indifference and must therefore pay the cost."

Coroner Severe In Indictment Of Homicide Record
Thinks Publicity Of Awful Record Is Only Way To
Stir Citizens To Realize Conditions
The Birmingham Age Herald , December 5, 1913

"Coroner Charles L. Spain reiterated last night with emphasis the homicidal statistics that he gave out in an interview in the Age Herald a few days ago. Yesterday the statements of Coroner Spain brought forth criticism credited to Commissioner A.O. Lane to the effect that Spain's figures are misleading and that all violent deaths were not homicides. "I want to say to Judge Lane that Jefferson County would be very badly in need of a Coroner if that official could not tell that a death from heart disease is not a homicide. Commissioner Lane infers that in my haste to present startling figures to the public I have counted all the persons who died from heart disease, apoplexy and other ailments as unlawful homicides. A statement of this nature cannot be taken seriously. All anyone has to do to observe the frequency of homicides is read the newspapers. It is very rare that a day or several days pass without some person being murdered in some part of the County but usually in Birmingham. The newspapers print the tragedies of this County every day and this news is read so it is useless for Judge Lane to attempt to convince the people of Birmingham and Jefferson County that this is a nice quiet peace loving community where everyone who dies usually passes away from heart failure, apoplexy and other kindred ailments. Judge Lane will find if he looks at the records in my office that some 300 odd persons of Jefferson County met death through the instrumentality of the pistol and knife in the last 11 months. He can call it heart failure if he cares to but I call it plain murder. I have nothing to hide in my office and as my job doesn't pay enough to fear removal and this curb the expression of my true sentiments. I suppose I have jarred some tender sensibilities by taking the public into my confidence on the true state of affairs in Jefferson County regarding crime. But I don't blame Judge Lane for trying to belittle the homicide statistics. I suppose if I were head of the Birmingham Police Department I would sincerely desire to have the number of murders as small as possible--especially as so few of the murderers are caught. However, as I am not the head of the Police Department but just a poorly paid Coroner I am going ahead attending to the business of my office the best way I can considering that I have at times several homicides to investigate at one time and will not falsify the records of the Coroner's office to curry official favor. The fact that there have been 300 homicides in the past year may be displeasing to advertise all over the County and I have no doubt that it is displeasing. It is certainly a shameful and deplorable state of affairs especially as it is the exception to the rule to punish anyone responsible for these homicides. But this advertising I believe will eventually awaken the voters of Jefferson County to some action and it is for this very reason that the records of my office are always open for inspection. I believe the greatest publicity should be given the fact of the large number of homicides in the County."

Judge Lane Issues Report
In Reply To Spain's Statement
Cites Figures To Prove Contention That
Birmingham Is Not As Bad As Claimed
73 Murders In Past 12 Months

(Dec. 1, 1912 to Dec. 1, 1913)
Shown By Report To Have Occurred In City
Five Pistol Duels, 11 Suicides, 12 Justifiable Homicides
And 28 Accidents

The Birmingham Age Herald, December 6, 1913

"Birmingham is not a blood and thunder, gore be-spattered, bullet swept, dagger littered city, Coroner C. L. Spain to the contrary says City Commissioner Lane. Judge Lane believes that inestimable harm is being done by the Coroner in his numerous newspaper interviews on the popularity of crime and bloodshed in this city and county. Judge Lane believes that a great part of the "300 murders" which the Coroner keeps flaunting in the face of the public are not unlawful homicides, but perfectly respectable demises of various kinds which do not in any way reflect on the moral or civic character of the community."

This edition of the newspaper includes an extensive list of deaths in the County which was compiled by Lane and which includes homicides as well as other violent and natural deaths to include suicides and accidents. This list includes a total of 134 homicides through the end of November, 1913.

But 134 Homicides In County In A Year
According To Lane
His Figures Show 73 In Greater Birmingham
And 61 Outside
The Facts Are Bad Enough He Says But Protests
Against Making Things Worse Than They Are

The Birmingham Age Herald, December 7, 1913

"In the entire County of Jefferson from December 1, 1912 to December 1, 1913 there were just 134 homicides according to the completed reports issued by City Commissioner Judge Lane yesterday. Judge Lane admits this is too many but he states it is far different from the "300 homicides" which Coroner Spain has been claiming for the County. I do not wish to be misunderstood in this matter Judge Lane said yesterday. I am not championing crime or defending our record. Heaven knows it has been bad enough, but what I am protesting against is making it worse than it is. I think Coroner Spain has made an honest mistake. I do not believe for a moment that he intentionally intends doing any harm to this community, but that does not get around the fact that he has done much harm by his repeated statements in the press holding this city up as a haven of criminals and giving figures and statements that are not facts."

Coroner Clings To Homicide Estimate
Believes Records Will Show Three Hundred
Killings In The County This Year

The Birmingham News, December 7, 1913

"It can't be helped if Judge Lane is one of the big guns of the Birmingham District. The figures will be brought out to show that what I have claimed is true--the records when properly worked up will show there were 300 homicides--killings in which some man or woman met death at the hands of another--during the year." Coroner Spain was smarting under criticism passed on his statements as to the number of homicides in Jefferson County when he made the above utterance.

"There would be no object in my giving Jefferson County a black eye," he continued. "I have hopes that by calling attention to the numerous crimes something will be done to bring about a change of conditions. There are many cases which I did not look into--in fact, I never had the time. Now comes along Judge Lane and makes answer to my statements. I have no reason to change my estimate of the number of homicides in Jefferson County for the year--the list of Judge Lane notwithstanding. I believe my records will show up differently from those presented by Judge Lane. If by reason of this controversy something can result that will bring about a change, I will be happy. The nature of the Coroner is such that there is no more profit in it, regardless of the number of investigations made: Its $100 per month, the salary and thats all."

Coroner Spain Grows Sarcastic
Investigation Of Killings Are Keeping Him
Very Busy These Days.

The Birmingham Age Herald, December 13, 1913

"Investigations are crowding Coroner Charles L. Spain these days, as for the past few days there has been a killing daily. "Of course, according to Judge Lane, all these killings are nothing but cases of apoplexy and heart failure," said Coroner Spain, "but I regret to state that I have to investigate them as plain, ordinary, sordid murders. I'd very much like to call all these cases polite names like apoplexy and heart failure, but as the majority of the investigations are with a jury those gentlemen might object, so on the docket daily the stenographer jots down one more usually with the words: 'Shot to death or stabbed to death, same being done unlawfully and against the dignity of the state of Alabama.' I hope to investigate three homicides tomorrow and catch up with my work. I also intend to work all day Sunday on an inquest."

After mid-December, 1913, despite an extensive review of later editions of both major newspapers, no additional stories relating to arguments about homicide rates could be found. This sudden discontinuation of vitriolic arguments suggests that a "truce" had been called for by Commissioner Lane and Coroner Spain. The most likely reasons for this having occurred can be explained by a statistical analysis of pertinent data.

So how can we attempt to deconstruct the statements of Coroner Spain, who publicly insisted on more than one occasion that there were "300 homicides" in Jefferson County in 1913, that similar numbers of homicides had occurred in recent past years and that the response by Lane that Spain was mistaken with his greatly inflated count of the number of homicides which had actually been committed? One easy way to do this would be to find the coroner's docket book for the year 1913 and to manually count the number of listed entries for individual homicides as has been done for other years where records are available. Of course, things are never that simple as that specific docket book, as well as several others from that era, are missing. It is therefore necessary to review and tabulate the numbers of homicides listed in the records that are available for years prior to and after 1913 in order to establish an average rate and to note if there are indications of any statistically significant or excessive spikes in the rates in any particular year. Coroner Spain's insistence that the homicide rate of 1913 was not much different from previous years would also become important. This statement was also considered not only incorrect at the time, but also highly inflammatory in regard to the perception of the quality of life in Jefferson County and the City of Birmingham at a time when the establishment of more business and industry in the area was being vigorously pursued.

We can also use the available statistical data to help decide if some of the derogatory descriptive terms applied to the "Magic City" in the past are indicative of the truth or are mere hyperbole. A review of the available documented statistics regarding the number of homicides investigated by the coroner during this era on a 12 month calendar year basis revealed the following data:

Homicides in Jefferson County

1911: 156	1922: 137
1912: 161	1923: 134
1913: 134 (as compiled by A. O. Lane. Official records missing).	1924: 150
1914-15: Records missing.	1925: 131
1916-17: 132	1926: 127
1918: 94	1927: 154
1919: 111	1928: 130
1920: 112	1929: 113
1921: 136	1930: 116

Average yearly rate of homicides over a 17 year period from 1911 through 1930 where figures are available: 131

It is notable that a comparison of the relatively consistent yearly homicide rates actually reflect a decreasing per capita rate when the regular and continuous increase in the overall population within Jefferson County during this period is taken into consideration.

Verdict

Coroner Spain was obviously mistaken when he issued his strongly worded public statements indicating that, in his opinion, there had been without doubt, "300 homicides" committed in Jefferson County within an 11 month period in 1913. This error was compounded by his insistence that similar rates of murder had occurred in recent previous years. He insisted that his statistics could be validated by reviewing the numbers of homicides documented in the files in his office. Spain had been newly elected to the office of coroner and assumed this position on January 19, 1913.

It is doubtful that Spain intentionally provided erroneous and inflated data and was, most likely, overwhelmed by the number of deaths that he was called upon to investigate. He apparently had not closely checked the available records in order to determine the actual number of homicides which had occurred during this time period or in recent past years. After independent data was presented by Lane, it is believed that Spain must have performed an actual count of homicides based on his records and found that he had grossly overstated the number of murders which had occurred so far in 1913 by twofold. Spain was probably embarrassed by his repeated publicly stated erroneous statistics for this and prior years, to include available records for the full year of 1912 which indicated that there were 161 homicides committed in Jefferson County.

This evaluation, based on statistical analysis, may explain the apparent "truce" which was reached between Spain and Lane and which is also supported by the sudden and complete cessation of their recent, almost daily arguments regarding homicide rates in the newspapers. Coroner Spain would leave office in 1917 after serving a single term.

The following newspaper article regarding the demographics of deaths in Jefferson County was published in 1920 which included a number of questionable statements of alleged facts. Although some of the noted statistics regarding homicides for several earlier years differ somewhat from the actual later counts made from docket books, there is no evidence of radical deviation between them. The disparity between these numbers may be due to the reporter not reviewing or accounting for the separate records of the Bessemer Division of the county coroner's office which were maintained in that city. This article also sheds some light on statistics for several early years where docket books were missing.

What was totally unexpected and questionable was a statement relating to the number of homicides which were deemed to be "justifiable" in 1919. If true, the ratio of justifiable to non-justifiable homicides in these early years is almost completely reversed from that of the period extending from the mid 20th century to the current time. However, as based on a notation in the same article indicating that there were 137 "unjustifiable" homicides in 1912, the word "justifiable" relating to the 1919 statistics may represent a typographical error where the letters "un" were inadvertently left off. It is hard to believe that the legal approach to the coroner's rulings on homicides could have undergone an almost complete reversal over a period of only several years. It is difficult to determine the veracity of these statistics due to the loss of early docket books and the fact that final legal determinations were not often noted in many of the existing docket book entries. In addition, the noted change in the racial composition of perpetrators and victims of homicides was another piece of information which may have been exaggerated and which was not apparent in a review of the later available statistics.

Another statement regarding a purported average rate of "2 homicides occurring every three days" in earlier years suggests an average yearly rate of approximately 242 homicides which can be considered to be an overestimate of the actual numbers. The relative rarity of deaths attributed to narcotics is certainly remarkable when compared to the modern epidemic of drug abuse.

CORONER SUBMITS REPORT FOR YEAR
Homicides Show Big Decrease Over Years When Saloons Were Open

The Birmingham Age-Herald, January 22, 1920

"There were 146 killings in Jefferson County last year, according to the annual report of the coroner. One hundred and ten of those were declared to be cases of justifiable homicide. Twelve suicides are on the list for the year, 263 deaths by accident, and 311 from natural causes, all being investigated by the coroner.

This report shows a small increase over the preceding year, but is far from coming up to the years when Birmingham averaged about two murders every three days. The year 1912 was not a particularly violent year as far as the murders are concerned, but it held its own among the others, showing a report of 137 unjustifiable homicides. In that year there were twenty-five suicides, twice the number of the year 1910. Many were the methods that were used, but the most usual were pistols and gas.

Saloons were at their height at that time and drinking killed fifteen men and women. Morphine and cocaine were responsible for three deaths while there were seven cases on the docket where the person died from starvation. Two separate cases are marked "death from delirium tremens." It is interesting to note that the majority of the other cases investigated by the coroner that year were caused by acute indigestion and hemorrhage of the lungs. One peculiar case has the following verdict: "Death while falling and breaking his neck while under the influence of liquor."

Going back still further among the docket books, the month of April, in 1909, was taken as an example to use for a comparison. In that month there were 18 murders, 1 suicide, 1 death by alcohol and 1 by "dope." The same month in 1906 shows 12 murders, 1 suicide and 1 death by alcohol.

Crime was certainly not on the wane in those days, and some of the old officials of the courthouse say that shootings seemed to have been very popular. Crime as far as the murders go has changed in one respect, for in the days of 1909, 1910, 1911 and 1912, the majority were where the principals were both white. In the past year most of the cases handled by the coroner were those involving negroes."

Numbers

Previous statements relating to the rapid population growth within the City of Birmingham and all of Jefferson County as industrialization expanded in this area can be better appreciated by looking at population based on census data. Numbers presented are rounded to the closest thousand.

Population

YEAR	JEFFERSON COUNTY	CITY OF BIRMINGHAM
1880	23,000	3,100
1890	89,000	26,000
1900	140,000	38,000
1910	226,000	133,000
1920	310,000	179,000
1930	431,000	260,000
1940	460,000	268,000

There was an exponential increase in population during the census periods extending from 1900 through 1940.7 Thereafter, from the mid to late 20th century the population of Jefferson County leveled out to a yearly average of 640,000 from 1950 through 2010.7,8

Especially notable is the extremely rapid population growth during the period 1910--1930 which saw an average increase of 9,300 persons per year.

Per Capita Comparisons

In an attempt to discover whether Birmingham was truly a "Hell Hole" and was as "Bad" as it had been described during the early 20th century it is helpful to reassess some of the available statistics on a per capita basis This method also allows for comparison of rates from this earlier era with those of the latter part of the 20th century in an attempt to discover during which period a citizen had a greater chance of meeting a violent demise at the hands of another person.

As noted, homicides per capita are the number of murders per 100,000 persons in a given time and in a set area. Using appropriate calculations the following table can be devised showing a sampling of figures for population, homicides and per capita rates for all of Jefferson County. (Note: All population numbers in all tables noted below are rounded to the closest thousand).

Year	Population	Total Homicides	Per Capita Homicide Rate
1911	226,000	156	69
1920	310,000	112	36
1930	431,000	116	26

It is clear from looking at these figures that a person within Jefferson County stood *greater than twice* the chance of becoming a victim of homicide in 1911 than he or she would have had in 1930 on a per capita basis. So far, the statistics which have been analyzed are derived from all of Jefferson County in regard to population and homicide rate data. However, it is enlightening to take a "snapshot" of similar statistics limited to the City of Birmingham for one year. In 1926, Birmingham rated number 3 on a list of cities with a per capita homicide rate greater than 18. With an estimated population of 215,000 during this mid census year, the city had a rounded per capita rate of 59 based on 127 homicides which had occurred within the city limits that year. Certainly a dangerous time for a city resident or visitor.

The Greater Birmingham area during the period 1910 through 1930 can be considered to have been a medium sized population region compared to larger urban centers of the time such as New York City and Chicago. A review of population numbers and homicide rates from those cities are revealing and shed light on the previous statement that large urban centers are never included in the "top ten" lists of cities with high per capita homicide rates, while the actual numbers of homicides in those localities far exceed those of the smaller cities which are often repeatedly included on such lists.

A review of data relating to these two large cities allows for a comparison of the disparate per capita and numerical rates. The total number of homicides for the dates shown vary to a minor extent between several available sources, Population and per capita rates of homicide are consistent among demographic tables found on various internet sites.

As in Birmingham in the early 1990s, the nationwide crack cocaine epidemic was a major factor in driving homicide rates to their highest numerical levels in history. In New York City, the 1990 per capita rate exceeded 30, only to fall to markedly lower rates than ever before in recent years.

Another outlier is Chicago in 2016 where a marked increase in the number of homicides, along with a large decrease in population, resulted in a statistically significant increase in the per capita rates of homicide for several recent years. This is opposed to New York City where a 13% decrease in homicides was achieved in 2016 in comparison to 2015.

New York City

Year	Population	Total Homicides	Per Capita Rate
1911	4,767,000	281	7
1920	5,620,000	215	6
1930	6,930,000	421	7
1990	7,322,000	2,245	30
2016	8,550,000	334	4

Chicago

Year	Population	Total Homicides	Per Capita Rate
1910	2,185,000	412	9
1920	2,702,000	407	11
1930	3,376,000	444	15
1990	2,784,000	849	30
2016	2,696,000	762	28

Obviously, per capita homicide rates for these large cities are appreciably exceeded by those previously shown for Jefferson County and the city of Birmingham during the same time periods in the early part of the century, while the pure number of homicides greatly exceed the Jefferson County numbers in all of the noted years. Statistics from the early 20th century relating to additional parameters associated with homicides in Jefferson County are also available. This information was compiled from the records of those cases which came under the investigative purview of the coroner. Much of this data remained remarkably consistent on a per capita basis over a period of many years with variations in total numbers being reflective of increasing population over time. Some examples are noted as follows with additional pertinent statistics included in other chapters.

Place of Occurrence of Homicides
1911

Birmingham City Limits: 86
Other Jefferson County: 70
Total: 156

Statistical Comparisons

In an attempt to make valid comparisons between the alleged increased homicide rates and poor living conditions within Birmingham and Jefferson County in the early 20th century, and with the reported increased numbers of homicides in the early 1990's, it is instructive to compare the per capita rates of homicide between these periods in order to see what conclusions can be drawn.

Comparing two of the highest yearly numerical and per capita homicide rates in Jefferson County during the early part of the 20th century with the year with the highest number of homicides committed in the modern era reveals the following information:

1911
Population	Total Homicides	Per Capita Homicide Rate
226,000	156	69

1926
Population	Total Homicides	Per Capita Homicide Rate
370,000 (Est.)	127	34

1991
Population	Total Homicides	Per Capita Homicide Rate
652,000	193	30

This comparison indicates that although the total number of homicides was greater in 1991 than in the earlier noted years, the chances of being murdered in Jefferson County in 1911 on a *per capita basis*, was more than twice as great as it was in 1991 despite the increase in the number of homicides which were committed. Similar high per capita homicide rates are found for several years preceding and following 1911 and continuing until sharp increases in the population decreased the per capita rates.

There are certain caveats to be considered when comparing murder rates between different time periods. The great majority of homicides which have been committed over the years in Jefferson County have taken place within the city limits of Birmingham. In the four year period extending from 1990 through 1993 there was an average of 179 homicides committed per year. Many of these deaths were related to the then ongoing turf wars associated with crack cocaine distribution. These deaths often involved a subset of criminals and which offers some substantiation of the old adage that persons who live violently often die in a similar fashion. No matter which century, the social environment of these denizens was typically confined to after dark and which was described by Sante as:

> *"Night is the repository of unfinished business,*
> *It is the text of its secret history,*
> *the monument to its victims and failures, its predators and police.*
> *It is the time of inversion and misrule,*
> *the province of vice and intemperance, of misery and blight.*
> *The clock is directed by a moral spring,*
> *And it binds pleasure and harm inextricably together in the night.*
> *Night is forgotten and endlessly repeated;*
> *it is glorious and it sits next door to death."*[9]

These are the numbers. They are the statistics based on mathematical calculations. However, when the social commentary as expressed by Sante and Lane are taken into consideration, the question arises as to whether these statistics are representative and applicable to a local population as a whole, either in the early 20th century or currently. Do these numbers truly reflect the equal opportunity for all members of a society to suffer a sudden violent death? Is the statistical chance of mayhem to be visited upon a law abiding citizen who goes directly home from work each day the same as for those members of a community who, in 1911, chose to frequent the dives of downtown Birmingham or the "blind tigers" of the west Jefferson County mining camps? Or was that any different for those individuals who chose to partake of the dangerous drug "wars" and culture in the early 1990s or who were innocent bystanders who became victims due to their socioeconomic status?

Although out of the time scope of this book, it is important to raise the question of how do we, as a society, try to explain and deal with the underlying causes for the self-destructive behavior of a new generation in the 21st century who abuse extremely potent drugs and who must realize that their chances for imminent death are as high as those for playing "Russian Roulette" with a gun!

In any discussion regarding homicide rates during the early 20th century and those of current times, several associated issues must be taken into consideration and factored into any analysis. As noted by Roger Lane:

> *"Two of the most important factors affecting the real rates*
> *(of homicide) have tended to pull them in opposite directions.*
> *One of these is the enormous advance made in medicine,*
> *especially in the treatment of traumatic injuries;*
> *the other is the continued growth of a weapons,*
> *particularly guns, culture."*[10]

A considerable number of early 20th century victims of fatal violence in Jefferson County would not have died in current times. The quick response and provision of medical aid by trained paramedics, along with the rapid transportation of victims, especially within the City of Birmingham, directly to an appropriate modern emergency medical facility has led to an appreciable decrease in mortality rates in the modern era. This is especially notable when taking into consideration the limited vehicular transportation and road system during the first part of the 20th century. This was especially so with those cases of injury occurring in the more rural areas, to include the numerous isolated coal mining camps within western Jefferson County. This lack of timely transportation of those injured following accidents in the mines and from other forms of violence was a factor that certainly increased mortality rates.

The steady decrease in the number of deaths after sustaining severe injuries can, perhaps, be best appreciated by briefly reviewing the history of military medicine. From the days of Napoleon's Army in the early 1800's to today, there has been a progression of improvements in medical and surgical techniques. Coupled with advances in technology which have allowed for the ever more rapid transportation of persons to medical facilities has led to improved survival of those who have been seriously injured.

We have advanced from horse drawn carts proceeding down muddy roads to medical facilities with limited capabilities far in the rear of the battle zone to the current extraction of the injured by helicopter and with rapid transportation to state of the art hospitals close to the front lines of battle which provide services that would amaze even those medical personnel of the Vietnam war era. The decrease in the number of wartime deaths is evident. This pronounced change in mortality rates is also reflected in the morbidity rates, i.e., the increased number of individuals who have survived after sustaining severe head injuries and/or multiple traumatic limb amputations. In earlier times such wounds would have almost guaranteed a rapid demise from such trauma or, at best, would have led to delayed death from infection and other complications shortly after their infliction. This inversion of morbidity and mortality rates over time, be they related to the "Butcher's Bill" of war or to those of their civilian counterparts, is a clear reflection of the advances in transportation, rapid appropriate treatment and medical technology.

In assessing death rates there is also the distinct possibility of an understatement of the actual number of homicides during the early

20th century due to the lack of postmortem examinations performed by competent, trained physicians as well as the questionable investigative and forensic science capabilities of the coroners and police officials of that time. In this regard, as suggested by Lane:

> "...in understanding the level of homicide in the 19th as compared to the 20th century, (it) is not merely misleading but perhaps radically so. While the "dark figure" is by definition unknowable for any era, the evidence concerning official (incompetence) and even cover-up suggests that it was far greater then than now."[11]

It is fair to say that Lane's opinion can also be applied to the noted homicide rates in Jefferson County in the early 20th century. These figures can be considered as being conservative in comparison to the more exact numbers compiled in the late 20th and early 21st centuries in conjunction with the more advanced and competent medical-legal death investigative system in place.

The statistics regarding Jefferson County presented and discussed in this chapter deal only with mortality rates. As with military combat related morbidity rates where soldiers sustain wounds and recover, typically at a rate well over three times as great as for those who die, it is believed that non-fatal assaults, both reported and unreported, similarly exceed the number of civilian homicides in any community.

CHAPTER 3

PASSION

"Well love, love, love
Love, oh careless love,
Well it caused me to weep,
And it caused me to moan,
And it caused me to leave my happy home."

—*Careless Love*

PASSION: A term which "implies strong, possibly violent human emotions which are often of an impetuous kind. An intense feeling that is at fever pitch."[1]

This word is felt to be the best choice for this chapter's title as it encompasses other terms such as desire, love, lust, jealousy, betrayal, rage and revenge. These terms alone, closely linked as they are to our emotions and associations with other persons, are a part of human nature and play varying roles in our daily lives. Most of our "passionate" responses are of a relatively minor and limited nature and quickly pass as we move on to new interactions with others. However, when more ardent emotions are accompanied by physical actions, these simple words may help to explain some of the complex factors associated with many violent deaths.

Passion, with its synonyms and related terms, is not limited to the incidents noted in this chapter. More often than not they are found to be descriptive words denoting basic motivating factors which are often accentuated by the presence of various intoxicants. Such human behaviors, and their associated outcomes, are to be found in various settings throughout this book.

A.J. MOTHERSHED KILLS J.J. HAMBRICK
AT CORNER OF THE WOODWARD BUILDING
Recent Family Troubles Are Given
as the Cause of the Killing
Mothershed Did Not Attempt To Escape With Statement,
"You Will Ruin No More Homes,"
He Deliberately Shoots Hambrick Twice
Alleged Intimacy
The Birmingham Age-Herald, December 19, 1903

"With the statement "You will never ruin another home," A.J. Mothershed of Pratt City shot and killed J.J. Hambrick, also of Pratt City, last night near the corner of the Woodward building. Mothershed surrendered to Policemen McDonald and Jones and was placed in the city jail on a charge of murder.

The shooting was the result of family troubles. The cause is best told by Mothershed's words a minute after the shooting. He said: "He robbed me of my happy home. I am the man that did the shooting. I don't care if they hang me or what they do to me. If I had a cannon I would have shot him to pieces. He robbed my home. I have not known the man but two hours. His name is Hambrick, so people tell me."

The shooting occurred when the streets were crowded and it seems a wonder that some one was not injured or killed by one of the bullets. Two shots were fired by Mothershed, and either would have proved fatal. Hambrick was standing leaning against the telegraph pole on the Twentieth street side of the Woodward building. Mothershed walked up, spoke a few words to Hambrick, deliberately drew his pistol from his pocket, rested his right hand on his left arm and fired his first shot. It struck Hambrick in the back just under the left shoulder blade and came out near the heart on the left side of the chest. Hambrick wheeled as the first shot was fired and Mothershed fired a second time. The second bullet entered the right side. It did not come out. Hambrick ran into Parker's drug store and got nearly to the door which leads to the lobby of the building. Here he wheeled and fell. He never spoke after he was shot. He lay on the floor and groaned constantly until he died in about five or six minutes.

Mothershed walked into the drug store twirling the pistol around on his finger. He was perfectly cool and stood at the cigar counter until the policemen arrived, when he held up his weapon and said he was the man who did the shooting. Mothershed is a carpenter and lives with his wife and children in Pratt City. He was working on a contract at Littleton and was only in Birmingham about two or three times a month.

There are other reports which differ slightly from this which it is said that Mothershed walked up to Hambrick and said: "You will never ruin another home or make any more orphans," and then shot him. After reaching the city jail Mothershed sent for attorneys John Shugart and Wade Mothershed and asked them to defend him. He refused absolutely to make any statement at the jail about the shooting, and the only information obtained from him was through

Wade Mothershed, who is not related to the man in jail. He said that the prisoner had merely stated that the shooting was about his wife.

It seems that two or three days ago Mothershed returned to Birmingham for a visit of a few days and learned of the intimacy between his wife and Hambrick. He consulted Chief Phillips of Pratt City, Attorney Shugart and others. At one of the consultations he broke down and cried for some time and seemed completely prostrated. He never made a threat against Hambrick but seemed to be dazed to some extent. According to the best information obtainable Hambrick and Mrs. Mothershed were found together in her room at the home in Pratt City. It seems that several days ago one of the neighbors went to the Mothershed residence to see Mrs. Mothershed. She asked one of the children where its mother was and received the reply that she was in that room. The child pointed to its mother's room. The neighbor walked into the room without knocking, as the child had told her that there was no one in there except its mother. She discovered Hambrick and Mrs. Mothershed together. It is also stated that neighbors had seen Hambrick go to the house. According to the statements of Pratt City people his visits had been going on some time, but Mothershed knew nothing of it as he spent most of his time in Littleton.

Hambrick leaves a mother, a sister and a brother. The deceased had been in Birmingham many years and was working as a switchman in Pratt City. No weapons were found on him. He had $6.25 in silver in his pockets. Mothershed used a .38 calibre latest improved pistol. Coroner Paris was notified, and will probably hold an inquest this morning."

MOTHERSHED SENT TO THE COUNTY JAIL
Coroner Paris Swears Out Warrant Charging Murder
No Developments in Cause of Shooting
Coroner Anxious to Know if the Courts
Will Term the Killing Justifiable

The Birmingham Age-Herald, December 20, 1903

"A.J. Mothershed, who shot and killed John J. Hambrick on the Woodward building corner was carried to the county jail on a warrant charging murder. The warrant was sworn out by Coroner Paris after he had talked to Mothershed and heard statements from several witnesses to the shooting. Coroner Paris said he had no course open except to send the man to jail, as he was a self-confessed murderer. He said he would like to know if the courts considered the killing justifiable. There were no additional facts about the shooting or the cause brought out yesterday. Since returning to the city Mothershed has not been living with his wife."

MURDER CHARGES AGAINST WHITE MEN
Defendants Must Remain In County Jail
Until Criminal Court Reconvenes Early In September
The Birmingham Age-Herald, July 13, 1904

"A.J. Mothershed and several more white men, charged with murder in the first degree, will probably be inmates of the county jail for sometime yet to come. The criminal court has adjourned for the summer, and will not convene until the middle of September. It is not known when the next capital docket will be set for trial when court reconvenes. Several of the defendants have applied for bail, but have been denied by the courts."

Postscript

It is known that Mothershed was held in the Jefferson County jail for a period of time extending into the early part of 1905 due to various delays including the retirement of a judge and the delay in replacing him and the trying of other existing cases on the docket ahead of his. The final legal consequences for Mothershed could not be determined. Possibly, the case against him was either dismissed or he was allowed to plead to a lesser offense such as manslaughter and that outcome was not prominently reported, if at all, in the newspapers. Another possibility is that he died from natural causes while in custody.

This was one of those instances noted previously where the coroner did not wish to make an independent determination as to whether a particular murder was justifiable or not due to the circumstances surrounding the incident and the questionable actions of both the deceased individual and the defendant. Public mores of that time which, of course, also extended into the legal community, were such that the extreme violent actions of a "wronged" husband, although technically criminal in nature, were believed in some cases to be socially acceptable, if not completely legally excusable, especially within many southern states of the union.

MURDER CAUSED BY JEALOUSY
Tom Myrick Accused of Killing Will Deavers
Arrested at Jefferson
Deavers Was to Marry Girl on Night He Was Slain, But Myrick is Said to Have Taken Her
The Birmingham Age Herald, December 26, 1903

"Jim Myrick, a miner who lived at Jefferson, was arrested yesterday afternoon on a charge of murder. He is accused of cutting the throat of Will Deavers, whose body was found stretched across the pavement in front of the Country club at North Birmingham on Thursday evening. Myrick is in the county jail.

According to the evidence the killing was a result of jealousy on the part of the dead man. It seems that the prisoner and the dead man were room mates at the mine at Jefferson and have been friends for some time. About a week ago the dead man came to Birmingham to see the woman in the case, and he was to have married her Thursday night. He has been a regular visitor at the residence near Sayreton, and Thursday morning they came to the city for Christmas and also to get married.

Late Thursday afternoon Deavers and the girl met Myrick, and according to the evidence the girl took up with him and they were together a great deal. She had a friend with her and the four boarded a North Birmingham car. The young lady of Deaver's choice was sitting by him, but he got up to give a lady his seat. Later it was vacated and he sat down again. He attempted to talk to his friend but she would not listen to him.

Myrick and Deavers had some words, and it is stated that the former threatened to kill the latter, saying that he had been following him all day and he was tired of it. After getting off the car at North Birmingham the two men engaged in a fight and Deaver's throat was cut from ear to ear. His head was almost severed from his body. The remains are still at Warner-Smiley's undertaking establishment, where they are being held until Coroner Paris is through with the investigation."

Docket Entry:
Date: February 26, 1909
Deceased: Jim Brown, Col.
Address: Bessemer
Cause Of Death: Gunshot wound.
Remarks: Found that deceas was carried from Birmingham to Bessemer Ala to be tried for assault on Jim Robinson girl and when Jim Robinson walked in sheriffs office at Bess. Jim Brown was seated handcuffed to another prisoner. Jim Robinson pull a 38 special and fired on him killing him instantly. Jim Robinson give up to sheriff and was bound over to gran jury with bale. I did not make any investigation as the slayer was all ready in jail.

ENRAGED FATHER KILLS HANDCUFFED NEGRO IN COURT
J.M. Robinson Shoots Jim Brown, Who Was Awaiting Preliminary Hearing Attacked His Daughter More Than A Week Ago Robinson is Brought to County Jail, Declines to Make Statement Other Than That He Has No Regrets Over Killing

The Birmingham Age-Herald, February 27, 1909

"This morning at 11 o'clock the city was thrown into excitement by the rapid firing of a pistol in Rebie hall and when the crowd rushed upstairs it was found that J.M. Robinson, whose daughter was attacked on February 15, near the pipe works, by a negro, Jim Brown, had shot and killed Brown as he was sitting in Deputy Sheriff George W. Jones office handcuffed to another negro, and waiting for his trial to take place.

The officers state that Robinson came into the office and asked officer Jones when the trial would take place and that Mr. Jones stated as soon as the justice could get to the court room. As Robinson turned he caught sight of Brown sitting in a chair and he quickly drew his pistol, a .38 special and began firing. Four shots were fired, three before the bystanders could get hold of Robinson and one while they were trying to take the pistol from his hand. Brown died with a bullet through his heart and an arm broken having been dragged into the corner by the man at his side. Robinson was taken to the clerk's office where he was later joined by his daughter, Miss Dessie Robinson, who had been waiting for court to convene so she could testify in the case. Robinson...was taken to the Birmingham jail on a warrant charging murder.

    The story of the causes leading up to the killing is as follows; On February 15, Miss Robinson, who was her father's housekeeper was preparing dinner in the kitchen when all at once a burly negro grabbed her by the throat and struck her with a broom handle. Miss Robinson screamed for her father and he came running from the store, and thinking that the negro was only a thief he knocked him down with a shovel and dragged him out of doors. Officers were telephoned for and in a short time Deputy George Jones took charge of the negro who proved to be Jim Brown. After the officer had hurried away with the negro the father found that the negro had laid violent hands on his daughter, who had been so wrought up that she had not told of the attack. Robinson at once came to Bessemer on a car but the officers had gone to Birmingham with Brown. Not until this morning had the father seen the negro and it is believed that when he saw him he became so infuriated that he drew his gun and killed him. The coroner will investigate the killing Saturday morning.

Robinson lived in Talladega for a long number of years prior to his removal to Bessemer. He was a deputy sheriff there for several years. During his residence there he was thrice tried for murder and thrice acquitted. One time was for the killing of a white man and the other two grew out of the killing of negroes.

Sheriff W. R. Middleton of Talladega County was in Birmingham yesterday and called at Sheriff Higdon's office shortly after Robinson's removal to the county jail. He and Robinson are old friends and as soon as he learned of the late trouble he went to the jail to see him. In talking of Robinson he referred to him as a man without fear, and the only surprise he expressed at his killing the negro was that he had not done so prior to yesterday. At the jail Robinson stated he did not wish to make any statement beyond the fact that he had no regrets for his action."

Postscript

No further information could be found regarding the outcome of this case, however, it is most likely that Robinson either received a "no-bill" from the grand jury or was acquitted at a trial.

WALTER DIXON SHOT BY HARDEMAN AND INSTANTLY KILLED
Daughter of Latter is Witness of Shooting
Below Bessemer
Hardeman Has Not Yet Surrendered
Leaves Word He Will Give Himself Up This Morning--Resented Dixon's Attentions to Daughter--Inquest Today
The Birmingham Age-Herald, September 23, 1912

"Because he insisted on courting the daughter of Bob Hardeman after being warned by Mr. Hardeman that his attentions to the girl were undesirable, Walter Dixon was shot and instantly killed with a Savage rifle in the hands of Mr. Harmed late last night as Dixon was escorting the girl home from church.

Three or four months ago Dixon is alleged to have shot and killed Walter Dagnon at Johns, Ala. It is claimed that Dixon had been paying attention to the Hardeman girl for some time and a short while ago Mr. Hardeman ordered him away from the house and warned him to stay away from Miss Hardeman.

It was late at night and Dixon and the girl were nearing the Hardeman home when suddenly Mr. Hardeman is said to have stepped into the road in front of them. Without a word he threw his rifle to his shoulder and fired. Dixon fell to the ground. A bullet had entered the left side and passed out the right side just under the back of the armpit. Coroner Brasher visited the scene of the shooting and he will hold an inquest Monday morning."

BOB HARDYMAN SURRENDERS FOR KILLING WALTER DIXON
States He Shot Dixon In Self Defense
When He Found Him Mistreating Daughter
The Birmingham Age-Herald, September 24, 1912

"Following the shooting of Walter Dixon at Blue Creek late Saturday evening Robert Hardyman, a miner who works at the Virginia mines, yesterday morning appeared at the sheriff's office in Bessemer and gave himself up, stating that he had killed Dixon in self-defense. Later in the day Coroner B.L. Brasher issued a warrant against Hardyman, charging him with murder and holding him under a bond of $1000.

Hardyman said yesterday. "I killed Walter Dixon in self-defense. I discovered him mistreating my daughter, Zooma, who he was escorting home from Adger, where they had gone to church, and killed him. He saw me and attempted to draw his gun first. I shot before he could get it from his pocket."

Zooma Hardyman corroborated her father's story. She stated that she had met Dixon in Adger where she and three other girls had gone to a revival meeting held there; he had asked her permission to escort her home and she had consented. According to a statement of the elder Hardyman, when Dixon fell dying to the ground, the girl cried that she was glad to see him die.

Dixon was 25 years of age and the proprietor of a pool room at Blue Creek. It is said that he had only been there for a few months, having been in the county jail charged with the murder of John Dagman, a constable at Johns, Ala. Dixon had secured his release on bond and was awaiting trial when killed. Hardyman is a pumper at the Virginia mines, and has a family of seven daughters and one son. The entire family lives in a house of three rooms at the mining camp.

According to reports, Hardyman had ordered Dixon to stay away from his home and not to go with any of his daughters, but Dixon willfully disregarded this. Hardyman said that he heard from Zooma's sisters that she had started home with Dixon and then he had taken his shotgun and gone to meet them. The killing followed.

The coroner has ordered all of the witnesses in the case to go before the grand jury at once. The funeral of Walter Dixon will be held this morning from Bessemer. The shooting caused very little disturbance in the neighborhood in which it occurred."

The Birmingham Age-Herald, September 27, 1912

"Assistant Solicitor Hugh Locke...assisted in the investigations of the many cases that were examined by the grand jury. Among the true bills returned were 10 charging murder in the first degree. "No bills" were returned in the case of Robert Hardyman, who shot and killed Walter Dixon last Saturday night near Adger."

Postscript

As noted in the Prologue, the story about the search for the burial location of Joe Calia may be recalled. The Italian immigrant was shot and killed by his father-in-law in Adger in 1916. In newspaper articles of that time, his father-in-law was identified as "Bob Hardyman" and was described as an individual who was "generally not known to be a nice person," and who had been "charged with killing a man three years earlier.

Robert Hardyman was apparently a man who was not to be trifled with, especially as it related to his seven daughters. As with Calia, his propensity for violence was clearly shown with the murder of Walter Dixon. The refusal of the legal "system," to include a grand jury of his peers, to indict Hardyman for committing any crime in either case speaks to the accepted mores of that time, especially as they related to the "protection" of female relatives.

POLICEMAN DYING AND WOMAN DEAD
FOLLOWING AFFRAY
J.A. Moore Still Conscious at St. Vincent's
Little Hope is Entertained For Him
Lucille Spraggins' Body is Being Held by Undertakers
Shooting Affray Occurred at the Woman's Home on the Southside At an Early Hour Friday Morning

The Birmingham News December 5, 1913

"J.A. Moore, a policeman who was shot at the home of Lucille Spraggins, 1527 Avenue H early Friday morning is alive and conscious at St. Vincent's. There is no hope entertained that he will recover according to the hospital authorities. Mr. Moore was shot once through the left chest. The wound cannot prove other than fatal.

Coroner Spain is investigating a rumor that Mr. Moore and Mrs. Spraggins have been intimate for some time and that Mr. Moore was a frequent visitor at her home and that Moore did not go to the house in the discharge of his duty, however, he is inclined to believe the police account. The body of Lucille Spraggins who was killed in the duel is being held by Shaw Undertaking Company pending the success of efforts to locate relatives. Her only known survivor is a daughter Ruth, age 7, who is in the Convent of Mercy at Selma. The girl does not yet know she is motherless.

According to reports at police headquarters, Officers Wilson and Moore were on their regular rounds Friday morning and heard loud talking in the Spraggins home. Moore said he was going in to investigate and asked Wilson to stand at the front door. Wilson heard someone arguing with Moore in the hall and trying to keep him from entering the room. It is believed that Moore answered "It makes no difference, I am going in there,"

The Officer entered the first door to the left where the talking was heard. It is said several persons came out of the room and left the house, Wilson making no effort to stop them. A few seconds later, Wilson heard a shot followed by several others. He went in and found Mrs. Spraggins on the floor alive but unconscious. Moore was lying full length on the floor, a bullet in his heart. Moore gasped, "she shot first", then became unconscious. The woman was unable to speak and an ambulance carried both Mrs. Spraggins and Mr. Moore to the infirmary. Mrs. Spraggins died on the way to the hospital without speaking. Moore repeated statements made of Officer Wilson that she shot first and investigation was made at the Spraggins house on Friday morning by police officials and Spain. Only one of the bedrooms seems to have been occupied. This room is the one used by Mrs. Spraggins and was in wild disorder. Four or five chairs were gathered in the room and evidently some kind of a party had been going on there with empty beer bottles and one half empty and one empty whiskey bottles scattered around the room. Three bullet holes showed in the walls, two of them were near the ceiling and on the South wall and one about four feet from the floor on the West wall.

The guns show that Mrs. Spraggins had fired four shots, all that were in the magazine. The body of Mrs. Spraggins at the undertaker showed she was hit twice, both times in the small of the back. The pistol was evidently fired at close range as there were powder marks from both shots on her skin and both bullets penetrated all the way through the body and came out through the groin.

Coroner Hears Rumors

After his investigation, Coroner Spain said "I can't tell as yet what the facts are at present. I can do nothing more than believe the report of the officers in the statement of Mr. Moore, but there are numerous rumors current which I must run down and investigate before I can give an opinion. I have been told Mr. Moore was a frequent visitor to Miss Spraggins and I don't know whether Mr. Moore went to the house last night in discharge of his duty or not."

The police records say distinctly Mr. Moore visited the house in the discharge of his duty. Mrs. Spraggins was well known to the police. The police allege the present home, as well as former homes of Mrs. Spraggins, was a disorderly house. Mr. Moore, 27 years old, has been on the force for five years. He is well liked by the other members of the force and according to the Chief, he is an efficient and capable officer. His father is a member of the police force also."

Death of Officer Brings Him Into Probe of Killing
Funeral Services Over Body of Moore
to be Held Sunday Morning
No Relatives of Woman Have been Located Yet
Coroner and Police Drop Case
Following Death of J.A. Moore

The Birmingham News, December 6, 1913

"The death of Mr. Moore will stop all official investigations. It is taken for granted by the authorities that the shots were fired by Mr. Moore and Mrs. Spraggins. The coroner spent all Friday investigating the affair. It was developed by him that Mr. Moore was an old friend of Mrs. Spraggins and a frequent visitor at her home. There were several men in the house when the officers arrived, but no attempt was made to stop them as they left before the shooting began.

Coroner Spain said now that the policeman is dead there will be no jury inquest into the killing of Lucille Spraggins. "I spent the day investigating the killing of the Spraggins woman and the facts uncovered are not entirely creditable to the deceased policeman. It is claimed that this woman lived in mortal fear of Officer Moore and had moved her residence several times."

Docket Entry:
I, C.L. Spain, Coroner of Jefferson County certify that on Dec. 4th, 1913 I held a preliminary investigation inquest on the body of Lucille Spraggins, White, with the following result: Deceased came to her death by gunshot wounds at the hands of Officer J.A. Moore, same being unlawfully done against the peace and dignity of the State of Ala.

Docket Entry:
I. C.L. Spain, Coroner of Jefferson County certify that on Dec. 5th, Court House, I held a preliminary investigation inquest on the body of Officer J.A. Moore, White, with the following result: Deceased came to his death by gun shot wounds at the hands of Lucille Spraggins, same being a justifiable homicide.

Postscript

Despite the coroner's official rulings, the questionable circumstances and unanswered questions surrounding the deaths of Spraggins and Officer Moore, his name can be found on the memorial to police officers killed in the line of duty in Jefferson County.

The many foreign immigrants who crowded into the Birmingham area in the early part of the 20th century were mainly drawn from Italian, Greek and Eastern European ethnic groups. Although one may think of the appreciable increase in the local Hispanic population as being a late 20th century phenomenon, the coroner's records are indicative of a small, but active community during these earlier years.

It may be remembered that the underlying motive for the revenge assassination of Father James Coyle in 1921 was related to his performance of a secret marriage ceremony of his killer's daughter to a Puerto Rican man.

The defense of the admitted murderer, a white Baptist minister and member of the Ku Klux Klan, was heavily influenced by the presentation of the dark-skinned son-in-law before the jury where the courtroom lighting was intentionally turned down. Widespread anti-Catholic sentiment during that time only added to the preordained outcome of the trial with its not guilty verdict.

Years later, some then unknowable and unintended consequences for several major and minor players in this affair would take place. These matters are presented and discussed in a following chapter.

MURDER AND SUICIDE IN NORTHERN PART OF COUNTY
Miss Sadie Dean Shot by Alvin Dorman, Who Cuts His Throat Immediately Afterward

The Birmingham Age-Herald, November 17, 1914

"Funeral services were conducted yesterday at the Hopewell Church cemetery, near Bradford mines in the Northern part of the county over the remains of Miss Sadie Dean, aged 19 years, and Alvin Dorman. Both deaths were the result of a tragedy enacted on the county road Sunday afternoon.

According to reports, Alvin Dorman, who it is stated, was unbalanced, met Miss Dean with her father and a younger sister coming from church. Just as her parent was entering the yard of his home Dorman is alleged to have stepped out of a thicket and faced Miss Dean with a double barrel shotgun in his hands. Dorman cooly announced that he was going to kill Miss Dean and despite the despairing entreaties of his victim and the frantic blows of an umbrella from a younger sister, the maniac fired both barrels. Miss Dean fell dead in the road.

Immediately following the shooting Dorman drew a razor from his pocket and slashed violently at his throat. He fell bleeding profusely by the side of his victim and expired in a few minutes. Both young people were members of well known families about Bradford mines."

BESSEMER MAN SHOT TO DEATH
Body Found in Woods At Car
Foul Play Theory Held In Killing of Cut-Off Resident
Four Wounds in Back and Leg Prove Fatal
in Night to L.K. Horton
Car Lights Still On. Is Located Close By
Officers Know of No Motive For Shooting
of Slag Company Worker

The Birmingham News, August 3, 1931

"Shot in the back apparently as he fled from his assailant in a lonely patch of woods near Muscoda, L.K. Horton of Bessemer was fatally wounded Sunday night. His body was found in a clump of brush beside a country road about 100 yards from his parked automobile. County Investigator McCollum said the man had been shot four times. Two bullets entered his right leg and two entered his back."

Office of Coroner
Jefferson County

Official Post Mortem Of: L.K. Horton
Col. White. Sex: Male
Held At: Brown's Morgue
Year: 1931. Month: 8 Day: 3 Hour: 11 A.M.
Post Mortem Findings: Gun shot wounds of left shoulder, left leg in thigh and calf and left groin.

County Commission Agent's
Investigation into the Death of L.K. Horton

This investigation came to be heard before T.J. McCollum, County Commission Agent on Aug. 3-5, 1931 at the Courthouse at Bessemer, Alabama.
Present at Investigation:
T.J. McCollum, County Agent
Arthur Green, Asst. Deputy Solicitor
William Kemp, Special Investigator
W.K. Schanz, Court Reporter

G. M. CULPEPPER
Examined by Mr. Green:
Q. Mr. Culpepper, you know we are investigating this killing; we want to see what you know about it.
A. Not a thing in the world.
Q. Do you want to tell us the truth about it?
A. Yes, sir; I want to tell the truth about it.
Q. Did you know Mr. Horton?
A. I met the man one time.
Q. Did you know Mrs. Horton?
A. No, sir.
Q. Have you ever been to their home?
A. No, sir.
Q. Do you know where she lives?
A. No, sir.

Q. Tell us the truth about this now. Have you ever been intimate with Mrs. Horton?
A. No, sir.
Q. Did you ever call on her?
A. No, sir.
Q. Ever speak to her about seeing her?
A. No, sir.
Q. You wouldn't even know her to see her?
A. No, sir; that is right.
Q. And the occasion of you meeting with Horton was that he came around to your place of business?
A. Yes, sir.
Q. What was the occasion of his coming around?
A. He came around; he said someone was at his house, he thought it was me.
Q. What did he say?
A. He asked if I was at his house; I told him I wasn't.
Q. What conversation did you have with him?
A. He said somebody was there and he heard it was me. I told him, well, he was mistaken, I didn't do such stuff as that at all; I didn't even know nobody by that name.
Q. You never have taken his wife out?
A. No, sir.
Q. Or never have been with her in any way?
A. No, sir.

ADA BELL GOLSTON c.
Examined by Mr. Kemp:
Q. Where do you work?
A. I work for Mrs. Cora Horton.
Q. Do you know Mr. Culpepper?
A. Well, I saw him about three or four times, but what his name, I don't know.
Q. Did he get out of the car and go into the house?
A. He was in the house, yes, sir.
Q. Was you present here about two months ago when Mr. Culpepper come there and come into the house, and a few minutes later Mr. Horton come up?
A. Yes, sir.
Q. Just what happened when he come up there, when Mr. Horton come up?

A. Well, it looked like he was going to get into something or other, start fussing and fighting, and I run upstairs, and he run Mr. Culpepper out.
Q. Did you see a pistol on Mr. Culpepper that day?
A. I sure did.
Q. Well, now, about two months ago did Mrs. Horton go off for three or four days?
A. She said she was going to see her sister, but she told me she went to Montgomery.
Q. Who did she say she was with?
A. Mr. Culpepper.
Q. Wait a minute. Has she ever been away a day and a night at a time since then?
A. Yes, sir; she went to Birmingham and stayed one night; she told me; I am gwine by what she said.
Q. Did she say she stayed with Mr. Culpepper?
A. Yes, sir.
Q. That has been going on practically the year you have been working there?
A. Yes, sir; during some of it, not all.
Q. Has she ever told you not to mention Mr. Culpepper to her husband?
A. Yes, sir; she sure did.
Q. Has she ever told you since her husband has been killed not to say anything to the officers?
A. No, sir; she ain't told me nothing about that. I don't reckon she thought nothing like that was going to happen.

Examined By Mr. Green:
Q. Did Mrs. Horton ever tell you anything about going with him, or what she wanted you to keep your mouth shut for?
A. Yes, sir.
Q. What did she tell you?
A. She said Now, Ada don't never say nothing about this, because you get your own self messed up.
Q. How do you know she ever went with him?
A. Because she would tell me when she got back home.
Q. How did they pay you?
A. The paid me $1.50 a week.
Q. Have you ever heard Mrs. Horton say anything about killing her husband for the insurance?
A. I have never heard of that, but they kept at it about the insurance paper.

Q. What did Mrs. Horton tell you about coming up here?
A. She told me that I could come up here and tell anything he would kill me.
Q. Is that what she told you?
A. Yes, sir. She always said you don't know nothing on me but hear me talking these things; you go up there and tell anything on me Mr. Culpepper will kill you. I want to get out. Will you please let me out; I don't want to talk no more.

MRS. CORA HORTON

This witness was brought up to the Solicitor's office after G.M. Culpepper had killed himself in the inner office of the Solicitor, and was left in the outer office until the inner office was cleared of all people except Mr. Green, Deputy Solicitor, Mr. T.J. McCollum, County Agent, Mr. W.T. Kemp, Special Investigator and Wm. K. Schanz, Court Reporter, and the dead body of G.M. Culpepper laying on the floor. Upon the witness being brought into the room, she refused to look upon the body, and asked that she be taken from the room thence would tell all. She was taken to the Court Reporter's office, across the hall, and…the following evidence was given:
Examined by Mr. Green:
Q. You realize that someone killed your husband. You want to make a statement about it, as I understand you to say. Tell us in your own words what you know about it, Mrs. Horton. As I understand, you and your husband had some trouble; he had been drinking a lot of liquor; he has not treated you well; is that it?
A. No sir, I wouldn't say that, but he drank a lot of whiskey.
Q. Tell us what started you with Culpepper, your affair?
A. I guess it has been about a year ago.
Q. When did you all plan to kill your husband?
A. I hadn't planned to kill him; he done it himself.
Q. Mr. Culpepper did?
A. I didn't plan it at all.
Q. What did he tell you about killing your husband?
A. I don't know how he was going to kill him; he said he was going to kill him.
Q. Tell us the truth about it now, as we are investigating it; we want to get the whole thing
A. Oh, well, he has been trying to do this; he has tried to poison him in every way that he could thought of; he has been planning this.
Q. When did he first talk to you about poisoning your husband; how long ago?
A. Five or six weeks.

Q. Lets get back to the murder; when did he tell you this time he was going to kill him before he was killed?
A. I think it was Friday.
Q. What did you say?
A. I told him he was going to get himself in trouble, and me too.
Q. You are not now telling us the truth. He made a statement there before he died involving you in it. Telling us you and him had made some kind of plans and what those plans were.
A. There wasn't any plans made. I am telling you the truth from my heart.
Q. What was the occasion of you telling this maid not to say anything about it?
A. I didn't tell her nothing of the kind.
Q. You didn't tell her not to say anything about your affair to anybody in the Solicitor's office?
A. No, sir. I didn't tell her anything of the kind.
Q. Did he tell you that he was going to kill your husband?
A. He said he was planning to; he had been trying to do it.
Q. How did he tell you he was going to do it this time?
A. He said he would hit him with an iron bar.
Q. Hit with him with an iron bar?
A. Yes, sir. He didn't say nothing about no shooting.
Q. Now, listen; you discussed your insurance policy with Culpepper.
A. I never did say what amount it was. Culpepper heard my husband say that he had ten thousand dollars. It was a sad mistake.
Q. Didn't you all discuss this, what would become of the insurance in case your husband was killed?
A. Who would get it?
Q. Yes.
A. He knowed it was made to me.
Q. Wasn't it then that you and Culpepper plotted and planned the death of your husband, that Culpepper was going to have him put away?
A. Have him put away?
Q. Yes; have him killed?
A. No.
Q. What did Culpepper tell you that he was going to kill him, how?
A. Culpepper has tried every way to kill him; I didn't want him to do it.
Q. How many times had he told you, on how many different occasions did he tell you that he was planning the death of your husband?
A. I don't know.

Q. Give us an idea?
A. I couldn't tell you.
Q. Was it ten time?
A. Ten times, about.
Q. Now, listen, he planned to poison him, didn't he, on one occasion?
A. That is what he told me.
Q. And he planned to knock him on the head with an iron bar?
A. Yes, sir; that is what he said.
Q. What other means did he tell you he was going to kill him?
A. That is all I know. Poison, and the bar. I never hear him say he would us a gun.
Q. Did he tell you why he hadn't killed your husband?
A. I don't know that he did say why; he didn't have no chance.

By Mr. McCollum:
Q. When was the next time that Culpepper told you about the poison plan not working and he not drinking that whiskey?
A. He said he thought what was in it would kill him.
Q. When was the last time he told you about killing him with the iron bar?
A. He always said he never expected to shoot him
Q. How did he tell you Friday?
A. He said he would meet him in the road and just knock his brains out.
Q. There on the public street?
A. I reckon so.
Q. You know that Culpepper was planning to kill him; you knew the next morning; You knew it when you heard your husband being killed, that Culpepper did it?
A. Well, I don't know.
Q Your own children accuse you of helping kill your husband; Your son told you that you helped kill his father?
A. Well, I don't know.
Q. Then I understand you to say that you claim that you didn't help kill your husband that night; getting down to the main facts of the case; you didn't take part in the killing; you didn't care whether he was killed or not, but you didn't plan it yourself; is that what you say?
A. No, sir.
Q. But you didn't care whether Culpepper killed him or not?
A. Well, I didn't want him to.
Q. You never told your husband to watch out for Culpepper; you never warned him to be on his guard, and never told your husband?

A. I told my husband that Culpepper threatened to kill him; he knew that.
Q. You had been intimate with Culpepper for how long; how long have you had these affairs with him; since when?
A. Oh, I don't know; about a year, I guess.
Q. And about how often would it be; once or twice a week?
A. Oh, no.
Q. Once a week?
A. I would see him sometimes.
Q. You know what has happened. There are two men killed, and you are the cause of it, absolutely the cause of it. Your three sons know all about it; they are the ones that has furnished me the information that I have worked the case up on. If I were you I would get my conscience clear; I would clear myself.
A. I told you everything I knew.
Q. I have seen a whole lot of cases like this; I have never seen one that anybody could go along until they told the truth.
A. I have told you what I know about it.
Q. No, you haven't.
A. What else is there to tell? I knew that he was planning to do this.
Q. You knew when your husband was found over there shot and killed, you knew who done it; back down in your heart you knew exactly who done it?
A. Well, I don't know whether he done it or the other man; I don't know it now.
Q. You knew who was responsible for it?
A. Him or the other man did it.
Q. Well, if the other man did it, he done it on the suggestion of Mr. Culpepper, and you knew that. You knew it was going to happen; you knew your husband laid out there Saturday night.
A. Well, I didn't; I sure didn't.
Q. I understood you said that the man that went to work with Mr. Culpepper is the man that told you that he said he was going to get to help him kill your husband. Did he tell you that?
A. He said he was going to get him to get him out; I don't know whether he said he was trying to kill him.
Q. Now, Mrs. Horton, listen; how much money, what did Culpepper tell you as to what he was going to give Blansett to help him kill him?
A. He never mentioned anything like that to me.
Q. Blansett is the man that shot Horton?
A. He is?

Q. Yes. He was shot with that .38. We have the .38 pistol now. Can you tell us what you knew of the arrangements Culpepper had with Blansett?
A. I sure cant; He never would talk about that man.
Q. Listen to me right good. You are not treating yourself right. Are you listening to me? I kind of feel that you were led into this, and I am very anxious to do all I can to get Blansett. The two men that were most guilty is Culpepper and Blansett, and Blansett was the man with Culpepper when this man was shot, and he helped shoot him.

At this point, Blansett was brought into the room.
HIRAM BLANSETT
Examined by Mr. Green:
Q. Sit down here, Blansett. You still say you never had a .38?
A. Never had.
Q. You never saw the pistol that Mr. Kemp has in his hand?
A. No, sir.
Q. Isn't it a fact that one of the reasons he (Culpepper) got you the job was to help kill this woman's husband?
A. I don't know nothing about that.
Q. Did he ever talk to you about the insurance her husband carried on his life?
A. No, sir.
Q. Blansett, I want to tell you just what I believe. We are very sympathetic with a man charged with a crime; we have a right to be fair with him. We have got you hooked dead to right; ain't any question about it. We know Culpepper got you in it. He got you into this just like he got Mrs. Horton. He got to frigging this woman and you were hard up, out of a job, needed money. If you believe us and will tell the truth about it, it will go a long way to help you out. I was sorry to see Culpepper take the stand as he did. I was going to help him. Unless you tell the truth, you are going to the electric chair as sure as your name is Blansett.
A. I will just have to go; I don't know anything about it.
Q. It don't make any difference to me. I am trying to be fair with you. Now listen to me. You have got a lot of sense. Now, listen: Culpepper told Mrs. Horton that he finally got a man that was going to help him pull the job. Culpepper told her how he tried to poison him and how he tried to break his neck with an iron bar. He told her on Friday that you were the man he was going to get to do it, and Mrs. Horton told it. Now, listen, you can't get by with it. Now, listen: this man was shot with a .38; we got the bullets you had; Culpepper told us here before

he died just exactly how the thing occurred. Now, those are the facts, and how are you going to get around them?

A. I don't know nothing about it.

Q. What I am telling you and what I am telling Mrs. Horton, Culpepper is the man that got you to do it. We want to know the reason why you did it. We want to do all we can to help you if we can. We want to keep you from the electric chair. As far as I am concerned I don't car whether you did it or didn't; it doesn't make any difference. I am not hard boiled; we have got sympathy for a human being. It don't do us one bit of good to see you put in the electric chair. We have never electrocuted a man yet; we don't believe in it. Nine times out of ten they come clean and then we recommend them to the mercy of the Court. All we want is the truth.

A. I have told you the truth; I don't know anything.

Q. That is exactly the position that Culpepper took. He got this woman in it; into this trouble, and he has got you into this trouble, you would never have known Horton but for him, or known anything about it.

A. I don't know nothing yet.

By Mr. Kemp:

Q. I say, you didn't have any more to do with the killing out here last Sunday night of Mr. Horton than you had something to do with this pistol I just showed you a while ago?

A. I have not seen either one of them.

Q. You know just as much about this .38 pistol as you do about the killing out there?

A. Yes, sir.

By Mr. Green:

Q. I feel sorry for you, Blansett. I mean it. I am not lying to you a bit. I am not trying to catch you or trying to fool you, or anything like that. You got my sympathy. You got the same sympathy I had for Culpepper. I don't know what made Culpepper do it; I can't imagine a man having that diseased mind except probably his lust for intercourse. I told Mrs. Horton to defend herself in the paper, and let the paper know just what led on to it. I want to get your reaction; I just want to see what led you into it.

A. I don't know nothing about it.

Q. None of the officers have whipped you, or anything like that?

A. When?

Q. Since you were in jail?

A. No, sir.

Q. I mean, nobody has been rough to you?

A. No, sir.
Q. Did you send any word to any lawyers?
A. No, sir.
End of abridged interrogation notes.2

BLANSETT ACQUITTED
The Birmingham News, October 29, 1931

"Hiram Blansett was acquitted of the murder of L.K. Horton in the verdict of a Bessemer jury. The State attempted to prove his death was the result of a conspiracy. Several witnesses corroborated Blansett's testimony that on the night of the slaying he attended church and then went home."

Postscript

There was no information found to indicate that an attempt to prosecute Cora Horton for conspiracy in the death of her husband was ever considered by the authorities. The acquittal of Hiram Blansett, along with the suicide of G.M. Culpepper, would have made it essentially impossible for prosecutors to pursue such charges against her. Culpepper likely knew he would be arrested, tried, likely convicted and possibly executed for his involvement in the premeditated murder of Horton, whether or not he or Blansett actually pulled the trigger.

Blansett Rites Set
Body of Bessemer Man Sent To Purvis, Miss.
The Birmingham Age-Herald, June 10, 1936

"Funeral services for Hiram Blansett, 34, who died at his home Monday night after a few hours illness, will be held in Purvis, Miss. He is survived by his widow, father and other relatives."

CHAPTER 4

RACE

*"Southern trees bear a strange fruit,
Blood on the leaves and blood at the root.
Black body swinging in the Southern breeze,
Strange fruit hanging from the poplar trees."*

---*Strange Fruit*
Abel Meeropol

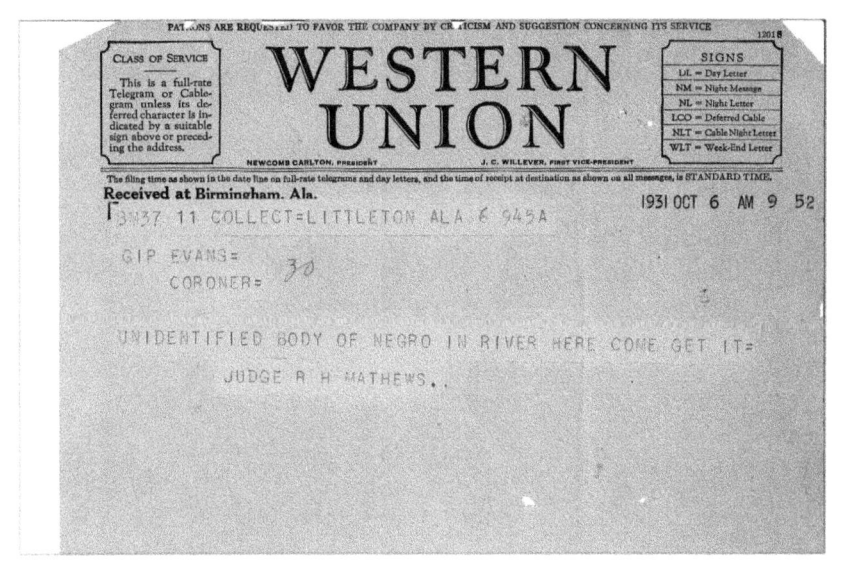

COMMISSION OF JEFFERSON COUNTY

W. D. BISHOP, PRESIDENT
W. E. CORNING   J. B. VINES

BESSEMER, ALABAMA

OFFICE OF
T. J. McCOLLUM, AGENT

October 11, 1931.

Mr. Cip M. Evans,
County Commission Agent,
Birmingham, Alabama.

Dear Sir:

In regard to the body of negro found in river near Littleton, Alabama, on the 6th day of October, 1931.

I answered call and investigated with the following results:

Gunshot wound of chest on left side, just below heart; body securely tied with barbed wire and fifty pound knuckle iron attached with wire and sunk in river; body nude.

I judge body had been in river between ten to fifteen days. Body was swollen and bloated beyond recognition.

Removed body from river with aid of some negroes and thought best to bury there as body would not go in pauper box. It was too large and so decomposed would not permit of moving.

Had negro by name of John Sanders dig grave in Banner Cemetery, which is just a short way from where the body was found.

Came to Pinkney City and had Bell Undertaking Co. furnish outside box and enter same in Banner Cemetery.

Expense on this investigation was as follows:

Opening Grave		$5.00
Outside box		6.50
Truck		5.00
	Total	16.50.

Hoping this meets with your approval, I beg to remain,

Yours very truly,

County Commission Agent.

tjm-s

It is not my intent to present an in-depth review of the well known, specific and abundant information regarding race relations during the early 20th century in this country, the deep South or within Alabama. This material has already been published in innumerable academic studies, news articles and books over many years. Rather, it is an attempt to examine this era in Jefferson County and Birmingham as seen through the available coroner's records and local newspaper accounts of that time.

Not without reason did the Magic City also become known as the most racially segregated city in the United States and to receive the sobriquet "Johannesburg of America." During the first quarter of the 20th century, both major Birmingham newspapers routinely published articles drawn from other news sources around the country in which there were recounted numerous instances of the mob lynchings of blacks, often purportedly following alleged acts against white individuals which were perceived to be either criminal in nature or just being socially incorrect as in speaking disrespectfully to a white person, especially a female. Although a large number of these incidents did occur within what can be defined as the "Deep South', i.e., in those States which had seceded from the Union during the Civil War, they were certainly not confined to that region. Numerous such incidents happened in many Northern, mid-Western and South-Western locations, with one of the most egregious large scale mob actions taking place in Tulsa, Oklahoma in 1921. News articles, which often included gruesome details, were reproduced from their original sources. Although there did not appear to be local editorial support for these actions, neither was there any indication of moral indignation or denouncement of such occurrences. It almost seems as if the regular printing of such stories, usually on the front page of the local newspapers, was purposely done as if to send a public message regarding the racial "rules" of that time as well as to what the potential outcome of such digressions might be.

As noted by Leon Litwack in his book "Trouble In Mind--Black Southerners In The Age Of Jim Crow," "a white churchman in Birmingham observed in 1905: "I have beheld the spirit of intolerance, of race contempt and race hatred growing, and it is emphatically more vigorous and venomous than it was half a decade ago." Edward L. Ayers in his book "Vengeance and Justice--Crime and Punishment in the 19th Century American South" added that: "Given an opportunity to act brutally, the sad fact seems to be that at least some people will." Legal officials, newspapers, and public opinion within the postwar South gave that sanction, both tacitly and explicitly, and white men took advantage of the opening. As E.L. Godkin of The Nation wrote in 1893, "man is the one animal that is capable of getting enjoyment out of the torture and death of members of its own species. We venture to assert that seven-eighths of every lynching party is composed of pure, sporting mob, which goes nigger-hunting, just as it goes to a cockfight or a prize-fight, for the gratification of the lowest and most degraded instincts of humanity...They do not care a straw about seeing justice--even wild justice--done on a malefactor."

During the course of research for this book, to include the review of thousands of the Jefferson County coroner's records and microfilmed newspapers, evidence of a number of cases of overt public mob lynchings in the Jefferson County area were found, several of which are presented in this chapter. Surprisingly, one highly publicized act was not committed by a mob of native white supremacists, but by a group comprised of more recently arrived and marginalized immigrants. Records and reports of other likely racially motivated homicides were discovered, one example of which is evidenced by the unpublicized and unsolved murder and attempt at disposal of an individual's remains as depicted in the telegram and letter which are reproduced at the beginning of this chapter.

It has been noted that more lynchings took place in Jefferson County than in any other county in Alabama from the post civil war period to the 1930s. Although many of these incidents had distinct racial motivations, a number of the cases which took place during the early 1900s were more directly related to the ongoing issues associated with union organizing in the industrial workplace and especially within the coal mines. As will be presented in the chapters titled Work, Mines and Prison, it is difficult to specifically separate the human interactions which took place and which intersected in many large and small ways during this time period. These not only included the workers themselves, but also involved the industrialists, law enforcement, military personnel and violent strikebreakers.

NEWS OF LYNCHING SHOCKS BESSEMER
Coroner's Jury Will Make Investigation Tomorrow
NEGRO'S BODY IN CREEK

The Birmingham Age-Herald, April 27, 1909

"The news of this morning that a lynching had taken place near the corporate limits of Bessemer was startling to the people of this city, as few knew of any crime having been committed in this part of the county. At an early hour this morning Coroner W.L. Brasher, accompanied by deputy sheriffs, undertakers, newspaper men and others, left for the scene of the lynching, and while no one knew just where the negro had been taken from the deputized officer, they had an idea that it was on the Parkwood road. After considerable searching for a lifeless body hanging to a tree, a newspaper man saw a white cloth on a twig, way down in the woods and a moment later the body of the negro was found in a small branch, the water running over it.

Lying flat on his back, with hands tied in front he had been shot to death, and not hanged as first reported. The body was riddled with bullets, head, limbs and body being shot to pieces, while scattered in every direction were the empty shells that told how John Thomas had met his death. After viewing the body the coroner ordered it placed in a wagon and taken to Bessemer, where it was viewed by hundreds of those curious to see how he met his death. Thomas seemed to be a negro of about 22 or 23 years of age, with a mean, vicious countenance and roughly clad.

Later in the day Andrew Roy, who had the negro when he was met by the mob gave a detailed account of the crime, the confession of the negro, the start to Bessemer, the stopping at Roy's home to get supper, the journey resumed and the dark road, to the place where 50 men, masked and stern, demanded that Roy surrender the negro. The horrible details were revolting in the extreme, and a wave of horror and sympathy ran through the veins when the brutal act was told.

The negro's confession that he committed the crime, that he was a convict for years for the same offense, that he had killed his man and shot at others, and the glee with which he told of his crimes all went to enrage the men who witnessed and heard what had been done. After a short trial, the issuance of the warrant and the departure of the deputy with the negro so worked upon the minds of the men about the camp that it was but a little step to the point where the populace decided to take the law into their own hands.

The general feeling here is that the report that the lynching took place at Bessemer is not fair to the good name of the city, for the original crime was committed 12 miles from Bessemer, and the shooting of the negro took place several miles from the city, not a citizen of the city knowing anything of the occurrence until hours after it was committed. The men were largely Shelby county men for the place where the crime was committed was just on the line. The coroner's jury will be impaneled and an effort be made to locate those who shot the negro to death, although there is little hope of this being done."

Any thoughts that may have been held during this time period as to perceived threats of mayhem and murder which might be visited upon the "peaceful" white citizens of the community by black criminals can be tempered by a review of actual homicide statistics based on racial makeup. This analysis was aided by the consistent documentation of the race of both perpetrators and victims in the coroner's records, a practice which continued into the 1960's.

By the parenthetical use of the letters "c" or "col" for blacks and "w" for whites following the names of the principals involved in each incident, it is possible to obtain a highly specific tally of the race of both victims and perpetrators in the majority of homicides, as well as for other types of deaths, with the exception of those cases where a perpetrator was not initially identified. This attention to a detail of apparent import to the white officials and southern society at that time can be likened to the similar attention paid to the specific documentation and categorization of certain citizens by religion, race and sexual orientation as practiced during the German Third Reich.

As noted by Roger Lane in his book titled "Roots Of Violence In Black Philadelphia 1860--1900," "In some cases there were clear unwritten rules that governed relations between the races. Undertakers, for example, with virtually no exceptions, dealt with the bodies of their own." Such racial separation in death is still found today as it is, for the most part, in our churches.

As indicated in a previous chapter, although relatively rare, there were occasions where the coroner rendered a verdict of non-justifiable homicide in cases where the victims were black and the perpetrators were known to be white.

Docket Entry:
I, J,R.T. Rives, Assistant Coroner, certify that on December 4th, 1917, I held a preliminary investigation inquest on the body of Dewitt Fletcher, Col., with the following result. I was called to Republic Road, near Artesian Wells, #7 Mines, and it was found he came to his death from a pistol shot wound of the back of the head, the same being an unlawful homicide and against the peace and dignity of The State of Alabama, at the hands of two white men.

The following is an example of an annual breakdown of homicides by race of perpetrators and victims. Yearly rates and ratios of this type remained remarkably consistent over a number of decades during the first half of the 20th century with increases in total numbers being reflective of population growth. The relatively high ratio of homicides occurring in areas of Jefferson County outside the Birmingham city limits is also reflective of the demographics of that time. Comparison of these ratios to those of the latter half of the 20th century reveals greatly reduced homicide rates outside of Birmingham due to the steadily decreasing mining and industrial activities within the western portion of the county following World War II with the annual number of homicides occurring in suburban Jefferson County in recent years having often been reported in the high single digits.

1911
Homicide Data By Race

Total Homicides in Jefferson County: 156
Perpetrator/Victim
Black/Black: 79
White/White: 24
Black/White: 1
White/Black: 26
Unknown/White: 6
Unknown/Black: 20

Place of Occurrence:
Birmingham City Limits: 86
Other Jefferson County: 70

During the early years of the 20th century, and coinciding with the influx of large numbers of foreign immigrants into the area who were searching for work in the mines, foundries and as service providers, there was a distinct attempt to separately categorize the newcomers from the native white population, even in death. Despite genetic racial classification and appearance as Caucasian, those individuals of non-Northern European descent were often differentiated in the official records by their place or country of origin. This practice appears to have ended in the early 1920's when the last such entries were found.

Docket Entry:
I, B.L. Brasher, Coroner of Jefferson County, certify that on Mar. 13, 1910, Bessemer, Ala., I held a preliminary Coroner inquest on the body of Harry Barto, Italian, with the following result: I found the deceased came to his death by gunshot wound of the left side, at the hands of D.E. Antonia, same being unlawfully done and against the peace and dignity of the State of Alabama.

Docket Entry:
Date: December 3, 1911
Deceased: Frank DeMarco, Italian
Defendant: Walter Chambers, White
Cause of Death: Gunshot wounds, same being Manslaughter.

Docket Entry:
Date: July 11, 1912
Deceased: George Argeros, Greek
Defendant: H.D. Perkins, White
Cause of Death: Gunshot wounds

Docket Entry:
Date: July 2, 1911
Deceased: Annie Pastor, Slavish
Address: Brookside
Cause of Death: By taking poison, Same being suicide intent.

CAPT. B.H. YOUNG VICTIM OF DRUNK NEGRO'S PISTOL
Two Bullets Fired Into One of the Most Popular Officers in the County
A Reward of One Hundred Dollars Is Offered By the Sheriff for Capture of Fred Spencer, Negro Who Did The Shooting

The Birmingham Age-Herald, April 28, 1910

"Bessemer, April 27,--(Special.)--As a result of a cold-blooded, murderous assault by a drunken negro at Dolomite this afternoon, Capt. B.H. Young of Bessemer, one of the most popular deputies in the sheriff's department, is at the point of death, his entire body paralyzed from a bullet wound in the neck and another one just under the nose. The shooting happened shortly before 5 o'clock and was sudden and cruel. The negro, Fred Spencer, had been drinking during the day and had frightened the people about Dolomite. He shot a negro woman three times, but it is not thought any of her wounds will prove fatal.

In the meantime a request had been made upon the sheriff's office for someone to come out and arrest the negro. Capt. Young was serving papers in Dolomite and was on his way to the negro quarters when he came face to face with Spencer. Captain Young had known nothing of the trouble which Spencer had been creating during the day and had no idea when he was walking toward the negro that murder was lurking in his mind. As he reached the negro the latter said, "Well, I guess you've come to get me," and suddenly drawing a pistol fired twice in rapid succession. Captain Young dropped to the ground unconscious while the negro made his escape. The scene of the shooting was immediately behind the Parson's pool room at Dolomite.

A posse of deputies was rushed to the scene from Birmingham in an automobile. Bloodhounds were taken from Bessemer to Dolomite and the trail taken. It was followed for about two miles when it was lost in a macadamized road. The supposition is that the negro boarded a wagon here and travelled for a little distance. All of the afternoon and until late in the night a large posse scoured the woods around Dolomite in search of the negro without success.

Captain Young has long been regarded as one of the best men of the sheriff's department. He was widely known, especially around Bessemer, and has a long line of intimate friends who are greatly wrought up over the affair. Should the negro be captured by his friends short work will probably be made of him. Description of the negro is that of one of dark ginger color, weight about 140 pounds, age 23, right hand crippled. He wore a wide brimmed, black Stetson hat and a new yellow shirt, which he had bought only a few minutes before the shooting. He did not wear a coat. Dr. E.W. Gwin waited upon Captain Young and did everything possible to relieve him. Later in the afternoon he was removed to Bessemer, where it was stated that his condition was extremely low. This is the first serious shooting affray in which a member of the sheriff's department has been wounded during Higdon's term as sheriff.

Up to an early hour this morning Spencer was still at large. He is thought to be hiding somewhere in the woods about Wilkes, between Dolomite and Ensley. A posse of citizens and deputy sheriffs are on his trail red hot with a pack of bloodhounds and his capture is hourly expected. It is feared that the infuriated posse of citizens will lynch the negro if he is found.The killing of Captain Young has aroused much feeling and the life of Spencer is not only in danger but there is said to be a probability of a race war in the community where the killing occurred. Captain Young was still living at an early hour this morning but he is not expected to recover."

CAPT. YOUNG DIES IN AWFUL AGONY
Wound Causes the Veteran to Choke to Death
HAD ROMANTIC CAREER
The Birmingham Age-Herald, April 30, 1910

"Capt. B.H. Young died tonight after hours of intense suffering. He took a sudden turn for the worse this afternoon and slowly choked to death. He had several internal hemorrhages and the blood, collecting in his throat, cut off his breath, and he died in intense agony. Three of Mr. Young's daughters and his son were at his bedside when death came, and a heartrending scene took place as the children watched the father suffocate.

Captain Young has had a most romantic career. At an early age Mr. Young enlisted in the Confederate army and served throughout the war with distinction, being present in most of the battles in Alabama. When the war was over he returned to his home and was instrumental in removing carpetbag rule from his county and Alabama. He was a member of the famous Ku Klux Klan and at one time had 46 indictments against him for his work. For the past four years he has been employed in the sheriff's office and many of the deputies feel a personal loss in his death.

All Bessemer is grief stricken at the death of Captain Young and prominent men have taken pains to show their regret and sympathy to the family. Affairs will be practically suspended during the funeral tomorrow which is expected to be one of the largest ever seen in Bessemer. Nothing has been heard of Spencer, his murderer, although posses are yet searching for him. The entire force at Bessemer has been working on the case since the shooting and is confident that the negro will be found."

YOUNG'S FUNERAL LARGELY ATTENDED
Was Among Bessemer's Most Popular Men
The Birmingham Age-Herald, May 1, 1910

"The funeral of Capt. B.H. Young took place this afternoon. The funeral was a large one and was attended by many out-of-town people. Colonel Higdon was present with five of his deputies. George W. Jones and his deputies were there and practically all of the officials of Bessemer. Confederate veterans acted as pallbearers. It is peculiar that after having been shot many times in battle Captain Young should at last succumb to a bullet."

TWO STORIES TOLD OF NEGRO'S DEATH
Coroner Thinks Lynching Occurred Near Dolomite
BODY FULL OF BULLETS
Wylam Police, However, Believe Man Was Called From His House and Murdered By Negroes— Investigation To Be Made

The Birmingham Age-Herald, May 3, 1910

"Early yesterday morning, between midnight and 6 a.m., a negro named Jim Hatter was mysteriously shot and killed near the side of the road between Wylam and Dolomite. The authorities appear to be divided as to their theories regarding the case, the Ensley and Wylam police holding to the belief that robbery was the motive, while from the facts which Coroner B.L. Brasher has been able to gather the county official is lead to believe that in the death of the negro there is a case of lynching. The two stories are so widely different that one would be inclined to scout the idea that they have to do with the same killing and apparently an official investigation, alone, will clear up the case.

Coroner Brasher returned late last night from the community where the crime occurred and circumstances which he gathered lead to the lynching theory. The coroner declares that information which he gathered to the effect that sometime after midnight Monday morning a crowd of men went to Hatter's home and tried to make the negro come out of his house. It seems the negro declined to obey the order, according to the coroner's story, and it is declared by witnesses that the crowd of men entered Hatter's home and dragged him out of bed. Taking him forcibly from his room, it is stated that they led him down the road some distance and murdered him, fairly riddling the body with bullets. The coroner states there are fully 25 bullet holes in the negro's corpse. The statement by Hatter's wife is that she could not tell whether the men who came to the house were white men or negroes. When Hatter's body was found it bore no clothing except an undershirt.

As to the circumstances which led up to the supposed lynching, the coroner states that the story furnished him is that Hatter had been hiding Bert Spencer, the negro who stands charged with the murder of Deputy Sheriff Young a few days ago. It is said that Hatter had been carrying food to Spencer and that when asked about it he declared that he was carrying it to one of his friends in the mine. However, the story goes that an investigation was made and the "friend" denied that Hatter had brought him any food. These facts lead to the belief that the crowd of men went to Hatter's home with a view of forcing him to tell where Spencer was hiding, and Coroner Brasher states that he supposes from the facts as stated to him, that Hatter refused to give the midnight visitors any information, wherewith they took him out and dealt summarily with him. The wife of Hatter appears to know little or nothing about the affair, or if she does she is not disposed to tell it. Her only statement regarding the supposed posse, is that she "believes" the men who came after Hatter were not negroes.

The theory to which the Wylam police cling is that Hatter was shot and killed by negroes and that robbery was the motive. Regarding the killing it seems that the police have evidence that Hatter was called out of his house shortly after midnight and that he was not forcibly taken away. They seem to believe that Hatter went off with the negroes willingly. It will thus be seen that the stories vary widely and apparently there are two sets of negroes dealing out different versions. The coroner states that he will conduct an official investigation of the killing at the Ensley hall Friday morning."

Postscript

The killer of Captain B.H. Young was apparently never apprehended and likely escaped from this area. Additional newspaper accounts from this time period relating to this case were not found, nor is there an entry noting the legal execution of an individual by the name of Spencer. Results of the inquest into the death of Jim Hatter were not found and there is no evidence that anyone was arrested for that crime. The attention of Coroner Brasher and the news media to these matters may have been diverted due to the major mine disaster at Palos which killed over 60 men in early May, 1910. The name of Deputy B.H. Young is not included on the Jefferson County Peace Officer's memorial.

FRENZIED ITALIANS LYNCH NEGRO ON PROMINENT BESSEMER STREET
Angry Men Were in Funeral Procession
of Negro's Victim
Body Is Riddled By Numerous Shots
The Negro Was Handcuffed and in Charge of Officers
When the Funeral Procession Came Down the Street
The Birmingham Age-Herald, January 29, 1912

"Friends of Joseph Gagliano, a prominent Italian who was foully murdered Friday night, frenzied at the sight of the handcuffed negro suspected of having committed the crime, leaped from the ranks of the funeral procession this afternoon and shot John Chandler to death. The negro fell with his weight to the ground, and while Deputy Parker was endeavoring to prevent the rescue of the man believed to have killed his prisoner, other Italians fired a score of shots into the negro's prostrate body. With gore dripping from 20 wounds, the corpse was carried to and undertaking establishment.

It was the most sensational occurrence in the history of this city. For half an hour the most prominent corner of Bessemer was the scene of wildest excitement. Women shrieked shrilly in a strange tongue. From every section citizens aroused by the sound of shot, came running. Under the feet of the veritable mob, its blood dyeing crimson on the pavement, was the body of Chandler about whose wrists the law had clamped its chain. In prominent view all the while was the coffin containing the remains of the dead Italian of its vengeance for whose death the law had just been deprived. When peace was restored, the funeral procession moved onward. With their own peculiar rites, the Italians deposited in the earth the ashes of Gagliano.

During the morning Coroner Brasher investigated the death of Gagliano, and the three negroes held for the crime. John Chandler, Forney Smith and Charles Paige were ordered to the county jail. Deputy Parker, in charge of Chandler, and Deputy Herron, in charge of Smith and Paige, were awaiting the arrival of a car. As the car reached the scene of the funeral procession, the deputies, with their prisoners, broke through the procession for the purpose of gaining the car before its departure. "We had stepped from the curbstone," states Deputy Parker, "when four shots in rapid succession rang out sharply. Chandler pitched to the ground a dead man. Reaching to the rear, I clasped my arm about the waist of the man who had fired the shots into the negro's back, and with my free hand took charge of his gun. Just at that moment I found myself in the clutch of half a dozen men, each of whom was endeavoring to release my prisoner. Other officers came running to my assistance, and I was able to hold my man. He was Louis Gagliano, the brother of Joseph Gagliano, whose funeral the Italians were preparing to attend. A moment later peace was apparently restored. But as the Italians backed from me they came upon the body of Chandler. Instantly frenzied cries again rendered the air, and a score of pistol shots rang out."

Throughout Bessemer excitement reigned for hours. Practically the entire male population was on the scene of the crime. A string of curious filed through the doorway of Jacob's undertaking establishment. A thousand men, it is probable, gazed upon the bloody, mangled face of Chandler, and beheld the gaping pistol wounds still open on his breast.

Joseph Gagliano was brutally shot without cause Friday night. He conducted a grocery store on Carolina avenue. He was highly regarded by the people of Bessemer. On the night of the murder a negro entered his store and made a small purchase. Gagliano reminded him as he was returning to the door that he had not paid the amount due. The negro, it is said, aimed a revolver at his heart and fired. Officers soon arrested Chandler, Smith and Paige, and it is stated that the evidence indicated the first name as the culprit. Peculiar is the fact that Chandler, not long since, was employed by the city as a guard of convicts."

CORONER PROBES BESSEMER LYNCHING
Fails to Fix Blame for the Negro's Death
M'Adory Disagrees
Coroner States Gagliano Should Be Released and Sheriff Refuses to Do So--
Mr. Brasher Makes Statement

The Birmingham Age-Herald, January 31, 1912

"The case of the Bessemer lynching Sunday has assumed quite a complex aspect. The coroner's jury yesterday impanelled to investigate the case and fix the blame of the episode, rendered a verdict that "John Prentiss, alias Chandler came to his death from gunshot wounds in the hands of Italians whose names are unknown to the jury." They did not involve the name of Louis Gagliano, the Italian who is in the county jail charged with having fired the first shots at the negro, and refused to involve the names of anyone else. Coroner Brasher last night stated emphatically that he thought that the Italian held in jail should be released from custody on the strength of the evidence introduced at the inquest. Sheriff McAdory stated equally as emphatically that he would hold Gagliano for a preliminary trial and was going to push the case as far as any official could.

There seems to be some spirit of resentment against Coroner Brasher for holding the inquest in the star chamber mode, but the coroner defends himself by saying that it has been his policy since he has been coroner to hold such inquests behind closed doors. He states that in his opinion the coroner's jury is an inquisitional body and the deliberations of it should be as secret as those of the grand jury. He stated that Deputy Sheriff Parker refused to swear before the jury that Louis Gagliano shot Chandler as has been claimed. Coroner Brasher said: "Mr. Parker was asked if Gagliano shot Chandler, to which Parker replied that the Italian pressed the pistol to the back of the negro. He would not swear, though, that Gagliano fired. Parker said after the shooting he procured Gagliano's pistol and found four empty chambers. 'How many bullet holes were there in the negro's back?' 'Fourteen,' Mr. Parker replied."

Coroner Brasher stated that two witnesses at the inquest swore that Gagliano was in the funeral procession and did not leave his carriage until after several shots had been fired. Sheriff McAdory states Gagliano was not in the procession at all, but had been lurking near where the shooting took place for several hours."

GAGLIANO FREED OF CHARGE OF MURDER
Not Guilty of Participating in Lynching
of Negro at Bessemer

The Birmingham Age-Herald, May 26, 1915

"After a few hours deliberation the jury in the case of Louis Gagliano, charged with murder in the first degree, returned a verdict of "not guilty" and the defendant was discharged.

Gagliano was indicted for the murder of John Chandler, negro, who was shot to death while in custody of county officers at Bessemer three years ago. The killing occurred while the funeral of Frank Gagliano, a brother of the defendant, was in progress. It is stated that a number of persons attending the funeral rushed at the negro with drawn revolvers and he was shot to death. Gagliano was arrested and indicted for the murder. After being in jail one year he was released on a $10,000 bond and nearly three years after the crime, the accused was given a trial and was acquitted.

Gagliano denied the killing and proved that he was in a carriage when the fusillade that killed the negro commenced. Many of the leading Italians of the district attended the trial and much satisfaction was expressed at the finding of the jury."

MAN KILLED WHILE RESISTING ARREST
In Scuffle With Policeman Pistol is Discharged
and Waiter is Mortally Wounded

The Birmingham Age-Herald, November 23, 1920

"Peter Kalopsis, a waiter at the City restaurant Fourth avenue and Eighteenth street, was shot and mortally wounded by Police Officer G.M. Bragan while resisting arrest. Officers Bragan and Flanders had gone to a negro house for the purpose of arresting Kalopsis, who was charged with illicit cohabitation with a negro woman. It is said by officers that he had been previously convicted on this charge.

Officer Flanders went to the front door and Bragan was stationed at the back door when Kalopsis attempted to make his escape. When he saw the officer it is said that he made a fake stumble and when the officer stopped Kalopsis caught him around the neck with one arm and took hold of the officer's revolver with the other. In the scuffle the revolver was discharged and the bullet entered Kalopsis' abdomen. The wounded man was taken to the hospital, where he died shortly afterward."

In a practical sense, and on a daily basis, there was cooperation between the races and legal authorities. Although seasoned with a degree of apparent paternalism and superiority, coroner's records and newspaper accounts occasionally hinted at such interactions.

Docket Entry:
I, B.L. Brasher, Coroner of Jefferson County, certify that on Nov. 16, 1910, Ensley, Ala., I held a preliminary investigation on the body of B. L. Pulham, Col, with the following result: I found deceased came to his death from a hemmerhage.
Remarks: I was asked by the citizens and officers of Ensley, Ala, who knew him well to make a thorough investigation to show whether there was any foul play, as he was in good health and a good negro. They asked me to call two doctors, Dr. Johnson and Dr. Field. Total Coroners fees: $6.30

On the other hand, the raw abject racism in existence during this era is unabashedly reflected in the following record of investigation.

County Commission Agent's Investigation
Over Death Of Josh Bagby

"This inquest came to be heard before County Commission Agent T.J. McCollum, in the Courthouse at Bessemer, Alabama, on Thursday morning, October 13, 1931.
Present at Inquest:
T.J. McCollum, Agent
Robert Ragsdale, Special Investigator
Wm. K. Schanze, Court Reporter

Allen Eastis
Examined by Mr. McCollum:
Q. All right. Just go ahead and tell...just the way it occurred. Just start where his car hit these people and they came after you to arrest him, and on up to the time that you shot him.
A. I was sitting in the Liberty Cafe in Brighton and Mr. Al Moran and his wife and Mrs. Naylor drove up there in front of the cafe, and he told me to come out and get in the car. I went out and got in the car...and he said a nigger ran into my car up here, and Mr. Naylor is up there holding him, and he seems to be drinking; I want you to go up there and arrest him. So he went right up the road about a block and his wife said Well, there comes the nigger now; and the nigger passed us in a Dodge. So I just told him Well, run in this street here and turn around and we will catch him. I watched the nigger, but before Mr. Moran could turn around the nigger turned in front of Huffman's store and went up Edwards Street. I said Cut through here and cut him off. I hollered at him to stop and he did stop. I just got out of their car and got in his, and asked him to turn around. He didn't say nothing. I said Turn this car around, boy. Instead of that he throwed it in second and shot the gas to it. I never had shut the door on his car. I told him to stop it. He said, Why god-damn you, you god-damn son-of-a-bitch, I ain't going to let you do me no such god-damn way. I said Stop this car, Boy, and he was trying to push me out the door; and he reached down, he had an automobile crank in the floor-board of his car, and he reached down to get that crank, and I shot him.
Q. Was he still cussing you?
A. Yes, Sir.
Q. Cussing you and all other white folks?
A. He didn't even flinch from that shot. I said Stop this car, Boy; and he said Why god-damn you; god-damn all you white folks, you god-damn son-of-a-bitch.
Q. That was after you had shot him the first time?
A. Yes. So I just shot him again, and shot him through the head. He fell over. I reached over and cut the ignition off, and pulled the emergency brake up but it wouldn't hold; and then I had to guide the car, I guess fifteen or twenty feet down the road; and then I reached over him and put my foot on the brake and stopped it.
Q. Well, he also cussed out those other people, didn't he Allen?
A. Yes, Sir. There was a lot of people up there where the wreck happened; a lot of women folks that heard him cussing.
By Mr. Ragsdale:

Q. You are Chief of Police over there?
A. Yes, Sir.
Q. You were just fixing to arrest this nigger, and take him to jail?
A. Yes, Sir; I had arrested him.
By Mr. McCollum:
Q. I have not yet got his name yet.
A. You haven't?
A. No, Sir. I think there are some people coming up this morning from Birmingham to see about him; I think he is a Birmingham nigger. I guess we will get his identity when they come out.
By Mr. Ragsdale:
Q. When you shot this nigger he was reaching for that automobile crank to hit you?
A. Yes, Sir,
Q. He was trying to push you out of the car all the time while the car was running?
A. Yes, Sir; all the time while the car was running he was trying to push me out. I seen I was going to have to do something. That's how them seven holes when that one shot was made, because when he stooped to get that crank, he was trying to get it under the steering wheel, and that throwed all his muscles out."

As noted, quasi-judicial verdicts or rulings of "justifiable" homicide were often made by the coroner. However, when a particularly egregious incident occurred, especially a murder with racial overtones and under circumstances leading to front page publicity in both daily newspapers, a different legal approach by officials would be required.

In order to support the status quo of white supremacy, and in an attempt to assuage any public discontent based on a perception of unfairness or favoritism, it was necessary to escalate legal decision making to a level above the Coroner and District Attorney. However, it was also important to try to avoid a public hearing in the form of a jury trial with its presentation of evidence and information which might lead to embarrassment of officials and with possible unintended societal consequences. The ideal forum which provided for a quick and minimally publicized "favorable" and unquestioned outcome would be the Grand Jury. Ideally, the Grand Jury was to be made up of a so-called group of "peers" within the community, although black individuals and women were excluded from membership. They would, after hearing evidence presented only from the prosecutor's standpoint, render a legal opinion as to whether or not charges should be filed against an individual accused of a crime and, therefore, if a public jury trial would be required to settle the legal issue of guilt or innocence.

NEGRO IN ATTACK CASE IS SLAIN BY VICTIM'S FATHER
Parent Of Girl, 7, Fires Four Shots In Courthouse After Defendant Gets 99-Year Sentence
Pistol Shots Bring Anti-Climax To Trial

The Birmingham Age Herald, May 12, 1938

"The father of a 7-year-old girl, who had just heard a Negro youth sentenced to 99 years on a charge of having carnal knowledge of the child, shot the Negro to death in the corridor of the Jefferson County Courthouse.

H.E.Colburn, Birmingham mechanic, was reported by officers and other witnesses to have stepped from the vicinity of a telephone booth on the sixth floor of the courthouse and shot the Negro, Joe Lewis Smith, 20, four times while Smith was being taken to the jail.

Immediately after the shooting Colburn gave himself up to officers, three of whom were standing beside the Negro at the time he was shot. Coroner Gip M. Evans returned a finding of unlawful homicide and ordered Colburn held. He was taken to the City Jail for the night. Court attaches said that during the trial of Smith they had searched Colburn "several times to make sure he was not armed."

After four hours of deliberation, the jury had returned a verdict finding the Negro guilty and fixing his punishment at 99 years in the penitentiary. Judge McElroy instructed officers to take the Negro to the County Jail. The officers took the Negro out of the courtroom and started down the corridor with him to a door which led to the elevator to the jail. At that moment, the father of the 7-year-old girl appeared in the hallway and opened fire on the Negro.

Colburn, in the presence of a reporter for the Birmingham Age-Herald, fired four shots into the Negro's body and then surrendered to officers who had been guarding Smith. When the jury returned the verdict of 99 years, Judge McElroy instructed officers in the court to find out where the girl's father was. A few moments later the sound of pistol shots were heard in the corridor of the courthouse, and the Negro fell in a pool of blood in front of the office of the Criminal Court clerk on the sixth floor.

Detective Espy said Colburn hid in a telephone booth in the hallway until the Negro was taken out of the courtroom and emerged from the booth with a pistol in his hand and fired. Colburn, after the shooting, refused to make any statement for publication, but was heard to call a friend of his over the telephone and say, "I got the Nigger."

A story in The Birmingham News on the same date also indicated that:

"The jury in the case deliberated for four hours before finding the Negro guilty of molesting the child last Christmas eve. Testimony had revealed that Smith had been employed by the Colburns to guard their daughter and three year old son in the Colburn apartment while the parents went downtown to buy Christmas presents for the children. The girl had been asleep in the bedroom when the Negro molested her. The Negro did not take the stand in his own defense during the trial. He had been treated for two social diseases from September, 1936 to November, 1937."

EXONERATED
Grand Jury Frees Courthouse Killer
Father Who Shot Abuser Of Girl Given No-Bill

The Birmingham Age-Herald, June 10, 1938

"H.E. Colburn, held in the County Jail since May 11 for the Courthouse slaying of a young Negro convicted and sentenced to 99 years in prison for abusing Colburn's seven-year-old daughter, was a free man today—exonerated by a grand jury which heard only the prosecution side of the evidence.

The 31 year-old mechanic was released from jail immediately after the grand jury returned a no-bill in the case. He had been held without bail on a murder warrant. Courthouse officials said the grand jury's action would not prevent any future grand jury from indicting Colburn if it saw fit, but it was generally believed that the case is ended."

Postscript

The judicial outcome of this incident of retribution, with its premeditated assassination of the defendant, and its description in the print media, is not surprising given the racial tenor in existence during those times.

Almost all entries in the records and newspaper clippings contained within the coroner's file concerning this case indicate that the defendant, John Lewis Smith, was 20 years old. However, although a specific date of birth is not entered on the copy his death certificate, the notation in the age block is "16". Although an error in Smith's age of a year younger or older might be possible and reasonably acceptable, the four year age difference is questionable. The younger noted age is supported as being his true age by his trade being listed as "School Boy" on the certificate. This is not an occupation which would normally be attributed to a 20 year old.

The informant for data included on the death certificate is noted to be "Mauda Hill" and his mother's name as "Mauda Cook." This named individual was apparently the deceased's mother whom he was noted to be living with in Birmingham. It would be assumed that she would have been aware of her son's true age. Smith's remains were removed to his place of birth in Talbotton, Georgia for burial. Attempts to locate his gravesite for the purpose of attempting to determine his true birth date were unsuccessful.

Leon Litwack noted that:
"Through the first four decades of the twentieth century, the essential mechanisms, attitudes and assumptions governing race relations and the subordination of black southerness remained largely intact. The same patterns of discrimination, segregation, unequal justice, and racial violence persisted. Sporadic breakthroughs were made by individual blacks, and the New Deal injected a measure of hope, but the great mass of black men and women in the South still lived out their lives in a severely restricted, isolated and relatively static world. More than A million black Americans fought in World War II, as they had in World War I, to make the world safe for democracy. After the war even larger numbers developed new strategies And tactics to make the United States safe for themselves. On some new battlefields—Montgomery, Selma, Birmingham, Jackson, Little Rock, Detroit, Boston, Chicago, Los Angeles— still another struggle would be waged over the meaning of freedom. That struggle still persists."[1]

CHAPTER 5

MINES

"You load sixteen tons and what do you get?
Another day older and deeper in debt.
St. Peter don't you call me 'cause I can't go.
I owe my soul to the company store."

---Sixteen Tons

"After Damp" can be defined as a deadly gas which is comprised primarily of carbon monoxide and carbon dioxide that followed a dynamite blast gone awry. Exposure to afterdamp caused miners to lose consciousness in seconds and could cause death in minutes.

MORE THAN 100 MEN ENTOMBED IN MINES

FRIGHTFUL CATASTROPHE AT VIRGINIA CITY
Workmen Heroically Struggle to Reach Their Comrades
in The Mine Before They Perish From Foul Gases
Caused by The Explosion

SCORES OF MINERS ARE SUPPOSED TO HAVE DIED IN TERRIBLE AGONY

With Pick and Shovel Dozens of Men Are Racing Madly
With the Grim Monster, Death
Parties from Pratt City, Ensley and Bessemer
Rush to the Scene to Assist in Gruesome Task
Gray Explains The Catastrophe--
"Windy Shot" Probably Causes The Trouble
Men Fear "After Damp"
The Birmingham Age-Herald, February 21, 1905

"The scene at the Virginia Mines today where a terrific explosion yesterday imprisoned 160 men 100 feet below the surface, was the most gruesome and harrowing that that has ever been witnessed in this section of Alabama.

The corpses are frightfully mangled and disfigured and identification almost impossible. Many of them are so badly bruised and discolored the negroes cannot be told from white men. All day long at the mouth of the mine the mourning and wailing of women and children whose unfortunate relatives were in the mines has been the most heartrending feature of the disaster. One hundred families and 360 children are left destitute and without means of support by the calamity. As the bodies of the victims which in many cases have been gathered together a piece at a time, are brought to the surface, they are placed in rows on a rough improvised platform. Coroner Paris is busy inquiring into the disaster, having already empaneled a jury,"

76 BODIES RECOVERED FROM RUINS
RESCUERS ARE OVERCOME BY ODORS
MANY FUNERALS WILL BE HELD TODAY
Work of Rescuers is Retarded by Foul Gases Accumulating in the Mine
Sickening Sights are Witnessed as Relatives Claim Bodies at the Morgue
Every Corpse Save One Bruised And Lacerated

The Birmingham Age-Herald, February 23, 1905

"The aftermath of the Virginia mines disaster, the claiming and disposition of the dead, is by far the saddest feature of this shocking tragedy. The scenes around the improvised morgue, the seething throng of people and the unspeakable grid of the bereaved relatives and friends of the victims of the frightful catastrophe, have converted Bessemer into a city of the dead.

As rapidly as the bodies are received on the train from Virginia mines they are washed, embalmed and placed into caskets and turned over to their relatives and friends. Many times today has a funeral procession, followed by friends and relatives wended its way out of the city and over the hills and mountains back to Virginia, to some funeral pile, where the stricken ones are left alone in their sorrow to mourn over the bruised and bleeding clay, all that is human of what three days ago were manly and joyous, husband, brothers, sons and sweethearts.

Every passenger train coming into Bessemer today has brought a shipment of caskets which were ordered by wire from other cities. On both sides of the the morgue these caskets have been piled several feet high. The street is lined with hearses and dead wagons to bear away the dead as soon as they are laid into the caskets. The officers guarding the doors of the temporary morgue have had their patience taxed in restraining the anxious relatives and friends, many of whom have come from distance states to claim the corpse of the loved ones who perished in the disaster.

So far all the bodies that have reached Bessemer have been identified save one. This is the body of a negro and is supposed to be William Howard. Owing to the many mangled bodies some difficulty was expected in many instances in the identification. The removal of the clothing from the bodies disclosed many horrible and sickening sights which had been hidden from the eyes of the rescuing parties at the slope of the ill-fated mine. In many instances the head and limbs of the victims had almost been severed from their bodies and many horrible and gaping injuries added horror to the sights revealed to the undertakers and their helpers. In removing the clothing from the bodies, $70 dollars was found in the clothes of one of the Italian miners.

Notwithstanding the mangled and charred forms of the unfortunate victims, the finely developed forms of the dead cannot but impress the fact the miners at Virginia were fine specimens of manhood. The frame and muscles of the men, developed by years of experience in digging coal, have given to the miners constitutions that could have withstood hard and persistent attacks of illness

Every effort has been made to keep back the morbid curiosity seekers, but in spite of all hundreds managed to evade the officers and got inside of the morgue. The scene inside the building was gruesome to the very extreme. On one side of the room, the bodies of the white miners were laid side by side. While the other side was used for those of the colored. Nearly all the faces bespoke unutterable agony and most of the hands were frightfully burned; evidently in the effort to ward off the flames from their faces. A few looked placid and serene, but the majority were horribly mangled. One man was headless while the other one had had the top of his scalp completely torn off. Many were perfectly limp, having had every bone in their bodies broken. With distorted features, broken and mangled limbs, the bodies presented a frightful spectacle. It was a sight to shudder at."

CORONER'S JURY RETURNS VERDICT
Four Men Charged With Criminal Negligence
In Connection With Virginia Mines Disaster

The Birmingham Age-Herald, April 18, 1905

"The jury empaneled by Coroner W.D. Paris to investigate the Virginia Mines disaster, yesterday afternoon returned a verdict which charges four men with "criminal negligence." They are E.T. Shuler, G.H. Shuler, Amos W. Reed and Sam Hartley, operators, managers and mine foreman, respectively. The inquest was held over the remains of John Brown, one of the victims of the disaster, but a like verdict was returned in the case of each of the 111 men who met his death in the ill-fated mines. "We the jury...(find that) said explosion was caused by the collection of dust that was allowed to accumulate...although the state mine inspector had repeatedly warned them of the dangerous condition of the mines for over a year prior to the explosion and that the said John Brown came to his death in an unlawful manner by willful and criminal negligence...of the operator, managers and mine foreman of said mine against the peace and dignity of the state of Alabama," The grand jury which is now in session may also investigate the disaster."

Postscript

This was the first major mining disaster which had occurred in the early 20th century in what is now the Hueytown area of western Jefferson County. The final death toll was 112. As was common at that time, both coroner's records and newspaper accounts listed the victims by race, noting that 65 Whites and Italians and 27 Negroes had been killed.

No information could be readily found to indicate if the men found "criminally negligent" by the coroner's jury, or the company itself, ever faced further legal action, although with the power held by the mine owners at that time, it is doubtful. Most likely, a nominal sum of money was paid to the surviving relatives. The cause of the explosion was believed to have been due to a "Windy Shot" which can be defined as the result of using too much black powder or when the charge is improperly tamped down before setting off the localized explosion. "Windy Shots" would spew sparks into the mine, frequently igniting methane gas, coal dust, or both. These massive explosions could rapidly travel through miles of tunnels and kill and maim miners long distances from the initial blast.

It is not possible to completely separate material relating to "legitimate" coal mining operations and the associated major disasters from those issues concerning prisons and general industrial work in Jefferson County during the early 20th century. Living and working conditions for both voluntarily employed miners and forced contract prison laborers were terrible. Although the hired miners were not physically shackled and could technically leave if they wanted to, the existing system of debt bondage, along with their essential confinement to rural encampments close to the mines, insured their "captivity" almost as much as if they wore a ball and chain. The proposition of "freedom" between the two groups could only be considered a matter of relative degree. The complex factors relating to the debt bondage endured by the freely employed miners, the deprivations associated with forced prison labor and the unionization efforts of miners and other industrial workers are all interwoven. The inability to isolate these interrelated matters from one another will become evident in this and the following two chapters.

The miner's continuing servitude was guaranteed by the scrip system where workers were not paid in cash, but with non-transferable credit vouchers which could only be exchanged for goods and equipment sold at the company store. Detailed bookkeeping by the employer insured that any advances for necessities would be automatically deducted on the next payday. Any remaining compensation due would be paid in scrip. In addition, workers lived in company owned housing for which rent was also deducted from their pay. This system made it impossible for workers to amass any appreciable cash savings. This lack of actual money, coupled with inadequate means of transportation, made regular travel to the "distant" cities of Bessemer and Birmingham rare excursions. Only massive and repetitive strike activity by members of the United Mine Workers union would finally end this system of peonage long after forced prison labor had been banned.

From the late 19th century to just prior to World War II, Alabama coal miners initiated hundreds of strikes with many taking place in the 1930s. Hard hit by the Great Depression, Jefferson County's unemployment rate had reached 32 percent by 1930 and coal and iron production had plummeted. Local coal operators refused to negotiate miner's grievances with national unions. A February, 1934 strike involved two thousand employees at seven mines. Picketing, demonstrations, armed marches and strikes continued into 1939, when twenty thousand miners struck for 47 days, shutting down the entire Alabama coal mining industry.

Much coal mining had originally been performed close to the city of Birmingham in areas such as Pratt City in the late 19th and early 20th centuries, mainly with contract prison labor. However, most heavy mining, along with worker settlements and prison camps, soon gravitated to the larger and more easily accessible deposits located in West Jefferson County.

GREATEST MINE EXPLOSION IN HISTORY OF STATE COSTS MANY MEN THEIR LIVES
Face Of Cliff Was Blackened By Explosion
The Birmingham Age-Herald, May 6, 1910

The Palos Mine No. 3 was situated on the east bank of the Warrior River, about 20 miles west of Birmingham. The force of the explosion was evidenced by the following which was taken from newspaper and eyewitness accounts: "Sam Goolsby, a rural mail carrier to the mines, was killed while walking on the track in front of the mine. He was knocked 30 feet into the river and was horribly burned. The flame from the opening seemed to engulf him entirely, although he was probably 200 feet from the mouth of the slope. He leaves a wife and ten children."

Postscript

Eighty-four individuals lost their lives in this disaster and the cause of the explosion was never determined. As was the usual practice during this era, the deceased miners were separately listed in the coroner's record by race. The identity of at least seven black miners were initially listed as "unknown." The coroner's docket entry for this disaster was unique in that the ages, known or approximated for the victims, were also listed.

Although the included data revealed that the average age of both black and white victims was 27 years old, individual entries reveal a more personal and disheartening picture. Along with multiple victims in their late teenage years, the following individuals were also listed: M. Spruell, age 13; his brother Albert, age 15 and Ralph Setzer, age 14. In addition, three Stansbury brothers; Fred--21, Bob--22, and Con, age 18 years old were included along with several other pairs of men with the same last names who died in the blast.

In the days before the introduction and enforcement of child labor laws, it was common for younger individuals to be employed in the mines, usually involved in leading mule driven cars laden with coal out of the shafts or performing other ancillary work such as greasing the axles of the cars.

Sporadic, relatively large mining disasters continued to occur in Jefferson County into the mid 1930s.

DOLOMITE MINE BLAST DEATHS TOTAL 84
20 White Miners Among Dead: More Than 60 Injured
Bessemer Turned Into Morgue;
All Embalmers Busy

The Birmingham News, November 23, 1922

"The explosion occurred simultaneously with the crash of three "skip" cars, which ran "wild" down the slope to the mine "yards," approximately 1,100 feet from the entrance. These cars, breaking cable, while they were being hauled up the slope to the entrance crashed downward severing an electric circuit. This caused a spark and as the cars crashed into the "yards" where loaded coal cars were assembled before being hauled to the surface, the explosion occurred.

So great was the blast that the flames blazed upward all the way to the mine entrance, approximately 1,000 feet and continued on 300 feet further to the main tipple, setting this afire. Approximately 50 men were working in the "yards" at the time and all of these men were either killed or injured."

Postscript

An undated letter included in the coroner's file shows a typewritten list of 83 men killed in this disaster. This is followed by pencil entries of the names of 7 additional individuals, for a total of 90 victims. The latter group probably represents either injured persons who died later or remains recovered at a later date.

50 MINERS KILLED AT OVERTON
Most Of Those In The Mine Believed Killed By Blast
Nine White Men Are Victims
Widows and Fatherless, After Constant Vigil, Identify Dead Miners

The Birmingham News, December 10, 1925
Charleston West Virginia Daily Mail, December 11, 1925

"The cause of the blast had not been officially determined. Some of the mine workers believed it was caused by a miner striking a match which is forbidden or by a "windy shot." It is believed that most of the bodies unrecovered are those of negro workers. Relatives of the victims were not allowed to view the bodies. Identification was being carried out with greatest difficulty. Of the fifty-three men killed outright, only two were unmarried and most of them were parents of large families,"

MULGA MINE YIELDS 33 BODIES
Most Victims Are Killed By "After Damp," But Some Are Crushed

The Birmingham News, October 16, 1937

Although this was one of the last major mining disasters to occur in Jefferson County, numerous accidents which affected smaller groups of men, as well as individual miners, regularly occurred and were due to various causes. Those incidents involving many fatalities received prominent media attention. Accidents involving a few deaths seemed routine, were accepted as "the cost of doing business" and received minimal, if any, publicity. A sampling of these "minor" incidents in the early part of the century illustrate the constant dangers associated with the coal mining industry. Although there were fewer major disasters later in the century, individual fatalities would continue to occur on an irregular basis well into the 1950's.

Docket Entry:
Date: May 25, 1909
Deceased: Jim Morris, Col.
Cause Of Death: Explosion
Notes: I found deceas had been blasting down some iron ore and had blasted a rock down that was too large to burst with a hamer so he put in 3 pot shots and fired them off and deceas thought all 3 of shots went off and deceas went and set down on the rock and another shot went off and killed him instantly.

Docket Entry:
Date: February 9, 1911
Deceased: Rufus Dubose, Col.
Cause Of Death: Coming into contact with a live wire while riding on top of a motor car in the mines at Dolomite as motor was turning a curve.

Docket Entry:
Date: January 24, 1912
Deceased: W.W. Johnson, White
Cause Of Death: From trying to thaw dynamite by fire in said mines.

Docket Entry:
Date: October 11, 1917
I, J.R.T. Rives, Assistant Coroner, certify that I was called to Banner Mines to investigate the death of Claude Johnson, Col., Herman Beard, Col., Bob Patterson, White, Tom Stewart, Col., and it was found they came to their death from injuries received when car broke loose at mouth of mine and it ran back on them.

Docket Entry:
Date: November 12, 1923
Deceased: Tony Bartalony, White
Cause Of Death: By being blown up in mines.

Docket Entry:
Date: October 6, 1937
Deceased: James Dycus, W and Toney Lewis, C.
Cause Of Death: Crushed by falling rock. Removed a prop to allow mule to pass and rock fell.

A number of coroner docket entries relating to mining accidents include commentary, usually very short, but which specifically assigns blame for the causation of various accidents and which is attributed to supervisors, higher management or to the miners themselves. It is believed that such officially noted culpability on the part of mining company officials would hopefully insure that some degree of compensation, however minimal, would be provided to the victim's families in those years which preceded modern worker safety and compensation laws.

Docket Entry:
Date: February 2, 1909
Address: Short Creek Mine
Cause Of Death: Explosion
Deceased: 18 victims (separated on list by race--5 white and 13 colored).
Note: Found said explosion from the investigation of what I could get from the miners who worked in those mines it must have been caused by a windy shot, said shot being made by someone that did not understand mining and said blame lays on the mine forman for allowing green men to be allowed to put on shots.

Docket Entry:
Date: July 1, 1910
Deceased: John Eppes, Col.
Cause Of Death: Came to his death on his own negligence having been an experienced miner for 11 years, he should have known the danger he was in.

Docket Entry:
Date: February 17, 1911
Deceased: I.M. Horton, White
Cause Of Death: From being struck by a rock which was dumped above and came back down the slope. Note: We believe that this could be remedied and believe that this death is caused by negligence of the company.

Docket Entry:
Date: June 24, 1911
Deceased: Willie Cole, Col.
Cause Of Death: Being run over by a car or cars owned and operated by the Sloss-Sheffield Coal and Iron Co. Note: By gross neglect on the part of the company, in not having a boss driver to look at the boys who work in the said mines and we feel that the officials should be held responsible for his death.

Docket Entry:
Date: September 10, 1918
I, J.R.T. Rives, Asst. Coroner certify that I held a preliminary investigation inquest on the body of John Francis Pennington, white, Turner Byars, Henry Truss, C.A. Young, Col., with the following result. I was called to Mary Lee Mines to investigate the death of the above and it was found that they came to their death from drowning, same being an Act of God.

Violence in the workplace is certainly not a modern phenomenon. Coroner docket entries note a number of known incidents of homicide which occurred in the mines, as well as in the mining camps near them. Few entries indicate the reasons for such assaults, but it is assumed that the usual factors of jealousy, retribution or some other form of animosity were involved. It is also certain that an unknown number of additional homicides occurred in the mines and were attributed to "accidental" means such as "falling rock" and were just dismissed or covered up by mine managers and supervisors. This is especially believed to have occurred in the convict mines where life was cheap and managers didn't want to slow down the progress of work by inviting inquiries by the coroner or some law enforcement agents who, just as soon, would rather not know about such incidents unless their occurrence was obvious, egregious and could not be denied.

Docket Entry:
Date: March 27, 1909
Deceased: Charley Kenedy, Col.
Defendant: John Williams, Col.
Cause Of Death:By being struck on the head with sledg hamer causing instant death. Remarks: Both men were convicks at Baner Mines at time of the killing.

Docket Entry.
Date: May 14, 1911
Address: Maxine Mines
Deceased: John E. Elliott, White
Defendant: Unknown
Cause Of Death: Gunshot wound at the hands of parties unknown to jury.

Docket Entry:
Date: October 30, 1915
Address: Bessie Coal Mines
Deceased: Mack Henry, Col.
Defendant: Frank Coats and Will Stepson
Cause Of Death: By hitting him in the head with a coal pick.

Docket Entry:
Date: March 31, 1917
Address: Sayreton Mines
Deceased: Dan Childs, Col.
Defendant: J. G. Meagher, White
Cause Of Death: By being struck over the head with an iron bar, same being justifiable homicide.

Docket Entry:
Date: July 11, 1922
Address: Banner Mines
Deceased: Will Jackson, Col.
Defendant: Herbert Meadows, Col.
Cause Of Death: By powder explosion while trying to throw same on Herbert Meadows, same being a justifiable homicide.

Statistics

Following 1909, coroner's records, with a few exceptions for missing data, provide an overview of the annual number of accidental mining fatalities occurring in Jefferson County in the early 20th century.

The nineteen years which yield almost complete records of these deaths show a minimum documented yearly average of 47 fatalities for the inclusive years. These annual numbers are minimally inflated by the irregularly occurring larger mining disasters at the Virginia mine in 1905, Palos in 1910, the Banner mine in 1911, the Dolomite disaster in 1922 and the Overton blast in 1925. The last large mining disaster which occurred in Jefferson County, and which is not reflected in these statistics, took place in Mulga when 33 miners died in an explosion in 1937.

Minimum Number Of Known Accidental Mining Fatalities Per Listed Year In Jefferson County

1905---112
1910---84
1911---155
1912---24
1916---30*
1917---15
1918---26
1919---36
1920---20
1921---24

1922---110
1923---26
1924---18
1925---84
1926---34
1927---34
1928---17
1929---22
1930---24

Total Deaths = 895/19 years = 47 average annual number of deaths for inclusive years shown.
*Minimum number of fatalities available for 1916 from newspaper accounts of the Bessie mine disaster. Coroner's records missing.

"Natural Causes"

As they are considered to be due to "natural causes," coroner's records rarely included examples of deaths associated with chronic exposure to elements encountered by those individuals who had worked in the coal mines for many years. Such deaths did not come under the jurisdiction of the coroner.

During the period of my training in pathology at the Veterans Administration Hospital in Birmingham in the early 1970's, I had the opportunity to observe the anatomical results of the chronic exposure to coal dust. This was especially true for those men who had worked in Alabama's mines during the earlier part of the 20th century when personal protective equipment in the form of respirators, filtering masks and dust monitors were unheard of and prior to the increased use of machinery to perform much of the heavy mining work. In addition, the type of coal mined in this area was geologically of the "soft" bituminous variety which contain more toxic impurities than the harder anthracite coal mined mainly from deposits in the Pennsylvania region of the country.

These few elderly men, who had survived into their 80's and early 90's, albeit minimally physically active due to their age and respiratory insufficiency, were remarkable examples of the destructive effects of their unprotected long term exposure to anthracite coal dust. The term "Black Lung" was truly applicable as their lung tissue can only properly be described as being "black as coal" in contrast to the light pink-tan coloration and spongy appearance of normal lung tissue. In addition, lung sacs, or alveoli, had been destroyed in a diffuse fashion resulting in large spaces. This severe emphysematous change would have made breathing and adequate oxygen exchange very difficult, especially upon even slight physical exertion. Such difficulty in respiration often renders the individual extremely anxious as he fights to sustain an adequate level of oxygen within his system---an impossible task in the face of extensively disrupted lung tissue.

Although the number of cases of Black Lung disease had been radically reduced by the mid 20th century, there has been a recent pronounced resurgence of the condition, especially in the Appalachian region where underground mining is still common.

Numerous lives were lost over many years---either quickly in violent explosions or due to chronic debilitation. It was at the cost of the expendable lives of thousands of men and the generation of untold grief and deprivation of their kin. Not just in Jefferson County, but worldwide in the quest for "King Coal."

The once booming mining camps and small cities of west Jefferson County disappeared many years ago with the closure of most of the old below ground mines. What open surface mining remains today employs relatively few men, who with their massive machines can collect more coal in one day than it took hundreds of men to remove from below the ground in a week. The names and history of these small bustling towns are almost unknown to most current citizens of Jefferson County: Praco, Maxine, Flat Top, Labuco, Powhattan and Littleton (site of the worst mining disaster in Alabama history) and many others, are now essentially ghost towns. There are relatively few remaining residents in many of these areas. The demise of the more remote sites was hastened due to the lack of modern utilities such as running water, electricity and indoor plumbing. These formerly heavily populated areas are now overgrown with vegetation---gone back to their native condition. Probing these modern archaeological remains yields parts of an occasional brick foundation of a dwelling. All wood has rotted away or has been reclaimed. Also to be found are rusted cans, bottles and the remnants of dolls and cheap metal toys. There was nothing of great monetary value owned by those residents to leave behind. The only thing of any worth here was the coal which was paid for with the bodies and souls of thousands of human beings, both legally imprisoned and technically "free," who toiled here over many years, the interest compounded by the tears of their relatives.

Perhaps the singer Loretta Lynn summed it up best:

"Not much left but the floor,
Nothing lives here anymore.
Except the memories of a coal miner's daughter,"

---Coal Miner's Daughter

CHAPTER 6

PRISON

*"On this old rock pile with a ball and chain,
They call me by a number, not a name.
Gotta' do my time, gotta' do my time,
With an aching heart and a worried mind."*

—Doin' My Time

Note: The "Gob" is a term for that part of a mine from which the coal has been removed and the space more or less filled up with waste material.

*—-An imagined dialogue in the mind of
Joe L. Thomas, convict, #2 Prison, Pratt City*

"Goin' deep into the Gob tonight. Got to get out of here now! Been here a year for a crime I didn't do and get beat when I say so. I know the layout and manways of this damn mine like the back of my hand! Gonna' stay down here tonight when everyone quits. They won't miss me 'till after supper when they do last head count while they put the chains on. Then they'll raise hell and come down here with the damn dogs lookin' for me. But I know how to beat them hellhounds! Go through some water and crawl the undercuts along the walls. I'll backtrack the breakthroughs a few times to confuse them and then just sit tight. By the time they get down here I'll be so damn deep in this mine, they'll never find me!

It's black down here but I know all the turns and holes in the dark. Been planning this for six months now, mapping all the passages in my mind's eye and I can feel the turns I gotta' make by hand. Got enough biscuits and some dried fatback hid to last me about a week. They'll figure I run off by then, probably the first night, and give up lookin' for me down here and pull the night guard off the slope in a couple of days. That's when I'll work my way out and be gone. Ha! I'll be able to hear them working during the day so I'll know when its night. Gonna' beat those cracker bastards!

Think its been almost a week now. Don't hear the dogs. Out of food and can't drink that acid water seepin' down the walls no more. Feelin' sort of sick and weak, so I gotta' make my move now! Gotta' remember to work my way backwards. Slide along the wall to the first right cut-off and turn there. Feel down past the next left and then go to the next left opening and turn there. Long wall from there with no turns 'till the big gallery on the left side.

   Damn! Hit a dead end! This ain't right! Must have turned the wrong way at the big opening. Should have gone right! Took me deeper into this hellhole! Got to backtrack now and find it. Got to get some sleep first then try again. I'll be ok.

   Can't figure this! Keep hitting dead ends and now I'm confused. Got to sit down and think this through. Got to get out! Even been callin' for help when I hear them workin', but they too far away and there's too much noise for them to hear me. Feelin' too weak to call out loud anyways. Ain't ate nothin' in a few days. Just gonna' rest now. They'll find me."

Docket Entry:
Date: December 5, 1910
Deceased: Joe L. Thomas, Col.
Address: #2 Prison, Pratt City.
Cause Of Death: From exposure as he had been in "Gob" of mine for two or three weeks, trying to escape.
Remarks: Deceased was a County Convict from Conecuh County, sent for burglary Oct. 18, 1909. Sentence expires March 17, 1911. Had been in the mines 1 year and a few days when he hid out in the "Gob." For past two weeks thought the man had escaped and sent in report to that effect. Made several searches of the "Gob" to find him, since he had been hid out he has been gone five weeks.

   The case of Joe Thomas was not the only one of such a nature to have occurred within the maze-like warrens of the prison mines. Several months before the remains of Thomas were found, a similar incident at another mine was documented by the coroner:

Docket Entry:
Date: October 1, 1910
Deceased: Unknown negro--supposed to be Will Lindsay.
Address: #3 Prison, Ensley.
Cause Of Death: Unknown causes.
Remarks: Will Lindsay, col. escaped from #3 mines in 1909 July 9th, sent from Shelby Co., Ala. Was 5 feet 7 1/2 inches tall, age 41, wt. 155. J.W. Wosler says body was partly under water, seemed that body had been covered with water. This negro has never been heard of since his escape and is quite possible that in trying to make his escape, and got lost in abandoned part of mines, and died from starvation and bad air. The skeleton corresponds to description of Will Lindsay.

As noted by Douglas L. Blackmon:

"Forcing convicts to work as a part of their punishment was entirely legal; the 13th amendment to the U.S. Constitution, adopted in 1865, outlaws involuntary servitude—except for "duly convicted" prisoners. Convict leasing in other states never reached the scale of Alabama's program. By the turn of the century, most states had ended the practice or soon would because of opposition on humanitarian grounds and From organized labor. But in Alabama, industrialization was generating a ravenous appetite for the state's coal and iron ore. Convicts provided an ideal captive work force: cheap, usually docile, unable to organize and available when free laborers went on strike,"[1]

C.V. Harris wrote that:

"Convict labor was useful to employers mainly because of its regularity. Convicts could not work three days and loaf four nor "take off" for picnics, funerals and excursions. Further, convicts were invaluable in suppressing unionism. During any strike, the convict miners continued to grind out their daily quota of coal."[2]

Blackmon further indicated that:

"Under the convict leasing system, government officials agreed with a company such as Tennessee Coal to provide a specific number of prisoners for labor. State officials signed contracts to supply companies with large blocks of men--often hundreds at a time--who had committed felonies. Companies entered into separate deals with county sheriffs to obtain thousands more prisoners who had been convicted of misdemeanors. The companies built their own prisons, fed and clothed the convicts and supplied guards as they saw fit. Sheriffs, deputies and some court officials derived most of their compensation from fees charged to convicts for each stop in their own arrest, conviction and shipment to a private company. That gave sheriffs an incentive to arrest and obtain convictions of as many people as possible. They also had an incentive to feed the prisoners as little as possible since they could pocket the difference between what the state paid them and what they spent to maintain the convicts while in their custody."[3]

In regard to the Pratt Mines complex an observer for a special Alabama legislative committee in 1897 wrote a report describing 1,117 convicts, many "wholly unfit for the work at labor in the shaft. The men worked standing in pools of putrid water. Gas from the miner's headlamps and smoke from the blasts of dynamite and gunpowder choked the mine."4 The convict board's death registers show that in the final decade of the 19th century, large numbers of men died when diarrhea and dysentery periodically swept through the Pratt Mines. Citing inadequate food, beatings of miners and unsanitary conditions, state inspectors periodically issued reports criticizing the mine's operators. An 1890 report from the convict inspectors board described "more sickness" at the Pratt Mines "than any other place." Even earlier, Chaplain J.B. Anderson in his Biennial Report of the Alabama Penitentiary in 1882 must have caused some discomfort among legislators when he declared: "This neglect of, and cruelty to convicts may go on for a time yet, but sooner or later curses of the Almighty God will be showered down upon the proud Commonwealth. Unless the present system is changed, the Judge of all the earth will see that retributive justice is meted out in due season to the State of Alabama."5

Edward L. Ayers noted that:

*"Because prison officials so often had something to hide, these reports...were models of obfuscation and officialese. Reports in Alabama give glowing accounts of the "good order" of the convict camps, yet a mere glance at the statistical tables accompanying these Reports show that up to 40 percent of the prisoners were dying. Fragmentary and missing reports were not so much mistakes as they were a part of a built-in Incompetence, a purposeful confusion. By 1890, the death rate of Alabama's leased county convicts had become twice as high as that of the notorious state convict lease system. The boundary between the two systems often became indistinguishable."*6

Blackmon wrote that:
*"Men were priced depending on their health and their ability to dig coal. Under state rules adopted in 1901, a "first class" prisoner had to cut and load into mine cars four tons of coal a day to avoid being whipped. The weakest inmates, labeled "fourth class" or "dead hands," were required to produce at least one ton a day. As revenues from the lease system rose, companies Took over nearly all of the penal functions of the state. Company guards were empowered to shoot prisoners attempting to flee and, well into the 20th century, to strip disobedient convicts naked and whip them."*7

Ayers also noted that:

> "In comparison with manufacturing enterprises within the penitentiaries of the North, the profitability of the lease system was real and sustained. Substantially lower overhead, more profitable products, longer hours, and The more brutal exploitation made possible by a disregard for the prisoner's health and welfare generated considerable short-term profits for the state as well as for the businessman lucky enough and callous enough to lease convicts."[8]

C.V. Harris indicated that:

> "From 1891 to 1913, the Jefferson County Commissioners leased most of the county convicts to the Tennessee Coal, Iron and Railroad Company, the Sloss-Sheffield Steel and Iron Company and the Pratt Consolidated Coal Company. These coal mining corporations hired Convicts not only from Jefferson County but also from other counties in Alabama and from the state penitentiary. Thus the convict lease system funneled a large proportion Of Alabama's convicts into the Birmingham mineral district. Between 1906 and 1911, the coal mines employed an average of 1,500 state and county convicts per year."[9]

As previously noted in the chapter on Mines, all mine workers were continually exposed to dangerous conditions which led to numerous accidental injuries and deaths. If anything, conditions faced by prisoners showed an almost compete disregard for their safety and working conditions.

Docket Entry:
Date: July 20, 1909
Deceased: Joe Hinson
Address: Pratt Mines #11
Cause Of Death: By coming in contact with a live ware, killing him instantly.
Killed while working in mine for the Tennessee people.
Remarks: Joe Hinson lived at East Lake and was sent to Prisen for cutting a mans head of With an ax about a dog.

Docket Entry:
Date: October 20, 1911
Deceased: Henry Carter, Alias Henry Collins, Col.
Address: #12 Prison
Cause Of Death: By falling rock in the mines. Unavoidable accident.

On occasion, a detailed history regarding a deceased inmate was included in the coroner's docket entry.

Docket Entry:
Date: April 22, 1910
Deceased: Matt Dunn, Col.
Address: #12 Prison
Cause Of Death: By getting crushed between a mining car and rib.
Remarks: Was sent from Pickens County. Age 26, height 5 feet 3 inches, race--negro, sex--male.   Complexion--black. Hair--black. Eyes--black. Teeth--bad. Occupation--farmer. Was single. Other relatives-father--1 brother--2 sisters who live in Pickens County. Habits--bad. Education--none. Charged for murder in first degree, life sentence. Never sentenced before. Wore #8 shoe.

Due to overcrowding and poor hygienic conditions, various diseases and debilitation led to the deaths of numerous prisoners, especially during the late 19th and early 20th centuries. Notations of these "natural" deaths were typically absent from the coroner's records, as they were not believed to come under his jurisdiction. State statutes pertaining to the office of the Coroner simply indicated that the coroner could take jurisdiction and investigate a death when there was some indication or suspicion that a death was due to violence. Lacking evidence of such, there was no allowance for the investigation of non-violent deaths, even when they occurred in the hellish conditions of the prison mines and work camps, although on rare occasions an entry relating to a natural death while imprisoned could be found.

Docket Entry:
Date: July 3, 1910
Deceased: Archey Hargiane, Col.
Address: #2 Prison
Cause Of Death: I found deceas died from some Internal diseas. Died very Sudent. Dont No the Real Cause. He had cifalus Trouble.
Remarks: Sent up from Hail county, Ala. Gran Larceny.

Work within the prison system could also lead to the accidental deaths of prison guards in the course of their duties.

Docket Entry:
Date: August 7, 1909
Deceased: Clarence C. Cork
Address: Flat Top
Cause Of Death: I found deceas came to his death By Being drowned In Little Warrior River While Chasing an Escaped convick. Dont No How deceas Got off of the mule he was riding.

Terrible living conditions and lack of adequate medical care were not limited to those men confined within the state sanctioned prison mines. A newspaper article relating the poor conditions existing in the Birmingham city jail, and employing the theatrical writing style of that time, attempted to bring this issue to public attention.

WHITE WOMAN DIES IN CITY JAIL CELL
Annie Summers Was "Dope Fiend" and
Has No Relatives Known Here

The Birmingham Age-Herald, August 11, 1913

"The eternal sleep came suddenly to one Annie Summers yesterday afternoon. It did not come peacefully, but after an hour of torture in which Annie suffered terribly for all her past misdeeds, her emaciated form quivered convulsively and then was still.

Death to Annie Summers came in the city jail where she was confined in a cell where roaches and huge water bugs and the slime and smells were horrible. There was no loving hand to rub the brow of Annie as she lay. She was not soothed by the knowledge that loving relatives were at her bedside; for only a negro "trusty" was present and the accompanying ode to her death was the wild song of the bawdy women mingling at times with the coarse, unrestrained laughter of negro wenches. Annie Summers died in the city without friends and without honor and was about 35 years old and looked twice that. She was not well known to the police. She was arrested Saturday night by Officer Alexander on Second avenue. The only charge against her was that she was a "dope fiend."

"There will be a thorough probe into the death of Annie Summers," said Chief of Police George Bodeker. "I will ask that a written report of the death be made to me at once by the wardens in charge. If there has been any negligence in letting this woman die without care the parties responsible will be exposed." City Physician Charles Whelan would say very little of the affair. Coroner C.L. Spain was notified of the death last night and will look into it this morning."

MORE THAN HUNDRED CONVICTS KILLED IN
DISASTER AT BANNER
Fatal Afterdamp Caused By Explosion
Yesterday Morning
Suffocates Scores And Frustrates The Rescuers In Work
All Hope Abandoned For Men Underground

Big Pile Of Dead Seen Huddled Together Near Opening
Sixty Men Escaped Alive Soon After Explosion Occurred
Large Percentage Of Mine Victims Were Negro Convicts
The Birmingham Age-Herald, April 9, 1911

"In addition to the positive identification of the two free white men, the rescuers were able to see many dead bodies strewn in every direction. Yesterday's explosion differs from those in the past years in Alabama in that there are practically no mourners at the openings. Usually there is a great crowd of widows and orphans waiting for loved ones but the men at Banner were convicts--for the most part without friends and whose relatives are scattered through the various counties of Alabama from which the convicts were sent. There were no loved ones to hurry to the scene immediately after the shock. The mourning must be done in the remote homes and hamlets from which the unfortunates were torn to pay the penalty for misdeeds."

GRUESOME STREAM OF BODIES NOW POURS STEADILY FROM THE MOUTH OF BANNER MINE

Total Dead Will Reach 128 Making It Most Disastrous
Explosion Which Ever Occurred In Alabama
Dead Mules Have Interfered With
The Work Of Getting The Bodies
The Birmingham-Age Herald, April 10, 1911

According to the Encyclopedia of Alabama:

"At precisely 6:30 in the morning on April 8, 1911, an explosion rocked the Banner Coal Mine, the pride of the Pratt Consolidated Coal Company located West of Highway 78 near Littleton in Northwestern Jefferson County. When the gas and dust settled, 128 miners lay dead in the dark corridors. Of the total killed, 125 were convicts leased to the company from state prisons. The economic interests involved could not be overridden (by legislative attempts to end the convict lease system), even by the shock of the Banner explosion, however, and the convict lease system continued until its abolishment in 1928."[10]

"Of the 128 dead, 114 were African American and 14 were white, 123 were convict workers and 5 were free. 72 of the dead convicts were from Jefferson County. One of those who died, Assistant foreman O.W. Spradling had escaped from the explosion but died from the effects of "after damp" after returning into the mine to help with rescue

> efforts. Most of the dead were buried in a trench dug by their fellow inmates in the on site convict cemetery. Damage to the mine itself was minimal and mining activity resumed a week after the accident. The coroner's inquest was held before a jury. They determined that the mine was in good condition and that the company was not at fault. The Banner Mine is now a strip mine and most of the underground works have been obliterated. The convict cemetery was relocated nearby."[11]

The use of forced labor was not limited to state and county convicts leased to private industry. Although with a much lower prisoner death rate, the City of Birmingham was a prolific employer of such a work force. As noted by C.V. Harris:

> "The determination of Birmingham whites to control negro vagrancy was a factor in a...type of government activity directed mainly towards Negroes—the operation of a convict labor system. Most citizens also believed that convicted lawbreakers, not taxpayers, should pay the expense of maintaining the police, court and prison systems and that if lawbreakers could not pay the fines and costs in cash, they should work them out."[12]

> "During most years, the city of Birmingham shackled its convicts in chain gangs, which cleaned and repaired streets ten hours a day. Prisoners on the street gang worked out their fines at the rate of fifty cents per day. Police Department reports frequently compared fines and convict earnings with department costs and payrolls and noted proudly how closely the department came to paying for itself. In 1907 and 1908, following especially vigorous anti-vagrancy drives, the Police Department congratulated itself upon showing a profit. Until 1911, the city kept its street gang in shackles day and night. In 1910 and 1911 protests against the practice came from the Jefferson County Medical Society and the Birmingham Pastors Union. In 1911 the City Commission provided extra watchmen in the jail so the prisoners could be relieved of their shackles while they slept, but were still shackled during the workdays."[13]

> "Birmingham citizens objected to the state convict lease system partly because it reduced the payroll spent in Birmingham and partly because of such inhumane features as heavy workloads, frequent beatings, poor food, miserable sanitary conditions, and the the appalling death rate of convicts in the mines. But the objection most persistently and prominently mentioned by Birmingham citizens was that the state convict lease system made Jefferson County the "dumping ground" for the worst convicts of the entire state."[14]

In his Pulitzer Prize winning book, "Slavery by Another Name," Douglas L. Blackmon details the life history and death of one convict, twenty-two year old Green Cottenham, arrested for vagrancy in Shelby County in 1908 and sentenced to a year of hard labor. The next day, Cottenham was sold to the U.S. Steel Corporation for the duration of his sentence and was:

> *"plunged into the darkness of a mine called Slope No. 12---one shaft in a vast subterranean labyrinth on the edge of Birmingham known as the Pratt Mines. There he was chained inside a long wooden barrack at night and required to spend nearly every waking hour digging and loading coal from the mine. Cottenham was subjected to the whip for failure to dig the requisite amount, at risk of physical torture for disobedience, and vulnerable to the sexual predations of other miners. Sexual abuse was rampant, in the darkness of the prison and isolation of the mine shaft. The lightless catacomb of black rock, packed with hundreds of desperate men slick with sweat and coated in pulverized coal, must have exceeded any vision of hell a boy born in the countryside of Alabama—even a child of slaves—-could have ever imagined. Waves of disease ripped through the population. Before the year was over, almost sixty men forced into Slope 12 were dead of disease, accidents or homicide. Most of the broken bodies, along with hundreds of others before and after, were dumped into shallow graves scattered among the refuse of the mine. Later I would discover atop a nearby rise another burial field where Green Cottenham was almost certainly was buried."*[15]

> *"Pratt Mines was a scene of nightmarish human suffering and brutal retaliation. Subject to squalid living conditions, poor medical treatment, scant food, and frequent floggings, hundreds died--the victims of mine explosions, rock falls, fires, neglect and, most commonly, recurring outbreaks of disease. If unclaimed by relatives, those who died were quickly interred in crude burial places adjacent to the prison camps or incinerated in one of the company's coke ovens. The private guards who staffed the slave labor mines and camps were vulgar, untrained, and often inebriated.*
> *Underfed and overworked convicts traveled from the Pratt Mines stockade to the mine through an underground manway before dawn each day, and back through the same tunnel after dark. Only on Sundays, when mining ceased for a day, would the prisoners see sunlight."*[16]

> *"Every African American in Alabama had been told stories about the vast prison mines at Pratt City. For a generation it loomed over the lives of black people, a mysterious hell in living earth buried beneath a licentious mining boomtown.*

> Men sent there for three months or six months instead disappeared for a year, or forever. The few men who straggled back to their homeplaces told of a whole city of mines, where shafts crisscrossed the subterranean world like a crazy quilt of streets with hundreds of underground "rooms," sometimes nearly intersecting with the shafts of other mines."[17]

> "Once deep in the mine, convicts were parceled in pairs into narrow "rooms" carved at right angles from the sides of the main shaft under the seam of coal. Many of the rooms were more like tunnels—some as tall as four feet but many barely two feet wide. The circumscribed chambers extended more than twenty-five feet from the mine shaft, forcing miners to slide on their stomachs a distance of five or more times the length of their bodies. The prisoner drove wedges into the coal to separate sections weighing a half ton or more. After enough slams of the sledge, the huge slabs of coal cracked free, sometimes for inexperienced convicts, landing in thunderous crashes inches from the prostrate miners. Sometimes only blasting powder--wrapped in newspaper to make simple cartridges and placed in holes drilled at the edge of the seam--could separate the coal from the surrounding rock. The miners hurried out of the room and back into the shaft seconds before the ceiling of coal collapsed with the explosion. Many men were caught by the falling coal and killed or maimed. Once broken free, the coal was hammered into fifty and hundred pound pieces and loaded into train cars. Once a day, another prisoner came by with a bucket containing portions of crude food."[18]

Blackmon also commented about the unmarked prison burial grounds associated with the Pratt Mines complex:

> "On an overgrown hillside five miles from the bustling downtown of contemporary Birmingham, I found my way to one of the only tangible relics of what Green Cottenham endured. The ground was all but completely obscured by the dense thicket. But beneath the undergrowth of privet, the faint outlines of hundreds upon hundreds of oval depressions marked the land. Spread in haphazard rows across the forest floor, there were sunken graves of the dead from nearby prison mines once operated by U.S. Steel.
> Here and there, antediluvian headstones jutted from the foliage.
> No signs marked the place. No paths led to it.
> No specific record of the internments survived.
> Here and in scores of other similarly crude graveyards, the final chapter of American slavery had been buried."[19]

It was incidents such as these which played a role in the prison lease system being abolished in 1928. On June 1st of that year the last convicts left the Flat Top mine.

A letter to the editor of The Birmingham News was printed in 2010 which took to task those who support the Sloss furnaces as a tourist site and who speak of this area's industrial past without telling the complete story:

Make Sloss a memorial for all who died there

"Upon reading the letter "Tour reveals real treasure," it became immediately clear the letter writer knows tragically little about what really went on at Sloss Furnaces while Birmingham forged itself into a city. Its not her fault. The ugly truth is not part of the Sloss Furnace tour.

To the letter writer and anyone else who might be quick to gush about "all those smokestacks in 1871," I would recommend Douglas Blackmon's 2009 Pulitzer Prize-winning expose: "Slavery by Another Name." In it, Blackmon exhumes the skeletons of countless leased convicts condemned to a living hell of coal mines and steel furnaces in the Birmingham area.

For several decades following Reconstruction, an unknowable multitude of black men were arrested on trumped-up charges, principally vagrancy, but their real "crime" was (that) they were black. These men, some only boys, were leased to the various coal companies, including Sloss. They were forced to toil upwards of 14 hours a day in the blistering heat of smelting chambers or in the poorly ventilated bowels of coal mines, where they were underfed and underclothed; often, they were made to work naked.

At night, they were chained inside barracks without heat or plumbing. They were routinely beaten--sometimes to death--and denied even the most basic medical care when they survived the beatings, or when they suffered the myriad health problems that were the direct consequence of the living conditions forced on them. The death toll was monstrous.

I could go on, but instead will suggest that "Slavery by Another Name" be required reading for anyone who has ever lived in the Birmingham area. For me, it is a moral imperative. Sloss Furnaces should also be a memorial, and I urge its operators in the strongest terms to openly represent it as such. It is no small irony that each October, Sloss becomes a haunted furnace.

Jonathan K. Horn
Sylvan Springs"

"Unlawfully Done"

Docket Entry:
Date: June 14, 1917
Deceased: J.A. Reynolds, White
Address: Maxine Camp #5
Defendant: J.N. Hooper
Cause Of Death: Pistol shot wound, same being unlawfully done and against the peace and dignity of the State of Alabama.

'I just want to clear the record'
The Birmingham News, January 2, 1983

"it was a bitterly cold night in 1916. A man knocked on the front door of the modest home of J.A. Reynolds Sr. in Adamsville. Reynolds opened the door and was asked by a man if he could buy a pint of home-brew. In those days almost everybody in western Jefferson County earned his living in the mines, but there was a strike going on, and Reynolds apparently was trying to make ends meet anyway he could. Besides, it was almost Christmas. Despite pleas from his wife, Minnie, not to sell it to the man, Reynolds sold the home-brew anyway. As soon as the money changed hands, a deputy with the Jefferson County Sheriff's office stepped from the darkness and informed Reynolds he was under arrest.

J.A. Reynolds was just 2 months old in December, 1916. But he has heard his mother talk about the night they led his father away. He knows his father was charged at the Jefferson County Jail with selling alcohol illegally. He knows his father was tried. As far as Reynolds knows, his father was found innocent. That's why he can't understand why J.A. Reynolds Sr. died a "convict" in a prison mining camp. And that's why Reynolds is determined to clear his father's name.

Reynolds never had worried much about the father he never got a chance to know, until he visited his elderly mother in California. During the visit, Reynolds said his daughter asked his mother how Reynolds' father had died. His mother was too embarrassed to tell the truth: That Reynolds was shot by a prison guard in 1917, while truing to escape from Maxine Mine No. 5 near the Praco community. Instead of the truth, his mother told the daughter that J.A. Reynolds Sr. had died of a heart attack, Reynolds recalls. "That made me mad so I decided to set out and find the truth. When a man's been in prison...his family's degraded about as much as he was. I'd always heard my daddy was in prison, and I figured he was guilty. It didn't mean nothing to me. But when my daughter asked my mother, and embarrassed her, and she had to tell a lie, I didn't like it."

With that, Reynolds began a search to learn what did happen to his father. And that search has convinced him that J.A. Reynolds Sr. died an innocent man. After poring through musty court records and other documents, after checking with officials of the State of Alabama and Jefferson County, he can find no record that his father was ever convicted of any crime. Why he wound up in a prison mine, why he died there and why his death certificate lists his occupation as "convict" is a mystery lost in the passage of time.

Reynolds produces records that show that on Dec. 22, 1916, the elder Reynolds was arrested for selling a pint of home-brew to another man and lodged in Jefferson County Jail. Bond was set at $300, but he apparently could not make bail. The elder Reynolds pleaded innocent to the charge on Feb. 21, 1917, and two days later he was brought to trial. Court records indicate that Reynolds was found innocent of the charge. Thats where the mystery begins. Reynolds apparently never was freed. Reynolds Jr. said his mother had told him about coming home to him and his brother, 2 at the time, and wondering why her husband wasn't released immediately. "Back then you didn't ask no questions…She had to take care of us. Momma didn't even know where they'd sent him."

Four months later was the next time she heard about her husband. He was dead, killed by a prison guard at the Maxine Mine. In those days, convict labor was used on a lease arrangement between companies and the county. Somehow, Reynolds Sr. wound up one of those working at the Maxine mine. The account of his death was reported on June 15, 1917, in The Birmingham News and the then-Birmingham Age-Herald. Both reported a "J.A. Randols" was killed trying to escape. The elder Reynolds was shot in the back, according to an old Hillman Hospital document.

A report filed by G.L. Spain, then a county coroner, said the victim was shot by J.N. Hooper, a guard at the mine. "Now that I have proven that my father was innocent, I want the record set straight and his death certificate corrected," Reynolds said. In November, 1981 a reply from the director of the bureau of vital statistics for the county indicated that "We wish to advise that corrections such as you have requested cannot be made on long-established records as the occupation as shown does not belie the fact of death on the fate given."

In an effort to further support his claim that his father was ruled innocent, Reynolds' daughter wrote a letter to the Alabama Board of Pardons and Paroles inquiring if any state records indicated her grandfather was in fact a convict. A letter from the state indicated that they "could find no record of a criminal conviction in this case in Jefferson County. In addition, the Board of Corrections...can find no record of Mr. Reynolds ever having been a state prisoner."

Reynolds says he is satisfied that he has proven his father innocent, but he still wants to find out the truth about what happened at the time the shooting took place at the mine. "I'm a God-fearing man. I believe God left me here to straighten this out. If there is a heaven or a hell, maybe my poor old mother will be able to see him (the father) someday and tell him he is cleared. I just want to clear the record. For my grandkids."

Postscript

The above noted docket entry, as well as the story of this case and its aftermath as reported in The Birmingham News by Lou Isaacson, reflects an extremely rare example of a case where the Jefferson County Coroner had ruled that the shooting death of an alleged escapee from a prison work camp at the hands of a guard was "unlawfully done." This official statement was rather remarkable due to the fact that it was one of the few such cases that I came across during my research where any prison guard, law enforcement officer or railroad police agent employed deadly force against an individual and where such a "ruling" was made.

My attention was first drawn to this case when an inquiry was made by the son of the deceased. That the shooting death of J.A. Reynolds, a white man who had been incarcerated at a prison camp for allegedly illegally selling "home-brew" to a police officer received such an official documented sanction suggests a statement of protest on the part of the coroner. Most likely it reflects his strong personal opinion that, at least in this case, the act was a rather egregious example of an unwarranted application of deadly force against a fleeing unarmed man. Perhaps the coroner had discovered the background relating to Reynolds' questionable imprisonment following his acquittal on the charges lodged against him.

Despite extensive research within newspaper archives by Reynolds' son and myself, we were unable to discover any additional information about the case to suggest that any legal action against the prison guard was pursued within the judicial system despite this rare accusation made against him by the coroner.

In attempting to understand the rarity of the Reynolds case one must take into consideration the routine practice during this era (and continuing for many years thereafter) of the quasi-judicial "rulings" that deaths of individuals at the hands of any law enforcement agent, no matter what the circumstances, were more often than not, ruled as being "justifiable." Although the underlying reasons for Reynolds having been incarcerated following his acquittal of the charges are unknown, it should be remembered that the system of convict labor in Alabama and its individual counties was a world and law unto itself. An inappropriate comment by Reynolds to the wrong person could have led to his continued imprisonment. It is also notable that Reynolds was white. Whether this fact played a part in the coroner's decision is unknown. Similar shootings of a number of black prison camp escapees were, without exception, ruled "Justifiable."

Docket Entry:
Date: July 29, 1911
Deceased: Frank Miller, Col.
Defendant: J.B. Tomne and W.B. Cardin
Cause Of Death: Shot while trying to escape from #12 Prison Being Justifiable Homicide.

Docket Entry:
Date: May 19, 1931
Deceased: Willie James, Col.
Defendant: Convict Guard K.P. Duncan
Cause Of Death: Gunshot wounds of head and body.
Remarks: Was attempting to escape from the crew.

However, the legally justified killings of escaping white convicts were not unknown.

FELONS MAKE A DARING DASH FOR FREEDOM
Five Men Blew Their Way Out of Pratt Mines Prison With Dynamite
Withering Fire From Guards Cut Them Down
Gang Was Led By Tom Fay, Member of Famous Miller-Duncan Gang
Two of the Men Are Probably Fatally Hurt

The Birmingham Age-Herald, September 5, 1903

"As a result of a desperate dash for liberty by five convicts from the camps at Slope No. 2, Pratt City, early yesterday morning, two of them are probably fatally wounded, two badly wounded and a fifth is at liberty. The escaping gang ran face to face with two of the prison yard guards, who opened fire with pistols and shotguns and brought four of them to the ground before they could climb the fence and reach the woods. The fifth escaped in the excitement and has not been heard from since.

The gang was led by Tom Fay, the youngest member of the famous Miller-Duncan gang of safe blowers and murderers. The wounded convicts are:

John Brewer, shot through body and in back, fatally wounded.

Richard Kennybrook, fatally shot in bowels and kidneys.

Tom Fay, shot in leg, not fatal.

Tom Melvin, shot in foot, not fatal.

James Amory, escaped, and it is thought he was not wounded, He has not been recaptured.

The convicts used dynamite in effecting the escape. They secured a large amount of it from an unknown source, and with matches and fuses they were prepared to blow their way to liberty. The first fuse was lighted by Tom Fay, and the dynamite blew out the entire end of the water closet to the building in which they were confined. There were fifty men confined in the building, but the opening made by the dynamite was not large enough for more than two men to pass out at a time. The debris had not ceased to fall ere Fay, followed closely by the other four men, dashed through the opening only to be met by the two guards who were armed with rifles and pistols.

The guards fired shot after shot with telling effect and all but these five convicts remained in the room and lay down to escape the rain of bullets which was pouring through the opening. Fay was the first of the convicts to falter. He received a flesh wound in the calf of his leg and it brought him to the ground. The other four continued in their flight and a desperate fight took place between them and the guards.

The convicts had sticks of dynamite and fuses which they lighted and threw towards the guards. Two of these pieces exploded and Kennybrook was in the act of lighting a third stick when he was shot by one of the guards. He fell on the ground and was unable to move. The escape was well planned and daring. Fay evidently led the gang. The authorities are at a loss to know where the convicts got the dynamite and fuses. The sticks which exploded were harmless and did not stop the guards, as was intended."

Other types of custodial related deaths were intermittently recorded over the years.

MEN BURNED TO DEATH IN THE PRATT CITY JAIL
At Least Five Prisoners Perish in Fire
Which Consumed Entire Building
Jack Kelley, A White Man, Was Among The Victims
The Birmingham Age-Herald, January 14, 1904

"The Pratt City jail was destroyed by fire at an early hour this morning and Jack Kelley, a white prisoner, and three or more negro prisoners, were burned to death. The jail was a wooden structure. It was discovered to be on fire about 1 o'clock. There were about twenty-five prisoners in the jail. Wild confusion prevailed and about twenty of the prisoners made their escape, some of them with their garments on fire. The only prisoner who perished that had been identified was Kelley. He worked for the Birmingham Southern railroad and was only locked up about 11 o'clock last night on a charge of drunkenness. He was 50 years of age and leaves a wife."

NEGRO CREMATED IN WARRIOR CITY JAIL
Futile Efforts Made To Save Negro From Horrible Death
The Birmingham Age-Herald, January 23, 1918

"Richard Gilbert, Negro, was cremated when fire destroyed the jail at Warrior yesterday morning. Gilbert was arrested on a charge of stealing meat Monday afternoon and on account of the bad weather Deputy Sheriff Cowheart was allowed to place him in the Warrior jail. He was to have been brought to Birmingham today. Immediately after the alarm was given, hundreds of spectators appeared upon the scene and with makeshift appliances did all in their power to save the negro. The negro was confined in a steel cage in the front part of the jail and from all information at hand the origin of the fire was in the rear of the building. Attempts were made to pass the doomed negro an ax with which to try to free himself, but all attempts were futile, the ceiling of his cell crashing down upon him and killing him instantly at the time when assistance was almost at hand. The Coroner's investigation will be held this morning."

Postscript

The belief that what was originally reported in the newspaper as a fire death of unknown origin was dispelled by the Coroner's docket entry: "I, J.C. Hartsfield, Deputy Coroner, was called to Warrior to investigate the death of Dick Gilbert, Col., and it was found he came to his death by being burnt up when the Jail at Warrior was set on fire, by unknown party or parties."

Docket Entry:
Date: January 30, 1917
Deceased: Elbert H. Taylor, Alias Thunder, Col.
Cause Of Death: By jumping out of window of City Hall while trying to escape.

Docket Entry:
Date: May 8, 1918
Deceased: Richard Cosby Barnard, White
Address: County Jail
Cause Of Death: By cutting his jugular vein at his own hands, same being done with suicidal intent.

> *"These walls and bars can't hold a dreamin' man*
> *So I'll be home to tuck the babies in*
> *They can chain my body but not my mind*
> *And I'll break out again tonight."*
>
> *---I'll Break Out Again Tonight*

CHAPTER 7

WORK

*"Daddy died a miner and grandpa he did too,
I'll bet this coal will kill me before my working days are through
And a hole this dark and dirty an early grave I find.
And I plan to make a union for the ones I leave behind."*

—*Fire In The Hole*

--"Communism? I don't want nothing that belongs to no other man. Just want to make a living wage on my own."

--"When I returned from the war and went back into the TCI mine I was older and those long 12 hour days were hard. The pay was barely enough to feed my family with nothing left over for anything else. So we went on strike again and again for more pay and the eight hour day. They starved us out by bringing in convicts and scab workers to do the job."

--I ain't got nothing against the Black man, as long as they go their way and I go mine. Black boy pulled me out from under the coal seam when it come down on us last week and I'd do the same for him!"

--"Like to get one of them newfangled respirators they're using up in Kentucky. Might keep me from dying young and hard from the Black Lung like my grandpa and my wife's daddy. At least maybe keep me from coughing up this coal dust all the time.
---A compilation of remarks from industrial workers
and miners from across the United States
1908-1936 [1]

The information presented in the previous chapters on Mines and Prison finds its culmination in this section on Work. Within this triad is found the interaction and expansion of these interrelated matters with the added factors of labor strife and unionization efforts which extended over a period of at least fifty years and which affected workers in Alabama as well as in many other parts of this country to varying degrees. The story of the industrial revolution and its associated growing pains is vast and has been extensively depicted by written word and in movies. It is a difficult task to adequately tell the story of labor in the Birmingham--Jefferson County region during the early 20th century, no less to present more than a brief overview of the larger picture as it affected our entire society and millions of individuals. What and how much information could be included in order to highlight the pertinent historical material relating to these true life and death issues which took place daily within the Magic and Marvel cities?

In reviewing local labor relations, it is seen that a "witches' brew" of politics, the power of factory and mine owners, both local and far removed, as well as racial and class factors all came into play. It cannot be denied that the unionization of workers countrywide was necessary to address the dangerous conditions which existed in the mines and factories of that era, as well as with the issues of long working hours and low pay. However, major changes would not be easily made without much violence and deprivation between all of those involved, especially by the individual workers.

"During the early days of the industrial revolution, the old personal relationships between worker and manager had disappeared. But nobody had yet invented peaceful ways to settle labor disputes between classes of people who rarely saw or spoke to one another. In the absence of discourse, disputes often turned violent, especially during hard times when large numbers of men were fired or had their wages cut. From 1934 to 1936, with a deepening depression, the whole United States was swept with an unprecedented wave of violent strikes, and an industrial center like Birmingham was a prime place for such violence."[2]

As noted by F.L. Allen, following World War I:

"The nation at war had formed the habit of summary action, and it was not soon unlearned. The circumstances had changed, that was all. Employers who had watched with resentment the rising scale of wages paid to labor, under the encouragement of a government that wanted no disaffection in the ranks of the workers now felt their chance had come. The Germans were beaten; the next thing to do was teach

> *labor a lesson. Labor agitators were a bunch of Bolsheviks, anyhow, and it was about time that a man had a chance to make a decent profit in his business. Meanwhile labor, facing a steadily mounting cost of living, and realizing that it was no longer unpatriotic to strike for higher wages, decided to teach the silkstockinged profiteering employer a lesson in his turn. The result was a bitter series of strikes and lockouts. Nor was there little radicalism among steel strikers. Their strike was a protest against low wages and long hours. A considerable proportion of them worked a twelve hour day. In 1919, the great steel strike had been in progress only a few weeks when a great coal strike impended. In this case nobody needed to point out to the public the red specter lurking behind the striking miners. The miners had already succeeded in pinning the Bolshevist label on themselves by their enthusiastic vote for nationalization; and to the indiscriminating newspaper reader, public control of the mining industry was all of a piece with communism, anarchism, bomb-throwing and general red ruin.*
> *Here was a new threat to the republic.*
> *Something must be done.*
> *The government must act."3*

My personal introduction to the labor issues of that earlier time came by way of my maternal grandmother who indicated that she had always been proud of being arrested in New York City for joining a demonstration in the street following the Triangle Shirtwaist factory fire in 1911.4 This tragedy, in which 145 workers, mainly young immigrant women, died when they could not escape the building because the fire exits had been purposely locked by the owners, became a watershed event leading to mandated improved safety practices in the workplace.

To gain some idea of the scale of industrial production in Jefferson County by the mid 1890s, Blackmon noted that:

> *"The number of free laborers surged past ten thousand, as the (Pratt) company's thirty coal mines—including the fourteen on the outskirts of Birmingham—generated nineteen thousand tons a day in 1900. To provide the most critical raw materials in iron and steel production, TCI—as Tennessee Coal, Iron and Railroad was commonly known-- operated 3,722 coke ovens and four quarries producing one hundred railroad cars of limestone and dolomite every day. Twenty blast furnaces smelted 3,550 tons of pig iron each day. More than two*

> *dozen furnaces generated 830,000 tons of iron and steel, shipped to thirty-five states and eight foreign countries. TCI owned in excess of 400,000 acres of mineral lands. Responding to booming demand, TCI invested heavily in its Pratt Mines complex and dozens of other sites across the seemingly boundless coalfields surrounding Birmingham.*
> *A thriving, permanent town called Pratt City sprang up nearby, with a bustling commercial district, bars, brothels, streetcars, churches and an overwhelmingly black population. Six miles to the west, another town, Ensley, grew around the company's mushrooming pig iron plant and six open-hearth blast furnaces each topped with a looming red smokestack perpetually billowing with cinders and toxins. Thousands of miners and their family members were packed into shacks, tenements, and company houses nearby. The acrid smell of coal smoke never dissipated.*"[5]

In regard to early attempts at worker organization, the use of convict labor and the racial overtones of the time, Blackmon wrote that:

> "*Like Pratt City, the mines at Flat Top and Coalburg were packed with black men forced underground at gunpoint. The others filled each day with white men paid by the hour who despised the black convicts, partly out of the habit of despising African Americans but more now for the crippling damage their presence did to the free miners' pleas for better wages and working conditions. By midsummer of 1908, U.S. Steel and other mine owners in Birmingham were moving toward a bitter climax in their struggle with the United Mine Workers. Seven thousand free miners were on strike—this time joined by five hundred free black miners, many of whom had been brought in as strikebreakers during earlier labor unrest and had never been welcomed by a union run by white men. Now hundreds of miners swarmed the entryways of the mines, harassing any workers who entered and threatening to break free convicts as they moved from the mines to their prison. The homes in Pratt City of some leading company officials, as well as miners who continued to work, were dynamited in the night. The specter of black and white miners unified against the coal companies was terrifying to the elite of Birmingham—and across the South. Mine owners responded with an aggressive campaign to divide the union along racial lines.*"[6]

As noted by Brian Kelly:

> "Birmingham's exceptionalism lay in the fact that its coal miners—unlike most of their counterparts elsewhere in Southern industry--succeeded in giving area employers a run for their money. Five times between 1890 and 1929 black and white union miners overcame formidable obstacles to mount district wide strikes against the South's most powerful industrial employers. Twice in the first two decades of the twentieth century state officials declared martial law in the Birmingham district and dispatched troops to put down strikes approaching insurrectionary levels." A strike in 1904 "lasted over two years, exacting a heavy toll on the UMW's power and sapping the morale of its members. Relying heavily on convict labor to guarantee a steady supply of coal, the mine owners managed to maintain their operations without any serious disruption in output. On July 6, 1908, four thousand black and white Alabama coal miners had gone on strike after commercial operators in the Birmingham district demanded a 17 percent reduction in wages. The strike was an all-or-nothing affair for District 20 of the United Mine Workers, a last-ditch attempt to hold on to some semblance of organization in the Alabama coalfields after a half-decade of debilitating, increasingly defensive skirmishes with local operators. The operator's demand for a sharp wage reduction was understood by the UMW as a final effort to dislodge the union from Alabama."[7]

"The managers of industrial and coal mining interests were conscious of-- even obsessed with—the strategic import of race. At the nadir of UMW influence in the years following the 1908 strike, they patched together a system of labor relations that grafted the most advanced model of labor management in the world onto more traditional methods rooted in the region's slave past. In the coal camps and mine villages scattered throughout the Birmingham district an ambitious reform program inspired by northern-based welfare capitalism coexisted with convict labor, the company "shack rouster," and the whip. The centerpiece of the operators' project was a system of racial paternalism that aimed to take advantage of existing racial divisions and the relative vulnerability of black workers under Jim Crow to erect a prominent barrier against unionization. Such tortured public posturing could be maintained only in the absence of an effective mine workers' organization. The operator's system

*began to crack, however, and finally collapse, under powerful pressures brought on by World War I. From 1917 onward they faced a renewed interracial challenge, culminating in the district-wide coal strike of 1920-21. The employers' panicked reaction to the revival of interracial unionism, culminating in the resurrection of Klan-style vigilantism and military suppression of the UMW, reveals much about the essence of white supremacy in the industrial South that a narrow focus on workplace racial "identity" would otherwise miss."8
"From the beginning of the 1908 strike, heavily armed "deputies were deployed throughout the district, and by the end of the deployed throughout the district, and by the end of the month some sixty "Texas sharpshooters" had been imported from the west and deputized by the companies. Operators calculated that their best chances for undermining the strike lay in driving a wedge between the "ignorant whites and blacks who have been idling away these many weeks," and the "better class of white union miners" who they supposed "would return to work at once but are afraid of assassination."9*

Unless you are very familiar with this part of Jefferson County, you will find it difficult to locate a remnant of the two lane "Old 78 Highway" that runs parallel to the current four lane U.S. Highway 78. This formerly busy route for automobiles and trucks traveling to points north of Alabama has been eclipsed by the opening of the segment of nearby interstate highway and now has mostly been reduced to carrying local traffic.

The pastoral landscape of this region belies the intense activities and violent emotions which played out in this now relatively depopulated area during the early part of the 20th century. There are no obvious indications of the prior existence of the once bustling coal mining town of Littleton which has been reduced to a few remaining homes. With knowledge of this background, one experiences a haunting feeling of quiet and desolation while traveling the nearby Banner Mines Road which leads to the site of the worst mining disaster in Alabama history. There is no sign or memorial which indicates the burial site of the many convict laborers who died in that explosion. Their remains were first interred in the Banner Mines cemetery, but were later reburied in a mass grave at a now forgotten location. The underground mines, as well as the open pit mines which followed, have now been "reclaimed" and covered over. A traveler not knowledgeable of the past history of this place would find it hard to believe the difficult physical and social conditions which had existed here.

WITH 1000 VOLLEYS RANG MOUNTAIN AROUND JEFFERSON
Deputy Gardner Falls Mortally Wounded and Rioters Have Losses
Train Leaves Hamlet In Hail of Bullets

The Birmingham Age-Herald, July 18, 1908

"After a most exciting battle, which knows few equals in Alabama since the civil war, a train load of 30 deputies escaped through a tunnel in the mountain yesterday, leaving Jefferson, the little junction beyond Brookside, in the hands of nearly a thousand sympathizers of the striking miners. The deputies carried with them Charles Gardner, perhaps fatally wounded by the first shot, and the "other side" is probably nursing a half dozen or more seriously wounded men.

The battle at Jefferson, from authentic descriptions brought to Birmingham, would make a picture worth painting. A train loaded with men blazing forth volley after volley from Winchester rifles; the hills on each side and the slope above the tunnel in front literally swarming with armed men, constantly firing from behind rocks and trees, were the picturesque and awe-inspiring circumstances.

More than 1000 shots were fired during the skirmish. The deputies, who were heavily armed had exhausted their ammunition, and the hills were still ablaze with firing when the engine pulled out through the tunnel and sped away to Blossburg.

The history of the difficulty begins early yesterday morning. Deputy Courson left Jasper on a special train carrying strikebreakers and other deputies. On arrival at Adamsville they were met by a large crowd of some 700 men, who are said to have attempted to entice the strike-breakers to join their ranks. However, the men were delivered at the mines. The train made a loop back to Birmingham and out again towards Blossburg. Jefferson is only a junction where a branch line runs out to Blossburg and the main line goes through a tunnel. The mountain surrounds it on all sides. Returning to Birmingham the train started out with another load of deputies at noon. On this train were George Courson, Maj. S.D. Dodge of Ensley and 16 deputies including Charles Gardner. Just beyond

Pratt City the train was rocked and the deputies, jumping off, fired several times, captured four prisoners and proceeded towards Blossburg with their prisoners. Before their arrival at Jefferson, a party of strike-breakers located there, becoming frightened by the threats, prepared to board the train.

Just as Mr. Gardner was swinging up the step a gun was fired from the switch tower, burying 13 shot in his back, neck and head. He was carried to the train for dead, and the battle began. For some 15 minutes the firing continued. The deputies believe they shot four men, and are not certain about others. The "sympathizers," who were on the hill, overshot their mark, and, although the windows were shattered and the car peppered with shot, none of the deputies were injured. This was the final violence of the day. It is believed that it was begun by a negro. While there were no other serious disturbances yesterday, several houses were dynamited in Pratt City."

Postscript

In the entry on the Officer Down Memorial Page (https://odmp.org/officer/18796-deputy-sheriff-robert-gardner) it is noted in the incident details section that "Deputy Gardner was shot and killed during a clash with a group of strikers who were picketing a coal mine. Deputy Gardner and 12 other deputies were escorting strike breakers across the picket lines when they were fired upon. Deputy Gardner and 12 of the miners were shot and killed during the ensuing shootout."

The origin of this entry is unknown. It is obviously erroneous as review of newspaper accounts written at that time indicate only that the miners "had losses." There is no indication that any of the striking workers were killed. It is impossible to believe that there would be no mention whatsoever in the newspapers of the deaths of 12 miners had such an incident actually occurred. Such a number of fatalities would likely have received front page attention not only locally, but nationwide during this period of widespread labor strife.

Just over a week following the lynching of the black union militant William Millin in Brighton,

> "the union miner Jake Burros was hanged from a tree after being arrested for allegedly dynamiting the house of a strike breaker. With tensions mounting, a delegation of prominent Birmingham citizens threatened the UMW

vice-president John P. White that unless the strike was ended they would "make Springfield, Illinois (where a vicious race riot had taken place only weeks earlier) look like six cents." Governor Comer became increasingly adamant that the strike must be defeated, dispatching troops to the strike zone and concentrating his remarks on the danger it posed to white supremacy. With the threat of racial conflagration looming over them, the UMW leadership began to fold under the pressure. Union officials declared the strike over.
The UMW had suffered a colossal defeat in Alabama, a debacle that sealed the fate not only of industrial unionism in the coalfields but of any possibility that black workers might extend their challenge to the racial status quo. The UMW was was shattered beyond recovery, at least in the here and now. For as far into the future as anyone could see, Alabama operators would have things their way."[10]

The 1920 Alabama Coal Strike

As noted in Wikipedia:

"The strike was authorized by UMW president John L. Lewis, and as many as 15,000 of the 27,000 coal miners in the state stopped work. The striker's first major confrontation happened on September 16, in Patton Junction in Walker County, where strikers killed the general manager of the Corona Coal Company, along with a company guard.
But African Americans bore the brunt of the violence: among many such threatening incidents, black miner Henry Junius was found in a shallow grave outside of Roebuck a few weeks into the strike. At least thirteen houses of strikebreakers were dynamited between September and December. Also in December state troopers terrorized the small black business district in Pratt City with random machine gun fire. The Alabama State Militia and the state police had been called out by the governor, Thomas Kilby, known as the "business governor." Once on site, state troop commanders typically placed themselves at the service of the coal companies.
    By February thousands of workers had been evicted from their company houses and left homeless. Towards the end of February the enormous expense of conducting the strike with no progress led the union to seek a resolution. None other than Governor Kilby was accepted as arbitrator. Kilby's settlement flatly refused union recognition and any wage increases, and he refused to reinstate striking miners. The national UMW chose to adhere to Kilby's decision. The union closed its state offices, and the strike prevented any union advances in the state for another ten years. At least

> 16 people were killed in the strike, more than half of them black, with an uncounted number of wounded."

As noted by R.P. Ingalls:

> "When police action failed to stop radical activity vigilantes resorted to physical attacks. Birmingham had long been noted as a particularly violent place. The city had also featured a do-it-yourself approach to law, and during the 1920s it had one of the country's most powerful chapters of the Ku Klux Klan. At its height in the mid-twenties, the Robert E. Lee Klan No.1 included almost half of the city's voters and many of the judicial, political, and police officials.
> The Lee Klan also engaged in a number of floggings. As late as 1934 the Lee Klan was still active, and Birmingham Klansmen attending a statewide convention were told, "the klan will either run communism out of the country or will itself be run out..." During the mid-1930's Widely circulated leaflet warned:
>
> "NEGROES BEWARE. DO NOT ATTEND COMMUNIST MEETINGS."
> Signed by the Birmingham Klan,
> the handout concluded: The Ku Klux Klan is watching you.
> TAKE HEED.
> Tell the communist leaders to leave."
> In addition to the Ku Klux Klan, new Klan-like organizations, especially the White Legion, joined the fight against the radical menace in Birmingham. The city's police chief claimed in 1934 that 1,500 members of the White Legion were massed to help enforce an order barring a May Day rally by communists."[11]

> "The setting for the outbreak of antiradical violence was shaped by the depression which struck Birmingham especially hard. In 1933 the Roosevelt administration found Birmingham "the worst hit town in the country." The following year, the The following year, the city was compared to a "paralyzed giant." Of the city's 800 industrial plants, not more than half were working. The coal and iron shafts...stand deserted. Jobless men walk the streets of Birmingham and fill the parks in greater numbers than in any other city of the South."[12]

STARVATION DEATH QUICK AND CERTAIN
Many without Food In County Now Face Hunger— More Deadly Than Disease

The Birmingham News, March 8, 1936

"Starvation may write a new death certificate for Birmingham before the week is over. Like tuberculosis, it works insidiously, and thrives in cases of malnutrition. Its results are certain and relentless, and the process of starving to death, according to a widely known Birmingham physician, is a matter of hours only once food is denied.

Some 20,000 residents of Jefferson County, therefore, face actual starvation this week. Some of them without food Sunday, already are starving. Starvation and its running mate--disease--have a fertile field in which to work among the thousands in Birmingham and Alabama whose sole means of sustenance, the State Department of Public Welfare, has been taken from them. Cupboards were bare, in many of these cases, Saturday night. Many more will be without food Sunday, and practically the entire number will be desperately in need of food by Monday. Relief officials candidly described the situation as "critical," and declared they were unable to see even the slightest ray of hope in probably immediate developments.

As matters stood Saturday, nothing had been done and nothing was being done because the problem has been checked up to the Legislature, which adjourned after four weeks of its special session until Tuesday. Hundreds of hungry persons, apparently in a daze and unable to comprehend the terrible actuality that faced them, continued to call in person and over the telephone to the DPW. No word of encouragement was available there, because the DPW has been closed a week.

The story has been told to the members of the Legislature, but the Legislature has not enacted a law to enable the State of Alabama to attach $153,000 in federal funds made available to take care of the destitute in Alabama. Yet the approximately 20,000 in Jefferson County, and more than 75,000 in the state, continue to look hopefully toward Montgomery.

Those in more desperate straits were borrowing from their neighbors where they could. Others were making frantic appeals to church and fraternal organizations. Still others were fighting the gnawing pangs of hunger. Tuesday, when the Legislature reconvenes, is a long time off, to them, even if it were possible to feed them that day."

Statistics

In an attempt to gauge the extent of work related deaths in Jefferson County during the early 20th century it is helpful to review available statistics based on information derived from the coroner's docket books. The following table lists the numbers of industrial accidental deaths per year from 1911 through 1930. These numbers exclude railroad and mine related accidental deaths which are enumerated in the appropriate chapters. Several early years have been excluded due to the absence of complete records.

1911---57	1921—-129	1927---175
1912---82	1922—-116	1928—148
1916---81	1923—-140	1929---206
1917---86	1924—-148	1930---121
1918---139	1925—-165	
1920---148	1926—-167	

Total deaths = 2,108 / 16 years = Avg. 132 per year (rounded).

The pattern of a steadily increasing number of accidental deaths within local work settings over the period of the years shown coincides with the expanding industrialization within this area and the increased number of workers. It is unknown whether the gradual implementation of improved safety practices over this period of time played a role in preventing the death rate from being even higher, however, it is obvious that the heavy industrial workplace remained a dangerous one. It should be noted that these figures represent mortality rates. The number of those workers who sustained serious life threatening and crippling injuries, but who survived, is unknown. The sharp decrease in the number of fatalities in 1930, as compared with several immediately preceding years, is consistent with the sudden massive drop in employment at the start of the Great Depression. Statistics for later years within the 1930s are unavailable due to the absence of many coroner's files and docket books for that period.

In comparison with the early 20th century, the numbers of workplace fatalities in the 21st century has shown a major decrease nationwide. This is due to the implementation of extensive legally mandated and enforced safety standards and practices in the workplace. However, the major decrease in heavy industry in

America must also be taken into consideration. Therefore, a review of death rates between these two time periods would not be comparable.

A listing of sterile statistics does not adequately portray the circumstances of how these deaths came about. Nor can they ever provide an indication of the social and financial effects and hardships on the families of the victims, especially in the years preceding the social "safety nets," such as workmen's compensation, that we now take for granted. The following docket entries provide some idea of the varied dangerous circumstances typically faced by the industrial workers of that time.

Docket Entry:
Date: July 18, 1910
Deceased: W.J. Cusick, White
Address: Ensley
Cause Of Death: Falling from the roof of the old open hearth at Ensley, Ala.
Remarks: Same being negligence on the part of the foreman by sending an inexperienced man on the building.

Docket Entry:
Date: September 3, 1910
Deceased: W.M. Duckworth, White
Address: Ensley
Verdict By: Jury
Cause Of Death: From being caught between a column and an electric crain at the TCI RR Co's steel plant.
Remarks: Negligence on part of the company by not having a watchman to caution their employees in case of danger.

Docket Entry:
Date: October 4, 1910
Deceased: Thomas Furnace and John Plotz, White
Cause Of Death: Overcome by gas.
Remarks: Negligence on part of Republic Iron Steel Co. by not having a guard with laborers when they are in boilers.

Docket Entry:
Date: September 25, 1911
Deceased: Bob Branch, Col.
Address: Woodlawn Furnace, Bessemer
Cause Of Death: A powder explosion caused by loading hole when too hot.

Docket Entry:
Date: December 30, 1913
Deceased: Jack Morgan, Col.
Address: Bucki Cotton Oil Co.
Cause Of Death: By being smothered to death by cotton seed.
Remarks: It is unknown as to how deceased became covered up with cotton seed.

Docket Entry:
Date: January 1, 1914
Deceased: Luke V. McCabe, W., Collagaro Mulocco, an Italian, Charlie Austin, Col., and an unidentified negro.
Address: Vanderbuilt Furnace
Cause Of Death: By being burnt by gas and hot ashes occurring through the down corner valve.
Remarks: We, the jury, also find it negligence on the part of the Woodward Coal and Iron furnace…that they allowed the dust bell to be capable of less resistance than the safety caps.

Docket Entry:
Date: June 2, 1916
Deceased: Bob Brown alias Bob Robinson
Address: 4th Avenue and 22nd Street
Cause Of Death: By being crushed by earth while working in excavation for foundation of Birmingham News building.

Docket Entry:
Date: October 20, 1917
Deceased: Claude McCauley, White
Address: Steel Mill, Ensley
Cause Of Death: From burns caused by sparks from the steel mill, same being accidental.

Docket Entry:
Date: October 25, 1917
Deceased: Richard Foster, Col.
Address: City Sloss furnace
Cause Of Death: Found he was completely burned up, only a few bones left, same being accidental.

Docket Entry:
Date: January 17, 1919
Deceased: Samuel E. Hortley, Wh.
Cause Of Death: By being flung to death by clothing getting caught on gasoline engine.

Docket Entry:
Date: February 7, 1919
Deceased: James Ivory, Col., Will Youngblood, Col., Ben Austin, White.
Address: T.C.I. Hospital
Cause Of Death: From burning of entire body by furnace blow out. Same being accidental.

Docket Entry:
Date: November 30, 1922
Deceased: Robert Maunck, Col.
Cause Of Death: By amputation of both limbs, caught in a rock crusher.

Docket Entry:
Date: June 16, 1925
Deceased: John Hugh Boyle, Wh.
Cause Of Death: By his body being partly severed when he was caught in saw mill.

Docket Entry:
Date: September 11, 1926
Deceased: Fred Busby, white., Andrew Conley, Col., and Sol Schular, Col.
Cause Of Death: By being badly mangled by dynamite explosion in rock quarry.

Docket Entry:
Date: September 25, 1929
Deceased: Henry Hicks, c.
Address: Courthouse
Cause Of Death: Traumatic fracture of skull.
Remarks: When he was hit on the head by falling timbers, on the new court house job, same being accidental.

Docket Entry:
Date: October 12, 1929
Deceased: Jim Ash, C.
Address: Ensley blast furnace
Cause Of Death: Fractured neck received when his head came in contact with a coke bucket, same being accidental.

    As the decade of the 1930s progressed, and upon the recognition by the Tennessee Coal and Iron Company of the Steel Workers Union, along with a new contract, antiradical violence ceased. The long, violent road towards the acceptance of unionization by industrial workers and changes in the workplace had certainly improved, but there was still a long way to go as the nation entered the World War II era. It would now be the turn of the auto, garment, railroad, waterfront and trucking teamsters unions across the country to take their turn in demanding better pay and safer working conditions as the country progressed through the war and towards the mid-twentieth century.

> *The mills*
> *That grind and grind*
> *That grind out new steel*
> *And grind away the lives*
> *Of men,--*
> *In the sunset*
> *Their stacks*
> *Are great black silhouettes*
> *Against the sky*
> *In the dawn*
> *They belch red fire.*
> *The mills,--*
> *Grinding out new steel,*
> *Old men.*
>
>   ---*Steel Mills*
>   Langston Hughes

CHAPTER 8

HOMICIDE

*"It could be a spoonful of water,
save you from the desert sand.
But one spoon of lead from my 45
save you from another man."*

—*Spoonful*
Howlin' Wolf

Essentially all homicides have some basis in factors related to passion, money, drugs, revenge or insanity, either singularly or in some combination. As noted by Sante: "You do not have to be glamorous to meet a violent end; it can happen any old way--by mistake, for failing to give somebody a cigarette, for loving too much or too little, for wearing the wrong hat."[1] The general information provided by Roger Lane in his history of violent death in Philadelphia in the 19th century can be compared to Jefferson County in the early 20th century where he noted that typically, homicide

> "resulted from a brawl or quarrel originating in a saloon but reaching a climax in the street. Drink was an important part of the culture of the city, enormously so among those subgroup in which most killings occurred. Other than the alcohol itself, whatever allegedly precipitated the trouble—a spilled drink, a careless remark, an argument about the merits of different steam engines--almost always seemed tragically out of proportion to the aftermath."[2]

> "Although the numbers of deaths attributed to suicide and accidents exceeded those due to homicides, they were at least reasonably, if not evenly, distributed through the ranks of social class. However, homicide, with some striking exceptions, was concentrated among low status or even marginal people and groups."[3]

As opposed to general statistics showing that in the mid-20th century, more murders occurred in the home than in all other places combined, Lane suggested that many homicides committed during the late 19th and early 20th centuries occurred outside of homes for two reasons. The first was that:

> "the kinds of people most likely to commit homicides, overwhelmingly poor and lower class, were perhaps less likely to be...found at home at all." Secondly, "a large number of people lived in shacks or airless cellars...and for transient bachelors, who were one of the most violence prone groups in the population, life in boarding-houses were the rule. The rate of literacy was not high by later standards and in the absence of radio, television, and even central heating, many men must have sought out the saloon for the simple comforts as well as the other forms of solace that it offered. The time spent in transit could be even more exciting or hazardous, with the streets full of animal activity, and all in open contact, none enclosed in moving metal shells."[4]

Statistics

In a previous chapter statistics were presented which depicted murder rates in Jefferson County over a multi-year period. These annual numbers of homicides which were documented in the coroner's records included those deemed to be both legally justifiable and non-justifiable. These figures also included those homicides committed by police officers, special deputies and prison guards in the course of their official duties. In addition, in the chapter related to race, data from the representative year of 1911 was presented which provided a breakdown of homicides by the races of perpetrators and victims. These documented rates and ratios in that year did not deviate significantly over the ensuing years to 1930.

It is helpful to review several statistically related aspects of homicides committed by members of the general population in order to attempt to assess various social factors which were related to these violent encounters. Specific statistics, along with an analysis relating to homicides committed by law enforcement officers, will be included in the next chapter.

Expanding on previously noted data, and in an attempt to better understand the rates of homicides in the years following World War I in Jefferson County, it was found that the documented numbers taken at face value do not deviate in a statistically significant fashion during the years 1918--1930, with an average annual rate of 127 murders over that period of time. However, when interpreted in light of the changing demographics, to include the rapid and considerable local population growth during that time period, statistics reviewed on a per capita basis provide a distinctly different view of the local dynamics of homicide than on a purely numerical basis.

In summary, it was shown that despite the average annual number of homicides remaining numerically consistent during this period the per capita rate, as reflected by increased population, showed a statistically significant decrease, a process which has continued into the first part of the 21st century.

The presentation and analysis based only on numbers tells us little about fatal encounters, some mundane and others which garnered the rapt attention of the coroner, law enforcement and judicial officials, as well as the news media and the general population. A limited review of some of these incidents, as brief or, in some pertinent cases, as detailed as the available information allows, may provide some insight into the dynamics of homicide, legally justified or not, during this era.

Although official records include all homicides brought to the attention of the coroner, it was not unusual that during the research of these cases, that a number of incidents were found not to have been reported in either major newspaper of that time. This precluded the ability to learn more about certain cases. The lack of reporting may have been due to limitations on the speed of communications between officials and representatives of the news media, the rapidity of which we take for granted today. Or in some cases it might have been due to the lack of interest in reporting or publicizing certain incidents for various reasons, either on the part of the news media or by certain law enforcement officials and politicians.

In regard to the law enforcement, legal and judicial systems and their approach to the defense and prosecution of those persons accused of committing homicide, Lane, in another study of violence in Philadelphia, which is also applicable to Jefferson county, indicated that:

"The record of successful prosecutions was held down for many reasons, the most important being the fact that the plea of self-defense was hard to counter. The typical case was the result of a fight, usually between two or more drunken men. Given conflicting memories and witnesses, juries (both coroner and petit) often found it hard to tell who had done what first and to whom, and they seized on acquittal as the shortest way out of the fog of testimony."5

"While the law represented the official moral sense of the State, the unofficial function of the jury (or the coroner), was to register the moral sense of the community."6

Assassination, Feuds, Duels, Vigilantism, Betrayal and Revenge

APRIL'S RECORD IS ONE OF WORST IN HISTORY OF COUNTY
Coroner Called On to Investigate
40 Violent Deaths During Month
Twenty-Three Proved Outright Homicides
In Only Seven Cases Has Identity of Persons
Guilty of Homicide Been Established—
Officials Comment on Situation

The Birmingham Age-Herald, May 1, 1909

"Yesterday closed perhaps one of the most violent months in criminal circles that Jefferson county has ever experienced. With 23 homicides investigated by the coroner and 17 other violent deaths due to unnatural causes, besides shooting and cutting scrapes too numerous to enumerate, the record for the month of April is pronounced fairly appalling.

During the past four weeks Coroner Brasher and two assistants have been at work night and day investigating cases where deaths resulted from violence or from other unnatural causes and the coroner's report for the month reveals a terrible and bloody record. Coroner Brasher's words yesterday were that "it has come to a time when a negro's life in Jefferson county is not set a pin's fee," referring to the slaughter of the past month. The number of negro murders where the victims came to their death "from gunshot wounds at the hands of unknown parties," is the most noticeable feature of the list compiled by the coroner.

A free discussion of crime in Jefferson county with the county officials fails to fix the responsibility. It is submitted that the failure of authorities to apprehend murderers and other law-breakers has made the rougher element of negroes bold and defiant and that they run riot without fear of the law. To this both Chief of Police Bodeker and Sheriff Higdon answer that they are doing all within their power to catch the offenders of the law. Chief Bodeker has always contended that the police force of Birmingham is entirely too small to properly patrol the city.

Colonel Higdon points out that Jefferson county possibly has the roughest element of negroes in the country. He calls attention to the fact that the negro criminals hide off in the mining camps where they are rarely seen by others than their fellow workmen, and that their location and identification is very difficult. He also stated, and his statement is borne out by the coroner's report, that in a majority of the negro cases the murderer is unknown to the authorities because the negroes are not prone to turn states' evidence against those of their color.

Sheriff Higdon calls attention to what he considers a great evil. It is understood that on the first of every month the mining camps in Jefferson county are fairly flooded with catalogs sent out by the big arms companies. It is stated that pistols are advertised as low as 95 cents. Consequently practically every negro in the county has a revolver of some sort. It is also stated by Colonel Higdon that a whiskey house in another state is sending out circulars advertising "four quarts of whisky, a revolver and a bowie knife," all for a ridiculously low price. The sheriff states that when the negro drinks the awful whisky accompanying the premiums he is ready to use the pistol and knife. The general expression is that the county is standing face to face with a very knotty problem, but the ways and means of solving this problem do not seem to be forthcoming."

Docket Entry:
Date: August 10, 1910
Deceased: Albert Parks, Col.
Address: North Birmingham, Ala.
Cause Of Death: I found deceased came to his death from gun shot wound at the hands of Hugh Friel, Jr., white. I let the defendant go on the plea of self defense and protection of the citizens of North Birmingham, Ala.

NEGRO IS KILLED BY HUGH FRIEL, JR.
Young Man Was Released On $1000 Bond For Shooting Burglar Who Was Attempting To Escape From House

The Birmingham Age-Herald, August 10, 1910

"Hugh Friel, Jr., was arrested yesterday afternoon on a charge of murder. Friel shot and killed a negro burglar yesterday afternoon at North Birmingham. The dead negro is alleged to be Albert Park. His colleague, Andrew Lewis, was arrested by Officer Morrow and locked in the city jail charged with burglary and grand larceny.

Sergeant Tom Shirley described the shooting. He said: "We received a call that someone was robbing the house of Lige Adams, the negro janitor of the school house, and Officer Morrow, with several citizens, went to the place. The house was surrounded by citizens who came out voluntarily to help capture the burglars, who were still in the house. Some of the citizens were armed. The negroes refused to surrender. They then made a break through the crowd on the run and were getting away when young Friel, one of the crowd, drew his shotgun on one of the fleeing negroes and shot him in the back with a load of bird shot. The negro ran around the house and fell dead.

Coroner Brasher went to the scene and will hold a thorough investigation today. All who saw the shooting together with Deputy Wilson and Coroner Brasher, say that Friel was justified in the shooting, and it is expected that the coroner's jury will release him from all blame."

Postscript

Apparently Hugh Friel was not charged with the murder of Albert Park, however, Friel was to meet his own violent demise years later as noted in the following coroner's docket entry:

Date: January 15, 1918
Deceased: Hugh Friel, Jr., and W.P. Brown, White
Address: So. Cement Plant
Cause Of Death: From suffocation and smothering in the cement crusher, same being accidental.

The public and official acceptance of the legally justified homicide of unarmed "fleeing felons," would continue until changes in laws and municipal rules pertaining to the use of deadly force by police officers in Birmingham were made in the late 1970s.

Docket Entry:
Date: August 26, 1911
Deceased: Will Howard, Col.
Address: 600 S. 20St, City.
Defendant: E.N. Brittingham, White.
Cause Of Death: Gun Shot Wounds
Remarks: Same being justifiable homicide by protecting his home and property.
Was shot near the Jewish cemetery at Enon Ridge, Aug. 22, 1911.

The violent crime and murder rates in Jefferson county, and especially within the city limits of Birmingham, reached "epic" proportions as noted in newspaper accounts of the time. Statements as to the perceived root causes of this criminal activity continued to be publicly espoused by Coroner Charles L. Spain during his term of office.

As recounted in earlier chapters, Coroner Spain would continue to take every opportunity to publicly castigate citizens, as well as some politicians, for their perceived irresponsibility which he felt had led to both the exceedingly high crime and homicide rates, as well as for the failure to provide for an adequately manned police force to deal with these pressing issues.

PEOPLE OF BIRMINGHAM
TO BLAME FOR MURDERS
CARPENTER NOT ARRESTED
Police believe John Camp's Murderer is Hiding Somewhere in Birmingham--
Coroner Spain Severely Scores Citizens of Birmingham, Whom He Says Are Directly Responsible for "Wild West" Conditions Here
The Birmingham Age-Herald, October 6, 1913
"At a late hour last night the negro Millard Carpenter, who shot and killed John T. Camp, the well known transfer man, was still at large. It is the general opinion here that he is hiding in one of the numerous negro dives. The entire police department is on watch.

It is not thought at police headquarters that the negro will be captured alive.

Throughout yesterday an absorbing topic of conversation was the murder of Mr. Camp, who was one of the most prominent business men in the city, and very popular. Indignation was fully expressed and it was recounted that in the last two weeks there have been killings daily, and not one of the guilty persons had been arrested. "It is a murder here and a murder there," said County Coroner C.L. Spain, "and the worst part of it is that not 1 per cent of the guilty parties are ever caught and punished. I am not offering a criticism of the police department. Undoubtedly with the extremely small force allowed Chief Bodeker by the city commissioners he is getting as good results as could be expected, but the question remains, are the taxpayers of this great city satisfied to place a premium on murder by having an inadequate police force to prevent such crimes or to catch the guilty persons after such crimes have been committed.
Somebody is responsible for the fact that human life is held so cheap in this city. It is a condition that should bring the blush of shame to the cheeks of the citizens who have the welfare of the city at heart. The causes of all this killing I have found in my investigations are mostly due to the fact that about every other man in Jefferson county carries a pistol and will use it quicker and upon slighter provocation than was the vogue in the west 50 years ago. Other causes are that cocaine and the cheapest grades of liquor are easily accessible to the negroes. A negro full of 'turkey-trot' gin and 'dope,' and with a .44 caliber pistol can do a whole lot of damage in a few minutes, as the records of my office show. No police department can enforce the laws if the citizens do not wish the laws enforced and I cannot imagine that where the great majority of the citizens are themselves 'pistol-toters' that the desire to enforce the law is very great. It is easily to be seen that Birmingham is not urging a strict enforcement of the law because it was representatives from Birmingham who went to the legislature and forced through an iniquitous bill curbing the powers of the coroner in his investi- gations. I repeat that it is up to the citizens of Birmingham to prevent the history of this city being written with a pen dripping with the blood of the victims of the assassins' bullet or knife. A stop to these terrible conditions of affairs is due and it is due now."

Culpepper Exum, president of the city commission ordered Chief of Police Bodeker to spare no expense in the endeavor to arrest Carpenter and offered a $50 reward for the negro, dead or alive."

CARPENTER DIES ON GALLOWS FOR THE MURDER OF CAMP
Execution Witnessed by Mrs. Camp and Her Daughter
Negro Dies Calmly and Apparently Unafraid
The Birmingham Age-Herald, August 7, 1915

"In the presence of a large crowd, which included the widow of J.T. Camp, his daughter, his brother and a friend of Mrs. Camp, Millard Carpenter, negro slayer of J.T. Camp, president of the Camp Transfer company, was hanged in the yard of the Jefferson county jail yesterday morning. The trap was sprung by Sheriff Batson and 10:56 and 18 minutes later Carpenter was pronounced dead by the attending physicians. He met his death without a tremor and was repeating in an audible voice the prayers for the dying. Rev. Father Malone of St. Paul's church accompanied the doomed man on the gallows and offered the prayers of the church while the last preparation was being made and as the trap fell that sent the negro's soul into eternity.

He was a large, well built negro, and his vitality was attested by the fact that it was 18 minutes before the physicians pronounced him dead. His body was taken in charge by the county and buried in the potter's field. The crime for which Carpenter was hanged occurred in 1913, which following a dispute over an amount of wages, Carpenter shot and killed Camp, by whom he was employed. The negro made his escape but was captured at Pine Bluff, Ark., and brought back to Jefferson county where he was tried and convicted. He claimed provocation and self-defense."

SPAIN ATTRIBUTES MURDERS TO LACK OF LAW ENFORCEMENT
SAYS VAGRANCY LAWS ARE DISREGARDED
The Birmingham Age-Herald, October 14, 1913

"Lack of law enforcement and the indiscriminate sale of cheap liquors and drugs," said Coroner Charles L. Spain, "is responsible for the present defiant attitude of the negro in Birmingham. There is a change of attitude in the negro in at the present time. They are defiant of law and order and will kill on the slightest provocation. The blame for this vests almost entirely on the greed for sordid gain on the part of a few sorry white people. If the law was properly enforced the druggist who sells cocaine would be placed in the penitentiary. The sale of cheap whiskey and gin to negroes would be stopped and the lounging negro vagrants would all be placed in jail. A condition of affairs exists on Eighteenth street, between First and Fourth avenues that is deplorable. Here on both sides of the street are found negro loungers and hangers-on who have no visible means of support and who obstruct the sidewalk in front of pool rooms and bar rooms. These negroes must live. Where do they get the money to play pool and drink? They do not work, and therefore they must steal and when a negro steals he will kill. The police should arrest and place in jail all negroes who cannot show that they are working at some substantial calling. On Twentieth street, between Third and Fourth avenues, the same condition practically exists, only here it is white men who are hangers-on and vagrants. The infest the saloons and poolrooms and obstruct the sidewalks leering at all who pass by. These men do not work. They must live and their mode of living is not open to investigation. It is of such riffraff that the record of homicides in Jefferson county is made what it is. The negro problem is a hard one to face, but the problem of white people making money off the negroes by selling them poison is a much harder one to face. It is to the indiscriminate sale of cheap liquors and drugs, more than 'pistol toting' that the lust to kill continues its grisly toll in Jefferson county."

Serial Axe Attacks

A series of attacks against individuals, many of whom were immigrant Italian storekeepers, occurred sporadically over a period of years, mainly from 1919 through 1923. Law enforcement officials believed many, but certainly not all of these attacks, were committed by the same person or group of criminals. Very few of these cases were ever solved, however, these incidents seemed to rapidly decrease following the front page attention paid to them as a group by the two major newspapers. This occurred after the number, similarity and increasing severity of the crimes was finally realized by the news media.

JOE MONTIONE, ITALIAN MERCHANT AND WIFE MYSTERIOUSLY MURDERED
Victims Struck on Head With Axe; Assailant Sets Fire to House and Escapes
No Clue as to Identity of Murderer Left Behind

The Birmingham Age-Herald, December 22, 1921

"Joe Montione, Italian merchant at 3224 Church street, North Birmingham, and his wife, Susie Montione, are dead as a result of injuries inflicted yesterday morning in one of the most fiendish crimes in the annals of local police records. Both were struck on the head with a short handle ax, Mrs. Montione being killed instantly and Joe Montione dying at the Norwood infirmary.

Montione was supposedly leaning over a basket of onions in his store when felled to the floor by the blow from the ax. Indications are that he was then dragged to the bedroom in the rear of the store, where Mrs. Montione was sleeping with her 7-month's-old baby, Pete. Upon discovering Mrs. Montione in bed, it is thought the assailant struck her with an ax before she had chance to give an outcry. It is believed by police the murderer then set fire to the bed to conceal the crime.

Both Joe and Susie Montione were discovered by Virgil Price, a negro woman, who lives next door. She had noticed smoke issuing from the windows of the building, and upon entering discovered Montione and his wife unconscious, the bed on which Mrs. Montione was lying in flames and the cradle in which the Montione's baby was asleep in danger of burning.

While robbery is believed by the police to have been the motive for the double crime, no tangible clue was left except a short-handled ax found in the store."

SOUTHSIDE MAN AND WIFE VICTIMS OF AX MURDERER
MRS. G.S. CRAWFORD SLAIN AND HUSBAND NEAR DEATH RESULT OF FIENDISH ATTACK
Babe Unharmed in Bed Nearby-- Woman Killed in Room Adjoining Husband's Grocery at Ave. D and Fifteenth Street

The Birmingham Age-Herald January 11, 1922

"Mrs. G.S. Crawford is dead and her husband is reported dying at the St. Vincent hospital, victims of a murderous assault committed in the bedroom of their home adjoining Crawford's grocery about 10 o'clock last night. Investigation by city police and detectives revealed the second crime of its nature within a month in Birmingham, the gruesome wounds of both victims indicating another ax murder had been committed in the city. The ransacked premises prove a motive of robbery.

Mrs. Crawford's neck was cut from ear to ear and the top of her head completely crushed. Crawford is injured by the blow of a weapon on his skull, which is thought to be fractured. A 2-year-old baby in a bed four feet from the bodies was unharmed. The bedroom had been completely ransacked and all money had been removed from the money sack which was under Crawford's pillow. The murder was discovered when (police officers) entered the rooms of the home, which adjoined the grocery store, and found their bodies lying in the middle of the bedroom in large pools of blood. Crawford is thought to have been possibly asleep at the time and Mrs. Crawford in the act of waiting on the supposed customer who proved to be her murderer.

"Mother, don't leave me," the baby cried when the undertakers were picking up the body. The child had looked on with awed silence while the officers and detectives made their search and investigations. Police are at a loss as to the identity of the murderers. Coroner J.D. Russum arrived upon the scene shortly after it was reported. He took charge of the child. The case parallels in almost exact detail the murder of Joe Montione and Susie Montione."

Joe Crawford, the night watchman, stated that he had heard Crawford speak of having trouble with the negroes who resided in that vicinity and that Crawford had always carried a gun. The store is situated in a negro section of the city and few white people reside in the vicinity."

CITY STIRRED BY RECENT ACTS OF AX MANIAC
Similarity in Bloody Crimes Points to Some Fiend
as Man Guilty of Deadly Series Here
Officers Comb City In Search of Ax Wielder—
Several Arrests Made
The Birmingham Age-Herald, January 27, 1922

GROCERS OF CITY ARMING FOR SELF-DEFENSE
Citizens Suggest Guns and Guards to Thwart Axman
Bold Citizen Guards Are Suggested as One Means of Giving Protection-- Total of Nineteen Murders in 1921 in Birmingham Never Solved

The Birmingham Age-Herald, January 28, 1922

"Guns and guards! Birmingham citizenry and Birmingham's small store owners seem to be united on the idea that guns and guards will prevent future ax murders in the city and make the streets and stores of Birmingham safe for human life. The store owners are arming themselves. They are buying revolvers of large calibre; shotguns, some of the sawed-off and riot guns, and in some instances high-powered rifles. The Ku Klux Klan has taken a hand and no one knows what may be concealed beneath their white robes."

STOREKEEPER AND WIFE AXE VICTIMS, BOTH NEAR DEATH
Couple, With Skulls Crushed, Are Found In Grocery, Where They Lay All Night In Cold, Shortly After Daybreak; Assailants Escape, Leaving Axe
Three White Men, Suspected of Assaulting Mr. & Mrs. Luig Vitellaro, Were Arrested by City Detectives and Taken to Central Station

The Birmingham News, January 24, 1923

"Luig Vitellaro, 42, grocer, and his wife, Josephine, 32, were added to Birmingham's rapidly growing list of axe assaults when they were found with their skulls crushed in the Vitellaro store at 2431 Eighth Avenue, North, where they had lain all night in pools of blood. Both had been struck with the sharp blade of an axe and are believed to be fatally injured. The bodies were discovered by Andrew Hightower, negro employee of the Ivy Leaf Coal Company when he entered the store to make a purchase. Hightower immediately spread an alarm and police and ambulances were quickly called. Both victims were taken to General Hospital and were reported to be in serious condition with little hope held for their recovery.

Robbery, according to police, was the motive, as Vitellaro's pockets had been turned and their living rooms in the rear, thoroughly ransacked. Dresser drawers had been taken out and upturned and a mattress in the bed, where friends of Vitellaro say he usually kept between $200 and $300, cut open. Vitellaro apparently was struck from the rear--possibly as he leaned over to fill a sack of groceries--and knocked unconscious with the first blow, while Mrs. Vitellaro evidently was attacked when she rushed from their rooms in the assistance of her husband as she was clad only in nightclothes. Her body bore many bruises as if she had grappled with the intruder. Beyond the finding of the axe and a blood-stained knife which was picked up near Mrs. Vitellaro, police were without further clews. It is believed that the robber, or robbers, were acquainted with the habits of the couple."

VITELLARO, VICTIM OF AXE ATTACKER, DIES IN HOSPITAL
STOREKEEPER EXPIRES SUDDENLY WITHOUT CLEARING UP MYSTERY
The Birmingham News, January 30, 1923

"Luig Vitellaro's name was added to the death list of axe victims when he died one week after being struck down in his store. Mrs. Vitellaro died the day following the assault. Vitellaro was 42 years old, and his death is the twelfth casualty in the axe crime wave. He was the twenty-eighth person assaulted. Although Vitellaro regained consciousness and was able to converse with his fellow countrymen, officials investigating the assault were unable to obtain a statement from him regarding the identity of his assailants. City detectives who visited Vitellaro stated that the patient showed no inclination to talk about the assault and turned away, feigning sleep when questioned."

WOMAN FATALLY INJURED AS FIEND WIELDS MEAT AXE
Another Is Seriously Injured As Negro Invades Store On First Night Proprietor Is Absent In Nearly Three Years; One Suspect Is Arrested
The Birmingham News, October 24, 1923

"For nearly three years Bernard Vigilant, Southside grocer, considered one of the wealthiest Italians of the Birmingham district, spent his evenings at home with his beautiful wife, Juliet, and family. Monday night, due to her insistence, he left them for the first time in that period to witness a performance of "The Fool," at the Jefferson Theater. When he returned at 11:15 o'clock, he found his wife lying on the floor, suffering from a blow on the head and a slashed throat, and his mother-in-law, Mrs. Elizabeth Romeo, 65, mortally injured and his house and grocery ransacked as a result of the work of Birmingham's noted axe murderer, or one who is following in his footsteps."

AX MURDER LIST IS INCREASED TO 15
Mrs. Vigilante Dies Without Opportunity Of Trying To Identify Assailant

The Birmingham Age-Herald, October 25, 1923

"Birmingham's long list of ax murders was increased to 15 when Mrs. Julia Vigilante, 26, died at St. Vincent's hospital from wounds inflicted by a negro assailant who struck her down with a meat cleaver and then cut her throat, following his heinous work by slaying Mrs. Frank Romeo, 65, Mrs. Vigilante's mother, as she slept in her bed at their store, 204 Twenty-Fourth Street, South, sometime Monday night. Mrs. Romeo succumbed to her wounds Tuesday morning without regaining consciousness. The negro attacked Mrs. Vigilante after he had purchased some fruit, and as she reached on a shelf for some smoking tobacco, struck her down.

Jim Taylor, negro, arrested after the bloodhounds had trailed him to his home, was in the city jail pending the action of the police. It was hoped that he could have been taken before Mrs. Vigilante for identification, but now it is just what all other ax murder cases have resolved themselves into--a case of circumstantial evidence."

Postscript

Although the appreciable number of assaults and murders which were committed with an instrument which may now seem to be an odd choice of a weapon, it should be remembered that various types of axes were much more prevalent, readily available and were used daily by many people as tools during the earlier part of the 20th century.

There seemed to have been a tendency for newspaper reporters to suggest that many of these homicides were committed by either one person, or at the most several individuals, during the multi-year course of robberies of grocery store owners. However, "reading between the lines" of some articles which specifically related to attacks on several Italian individuals might suggest that some were victims of internecine warfare or the real threat of extortion by fellow countrymen, e.g., the "Black Hand" criminal gangs, which were found across America at that time in those cities with large immigrant populations and who demanded payment for the "protection" of these storekeepers. That such situations had likely occurred is suggested by those instances where surviving victims refused to provide detailed information about their assailants to police or to positively identify suspects brought before them.

Information regarding these fatal ax attacks, as well as non-fatal assaults and murders not involving store owners but where injuries were believed to be inflicted with axes, were recounted in great detail by Jeremy W. Gray in his book "The Infamous Birmingham Axe Murders. Prohibition Gangsters & Vigilante Justice."[7]

Self-Protection

Docket Entry:
I, Coroner J.D. Russum, Jefferson county, certify that on January 25th, 1924, I held a preliminary investigation on the body of Joe Jackson, (C) with the following results: I was called to McMillon Undertaking Company to investigate the death of Joe Jackson and it was found that deceased came to his death by gunshot wounds of the back and hip at the hands of one Joe Ferlisi, (W) same being a justifiable homicide.
For issuing 5 subpoenas $1.25
For serving 5 subpoenas $2.50 $3.75

Although a number of immigrant grocers and other storekeepers became the prey of robbers and either suffered death or serious injuries at their hands, there were a few individuals who prepared for and stood up to such assaults. The Ferlisi family, longtime grocers in the North Birmingham area, became legendary in regard to their refusal to be victimized and established and practiced procedures to thwart robberies of their small stores. A number of criminals who sporadically attempted to commit such crimes against them met a sudden, violent demise over a period of many years which extended into the mid 1970s when the Ferlisi family decided to close their last store.

It is interesting to note that the mere knowledge of their readiness to respond with deadly force was sufficient to prevent any person in the local area who knew them from even contemplating the commission of an armed robbery of the Ferlisi store. It was always individuals from other areas who had no knowledge of this family and their preparations, worthy of a trained military combat team, who would make the always fatal mistake of attempting to rob them. Although they did not boast of what they felt they had to do under these circumstances, one family member told me that they would be "damned if we would allow someone to rob us of our hard earned money."

Justifiable Vigilante Justice

In the mid 1920s there occurred a spate of cases of homicide investigated and recorded by the coroner wherein individuals were found under circumstances which suggested that they had been engaged in some type of criminal activity and had been shot and killed by some person or persons who were never identified. However, this fact and the lack of detailed information regarding the circumstances surrounding these deaths, did not deter the coroner from making an official ruling of "justifiable homicide," without the calling of a coroner's jury and which usually obviated any further investigation by authorities.

No indication of the knowledge of or reporting of any of the following deaths by the news media could be found.

Docket Entry:
Date: December 16, 1924
Deceased: John King, Col.
Address: Jordan Und. Co.
Defendant: Party or parties unknown.
Verdict By: Coroner
Cause Of Death: Gunshot wounds of neck while he was stealing coal off a moving freight train, same being a justifiable homicide.

Docket Entry:
Date: December 24, 1924.
Deceased: Zeak Hicks, Col.
Address: Southern Und. Co.
Defendant: Party or parties unknown.
Verdict By: Coroner.
Cause Of Death: Gunshot wounds of abdomen, left shoulder and mouth...while stealing coal.

Docket Entry:
Date: December 26, 1924.
Deceased: Willie Rogers, Col.
Address: Welch Brothers Und. Co.
Defendant: Unknown.
Verdict By: Coroner.
Cause Of Death: Gunshot wounds of hips while stealing coal.

Docket Entry:
Date: February 21, 1925.
Deceased: Henry Brown, Col.
Address: Joe Young Funeral Home
Defendant: Unknown.
Verdict By: Coroner.
Cause Of Death: Gunshot wounds of chest, left hip and right leg, same being a justifiable homicide. No witnesses.

Docket Entry:
Date: April 3, 1925.
Deceased: Willie Zinnerman, Col.
Address: Davenport & Harris Funeral Home.
Defendant: Unknown.
Verdict By: Coroner.
Cause Of Death: Gunshot wounds of body at the hands of parties unknown, same being a justifiable homicide.

VIGILANTE KILLS NEGRO AS STORE LOOTING IS SEEN
Fountain Heights Group Member Shoots From Across Street
The Birmingham Age-Herald, October 1, 1937

"An unidentified negro was shot and killed last Friday night at the Pierson Grocery Company, 1531 Twelfth Court North and terrorized inhabitants of Fountain Heights hoped that this would at last put a stop to the series of burglaries and intrusions in that section which four months ago caused them to form a vigilante group.

The negro fell victim to the deadly arm of Charles A. Pierson, owner of the store, himself one of the organizers of the vigilante group. Pierson told officers that he shot the negro with a shotgun after watching him toss about 20 cartons of cigarets through a window in the store and then jump out to flee with the loot. Officers were told by Pierson that he took careful aim and fired, hitting the negro twice. The negro fell dead just outside the store.

For more than a half year Fountain Heights has been subjected to a series of burglaries. In the past two weeks alone, five Hill grocery stores and a restaurant had been burglarized. But the depredations were not alone confined to stores. Frightened residents on numerous occasions reported to police their homes had been entered in the middle of the night. But always the intruder managed to escape before police arrived. So residents of the section took to carrying arms and patrolling the district at night.

Friday night, warned by a method which he asked not to be made public, Mr. Pierson discovered that his store was being burglarized. Awakened in his home, just three doors removed from his store, he grabbed a shotgun and dashed to a position across the street from the store. It was then, he said, he saw his store being looted. Entry to the store was grained by a brick being thrown through the window."

VIGILANTE CLEARED AS THIEF IS KILLED
Fountain Heights Man Slays Negro Burglar As He Emerges From Store
The Birmingham Age-Herald, October 3, 1937

"Coroner Evans Saturday returned a finding of justifiable homicide in the killing Friday night of an unidentified Negro burglar by Charles Pierson as the thief emerged from Pierson's grocery store laden with loot. Pierson, one of the organizers of a group of vigilantes in the Fountain Heights community several months ago, after the neighborhood had been harassed by Negro marauders, told police he was awakened by a burglar alarm connected from his store to the bedroom of his home. Grabbing his 12-gauge shotgun, he arrived to find a Negro coming out the front window with 20 cartons of cigarets. Pierson ordered the Negro to halt and fired twice when he failed to obey. The Negro fell dead with wounds in the shoulder and stomach. It was found that the burglar had taken about 75 pennies from the store in addition to the cigarets.

The Fountain Heights vigilante group was formed about four months ago after a series of nocturnal raids, in one of which a minister's wife was terrorized by a Negro burglar. Determined to break up the burglaries, members of the committee patrolled the streets for many nights and residences and places of businesses were equipped with burglar alarms. While the vigilantes were in the field there was one night chase in which a number of shots were fired at a fleeing Negro."

No Legal Recourse

On occasion, physical altercations between two individuals led to the deaths of both parties. Obviously, no further legal action was possible or required on the part of the authorities other than being duly, and briefly, noted in the records of the coroner.

Docket Entry:
Date: March 5, 1911
Deceased: L.E. Marbut, White
Address: Rising Station
Defendant: C.J. Strong
Remarks: I found deceased came to his death from gun shot wound at the hands of C.J. Strong, white. Same being the result of a duel.

Docket Entry:
Date: March 5, 1911
Deceased: C.J. Strong, White
Address: Rising Station
Defendant: L.E. Marbut
Remarks: I found deceased came to his death from gun shot wound at the hands of L.E. Marbut, white. Same being the result of a duel.

Docket Entry:
Date: September 16, 1912
Deceased: Frank Holiday and Sid Nunn
Address: 200 South 20th St., City.
Cause Of Death: Gun shot wounds. Both parties being dead.

Docket Entry:
Date: September 10, 1918
Deceased: Jeff Anderson & Viola Rodgers, Col.
Address: Hillman Hospital
Cause Of Death: Gun shot wounds. By being shot with a pistol at the hands of each other.

Docket Entry:
Date: April 8, 1928
Deceased: Daniel Smith, Col.
Address: Bradford's Undertaking Company
Cause Of Death: Gun shot wounds of the right side of neck at the hands of Adie Worthington, same being a justifiable homicide.

Docket Entry:
Date: April 10, 1928
Deceased: Adie Worthington, Col.
Address: Jordan's Undertaking Company
Cause Of Death: Stab wounds of the left chest.
Remarks: Both parties dead.

LEWISBURG

The previous, roughly chronological review of several notable cases mainly revolve around incidents involving a limited number of participants, usually a single perpetrator and victim. However, in order to appreciate a degree of murderous depravity unparalleled in the history of Jefferson County, if not the entire state of Alabama, it is necessary to return to the period starting approximately in 1904 and culminating in 1913. Not before or since that time, possibly with the exception of the Phenix City debacle of the early 1950s, have there been as many murders and continuing terrorism visited upon a localized group of citizens of this state.

The extent and complexity of this gang related rampage, which went unaddressed by local law enforcement and judicial authorities for years, either through a combination of ineptitude, acceptance, graft or direct involvement would, in 1911, finally force higher authorities at the state level, to include the governor, to intervene in a situation which had reached crisis proportions.

The Saga Of "Bloody Beat 22" And The New Georgia Desperadoes
"A Carnival of Bloodshed"

Much of the relatively dense population during the early 20th century in the area in northern Jefferson County known as Lewisburg, as well as its environs of Upper and Lower Coalburg, Arcadia and Newcastle have long been relocated. Their presence at that time was predicated on the massive deep coal mining activities being conducted in that region. With the sudden end of the convict labor system and the gradual movement of mining activities to other areas of the county, the population in this region was rapidly, at least temporarily, reduced. Families of the original citizens who remained in the area are now mainly located within and immediately around the city of Fultondale which was incorporated in 1947, as well as within the adjacent city of Gardendale and its environs. The fact that many of the described depredations occurred in areas such as Walker Chapel is unknown to most of the people who currently live there, other than those long term residents who may have been told of such matters in stories passed down by older relatives or neighbors. Much of the region outside of the current populated areas is now open space or includes the sites of industrial and other business activities, as well as being crossed by interstate highways.

Here is the story of this chapter of criminal activity, social upheaval and the imposition of ultimate punishment as noted in selected newspaper accounts of the time. I have edited a number of these reports from their extended original versions with deletion of material which was repetitive or not felt to be directly related to the pertinent issues, however, the dialogue and terminology used is reprinted verbatim. It is only through a review of these documents that a full comprehension of the effects of this matter on the society of that time can be fully appreciated.

If Birmingham had been repetitively described in the early 20th century as being like the "Wild West," then the area known as Lewisburg and its immediate environs, could be considered to be its "Dodge City," As noted in the current online version of Bhamwiki, "Bloody Beat 22 was a perforative nickname for the Lewisburg community, which had become notorious for lawlessness in the early

1910s. Mining activity at Lewisburg and nearby Newcastle gave rise to a row of saloons and whiskey houses at the intersection of Stouts Road and Walker Chapel Road. They, in turn, gave rise to any number of fights and feuds that made the stretch resemble a "Wild West" town. A gang led by brothers Arthur and Walter Jones, along with Will Watson, Teck Duncan and Deputy Sheriff Henry Cole were blamed for most of the murders that beset the community."

One of the earlier homicides later attributed to members of this gang occurred in January, 1909. The murder of William Rhea remained unsolved for two years and was reflected in the following coroner's report:

Docket Entry:
Date: January 12, 1909.
Deceased: William Harry Rhea.
Address: Arcadia Mines.
Cause Of Death: Ambushed

RHEA MURDERED:
Slayer Unknown
Killed Near Scene of Father-in laws Death
Died Without Struggle
Officers Have Been Unable to Find the Slightest Clew--
Had Falling Out With Miners During Strike

The Birmingham Age-Herald, January 14, 1909

"Jefferson county had another murder committed in its confines Tuesday afternoon in which all indications are that the murderer will never be captured. W.H. Rhea, who was a union miner until the recent strike was declared, was found dead in the road with a bullet in his body, about a mile and a half from Arcadia and a short distance from his home. The body was found within a few yards of the place where Mr. Faulk, the father-in-law of the dead man, was murdered about a year ago.

Coroner W.L. Brasher...made an investigation of the affair. The body was lying face downward, the bullet having penetrated the right breast and lodged in the back. This bullet was extracted from the body by Coroner Brasher, who used his pocket knife. It is said that a physician residing near the scene refused to come when sent for by the Coroner.

All evidence pointed to Rhea having been shot from ambush. There were no indications of any struggle while there was also no sign of any person having hid in the neighboring bushes. To all appearances Rhea's slayer had simply shot him down with absolutely no warning. On the body of the dead man was found a .45 Colt's revolver, all chambers loaded, and 26 cartridges. The bullet which had caused his death was from a 44-calibre Winchester rifle. A widow and one child survive Rhea, his widow going through the awful experience of having her father and husband mysteriously murdered within a year of each other, with never a clue to their murderers.

It is generally believed by the officers that the killing grew out of a feud which reached fever heat when the strike was declared last summer. Rhea was a miner and belonged to the union, but it was said a falling out had developed between a number of the miners and Faulk and Rhea. Faulk was found murdered and shortly afterward the strike was declared. Rhea refused to go out and his life was threatened."

THREE HELD FOR MURDER OF RHEA
The Birmingham Age-Herald, January 20, 1909

"Lester Carter, Arthur Jones and Walter Jones, all of whom live in the vicinity of Arcadia, have been arrested...and are confined in the county jail with charges of assault and battery and murder docketed against them. The murder warrants were sworn out by Coroner Brasher...and are in connection with the murder of W.H. Rhea, who was assassinated several days ago a few hundred yards from his home."

Although identified as suspects shortly after the murder and arrested, these men would be released from custody due to their alibis and the lack of evidence. This would be one of the first cases which would, eventually, lead to the downfall of the Lewisburg gang.

REIGN OF TERROR CAUSED BY MANY ASSASSINATIONS
Six Negroes Killed In Six Days in Vicinity of Lewisburg
Half Dozen White Men In 18 Months
Lives of Deputies Are Threatened
Sheriff Urges Governor to Offer Reward—
Officers Visit the Scene

The Birmingham Age-Herald, November 3, 1911

"Is the mining district north of Birmingham, around Lewisburg, Coalburg and Arcadia, becoming converted into a veritable Dead Man's Gulch? Such seems to be the case from developments which have come to light within the past few days. Deputy sheriffs, at the threatened forfeit of their lives, guaranteed by occurrences of the immediate past, are barred from making investigations and arrests. "Black Hand" letters have been received by them, one in particular warning them to cease their activities in that direction. Instead of deterring them from further pursuing their investigations, it has only served to spur them on to run down the perpetrators of these outrages.

The sheriff will advance no theory concerning the assassinations, and states he is at a complete loss as to how to account for things which have been done. He is extremely active, however, in setting into motion forces which sooner or later must bring these desperadoes to justice. He is being assisted by the law abiding people of that community who want to stop crime there."

LEWISBURG ADDS ANOTHER KILLING TO LIST OF CRIMES
Constable W.W. Ellard Is Killed and Son Ralph Is Injured
Hagan Says It Was In Self-Defense
Shooting Occurred in Hagan's Drug Store-- Developments May Show Who Is Ringleader in Famous Clique

The Birmingham Age-Herald, November 13, 1911

"What is believed to be the beginning of the end of the awful clique in the Lewisburg-Coalburg-Arcadia district known as the "New Georgia Desperadoes" occurred last night with the killing of Will Ellard, Constable for that beat. Ellard is said to have been killed by Tom Hagan and Bob Payne, the former a young druggist of Lewisburg and the latter the bank boss of the Mary Lee mines.

According to information obtained, Ellard entered Hagan's store and walked behind the prescription case where Hagan and Payne were sitting. Walking up to Payne, Ellard is said to have said: "Payne, I always thought you were a friend of mine, but from what I understand, you have been saying things behind my back no friend would say of another." Payne is said to have denied the allegation and Ellard is accredited with having called him a liar. Ellard then started for Payne, and Payne tried to get out of the way when Ellard grabbed him and they clinched. During the melee Payne is said to have fired two shots and then left Hagan in the store alone with Ellard. Then Ellard is said to have started at Hagan, when Hagan grabbed Ellard's pistol from the floor where it had fallen and shot him. Hagan claims self defense

Immediately after the shooting Hagan hastened from the store and made his way across the mountain where he procured a horse and rode to the county jail and gave himself up to Warden Brown. Hagan Makes Statement:

"Just before Ellard came into the store and began on Payne, John Elliott came to me and asked if I was a friend of Ellard. I told him that I was, and he asked me to go out to the mines and intervene between him and another man whom Elliott said Ellard was trying to kill. I smelled something fishy about the matter and would not go. To be frank, I believe they intended to lure me from my store and kill me as they did Lawrence Evans and Broom some time ago. Ellard was the ringleader of the clique out there who has been giving so much trouble and he had it in for Payne and myself because we would not clique with them."

Hagan talked about the clique in that district which elicited such as caustic report from the recent grand jury, and which has baffled the sheriffs for years. He stated positively that he would do all in his power to break up the way of doing things out there, and was anxious to have conditions so that law and order could be maintained there. Hagan is said to bear an excellent reputation everywhere. From the evidence given to reporters at the scene of the trouble last night by eyewitnesses and others is seems that Hagan acted purely in self defense.

When the information given deputies at the jail last night is finally sifted down, a thunderclap which will shake the entire county will probably be heard. It was hinted that Ellard was the author of the black hand letters recently written deputy sheriffs regarding their activities in the many unsolved murder mysteries in that region.

During the melee at the store a showcase was turned over and several shots were fired. Ellard's little 8-year-old son, Ralph, who had run in, in an effort to get his father home, received a wound in the thigh. He was not seriously injured and his wound is accepted by all as being purely accidental. Ellard was shot in the front of the neck, in the hand, in the wrist and in the abdomen. He died within a short time after being shot."

FELIX ELLARD KILLED BY UNKNOWN ASSASSINS AT LEWISBURG YESTERDAY
Men Behind Bushes Along The Roadside
No One Last Night Was Able To Make Any Suggestion That Might Lead to The Detection of the Guilty

The Birmingham Age-Herald, March 19, 1912

"Felix J. Ellard, aged 57 years, father of Constable W.W. Ellard, who was killed at Lewisburg several months ago, was mysteriously shot and killed from ambush. Presumably two loads of buckshot fired from a double barreled shotgun took effect in his left side and back. The left side of his face was badly riddled.

Ellard was returning from East Birmingham. He had reached a point about two miles from his home, along a lonely stretch of the road, when the shots were fired. It is supposed that the shots frightened the horse which he was driving and it ran away. The horse was seen coming home by Ellard's only living son, Claude Ellard, aged 19 years. The latter not knowing the meaning of the horse's coming home alone, got in the buggy and drove back to find his father in a pool of his own blood, breathing his last. Claude told a deputy: "They got my brother and they got my father. I guess I am the next one, and I am ready to go."

From appearances about the place it is thought that there were at least two men in the ambushing party. They selected the most advantageous spot on the lone road to Ellard's home. The ground back of the ambush was dug up by the boot heels, showing that they were evidently there for some time. The top of the bushes with which they had built their snug barricade was perforated with buckshot, showing that they dared not show their gun above the top of the brush heap. There is no speculation regarding the identity of the assassins. Everyone talks freely of the shooting, but no one has any ideas regarding who did it.

Made Enemies In His Recent Crusade

Mrs. Dement, wife of Judge Dement, stated that she was of the opinion that Ellard was murdered by some enemy he had made in his recent crusade against the lawbreakers of the community.

Deputy Sheriff Jordan called the superintendent of mines of the Tennessee Coal, Iron and Railroad Company, asking for the loan of bloodhounds, which request was granted. Deputies Jordan and Friedman left Lewisburg then for Prison No. 2 of the Pratt mines, and secured the dogs. Among the dogs was an offspring of the famous "Scout," one of the most renowned dogs ever owned in Alabama. When they reached the scene of the shooting they immediately took up the trail and scampered off in the general direction of Arcadia and Upper Coalburg. When last seen they were still pursuing that general direction, and it was thought here at the time that the murderers would be caught before daylight.

FIRST ARREST MADE FOR ELLARD KILLING
TECK DUNCAN IS ARRESTED
UPON MURDER CHARGE

Assassination of Felix J. Ellard On Ellard Road Near Lewisburg Is Laid at His Door
WAS STAR WITNESS IN CASE OF ARTHUR JONES
Automobile Full of Detectives and Deputies, Headed by Sheriff McAdory and Chief Bodeker, Goes to Lewisburg to Make Further Investigation Into the Murder of Ellard

The Birmingham News, March 20, 1912

"Teck A. Duncan, of Coalburg, near Cat Mountain, ten miles west of Birmingham, was arrested this morning by City Detectives Cole and Goldstein and Policemen Moser and Bagley. He was taken to the county jail and opposite his name on the docket is the charge, "murder of Felix J. Ellard."

JONES BROTHERS CONFESS TO SERIES OF HORRIBLE CRIMES AT LEWISBURG
Confess To Seven Murders
Some Victims Shot From Fear and Others Were Assassinated for the Pure Fun of It
Light Turned On Bloody Carnival
History of the Awful Reign of Lawlessness and What Has Been Done By Officers to Round Up the Bloodthirsty Gang

Walter Jones Confessed to the Killing of Lawrence B. Evans, White, and Will Spencer, Lewis Lowery and Shep Chaney, Colored. Arthur Jones Confessed to the Killing of Will Rhea, White, and John Holland, Colored. They both confessed to the murder of George Shoemaker, White.

The Birmingham Age-Herald, April 14, 1912

"An awful story of cold-blooded crime was revealed yesterday, when Arthur and Walter Jones, two white men under indictment for the murder of a negro named Holland, confessed that they had killed with their own hands a half dozen persons and were implicated in the deaths of many others. Their confessions were made voluntarily. Previous to the confession Solicitor Heflin informed both men that no hope of immunity or clemency from the state could be given them. They told their gruesome story warily and with much craftiness, implicating themselves only when they learned that the coroner's jury was in possession of damaging testimony against them or that a confession had been made by others of their gang.

A startling feature of the confession was that both the self-confessed murderers charged Felix J. Ellard, deceased, with being the instigator and abettor of the carnival of crime that had terrorized the western part of Jefferson county for a period extending back to the 1904 strike. They accused old man Ellard of offering money for the "removal" of Dearmond and others who were subsequently killed; with ordering the execution of anyone of their member who showed the least sign of being "featheregged" and that Ellard saw to it that a complete alibi was established in the event of capture and trial of any of their gang.

They told of the cold-blooded assassination of negroes, many of them wanton and without motive except the lust for human blood, and of a number of killings for the purpose of revelry when often a few pence constituted their only gain. Terrible stories have been recorded from time to time of crimes committed with gain or revenge for a motive, but the Jones boys in their confession told of crime after crime that had been committed in Lewisburg without the motive of fear, revenge or profit.

The seeming immunity from punishment rendered the perpetrators bold and from killing for fear they went to killing for the mere fun of it. Human beings were used for targets to test marksmanship and men were slain in order that someone might carve a notch on his pistol. So long as the gang stayed together a conviction was impossible. At the coroner's inquest, held over the victims, none dared testify and if perchance suspicion was strong enough to justify an arrest, money and influence, and again the dread of testifying prevented the introduction of damaging evidence and the accused would not only be discharged but either fully vindicated or justified.

But as often the case, it was a disagreement among themselves that brought about their undoing. The nemesis that brought them to bay was the fact that several of the gang had been "spotted" for removal. Then it was that the skein began to unravel, and one after the other crimes were traced back to a net of undeniable evidence woven around the guilty parties, and they were confronted with their crimes, and as a result came the confessions.

The full confession of Claude Ellard, the preacher son of Felix Ellard, to the murder of Will Rhea, in which he implicated Arthur Jones and others, probably led to the confessions and other information that is in the possession of the coroner's jury. There is little doubt but that the whole situation will now be cleared up, the guilty ones punished and the name of Lewisburg be no longer a reproach.

A clue here and there resolved itself into a tangible certainty and crimes that were almost forgotten were revealed. Through it all was seen the form of Felix Ellard and the very jury empaneled to investigate his unlawful death was made acquainted with the terrible record of his life.

Partial List of Murders Committed in "Bloody Beat"

John DeArmon, white, shot and killed at Arcadia, June 26, 1908.

Lawrence Evans, white, shot from ambush near Mary Lee Mines, October 2, 1911.

Will Rhea, white, shot from ambush at Arcadia, June 26, 1908.

George Shoemaker, white, shot and killed at Upper Coalburg, January, 1905.

Will Spencer, negro, killed while seated in his own house at Lower Coalburg.

Shep Chaney, negro, killed while working night shift in Arcadia mines, Nov., 1911.

Sam Thomas, negro, shot and killed while fishing in creek at Coalburg, July, 1911.

Lucius Lowrey, negro, shot and robbed in own house and his body burned to conceal crime.

Peter Jackson, negro, shot and robbed on highway between Upper and Lower Coalburg

Alex White, negro, shot and robbed on highway.

George Buchanan, shot at same time, but recovered.

Hansome Woodruff, negro, shot and killed, motive unknown.

Robert Malone, negro, shot and robbed on Coalburg road, January, 1911.

Oliver Duckett, negro, shot from ambush at Arcadia mines.

Luther Broom, white, killed on the porch of Hagan's drug store, March, 1910.

Will Ellard, white, killed in Hagan's drug store, November, 1911.

Felix J. Ellard, shot from ambush, March 18, 1912.

A number of other killings known to have been committed but are withheld from publication by those working on the cases."

CORONER'S JURY REPORTS ON FOURTEEN MURDERS COMMITTED IN BLOODY BEAT
Fourteen Verdicts Charge First Degree Murder Against 12 Men
Find That Alibis Were Arranged For Murders Before Commission of Crimes--
Deplorable Situation Around Lewisburg

The Birmingham Age-Herald, April 20, 1912

"That human life was taken to satisfy either fancied grievance or passing whim and that not only was there an organization to kill, but also an organization to commit perjury on behalf of the guilty parties, was stated yesterday in a partial report by the coroner's jury impaneled to investigate the numerous murders alleged to have been committed in the Lewisburg district.

According to the report the investigation revealed a frightful state of affairs in the Lewisburg district. Crimes from assassination to petty theft were disclosed to the jury, and it was found that the perpetrators not only inaugurated a carnival of blood but were directed by men of sufficient intelligence to enable them to commit their crimes with comparative safety.

On the bloody list of murders the findings of the jury charge Arthur and Walter Jones with either being the actual murderers or accessories to seven murders each. Burn Kittrel is charged with three to his credit. Ed Kittrel two, John Miller, Will Watson, John Wade, Houston Sullivan and Claude Ellard with one each. All these are white men and are confined in the county jail. Others are implicated in many of the crimes, but for reasons their names are withheld.

The coroner's jury report detailed the multiple murders which had been committed over a period of at least five years and attributed these killings to a number of perpetrators. The strong wording of recommendations issued in this report also appears to be the first publicly stated chastisement of the chronic inaction of local law enforcement officials to respond to these crimes when they first occurred. Included in the report is a statement that "The lengths to which lawlessness in this community has gone show conclusively to our minds the necessity of prompt and effective investigation and speedy prosecution of all homicides, and of a fund for the purpose of securing competent aid in making such investigations. Had the first homicide in this community been vigorously investigated and the perpetrators arraigned before the bar of justice, the carnival of bloodshed which has since shocked this entire state would in all probability have been stopped in its inception. The commission of one homicide unpunished led to the commission of another. Out of this one arose yet another, until it seemed that the taking of human life became but a game or a hunt in which, unlike that of animals, there was no closed season."

DEPUTY HENRY COLE IS IN JAIL CHARGED WITH KILLING FELIX J. ELLARD
Cole Not Worried Over His Situation
Says If They Have Anything on Him It Is a "Frame Up"-- Can Easily Prove His Innocence

The Birmingham Age-Herald, April 21, 1912

"Since the early stages of the recent investigation of conditions about Lewisburg and Coalburg it has been common talk among officers that Deputy Cole was suspected of being implicated in the killing of Felix Ellard.

At the county jail last night Cole said regarding his arrest to an Age-Herald reporter: "I don't know what dope they have on me, if any, but whatever they have, it is a frame up. Of that I have no doubt. I did not kill Felix Ellard and don't know who did it."

Cole appeared last night to be perfectly of his ease, smoking and reclining in his chair in apparent comfort. He discussed his case with alacrity and did not seem to mind in the least answering questions propounded by the newspaper man. He seemed a bit puzzled, however, as to what the charge against him was based upon, but it did not seem to worry him. "I will have no trouble in proving my absolute innocence of what I am charged with. I can prove just where I was every minute of the day that Felix Ellard was killed."

ARTHUR JONES GOES ON TRIAL THIS MORNING
Case of Henry Cole Comes Up Tomorrow
Jones Boy, Who Goes On Trial Today, Is Charged With Murder of Holland Negro

The Birmingham Age-Herald, May 7, 1912

"The interest in the trial of the Lewisburg cases was manifest at the Jefferson county courthouse by the large number of witnesses from the Lewisburg district, both for the prosecution and defense. Arthur Jones, charged with the murder of John Holland, a negro, will go on trial this morning. The case against Walter Jones, charged with the same offense, is set for Wednesday morning, the Will Watson case going over until Thursday morning. These three white men were indicted for the killing of the negro Holland.

Seldom in the history of the county has such widespread interest been taken as is manifested in the Lewisburg cases now on trial.

Not far behind the cases against the Jones boys, in point of interest is that of Deputy Sheriff Henry Cole, which was passed by the state until Wednesday.

A pathetic feature of the trial was the presence of the wives of the men accused of the Lewisburg tragedies, several of whom bore infants in their arms. The killing of John Holland and its subsequent developments, which resulted in the arrest of the men who are now on trial, was the beginning of the investigations which have brought to light many of the Lewisburg mysteries. The clew to the Holland killing was given to Sheriff McAdory last June and was closely followed up until the men suspected were lodged in jail, and the investigations then began that led to the fathoming of the other crimes."

ARTHUR JONES DESCRIBES HOW HE SHOT AND KILLED THE NEGRO, JOHN HOLLAND
Dramatic Stories Related in First Lewisburg Case
Wade Tells of Negro's Death
Presence of the Prisoner's Mother Was Pathetic Feature of Big Trial

The Birmingham Age-Herald, May 8, 1912

"Gentlemen of the jury, the only way you can stop the shedding of human blood is to hang those who are guilty of this most heinous crime, the only way you can remove the blot on the fair name of Jefferson county is to apply the extreme penalty to him who willfully takes a human life. If you believe the defendant has established his innocence from the evidence you have heard turn him loose, if you believe from the evidence that the defendant is guilty, then do your duty, uphold the law, and by your verdict place the noose around the neck of Arthur Jones for the willful murder of John Holland.

(Jones)...while not denying the shooting of Holland, only did so when he thought his own life was in danger. Mr. Heflin reviewed the testimony at length and denied that any element of self-defense had entered into the killing of Holland...and stated that the evidence showed that Jones killed Holland wantonly or to pay an obligation he owed Will Watson, a white man who was arrested at the instance of the negro.

A feature of the trial was the testimony of John Wade, who testified that he was present when the negro Holland was killed and he gave all the details of the circumstances that led up to the killing. The testimony was exceedingly dramatic and caused quite a sensation in the courtroom. His story was unshaken on cross examination in describing the details of the killing. On the table in front of the jury was a package containing a few bones and portions of clothing said to have been worn by Holland on the day he disappeared. Deputy Sheriff Fred McDuff…testified to the finding of the bones of the negro Holland, his hat and a portion of his shoe. Mr. McDuff identified a shotgun and a revolver which were found at the home of Arthur Jones…later identified as belonging to the deceased negro.

Julia Holland, mother of the deceased negro…testified that her son left home on June 16, 1911, and that she had never seen him since that day. She stated that a white man came to her house and said Walter Jones wanted her son to go with him to condition some chickens. She described the white man, and when confronted with John Wade identified him as the person who had come for her son. She also identified the hat and portions of clothing that were found by the deputies near the place where Holland was supposed to have been killed. She testified that her son had had some trouble with Will Watson, a white man, about the stealing of some chickens.

Wade stated that he was sent to Holland's home to get the negro to come to the woods to meet Walter Jones, presumably to talk about some chickens. He testified that he and the negro were met by the two Jones boys and Will Watson and a conversation about chickens took place. He said Walter Jones took the shotgun from the negro and extracted the shells. At this time, he states that he saw the negro put his hand in his pocket and Arthur Jones raise his Winchester and shoot Holland in the head, the negro dying almost immediately. He stated he and Watson dragged the negro's body into the woods and left it.

Arthur Syphus testified to a conversation that he had with Arthur Jones relative to the killing of Holland. He said that Jones told him that he had killed that "negro chicken conditioner," and that the trouble grew out of a dispute between him and Will Watson and the negro about an alleged charge of chicken stealing."

ARTHUR JONES FOUND GUILTY OF MURDERING JOHN HOLLAND AND SENTENCED TO BE HANGED
Doomed Man Displays No Emotion At Verdict
First White Man in History of County to Die for Killing Negro
Death-Like Silence As Verdict Is Read

The Birmingham Age-Herald, May 9, 1912

"For the first time in the history of Jefferson county a white man is to hang for the murder of a negro unless Providence, the supreme court, or the governor interferes. By a verdict of a jury of his peers, Arthur Jones, a white man, is to hang by his neck until dead for the murder of John Holland, a negro miner, who was killed on Cat mountain near Lewisburg about a year ago.

Amid a death-like silence and with intense interest depicted on the faces of everyone present, the jury filed into the court room and stood before the railing that separates the spectators from the court officials. "Have you gentlemen arrived at a verdict?" asked Judge Cahalan. "We have," replied the foreman. "Hand your verdict to the clerk." Chief Deputy Clerk Dave Williams received the papers from the foreman and in a clear, penetrating voice read the verdict: "We, the jury, find the defendant, Arthur Jones, guilty of murder in the first degree as charged in the indictment, and fix his punishment at death." The defendant, Arthur Jones, was in court when the verdict was read and displayed the same coolness that has characterized his conduct during his days of his trial for life and liberty. His brother, Walter, whose trial for the same offense was in progress when the jury announced that they were ready to report, was seated across the table from the defendant. As the dread sentence was read out, beyond a quick glance at each other, the two men displayed no emotion and neither spoke."

WALTER JONES ON TRIAL FOR MURDER OF JOHN HOLLAND
Accused of Same Crime of Which His Brother Is Convicted
Same Witnesses Introduced as in Trial of Arthur Jones-- Wade Repeats Story of Negro's Death

The Birmingham Age-Herald, May 9, 1912

"The evidence in the case of Walter Jones, brother of Arthur Jones, who received the death penalty for the killing of John Holland as concluded yesterday. When the arguments began, Assistant Solicitor Hugh Locke opened for the state. He was followed by Charles D. Comstock for the defense. Borden Burr made the closing argument for the state. The same witnesses were used by the state as in the case of Arthur Jones. These witnesses offered practically the same testimony that was offered in the case against Arthur Jones and though subjected to a sharp cross-examination by attorney Comstock were not shaken in their testimony.

WALTER JONES IS SENTENCED TO LIFE IMPRISONMENT
Guilty of First Degree Murder for Killing of Holland
Prisoner Calm As Verdict Is Read
Second Jones Brother to Be Convicted
This Week for Murder of Negro at Lewisburg,
First Receiving the Death Penalty

The Birmingham Age-Herald, May 11, 1912

"That a white man can be convicted in Jefferson county for the murder of a negro was again exemplified in the criminal court yesterday when the jury who heard the testimony in the case of Walter Jones, white, charged with the killing of John Holland, a negro, returned a verdict of guilty and fixed the punishment at life imprisonment in the penitentiary. The prisoner, Walter Jones, received the verdict with the utmost composure and, beyond a quizzical glance at the jurors as they stood before the bench, gave no evidence of being in the least disturbed. The trial of another white man, Will Watson, charged with the same killing, is now in progress."

REMARKABLE RECORD MADE BY COURTS IN TRIAL OF LEWISBURG CASES LAST WEEK

WILL WATSON FOUND GUILTY AND MUST DIE ON THE GALLOWS
Story of Heinous Crime In Woods
John Holland Was Lured From Home By Four Men and Never Seen Again---Teck Duncan's Statement

> For the murder of the negro John Holland,
> the following convictions have been had in the
> criminal court of Jefferson county:
> Arthur Jones, death
> Walter Jones, life imprisonment
> Will Watson, death
> John Wade, the fourth white man indicted
> with the same offense, is yet to be tried.

The Birmingham Age-Herald, May 12, 1912

"Three times in the past week the death sentence was pronounced in the criminal court of Jefferson county. Twice the dread penalty was imposed on white men for the murder of a negro. Intense as the feeling in the early part of the week when the Jones boys were tried and each jury decided their fate, yet the feeling was stronger yesterday when the jury which had been deliberating on the verdict to be rendered in the case of Will Watson, charged with being an accessory to the killing of Holland filed into the courtroom and announced they had reached a verdict. The silence was almost oppressive as the clerk received the verdict. The hope that the long deliberation of the jury had raised in the mind of the accused was plainly apparent as he sat nervously drumming the table with his left hand. He watched with eagerness every movement of the clerk as he prepared to read the verdict. The firm, strong voice of Dave Williams rang out and the finding of the jury became known: "We, the jury, find the defendant, Will Watson, guilty of murder in the first degree as charged in the indictment and fix his punishment at death."

As Judge Cahalan qualified each juryman individually, the prisoner seemed scarcely to realize his fate. At the conclusion he jumped to his feet and excitedly exclaimed: "You have condemned an innocent man." His voice was harsh, his manner resentful. His actions, when the verdict was read, were in striking contrast to those of the Jones boys, each of whom received the verdict that meant their life or liberty with the utmost composure. Watson was plainly disturbed and evidently disappointed. It was predicted an acquittal would be the verdict, and as time passed the rumor gained ground. But at no time was an acquittal considered. The delay was caused by a discussion on life imprisonment or death, and the extreme penalty prevailed.

The killing of the negro John Holland on Cat mountain will go down in history as one of the blackest crimes in the criminal records of the state. Four white men played a shameful part in the death of Holland, but to the credit of the white race those four white men were hunted down and brought before the law of justice, where a jury of their peers meted out to them the highest punishment the law provides for their participation in the heinous crime.

The man is not born who could listen to the sickening details of the crime as told to the coroner's jury, the grand jury and the petit jury and not give his hearty commendation to the findings of those men who sat in the jury box, unless he be devoid of every spark of right and justice, or blinded by prejudice and passion. The juries of Jefferson county are selected from the highest type of its citizenship, and... have declared in the strongest possible manner that the blood of its humblest citizen cannot be shed with impunity.

The Sheriff was informed by his deputies that Teck Duncan desired to make a statement in regard to the disappearance of Holland. Duncan...threw the first ray of light on the killing of Holland, from which so much has been accomplished in cleaning up the conditions at Lewisburg. In fact it was Duncan who first threw the net that entangled Walter and Arthur Jones, Will Watson and John Wade in its meshes and started the chain of evidence that later brought to light so many of the murder mysteries that had baffled the officials and shocked the community and state. Duncan is not unmindful of the service he has rendered and in his characteristic manner says that instead of being confined in the county jail, he ought to be furnished a suite of rooms at the Hillman hotel by the county, considering the service he has rendered the state.

Duncan related the Holland killing as it had been told to him by the Jones boys and others that either knew of it or had taken a part in the killing. His statement was later substantiated by the confessions of Arthur and Walter Jones and by the evidence given by John Wade. While full credit must be given to Duncan it must be remembered that it was the work of Deputy Sheriffs Chris Hartsfield, Fred McDuff and Henry Cole, who had followed persistently a few slight clues which led to Duncan's disclosure, and these three deputies are due the credit of unearthing the first clue that lead to the Lewisburg murders."

QUIETLY JONES HEARS
THE DEATH VERDICT PRONOUNCED
TWO JONES BROTHERS NOW CONDEMNED TO DIE FOR LEWISBURG CRIMES, WHICH STARTLED STATE

The Birmingham Age-Herald, June 1, 1912

"With stoicism rivaling that of an old time Indian, Walter Jones, charged with the murder of Lawrence B. Evans and others in the Lewisburg vicinity, yesterday heard the verdict of the jury condemning him to death at the end of a rope. The prisoner did not display any nervousness whatever when the verdict was read, seemingly accepting it as a matter of course.

Walter Jones now stands convicted of the murder of John Holland, a negro, at Lewisburg and is under life sentence for that crime. His brother Arthur, was convicted of the same crime and condemned to die. Both brothers are now condemned to hang by the neck until dead for murders committed in "Bloody Beat 22."

TECK DUNCAN IS FOUND GUILTY
AND CONDEMNED TO LIFE IMPRISONMENT
Was First Man to Be Tried for Murder of Felix J. Ellard Is Fifth of Famous Lewisburg Cases to Be Tried, All of Which Resulted in Convictions as Charged

The Birmingham Age-Herald June 7, 1912

"Life imprisonment in the penitentiary was the verdict returned by the jury in the case of Teck Duncan charged with the murder of Felix J. Ellard. This was the fifth of the Lewisburg cases to be tried in the criminal court of Jefferson county, and for the fifth time a jury has returned a verdict of guilty as charged in the indictment. Three times has the death penalty been the findings of the jury and twice has imprisonment for life been imposed. Henry Cole, who was indicted with Duncan for the Ellard murder, goes on trial on the 17th of the present month."

At this time, the Age-Herald printed the report of the grand jury which, in part, addressed issues related to Lewisburg.

The Birmingham Age-Herald, June 8, 1912

Bloody Beat 22

"We have found 30 true bills in Beat 22 and 56 murder cases; five no bills, and have examined 247 witnesses. As to the thoroughness with which we have gone into this matter, we call attention to the recent convictions, being three for death sentences, two for life sentences, and no acquittals. We found from evidence before us that absolute fear of a certain lawless element has heretofore caused good citizens of this district to absolutely commit perjury rather than give evidence against murderers, and these witnesses would not testify until the ring leaders and a majority of these murderers were safely locked behind jail doors and a network of evidence had been woven around them which practically amounted to a guarantee that they would never gain enjoy even a few hours of freedom. We found that these murderers had professional alibi witnesses and bondsmen and killed absolutely without cause and, we believe, in some instances, merely to have the pleasure of seeing a negro jump when one of these crack marksmen had shot true to the mark and struck a vital spot. We believe that the professional bond making machinery for this lawless crowd has been destroyed. We further believe conditions will now be better in these beats, but we most earnestly urge a close and vigilant surveillance of these beats by our officers and especially with regard to keeping down "blind tigers." We found that a large number of these crimes were committed when the murderers were under the influence of liquor."

JESTS PASSED AS TWO MEN ARE SENTENCED TO DEATH
Dramatic Scene in Criminal Court Room Yesterday as Judge Frank Cahalan Utters Words That Send to the Gallows Will Watson And Arthur Jones Who Killed Negro John Holland

The Birmingham Age-Herald, June 9, 1912

"The judgement and sentence of the law is that you, Will Watson, on the 19th day of July, 1912, be taken to a place appointed by law, and there, by the sheriff of the county or his deputy, be hanged by the neck until dead."

These dread words were meted out by Judge Frank Cahalan of the criminal court yesterday. The same language was used in sentencing Arthur Jones. Both were white men and both convicted and sentenced to death for the murder of a negro, John Holland. Judge Cahalan called the two men before him. Speaking to Arthur Jones he asked: "Have you anything to say why the sentence of the law should not be passed upon you?" "Nothing, except I am not guilty," replied Jones. "Have you anything to say why sentence of the law should not be passed upon you?" was asked of Watson. "I am perfectly innocent of the charges," replied Watson, "and am in the hands of the Lord." Addressing both men, Judge Cahalan said: "I would not for a moment dispel any hope you may have of escaping punishment by appeal or otherwise, but I earnestly recommend that you pass the time between now and the date of execution in seeking spiritual consolation and preparing to meet your maker and may He who is all merciful have pity and mercy upon your souls."

The scene was most dramatic. The court was crowded. In addition to the two men who were sentenced, Teck Duncan and Walter Jones, both convicted of murder were present in the court room. The attitude of Walter Jones, who also has received the death penalty, was one of perfect indifference. Teck Duncan appeared to be amused at the proceedings. When Watson took his seat after being sentenced, Duncan jested with him about his approaching doom. The same degree of calmness that has characterized Arthur Jones during his incarceration and trial never deserted him and he received the sentence of death with the utmost composure. Watson was plainly disturbed and affected by the awful edict."

JAIL DELIVERY PLOT FRUSTRATED YESTERDAY
Saw Found By Sheriff's Office And Bars Are Found Cut In Cells of Crossland and Walter Jones
The Birmingham Age-Herald, June 28, 1912

"A mysterious plot to escape from the County jail, in which are involved Walter Jones and a man named Crossland, both under sentence of death, was frustrated by the sheriff's office. A saw was found with which several bars in the jail had been sawed into and it is believed that with three more hours of darkness two of Jefferson county's most notorious criminals would have escaped from the county jail and in all probability would have been well on the way to freedom before their escapes would have been discovered. Other prisoners, too, would have profited by the successful termination of the plot.

Sheriff McAdory received information that led him to make an immediate investigation of certain cells in the jail and the search was rewarded by the finding of a hack saw frame and five new blades up between the top of the jail and the roof, and a broken saw blade was found in the cell occupied by Walter Jones and Crossland. In Walter Jones' part of the cell one whole bar and a half had been sawed into and in Crossland's one bar was three quarters of the way through. The two prisoners were moved down into cells close to the door, where they can be closely watched. "We have no clew at present as to whom the party might be who carried the saws into the prisoners. The jail will be repaired at once and the guards reinforced. The saw frame could have been carried into the jail piece by piece."

WALTER JONES, UNDER SENTENCE OF DEATH, AGAIN TRIES TO ESCAPE FROM JAIL
He and Prisoner Wilkerson Saw Hole in Their Cell Roof
Warden Tipped By Another Prisoner
Jail Surrounded By Police and Deputy Sheriffs
Then Found Prisoners Sawing Hole in Wooden Jail Roof

The Birmingham Age-Herald, September 9, 1912

"With a sentence of death hanging over him, Walter Jones made his third attempt to escape from the county jail last night and but for a tip given Warden Gilbert by another prisoner, Jones and Harry Wilkerson, a young white boy confined on a charge of forgery, would have made good their escape. According to a statement made by Wilkerson, he has been busy sawing a hole in the iron roof for the past week. The hole was completed and Jones and Wilkerson removed the piece of iron and quietly slipped through the hole in the roof of the cell. This left them in a small attic with nothing but a wooden roof between them and liberty. It was while the two escapes were sawing a hole in the wooden roof that the tip was given and Warden Gilbert immediately sent out the alarm.

A number of officers from the central police station answered the call and inside a few minutes about 25 policemen were on the scene watching every corner of the jail for the two men. The hole in the roof of the jail was a "piece of work" that would have done credit to a master mechanic and it was in the small attic above the hole that the officers soon found Jones and Wilkerson.

"Bish" Gilbert, night warden, stated that he heard sounds coming from inside the jail several times during the week, but after thorough investigation was unable to locate them. Wilkerson was not the least bit abashed when pulled out of the attic. "Just took me a week to do the job," he said, "and if we had had a few more minutes you would never have heard from us again." The young man then went back into the attic and handed Chief Deputy Walter Metcalfe the three steel files which he had sawed the hole with. Jones would not say a word about his attempt to get away and was confined to a cell on the ground floor. This is Walter's third attempt to escape from the jail and his nearest approach to success."

DEPUTY HENRY COLE IS GIVEN TEN YEARS IN SUNDAY VERDICT
Defendant Taken to Jail and Cannot Be Allowed Bond Pending Appeal Was Found Guilty of Manslaughter Killing of Albert Nix Occurred at Sumpter In Blue Creek Region in 1907— Cole's Friends Surprised

The Birmingham Age-Herald, November 25, 1912

"The jury in the case of Henry Cole, deputy sheriff, charged with the murder of Albert Nix in April, 1907, brought in a verdict yesterday finding the defendant guilty of manslaughter in the first degree and fixing his punishment at ten years in prison. Immediately after returning the verdict Cole was taken into custody and confined in the county jail. He was apparently greatly crushed by the verdict for evidently he and his friends had not expected this outcome.

The jury yesterday in bringing in a verdict for manslaughter in the first degree gave the highest legal punishment for that offense. The fact that Cole was given ten years means that he must remain in custody while his appeal is being prepared and the decision is handed down by the supreme court. The case had never gone to trial before. Much interest has been attached to this case because of the fact that Cole was also charged with the murder of Felix J. Ellard, one of the series of sensational killings in the Lewisburg district."

SLEUTHS ARE HOT ON A COLD TRAIL
Newly Made Grave Near Lewisburg
Sent Cold Chills Down Backs

The Birmingham Age-Herald, November 30, 1912

"Another tragedy at Lewisburg," was the word that flashed around the sheriff's office yesterday afternoon. A message from W.L. Walker, a dairyman, who had been hunting near the DuPont Powder works between Boyles and Lewisburg caused the men sitting around the sheriff's office to rush to the scene in automobiles, prepared for the worst. They were to meet Coroner Brasher at the spot. Walker...had discovered a newly made grave. There was no stone-- not even a twig, to indicate whose bones rested in the gruesome sepulcher. Was it the aftermath of another "Bloody Beat 22" murder? Apparently yes.

Arriving at the scene, Mr. Metcalfe took but a few seconds to station his men in advantageous positions to swoop down on the mysterious tomb. Arrayed in a brand new overcoat, Coroner Brasher aided in superintending the maneuvers. Exercising all caution the five men carefully stole nearer and nearer to the grave. Hartsfield was in his customary place in the front ranks. There was not a sound. Closer and closer they came to the scene of the expected crime.

Suddenly the men on the skirmishing line jumped to one side and retreated a few steps. However, they had only been startled by Coroner Brasher falling over a barbed wire fence, tearing his new overcoat to shreds. A discussion was held. Then Hartsfield led the troops again toward The Great Mysterious. Their courage renewed, the five men walked up to the grave, and after many excuses began to unearth the body. After a few minutes of slow digging, to the horrified vision of the five sleuths appeared the body of a cow, a nice black Jersey cow. "Humph," said Coroner Brasher, smoothing out the tatters of his new coat. "Just what I thought," said Chief Metcalfe. Steele, McDuff and Hartsfield merely wiped the mud from their boots. The trip back to Birmingham was made in record time. The theory is that some person after stealing the cow and appropriating a few choice cuts of the meat, buried the body in the grave to escape suspicion."

AUTOPSY INDICATES DEPUTY SHERIFF HENRY COLE DEAD FROM MORPHINE POISONING
Unusual Career Is Ended
Was Taken Very Ill In Jail Yesterday Morning
Doctors Said At Once He Would Die
Recently Given Ten Years for Nix Killing and Indicted on Charges of Murdering Felix J. Ellard at Lewisburg

The Birmingham Age-Herald, December 20, 1912

"That Deputy Sheriff Henry Cole died yesterday afternoon at the Hillman hospital probably from the effects of morphine poisoning was the startling evidence produced at an autopsy held over the body last night.

Mr. Cole had been confined in the county jail for some time on a charge of killing Felix Ellard at Lewisburg last spring. For five hours Mr. Cole lingered between life and death, his breath coming at irregular intervals, and very slowly. He died at 6:45 o'clock. Solicitor H.P. Heflin and Coroner B.L. Brasher ordered an autopsy held over the body at once, as there had been signs of morphine poisoning. It was at first thought that Mr. Cole had died from apoplexy, or blood clot on the brain, but the autopsy revealed that the brain was in perfect condition, and that there was no trace of a blood clot. Coroner Brasher stated after the autopsy: "There was no blood clot, but there were strong signs of morphine poisoning." As Mr. Cole had been in apparently good physical condition, although greatly unstrung and nervous, it is believed he died from morphine poisoning.

The autopsy last night was the first step in solving the mystery surrounding the death of Mr. Cole. As it has been practically assured that he died from poison, the next step will be to find whether he died by his own hand. Dr. McLester will analyzer the contents of the stomach of the dead man for poison and it will probably be several days before he completes his work.

Henry Cole, convicted of the murder of Albert Nix and charged with the killing of Felix J. Ellard at Lewisburg, died in the Hillman hospital, bringing to an end what is regarded as one of the most unusual careers in Jefferson county. Mr. Cole, or "Uncle Henry," as he was widely known, was removed from the county jail where he had been held a prisoner pending trial, to the Hillman hospital.

According to officials he had been in poor health and despondent for several weeks

He was first noticed as being seriously ill yesterday morning by John Wade, who occupied the same cell. Wade said that Cole had complained of feeling badly. About 9 o'clock Cole asked Wade if he could hear the negro prisoners singing in the jail. "The music sounds sweeter than ever before," said Cole. When Wade got up yesterday morning he…noticed that Cole was breathing very heavily and told Day Warden Griffith that Cole appeared to be very sick.

Dr. R.H. Hamrick stated at once that there was no hope of recovery. He stated that there were signs of morphine poisoning. A number of people were of the opinion that Mr. Cole had poisoned himself. When asked about this theory Sheriff McAdory stated: "I examined every piece of clothing of Uncle Henry, went through his suitcase and trunk in an effort to find poison and could not find no trace whatever." The sheriff stated that…a doctor was called upon the request of Mr. Cole and some medicine was administered . Mr. Cole's daughter visited him Wednesday afternoon and remained with him for some time.

For the past two weeks Cole had been despondent, unstrung and nervous. Convicted of killing Albert Nix, he was given a 10-year sentence in the penitentiary. This action was immediately followed by Judge Fort's refusal of a new trial. It is said that Cole had also been told of Teck Duncan's alleged confession and that he had brooded over this matter; that he had been told more witnesses had been secured against him in the Ellard case and that he believed a "frame up" had been fixed against him. The iron nerve with which he had carried himself through many dangerous situations and which had pulled him out of many a tight hole, finally gave way and he became ill. Mr. Cole frequently talked of his troubles to the officials around the jail. It is said that he recently asked "how much morphine a person could take to make him sleep."

Mr. Cole was 57 years of age. He is survived by a widow, two daughters and one son. He was born near Jasper, in Walker county and served as a deputy sheriff in Bibb county. He has served as deputy sheriff in Jefferson county for many years, having a remarkable and varied experience. In a statement made to Sheriff McAdory several days ago, Cole denied having killed as many men as he is accused of. His statement was that during his term as deputy, 22 years of service, he had killed eight men and that he was compelled to shoot in self-defense in each instance. "I killed Thrasher, Nix, Morrison and Pickens and four negroes, but I swear that is every one I ever killed, and I had to shoot each time," was the statement of Cole. "They accuse me of killing Painter along with Thrasher, but I didn't shoot him."

During the trial for the killing of Albert Nix, Cole was confident of acquittal. The trial grew out of the shooting of Nix in Blue Creek in 1909. Cole, as deputy sheriff, had gone to the Nix home with a warrant for the arrest of Mrs. Nix on a charge of abducting her children by a former marriage. Trouble insued and Nix was killed. The jury in the case was out for about one day and returned a verdict of guilty, fixing Cole's penalty at 10 years in the penitentiary. Cole at the time of his conviction was held in the county jail on an indictment of the grand jury for the assassination of Felix Ellard at Lewisburg last spring. Interment will take place in Elmwood cemetery."

MORPHINE KILLED COLE; HOW HE GOT IT IS A MYSTERY
The Birmingham Age-Herald, January 11, 1913

"The coroner's jury investigating the death of Henry Cole returned a verdict to the effect that the former deputy sheriff met his death by morphine poisoning but that the jury could not decide how he obtained the poison. How Cole obtained the poison is still a mystery and is a point that the coroner's jury would like for the grand jury to investigate. It is still a matter of mystery whether he committed suicide or whether someone on the outside gave him the poison."

JONES SENTENCE MAY BE COMMUTED
Petition Being Circulated
to Save Arthur Jones From Hanging
The Birmingham Age-Herald February 9, 1913

"Commutation of the death sentence inflicted on Arthur Jones for the murder of John Holland, will be requested by the citizens of Jefferson County. It is understood a petition is being circulated now and will be presented to Governor O'Neal soon.

The supreme court this week affirmed the verdict of guilty and set March 21 as the date for the execution of Jones and William Watson, who was convicted in the same case. C. Henry Cole, deputy sheriff, who died in the Jefferson county jail while confined on a charge of murder, signed the petition before the supreme court passed on the case. He realized that the case would be affirmed and placed his signature to the petition a few days before he died,"

SENSATIONAL REPORT FILED BY GRAND JURY MINORITY
Claim Sheriff M'Adory and Deputy Metcalfe Should Have Been Indicted by the Grand Jury
Gamblers And The Owners Of Places Get "Square Deal"
Extraordinary Grand Jury Is Recommended
Minority Report Made By Five Members

The Birmingham Age-Herald, February 21, 1913

"Five members submit minority report and give it as their opinion that Walter L. Metcalf should have been indicted as a principal or accessory before the fact to the murder of Felix J. Ellard, and that Sheriff Walter K. McAdory should have been indicted for aiding, shielding and protecting Henry Cole and W.L. Metcalf from arrest and punishment."

METCALF INDICTED ON CHARGE OF BEING AN ACCESSORY AFTER THE FACT

The Birmingham Age-Herald, February 21, 1913

"Alleging that he was an "accessory after the fact" the grand jury returned an indictment against Walter L. Metcalf, chief deputy sheriff of Jefferson county and he was placed under a $500 bond to appear before the criminal court in answer to the charge.

The indictment is very lengthy and contains three counts. The indictment alleges that Mr. Metcalf had prevented Teck Duncan from making certain disclosures regarding the killing of Felix J. Ellard and that he allowed Henry Cole to interview Duncan at a time when they were both under investigation for the Ellard killing and that he allowed Cole to serve subpoenas while he was under suspicion of being implicated in the crime.

The silence was marked as the deputy clerk of the criminal court read a brief report signed by five members of the grand jury, who expressed dissatisfaction at the finding of the majority in the investigation of the sheriff's office in connection with the killing of

Felix J. Ellard and gave it as their opinion that Chief Deputy W.L. Metcalf should have been indicted for a higher crime and that Sheriff McAdory should have been indicted for shielding and protecting Henry Cole and W.L. Metcalf from arrest."

ELEVEN MEMBERS OF WATSON JURY ASK CLEMENCY OF O'NEAL
Every Effort Being Made to Save Condemned Man From Gallows
Preparations for Execution Tomorrow Practically Complete-- Witnesses All Summoned— Watson Is Hopeful of Commutation

The Birmingham Age-Herald, March 20, 1913

"Eleven members of the petit jury that convicted Will Watson of the murder of John Holland, negro, and gave him the death penalty have signed a special petition requesting Governor O'Neal to commute his sentence to life imprisonment. The twelfth juror is out of the state and consequently could not be reached. Watson's brother stated that they were relying solely on the assistance of the public to save the condemned man from the gallows, and said that the sentiment seemed all in favor of the sentence being commuted to life imprisonment.

Julius Davidson, who defended Watson, has never ceased working in his behalf and...has been largely instrumental in getting the petitions asking for executive clemency signed by the people of the county. He states that over 13,000 names have been secured. He also states that a number of prominent business and professional men, including two members of the legislature, have offered to go to Montgomery to intercede in behalf of Watson. When seen yesterday Watson was very hopeful, and while evidently under a great strain was comparatively calm. He protests his innocence and seems to be fairly confident that he will be reprieved.

It is understood that the mother of Arthur Jones will go to Montgomery and ask for clemency for her sons. At the sheriff's office the preparations have been practically made for the hanging of Will Watson and Arthur Jones, and notices have been sent to the witnesses required by law to be present. None others will be admitted to the jail yard except the representatives of the press.

There is a marked difference in the demeanor of the two men, Watson since being in jail has become very religious and has taken part in the religious services held in the jail. He has written a poem addressed to his wife and children. He has never lost hope of reprieve and although within the shadow of the gallows still has hope. Arthur Jones seems to be keenly aware of the seriousness of his position. His pale countenance and nervous movement of his eyes show that he realizes how near death he is and that only executive clemency can save him. While he knows that his friends are doing all they can for him, he does not appear to have the hope that has buoyed up Watson since their trial and conviction.

This afternoon the final appeal will be made to Governor O'Neal and on that final appeal rests their life or death. Should the appeals for clemency be refused on Friday morning, March 21, they will be hanged by the neck until dead."

TEARS ARE SHED BY JONES AND WATSON AT FAMILIES' VISIT
Sobbing of Little Daughter Causes Watson to Break Down Completely

The Birmingham News, March 20, 1913

"Little girl, you have been praying for papa, haven't you?" Amid a flow of tears, William Watson, condemned to die, was permitted to come out of the death cell at the county jail, in the presence of the sheriff, deputies and representatives of The Birmingham News, and have a last talk with his wife, his sister and his two little children. The tears did not abate for several minutes. The wife informed her husband that on the fast train during the afternoon she would on bended knee before the Chief Executive of the State plead for mercy and a commutation of sentence. The sisters of the Jones brothers were permitted to come into the jail and another scene of tears was enacted, the Jones brothers being almost prostrated.

There will be no double execution in the jail yard. The two men condemned will be hanged separately, as requested by the men. Sheriff McAdory...announces positively that only those permitted under the law to witness the executions will be allowed in the jail yard. There will be no show made of the gruesome event. No photographers nor kodaks will be allowed in the jail yard. Several deputy sheriffs are now stationed outside the jail and four or five additional men on the inside, to guard against any attempt to escape or rescue of the condemned men.

Following is a letter written by former Coroner Brasher to Governor Emmet O'Neal yesterday:

In re: Arthur Jones and Will Watson. I investigated the these cases eighteen days. From the testimony and evidence and knowing the witnesses as I do and from personal knowledge of the affair, it is my opinion that executive clemency should be used. I therefore recommend a reprieve to life imprisonment.

                B.L. BRASHER
          Ex-Coroner of Jefferson County"

JONES AND WATSON MEET DEATH CALMLY TWO ARE EXECUTED

White Men Pay Extreme Penalty For Murder
Of John Holland Near Coalburg in 1911
Pitiful Scenes When Wives And Children Say Farewell
Neither Man Breaks Down Under Terrific Strain---
Watson Makes Statement From Edge Of Gallows
Denying He Was Present When Shooting Occurred

The Birmingham Age-Herald, March 22, 1913

"One of the few times in the history of the state a white man has paid the extreme penalty of the law for the murder of a negro. Possibly for the first time in the history of the south have two white men been hanged for the killing of a single member of the African race. Yesterday morning between the hours of 11 and 12 o'clock Arthur Jones and Will Watson, charged, convicted and condemned for the murder of John Holland were executed in the yard of the jail of Jefferson County, and each man met his fate bravely. And both men confessed complicity in the crime for which they were hanged.

Crowds of morbidly curious began gathering around the railing of the courthouse grounds as early as 8 o'clock and by 9:30 it was necessary to stretch a rope across the alleyway leading to the jail entrance. It was a crowd of high and low degree. Attracted by the tragedy being enacted within the grim walls of the jail the prosperous business man rubbed elbows with a messenger boy on the one side and a negro on the other. The news that Governor O'Neal had refused to extend the executive clemency was broken to Watson and Jones about 7 o'clock yesterday morning.

Standing on the edge of the scaffold he said: "I wish to say one thing, boys. I do not feel I ought to be hanged for this...I am going to come clean with the truth and tell all I know. My first trouble came up in the John Holland case. He went around and accused me of stealing his chickens. He told it all over the neighborhood and said that he caught me in his chicken yard. There was not a word of truth in it. I have taken no life. I guess that is about all."

The crime for where the two white men paid the extreme penalty yesterday was one of the blackest in the history of Jefferson county. It showed a conspiracy on the part of four white men to inveigle their victim into the woods and there shoot him down like a dog. The crime was committed near Coalburg in the western part of the county on June 18, 1911, but was not brought to light until the spring of the following year. Arthur Jones was tried first and was given the death penalty; Walter Jones received life imprisonment, but a few weeks later was sentenced to hang for the murder of Lawrence B. Evans, and Will Watson was tried and found guilty of murder in the first degree and sentenced to be hung. Strenuous efforts were made to save Watson from the gallows, many believing that the punishment was too severe and the Governor was urged to commute the sentence to life imprisonment. But the pardon board and the governor refused to interfere and the law was fully carried out."

WALTER JONES DIES ON GALLOWS FOR MURDER OF L.B. EVANS IN 1911
Never Confessed And Protested Innocence In Final Statement From The Scaffold
Pathetic Scene As Relatives Bid Him Farewell Forever
Just Before Beginning March To The Gallows He Gives Bible To Condemned Negro And Offers What Consolation He Can

The Birmingham Age-Herald, April 5, 1913

"With the same degree of calmness and courage that characterized the execution of his brother Arthur two weeks ago, Walter Jones met his death on the gallows in the jail yard yesterday at noon for the murder of Lawrence B. Evans."

SENSATIONAL ALLEGATIONS BY DUNCAN IN METCALFE TRIAL
Chief Deputy Charged With Complicity in the Killing of Felix Ellard by Teck Duncan
Duncan Reiterates Former Statements That He Had Been Offered Inducements to Kill Ellard
To Be Cross Examined This Morning

The Birmingham Age-Herald, April 19, 1913

"Sensational allegations were made yesterday by Teck Duncan, while testifying at the trial of Walter Metcalfe, chief deputy sheriff, who was indicted by a recent grand jury on a charge of being an accessory after the fact to the murder of Felix J. Ellard. He reiterated former statements that he had been offered inducements to kill Ellard and implicated Mr. Metcalfe in an alleged plot between the late Henry Cole, himself and the chief deputy. He made a long statement as to alleged details of the plot to kill Ellard and of the gruesome incidents of the assassination, describing in detail how he laid in wait for his victim and how he shot him in cold blood. He denied, however, that he shot Ellard from ambush but said that he met him face to face and that Ellard drew a large pistol and attempted to shoot him.

During the trial Duncan was allowed in the corridor where many of his former friends and neighbors were seated and chatted quite freely with them. He was smoking a cigar most of the time and seemed in the best of spirits.

CRIMINAL JUDGES FIND METCALFE IS NOT GUILTY
Only Evidence Tending to Convict Him Was That of Teck Duncan,
Whom Judges Say They Cannot Believe--
Mr. Metcalfe Makes Statement About Verdict

The Birmingham Age-Herald, April 24, 1913

"Declaring that the only evidence introduced by the state tending to connect Walter Metcalfe with the crime as charged in the indictment was that of Teck Duncan and that they could not for several reasons believe his testimony. Judges Greene and Fort declared the defendant not guilty as he was charged. There was no demonstration on the part of the spectators but as the concluding words were spoken friend crowded around Mr. Metcalfe and shook his hand and expressed their satisfaction over the verdict.

The decision of the judges was as follows: "In our opinion all the evidence introduced in this case, except the testimony of Teck Duncan, is consistent with the innocence of the defendant, therefore, to convict the defendant we must believe that part of Duncan's testimony to connect the defendant with the commission of the offense charged. In addition to evidence tending to show threats on the part of the defendant on account of the defendant's testimony against him in his trial for murder, he has been impeached in every way known to the law: 1. By conviction of a crime involving moral turpitude. 2. By statements made by him materially different from parts of his testimony in this trial; and, 3. By proof of a notoriously bad character for truth and veracity, we cannot believe the testimony of Duncan and therefore we find the defendant not guilty."

TECK DUNCAN DIGS COAL LIKE OTHERS
Given New Striped Suit and Pick and Shovel at Flat Top
The Birmingham Age-Herald, June 17, 1913

"Teck Duncan, the Jefferson county life convict who recently acquired considerable notoriety as a result of his connection with the crimes at Lewisburg, is, despite statements to the contrary, an ordinary convict, decorated in stripes and with a pick and shovel, according to a declaration of L.F. Greer, Inspector for the state convict bureau. While in Birmingham last night Mr. Greer said: "Some days ago I read in the Age-Herald an interview in which Duncan is alleged to have stated that he would be put in charge of the air shaft at Flat Top, and would serve in the capacity of a minor boss. This statement, had it been true, could have been judged significant in view of the confession of Duncan which tended to involve certain county officials in the murder of Felix Ellard. Now as a matter of fact, when Duncan reached Flat Top he was given a brand new suit of stripes and a No. 2 shovel and pick. He is digging coal and is performing his task as is every other convict." Mr. Greer has just completed an inspection of the four mines in which state convicts are employed. He declared that conditions were unusually good, and that from none of the men had there come a word of complaint."

"Bloody Beat 22"---Postscript

Although not directly stated or alluded to in related newspaper accounts of that time, it is my contention that the long existing state of lawlessness in the Lewisburg area had caught the attention of powerful local businessmen and politicians. It had finally reached the point where these men perceived that this continuing "out of control" situation was resulting in bad publicity and was detrimental to their on-going plans to bring more and larger business and industrial interests into burgeoning Jefferson county. It is almost certain that such a response on their part would have been necessary to force change in the status quo by bringing political pressure to bear from a higher level of government on this deteriorating situation. Such involvement was initially publicly attributed to the actions of a local law enforcement association. This included importing outside nationally known private investigators and appointing special prosecutors, initiating coroner and grand jury investigations, as well as arranging for involvement and personal visits by the governor. As shown, these activities would result in far-reaching ramifications for the affected citizens, as well as for those persons accused of committing the crimes. Such extensive, as well as expensive efforts, could not have been undertaken without pressure being applied on public officials by powerful men; those decision makers who can direct such activities from behind the scenes and who do not pursue, or welcome, public attention.

Revenge?

On their face, the executions of Walter Jones and Will Watson for the murder of a black man during this era are more than just curious and, given the tenor of the times, almost inconceivable. It has been shown that local law enforcement and judicial authorities, along with high ranking political figures, had been severely embarrassed by their previous inaction and incompetency related to the "Bloody Beat 22" debacle which had been brought to the public's attention. In light of this, I believe that there is a strong possibility that these officials saw the proven murder of John Holland to provide an opportunity, once and for all, to bring leading members of the Lewisburg gang to justice for their crimes.

Such a vehicle for their punishment appears to have been found despite the racial overtones which went against the prevailing white supremacy belief system of that time. The chance to finally break up this notorious gang, and to execute several of its leaders, likely presented too much of an opportunity to pass up. It also helps to explain the lack of intervention by the Alabama Supreme Court, the Pardons Board, as well as by the governor, despite the racial disparities of that era.

It is thought that from the beginning, following their arrests and incarceration for the murder of John Holland, that Arthur Jones and Will Watson most likely believed that due to the fact that a white man had never been executed for the murder of a black individual in the history of the state of Alabama, that they would never pay the ultimate penalty for this crime. Although they probably believed that they might be convicted of the murder of Holland based on the evidence, Jones and Watson (and their attorneys) likely felt that they were fortunate to have been charged with this particular crime and not for the murder of one of their white victims. They may have surmised that they would probably receive a sentence of life imprisonment or, in the worst case the death penalty, a punishment that most likely would be reduced either by the appeals court or by commutation by Governor O'Neal, possibly at the last minute, and that such actions would result from behind the scenes decisions made by those officials who could effect such judgements. However, following the adverse public opinion and their embarrassment during the investigations, these men may have seen the executions as an opportunity to visit a final "revenge" of their own on at least the leading men who had caused them such serious trouble and, perhaps, may have threatened their future political and monetary fortunes.

An additional benefit of such a seemingly "fair" and even-handed application of the legal process, as trumpeted by the news media, had the dividend of being employed to publicly suggest a change in the long time racial status quo. Societal change was now slowly gathering momentum as reactions to summary mob "justice" and lynchings were beginning to alter public acceptance of these common extrajudicial activities. There was an increasing demand for the employment of the established rule of law, rather than vigilantism.

Despite the extensive investigations of the multiple murders associated with "Bloody Beat 22," to include the coroner and grand jury activities, high level political involvement, public and news media approbation, as well as accusations of suspected direct and indirect involvement in crimes by law enforcement officials and the outcome of several trials of principal actors, the final surprising and rather remarkable chapter of this saga was yet to be written.

Where capital punishment was dispensed by the government on a regularly recurring basis when crimes such as murder, robbery and rape had been committed by black perpetrators against white victims, it was an extraordinary occasion when these roles and consequences were reversed, as occurred at the culmination of the Lewisburg "troubles." So rare was such a final outcome that the related commentary reported in the major local newspapers bordered on disbelief. As the executions neared and seemed more certain to actually take place, there was an outpouring of renewed attention by the news media. There were reports of public petitions for clemency, to include apparent "second guessing" of the penalty recommended by the same members of the jury which had convicted one of these men and who may have always thought that their decision would be overturned by the appeals court or clemency provided by the governor, especially in light of the fact that these were white men who had been found guilty of the murder of a black individual.

Other matters related to the "Bloody Beat 22" story would play out in the period around and following the executions of Arthur and Walter Jones and Will Watson. Several months prior to their deaths, former Deputy Sheriff Henry Cole apparently committed suicide by taking an overdose of morphine while incarcerated in the county jail. Cole was despondent following his conviction of a murder that occurred several years earlier and was, at the time of his death, awaiting trial for his alleged involvement in the murder of Felix Ellard. It was never determined how Cole obtained the morphine, a drug readily and legally available to the public at that time.

Allegations by Teck Duncan were made against Chief Deputy Sheriff Walter Metcalfe in regard to his (and Sheriff McAdory's) alleged involvement as "accessories" to the murder and coverup of the death of Felix Ellard. These charges against Metcalfe were brought to a trial before three judges where he was found not guilty mainly due to questions regarding the veracity of Teck Duncan's testimony and the lack of any additional evidence against Metcalfe.

Although the worst of the criminal activities in "Bloody Beat 22" may have ended around 1913 with the convictions and executions of several of the major participants, the Lewisburg area would still remain quite raucous until the initiation of national prohibition of alcohol in 1918, along with decreasing coal mining activity in that area.

HUMAN BONES BRING MEMORIES OF PAST IN BLOODY SECTION
Gruesome Remains of Victim Found in Shaft Near Arcadia
Brought To City For Investigation
Crushed Skull Indicated to Officers That This Man Had Gone the Way of Many Others

The Birmingham Age-Herald, December 10, 1913

"An echo of the notorious Lewisburg murders of two years ago filled the ears of Coroner Charles L. Spain, Chief Deputy Walter Metcalfe and Deputies McDuff and Hartsfield as they gazed upon the bones of a murdered man discovered in an old coal shaft between Coalburg and Arcadia, scarcely a quarter of a mile in the rear of the home of the Jones boys. The gruesome discovery was made by Superintendent Haskins of the Coalburg mines, while on a prospecting trip.

As soon as the bones were discovered on a ledge near the entrance of an abandoned coal shaft the sheriff's office in Birmingham was communicated with. An official survey of the bones which were scattered about revealed a skull, which had been fractured apparently by a heavy blow. This tended to confirm the suspicion in the coroner's mind that here were the remains of another victim of the vengeance of the notorious clique of assassins.

Under the regime of lawlessness over a score of men were murdered and the bones discovered yesterday, are thought to be the remains of one of the many citizens who "disappeared" in those hazardous times. It had been thought at the sheriff's office that memories of the Lewisburg cases were forgotten, but from time to time incidents spring up unexpectedly which bring echoes of the bloody past in that section. A few weeks ago Burns Kittrell, a former member of the Jones gang, and out on bond, was killed at the mining disaster at Acton mines; yesterday the bones of an unknown victim of the feud were discovered and it is expected that at various times incidents will arise that will set tongues a wagging on the bloody doings of other days."

Postscript

While there may be many questions about these matters which will remain unanswered, one of the final acts in this "play of life" ends with the demise of Teck Duncan, the individual who played a major role in initiating the chain of events which would lead to the downfall of the Lewisburg gang. Although it is difficult to view him as a "hero" of any kind, the outcome for Duncan can be viewed as a reflection of the forced convict labor system in the coal mines under the terrible and dangerous conditions which have been noted in a prior chapter.

TECK DUNCAN SUCCUMBS TO ATTACK OF PNEUMONIA

The Birmingham Age-Herald, December 18, 1913

"Teck A. Duncan, the most noted character in the Lewisburg murder investigations, and who was sentenced to life imprisonment for the murder of Felix J. Ellard, died yesterday morning at Wetumpka after a brief illness of pneumonia. He is survived by his widow and three small children, four brothers and one sister. He was 36 years of age.

Duncan was tried for the murder of Ellard and convicted. His attorney gave notice of appeal, but the appeal was withdrawn and he confessed to the killing but implicated several others in the crime. He was sent to the mines to serve his sentence and a few months ago lost an arm in a mine accident, and was transferred to Wetumpka, where he contracted his fatal illness.

Duncan was a unique character in many ways and claimed the credit for disclosing the John Holland murder which led to the investigation of the conditions of "Bloody Beat 22" and the arrest and conviction of white men of which three were sentenced to death and hanged. During the several trials of the Lewisburg cases Duncan was brought to Birmingham and despite the fact that he was a life prisoner was always cheerful. On one occasion he stated that on account of the service he had rendered the state he "ought to have rooms at the Hillman instead of being in jail."

CHAPTER 9

POLICE

"Boys, there's more justice in the end of this nightstick than there is in all of the courts of the land."[1]

—-Alexander "Clubber" Williams, Inspector, New York City Police Department. ca. 1890s.

The arrival of the 20th century brought with it not only increasing industrialization, but also the requirement for large numbers of individuals needed to provide the manpower for production in the factories and mines, along with others who would provide all of the ancillary services essential for the support of a growing community. There were jobs available for all who wanted to work. These numerous non-industrial vocations and professions would include law enforcement agents. Such positions were not limited to municipal police and deputy sheriffs, but also extended to "special deputies" employed by many factories and mines as well as designated "special agents" employed by the railroads serving the area, all of whom had the force of law behind their official actions.

Although the existing major cities throughout the country were expanding their established systems of government and the services that they provided to their citizens, the smaller town of Birmingham was faced with its rapidly growing industrial base and population along with unique problems and associated "growing pains." City leaders attempted to meet this expansion and deal with such pressing issues as increasing the manpower and improving the professionalization of the existing police force.

In regard to the role of law enforcement officers in general at that time, Litwack noted that:

> "As enforcers of white supremacy the police assumed a pivotal role. Not only did they enforce vagrancy laws to solidify control of black labor; but also by virtue of their arrests they helped swell the black labor force exploited by local and state governments; in Talladega, Alabama, for example,

> police arrested a weekly quota of blacks to fill out the chain gangs. The use of excessive force by the police underscored the determination to remind blacks at every opportunity of their vulnerability and helplessness. If the police sometimes singled out young blacks for punishment, it was a way to check their tendency toward "impudence," to restrain their restlessness, and keep them in their place. The violence meted out by the police and sheriffs was no aberration but stemmed from ideological conviction—the still commonly accepted antebellum belief that blacks understood only force, that they worked and behaved best under the threat of the lash, and that their uncontrolled impulses required a special quality of discipline. Not only did the police deal severely with blacks accused of crimes against white persons or property, but they also chose to ignore black violence against blacks. When a black was arrested for killing another black, some prosecutors offered the defendant a lenient plea bargain, or, in the event of a conviction, some judges would hand down a less severe sentence."[2]

Relating to the law enforcement and judicial systems existing at that time, Litwack also noted that:

> "The cynicism manifested toward the police and the courts was captured in this observation attributed to a white chief of police: "If a nigger kills a white man, that's murder. If a white man kills a nigger, that's justifiable homicide. If a nigger kills another nigger, that's one less nigger."[3]

> "The subject of the police officer dominated conversations among young blacks and the stories invariably revolved around chases, harassment, clubbings, illegal arrests, and coerced confessions. But other tales also made the rounds, tales that did wonders for black pride and soon became legendary. With particular relish, some blacks recounted their success in outwitting law enforcement officers. Still others took delight in their exploits, even if caught."[4]

The rapid expansion of the population and of the industrial base along with the concomitant development of professional and other business services, would have a not unexpected downside. The increase in criminal activity by those individuals within the unskilled worker class and by the poor and unemployed, along with the increase in prostitution and both the legal and illicit production and sale of alcohol, sometimes poisonous, was to be expected. The extent of the attraction of a more professional, and dangerous criminal element to the area was not foreseen or adequately planned for.

The influx of large numbers of such experienced characters from the under-worlds of larger, established cities where they had honed such skills as breaking and entering businesses and safecracking, as well as employing their abilities as "con men" (and women) to prey on the local poorly educated and unsuspecting public, would reach epidemic proportions. During this time, there was little legal recourse to certain criminal activities when banks were not trusted and their failure, embezzlement or robbery meant the permanent and personal loss of any valuables or cash that a business might have on deposit or stored within their vaults. There were no guarantees of deposited funds by the Federal government. This led to many small businesses and large companies installing heavy expensive safes on their premises which, they were told by salesmen, could never be broken into. However, if expert lock pickers employing their practiced skills could not quietly break into a modern safe, then explosives could always be resorted to.

There was a harbinger of the imminent and rapid increase in serious criminal activities in the Magic City. Within a few months following the turn into the 20th century, an event would take place that would shock the community out of its complacency and into a realization of the changing times. This incident would lead to an awakening of the populace with a loss of the idealism and innocence that had been associated with the "gilded age" of the late 19th century. This particular criminal act would lead to the executions of two members of a burglary gang, one of whom it was believed, even by some law enforcement agents, was not directly responsible for the deaths of either of two police officers. It would lead to many years of continued investigations, a process that would eventually culminate in 1914 with an unrequited final outcome.

OFFICERS KIRKLEY AND ADAMS
SHOT BY SUSPECTED SAFECRACKERS
Two White Men Who Were Being Escorted to Police Headquarters Fire on the Officers and Escape
The Wounds Are Not Fatal

Safe of the Standard Oil Company Looted and Watchman Knocked in Head—- Nearly $300 in Cash Secured

The Birmingham Age-Herald, March 28, 1900

"Police Officers George W. Kirkley and J.H. Adams were shot and seriously wounded shortly before 12 o'clock last night by two unknown white men whom they had under surveillance as safe robbers. The attending physicians do not believe that the wounds of either of the officers is of a dangerous nature, though sufficiently serious to lay them both up for some time.

The shooting occurred at Third avenue and Twentieth street and both of the desperadoes made their escape. Early in the evening the safe of the Standard Oil Company at 709 Avenue F, was blown open and robbed. Several officers were detailed to make a search for the burglars. Among these were officers Adams and Kirkley. These two officers soon thereafter saw two white men coming east in First avenue. They followed them to Third and Twentieth, where the shooting took place. In speaking of the trouble, officer Adams said: "Kirkley and I were watching for the men who had blown open the safe. They passed us and we followed them. They went in the Glen Lea saloon and took a drink, and then going out the back door, Kirkley and I passed them about midway of the block and accosted them. We suspected they were the parties who had blown open the safe and began asking them questions. One of them said he worked at the Alabama Great Southern shops, but I knew that was not true, as I know the face of every man who works there. He then said he boarded at Mrs. Smith's in Twenty-first street, but I know of no such boarding house. Their actions and their answers were suspicious and I told them we would have to take them to the station house, but did not put them under arrest. We had started to the station, Kirkley and one of the men going in front, but had gone only a few steps when the one with me turned, and, with the remark, 'I'll kill you now,' fired his pistol at me, the ball entering my right shoulder. He fired several times. I was stunned by the bullet and fell up against a post to steady myself. As soon as I could draw my pistol I began firing at him, and did not stop until I had emptied it. I think I hit him at least one time. One went East in Third avenue while the other ran off in the other direction. ." Officer Kirkley corroborated Officer Adams' story in every detail up to the point where the shooting began.

Kirkley stated that "As I turned the man with me pointed his pistol at my body and fired, the ball taking effect in my abdomen. He fired several times at me and I emptied my pistol at him."

The wounded officers were taken to Hillman hospital. The wounds were then pronounced not dangerous, although that of Officer Adams is rather serious. The two men appear to be about 30 years of age and were well dressed. They answer the description of the cracksmen who have been operating in the district, and it is firmly believed that the officers had the right parties in tow, and that they, realizing they were caught, made a desperate break for liberty."

SENSATIONAL DEVELOPMENTS FOLLOW FAST UPON THE SHOOTING
Officers Scharber and Manasco Temporarily Suspended From the Service Charged With Cowardice by Chief Austin
Two Arrests Have Been Made
Satchel Containing Complete Cracksman's Outfit Found in Possession of One of the Men—Condition of the Officers

The Birmingham Age-Herald, March 29, 1900

"A series of sensational developments have followed the shooting of the two police officers by the suspected cracksmen, the most important is the suspension of Officers Scharber and Manasco on the charge of cowardice and arrest of two men supposed to be members of the gang of burglars who have been working around the city.

None less important, however, is the developments in the condition of the two wounded officers, who, it is feared, are wounded more seriously than was at first thought, the condition of Officer Kirkley being especially critical. The news of the shooting created intense excitement throughout the city and unlimited sympathy was expressed for the unfortunate officers who, in the discharge of their duty, became the victims of the murderous bullets which may yet cost them their lives.

A suspect named Lewis was arrested at a boarding house and then taken to police headquarters, where his two satchels were opened. In one of them it was found a complete cracksman's outfit, consisting of about thirty sticks of dynamite, a bottle of nitro-glycerine, two bundles of fuses, a dozen hanks of fishing line used in fixing a load, two chamoise money belts, two large cloth sacks to carry away booty, black cloth for masks, a small hammer, and a .38 calibre pistol. Lewis says he is a carpenter by profession and that he came here about three of four weeks ago for the purpose of getting work. Since his arrival it is charged that he has spent much money. A few evening ago his roommates saw him with $100. He denies any connection with any set of crooks, safe-crackers, robbers or anything else. He says he purchased the dynamite for the purpose of killing fish in the river. Another man was arrested as he was going into Higgins boarding house. Both men were taken to the Hillman hospital, where they were seen by the wounded officers, who stated that neither of them were the men who did the shooting. Lewis was later identified as an escaped convict from the Mississippi penitentiary where he was doing time for safecracking.

Officers Scharber and Manasco were relieved of their badges at the order of Chief Austin who preferred charges of cowardice against them. It was charged that the officers who had just gone off duty, were standing just across the street from where the shooting occurred, and that they absolutely made no effort to assist their brother officers or to stop the men who escaped. At a late hour last night the condition of Officer Kirkley was decidedly unfavorable, as it is now thought that the bullet passed through his liver. Officer Adams was resting easy."

BRAVE OFFICER KIRKLEY IS DEAD
Passed Away At Hillman Hospital at 7:15 O'clock Last Night—Died In Discharge of Duty
Police Department Wrapped in Gloom--
Was One of the Best Members of the Force--
He Leaves a Large Family

The Birmingham Age-Herald, March 30, 1900

"Poor Kirkley is dead. The brave officer who in the discharge of his duty was shot by an unknown desperado on Tuesday night, succumbed to his wound. Death came to Kirkley as the shadows of the night were gathering, and he died as he had lived--a brave and true and honest man. He fell as a soldier falls, at the place of duty, and today a red-handed assassin walks the earth unwhipped of justice, guilty of the crime which we are divinely taught appeals to heaven for vengeance. They are making poor Kirkley's shroud. The question is asked: When shall the gallows rope be knotted to avenge the deed of his infamous execution? When shall the black heart of the slayer be sullied by the law's awful decree? Crime has long dogged the city's way, but it never assumed blacker, fouler, more sickening form than when it struck poor Kirkley down just before the midnight hour.

Kirkley had been a member of the police force several years, and he was one of the most useful and trusted men. He was born in Georgia in 1854. His wife and five daughters survive him. The death of the brave officer has cast a gloom on the entire police department."

THE MURDERER OF KIRKLEY IS CAUGHT
Gang of Crooks Surrounded and Captured by Birmingham Detectives and Chattanooga Police
Detectives Bodeker and Disheroon Are Sure They Have The Right Men--
Shrewd Work on Part of the Officers

The Birmingham Age-Herald, March 31, 1900

"The police this morning arrested a gang of eight crooks, three of whom have been positively identified by officers as three of the gang implicated in the recent robberies of Birmingham, and in the shooting of Policemen Kirkley and Adams. Their names are Frank Duncan, John D. West and Tom Fay, and the Birmingham detectives are certain that West is the slayer of Policeman Kirkley. John West, who has an ugly scar on his throat, contradicted Duncan, saying that he heard the latter came to this city last Tuesday from Birmingham. All three told rambling and absurd stories as to their business, etc. Detective Bodeker is quite certain that Officer Adams will be able to identify two of the three men caught here as the parties who wounded him and killed Officer Kirkley. The description given by Adams fits Duncan and West to a nicety."

THE MURDERS IDENTIFIED
BY THE SLOWLY SINKING OFFICER
Policeman Adams Swears to the Men—
Intense Excitement
Captured Crooks are Frank Miller and Frank Duncan

Stoutly Deny Their Guilt
After Being Positively Recognized By the Dying Officer the Men Were Taken to the County Jail

The Birmingham Age-Herald, April 2, 1900

"Rational of mind and possessed of the knowledge that death was perhaps only a few hours off, and of the full importance of any statement that he might make, Policeman J.H. Adams last night positively identified two of the crooks who have been arrested by the police as the assailants of Officer Kirkley and himself last Tuesday night. The men who were identified by the dying officer are Frank Miller, alias John Manning, one of the gang arrested in Anniston, and Frank Duncan, one of the Chattanooga gang. There was no hesitancy, and in the presence of witnesses, the poor fellow who may not live to see the light of another day, declared that he would stand before the judgement bar and swear that the two prisoners who stood trembling before him, with manacled arms, were unmistakably the same men whom he and Kirkley had under surveillance on the fatal night. It was a solemn scene and a still more solemn declaration as the wounded man raised his hand and pointing his finger at Miller declared: "You are the man who shot me," and turning to Duncan continued: "And you are the man who was with him." His voice was strong, his eye was clear and a slightly perceptible smile of satisfaction lit up his haggard face as he gazed upon the man whose protests of innocence only brought forth more positive declarations of identity from the parched lips of the poor fellow, who seemed to realize that justice would be done. "I have never seen you before," said Miller. "But I have seen you," replied Adams. "You are surely mistaken," said Duncan. "No, I am not mistaken" came the reply, and the prisoners were hustled out into the hallway. The two accused men pleaded with the officers in charge that some terrible mistake had been made. "I am as innocent of the crime as you," said Duncan to Chief Austin, "and I do not believe you think me guilty." "I believe that you are both guilty," replied the chief, "and we have evidence sufficient to convict you, and will do so."

There is absolutely no fear of lynching, notwithstanding the fact that there is great feeling manifest throughout the city, and the law will be allowed to take its course."

"DUTCH HENRY" THE NOTED CROOK MAKES A PARTIAL CONFESSION
Admits That He Is One of the Men
Fears The Gallows
To Save His Neck He Would Tell The Truth
As The Coils of Evidence Grow Tighter He Confesses His Part in the Crime--Shrewd Work of the Police

The Birmingham Age-Herald, April 3, 1900

"Confronted with positive evidence of his guilt, and in the hope of mitigating the punishment that will surely be meted out to him, John Hendricks, alias "Dutch Henry," alias Frank Miller, one of the gang of safe robbers charged with the murderous assault upon Officers Kirkley and Adams, yesterday confessed to his part of the crime, and offered to unbosom himself of the whole story if his neck could be saved. His confession was voluntary…and came as a last resort from the desperate character, who, through the strong web of evidence with which he is surrounded saw in his mind's eye the vision of the gallows with himself dangling at the rope's end. Hendricks admitted his involvement and stated that he was in the charge of Adams and that he shot his pistol over his shoulder, but with no intention of committing murder. He further stated that if the officers would agree to save his neck he would tell the whole truth. There is still hope for Officer Adams, although the physicians fear that his wound will prove fatal."

ADAMS' WOUND PROVES FATAL
Brave Officer Gone to Join Kirkley in the Great Beyond
Died at 11:15 Last Night
Appeared Much Better During the Afternoon, But Relaxed Into a Stupor—
Made Dying Statement to Dr. Whelan

The Birmingham Age-Herald April 4, 1900

"Police Officer J.H. Adams, who was shot by John Hendricks, alias "Dutch Henry," a member of the desperate gang of safe blowers, died at the Hillman hospital. For eight days has the wounded policeman fought the grasp of death, but man's power is limited and for two days it has been known that poor Adams could not survive. He died, however, with the intense satisfaction of knowing that the cowardly assailant had been captured and his death in time would be avenged."

THE FUNERAL OF OFFICER ADAMS
Remains Rest Beside Those of His Brave Companion
Sad Scene At The Grave

The Birmingham Age-Herald, April 6, 1900

"The remains of Officer J.H. Adams were laid to rest by the side of his brave companion in Oak Hill cemetery. Two freshly made graves mark the place where the remains of the two men who were so foully murdered now lie in peace. Over the two graves will be erected a monument, a tribute from the citizens of Birmingham."

CRAZED WITH RAGE AND DESPAIR
FRANK MILLER ASSAULTS A GUARD
The Last Ray of Hope is Gone
and Death Stares Him in the Face
He Hangs This Morning
Governor Jelks Refuses to Interfere
And the Condemned Man Must Suffer
the Penalty of His Crime—
Becomes Sullen

The Birmingham Age-Herald, June 28, 1901

"Frank Miller, the murderer of Policeman Adams, will be hanged in the Jefferson County jail yard about 10:30 o'clock this morning. Governor Jelks finally decided yesterday afternoon that he would not interfere with the due process of the law; and therefore Miller will be Hanged until he is dead, dead, dead! Doomed because he is a and wild with passion because he is doomed, Miller assaulted one of his guards last night. It appears that in the ungovernable rage of his wild despair, when he knew all possible chance for temporary escape from the gallows had vanished, he threw a glass of water upon one of his guards and then struck the guard a blow in the face. The sheriff at once informed Miller that unless he kept absolutely quiet he would be handcuffed, his ankles would be strapped together, and he would be bound to the floor. This had a sobering effect upon the doomed man, raving and storming in the shadow of the gallows. It was further reported that Miller swore he would stand on the platform of the gallows and curse Sheriff Burgin. Yet it seems that Sheriff

Burgin has been kinder to and more considerate of the convicted murderer than any sheriff could be expected to act towards any condemned man; allowing Miller to order his meals from a cafe and permitting him to receive a liberal supply of whiskey, as a physician advised.

Everything is in readiness at the sheriff's office for the execution. The suit of black clothing which Miller will wear has been secured. He will go to the gallows dressed for his coffin."

FRANK MILLER EXPIATES HIS CRIME UPON THE GALLOWS AND DIES PROTESTING INNOCENCE
Marched to His Doom With Trembling and Fear and Plead for Time
Was A Notorious Criminal
One of the Slayers of Officers Adams and Kirkley Suffers the Death Penalty—
Alonzo Williams Also Hanged

The Birmingham Age-Herald, June 29, 1901

"Frank Miller and Alonzo Williams, two murderers, were hanged in the county jail yard yesterday, the first dropping to the rope's end at 10:55 o'clock and the other going down through the trap at 11:57.

The contrast between the manner in which the white man and the negro accepted death was the most remarkable feature of the two executions. The latter went to the gallows with a face wreathed in smiles and a soul apparently filled with the joy of his religion; which exhibited itself in the form of hysterical actions and words. Miller walked rather firmly to the gallows, but at the last minute, filled with the unmistakeable dread of death, he almost lost entire control of himself. As the last seconds of life were fleeting and as the black cap was cutting out the light of the world, Miller trembled and nearly fell to the floor of the scaffold. He gasped and begged for the very last minute the law would allow him, and as the trap was about to be sprung made futile efforts to get himself beyond the edge of the fatal drop door. When the trigger was suddenly pulled and Miller shot downward his neck was broken. The body hung straight and not a motion of any kind exhibited the usual muscular contraction that follows sudden death, other than the slight turning due to the twists of the hemp. With the negro the contrast was even more in evidence than in the manner of meeting death. As the floor of the scaffold swung from under the body a noise of a tightening of the rope was heard; the form fell whirring. As it did so the muscles of the legs pulled the feet upward as from the sudden jar; the hands and arms were drawn upward and towards the sides, and the fingers of the hands twitched as though they were clapping. There were one, two, three of these nerve movements and then the body hung limp and still until cut down.

The execution was witnessed by about two hundred persons in the jail yard and almost an equal number from the courthouse windows. A few men and boys climbed poles and the walls but were not allowed to retain their positions. A few women were in the court house, but none in the jail yard. Outside, for two blocks distance on either side, a crowd pushed and moved making efforts to view the body as it was brought out from the yard. For hours the crowd stood around the yard and talked of the execution.

The Crime For Which Miller Was Hanged

On the night of March 27, 1900, the safe of the Standard Oil Company was blown open and robbed by a gang of safecrackers. The night watchman, Joseph Clayton was shot in the foot and otherwise roughly handled, and about $300 was stolen from the safe. Clayton's foot afterwards had to be amputated from the effects of his injuries. It is said that Miller was present at the time and saved Clayton's life by preventing the others from killing him. The gang was said to have been composed of white men, among them the following: Frank Miller, Frank Duncan, Frank Edwards, John D. West, Thomas Fay, "New York Harry" and a man called "Sheeny Bugs." The first six were subsequently arrested and have all, except "Sheeny Bugs," been convicted. "New York Harry" succeeded in making his escape and "Sheeny Bugs" "gave away" the gang and in return was given his liberty.

The first trial was that of Miller and Duncan, which occurred in May, 1900. They were tried on the charge of killing Officer Adams, the other charge against them of killing Officer Kirkley being held up. They both were convicted, Miller being given the death penalty and Duncan being sentenced for life. At this trial Miller said that Duncan was not with him at the time of the shooting, but that the man who did the shooting and the man who was with him was New York Harry. Miller has since stoutly denied that he did the shooting, saying he was surprised when it started and that he ran, firing his pistol over his shoulder to frighten off his pursuers. Duncan also swore he was not present, and corroborated Miller's statement that New York Harry did the shooting. New York Harry was never found, and many people thought he was a myth.

Miller is said to be a noted safe blower, being credited with having been the first to introduce nitro-glycerine as a means of safe blowing. A bottle of this fluid was found in the pocket of an overcoat said to belong to Miller and it was testified to by some of the other members of the gang on their trials that the blowing of the Standard Oil Company's safe was done to settle a dispute as to whether a safe could be blown open with nitro-glycerine without making a noise.

"Wont you forgive me for the crime I have committed?" asked Frank Miller of R.O. Adams, brother of the murdered officer Adams, yesterday while standing on the scaffold, a few minutes before he was executed. Mr. Adams replied to him, "I have never said an unkind word against you, Miller. I never passed an opinion on the case of murder for which you were tried and convicted. I left this for the court to do, and it was they that said you were guilty, and not I."

Alonzo Williams killed two negroes, each under the same circumstances. He was hanged for killing Bob Callahan, whom he killed while serving a life sentence for killing another negro. Williams was originally confined in the Pratt mines for a non-capital offense, and while serving his time there he became enraged at a fellow convict and plunged a pick through his head, killing him almost instantly. He claimed that the deed was done in self-defense, but upon his trial he was convicted and sentenced to the penitentiary for life. After his return to Pratt Mines it was not long before he had a row with another fellow convict and this row culminated as did the other. Williams drove a pick through the other negro's head, producing instant death."

MURDERER FRANK DUNCAN SAWS THROUGH JAIL BARS TO LIBERTY
With Aid of Three Prisoners Noted Crook Escapes
Lock To His Cell Was Sawed From Outside
All Trace Lost of the Four Men When They Filed the Lock on the Gate and Set Foot In Alley
The Birmingham Age-Herald, January 21, 1902

"Frank Duncan, sentenced to hang for the murder of Policeman Kirkley, under life sentence for complicity in the killing of Policeman Adams, and professional safe blower, escaped from the Jefferson County jail some time between the hours of midnight and daylight Monday morning. Telegrams were sent in every direction, and officers were hurried to every point where it was thought probable he might pass. At midnight no trace of the fugitives had been found. The news of the escape of the prisoners quickly spread throughout the city and created the liveliest interest."

"Duncan has been in jail about two years, and on January 2, 1901, he, in company with Frank Miller, Frank Edwards and John West, made an attempt to escape from the jail, which nearly succeeded. They were just in the act of scaling the jail wall when they were discovered by a small negro boy who gave the alarm and they were retaken. Duncan profited by this experience and planned the escape Sunday night at an hour when all the prisoners and small negro boys in the jail yard and out of it were asleep. Just after the attempted escape of Miller and Duncan a night watchman was put inside the jail and kept there until Miller was hanged.

NOTED BURGLAR IN THE TOILS
New York Harry is Captured in Missouri
Wanted In Birmingham
Man Who is Supposed to Have Been Connected With the Killing of Policemen Adams and Kirkley, Has Been Fully Identified

The Birmingham Age-Herald, May 16, 1903

"A brief special to the Age-Herald from Kansas City last night stated that Garry Dowd, alias "Denver Harry," alias "New York Harry," who figured conspicuously by the latter name in the trial of Frank Miller and Frank Duncan for the murder of Policemen Adams and Kirkley, has been arrested in Macon, Mo. If the man arrested is the right one the capture is a most important one, as Dowd has been wanted for years in many cities.

"New York Harry is about 45 years of age and from childhood has been a criminal, It is thought he had something to do with the killing of the two Birmingham policemen at Third avenue and Twentieth street about three years ago. He was never arrested in Birmingham, but Miller while in jail stated to the officers that "New York Harry" fired the shots that killed the officers.

Dowd, or "New York Harry," as he is better known in Birmingham, is probably the most noted criminal who ever operated in the southern states. He is credited with a long list of crimes. A policeman stated last night that Dowd had killed at least fifteen men, and had blown up a large number of safes. From police publications Dowd killed two policemen in Joplin, Mo., under circumstances very similar to those of the murder of Policemen Kirkley and Adams in Birmingham. It is said he killed two officers in Chicago and also a detective. In all he is credited with killing six policemen, one detective, a flagman on a train and a number of citizens. The officers wonder at the manner in which has eluded capture. His deeds, they say, have been covered up and his hidings so well arranged that it seemed almost impossible to find him. He is said to be one of the most expert shots in the country and Frank Duncan, when in jail here, said there was not a better marksman anywhere than "New York Harry." Before Miller was hangers he contended and continued to assert, even while on the gallows, that "New York Harry" was the man who shot Officers Kirkley and Adams.

At a late hour last night the following special was received: Macon, Mo.,--Harry Dowd, alias "Denver Harry," under arrest here, is wanted at Birmingham, Ala. Dowd has been working in the coal mines near this city, and a letter found among his belongings led to his arrest."

FRANK DUNCAN IS HELD BY THE U.S. AUTHORITIES
Birmingham Officers Are Speeding on to Tavares, Fla., Where the Prisoner is Confined—
Duncan and Party Are Charged
With Numerous Postoffice Robberies in Florida
The Birmingham Age-Herald, October 3, 1904

"James Ward, thought to be Frank Duncan, was arrested in St. Augustine, who is held on a charge of robbing the United States post office at Leroy, Fla., and the bank of Tavares. Chief Jones of Tampa, secured a photograph and description of Frank Duncan and was convinced that Ward and Duncan were one and the same man. The robberies with which Ward is charged in this state would include the post offices at Bronson, Baxter, Crawford, Crystal River, Hernande, Lawfey, Levy, Levon, Martell, Otter Creek, Titusville, Tarpon Springs and Waldo. Besides these they are supposed to be connected with the cracking of safes at Tampa and Tavares."

OFFICERS THREATENED WITH BOTTLE OF NITRO-GLYCERINE
Frank Duncan Sustains His Reputation as a Very Dangerous Character
His Wife Smuggles The Deadly Explosive To Him Alabama Officers Coming to Birmingham With the Prisoner and Great Apprehension is Now Felt for Their Safety

The Birmingham Age-Herald, October 6, 1904

"Frank Duncan and his partner, Kid Stafford, were found guilty on the charge of blowing a safe and were given the full sentence by the judge, fifteen years in the Florida penitentiary. The judge suspended the sentence of Duncan and he was turned over to the Alabama authorities.

The prisoners were escorted back to the jail by deputies. As the men were standing in a corridor with the prisoners Duncan pulled a bottle of nitro-glycerine from his pocket and raising it aloof exclaimed in a most dramatic way: "Turn us loose or we all go to hell together." The sheriff ordered him shot. But Detective Ahn leveled his pistol at Stafford, who begged him not to shoot and sank to his knees like a craven coward. This took Duncan by surprise, who told the officers if they would not shoot his partner he would not throw the stuff, and the officers by threat to shoot made him place it gently on the floor. After Duncan had been foiled in his attempt he begged the officers to shoot him saying that he was ready to go. The excitement lasted about five minutes and during the time the officers thought their time had come.

Duncan's wife came up from Tampa and advised her husband to never hang, but kill himself. It is thought that she slipped him the bottle of nitro-glycerine. A little apprehension is expressed for the Alabama officers, who will leave tonight with the prisoner for Birmingham, as it is feared their confederates will wreck the train. The local officers felt much relieved when the prisoner was in other hands, as he was one of the most desperate characters ever confined in the jail here."

FRANK DUNCAN IN JAIL AND RELATES HIS EXPERIENCES SINCE HIS DARING ESCAPE
Famous Condemned Prisoner Tells How Escape Was Planned and Executed
Laughs At The Scare Given Florida Officers
Declares That He Never Killed Kirkley or Adams, But Was in His Room When He Heard the Shooting

The Birmingham Age-Herald, October 8, 1904

"By Frank Duncan (as related to a reporter through his lattice door last night.)

"Frank Duncan is my correct name and I am 37 years of age...I want to say candidly that I never killed either of these officers, and the only time I ever saw Officer Adams was when I was brought before him for identification upon my arrest.

"While I was in jail at Tavares the funniest think I have ever seen in my life came off. That was my play with the fake nitroglycerine bottle. As soon as I was in jail I thought of this scheme to make a getaway. I prepared the stuff out of molasses and water and had it in my pocket all the time I was in jail. As we got into the corridor of the jail--there were five officers with me--I jerked the fake bottle from my pocket and holding it aloft cried, "Here's the bottle of nitroglycerin. Unless you turn my partner and myself loose I will throw it and blow us all to h-ll together. Just at that moment there was a scatteration, and talk about making a quick getaway, those officers were the limit. They spread in all directions. One of them however, was so scared he couldn't move. After they had stopped shaking one of them yelled, 'shoot him, shoot him.' They had their guns leveled at Stafford, poor unfortunate boy, and seeing that the bluff had failed I told them I would lay the bottle down. I told them it was a fake and laid it on the stove. Then they got awful brave and talked about shooting me. I told them to go ahead and shoot , that I didn't care. They put me into a cell, and as I turned around Detective Ahn punched me in the face with his pistol. Before this great farce I was placed in a strong position to work it, as the Birmingham officers had just exploded a bottle of nitro-glycerin, which it is claimed was found in my valise. It made an awful and noise and blew a big hole in the ground. Everybody heard it and it had the effect I desired. The Birmingham officers all recognized me and they treated me very nicely all the way back. They did everything they could for my comfort and they are all perfect gentlemen. I tried not to give them the least trouble.

Going back to the crime for which the courts say I must hang, I want to say that I am not a murderer. So far as I know the statement made by Frank Miller on the gallows was correct. All the men believe that it was New York Harry who shot both men. If I hang it will be for a crime I did not commit. New York Harry's name is O'Dowd. Yes, I guess my wife will come to Birmingham. She generally comes as near me as possible when I am in trouble. Unfortunate woman. I have been in trouble near ever since we were married five years ago. The last time I saw her was in Tavares while in jail at that place."

"NEW YORK HARRY" CAUGHT IN ST. LOUIS
Famous Crook Beaten Into Insensibility in Desperate Battle
May Save Duncan's Neck
Both He and Frank Miller Claimed New York Harry Killed the Policemen, and said He Would Admit It

The Birmingham Age-Herald, October 24, 1904

"From the Cincinnati papers it appears that New York Harry, the noted crook who has been frequently charged with the murder of Policemen Kirkley and Adams, and on whom Duncan pins chances of escaping the gallows, has been caught in St. Louis. It will be remembered that several days ago five St. Louis detectives in attempting to capture a gang of supposed train robbers engaged in a desperate battle in that city, in which two detectives were were killed and one of the robbers was killed and two captured. One of these was New York Harry who was caught just outside the house and was forced to go into the room occupied by the robbers with the detectives. He was going under the name of Henry Adam, alias Harry Vaughn, but was recognized as New York Harry. This at least sets to rest the theory that no such man as New York Harry ever existed.

Frank Miller while on the gallows claimed that New York Harry committed the murder at Birmingham and said that if he was ever captured he would admit it. Frank Duncan has persistently claimed the same thing. It now rest with New York Harry to say whether or not he is the guilty man. He may be the means of saving Duncan's neck.

Alleged police killer Harry Vaughn, will face trial for the double murder of two officers in Birmingham as soon as he can be taken to that city from St. Louis where he is now in the city hospital, under police guard, and suffering from wounds received in a desperate battle with detectives. In this fight Vaughn was beaten into unconsciousness. Detectives John Shea and Thomas Dwyer were killed, and criminal Al Rose was shot to death. Detective James McCluskey was shot through the body and is in a critical condition, while C.C. Blair, another of the party of desperadoes, has four bullet wounds through the body and will likely die, thus escaping trial for the killing of the two officers named.

It is now developed that Vaughn is the man sought by the officers of Birmingham under the name of "New York Harry" Wester, whose record is as follows: "Thomas Dowd, alias Harry H. Vaughn, alias Petit, alias Graham, alias New York Harry, alias Harry O'Dowd, alias Denver Harry, aged 45."

A few months ago, 'Dutch John' Hendricks, safeblower, graduate chemist and student for the priesthood, was hanged in Birmingham for the murder of two policemen. His last words uttered upon the scaffold were: "I am innocent. 'New York Harry' killed both of those policemen, and if he is ever caught he will admit it, and you will know you have hung an innocent man."

Five Lives May Be Cost of Harry Vaughn's Arrest

Officers have been on the lookout for a gang of men suspected of train robbery. The suspected gang were located in a room in St. Louis. Vaughn left the room to take a walk. He was seized by officers, who then, fearing that the news would be carried to his friends, took Vaughn with them and undertook to arrest the other members of the gang. As the officers entered the room with Vaughn, Rose and Blair, the suspected men, opened fire with their heavy revolvers. Shea, Dwyer and McCluskey, detectives, were shot down. Vaughn tried to wrest himself free from officers Boyle and James to help his friends. The three wounded officers replied to the fusillade they met, while Boyle and James hammered Vaughn into insensibility. When he lay unconscious on the floor, Boyle and

James joined their comrades in pouring a rain of fire into the suspects. Rose was shot down and Blair fatally wounded."

FRANK DUNCAN FEELS HOPEFUL
Says if New York Harry is Caught He is Saved
Has Been Feeling Blue
If Report is True His Wife Will Probably Go to St. Louis
And Have a Talk With the Famous Criminal
The Birmingham Age-Herald, October 5, 1904

"Frank Duncan is highly hopeful now that it is believed by a number of people that New York Harry has been captured in St. Louis. "I am saved if the report is true," said the condemned man. "My wife knows New York Harry quite well and I have but no doubt but what she will go to St. Louis and confer with the chief of police of that place in my behalf. They tell me that New York Harry is quite a desperate man, but up to the time he and Frank Miller killed the two policemen, I have never heard of him taking the life of anyone."

There is an indictment against New York Harry in the hands of the sheriff of Jefferson county. The indictment does not charge murder, but does charge the criminal with highway robbery. It is understood that the solicitor of Jefferson county will exert all of his efforts to have New York Harry brought back to Birmingham for trial, but it is hardly probable, it is said, that he will be successful."

Duncan's hopes were dashed when later on the same day the following information was received from the St. Louis authorities:

NEW YORK HARRY STILL AT LARGE
Prisoner in St. Louis Not the Noted Safe Blower
Photograph Is Received
It Disposes of the Theory That Former Member
of Miller-Duncan Gang Has Been Caught
Duncan Hears the News
The Birmingham News, October 25, 1904

"Harry Vaughn, under arrest at St. Louis, is not "New York Harry" is revealed by this telegram from Chief of Police Kiely, of St. Louis, to the Birmingham News: Photo and description of Vaughn mailed. Confined Jefferson City 1897 to June 8th this Year." In other words,

Vaughn had been an inmate of the state prison at Jefferson City, Mo., from 1897 to the 8th of June of the current year, and hence he could not have been in Birmingham during the period of the operations of the Miller-Duncan gang in this city and vicinity.

Duncan was much elated yesterday afternoon over the possibility that New York Harry had been located. He was shown the photograph this morning and said that while there was some resemblance, he did not recognize the man as New York Harry."

MANY SIGN THE DUNCAN PETITION
Several Hundred Citizens Are for Commutation of Sentence
Prisoner Is Very Hopeful
The Birmingham Age-Herald, October, 30, 1904

"Several hundred names were added to the petitions being circulated asking the governor of Alabama to commute the sentence of Frank Duncan, condemned to die for taking the life of policeman George W. Kirkley. The attorneys, friends and sympathizers of Duncan expect to make the largest petition ever sent to the chief executive's office of Alabama. It will be sent in order that Governor Cunningham may have ample time in which to carefully consider it. Personal letters from influential men of Birmingham and the county will also be sent to the governor in behalf of the condemned man."

WIFE PLEADS FOR HUSBAND'S LIFE
Mrs. Frank Duncan Appears Before Governor Cunningham
Begs Him To Stay Sentence
With Tears and Sobs She Appears Before the Pardoning Board--
Policeman Kirkley's Wife Writes Letter to Governor
The Birmingham Age-Herald, November 4, 1904

"After fully investigating all the new evidence Acting Governor Cunningham announced that he would not interfere with the death sentence of Frank Duncan sentenced to hang next Friday. This removes every hope that the convicted man has.

Almost prostrating herself and with her body shaken and torn by the anguish of her situation, Mrs. Myrtle Duncan, wife of the condemned Birmingham murderer and safe blower, gave the acting governor of Alabama one of the most heart-rendering half hours of his whole life. With tears streaming down her browned and grief furrowed cheeks and words of pleading on her trembling lips, this earnest and persistent woman, "faithful unto death," cried for the life of her husband and begged the governor to stay the strong hand of the law and and save the condemned man from the cruel strangulation of the hangman's knot.

Mrs. Kirkley's Letter

Just here it was found that new and to some extent sensational evidence had been submitted in a letter from Mrs. G.W. Kirkley, wife of one of the policemen said to have been killed by Duncan and a partner. In the letter it was stated that Officer Kirkley said before he died that Duncan was not the man who shot him. It was addressed to the governor: "In behalf of Frank Duncan who is to be hanged the 25th for the supposed murder of my beloved husband, George W. Kirkley, I feel it is my duty as a Christian woman to tell your honor my husband's statement was this: The man Frank Duncan that was with him did not do the shooting, and that is all I can say." The letter was written in a masculine hand and signed by Mrs. Kirkley in a trembling and rather broken hand.

Surely no party of men ever had a more pitiful case to deal with. Not one of them but believed the penalty attached to the case was just and all felt that the law demanded the death sentence. But every man of them stood with bared head before the persistent love and energy of this woman. Her tears were like sharp pointed knives in their hearts and it would be a very safe guess that every one would have given much if he had been able to have given her some hope. Within half an hour the announcement was made that there would be no favorable recommendation, the language to the governor being: "Many citizens have petitioned for a commutation of this man's sentence. After carefully considering all of it we do not find sufficient evidence to authorize us to recommend that the verdict of the court be interfered with."

FRANK DUNCAN SAYS HE WILL DIE LIKE A BRAVE MAN
Famous Prisoner Will Be Hanged Before Noon Today
The Birmingham Age-Herald, November 25, 1904

"Frank Duncan will be hanged today on the charge of taking the life of Officer George W. Kirkley over four years ago. The execution will take place before noon in the Jefferson county jail yard. Duncan has professed religion and says he is ready to meet his maker. Although slightly nervous yesterday Duncan appeared to be holding his nerve very well. He declared that he would die game. "I will die like a brave man, which I think I am. I have been in a number of tight places during my career, but I have never shot at or killed a human being."

Only about one hundred tickets of admission to the execution have been issued from the sheriff's office. On the door of the office appears the following notice: "Please do not ask for passes. They are all out and we are not in the mood to be worried." Sheriff Burgin has issued the following: "Following are the assignments for duty on hanging day. Get to the place by 9:30 and stay there until the corpse is brought out and the crowd dispersed. This is one time that strict obedience will be demanded of each man, and any failure will call for a resignation. Admit no one without a pass, except policemen in uniform or with a badge and constables. Be sure they are what they claim to be."

WITHOUT FLINCH OR TREMOR DUNCAN GAMELY FACES DEATH
Famous Criminal Stoutly Proclaims His Innocence of Murder to Last Moment
"May God Forgive Me For What I Have Done"
Walked Upon the Gallows Without Assistance, Clearing Three Steps at a Time—
His Wife is Without Funds

The Birmingham Age-Herald, November 25, 1904

"Frank Duncan yesterday paid the penalty of death for the murder of Policeman George W. Kirkley on the streets of Birmingham over four years ago. Duncan's form dropped through the trap of the gallows at 11:37 o'clock and within eleven minutes from that time physicians pronounced him dead. His body was cut down and carried to the undertaking establishment of Lige Loy on Third Avenue and prepared for burial.

Before being hung Duncan said his remains would be taken to his old home in Pourtsmouth, Ohio for interment. He probably knew his wife was in destitute circumstances when he made the statement, but did not know that she could not raise funds with which to purchase tickets for herself and the body of her deceased husband. An effort will be made to secure from Mayor Drennen charity tickets for Mrs. Duncan and the corpse of her husband.

Duncan lived up to the promise he made several days ago--he died bravely. In fact, it is said by county authorities that Duncan displayed more nerve upon the gallows than has ever been shown by any condemned man in Jefferson county. He went upon the gallows, which by the way is the new steel one recently finished, unassisted. As he walked out of the county jail he was alone, and when he went upon the gallows, three steps at the time, fully 75 per cent of the crowd who was gathered in the jail yard to witness the execution thought that he was a deputy sheriff who went upon the scaffold to arrange the final detail of the gruesome task.

Duncan went through the ordeal without a flinch. Just before the black cap was adjusted over his face he took both hands, which were manacled, and smoothed down his hair. When the hangman was ready to adjust the noose about his neck he was not exactly on the trap. His attention was called to this and he stepped into position without uttering a sound. His body was taken to Loy's place immediately after the physicians had declared life extinct. Thousands of people crowded around the establishment during the afternoon. The undertaker decided to let the public view the remains. The first group to enter the place consisted of ten or twelve saleswomen, and for several hours the place was thronged with people.

Dr. W.P. McAdory was preparing to give Duncan a hypodermic of strychnine, but the prisoner refused, saying: "Never mind that, doctor." About 8 o'clock yesterday morning the crowds continued to gather around the jail and court house, and it was estimated that by 11 o'clock there were 2000 people lined along Twenty-first street. About 10:45 o'clock the jail door was opened and those having passes were admitted. The crowd on the outside of the jail was quite orderly. In the street there were a number of ladies in the crowd. All of the members of the Birmingham police department, policemen from towns in the district and constables and other courts officials were admitted.

Mrs. Duncan remained at Loy's all last night. She said that one of the last requests of her husband was that the public be not allowed to gaze upon him after death.

DUNCAN'S DYING STATEMENT

"I am truly glad to see so many of the brave policemen of Birmingham here to see me hung. It certainly takes bravery. I thank God today that I am able to meet anything that comes to me. I have been persecuted beyond all expression. The officers that worked up this case know that I am innocent. I know it; God knows it, and knows that I had nothing to do with this murder. Every man that had anything to do with this case knows it, and I am satisfied that there is not a man in Birmingham that actually believes that I am guilty. I have not got as much to account for today as my persecutors."

Attorney Shugart: "Tell them where you were at that night."

Duncan: "I was up over the restaurant--just where I have always told you I was."

Sheriff Burgin: "Is that all you have got to say, Frank?"

Duncan: "Yes, sir. I do hope the good people of Birmingham will sympathize with me in meeting this unmerited fate. That is all I have got to say, I ask God to forgive me for what I have done."

The drop fell at 11:36 a.m."

FAMOUS "NEW YORK HARRY" MUST COME HERE ON MURDER CHARGE
Bodeker Has Evidence to Convict Him of Kirkley and Adams Killing
Two Have Already Paid Death Penalty
Bodeker Contends Frank Duncan Was Hanged For Crime Which He Never Committed—
Dowd in the Atlanta Penitentiary

The Birmingham Age-Herald, February 4, 1912

"After a relentless search for 12 years, the man who is thought to be one of the real murderers of Police Officers George W. Kirkley and J.H. Adams is to be brought to Birmingham to face trial. Harry O. Dowd, alias James Scanlon, alias Thomas Dowd, alias Harry Pettit, alias "New York Harry," alias "Denver Harry," whom Chief of Police George Bodeker has always contended was the man who fired one of the fatal shots.

Harry O. Dowd, which is his right name, is...just finishing a five year sentence for safe blowing. He will be arrested as he leaves the gate of the federal prison. The crime which with Dowd is charged is one of the most atrocious recorded in the annals of Birmingham's police department, and at the time of its commission stirred the south. Officers Kirkley and Adams were attempting to arrest Dowd, Frank Duncan, John West, Tom Fay and "Dutch Henry" Miller on suspicion of having blown the safe of the Standard Oil company earlier in the night. At Third avenue and Twentieth street they intercepted the crowd of men, and when they commanded them to stop the officers were fired upon, both receiving wounds which caused their deaths. Officer Kirkley died two days later, on March 20, 1900 and Officer Adams died on April 3, 1900.

Detectives arrested Duncan and Miller, who were the leaders of the notorious gang of burglars and safe blowers. Miller and Duncan were subsequently hanged for the murder of the officers. Miller made a partial confession as to his part in the affair, but Duncan maintain his innocence to the time the trap was sprung and his neck broken.

At the time Duncan was sentenced to be hanged, Detective Bodeker insisted that it was his firm belief that Duncan was innocent of having killed the officers. He stated yesterday afternoon that he still believed that Frank Duncan was hanged for a crime which he had never committed.

While on the gallows to be hanged for the crime Duncan was handed the picture of Dowd by Bodeker. Duncan stated emphatically that the picture was that of the man who had fired one of the fatal shots. Detective Bodeker sustained Duncan's claim as to Dowd's guilt and his own innocence of the murder and has been working all these years, collecting the evidence with which to convict Dowd.

On the night of the shooting Dowd made his escape, but was arrested in January, 1908, brought to Birmingham, tried and acquitted for complicity in blowing the Standard Oil safe. At the time of his trial, Bodeker insisted that Dowd was one of the men who fired the fatal shots at the officers, but could not then produce the evidence to convict him, and Dowd was released. Dowd was sentence to five years for blowing the safe of the post office at Dunn, N.C. Post office Inspector Gregory worked up the case on him there and also made inquiries into his complicity in the shooting of the

Birmingham policemen. He conveyed his intelligence to Bodeker stating that he had evidence sufficient to convict Dowd and Bodeker stated that he had even additional evidence. That Dowd will hang for his crime, neither Gregory or Bodeker have the slightest doubt. They state that their evidence is absolutely conclusive."

COURTROOM PACKED WHEN PETITT TRIAL BEGINS BEFORE FORT
Defendant Accused of Being "New York Harry" and of Killing Officers

The Birmingham Age-Herald, January 28, 1914

"Former members of the so-called Miller and Duncan gang of safe-blowers were among the witnesses who testified for the state at the trial of Harry Petitt, alias "New York Harry," charged with the murder of Policeman G.W. Kirkley about 12 years ago. Much interest is being manifested in this trial and the courtroom was crowded with members of the legal fraternity, officials and spectators who listened with interest to the testimony of the alleged "pals" of the defendant, especially the details of the safeblowing at the office of the Standard Oil company and the events that are said to have followed.

Neither Frank Edwards nor Thomas West, self-confessed members of the gang, who were convicted and sentenced to terms of imprisonment and subsequently pardoned, would positively identify the defendant, West stating that he never knew anyone by the name of "New York Harry" but that a man who went by the name of "Denver Harry" was a member of the gang and that the prisoner resembled that person. Tom Fay, a third self-confessed member of the gang, also a pardoned convict, positively identified the defendant as "New York Harry," stating that he and the defendant came to Birmingham from Chattanooga together and joined the gang in the city.

The evidence was to the effect that the six men divided into pairs after the safeblowing and made their way by different routes to a rendezvous in the city. While four of the men were planning means of escape, shots were heard, presumably to be those that brought death to the two officers and that a few minutes later Miller and "Harry" appeared and stated they had got two "bulls" (policemen).

The state is contending that Frank Duncan, who was hanged for the murder of the two policemen, did not commit the crime, but that "NewYork Harry" was the murderer. Dr. Charles Whelan...testified as to the dying statement of Officer Adams, who he said identified Miller as the man who had shot him, and Duncan as the man who shot his partner, Kirkley."

MISTRIAL ENTERED IN NEW YORK HARRY CASE BY JUDGE FORT
Stood Seven To Five For Conviction
The Birmingham Age-Herald, February 1, 1914

"Agreeing that evidence was not sufficient to call for the death penalty or life imprisonment, the jury in the case of James Rooneyt, alias "New York Harry," failed to agree on a 10 years' sentence in the penitentiary and a mistrial was entered by Judge Fort and the jury discharged. At no time were any of the jurors willing to bring in a verdict of murder in the first degree, but the majority favored some punishment.

The jurors talked freely about their trying experience, some of them stating there was an honest difference of opinion among the jurors as to the guilt and innocence of the defendant. One juror said he was against a compromise verdict and that if the defendant was guilty he ought to be hanged. Post Office Inspector Gregory, who furnished practically all the witnesses for the state, would not express an opinion as to the outcome of the trial. He gathered up his bunch of ex-convicts that he had brought here to testify against the defendant and, like the Arab, folded his tent and departed.

The prisoner Rooney, was plainly disappointed. He stated that he was afraid that he would be convicted on "general principles" and that the jury might arrive at a compromise verdict and give him a term of years in the penitentiary. "I am much disappointed at the verdict," said Rooney, "for I fully expected an acquittal. With the exception of a few additional safeblowers brought here by Mr. Gregory, all of whom, by the way, have secured a pardon through his efforts, the evidence was practically the same as when I was tried for being a member of the Miller and Duncan gang and acquitted by a jury of this county. Just think of the power of Mr. Gregory, with all the machinery of the United States government at his command, and yet, the best he could do was to bring a bunch of ex-convicts, many of whom he had pardoned, to swear that I made certain confessions. I tell you that a man with a 25-year sentence hanging over him will swear anything to get a pardon. I don't say that Mr. Gregory offered a pardon to those fellows to swear against me, but when a convict is pardoned it is pretty generally known among the others the reason for the clemency. The statement that I ran all over the United States telling every 'crook' I met that I had been in trouble, is absurd--I know them too well--why, those fellows would hang their own father to get out of jail. I do not criticize the jury, for I am sure they were honest in their convictions, but it does seem to me that these gentlemen who voted to give me a sentence of 10 years must have been influenced by the testimony that I had been formerly convicted, and for which I paid the full penalty of the law, for if I was guilty of the murder for which I was tried, which God knows I am not, the punishment would hardly have been in keeping with the crime. I am very grateful to my attorneys for the fight they made to secure my freedom, especially as at this time I have not a penny in the world, and hope that my case will be again set at an early date. I feel that I will be acquitted."

Petitt Is Taken To Georgia By Inspector H.T. Gregory
Is Charged With Burglary
Man Who Was in Jail Two Years Awaiting Trial Hurried Out of State Without Even Being Permitted to Buy a Package of Tobacco,
When Murder Charge is Nolle Prossed

The Birmingham Age-Herald, May 19, 1914

"Denied one moment's liberty, James Rooney, alias "Harry Petitt," alias "New York Harry," was rearrested at the instance of Post Office Inspector H.T. Gregory, just as the order for his release was handed to Warden Bob McAdory. The two cases pending in the criminal court charging him with the murder of Policemen Kirkley and Adams were nolle prossed yesterday afternoon on motion of Circuit Solicitor Joseph R. Tate as none of the main witnesses against him answered to the call of the clerk. The state announced not ready and when asked by the court Mr. Tate stated he did not believe the witnesses could be gotten and agreed that the case be nolle prossed.

When the witnesses were called Inspector Gregory did not answer to his name but as soon as the defendant's attorneys secured the order for the release of Rooney he came up with two deputy sheriffs from Georgia and followed him to the warden's office. As soon as the release was handed to the warden Deputy Sheriff Chris Hartsfield placed Petitt under arrest and read a requisition from the governor of Georgia alleging that Rooney was wanted on a charge of burglary.

In such a hurry was the inspector to depart with his prisoner that when the deputy had some difficulty in placing the handcuffs on the wrists of Rooney he instructed the deputy to "bring him along" partially handcuffed and refused the request of the prisoner to buy a package of tobacco. Rooney stated that he knew absolutely nothing about the charge brought against him and that he had no chance with the powerful influence that Inspector Gregory could bring to bear to keep him in prison. He was very despondent over his rearrest, stating that he had neither friends or money and that on his release he expected to stay in Birmingham and make an honest living as he had several jobs offered him.

As the Georgia deputies left with their prisoner there were many expressions of regret and sympathy for the unfortunate fellow and the tactics of Inspector Gregory were strongly condemned. Warden Bob McAdory shook hands with Rooney and said: "I am sorry for you, Jim," and as the hand clasp was broken a "greenback" was left in the hand of the prisoner.

Rooney was charged with the murder of Policemen Kirkley and Adams who were killed in March, 1900, and has been in jail waiting trial for 26 months. The principal prosecutor of Rooney has been Inspector Gregory, who produced the principal testimony for the state at the trial of Rooney some months ago which resulted in a mistrial."

Postscript

Thus ends the known history of "New York Harry." Obviously, several government agencies were intent on keeping this individual incarcerated for as long as possible. Many people believed that he was responsible for shooting and killing at least one, if not both of the officers, in conjunction with Frank Miller who was convicted and hanged for the crime. A second member of the gang, Frank Duncan, who was also executed for this act, was believed by many, including numerous local law enforcement officers, to not have been directly involved in the murders of the officers and was not present when they occurred. If this was true, then the deathbed identification by Officer Adams of Duncan as one of the perpetrators was erroneous.

Adams' "certain" identification of Duncan as one of the perpetrators was sufficient to charge him with the crime at that time. Duncan's later escape from custody within the Jefferson County jail was a severe embarrassment to law enforcement officials and, perhaps, lends credence to Duncan's statement shortly before his execution that if he was hung he would be executed on "general principles." In any event, as there had been two persons who had been arrested by Officers Kirkley and Adams just prior to the shootings, then it may have been felt that at least two men would have to pay the ultimate price for the crime. Miller and Duncan would serve this purpose especially in light of the general belief at the time of the murders that "New York Harry" was likely an imaginary character.

ADMITTING REPORT
TO THE COUNTY INVESTIGATOR OF JEFFERSON COUNTY

Name of Hospital or Infirmary South Highlands Iny. Date 4-16-35

Name of person injured Mr. J. M. Early Sex Male Color White

Address 701 So. 47th St.

Name and address of relative or friend Mrs. J. M. Early (wife) Same address

Age 32 Civil state Married Occupation Motorcycle Cop

Time Admitted 9:00 A.M. 4/14/35 P.M. Ward 61 Died 2:45 a.m. Date 4/15/35 A.M. P.M.

Brought to Hospital by Ridouts

Name of person accompanying him

Address

How injured Shot in abdomen c automatic pistol.

By whom and address (In gun fight)

Where injured Irondale

Diagnosis Multiple Gun Shot wounds of abdomen, perforating Intestines - (Homicidal)

Doctors Gaines & Board

Name of Interne Gilbert Green Name of Nurse H. Warlick

Treatment on admission Morph. Sr. 1/4 - atropine Gro. 1/158

Disposition of Clothes and Valuables

Disposition of Body Luguire's

Investigating Officers

County Investigator notified by phone

Myrtle Hurley Clerk.

NOTE---Report all cases admitted whose injuries are due to gun shot, knife cut, razor cut and all other injuries from which persons are likely to die or do die.

Although certainly not an inclusive compilation of service related deaths of Birmingham police officers, deputy sheriffs and other law enforcement officers in Jefferson County during this era, the following cases provide examples of such deaths, some minimally publicized and others which demanded front page news coverage.

OFFICER WALTON SHOT TO DEATH BY A NEGRO
Fired on by Jim Webb, Whom He Had Gone to Arrest
Bullet Penetrated Policeman's Heart
Walton Fell Into the Arms of the Man
Who Accompanied Him,
Crying "He Has Killed Me"--The Murderer Wounded
The Birmingham Age-Herald, March 19, 1902

"Policeman William P. Walton, the oldest in point of service, and one of the most popular patrolmen on the police force, was shot through the heart and killed almost instantly last night by Jim Webb, a drunken negro he was trying to arrest. The policeman shot his murderer once through the arm before receiving the fatal wound. The negro was captured. Policeman Walton went to the home to to arrest the negro. He was accompanied by C.E. Cochran, who keeps a grocery store. Webb was wanted for assaulting John Brown, another negro, and was in a room on the second floor. Policeman Walton ascended the steps and pushed the door open. As he did so the negro shot once, the ball passing over the shoulders of both men. He fired a second time and the bullet struck Mr. Walton in the left chest above the heart. The third bullet passed through the officer's heart. Policeman Walton fired twice at the negro and then fell back in the arms of Mr. Cochran, saying: "He has killed me! He has killed me!" As he fell the policeman fired a third time, but his pistol pointed upward, and the trigger was pulled with the last convulsion of a dying man. The negro emptied his revolver at Mr. Cochran without effect. Before Mr. Walton fell Mr. Cochran shot four times at the negro over the shoulder of the policeman.

Policeman Walton fell at the head of the steps with his feet hanging over the top step. His overcoat is singed for an inch around where the bullets passed through showing how close the negro was when he fired. Webb was traced to the house of another negro by blood which flowed from the wound in his left arm. He undertook to conceal himself by crawling under the structure, but was dragged out. He surrendered to Chief Austin under promise that he would be protected.

Policeman Walton wore badge No. 1 of the department. He was born in Lincoln county, Georgia, in 1846, making him 56 years of age. He was one of the few men on the force who served through the civil war. He entered the Confederate army when about 16 years old and served through the rest of the war. Mr. Walton leaves six children."

JIM WEBB IS AT PEACE WITH GOD
Slayer of Policeman Walton to be Hanged Today
The Gallows Is Ready
The Birmingham Age-Herald, March 13, 1903

"Jim Webb, the negro who shot and killed Policeman W.P. Walton on March 18, 1902, will be hanged today at noon on the gallows in the yard gallows in the yard at the county jail. Webb sticks to the statement that he made at the trial that he thought he was shooting at a negro when the officer was killed by the bullet discharged from his pistol. Webb states that he was in a room when the door was broken down, and that he shot towards the door, thinking that a negro with whom he had quarreled was breaking it in.

During the past few days Webb has been praying great deal and last night the negroes in the colored department of the jail sang religious songs to the sing-song musical air peculiar to negroes. "I have made my peace with the Lord," said Webb. "On Sunday last I was baptized by immersion and it gave me strength. I don't think I will have any trouble walking up the steps o the gallows. I have got to die, and I will try to face it as best I can. Tomorrow morning I want to see my folks before they take me out to hang me. I think some preachers will come to see me, too."

None of the tickets of admission to the jail yard will be honored before 11 o'clock. Sheriff Burgin will pull the drop at 12 o'clock unless providentially hindered, in which case a deputy will officiate."

EXECUTION WAS QUICKLY DONE
Jim Webb, Who Killed Officer Walton, Hanged Yesterday
Condemned Man Gave No Evidence of Nervous Strain--
Stood Firm as Black Cap Was Adjusted.
Many Witness Hanging
The Birmingham Age-Herald, March 14, 1903

"Jim Webb, who shot and killed Policeman W.P. Walton, was hanged in the yard of the county jail. The drop fell at exactly 11:55 o'clock. Webb's neck was broken. His muscles convulsed violently for several minutes and his heart ceased pulsating at 12:06 1/2 o'clock. The corpse, still warm and limp, was taken from the gallows to the colored undertaking establishment at Charley Harris. The body will be buried in the negro cemetery at Woodlawn tomorrow afternoon.

About 350 people witnessed the execution of the murderer. Some of this number stood at the windows of the houses overlooking the jail. Half an hour before Webb ascended the steps to the gallows, fully 150 people had gathered in the jail yard, and in a pouring rain waited to see the condemned negro hanged. The gallows was erected in the corner of the yard, between the white jail and the hospital. It was in plain view of the windows of the City court and the windows in the court rooms were crowded. Almost 400 people stood on the outside of the yard, mostly negroes. Conspicuous among the crowd were policemen of Birmingham, Bessemer, Ensley and Pratt City. The sheriff had invited them to be present and they came to see the murderer of a popular fellow officer expiate the penalty of his crime.

At 11:45, when Deputy Sheriff William Love came out of the jail with the rope in his hand the jail yard contained about 250 people, including twenty-two members of a class of the Birmingham Medical College. The officer ascended the gallows and began arranging the rope. The rain continued to fall and umbrellas were lifted over the rope to prevent the part that had been soaped from becoming wet. At 11:52 Webb emerged from the jail door. Smilingly, he walked to his death. Reaching the steps he did not hesitate but ascended without any visible emotion. As he went up the steps Webb called out, "Is everybody here? I am ready to die." He had previously stated he did not wish to make any statement on the scaffold and when he reached the platform Deputy Sheriff Love quickly put the rope around his neck. As he did so, Webb said in a plaintive voice, "I'm walking my way to Zion, hallelujah." Further articulation could not be understood for the "black cap" was tied on his head. The feet and hands were severely fastened. The man stood firm. Almost before the crowd realized it, Sheriff Burgin pulled the lever, the drop fell and Webb's body shot downward. Webb had paid the penalty of his bloody deed."

The recurrent problem related to the mistaken identification of individuals suspected of committing crimes is as old as crime itself. Many innocent people have been arrested, tried, convicted and even executed based on such erroneous "positive" identifications made by other humans as has been more recently proven by the use of modern scientific technologies such as DNA testing.

Apparent misidentifications occurred in regard to the murders of several law enforcement officers in Jefferson County during the first decade of the twentieth century, two of which occurred in 1903 and all of which remained unsolved. The first case involved the arrest of a suspect who was originally noted in a newspaper headline to be "Identified As Right Man," but who later, along with the apparent case against him, mysteriously disappeared into history without a trace.

ENSLEY OFFICER SHOT BY NEGRO
Suspect Named "Jack" Mortally Wounds E.L. Bennett
Citizens Are Indignant
Policeman Starts to Arrest a Negro Suspect in Ensley Barroom and is Shot

The Birmingham Age-Herald, January 20, 1903

"Policeman E.L. Bennett was shot twice and mortally wounded tonight while attempting to arrest a negro in a saloon of tough reputation at Avenue B and Nineteenth street. The negro who fired the shots escaped and though the entire police force of Ensley and a number of citizens have been in search of him no trace of his whereabouts can be found. The negro is a comparative stranger in Ensley and was known as "Jack." The citizens of Ensley are indignant over what they consider the cold blooded murder of one of the city's most popular officers and if the man is caught it is feared trouble will result. The police promise that no violence will be done the prisoner.

Policeman Bennett did not know the negro but his suspicions were aroused by the man's actions and he decided to arrest him on suspicion. Entering the "dive" he approached the negro, telling him he was wanted. The negro quickly turned and drawing a small revolver fired two shots at the policeman. The stricken officer was taken to a drug store near by and then removed to the Cunningham hospital. Several prominent physicians were called in and it is their unanimous opinion that the wounds are fatal. The intestines were punctured and it is feared blood poison will set in.

The negro who shot Mr. Bennett is believed to have come from Warner mines and officers have been sent there for the purpose of locating him if possible. Policeman Bennett is one of the oldest and most efficient men on the force and is second in authority to the night captain. He has a wife and two little children."

OFFICER SHOT TO DEATH BY NEGRO
E.L. Bennett Killed by an Ensley Character Who Is Known as "Jack."
Had Iron Bar In His Pocket
Seemed Willing to Go When Arrested, But In Moment Pulled Gun and Fired Twice With Fatal Effect
Dead Man Had Family

The Birmingham News, January 20, 1903

"Policeman E.L. Bennett, one of the most valuable and popular officers of the Ensley force, died at the Cunningham Hospital at 7:30 this morning as the result of pistol wounds at the hands of a suspected negro, known locally as "Jack," whom Mr. Bennett arrested last night in a negro saloon on Avenue B and Nineteenth street.

Mr. Bennett was in the saloon about 9:00 o'clock in the course of his rounds, and seeing a heavy iron bar sticking out of the negro's coat pocket he approached him and drew it out, at the same time asking him what he meant by carrying such a weapon and telling him he would take him up for doing so. He did not think to search the negro for any other weapon and started out of the place with his prisoner, who apparently was willing to go, remarking to the officer as they reached the screen door near the front of the saloon: "All right, I'll go with you."

As he uttered this remark, witnesses state, he pulled a gun with his free right hand and fired two shots, one striking the officer to the right of the naval, the other penetrating his hand. The negro then jerked loose and fled, while Officer Bennett, in a dazed condition, walked up the street a few steps to the saloon on the corner, where he asked for help and lay down on the floor until an ambulance was sent for him.

At the hospital everything possible was done for his relief, but the wound in the abdomen was pronounced by the physicians as of a fatal nature, and after lingering through the night death ensued this morning. The dead officer leaves a wife and two children. The police used every effort last night to apprehend the negro. The officers believe they will be able to capture him. Mr. Bennett has been on the force for several years and was very popular in the city. His unfortunate death is a matter of regret to all his acquaintances, and much sympathy is expressed for his family."

OFFICER BENNETT DIES OF WOUNDS
A Reward of $100 Has Been Offered By City Of Ensley For Apprehension Of The Negro Murderer

The Birmingham Age-Herald, January 21, 1903

"Officer E.L. Bennett died this morning. Chief Camp of the Ensley police force has offered a $100 reward for the apprehension of the murderer. He has issued the following description of the negro: "Name, 'Jack,' height, 5 feet 8 inches to 5 feet 10 inches; weight, 165 to 170 pounds; dark brown small thin moustache; has what is called an 'evil eye,' that is, one eye has a nervous affection which causes it to jump or twitch almost continually. "Wore old blue overall pants, old coat with ragged sleeves, old dirty white hat."

OFFICER GOES FOR A SUSPECT
Third Negro Held at Pinckney as Officer Bennett's Slayer
The Dead Officer Buried
Many Friends Escorted Remains to Grave
Solemn Scenes at the Funeral
Wife and Children Receive Kindly Ministration

The Birmingham News, January 21, 1903

"Chief of Police C.F. Camp left Ensley this morning, going through the country to Pinckney, a little town near Blossburg, eight or ten miles west of Ensley where a negro suspected as the slayer of Officer E.L. Bennett, whose remains lie cold in death at his home in the city, has been arrested and is in custody. From the description given by those holding the suspected negro the chief thinks there is some probability of his being the man wanted.

Everything possible is being done to apprehend the slayer of the brave and popular officer, the full horror of whose tragic death has stirred the city deeply. A reward of $100 has been offered and no stone will be unturned by the officers in their efforts to find him.

Officer Bennett's funeral was held this morning from his late residence on Avenue I near Twenty-sixth street. The members of Towanda Tribe No. 48, Improved Order of Red Men, and those of the Ensley Odd Fellows' lodge, to which orders Mr. Bennett belonged for several years, escorted the remains in a body. The pallbearers were those of his of his personal friends from the police force and a few more intimate ones from private life. The service at the residence was conducted by Rev. George W. Read, of the Southern Methodist Church, of which Officer Bennett was a member. The remains were carried to Bessemer, where they were laid to rest in the family burying ground. The scene at Officer Bennett's home this morning was very sad and impressive. A great crowd gathered to do honor to the dead officer's memory. Ensley mourns with his loved ones and laments the loss of a true-hearted and noble man and officer."

The Birmingham Age-Herald, January 23, 1903

"A subscription is being signed by the leading business and professional men of this city to secure a reward of several hundred dollars to be offered for the capture of the negro known as "Jack," the murderer of Officer E.L. Bennett. The list was headed by $100 from Chief C.F. Camp, who returned today from Pinckney, where he went to identify a negro thought to be "Jack." But he returned without any success, as he proved to be the wrong one. Everything possible is being done, and it is believed that if he is captured he will be dealt roughly with by Ensley citizens."

BENNETT'S SLAYER CAUGHT IN ENSLEY
Negro Arrested After Desperate Struggle by Policeman Rush
Identified As Right Man
When Questioned by Chief Camp He Made Contradictory Statements and Seemed Ill at Ease--Arrest Was Kept Secret

The Birmingham Age-Herald, March 15, 1903

"Sam Holt, alias Sam Warren, alias Jack Warren, a negro, was arrested tonight, charged with the murder of Policeman Bennett, and the police say there is absolutely no question as to his identity. The arrest was made by Will Rush, who is known in Ensley as the boy policeman, and though the negro showed fight when apprehended, the officer finally over-powered him and carried him to jail. On account of numerous threats of lynching, the arrest was kept secret, and only a few persons were permitted to see the prisoner.

The police say Holt bears every mark of resemblance to the man who murdered the policeman, and that all of the men who were permitted to see him identified the negro positively as the man wanted. All of the scars described in the circular sent out were found on his body, and he carried a small pistol in a front pocket, from which the murderer of Policeman Bennett is said to have drawn his weapon.

The negro was discovered by Policeman Rush as he was walking down Nineteenth street. Rush stopped him. The negro attempted to draw a weapon, but the officer knocked him down and after a desperate struggle succeeded in putting the handcuffs on. When questioned, the negro made many contradictory statements and seemed ill at ease. In fact, the attendants at the jail say he was badly frightened, presumably at the threats of lynching which were made at the time Bennett was killed."

Postscript

Extensive research failed to reveal any additional information regarding this case. The record of executions which were conducted in Jefferson County did not indicate that an individual named Sam Holt or any of the aliases used by him, had been hanged for the murder of Officer Bennett, a certain result in those days where the killing of a police officer would end, almost without exception, in capital punishment being quickly meted out to a convicted offender.

There are several possible reasons for the lack of a documented outcome for this incident. Holt may have died from natural causes while in custody, committed suicide or escaped. More likely, in my opinion, during the course of the investigation it may have been shown that Holt had been wrongly identified and arrested as the killer and that he was later quietly released by the authorities who would not have wanted publicity related not only to a wrongful arrest, but also of their failure to capture the actual murderer.

Other notable factors relating to the murder of Officer Bennett came to light as I began to research the circumstances surrounding his death and the arrests of suspects. I originally came across this case by chance while reviewing newspaper microfilm records for information on another matter. I had previously gathered basic material regarding deaths of local police officers from what I believed to be the most comprehensive list of fatalities included on the Officer Down Memorial Page (www.odmp.org), which maintains a nationwide compilation of on-duty deaths of law enforcement officers by agency which have occurred over a period of more than 120 years. This web page failed to reveal an entry for Bennett. Related newspaper articles revealed that this officer was a member of the Ensley police department which was a separate entity until that city was incorporated into the city of Birmingham in 1910. Although some officers from the Ensley force may have been transferred into the Birmingham department at that time, it is most likely that any of Ensley's personnel records which might have existed were lost or destroyed. When information for the Jefferson County law enforcement memorial was being gathered there apparently were no existing records for the Ensley police department, nor were they found within the Birmingham police department archives. Therefore, there was no record of Bennett's death, other than the information found within the newspaper records of that time. Bennett's name is not currently included on the Jefferson County law enforcement memorial.

Another case of misidentification and the arrests of multiple suspects over a period of several years for the murder of a police officer, all of whom were eventually released, occurred later in the same year.

POLICEMAN MULLIN MURDERED BY NEGRO
Well Known Officer Shot Down While Attempting To Make An Arrest
Several Negroes Are Held By Police On Suspicion
Two Women Are Believed to Know Name of Murderer, But So Far They Have Professed Ignorance
Henry King Wanted

The Birmingham Age-Herald, September 28, 1903

"Policeman James H. Mullin was shot and killed by Henry King, a negro, last n night in the entrance to a barbecue stand on Second avenue between Twenty-sixth and Twenty-seventh streets. The policeman was at once carried to the city jail and died there in a few minutes. Every effort is now being made by the police department and sheriff's office to catch the negro. Several negroes have been arrested on suspicion, but police have doubts as to their having the right man.

Policeman Mullin had arrested the negro and was holding him by the belt. As they started across the street the negro is said to have suddenly drawn a revolver and placing it against the officer's breast fired. He then fled back toward the barbecue stand with the policeman in pursuit firing his revolver. Mullin emptied his weapon entirely, firing five times. Two negro women are in the city jail because they know something of the shooting, but they refuse to tell the name of the negro who did it. It was on the request of one of these women that the policeman went to arrest the man. The negro man beat the woman up badly and she is bruised from the effects of the fight. The women claim not to know the name of the negro who shot the policeman, but they will be placed in the "sweat box" this morning in hope to get the desired information. The woman, Annie Robinson, is a well known character in police circles, and her face is badly scarred from a burn.

As he was being lifted into the ambulance the dying man said: "All of them up there know who did it. Boys, I chased him into the barbecue store and he shot me. I am dying."

NEGRO HEMMED IN BY OFFICERS
Party of Police Said to Have Henry King Cornered In A House Near Gurney

The Birmingham Age-Herald, September 29, 1903

"A squad of a dozen policemen left Birmingham to scour the country between Birmingham and Selma in hopes of catching Henry, alias John King, the negro who shot and killed Policeman Mullin. The policemen are armed with Winchester, double-barreled shotguns and pistols, and they are prepared to remain on the search until they have exhausted every means of catching the negro.

Henry King, the negro who killed Policeman Mullin, had a career equaled by few in this county. He is wanted in Louisiana for murder; in Georgia for escaping from the penitentiary. He is also wanted for escaping from Coalburg, and for assault and battery on a policeman in Anniston. King was arrested here several years ago for grand larceny. At that time one of the worst gang of negroes which ever operated here was broken up. King was the leader of that gang. When the negro was caught at that time he made a desperate attempt to escape and crawled under a freight car, pulled his pistol and started to shoot policeman Nix, but the latter was too quick and made the negro lay his pistol down. Out of a wanton desire to get the best of a white man the negro took a pistol away from an old policeman in Anniston, beat him up badly and as a result the policeman lay in the hospital several weeks between life and death.

King is probably the smartest negro who ever operated in Birmingham. He is said to be unusually quick witted and daring. He is not afraid of anything or anyone. He has even dared the police to kill him. The woman, Annie Robinson, has followed King all over the county and he has been living with her for months. She was at last forced to confess who the negro was at an early hour yesterday. They are therefore certain the the negro who did the shooting is Henry, or John King."

NEGRO SUPPOSED TO BE SLAYER OF POLICEMAN MULLIN IS IN JAIL
Henry King Was Captured Near Gurnee Junction Crowd Surrounds Jail

The Birmingham Age-Herald, September 30, 1903

"Henry King, the negro whom the policemen went to Gurnee Junction to catch, was captured Monday night three miles from that place and brought to Birmingham yesterday. It seems certain that he is not the Henry King whom the policemen have arrested here before and who has such a long criminal record, but there are strong possibilities that he is the negro who shot and killed Policeman

James Mullin. The negro was captured without trouble. The negro states that he was not in Birmingham at all and knows nothing of the killing of Mullin. The police are by no means certain that he is the right negro, but he has been placed in the county jail and will be held until his actions have been thoroughly investigated and there is not the slightest doubt one way or another about the part he played in the shooting.

There was a large crowd at the depot, and still a larger one at the jail. More than 2000 people were packed around the jail, and it was feared that some demonstration would be made against the negro if it were learned he was the right one. Several policemen who knew the Henry King wanted in several places for different crimes state positively that this is not the same negro, although he has somewhat the same appearance and a number of scars which correspond somewhat to those of the other King. Annie Robinson and Henry King were brought face to face and the woman almost positively identified the man as the one who struck her and that she was almost willing to swear it was the same one. The police feel pretty confident that they have the right negro, but they will be better satisfied just as soon as they can trace his actions."

POLICE HAVE NOT THE RIGHT NEGRO
Almost Certain This Is the Wrong Henry King
Coroner Hears Testimony
Women Fail To Identify Negro as the One
They Wanted to Have Arrested for Assault and Battery
The Birmingham Age-Herald, October 1, 1903

"The coroner's jury yesterday heard the testimony of Annie Robinson and Lavenice White, the two negro women who were arrested on suspicion of knowing the murderer of Policeman James Mullin. The women both failed to identify Henry King as the negro who beat Annie Robinson. Several negroes were marched past them and then they were asked if any one of them was the negro who struck Annie Robinson. They both shook their heads and said they did not know a single man in the crowd, and had never seen any of them before.

The police are now almost certain that they have not got the right negro, but the prisoner will be held until there is not a shadow of a doubt. The only thing now that makes them believe there is the slightest chance for him to be the right negro, is that several persons have identified him as the man who once lived with Annie Robinson. If this is true then the women failed to recognize the negro merely to protect him. The police have no other clew which might lead to the arrest of the right negro."

WRONG NEGRO IS ARRESTED AGAIN
The Man Caught at Attalla
Proves Not To Be Henry King,
The Slayer of Policeman Mullin

The Birmingham Age-Herald, December 2, 1903

"Henry King, the negro wanted for killing Policeman James H. Mullin has not been arrested. The negro "Kink" Williams alias King Williams, alias Dick Morrow, who was caught yesterday at Attalla on suspicion proved to be the wrong man, although he was badly wanted by the police. The negro was brought to Birmingham yesterday and Sallie Joyce, a negro woman, identified him as the man who had beaten her about a year ago, and also as the one who shot a negro man in the eye here about the same time. She never identified him as Henry King, or the man who shot and killed Policeman Mullin.

Policeman Jim Ball, who knows King well and guarded him a long time in the mines, states positively that this negro arrested yesterday is not the right one, and several others who knew King have stated the same thing."

NEGRO IS SUPPOSED TO BE HENRY KING
Man Answering The Description Of The Murderer
Of Policeman Mullin Was Arrested In Atlanta

The Birmingham Age-Herald, January 28, 1904

"A special was received by the Age-Herald from Atlanta in which it was stated that Henry King, the negro who shot and killed Policeman James H. Mullin last September, had been arrested. Some credence is given to this being the right negro, as he is said to fill the description well, and to have had a pistol and a pair of brass knucks in his pocket when caught. The local police believe that King would never be caught without a pistol and other arms. The officers are sure that they have the right man".

Postscript

Obviously, this suspect was also shown not to be the "right man" and was released. The killer of Officer Mullin was never caught.

DEPUTY KILLED IN CRAP GAME
Abernathy Dies Soon After He Was Shot
Shooting Occurred at Littleton--
Two Negroes in Jail Charged With the Murder--
Deputy Sheriff Abernathy Highly Esteemed

The Birmingham Age-Herald, August 20, 1906

"Deputy Sheriff E.R. Abernathy of Blossburg, who was shot in raiding a negro crap game at Littleton about 2 o'clock yesterday morning, died from his wounds an hour later. He was shot in the breast and in the thigh. The negroes are in the county jail charged with murder. One of them, Will Johnson, alias Will Fley, was shot by Deputy Abernathy. It was he, according to C.W. Wood, alias "Shorty," the other negro prisoner, who killed the deputy. He states that Abernathy had covered the four negroes in the game with his pistol and was putting handcuffs on Johnson warning him that if he resisted he would kill him. Johnson did resist, Wood Says, and tried to grab the pistol and then Deputy Abernathy shot him, whereupon Johnson got his own pistol out and shot Deputy Abernathy. This statement does not account for the character of the wounds received by the deceased. One, it is said, was made by a small calibre bullet, while the other was inflicted by a bullet of large size.

Deputy Brent is expected from Littleton this morning with two additional witnesses, Joe W. Smith and W.L. Langered of Coalburg, both white. It is said that Smith will testify to the fact that Deputy Abernathy was killed by a white man who was in the crap game.

E.R. Abernathy has been a deputy at Blossburg for about five years and was recognized as a fearless and valuable officer. He was 35 years old and leaves a wife and four children. For several years the deceased was Mayor of Pinkney City."

Postscript

Research failed to reveal that anyone was held legally responsible for the death of Deputy Abernathy, possibly due to the conflicting statements provided by witnesses. The suspect Will Johnson is not included on the Jefferson County execution list and was likely released on this charge due to lack of evidence against him.

ANOTHER BRAVE COUNTY OFFICER IS SHOT DOWN BY LITTLETON RUFFIAN
The Birmingham Age-Herald, June 9, 1907

"The third county officer to meet his death at the hands of drunken assaillants at Littleton was killed yesterday afternoon. Fred Burke shot and instantly killed J.L. Hollis, one of the most popular constables in Jefferson. Drawing his gun, without any provocation, so far as is known, Burke fired once, the bullet entering just over the heart. The fellow first escaped, but was caught later in the woods nearby, after being wounded himself in the chase.

The affair was quite unfortunate, as the incensed man seemed to be giving vent to his wrath upon an innocent party. It appears that Burke had been acting the bravo all afternoon, walking the rounds and flashing his big gun. He paused for awhile in front of a hop jack stand where a large crowd was gathered, and made a good deal of disturbance. The hop jack man went out to quiet him, when Burke drew his gun and started to shoot, but the fellow begged pitifully and slipped back into his stand. At this point, Hollis came up to investigate the trouble, and seeing Burke the center of attention, walked up to him. Whether any words passed between them is not known, but before many seconds Burke again whipped out his gun and Hollis dropped dead in his tracks with a bullet through his heart. Burke made his way to the woods but the crowd set out in pursuit and brought him to a halt in the woods. It was learned that he gave resistance and had to be shot before captured.

Littleton is getting a bad reputation for fatal shootings, this being the third time within a year that an officer has met his death at the muzzle of a gun. The others were Constable Putnam and Deputy Sheriff Abernathy, both of whom were shot in exactly the same manner. Saturday night and hop jack stands are the time and scene of many unfortunate tragedies around the various mines. There was not a better known constable than Hollis in the whole county. He had been in charge of Beat 19 for many years and was a faithful officer. He was about 33 years of age and leaves a wife."

Postscript

According to the online Officer Down Memorial Page, "The 25-year-old suspect was convicted of second degree murder and sentenced to 22 years. He was paroled on December 23, 1910."

Shortly after the murder of Constable Hollis in the mining community of Littleton, an article appeared in the newspaper addressing the issue of violence in Birmingham and Jefferson County. Such soul searching and warnings of dire conditions would become a recurring subject for discussion by the news media and by officials, especially the elected coroners. Although in contrast, as indicated in this article, a defense of the community was also presented with an admission of the ongoing serious criminal activities, but with an attempt to put such conditions in perspective to the overall wholesomeness of the Magic City.

The Birmingham Age-Herald, June 19, 1907
By Burr Blackburn

"Is Birmingham a town of murderers and cut throats? Is it dangerous to walk the streets of the city represented in cartoon by a beautiful young lady of virtue and grace? By what sign shall she be known to the stranger that enters the gates?

It seems quite appropriate that these questions should be considered in the columns which present reports of the bloody crimes that daily occur in Birmingham. The one who searches out all the scenes of carnage, wreck and death might be led to think that the city is in the grasp of some terrible monster, were it not for the fact that, although abroad at all times of the night, he is never troubled, that her streets are peaceful and as quiet as they are clean and beautiful.

A prominent minister of Birmingham said the other day that while in another city visiting a well educated and respectable people, the editor of a southern weekly wondered how anyone dared to live in Birmingham, and was alarmed at the thought of spending a night in her hotels. He thought, judging from the criminal record, that the streets ran blood, and the very hearths are scenes of discords. He would fear to stick his head around a corner, that it might be chopped off with a razor, or to look a man in the eye, lest he draw a gun. The same minister said that it would be far from him to blame the newspapers for such a condition of the mans mind. On the contrary, he believed the newspapers would not be doing their duty if they did not give the horrid details and so impress them on the mind of the community as to increase their repugnance and to so widen the breach between murder and respect, that few will dare step across.

But in recent months so often have knife and pistol drawn blood and spread sorrow that a false impression has gone out from Birmingham, as if danger lurked to catch the respectable at every crossing, as did the foot pads once on the roads around London. This impression has been nowhere more plainly evinced than in the mind and versatile work of newspaper men of other cities. Some editors have come to value the story of a murder from Birmingham worth more than almost anything else, and with scarce-crow heads they often cry out, "Streets of Birmingham Run Living Blood," or "Murder and Terror Reap Saturday Night Harvest in Birmingham," and half a dozen other such blood-curdling declarations, blaring over the tale of a foul crime in one of Birmingham's low dens, or filthy districts where no man who values his life would think of going.

Let it be granted that men come to violent deaths in Birmingham nearly every day. Let it be granted that the scum of the earth fights and quarrels where it lies within the twelve mile square that goes by the name of Birmingham. Let it be granted that so many come to a sudden death out of the 150,000 that cover this little space. Then it may be said that on the bright side of the cloud, where few people point nowadays, life in Birmingham is a peaceful southern dream. Turn the eyes of strangers away from the darkened shadows, and let them see the clean streets, the clean hands and the noble purposes, the town of beauty and the men and women of character who are treading their paths hand in hand, full of the spirit of brotherly love, a band--no, an army--of honest workers. Are these beset with footpads, cut-throats and murderers? Rather they are greeted with smiles, hand grasps and friendly words.

Who is it that ever lived in Birmingham that could rest more than a moment in any other quarter of the globe? It is a city where life is safe. It is also a city where far above the average municipality, those who have no cause to fear, are in no wise to be feared. You find no Harry Thaw or Standford White tragedies coming from the highest families so far as respect goes. Society in Birmingham is not made up of the rich or the gaudy, but of the highly respectable. Neither does the class which can command respect hold itself aloof from the criminal element, but is to be found daily in the byways and hedges reclaiming those who have fallen. A man is only ostracized by his mistakes until they are corrected. Of course there be exceptions. When an innocent girl was shot on the streets the public outcry could be heard in other states. Officers have been shot and killed in the discharge of their duty, but it will be found from a careful study of the crimes of the past years that in most cases retribution seemed to come from the hand of Providence upon the victim. In nine murders out of ten the dead man, even though the victim of highwaymen, has been either drunk himself or quarreling with drunken scoundrels whom he should have shunned, or taking part in a crap game or other game of chance, or spending his life in idleness and dissipation. Now to this class of people Birmingham holds up a red flag and cries out, "Danger!" The city has far too many haunts and dens of the criminal, but about and around them are so many danger signs that the well meaning stranger can easily steer clear of them. Birmingham can no more be judged by the wicked than could San Francisco, the beautiful gate of the west, be judged by her China Town.

It has been said that Birmingham can give death to him who seeks trouble, and life to him who seeks good, quicker than any other southern city. Let the outside world know that she is not false who invites good people to come cast their lots with her and join in her peace and happiness."

WHOLESALE DEATH IN AWFUL MELEE
IN BLOOD-SPATTERED BLIND TIGER
Three White Men and Innocent Baby Girl Shot Down
When Officers Enter Ill-Fated Place On Third Avenue
One Dead Body Falls Against Child Crushing
Her Brains Out on Corner of Whiskey Case—
Policeman J.W. Little Among the Dead

The Birmingham Age-Herald, November 8, 1908

"Possibly the most tragic affair which ever occurred in Birmingham took place yesterday evening at the residence of J.W. Harris, 813 Third avenue, north, resulting in the violent death of four persons, all white, within the space of a very few minutes. The dead are:

Police Officer J.W. Little.

J.W. Harris, a former saloon keeper.

Womack, said to have been a partner of Harris.

Lillian Ruth Harris, the little 15 months-old daughter of Harris.

The circumstances of the death-dealing affair are the most horrifying imaginable. It grew out of an effort on the part of the police officers to apprehend a man wanted on a charge of drunkenness and disorderly conduct, although the man did not figure actively in the melee. The three men were killed as the result of bullet wounds. The little girl died after her brains were virtually mashed out on the corner of a case of whiskey when one of the wounded men fell upon her.

Ten minutes after the fatal affair occurred a partial account had spread all over town. The facts were not exaggerated, for no one knew of the violence of the shooting. However, a great number of persons in the downtown district rushed to the scene. The sight presented to the first view was blood-curdling. The room, which served as the kitchen of the house, was blood bespattered everywhere. The floor was fairly drenched with the life blood of the four dead and dying. In one corner near the stove lay the lifeless form of Officer Little. In another was the dying body of Womack, and near the front door of the room Harris lay expiring. Near the center of the room there sat a box of whiskey stained with the blood of the innocent little girl, who lay close by with a bullet wound in her abdomen and her head literally mashed to pieces.

Just what circumstances prompted the shooting are not known. However, Harris had been arrested some three or four times by Officers Little and Jones on charges of violating the prohibition law and it is known that he had remarked to others; in fact, he told Officer Little himself that if he ever entered his home again he would either have to carry him out dead or die himself. It is presumed by the police that Harris intended to carry out his threat, and that he began the shooting.

Accounts of the awful incident do not vary. Police Officer E.H. Jones, who went with Officer Little to the place, gave a detailed account of the affair to an Age-Herald reporter. Officer Jones stated that while it has been suspected that Harris was selling liquor at his home, it was not for the purposes of arresting him that he and Little went to Harris' residence, but to try and find John Enslen as charges of drunkenness and disorderly conduct had been preferred against him. Jones said that in order to prevent Enslen's escape it was decided that one would go to the front door and the other to the back door of the house. Jones went to the front door to ring the bell. Harris answered the door and when Jones told him that he had come to get Enslen he declined to let him inside the house. After some little remonstrance Harris agreed to allow Jones to look through the house stating Enslen was not there. He states that after searching the house and not finding Enslen he thanked Harris for his trouble and not seeing Officer Little at the back door he went out to get him in order that they might come back to town.

Mr. Jones states he went out the front door and passed around the house by way of an alley on his way to the back door. It is understood that in the meantime, Officer Little had succeeded in getting in the back door. Officer Jones said he heard about ten shots fired in quick succession in the house and that as soon as it was possible he ran into the house to Little's assistance. He states that when he entered the kitchen Officer Little cried: "Jones, I'm killed."

Mr. Jones states that both Officer Little and Harris had been shot and that the two, both in fainting condition, were trying to fire again. He says that they were within only a few feet of each other and both were flourishing their pistols. Mr. Jones says he grasped the two revolvers and pushed them toward the floor in order to keep the men from firing at him or at each other. He says that in doing this he leaned over considerably and that as he did so Womack walked up behind him and fired over his shoulder. Jones declares that he believes the bullet fired by Womack was intended for him, in as much as it barely grazed his back and entered Officer Little's right jaw. It was this bullet that very likely killed Officer Little, for when it struck him he sank to the floor and died almost immediately. Officer Jones stated that when Womack fired the shot he (Jones) turned and fired upon him. The bullet entered the breast squarely and Womack died within a very few minutes. It is understood that as Womack sank to the floor he fell upon the little girl and crushed her temple against the corner of the whiskey box. It was afterward discovered that a bullet had entered the little girl's abdomen, but it is thought that the frightful wound on the temple was primarily responsible for the child's death.

An examination of the bodies showed that Officer Little was shot in the leg, groin and right jaw; that Womack was shot in the breast;

that Harris was shot in the abdomen and under the left arm, and that the little girl was shot in the abdomen. All four pistols used in the affair were .38 calibre "specials."

The deceased officer is survived by a widow and five children. Chief Bodeker in speaking of him, said: "Officer Little was one of the best men who ever put on a policeman's uniform. He was a Christian gentleman and in all my experience with him I never heard him swear an oath. He was a hard working man, and a very sad incident was the fact that he was struggling to pay for his home at Rising by monthly payments."

Relative to the shooting Chief Bodeker said: "There is no one who regrets the occurrence more than I do. I especially regret the unfortunate death of the little child. The whole affair was a very deplorable one."

NEGROES SHOOT STOUTENBOROUGH
Occupants of Hack Open Fire

The Birmingham Age-Herald, December 24, 1911

"Yesterday morning about 12:30 o'clock Detective J.C. Stoughtenborough was shot and dangerously wounded by an unknown negro, three bullets striking him, one in the left arm, one in the left breast, and the other in the right hip.

It seems that Detective McCabe and Stoutenborough had been to Jonesboro to search a house where some stolen property was supposed to be located and were returning to town in their buggy when they met a hackman at Second avenue and Twelfth street, who pulled out of he road to let the buggy by, and then the hack fell over an embankment. Just after the buggy had passed, Mr. Stoutenborough got out and went back to help put the hack back on the road and when he flashed his electric light and asked if he could help, the negroes in the hack, a man and a woman, began shooting. The officer fired on them in return. The negroes got away before Officer McCabe could reach the wounded officer.

As soon as possible the officer was hurried to the Robinson hospital where his wounds were dressed. Fortunately Mr. Stoutenborough had a memorandum in his left pocket which probably saved his life, as the book deflected the bullet that struck him in the left breast causing it to pass out without striking any vital organ. The wound in the hip is a bad one. As soon as Mr. McCabe reached the spot he began firing, but did not hit the parties. Mr. Stoutenborough thinks he hit the man, as he was very near him when he fired.

Mr. Stoutenborough is a married man and has a family. He has been one of the plain clothes men for over a year and is a very popular officer. Ira Adams, the hackman, is in jail as it is thought he knows who the negroes in the hack were. A reward of $100 is offered for any clue leading to the arrest of the parties."

BESSEMER OFFICER DIES FROM WOUNDS
J.C. Stoutenborough Shot by Negroes
Are Still At Large

The Birmingham Age-Herald, December 28, 1911

"Officer J.C. Stoutenborough died last night at 1:20 o'clock at the Robinson hospital, where he was taken last Friday night after he was shot by an unknown negro near Jonesboro. A gloom has been cast over the city by the tragic death of the popular officer, who was admired and loved by all who knew him.

The wounded man was carried to the hospital where his wounds were dressed, they not being thought fatal until complications arose, which resulted in his death. John C. Stoutenborough was 32 years old. He leaves a wife and one child."

Postscript

The final outcome of this case could not be determined, however, it does not appear that anyone was ever arrested for the murder of this officer. Officer Stoutenborough's name is not currently included on the Jefferson County law enforcement memorial.

BIRMINGHAM WITNESSES ANOTHER BLOODY SUNDAY—FOUR ARE KILLED
DETECTIVE TULLY SHOT AND KILLED
IN DEADLY PISTOL DUEL WITH NEGRO
Pistol Duel Between Detectives and Negro
at Boyles Results Disastrously---
Death Comes While Officer Is on the Operating Table

Birmingham's Crime Record Of Yesterday

Detective Tully shot and killed by negro, Tom Harris.
Ben Clark, negro, shot and killed by Officer Leonard
M. Monas, a Greek, shot and killed
by nephew, Jim Monas
Tom Harris, negro, shot by Detectives Tully and Ray
Henry Gibbs, colored, probably fatally injured
by Officer Sellers
Sam Brady, colored, probably fatally injured by
accidental shots during Harris killing

The Birmingham Age-Herald, October 13, 1913

"Detective Hugh Tully was fatally shot through the stomach at Boyles by Tom Harris, a negro, who was fatally injured by the detective.

Sam Brady, a negro restaurant keeper, was also probably fatally shot in the melee. The shooting occurred in a negro "honk-adonk" across the street from the roadhouse at the Boyles car shops. From accounts of the affair it seems that Detectives Ray and Tully, in company with Officer Edward Lyons, went to arrest Tom Harris for the murder of Walter Williams, a negro, at West End. As the officers arrived a negro flagman pointed out Tom Harris to the detectives as he stood with arms akimbo on the counter of the lunch stand.

Before entering the negro restaurant Detective Ray detailed Officer Lyons to guard the rear of the place while he and Detective Tully went in the front. On entering the lunch room, which was dimly lighted, Detective Ray, looking at the Harris negro, said: "Nigger, I want you." The negro immediately backed away with his hand on his hip pocket, and Detective Tully rushed past Ray only to be met by the flash of the desperate negro's pistol. An animated pistol duel followed, mostly in the dark, as one of the flying bullets early in the affair put out the lamp. At least 15 shots were fired and when Officer Lyons entered the restaurant with his electric light he discovered Tully standing with empty pistol leaning on the counter breathing heavily. Detective Ray was standing near with empty pistol pointed at a crouching negro under a table. The negro Harris lay on his face pierced by many bullets apparently dead. "Eddie, I'm shot," said Detective Tully to Officer Lyons; take me as quickly you can to a hospital."

Leaving Ray to guard the wounded negroes in the restaurant, Officer Lyons bundled Detective Tully in Chief Bodeker's automobile and started for the infirmary. The six miles between Boyles and the Hillman Hospital was negotiated in less than ten minutes. No hope was held out for Tully, as he was shot right under the heart. At the St. Vincent hospital operating room a tragic scene was witnessed when Chief of Police Bodeker and detectives were talking to the wounded man. "Boys, if I've got to die, it is all right; If I live it is all right!" was the broken statement of Detective Tully. "I never realized that I was shot, except something like a punch. I walked right into him and I think I got him. Oh, God, my poor wife, my poor wife." The words of the detective were too much for even the hardened officers, who openly cried. "I am sorry, more sorry than I can say," said Chief Bodeker, "as Hugh Tully was one of my friends as well as one of the best officers on the force. This is a very great shock." At 2:30 o'clock this morning Chief Bodeker telephoned the Age-Herald: "Detective Hugh Tully died a few minutes ago. He is survived by his widow who he married about eight months ago. Tully was probably the best known man on the local police force. He was brave to a degree of recklessness. It was his impetuous rush last night that cost him his life. Detective Tully was shot by Thomas Harris, a negro of Sylacauga, who killed Walter Williams, another negro. Harris is still living and is here at the St. Vincent's hospital."

FUNERAL SERVICES FOR MR. TULLY WILL BE HELD TOMORROW
Interment Will Be in Oak Hill Cemetery
Was 43 Years Old; Native of Ireland

The Birmingham Age-Herald, October 14, 1913

"According to latest information, the negro murderer, Tom Harris, is still lying at the Southside jail. He has nine bullet wounds on his limbs and body, but there is some chance that he may recover. It is thought that he is responsible for other killings in the district."

Harris Succumbs to Wounds
The Birmingham Age-Herald, October 16, 1913

"Tom Harris, the negro murderer of Detective Hugh Tully and of Walter Williams, a negro, died yesterday morning in the Southside jail of bullet wounds received in the pistol duel with Detectives Tully and Ray."

CHIEF OF POLICE AND DETECTIVE ARE SHOT
T.B. Wallace of Bessemer Probably Fatally Hurt in Street Fight With Prisoner
The Birmingham News, February 27, 1916

"Chief T.B. Wallace and Detective J. Carl Goodwin, of the Bessemer police department, the former probably fatally injured, and Sam Lindsay, a white farmer near Morgan, is in jail, charged with assault with intent to murder in connection with the case. Wallace is shot through the left side, and it is feared that his lung is punctured. Goodwin is shot through the calf of his left leg. The shooting occurred on the corner of Third Avenue and Nineteenth Street. Immediately after the two officers were wounded with one discharge of Lindsay's 44-40 1871 revolver he was overpowered by Detective Ross and citizens and taken to jail. Feeling is high, but no violence is anticipated.

Lindsay is reported to have been intoxicated when he shot the two officers. Saturday night Detectives Ross and Goodwin say they found Lindsay sitting on the curbstone. He is said to have been holding his pistol in his hand as the officers approached. Lindsay was placed under arrest. The pistol was in Ross' overcoat pocket. After walking a short distance, Lindsay suddenly kicked Ross severely on the ankle, knocking his feet from under him. The officer and prisoner fell to the pavement with Lindsay on top. Wallace, Goodwin and others rushed to stop the struggle but the prisoner secured the pistol and discharged it one time. Goodwin fell as the report sounded and Wallace staggered away. Officer Ross grabbed the prisoner and struggled with him for possession of the weapon, finally overpowering him. Chief Wallace was taken to his home but an examination revealed the dangerous extent of his wound and he was carried to the hospital.

Sam Lindsay is a very large man physically. Following the shooting, it took nearly a dozen citizens to get him to jail. He was almost dragged.

DYING CHIEF IS SAID TO HAVE MADE STATEMENT
Bessemer Chief of Police Succumbs to the Wounds Received in Street Fight

The Birmingham News, February 29, 1916

"Chief of Police Thomas Benjamin Wallace, of Bessemer, who died at Elizabeth Duncan hospital this morning from a pistol wound received Saturday night during a scuffle with Sam Lindsay, a prisoner, is reported to have made a statement indicating that his wounds were not received accidentally. Chief Wallace knew he was in desperate condition Monday and that his life was despaired of. He made the statement to have it used as evidence.

Immediately after the shooting many rumors were afloat on the streets as to how the shooting occurred, some maintaining it was an accident, in that the pistol slipped from Detective Ross' overcoat pocket and exploded as it struck the sidewalk. Others were sure the revolver fell and was taken up by Lindsay and fired and other theories have been advanced and the statement made by the dying Chief of Police is expected to prove of great importance."

Postscript

The legal outcome regarding the alleged offender in this case is unknown. Chief Thomas had been a member of the Bessemer Police Department for 26 years.

J. CARL GOODWIN, BESSEMER POLICE OFFICER, KILLED
Shot by Unknown Negro Last Night-- Posse of Citizens Pursue Slayer

The Birmingham Age-Herald, June 16, 1918

"J.Carl Goodwin, one of the oldest men on the Bessemer police force was shot and instantly killed by an unknown negro last night. The negro made his escape. Goodwin had gone to a negro rooming house to get Pearl Caldwell, a negro for whom he held a warrant charging vagrancy. He went into the house and got Caldwell, and as they emerged through the door Goodwin saw a negro man on the porch whom he did not recognize. After looking him over Goodwin said, "That's a strange negro in town." Hardly had the words escaped his lips when the strange negro drew a revolver from his pocket and shot, the ball entering a vital spot of Goodwin's body. The officer dropped to the floor dead. Having shot the officer the negro ran. At a late hour last night he had not been captured. Immediately the news of the murder spread over town. A posse of citizens was organized to search for the slayer.

Goodwin was previously shot at the same time Chief of Police T.B. Wallace was killed in Bessemer about two years ago. He has been on the force for a great many years and was one of the most popular men in the department.

Great excitement prevailed in Bessemer following the murder, and the posse of citizens searching for him are determined that he shall not escape.

Postscript

The murderer of Officer Goodwin was not apprehended.

TWO POLICEMEN FATALLY WOUNDED BY NEGRO SOLDIER
Officer Evans Dead and Officer Phillips Dying as a Result of Shooting Affray
Assailant Killed

The Birmingham Age-Herald, February 16, 1919

"W.D. Evans, one of the most active members of the Birmingham police force, is dead; Officer A.W. Phillips is in critical condition and Albert Brown, a negro soldier, is dead as the result of a shooting affray that occurred between the officers and two negroes at Thirty-third street and Fifth avenue, north last night. The shooting occurred about a block north of where the Tidewater car line crosses the Louisville and Nashville railroad. Officer Evans, who was still alive when found, was lying about 10 feet from the negro, who was dead. Both of the men were lying between the railroad tracks. Officer Phillips, shot through the breast with a .38 calibre pistol, struggled to a telephone at a store three blocks away and telephoned to headquarters what had happened.

The shooting began when Officer Evans was searching the negroes who had emerged from a house alongside the railroad. They were carrying a small grip and the officers stopped them, inquired as to their business in that locality and told them that they would have to search them. While Officer Evans was searching one of the negroes, who was dressed in civilian clothes, Brown drew a pistol and fired upon Officer Evans, who fell fatally wounded, and then turning fired a shot at Officer Phillips which took effect in his breast. Although the officers were mortally wounded they both emptied their guns at the negroes, several shots of which took effect in the body and head of Brown. The other negro made his escape and it is not known whether he is wounded or not. When found the dead negro had a pistol in his right hand, his other hand was full of cartridges. The bullet that killed Officer Evans took effect just above the heart and no hopes were held for his recovery from the start. Officer Phillips was shot in the lower part of the breast. Although he is in critical condition slight hopes were being held for his recovery."

SUSPECTED PARTNER OF THE NEGRO WHO SHOT OFFICERS KILLED BY DEPUTY SHERIFF
The Birmingham Age-Herald, February 17, 1919

""Sam Moore, alias "Black Jack," a negro, believed to have been the partner of the negro soldier who Saturday night shot and killed Officer W.D. Evans and seriously wounded Officer A.W. Phillips, was yesterday afternoon, shot and killed by Deputy Sheriff Loo White, after the negro had attempted to shoot the deputy. Sheriff Hartsfield, with Deputies White, Pope, Harris and Hilliard, were searching for whisky, in negro quarters on Southside, when they saw eight negroes enter a house in Alley C, between Twentieth and Twenty-first streets. The officers entered the house and began making investigations. All of the negroes surrendered but "Black Jack," who walked out and off. The deputies ordered him to halt several times, which he did not do, after which Officer White ran after the negro and caught up with him, informing him that he was under arrest.

The negro cursed the officer, it is said, and ran his hand into his pocket, in which was found a double-barrel derringer, when Deputy White fired. The bullet went through the negro's neck. He was taken to Hillman hospital where he died. The negro answers a good description, given by Officer Phillips of the man who was with his assailant Saturday night."

Postscript

The name of Officer W.D. Evans was inadvertently not included on the memorial wall to Jefferson County law enforcement officers who have died in the line of duty.

NEGRO WOUNDS 15 AND IS SLAIN
County Officer Fights For Life In St. Vincent's
Police and Bystanders Among Injured After Bloody Siege of Man Who Cut City Health Inspector

The Birmingham Age-Herald, October 11, 1927

"Shot down by a charge from a gun in the hands of a crazed negro, Sam Williams, County Marshall, fought for his life at St. Vincent's Hospital, while nine other officers and four civilians were recovering from wounds received in a gun battle that waged for more than an hour in the heart of Birmingham Monday afternoon.

The body of Charles Pinkston, negro, riddled with more than 100 bullets was at a local undertaking parlor. Pinkston barricaded himself in an empty house at 1700 Avenue F and withstood the fire of almost half of the police force of the city after he had slashed George Kirchoff, city food and dairy inspector, with a knife. He shot Williams from the house before more than 100 officers and deputy sheriffs pitched the battle that ended in the negro's death. The negro had been reported for selling ice cream that did not come up to the requirements of the Health Department.

Kirchoff went to the Joyland Ice Cream Parlor at 613 South Fifteenth Street, which was operated by Pinkston. As Kirchoff stooped over the freezers to obtain samples, the negro crept up behind him and slashed him across the neck with a knife. In the fight that followed, Kirchoff was cut on the hands when he tried to take the knife from the crazed negro. The negro fled from the store, got his automobile and drove to the house on Seventeenth Street. Williams was sent by the sheriff to find and arrest the negro. As Williams sought entrance to the house, the negro, hidden behind the door, fired once, the charge from the shotgun striking Williams in the abdomen. Williams staggered into the back yard and fell. Officers arrived and took positions around the house. Detectives Lyons and Morris were standing just to the left of the house when the negro made his second appearance and was greeted with a fusilade of of shots from the officers' guns. The negro returned, firing several times. On the third shot Morris called, "I've been hit--I can't walk," and he hobbled toward the corner. Lyons went to his assistance just as the negro's gun belched forth again--this time H.H. Weir, W.F. Mitchell and V.W. Gore being the victims. In the meantime, thousands of people had gathered at the scene of the shooting and were hidden behind automobiles, trucks, fences and telegraph poles.

A lull occurred in the fighting while officers returned to headquarters to obtain tearbombs. Doodo Royal volunteered to throw the bombs in the house. Backing the armored police car in front of the house, Royal pulled the fuse plugs on the bomb, and with a neat underhand throw buried the missile into the middle of the front room. The bomb smoldered for a moment, while the form of the negro could be seen staggering about in the middle room. E.W. Jackson, standing behind a large truck, directly in front of the house, fired at the moving figure, as did former Deputy Sheriff Hinds, who was firing a shotgun from behind the front wheel of the truck. The negro staggered to the door amid a fusillade of shots, and returned the officers' fire, one of the bird shots from the negro's gun striking Jackson between the eyes. A few seconds later, Officer P.A. Stapp was struck in the forehead with a shot from the negro's gun. The firing lulled for a few moments while Royal again made his way to the front of the house, and with deadly accuracy threw another tear bomb into the house. The negro moved again, while officers poured bullets into the room, but this negro seemed bear a charmed life. A third tear bomb failed to dislodge him, and a fourth failed to explode.

Meanwhile, officers climbed to the roof of the adjoining house and poured five gallons of gasoline on the roof of the besieged house. They were ordered not to ignite the house, although the fire department was on the scene to prevent the spread of flames. Another exchange of shots definitely located the negro in the middle room of the house. Detectives Woody Sandefer and County Marshall Bob Greene climbed to the roof of the adjoining house from where they could look down into the room where the negro was hiding. Officers Norrell and Phillips crawled to the back of the house and broke the door down with an ax. While Sandefer and Greene poured a withering fire into the room, some of which struck the negro, Norrell and Phillips crawled into the house and shooting with both hands, pumped two complete rounds of ammunition into the negro's body.

Before the officers could prevent it, the negro's body was seized by the milling throng, and dragged face down to the police patrol, almost a block away. The combined efforts of more than a dozen officers were needed to take the negro's body from the mob. Cries of "Lynch him!" "String him up!" "Give us his body!" persisted even after the body had been loaded into the armored patrol. The patrol was driven several blocks from the scene of the riot and while more than a dozen officers stood guard, Coroner J.D. Russum went into the patrol wagon and pronounced the negro dead. The body was then taken to the alley behind the City Hall, where it was turned over to an undertaker. Nearly 100 bullets had been fired into the negro's body as it lay in the little room where he had made his frenzied stand."

BLOOD CRAZED NEGRO REVERTS TO SAVAGERY
Holds Police At Bay
From Barricaded Shanty Until Riddled;
Dragged Out Feet First, Distorted, Gory;
"I've Got His Pipe!" Yells Small Boy

The Birmingham Age-Herald, October 11, 1927
By James Saxon Childers

"Hurled back into the jungle by the first sight of blood squirting from the neck of an officer where only a moment before he had thrust his knife, a negro man fought the representatives of organized society until he himself was dragged feet first, a mangled mass, from behind a chimney and dumped, distorted and bloody beneath the feet of a crazed mob that screamed for him.

Shortly after 4 p.m., the negro entered a vacant shanty and there spat his defiance of lead for more than an hour during which time the shriek of ambulances, the bells of fire engines and the groans of wounded men added to the pandemonium. Almost immediately after the negro's entrance into the house the riot squad arrived. Automobiles emptied dozens of officers near the barricaded shanty. Motorcycle policemen darted their way through the huddled traffic. Detectives came in taxicabs, in private cars, upon the backs of motorcycles, all racing to take a position upon the line drawn around the tiny little brick house where periodically came forth a message of death.

Each time a victim fell before the gun of the negro, officers and those who merely looked on screamed, and some prayed that they might be the one to get in the payment of this enormous debt the negro rapidly was piling up. Hundreds of rounds were poured into the house before tear bombs were brought. Officers hurled these engines through windows that now were completely shot away, and through holes in doors that had been so smashed by shotguns and rifles that they were little more than wooden lacework. But the negro defied the gas, and while he must have suffered the agonies of hell he refused to come forth."

Monday's gun battle in many ways resembled an affray which occurred in Birmingham in Oct., 1924, in which a crazed Italian, suffering from a delusion of persecution, shut himself in a room at the Terminal Hotel and defied capture until he had been claimed by death. Tear bombs, fire equipment and armament of every description were resorted to before the fugitive was killed. Another similar occurrence took place in Feb., 1926, when another crazed negro, with an abundance of shells, held more than a dozen police at bay, after he had taken a position on the second floor of the old Postoffice Building, then used as a Public Library. Tear bombs finally brought the negro to terms after a siege of about three hours."

By Taylor Glenn

"Scenes common in days of distillery-infested mountains were reenacted when the city and county officers aided by scores of civilians, laid siege to the house at 1700 Avenue F, South in an effort to capture Charlie Pinkston, negro operator of an ice cream parlor. Rifles of every size, pistols long and short, tear gas bombs, inflammatory liquids, all were employed by the attacking forces before the holder of the house, finally bullet-riddled, was dragged into the streets by his captors. Never in the history of Birmingham, perhaps, had such a scene been enacted. It was like the days of the World War."

SAM WILLIAMS' WOUNDS FATAL; FUNERAL FRIDAY
County Marshall Shot In Battle
With Crazed, Besieged Negro
The Birmingham Age-Herald, October 14, 1927

"Funeral services for Sam L. Williams, Jefferson County marshal, who died Thursday at St. Vincent's Hospital of gunshot wounds in an attempt to arrest a crazed negro will be conducted Friday at Walker's Chapel Church. In the battle in which Mr. Williams was fatally wounded, at least 14 other officers and civilians were wounded. Mr. Williams was one of the first men shot in the gun battle which lasted for more than an hour."

Docket Entry:
Date: October 10, 1927.
Deceased: Charlie Pinkston, Col.
Address: Southern Undertaking.
Cause Of Death: Gunshot wounds of head and body.
Remarks: Charlie Pinkston was barricaded in an empty house at 1770 Ave. F. So.
Good Job.

MOTORSCOUT DIES IN BATTLE, HIS PAL IS HURT; TWO NEGROES HELD AS KILLERS IN GUN FIGHT POLICE OFFICER IS SLAIN AS HE STOPS UNLICENSED AUTO

Companion Slightly Wounded In Shooting
In Busy Bush Hill Street
E.T. Lewis Dies On Way To Infirmary
A.J. Dunn, Shot, Overpowers Assailant
And Keeps Irate Mob At Bay

The Birmingham News, March 4, 1928

"One motorcycle officer was slain and another wounded in a running gun battle with a negro in a roadster Saturday in the Graymont section of the city. Two negroes are in the county jail charged with murder as a result of the fight. The negroes charged with murder are Ravel Peoples, 28, and Madison Jenkins, 20. Peoples, charged with the actual shooting was captured by Officer Dunn in a sensational gun fight and hand-to-hand struggle after a chase of more than a mile through streets crowded with traffic. Officer Lewis was slain on Eighth Avenue, North, near Legion Field, when he rode alongside the car, which had no license, and which was driven by Peoples, and ordered the negro to stop. At pointblank range, Peoples fired, the bullet penetrating Officer Lewis' heart. As the officer fell from his machine, he attempted to draw his gun, but failed. The negroes then speeded up in an attempt to escape.

Officer Dunn...started out in pursuit, in the face of revolver fire from the car. Witnesses asserted that Jenkins held the wheel of the racing automobile, while Peoples turned and fired. Racing through traffic, the officer returned the fire as best he could, emptying his .44 caliber pistol without any apparent effect. Peoples had emptied his gun and reloaded, and again began firing. One bullet struck Officer Dunn in the left knee. The policeman began firing with a .38 caliber pistol, as the chase turned onto Bush Boulevard. A bullet fired by Officer Dunn punctured a tire. The automobile crashed into the curb. Peoples leaped from the machine and ran into an alley and Officer Dunn sprinted after the fugitive. Dunn had one bullet left in his gun. Peoples grappled with Duncan and in the struggle fired his gun, wounding Peoples in the cheek. Peoples jerked the gun from Dunn's hand. The negro snapped the empty gun several times, then struck the officer and knocked him down. Dunn seized a brick, hurled it at Peoples, knocking the negro down. Peoples was then beaten into submission by Officer Dunn with his gun. A large crowd that gathered threatened to start a riot. The crowd demanded that Dunn turn Peoples over to its custody. Dunn held the crowd back with his two empty guns protecting Peoples until assistance arrived. The officer said he believed the crowd would have lynched Peoples if it had reached him.

When Peoples was questioned at police headquarters, he said he shot Officer Lewis because the policeman ordered him to stop. The negro said he didn't know why he did it, that he was "just drunk."

DOOMED NEGROES MAKE FINAL PLEA
PARDON BOARD TAKES APPEAL
OF TWO UNDER ADVISEMENT

The Birmingham Age-Herald, July 17, 1928

"Ravel Peoples and Claude Scott, condemned Jefferson County negroes under sentence to be executed at Kilby Prison on the night of July 26, made their final appeals for commutation of their sentence at a special hearing before Gov. Bibb Graves and members of the State Board of Pardons. Peoples was found guilty of the murder of Traffic Officer Lewis, of Birmingham. At the hearing, the negro claimed that the officer fired at him first, wounding him, before he fired at the officer. This was denied, however, by Fred Cain,

Birmingham city detective and eye-witness to the shooting. Peoples claimed "bad liquor" was responsible for his act."

STATE SENDS MAN TO 'CHAIR'
Rabell Peoples, Negro, Pays For Slaying Policeman
The Birmingham News, July 20, 1928

"Rabell Peoples, Jefferson County negro, went to his death in the electric chair at Kilby Prison here shortly after midnight for the murder of E.T. Lewis, a Birmingham traffic officer. The first shock was applied at 12:21 a.m. and he was pronounced dead at 12:40 a.m. Peoples shot the officer when he was stopped for a traffic violation. He said he thought the officer was going to arrest him for a robbery which he confessed he had committed previous to the shooting."

POLICEMAN DIES, PAIR INDICTED
Case Set As Wounds Proves Fatal To F.J. Harris
Two Resigned to Fates Following Outcome of Robbery Effort
The Birmingham Age-Herald, February 9, 1935

"A speedy trial for Richard F. Darrafou, 25, and Wesley Vincent, 19, who were indicted by the Grand Jury on murder charges for the killing of Patrolman F.J. Harris was assured. When notified of the officer's death, Vincent, who admitted firing the fatal shot into Harris' back, fidgeted nervously in his county jail cell and said "If I get the death penalty, I figure it will be just what I deserve. Life doesn't mean anything to me now," Vincent continued as he sat twitching his hands nervously and staring out of his cell window. He was pale, unshaven and appeared upset over the officer's death. "I don't care whether I live or die, but I'm sorry as the devil about that man dying."

Darrafou is from Stockton, Calif., and Vincent from Shelton, Wash. Vincent, a former marine, said he had served with the U.S. Marine Corps two years and seven months, having received a "bad conduct" discharge for over-leave. Harris, 37, a widely known officer who had served at Five Points, died resulting from a .45 caliber bullet wound received in the back. Officers said Vincent admitted shooting Harris while the officer struggled with Darrafou during the attempted holdup of the Pickwick Club. Harris became a member of the police department in 1924. He is survived by the widow and two sons."

WESLEY VINCENT ELECTROCUTED
Chair Ends Career Of Boy Bandit
Youth Pays Penalty At Kilby For Slaying F.J. Harris
Mother Spends Part Of Last Day With Son
In Death House

The Birmingham Age-Herald, June 12, 1936

"Wesley Vincent, just turned 20, went to death in Kilby Prison's electric chair early Friday for the Roosevelt birthday dance slaying of Patrolman Forest Harris as Gabriel Waters and Tyrie Harrell, both Negroes, paid with their lives for killing white men over debt arguments.

Vincent, a 20-year-old youth whose mother had a "last chat" with him said he had faith enough in God to save him from a dreaded death. Surprising the governor and pardons board with a statement that he shot Patrolman Harris to "make him turn loose my buddy," Richard Darrafou, Vincent said that no one touched his arm causing the revolver to explode. Vincent and Richard Darrafou were condemned for killing a Birmingham policeman in a holdup there last year. Darrafou committed suicide as he and Vincent were cornered in an attempted jail break.

The young slayer's mother Mrs. Mae Vincent, who came all the way from Washington state to plead with Gov.Graves for her son's life spent a last afternoon with Vincent in the Kilby Prison death row. Mrs. Vincent, a slight, kindly-faced woman, said "Wesley always was a good boy and any trouble he got into can be blamed on the bad company into which he fell upon leaving home." A group of Birmingham, Ala., clubwomen financed the mother's trip from Washington."

"Special Agents"

As briefly noted at the beginning of this chapter, private business entities such as the Tennessee Coal, Iron and Railroad Company, the Southern and the Louisville and Nashville railroads, coal mines and other large industrial interests found it necessary to employ their own "special agents" to protect their resources from the rampant theft of materials and goods common to those times, most of which was transported throughout the country by the railroads. In addition, due to the inadequate manning of local police agencies, these appointed "special officers of the law" often became responsible for, and essential to, the provision of law enforcement and the keeping of peace and order in the numerous, often rowdy, mining and industrial camps throughout the county where many workers and their families lived under conditions of squalor. They were also called upon to provide security and to act as strikebreakers during worker protests which occurred often in this era. If overwhelmed, as occurred during several of the larger, violent strikes, additional men could be quickly "deputized" and placed on the company's payroll to assist. On several occasions, the only recourse to counter large gatherings of strikers who threatened or actually engaged in violence would be to call out the national guard.

    These "special agents" typically operated under the color of law, often receiving warrants for their police powers at the local political level. They were easily and quickly appointed as "special deputy sheriffs" by the local sheriff who, no doubt, was obliged to do so at the behest of managers of large business entities, as his own political fortunes were likely to be dependent on his protection of their interests. Individuals would not be allowed to be placed on the ballot for the office of sheriff, or for other political offices, unless they were approved by the party committee that made those decisions and who, in turn, took their "marching orders" from the local industrial and other large business owners.

    Although official approval of the activities of these agents was typically granted by the coroner when a death occurred at their hands, this was not always the case as indicated in several of the following docket entries. As in those rare instances where the coroner disputed the legality of deaths at the hands of regular police officers, the final judicial outcome of a number of these "special agent" related cases are unknown. It is believed, however, that few of the incidents involving these officers proceeded much further within the legal system where they were likely quietly disposed of at the level of the district attorney, grand jury or by a judge at a preliminary hearing, despite the coroner's initial opinion that a particular death at the hands of such a special officer was "unjustifiable." Few of these cases received additional attention in the newspapers as to their outcomes following their initial reporting, as the legal process was often postponed on multiple occasions and for extended periods of time. Although one can attribute these extensions to a busy legal system, the possibility certainly exists that these long delays for final decisions may have been intentional to allow for the public and the news media to lose interest in a particular matter.

Docket Entry:
Date: July 25, 1909
Deceased: Joe Wagner.
Address: Ensley.
Defendant: W.S. Russel.
Comments: I, B.L. Brasher, Coroner of Jefferson County, certify that I held a preliminary Coroner investigation inquest on the body of Joe Wagner at Ensley Ala with the following result:
I found deceas was Shot and Killed By one man W.S. Russel an officer of the Tenn People. Don't think under the Evidence that Russel was Justifiable and I ordered Him arrested for murder.
Total Coroner's Fees: $3.05.

Postscript

This case was not reported in the newspapers and the final legal outcome is unknown.

PATTON IS FATALLY WOUNDED IN BATTLE WITH TWO NEGROES
Kills One of Them After He Is Shot at Fossil
Comrades Get The Other Desperado
Wounded Man Was Well Known and Highly Esteemed in Bessemer District---
Former Chief of Detectives of City of Bessemer

The Birmingham Age-Herald, May 28, 1915

"W. S. Patton, former Chief of detectives of the city of Bessemer, and now a special officer of the Tennessee Coal, Iron and Railroad company was seriously if not fatally wounded by negroes resisting arrest at Fossil mines. The negroes, who are thought to be Harry Jefferies and Will Rogers, were killed, one by Mr. Patton after he was shot and the other by acting Chief Maddox and Detective Ross.

Elisha Casey, a negro, was shot and killed last night at Fossil and it is alleged that the two dead negroes did the killing. The negroes were located but when they saw the officers ran into a vacant house and barricaded the door, refusing to open it when summoned by the officers and threatening to kill anyone who approached. As is customary with officers, Detective Ross was left at the rear of the house while the other two officers broke down the front door and entered. As the officers scrambled into the room they saw the barrel of a gun protruding from a clothes closet. Patton threw up his revolver with a command for the negroes to come forth. Instead of obeying both opened fire.

The first bullet struck Patton in the abdomen knocking him to the floor. The second negro put another bullet into his side as he fell. With blood pouring from both wounds, Mr. Patton raised up on his left arm firing as fast as he could pull the trigger. His first shot took one of the negroes in the left eye, killing him instantly, but as he grew weaker his aim was poorer. In the meantime Mr. Maddox had been standing over Patton firing at the negroes. Several of his bullets took effect but not in vital parts. Upon his comrade's fall the remaining negro grew frightened and fled toward a back window. As he appeared Detective Ross fired and the negro fell dead.

Mr. Patton was rushed to Reeders hospital where an operation was performed in the hopes of saving his life, but little hope is held out for his recovery. He is about 40 years old and has a wife and several children. The wounding of Mr. Patton caused intense sorrow in Bessemer where he was well known, having resided here for years and having for a long time been connected with the Bessemer police department."

SPECIAL AGENT KILLS NEGRO; IS ARRESTED
The Birmingham Age-Herald, January 22, 1923

"A negro known only as "Geechie" to the police, was shot in the back and instantly killed in the yards of the Louisville and Nashville railroad at Railroad avenue and Fourteenth street by W.M. Dobbs, special agent for the railroad. Attempted theft of coal by deceased is alleged.

Dobbs was arrested and turned over to Coroner Russum, who is conducting an investigation of the affair. According to the statement of Dobbs, he saw the negro in the act of removing coal from a car and called on him to throw up his hands. He stated that instead of complying the negro attacked him but "turned his back" when he shot him."

Postscript

The legal outcome of this case was not noted in the coroner's file and could not be found in the newspapers. Despite the minor crime of theft of coal, the alleged violence towards the officer, who gave a questionable account of the circumstances and the fact that the victim was shot in the back, as well as his social status, most likely did not lead to any criminal charges being placed against Dobbs.

OFFICER IS KILLED IN GUN FIGHT
Fellow Railroad Agent Wounded In Battle On Train
NEGRO ALSO DIES AS PISTOLS BLAZE
Another Shot In Affray Aboard Moving Freight At Gate City

The Birmingham Post-Herald, May 11, 1938

"Pistols blazing across boxcar tops of an outbound Central of Georgia freight train late Tuesday night brought death to a railroad special agent and an unidentified Negro and placed another railroad special agent and a Negro in hospitals here, suffering critical gunshot wounds. The shooting occurred near the overhead bridge at Gate City. Both special agents were employees of Central of Georgia Railroad.

Special Agent Thomas A. Owens was killed in the battle. Special Agent W.A. Johnson, Jr., the other white man shot, was taken to St. Vincent's Hospital by Ridout ambulance, where he was reported in serious condition. Johnson was shot in the arm and in the abdomen. Johnson said he and Owens saw two Negroes get on the train in Woodlawn and that when they began to search for the Negroes to put them off, the Negroes opened fire while the train was in motion. Those slain in the gun battle which took place in a slag-filled gondola near midnight while the train was en route to Columbus, Ga., from Birmingham. (The unidentified) Negro hobo was identified as Orange Smith, alias "Buddy" Smith, 30, of Opelika. Identification was made from a circular sent by Sheriff Holt of Lee County. The circular listed the Negro was wanted in connection with investigation of burglary, grand larceny and robbery charges.

The officers, hired by the railroad to keep transients from hitching rides, saw the Negroes climb aboard. Starting from the back of the train, the two officers moved forward searching for the pair. As they jumped into the gondola the two Negroes were discovered crouching in a corner. Without warning one of the Negroes began firing and Owens fell mortally wounded, shot in the abdomen and head, before he had a chance to draw his gun. Johnson opened fire and killed the unidentified Negro who was wielding the gun. The other Negro, who apparently was unarmed, grappled with Johnson and was shot after he leaped from the car and attempted to escape."

Bullet Halts Boy's Trek—To His Home And Mother Louisville Youth Meets Disaster On Last Leg Of Jaunt From Hawaiian Islands; Railroad Special Agent Says He Shot During Attack By Hoboes

The Birmingham Post, July 27, 1938

"A bullet wound in his abdomen today had halted a 22-tear-old boy's cross-country trek to his mother and his home in Louisville, Ky. The halt may even be permanent for the youth, Homer Gray, lies in serious condition in Hillman Hospital. He was shot last night by Frank Benson, special agent for the Louisville & Nashville Railroad who said he found Gray and several hoboes congregated on the L & N. tracks above the underpass on the North Birmingham-Tarrant Road. Mr. Benson said he told the men to disperse but they advanced on him and pulled him to the ground. Lying supine, he said he shot the man directly on top of him, Homer Gray.

The story told today by the injured boys a different one. "I'm no hobo," he asserted, speaking with apparent pain and difficulty. "That freight I'd just got off out there was the first one I'd ever hopped in my life.Those other men that were out there--I didn't know them--I wasn't with them really. I wasn't in that scrap at all. That man shot me in the back. I wasn't even in the fight, didn't know what was going on, wasn't looking, in fact."

As a nurse daubed the cold sweat from his forehead he told he told his story how he had enlisted in the Army at the age of 20 and had been stationed in the Hawaiian Islands. He didn't like it there for "several reasons," asked for a special discharge after he had served two years in the islands. Meanwhile, no charges have yet been placed against either Agent Benson or Homer Gray.

Death Halts Trek Of Youth On Way To Visit Mother

The Birmingham Post-Herald, July 29, 1938

"Homer Gray, who trekked across the continent to see his mother in Louisville, died at Hillman Hospital yesterday victim of a gunshot wound.

Today authorities were trying to reach Homer's mother. As he lay at death's door in the ward at Hillman, Gray told a story typical of many told by youths of today who hitch-hike or "ride the rails." He was granted a special discharge from the U.S. Army. But his homeward trek was halted by death. Although he was in Hillman only two days, the case of Homer Gray found a soft spot in the hearts of the nurses and doctors. They sympathized, for his case was one of scores that flow in and out of the hospital each month. He persistently denied being a vagabond. He said he wasn't like ordinary men who hang around "jungles." The gang he was with started the trouble. He said he was going in the other direction when the shot was fired.

Meanwhile, it was announced the case would be turned over to the Jefferson County Grand Jury. County Investigator Gip M. Evans said he would withhold any decision in the case until the inquisitors convene. Today the body of Homer lay in the Hillman morgue unclaimed."

GRAND JURY GETS GRAY DEATH CASE
The Birmingham Post, July 29, 1938

"A Grand Jury will have to decide whether L. & N. Special Officer Frank F. Benson was justified in the shooting of Homer Gray, 21. Benson told Tarrant officers that he shot Gray during a scuffle with him and several other hoboes whom he had ordered to leave the L. & N. yards at Boyles.

Coroner Evans said he would not return a finding but would simply present the evidence he had to the Grand Jury and let them make a decision."

OFFICER IS CLEARED
Case Of Special Agent For L. & N. Railroad is No-Billed
The Birmingham Post, August, 1938

"Another case no-billed by the Grand Jury was that of Frank F. Vincent, special agent for the L. & N. Railroad, who shot and fatally wounded a youth in the railroad's yards at Boyles.

Solicitor George Lewis Bailes said the shooting of Homer Gray was found by the Grand Jury to have been justifiable. Gray was shot in the abdomen and died several days later in a local hospital."

Postscript

There are several aspects of this case which are worthy of further discussion:

1. In general, as the 20th century progressed, this incident provided an example of the increased practice of the coroner to present controversial cases to a Grand Jury for decisions regarding culpability, especially when they involved law enforcement officers.

2. The circumstances of this shooting incident were unclear based on statements from the officer and the victim. If the interpretation of the gunshot wounds by the pathologist at the autopsy are correct, then that would support the statement made by the victim that he was shot in the back and it is not consistent with statements made by the officer. If expert forensic pathology services had been available, it is most likely that this matter would have been resolved without question upon examination of the wounds and the decedent's clothing for the presence or absence of gunpowder deposits.

3. Perhaps because of the disparities of the statements and physical evidence, and in addition the standard practice of the times of almost always giving law enforcement officers the benefit of the doubt, the shooting was found to be "justifiable."

Conduct, Misconduct and Politics

The application and style of law enforcement which prevailed throughout Jefferson County during the early decades of the 20th century can politely be described as being of a "rough and ready" nature. The Birmingham Police Department as it existed at that time was an organization that was brutal, unprofessional and beleaguered by inadequate manning and funding. The agency would be used as a "political football" for many years and was constantly blamed for being a part of the cause of many of the city's problems relating to enforcement, crime rates and corruption. Many of the early officers were considered to be one step removed from the raucous citizenry that they were routinely called upon to attempt to control with varying degrees of success.

In Birmingham, as in other heavily industrialized cities in both the north and south, police officers had to be willing and able to successfully engage and deal with the many intoxicated and unruly people who possessed varying armaments and their will to use them. These individuals were drawn to the Magic City from the surrounding work camps, factories and mines in order to take advantage of the various "entertainments" offered there. These men (and some women) were often more than happy to test the ability of police officers to uphold the law and to attempt to best them in a physical confrontation.

The men who made up the early local police and sheriff's forces were, for the most part, comprised of white males native to the south. Blacks and most foreign newcomers to the area, with the exception of Irish men, need not apply. The Irish immigrants, who had proven themselves as formidable fighters in the armies of both sides in the Civil War, as well as police officers in the large urban centers of the northeast, had been recruited as law enforcement officers for many years.

Their propensity for being willing to physically fight and control disorderly elements was honed in those cities which included a large number of rowdy Irish immigrants. As noted by news columnist Peggy Noonan in regard to the means of transport of persons who had been arrested, "There was a reason they were called 'Paddy' wagons." It is notable that an appreciable number of such men were also employed by police agencies in the larger cities of the south despite the open anti-Catholic sentiments of that time.

Although granted exceptional powers of control and arrest of lawbreakers, complaints regarding the use of excessive force, as well as of unprofessionalism and misconduct on the part of some officers, were commonplace during the early years of the century.

INDICATIONS OF NEW POLICY IN THE POLICE COMMISSION
New Board Will be Very Strict About Breaches of Discipline
Will Dismiss All Men Who Are Caught Drinking
First Policeman Tried By the New Commission for Being Drunk Was Dismissed From the Force
Other Trials Held

The Birmingham Age-Herald, May 23, 1903

"Judging from the first trials held by the new police commission, it has inaugurated a new policy, in that every policeman who violates the rules and regulations of the department will be severely dealt with. The indications are that in all cases of drunkenness policemen will be dismissed from the force. The first case of absolute dismissal in many months took place when Policeman M.L. Broom was tried on a charge of drunkenness. He admitted taking two or three drinks of whiskey and then firing his pistol while on an Avondale street car… and seemed to be drunk."

CITIZENS RESENT RECKLESS FIRING ON CITY STREETS
Many Contend That Officers Should Be Disarmed While on Crowded Streets
Entirely Too Common Is General Comment
Bodeker Instructs Men Not Even To Fire in Air on Downtown Streets
New Pistol Law in Force In a Few Days

The Birmingham Age-Herald, June 26, 1908

"Recent street squabbles, pistol firing, killing negroes charged with misdemeanors, shooting innocent bystanders and other actions by the officers of the law have resulted in an outburst if disapproval against the habit in anyone of shooting on the streets, or of using guns at all. Mayor George H.Ward, when approached on this subject, said simply: "I don't think anybody ought to be shot unless he has done something to be shot for." That is taken to mean that a prisoner arrested for a misdemeanor should not be shot under any circumstances, that no less than a murderer should be shot down when trying to escape, and that the habit of shooting on the streets does not meet with the Mayor's approval.

This is the opinion of hundreds of business men. Chief Bodeker has made a statement disapproving all shooting while the streets are crowded. While most citizens declaim any knowledge of the provocation or circumstances in the recent shootings, they mean only to speak generally against the habit of shooting. "The shootings on the street must stop, unless, of course, the officer is protecting his own life, or endeavoring to apprehend a murderer. The shooting of the Mexican the other night might be deplored by no one more than myself. I was convinced after investigating the case, that the officer fired recklessly, and of course felt it my duty to prefer charges against him, besides suspending him until the police commission next meets.

I have instructed my men not even to fire in the air when they are in the crowded business sections of the city. It might be excusable for an officer to discharge his revolver in the air during the early hours of the morning when there are few people on the streets, but at other times it is dangerous."

Said Maj. Charles J. Allison, clerk of the United States court: "The manner in which officers shoot up our town is nothing less than outrageous. It should be corrected." Said Robert A. Brown of Woodlawn: "The matter of policemen and deputies shooting on the streets has almost become a practice, and the matter is one upon which no amount of condemnation would be excessive. The shooting of the Mexican a night or two ago recalls the instance when two officers took the liberty of indulging in a pistol duel on Third Avenue, the consequences of which was the wounding of a young woman who was passing along the sidewalk. There really ought to be some means by which such regardless men might be prosecuted by law."

George Brown, an attache of the United States marshall's office said: "They are too quick to use their guns because they can. Thats where the trouble lies. There ought to be some means by which this infliction on citizens could be remedied. A reckless shot upon the street might prove fatal to more than one life, and instead of protecting the people I cannot understand why an officer should shoot among them."

Edward H. Warner of the Green Undertaking company expressed his sentiments thus: "Reckless shooting on the part of anyone is to be greatly deplored, but when officers show a careless regard for human life there is a cause for protest. That men guilty of such acts should be disciplined I firmly believe the sentiment of all law abiding people. The undertakers of Birmingham handle practically all the accidents either by their ambulance or otherwise, and by experience know the great danger which the people of Birmingham are constantly being put to by the careless handling of guns." H.L. Jackson of West End, who had recently moved to Alabama from Chicago said: "I was standing at the corner of second avenue and nineteenth street when 'Hot Tamale Joe' was shot, and my opinion on the reckless shooting by officers is very strong. I had a similar experience in Chicago, a stray bullet fired by a policeman in that town clipping my hat. I think Chief Bodeker did right in suspending

Policeman Durden for investigation, and it is now up to the sheriff to do likewise."

POLICE START WAR ON CITY'S VAGRANTS
The Birmingham Age-Herald, January 21, 1911

"Chief Bodeker has begun a crusade against the negro loafers of the city and the beggars who are seen on the streets. The chief has issued instructions to the officers of the police department to see that the beggars are kept moving and that vagrants who hang around the pool rooms and soft drink stands of the city must be driven off or locked up.

The order issued yesterday to the department follows: "No boot-black stands will be allowed on the streets, sidewalks or alleys of the city of Birmingham. No beggars will be allowed to sit on the sidewalks and in the alleys. You must keep them moving. Also look after the vagrants around the pool rooms and soft drink stands. Arrest those you can convict and notify others that they must obtain work.

"BODEKER, Chief."

The chief is very indignant about the number of beggars sitting on the streets and the crowds of negro loafers that collect around the boot-black stands. He is determined to break it up. "There is nothing more unsightly than dirty beggars sitting on the sidewalk of the city," said the chief last night, in speaking of the coming crusade. "The majority of these are not deserving and at night can be found in the dives of the city spending for drink the money they have begged. The beggars who sit on the sidewalk make good money. I expect some of them average $10 or more a day. There is a city ordinance which prohibits this and I intend to break it up. Another class of people who are very annoying to the citizens are the crowds of loafers that collect around the boot-black stands and soft drink places. The most of these are vagrants, and I intend to break them up. I have issued such orders to the department and I expect to see them carried out. The beggars and loafers must go."

JUDGE LANE TELLS POLICEMEN
WHAT IS WANTED OF THEM
Blind Tigers, Mashers and Vagrants to Be Driven From The City
Officers Are Asked To Remember Oath

The Birmingham Age-Herald, April 17, 1911

"The prohibition laws of the city of Birmingham must be and shall be enforced. If you can't do it then we will get men who can," declared Commissioner of Public Safety A.O. Lane yesterday morning to the entire police department, 168 strong, assembled to hear his words in regard to enforcement of the law. "We have minimized the sale in the past few days and in the next few we will exterminate the illegal liquor traffic," he continued. "The flagrant violation of the prohibition laws of the city for a long time has been a burning shame and it is my sworn duty as commissioner to break it up and it must and shall be done."

Judge Lane made a forceful matter-of-fact speech to the police. He impressed upon the men three things: That they must break up the blind tigers, that they must drive the vagrants out of the city or to work and that they must move the "mashers" from the downtown corners. Judge Lane indicated that "It may be that the sale of liquor will be again legalized in the city. If this is true all will be well, but until the change is made it is essential that the law be enforced in that regard. There is another more flagrant violation of the law that is a disgrace to the community and must be stopped. Young girls who work find it necessary to stand on the corners waiting for cars and while there are annoyed by ungentlemanly vagrants who ogle them, I want you, whenever you see this, to instantly arrest the offender on a charge of disorderly conduct and put him in jail unless he makes bond. This must be stopped. It is a disgrace to the community and a reflection on the police department. There is another thing. You must invoke the law against vagrancy. A vagrant is the most worthless fellow upon the face of the earth. He neglects his duties and is an undesirable citizen. In this class are gamblers, who live by their wits. They depend on fleecing innocents who are foolish enough to pit their skill against superior skill. This custom must and shall be broken up. As I look into your faces I see the determination in all to co-operate with the new city government to restore the city to a high basis. It must no longer be Bad Birmingham. Birmingham is entitled to as good a name morally as she has commercially."

As noted previously, on relatively rare occasions, the coroner would find it expedient to deviate from the almost typical automatic practice of declaring that fatal encounters involving the police were legally justified. In those instances where potential egregious overreaction was suggested it was believed that a better course of action was to assign lesser charges, rather than to issue an initial ruling of simply justifiable or non-justifiable homicide, thereby forcing further legal action at a higher judicial level. As in this case, a coroner's jury returned a rarely encountered verdict of "manslaughter in the second degree." Such charges against these officers are indicative of the belief that they had possibly overstepped their bounds in applying deadly force but that their actions did not rise to the level of premeditated homicide and that there were alleged extenuating circumstances with aggressive actions being initiated by the victims against the officers.

Docket Entry:
Date: September 25, 1911
Deceased: Webb Lynn and Chester Lynn, W.
Address: Sayre Mines.
Defendant: H.L. Lawler and J.O. McBee, White.
Cause Of Death: Gunshot wound, same being manslaughter in the second degree.

TWO LYNN BOYS KILLED BY OFFICERS LAWLER AND M'BEE
Resisted Arrest for Trespassing on Forbidden Property
Lynn Family Has Remarkable History
Brother of Dead Boys Killed Short Time Ago
By Aleck Brewis, Who Was Also
In Trouble With the Deceased
The Birmingham Age-Herald, September 26, 1911

"While resisting arrest by Constable H.C. Lawler and Special Officer J.O. McBee at Sayre yesterday morning, Chester and Webb Lynn, two young men well known to the officers of Jefferson county, were instantly killed. The officers were just emerging with their prisoners from a little by-path into the big road when Chester Lynn is said to have clinched with Constable Lawler, pinioning his arms to his side, and at the same time attempting to draw the constable's pistol. Special Officer McBee, who had the other prisoner in charge, began firing and killed Chester with buckshot. The man fell to the ground being instantly killed.

During the excitement Webb Lynn had been momentarily forgotten and, seeing his chance, drew his pistol, which was concealed in his breast. He had it partly though the opening in his shirt when he was noticed by Constable Lawler. Before Lynn could get his pistol ready for action the officer fired a broadside of buckshot into him, the load taking effect in his body between the shoulder and hip on the right side. Lynn dropped to the ground without a murmur dead.

The boys were seen trespassing upon the land of the Sayre Mining and Manufacturing Co., from which they had been forbidden. The officers haled them and warned them to keep off. The boys are said to have replied that they were going on anyway, to which officers stated that if they did they would be arrested. "Well, come on and arrest us and we will make bond," one of the Lynn boys is said to have replied. The officers then proceeded to arrest them and were bringing them to the jail when the killing took place. The land had been marked with posters forbidding the Lynn boys coming on the premises under any circumstances, owing it is said, to an assault they are alleged to have made upon the company's superintendent some weeks ago.

Simultaneously with the killing Alec Prewis was in the sheriff's office obtaining a peace warrant for the Lynn boys. He alleged that they had shot into his house Saturday night. Chester Lynn, the first man killed, was arrested and placed in the county jail, charged with assault with intent to murder. He made bond and was released the following day. As he was leaving the jail he is said to have told Warden McAdory that he would be back again in a week.

As soon as he was notified of the killing, Coroner Brasher went to the scene and held an inquest. The coroner's jury returned a verdict against Constable Lawler and Special Officer McBee for manslaughter and bound them over to the grand jury under a $500 bond each, which was made on the spot."

Postscript

The legal outcome of this case against the officers is unknown, however, it is most likely that the grand jury returned a "no bill" against them due to the circumstances and the history of prior violent acts by both of the victims. As in other controversial cases, and where complaints may have been voiced by family members of deceased individuals, it was probably believed by officials to best place the onus of a decision regarding legal culpability on the part of the officers on citizens drawn from the entire county and comprising the grand jury. It should also be remembered that the original charge against the officers was returned by the coroner's jury, the members of which would have been chosen from white male individuals living close to the scene of the incident and possibly having a relationship with, or a fear of, Lynn family members. This practice of deferring final decision making to the grand jury would be employed more often as the century progressed, with coroner's juries being essentially discontinued in Jefferson County in the 1930s.

EXUM DISCHARGES THREE POLICEMEN
Were Charged With Reckless Firing
at Fleeing Negro on Street
The Birmingham Age-Herald, January 21, 1913

"Without uttering a word of defense, but on the contrary confessing to shooting upon the streets of Birmingham at a fleeing negro, three policemen stood before President Culpepper Exum and listened to words which discharged them from their positions. The officers were W.P. Taylor, Edward Lyons and B.J. Harrison. It will be recalled that while Commissioner Lane was absent from Birmingham the three officers gave chase to a fleeing negro charged with a felony. They fired at the negro in front of the Hillman hotel and the city hall, which act was witnessed not only by President Exum from his office but by many other citizens. The officers were immediately suspended. Mr. Exum...released the officers yesterday.

The policemen were accompanied to the office of Mr. Exum by Captain Eagan, acting chief. Mr. Exum...inquired of the officers whether they did the shooting and received an affirmative answer, excepting in the case of Officer Taylor, who affirmed that he had fired into the air. He added to Mr. Taylor: "I have good reports of you and regret exceedingly that I must in duty bound, inflict this punishment on you along with the other two officers who tell me they fired to hit. I wish that I could get my own consent to make your punishment somewhat lighter." Mr. Taylor thanked Mr. Exum for his words.

Mr. Exum than advised the officers that the city would hereafter do without their services. The officers did not say anything but turned and left the room. Mr. Exum regretted very much the necessity of releasing the officer but he felt it absolutely necessary to take that action."

OFFICER SAUNDERS HAS AN AWFUL TIME
Experience Yesterday Almost Equal to One of Opie Dildock's Adventures

The Birmingham Age-Herald, December 24, 1913

"Call Officer Saunders had an exciting few minutes yesterday afternoon on the east side of Twentieth street at the corner of Second alley, but he finally arrested his man--C.H. Lee of Jasper--and placed him in the city jail charged with carrying concealed weapons and resisting an officer. Several hundred persons gathered to witness the arrest of Mr. Lee, which bordered on the tragic throughout.

"I caught the call that there was a man on Twentieth street raising a fuss," said Officer Saunders, "and went out to get him. At Second alley I met the man, who had a billiard cue in his hand, and a large crowd about him. I saw he was greatly excited and taking him by the arm I started to walk him to the station. Here is where the trouble started. Without warning he shook me off and made a lick at me with his billiard cue. I caught the blow with my open hand and closed in. He reached into his breast pocket and drew out a .45-caibre derringer pistol but before he could use it I had wrenched it away and then with his other hand he started drawing a .38-calibre Smith & Wosson pistol, but I again got to him in time and took that away. I thought that would be about all but he had a razor left, but he did not have an opportunity to use it as I quickly removed the last of his playthings. He got as quiet as a lamb and we had no more trouble."

At the city jail, where Mr. Lee was searched, nearly $500 was found in his wallet. Officer Saunders stated that as Lee was in mighty bad company at the time of his arrest the chances were he would be extremely thankful in the morning for the way the city of Birmingham took care of his person and cash."

POLICEMAN FIRED FOR SHOOTING AT TRAFFIC VIOLATOR
Bullet Ricochets And Hits Woman Bystander In Midday Crowd

The Birmingham News, June 17, 1928

"Summary action in the case of a policeman who was too ready with his pistol on a crowded street erased the name of W.E. Coleman from the rolls of the Birmingham department Saturday night.

Coleman was discharged within six hours from the time he fired upon an alleged offending motorist who had failed to halt after an infraction of traffic laws. The dismissal of Coleman was announced by City Commissioner John Taylor, in charge of public safety immediately after all the facts had been presented to him.

The bullet fired at the offending car ricocheted and struck Mrs. R.G. Malloy, who was standing with her husband and sister at Third Avenue and Twentieth Street, North. The bullet struck Mrs. Malloy's leg. It was at 2:25 p.m. At 9 p.m. the policeman was asked for his badge.

The officials of Birmingham will not tolerate promiscuous shooting by policemen as voiced by Mr. Taylor, who declared officers and employees must be governed in all of their acts by common sense and the law. It is wholly outside the province or authority of a policeman to fire a pistol on streets in the downtown section or other places where human life is imperiled. The bullet had been fired, Coleman told his superiors, to halt a motorist who had driven through a red light, narrowly missing him. Chief of Police McDuff and Inspector Hawkins joined in denouncing, in no uncertain terms, the use of firearms in the downtown district. Inspector Hawkins issued this statement: "I have repeatedly warned officers they must not use firearms in the downtown section. The chance of a stray bullet striking a bystander is too great. Officer Coleman admitted to me that he forgot himself in the excitement of the moment and acted hastily. However, I repeat, shooting in the downtown district must not continue." Chief McDuff said: "Officer Coleman should have exercised more judgement than to have fired a pistol in the crowded downtown section. We will not tolerate such dangerous practices."

Officer Coleman had attempted to stop a man named Tom Garner, who was arrested after Coleman and Officer Goldstein had commandeered cars. Garner was later charged with reckless driving and driving while intoxicated. Coleman joined the police department in 1925, and has been a traffic officer since that time."

JURORS URGED TO HALT CRIME

The Birmingham Age-Herald, April 2, 1935

"Chief among the cases on the Grand Jury docket for investigation is the slaying of Fred H. McDuff, Jr., son of Sheriff Fred H. McDuff, who was killed Friday night in a restaurant at 1220

Arkadelphia Road. In a statement taken down by a court stenographer in his county jail cell, Hubert T. (Mike) Mulligan, Frisco Railroad special officer, admitted he shot McDuff, but declared the shooting was accidental. Mulligan told county and city officers that he and McDuff "staged" a quarrel and fight to frighten C.B.Bates, who was employed with Mulligan and McDuff as a special agent for the railroad company.

Mulligan, who is held on a charge of murder, said after he and McDuff had "staged" the "fake" quarrel, he whipped out his pistol and it discharged accidentally, causing McDuff's death. He declared he had no intention of killing McDuff and that he regretted the shooting."

Postscript

An indictment for murder in the second degree was returned against Mulligan by the Grand Jury and he was released on $5,000 bail. The final legal outcome could not be determined.

Black Officers?

Shortly after being appointed Birmingham Commissioner of Public Safety in 1937, Theophilus Eugene ("Bull") Connor would publicly broach the subject of possibly employing African-Americans as Birmingham police officers, albeit only in areas populated by black citizens. Based on Connor's radical racist polices and practices, it is surprising that he would have even entertained such an action and it may just have been a sop to concerns in the black community about the ever present suppression by white police officers. If he had truly considered doing this, he was quickly dissuaded from trying to implement such a policy.

CITY MAY HAVE NEGRO OFFICERS
Connor Considers Placing Them In Colored Area
The Birmingham News, September 19, 1938

"Commissioner of Public Safety Eugene (Bull) Connor today was considering placing Negro policemen in the heavily populated area around Fourth Avenue, North, and Seventeenth Street, in accord with the present policy of several other large Southern cities. The police official said he planned to contact heads of other police departments who have had the Negro officers in their towns, to "get their experiences and their reactions." He said that in the event the plan went through, the Negro would "have to be above reproach and with the greatest integrity."

"The Negro population around Fourth Avenue has always been a thorn in the side of the department, and if the Negro officers are placed there I think law and order will prevail far above its stages at the present time," Connor said. "The officers will have to be passed upon by the Civil Service Personnel Board just like other officers." He said he planned to confer with the higher officers in the Police Department to get their viewpoints."

Postscript

It would be 28 more years before the first black man was employed as an officer with the Birmingham Police Department.

Statistics

The compilation and analysis of statistics related to overall murder rates within the city of Birmingham as well as within the remainder of Jefferson County during the early 20th century, along with comparisons to other cities, were noted in a previous chapter. Data specifically related to deaths at the hands of police officers during the course of their official duties in the earlier era, and comparisons with the latter part of the 20th and the early 21st centuries, are presented in this chapter.

Information obtained from coroner's records which document police shooting deaths throughout Jefferson County from the years 1909 through 1939, with the exception of 1932 and 1933 where information was unavailable, reveals that during that inclusive period of 29 years there were a total of 235 homicides by law enforcement officers with a yearly average of 8 fatalities. The great majority of these deaths occurred within the Birmingham city limits. In the years prior to 1927 the rate did not exceed 11 incidents per year with the exception of 1909 when 16 deaths were recorded. However, a closer examination of annual rates reveals an anomalous period in the years 1927 through 1930 when there was a statistically significant increase in the number of police related homicides. It may be possible to attribute this increase to the difficult financial and social conditions of that time to include rising unemployment and petty theft rates which began to affect Birmingham several years prior to the stock market crash and the "official" start of the great depression in the fall of 1929. At that time it was said that "No Alabama city suffered as much as Birmingham. Services, both private and public, were stretched by the starving, sick, homeless, and unemployed."5

However, as it has already been shown in several case examples, political interest in curbing rising crime rates may have led to pressure not only on police departments to react, but also on "special agents" of the various railroad companies to employ deadly force, if necessary, to discourage theft. This approach would also show that Birmingham should not be considered as a safe haven for more unemployed men and families who were traveling throughout the country searching for work or public assistance. Men traveling illegally on the railways particularly received increased scrutiny with these "hoboes" being actively discouraged from setting up encampments or "hobo jungles" within Jefferson County.

In any event, there was no apparent outcry from the news media deploring or questioning the increased number of deaths at the hands of police officers during these years. This may, in turn, be attributed to the fact that the majority of the victims were poor black males. In addition, as will be presented, a seemingly inordinate number of these deaths were not reported in the newspapers. During this notable period the actual yearly police involved homicide rates were:

1926---10
1927---26
1928---16
1929---13
1930---26

Although the missing data from 1932-33 complicates an analysis, homicide rates during the pre-world war II years of 1931 and 1934-39, which include some of the worst years of the depression throughout the country, and especially as it affected Birmingham, immediately returned to, and remained at, the lower annual rates which preceded 1927.

The majority of law enforcement related homicides were committed by sworn officers employed by various municipal departments and the sheriff's office. A relatively small but still significant number occurred at the hands of other legally authorized persons to include "special agents" employed by railroads, mines and heavy industry, as well as by prison guards. An unknown factor associated with police shooting cases are statistics related to those incidents which did not result in fatalities.

A comparison of the numbers of police related shooting deaths from the early part of the 20th century to those of the period extending from 1981 through 2017 is revealing. This latter group of years followed legal procedural and policy changes which were implemented beginning in 1977 by municipal governments originating with Birmingham in regard to the so-called "fleeing felon" rule. This longstanding practice had permitted the legally "justifiable" homicide by police officers of even unarmed individuals who were alleged to have committed a felony and who were not only non-threatening to the officer or others but who were also running away from the scene of a crime.

In regard to the race of deceased individuals, a review of data revealed that of the deaths which are specifically accounted for in the available official records during the period 1909-1939, for a total of 37 years, there were 217 deaths which occurred at the hands of police officers and other "special agents." Of this total where race was documented the breakdown of 212 cases is:

Black---189 (85%)
White---23 (10%)

Of this total, at least 119 or 56% are known to have been committed by Birmingham police department officers.

In contrast, during the period 1981-2017, for a total of 36 years, there were 93 deaths. These statistics, in comparison with those for the earlier period and also taking the population increase into consideration, indicate that as previously shown with homicide rates in general, there was a distinctly significant statistical decrease in numerical as well as per capita rates of deaths incurred at the hands of law enforcement officers in the latter time period where the following racial breakdown was found:

Black---66 (71%)
White---27 (29%)

Of these, 46 deaths involved Birmingham police department officers (49%).[6]

In summary, statistics were presented in a previous chapter which showed numerical and per capita rates for all homicides in Jefferson County and separately in Birmingham for selected years. For various reasons it is misleading or not possible to accurately calculate and compare similar average per capita statistics as they relate to homicides committed by police officers over multi-year periods. However, certain conclusions can be drawn from the analysis of the known annual rates.

In the 29 year period from 1909-1939 there was an average annual rate of 8 homicides compared with the 36 year period from 1981-2017 which revealed an average of 2.6 deaths per year at the hands of officers. This clearly denotes a statistically significant decrease in the number of fatal police related encounters when these two time frames are compared.

Similar conclusions can be reached in regard to the number of police officers who were killed in the line of duty, which excludes traffic related accidents, during these separate eras. It was found that during the period 1900-1940 that there was a total of 39 homicides of officers within the Birmingham city limits which were mainly comprised of members of the Birmingham police department, while 9 deaths involved members of the Jefferson County sheriff's office. The remaining 8 deaths were of law enforcement officers employed by various smaller police departments. During the period 1980-2017 there was a total of 18 on-duty homicides of police officers. Of this number 8 were members of the Birmingham police department, 3 were deputy sheriffs and the remaining 7 were officers employed by various police departments within the county.7

The loss of any life is always tragic when it affects individuals, their relatives and friends. However, as was also shown in the analysis of overall homicide rates, the general picture emerges of a much more dangerous "Magic City" during the early 20th century as compared to recent years for both the general population and for law enforcement officers. A conservative estimate of a 50% per capita reduction of deaths within both groups is obtained when it is taken into consideration that the population of Jefferson County increased approximately threefold during the period from 1909 to 1980. A similar pronounced numerical decrease in these death rates is also seen during the period of 1980 to 2017.

Unreported

During the course of compiling material for possible inclusion in this chapter an extensive review of microfilmed newspaper articles from both The Birmingham Age-Herald and The Birmingham News was conducted. It became apparent that an appreciable number of deaths at the hands of police officers as well as various "special agents" that were documented in the coroner's records were not reported in either of these major newspapers.

Reports of some of these deaths may have been missed by me as many others received only brief mention in small articles which were found embedded far from the front pages. When a particular death was noted in one of the newspapers, a similar article could usually also be found in the other one, especially in regard to those incidents which had garnered much public attention. The lack of reporting of some of these deaths which had occurred in the more rural portions of the county may be explained by the lack of rapid communications that we now take for granted, however, the majority of the cases where a newspaper report was not found occurred within the city limits of Birmingham as shown by the coroner's records.

A major question which arises in relation to the numerous unreported deaths at the hands of law enforcement agents is that relating to intent. It appears that reporters working for both of the newspapers were well attuned to local activities, especially as they related to crime. Articles could be found on a daily basis where numerous minor acts of social misconduct were reported. It is difficult to accept that reporters from both papers would not have learned of so many of these deaths under those circumstances. Contact with their personal informants on the streets and among police agencies were likely just as important and as frequent then as they are today. Questions arise as to what the possible motives may have been to avoid publicizing such incidents. Was there some form of conspiracy between members of law enforcement agencies, the coroner and the press to avoid public attention to these deaths by intentionally not reporting many of them, especially as was seen during the years 1926-1930 when the number of police shooting deaths surged. Or was it just due to a lack of interest?

These become sort of "smoking gun" questions due to the fact that then, just as now, it is the coroner who is the only official who is initially aware of all violent deaths which have occurred within all jurisdictions within the county on any given day. It is he who is contacted every morning by news reporters to check on these matters as it is not possible for them to monitor all police radio transmissions 24 hours per day or to contact every law enforcement agency. And if the reporters during this earlier period had knowledge of such incidents from other "off-the-record" sources, did they also agree not to report them if it was requested? If so, who made the decisions not to do so?

This picture of apparent regular underreporting of these incidents by the main news media, especially during the period 1926-1930, is troubling. It is doubtful that the choice of not reporting many of these deaths was left to the discretion of individual low-level reporters, but must have required the direction, or at least the acquiescence of editors and the management of these media entities. As a possible defense, however, it should be noted that an unknown, but likely appreciable number of these unreported deaths, may have occurred during the late night or early morning hours and on weekends in parts of the city where much attention would not be paid by the public at large or the press. In addition, information obtained days after an incident had occurred may not have been considered timely news by reporters or editors. Also, it was not uncommon to find an appreciable delay between the dates of death in many cases and the date of the final decision by the coroner as to his "verdict" as to whether a particular homicide was found to be "justifiable" or not.

During the years 1909-1925, as well as including data from 1931 and 1935-1938, there were a total of 134 shooting deaths by all types of law enforcement agents within Jefferson County for a yearly average of approximately 6 deaths during this 23 year period. Of these 134 deaths, 42 (31%) were either unreported or could not be found within the newspaper archives. There were too few cases occurring in any of these individual years to allow conclusions to be drawn regarding any possible intent not to report them. In contrast, during the inclusive 5 year "surge" period of 1926-1930, there were a total of 91 police shooting deaths. Of these, 54 cases (59%) were unreported or could not be found in the newspapers. Even taking into consideration that possibly 10% of this total were inadvertently missed upon my review, the fact that approximately half of the total number of these cases were not reported strongly suggests that a concerted, if unofficial, effort by police, the coroner and news media representatives was undertaken during these years to avoid bringing the egregious increase in police shooting deaths to the public's attention.

Enforcers

In addition to purely numerical statistical data gleaned from a review of the coroner's office records relating to police shooting deaths, it was also possible to determine the names of the involved officers, as this was information which was routinely included in essentially all of the pertinent coroner docket entries as well as in related newspaper accounts. Although the names of their agency of employment were often not specified in the coroner's records, the use of titles such as "officer," "deputy," or "special agent," as well as the location of the incident if the person had died at the scene and not at a hospital, were details which allowed for the likely identification of their departments.

In an attempt to assess whether an individual officer was involved in multiple shooting incidents a comparison of names was performed. In a total of 217 cases reviewed it was found that the names of the great majority of involved officers appeared only once and on rare occasion twice over a period of years. The involvement of certain officers in multiple shooting incidents can be found in groups over the years 1909--1938 corresponding to a typical police officer's career, but especially during the period from 1926--1930 when the number of police shooting incidents surged. Obviously, data is not available for the number non-fatal shootings which occurred. Of the total of 217 deaths reviewed the racial breakdown of victims was as follows:
Black---189
White---23
Unknown---5

There were, however, a number of incidents where the names of individual officers reappear on a regular basis, earning them the sobriquet of "Enforcers." Although the actual rationale for their propensity for employing deadly force cannot be known for certain, it is possible that these particular men patrolled certain districts or "beats" where the rates of violent crime were higher than in other areas. In addition, in the days before patrol by officers in motor vehicles became routine, it was common for a policeman to patrol his beat on foot, sometimes with a partner, but usually alone. In his interactions with both the law abiding public and with the criminal element, he could not afford to appear indecisive or to come out second best in a physical altercation. Showing any sign of weakness or lack of resolve would mean an end to his perceived authority and would likely invite further aggression against him by the denizens of that area. Although an outward appearance of friendliness on the part of an officer might be shown, more important was the acknowledgement of respect and even fear of him by all citizens, whether it be shown with his fists, a nightstick, or if necessary, his gun.

Over separate periods during the early 20th century, records revealed the following individuals to have been involved in multiple incidents where deadly force was applied by the same officer more than twice:

Name	Agency	Date of Incident	Coroner Docket Entry Notes
J. C. Ballard	Birmingham P.D.	10/11/1924	GSW's of chest. Resisting arrest
		11/30/1928	GSW abdomen Resisted arrest.
		2/22/1930	GSW Head. Resisted arrest.
P.M. Bookout	Birmingham P.D.	3/8/1930	GSW Jaw and Chest Resisted arrest.
		3/10/1930	GSW of Legs. Made attack on Officer.

Resisted arrest		7/1/1930.	GSWs Body (Not reported in newspapers).

Note: Although perhaps coincidental, it is notable that Officer Bookout was involved in two fatal shootings within two days and three within one year.

P.L. Stapp	Birmingham P.D.	6/15/1930	GSW Chest. Shot at Officer Stapp.
		12/17/1930	GSW Body.
		1/11/1931	GSW Head and Body.
		12/29/1935.	GSW.

The Helton Family

Although there were a number of individual officers who engaged in fatal encounters with alleged criminals, there was only one group of men who could be classified as a family of "enforcers." Over a period of years ranging from 1909 through 1930 there were no less than nine separate incidents where multiple related members of the Helton family employed deadly force during the course of their law enforcement careers with the Birmingham Police Department, the Jefferson County Sheriff's Office and as special agents for private industry.

My knowledge of their well known reputation in Birmingham and Jefferson County as fearless officers who did not hesitate to engage with law breakers was confirmed by my personal conversations with John "Jack" Helton who was a Deputy Coroner with the Jefferson County Coroner's Office during the 1960s and 70s and who covered the Bessemer Division. Helton assured me that in addition to the recorded fatal incidents involving his grandfather, father and uncles that there were a number of additional shooting incidents in which they were involved which did not result in fatalities. There were also several incidents where Helton family members received non-fatal wounds during the course of shooting incidents and in one case the murder of one of the most aggressive members of the family occurred.

Coroner's records show the following fatal incidents and their dates of occurrence which involved the members of this family:

J.C. Helton	W.B. Helton	W.A. Helton	W.M. Helton	C.C. Helton
3/8/1909	9/26/1920	8/8/1926	3/11/1930	11/2/1927
	9/10/1927			11/14/1927
				3/8/1928
				3/10/1930

OFFICER IS KILLED IN THIEF HUNT
C.C. Helton, T.C.I. Agent, Shot To Death At Docena Cottage

ASSAILANT TAKES VICTIM'S WEAPON
Bloodhounds Taken Out By Deputies To Hunt For Slayer
The Birmingham Age-Herald, October 28, 1936

"C.C. Helton, special officer of the Tennessee Coal, Iron & Railroad Company, at Docena, was shot and killed in a cottage at the Docena village Tuesday while investigating a petty larceny case. Deputy sheriffs combed the surrounding area Tuesday night for Andrew Means, 16, Negro boy, resident of Capps Town near Wylam in connection with the shooting. Willie Geter and Sadie Geter, mother and stepfather of the boy, were held in the county jail for questioning.

Special Officer Helton was searching for a pair of shoes, reportedly stolen by a negro. The officer discovered a negro hiding in the attic of the cottage and as the officer climbed into the trapdoor he was shot through the head. Three more bullets were fired into Helton by his own gun and the assailant fled carrying a pair of shoes and officer Helton's gun. Several negroes standing outside the cottage heard the shots and saw a negro flee, but officers said that there were no eyewitnesses to the shooting.

Helton was widely known in Birmingham police circles, having served in the Birmingham police force from 1927 to 1930. Two of his cousins, W.B. Helton and John Helton, and an uncle are still with the department. C.C. Helton is survived by his widow and five children who reside at Docena."

Postscript

Newspaper records were searched through November, 1937 with no indication that Means had been apprehended.

The McDuff Family

Several McDuff family members were employed by various law enforcement agencies and as special agents within Jefferson County over a number of years. Fred McDuff, Sr., would serve as Chief Deputy Sheriff and would later be elected Sheriff and serve in that position from 1935--1939. As noted earlier in this chapter, and in a later one, several other members of the McDuff family would become involved in notable incidents of a sad nature.

DEPUTY M'DUFF FIRST TO KILL ALLEGED THUG IN CLEAN-UP CAMPAIGN
Rolls Into City With Body of Black Thrown Over Hood of His Auto---
Was a Question of Who Could Shoot First, and the Officer Won Out Handily

The Birmingham Age-Herald, December 11, 1920

"With the body of Walter Connell, a negro, alleged to be a highwayman, thrown over the automobile hood, Chief Deputy Sheriff Fred McDuff rolled into the courthouse yard yesterday morning about 11 o'clock. McDuff was quicker with a gun, so he is still alive. Back of Avondale park yesterday, on the road leading to Mountain Terrace, the negro, cornered and surprised, drew a gun on the officer. It was his last act. McDuff dropped the alleged felon with a bullet in the neck. He died almost instantly.

Deputies McDuff and Virgil Sandefer went out yesterday morning on their usual patrol of the highways, this having been their custom since the crime wave in Birmingham and Jefferson county reached its height. They saw the negro dodging towards a clump of bushes. He had a shotgun and remained concealed for a short time, but made his appearance again over the crest of the hill, having crawled away. Thinking the negro had spotted and recognized them, McDuff waited and watched with his rifle by his side. The negro, after awhile evidently thinking the coast was clear, came over the hill and towards the road. As he came within 25 yards of the officer, McDuff raised up and commanded the negro to throw up his hands. The order was ignored. The negro raised his shotgun and took aim. However, he was too slow and the officer fired. On examination of the negro's gun it was found that the safety was off. The negro had on typical highwayman clothes. The negro was not identified until yesterday afternoon when the wife of the man came into the coroner's office for a death certificate. She stated that someone told her that Connell had been killed and she came to town to see if it was so.

Although there had been a long series of night and day highway robberies, this is the first alleged highwayman to be killed, and officers are of the opinion it will curb the crime wave that has been sweeping this district. The road on which the shooting occurred has been a favorite spot with highwaymen as the road at this point runs through an unpopulated section. While the sheriff's force is patrolling the roads of the outlying districts outside of the city limits the city detective department is continuing its raids on vagrants. City officials are waging war on vagrants and expect to make it so warm for them here they will hunt a cooler clime. Officers continue to inspect the pool rooms daily. The outcome of these raids are being watched with interest by the citizens of Birmingham who are loud in their praise of the efforts being made by the officers to rid this city of the vagrants that infest it."

Legends

Throughout history society has, for many reasons, invented and developed "heroes" whose exploits, to varying degrees, have had their basis in a combination of known facts, embellishments, outright falsehoods and wishful thinking. The stories of such men and women date from antiquity to current times and can be found in a particular country, region or locality. They are present in all cultures around the world and may be depicted in such ways to include drawings on prehistoric cave walls, in religious books or by being passed down through descendants by word of mouth in the villages of Africa.

Some "legends" have been recalled for thousands of years while others have been more contemporary and memories of them have faded away with the passing of time. Modern anti-heroes such as John Dillinger, as well as Bonnie Parker and Clyde Barrow, also retain a place in modern western memory and they have often been depicted in books and movies as misguided individuals who took on "Robin Hood" roles during their lives and which followed them after their violent deaths, even though they actually were sociopathic criminals whose exploits led to the deaths of a number of police officers in the 1930s.

Certain local law enforcement agents also attained legendary status and notoriety in Birmingham and Jefferson County during the early part of the 20th century. Although forgotten for the most part now, some of their stories have been discovered in newspaper accounts of those times and samples are presented.

The public was interested in stories about local law enforcement "legends" and their crime fighting activities and the news media, in the form of the two major newspapers in Birmingham, were ready and willing to provide such salacious material for public consumption. This was presented in a style that was socially acceptable and consistent with that found throughout the country in the early 20th century, but to no greater degree than in the south. A number of these stories, as well as cartoons, contained blatantly racist material which was written, edited and published daily by the white men who controlled the local newspapers. As previously noted, the acceptance of this material by many members of the public at large is supportive of the comment made by the English writer L.P. Hartley who stated that "The past is a foreign country; they do things differently there."

Although it may seem easy today, using the "20-20 vision," of hindsight, to shake our heads in wonder at the past approach of the news media to certain social issues, it can be just as difficult for us to understand the complex factors which drove the mores and mindset of the majority of the public during those times. Although the past cannot be changed we can only reflect with some dismay, and to hold these earlier newsmen to be at least historically responsible for their spectacular failure to offer at least a modicum of disavowal for certain actions, or to have at least suggested reform from within their powerful forum during this era. However, it should also be remembered that these individuals were the products of their times, social class and the existing mores. They would not have been placed in, or have been allowed to keep their positions for long, if they had strayed from the accepted "status quo."

Some moderation of extreme beliefs began to be suggested within the print media starting in the late 1930s, but serious editorial demand for proactive social change would not begin in earnest until September 15, 1963.

CAPTAIN HAWKINS HAS NEVER FIRED A GUN IN BIRMINGHAM
But Once in Fort Payne, Single Handed, He Stopped a Mob and Killed a Dozen

The Birmingham Age-Herald, September 20, 1914

"Captain Robert H. Hawkins is the most feared man of the police department. "Old Blue Steel," as he is known to the criminal world, is a terrible bugaboo to the negro element as they openly tremble at his approach. Negro women to quiet their children just whisper, "Old Blue Steel will get you shore," and the wildest pickaninny is quickly reduced to extreme docility. And yet in the 15 years that he has been a police officer in Birmingham Captain Hawkins has never fired his pistol at any man. His record is unique in that respect.

Birmingham even to its most optimistic booster does not appear to be a "Sunday school" town and it is a well known fact that the police of this city have more danger to contend with than any other city of similar size in the United States. In the old "free, rough and ready" western days of Leadville and Cripple Creek human life was not cheaper or more wantonly taken than in the last 15 years in Birmingham. Approximately every member of the police department has killed one, two or more men in pistol battles during that period. Still Captain Hawkins, the most feared of the numerous brave men at police headquarters proudly boasts that he has never shot at anyone while a police officer in the city. He is justly proud of his record.

No one knows, not even Captain Hawkins as to how he acquired the nickname "Old Blue Steel." The first time it was led to the knowledge of Captain Hawkins was about 10 hears ago in "Buzzard's Roost"--a notorious section for negro "roughnecks"--on First and Second avenues between Twenty-sixth and Twenty-seventh streets. It was on a Sunday night. Captain Hawkins, then a patrolman and a partner Officer James Mullin, was stationed at "Buzzard's Roost." Hawkins had gone to supper and while he was absent a fight broke out in a negro "blind tiger" and in attempting to make an arrest Officer Mullin was shot and killed. A few minutes later Hawkins was told that his "buddie" had been killed in a negro dive and hastened to the scene. On his way he heard a negro say: "Wal dar shorely be sumpin' doin' now. 'Old Blue Steel' am here and hits no place for a good nigger." Another version of how the nickname first came into use was that a negro told an officer that a mistake had been made in killing Officer Mullin, as the murderer, the notorious Henry King, was after "Old Blue Steel."

Captain Hawkins was born at Pikeville, Tenn., about 55 years ago. He is married and has several children. He has a modest home on Avenue G and is a quiet, unassuming man. He became a member of the Birmingham police department in 1897 and was elected sergeant in 1908. In 1913, he was elected by the city commissioners to a captaincy and has served the city in that capacity ever since. He is a familiar figure about the downtown streets. His tall, gaunt form rapidly striding up the street in his trim uniform with a military salute for every acquaintance impresses. A few days ago he was given the morning shift, which means that he now goes on duty at 11 o'clock at night and works until 7 o'clock. It also means that "Old Blue Steel" is up all night guarding the property of the citizens. It means that no police officer can sleep on his beat and get away with it as Captain Hawkins has the reputation of appearing when least expected, and as he rides a bicycle he covers all parts of the city, so that even the bicycle scouts have to be "on the job" as the wily Captain may turn up on them at anytime.

Goldstein

Although few Jewish men were attracted to police work or were accepted within it during this era, one particular individual was employed by the Birmingham police force, rose to the rank of Detective and had a long and storied career within the department. His record was filled with both questionable and heroic actions as depicted in a series of newspaper articles from that time.

MAIL CARRIER IS SERIOUSLY SHOT BY POLICE SCOUT

The Birmingham Age-Herald, June 7, 1910

"Last night Police Scout Harry Goldstein shot and probably fatally wounded a negro mail carrier by the name of Jesse Boynes. Boynes was taken to St. Vincents hospital and it was stated that his wound was considered very serious. The ball entered his back near the spine and came out through the stomach.

Officer Goldstein told of the shooting this morning as follows: "I was at the corner of Fourteenth street and Sixth avenue when I saw a negro sneaking along the sidewalk near the store on the corner. Burson and I were together and we asked the negro what he was doing there that time of night. For answer he turned and started to run away from us at top speed. That looked suspicious and we gave chase. We shot into the air several times and tried to scare the negro into stopping. We told him that we were policemen and that he should stop. He ran to the alley and started to cross the street. He was gaining on us every minute and just as he got under the street light I told him to stop or I would kill him. I merely meant to scare him into surrender. Instead of surrendering he stopped directly under the light and started to pull his gun. I was in the lead of Burson and saw it was either his life or mine, so I threw my gun on him and shot him."

The shooting occurred about 1:20 o'clock this morning. Boynes is one of the best known negroes in town, being a United States mail carrier and a prominent negro lodge man. He was taken to the Hillman hospital first but was taken from there to St. Vincent's at his own request as he said his people had money to pay for his treatment."

GOLDSTEIN IS PUT UNDER $5000 BOND
The Birmingham Age-Herald, June 11, 1910

"Policeman Harry Goldstein was bound over under a bond of $5000 for the killing of Jesse Barnes, a negro mail carrier, whom the officer took for a burglar. Bond was made in a few minutes. Chief Bodeker being one of the bondsmen.

The principal witness for the defense was Police Scout J.B. Hurson, who was Goldstein's partner, and who was the only eyewitness to the shooting. His account bore out the statement of the defendant relative to the shooting--"that the negro had acted suspiciously and when they called to him to halt he ran; that when he reached the corner he stopped suddenly, turned toward them and endeavored to draw something, evidently a pistol, from his hip pocket and that at this movement, Goldstein shot at him, having previously shot in the air twice in an effort to halt the negro."

Principle evidence for the prosecution was the dying statement of the negro, this being in effect that he had thought the officers were trying to hold him up. A large number of negroes were placed on the stand, none of whom witnessed the affair. Their evidence differed materially regarding the number of shots and the time of the shooting."

Postscript

The fact that Goldstein was of patrol officer rank at the time of this incident and was later promoted to Detective suggests that charges against him were not sustained in regard to this incident. In addition, the coroner had made a ruling that the shooting of Boynes was "justifiable," even though there was indication that the bullet entered the victim's back.

GOLDSTEIN SAVES NEGRO
The Birmingham Age-Herald, February 20, 1912

"Real, live, sure enough melodrama was enacted yesterday morning at the Monarch livery stable, on First avenue, when city Detectives Ray and Goldstein cornered Will Brown, a negro, wanted for grand larceny. The negro was not especially willing to be arrested and is said to have attempted to jump from a window in the building 50 feet above the pavement. Ray was on the sidewall, Goldstein having pursued Brown to the top of the building. Three times he fired at him low, one of the bullets striking the negro in the leg just as he tried to jump from the window. Quick as a cat, Goldstein grabbed the falling man and held him suspended in the air, far above the pavement. However, Brown was a very large negro and it taxed every ounce of the detective's strength to keep him from falling to an almost certain death. A crowd soon congregated on the street below and some one hurried to Goldstein's assistance. Brown was taken to the city jail charged with grand larceny. It is alleged that he stole a pushcart and a case of eggs from Yielding Bros. store."

HARRY GOLDSTEIN SHOT IN HIS HAT
The Birmingham Age-Herald, August 12, 1912

"City Detective Harry Goldstein was seriously injured this morning, that is, serious to his hat. The bullet cut a nice clean hole in Goldstein's brand new hat.

The detective was at Pratt City attempting the clearing up of a mystery of an assault, and he had gone to the home of a negro in Pratt City, where he thought he might find a negro who could tell him something. But while the detective was waiting at the front door, the man went out the back, and someone fired at Goldstein from behind.

In a hot chase that followed, Goldstein bruised his left leg considerably when he stumbled and fell over a pile of chert. After this it was easy for the negro to make his getaway. Goldstein hired a taxicab and was brought to town."

GOLDSTEIN FREE OF BRIBE CHARGE
Detective Cleared By Jury In Federal Court
The Birmingham Age-Herald, November 28, 1925

"A federal jury, after only five minutes deliberation, returned a verdict of not guilty and exonerated Harry Goldstein, formerly of the Bodecker Detective agency of charges of attempting to bribe F.L. Britton, federal prohibition agent into using his influence to have an outstanding prohibition case nolle prossed.

The case began Friday morning and went to the jury Friday afternoon. The evidence tended to show that Goldstein paid Britton $400, with the understanding he would aid some of Goldstein's friends who were in trouble. The defense claimed that the bribe was not given and hinted it was a frame-up. Goldstein, when put on the stand by his attorney, John Altman, told the jury that Britton had asked him for some evidence in possession of the Bodecker agency. "I refused," he said, "and he told me I would probably knock him out of a promotion and that he would get me in the long run."

The government's evidence, according to its presentation to the court contained a flaw of an unaccounted hour's time between the time Britton was supposed to have received the money and the time he presented it to officials. It was upon this point the defense based part of its case, it was said."

More Goldstein
It is unknown if Abe Goldstein was related to Harry Goldstein.

CITY DETECTIVES ARE EXONERATED
Residence of Minister Entered By Mistake, Chief Says
The Birmingham Age-Herald, April 5, 1935

"City Commissioner W.D. Downs and Chief of Police E.L. Hollums said they had exonerated Detectives Abe Goldstein and M.W. Alexander of the city liquor squad, of blame in connection with an incident at the residence of the Rev. Donald A. Hyde, 2012 Ave. G Ensley. Chief Hollums said the detectives had a warrant to search a residence on Avenue F, Ensley and that the residence of the minister was entered by mistake.

Following the raids at the residence on Avenue F, which the officers conducted after leaving the minister's residence, they returned to the Rev. Mr. Hyde's residence and apologized. A formal demand for an investigation had been made by the Ensley Merchant's and Associated Business Men."

Early in his career, Birmingham police Detective J.T. Moser played a major role in the "Bloody Beat 22" affair. Both he and sheriff's deputy "Pap" Dinken were involved in many notable and notorious incidents and investigations during their long careers in law enforcement in Jefferson County during the early 20th century.

CITY DETECTIVE SHOT TO DEATH
J.T. MOSER VICTIM OF SLAYERS
Shooting Occurs Here As Officer Attempts To Arrest Pair
The Birmingham Age-Herald, February 1, 1939

"Birmingham Detective J.T. Moser was shot to death by one of two men who seized his pistol while the officer was questioning the pair "on suspicion" at a Southside street intersection. About two hours later two men identified by county officers as escapes from Speigner Prison, were arrested on Montgomery Highway several miles south of Birmingham and placed in County jail on charges of murder in connection with Moser's death. The arrest made by a lone deputy, came after a spectacular chase in which city, county and state officers took part.

Captured by Sheriff's Deputy "Pap" Dinken, near Calera, the men were Robert Oglesby, 27, and William C. Williams, both escapes from Speigner Prison. Detective Moser was shot by one of the two men who seized the officer's gun while he was questioning them at Twelfth Street and Sixth Avenue South. The detective's assailant fired two shots at a companion who had accompanied Moser, shoved the wounded officer into the gutter and fled in the police car. Detective Moser was taken to South Highlands Infirmary where he was pronounced dead on arrival. The detective was struck just below the heart.

In describing the capture of the two men, Dinken said he went down the Boothton Road on a "hunch" that the two men would head that way. Dinken said that shortly after the car with the two men came over the hill and crashed into his own car. The deputy said he came around the car pointing his gun at the men and ordered them to put up their hands. Oglesby, whom Dinken said was the driver of the car, got out and held up his hands. The other man was slumped over in the seat and when he went up to him, the man pulled a gun on him. Dinken said he fired close to the man's ear and the man then surrendered his gun.

Detective Moser entered the police department in 1910. He was working on his day off when he was slain. Officers recalled that at many times in the past he had solved cases by working on his off days with "Squab," a Negro who is reported the only one of his race ever to hold a special officer's commission with the city. This strange "partnership," which led to the solution of a number of important cases here, ended when "Squab," whose real name was A. Van Ross, was killed in an automobile accident two years ago. There was a close attachment between the two men. When "Squab," his body broken in the accident was brought into Hillman Hospital in the middle of the night, his only words were, "Send for Mr. Mose, send for Mr. Mose." And Mr. Moser, aroused from his sleep, donned his clothes and sat by the side of "Squab" for the rest of the night. Hospital attendants said "Squab" quieted down as soon as Detective Moser appeared and seemed immediately to lose his fear of the death he knew was closing in on him."

MOSER KILLER DENIED MERCY
Chair Death Scheduled Friday For Slayer Of Detective
The Birmingham Age-Herald, June 13, 1940

"Willie C. Williams, whose crime career spans 16 of his 29 years, lost today an attempt to avoid death in the electric chair, although he succeeded in 1934. Williams, convicted of slaying Birmingham City Detective J.T. Moser after escaping from Speigner Prison, was denied clemency by Gov. Frank M. Dixon. His electrocution is scheduled at Kilby Prison Friday.

First convicted of burglary in 1924, and even before that a reform school inmate, Williams was serving a life term for robbery when he escaped. Former Gov. B.M. Miller commuted Wiliiams' sentence from death to life imprisonment in the robbery in 1934. Counsel for Williams insisted he was "not a cold-blooded killer." The convict himself told Dixon that Moser was shot as they scuffled over the officer's gun, and asserted that the detective, who stopped Williams and a companion to question them, "never told me he was an officer." Pleading for his life, Williams testified he could have killed the officer who finally apprehended him had he been intent upon malicious slaying. A charge that liquor was sold freely around Speigner Prison was made by the prisoner, who said he "never would have left Speigner if I hadn't been full of whiskey." He claimed he also was drinking when Moser was shot and presented witnesses who testified "he doesn't have any sense when he gets liquor in him."

OFFICER'S SLAYER IS ELECTROCUTED
The Birmingham Age-Herald, June 14, 1940

"The electric chair which he escaped by commutation of a death sentence for robbery in 1934 claimed the life of Willie C. Williams, 29, early today for murder. Williams was executed for the slaying of Detective J.T. Moser who had arrested him while he was a fugitive from Speigner Prison, where he was serving life for a robbery committed in Mobile."

This chapter concludes with a review of the ultimate purported local law enforcement "legend."

Alius Brown And His Wonder Horse
Real, Myth or Exaggerated Hybrid?

Litwack references the autobiography of W.C. Handy, the self-proclaimed "Father of the Blues," as his source for what they both presented as factual material.

Litwack noted that:

> "Alius Brown, the high sheriff of Jefferson County, Alabama, achieved a reputation in the late nineteenth century for ruthlessness and efficiency. His claim to distinction rested largely on the remarkable white horse he rode, and the stories about that horse's powers reverberated through black Birmingham and in the countryside. The sheriff reportedly never had to shoot at a fleeing black man. He only needed to get down from the horse and let this extraordinary animal pursue him. It would set out after the black fugitive "like a hound dog after a rabbit" and quickly overtake him, then clasp the fugitive's arm in his teeth and return him to Sheriff Brown. In the early 1890s, at a pipe works in Bessemer, only a few miles from Birmingham, black laborers sang,
>
> "Here comes Alius Brown, baby,
> Ridin' after me,
> Ridin' after me, baby
> Ridin' after me.
> Here comes Alius Brown
> Ridin' after me;
> I'm goin' back to 'Birn-in-ham.'"[8]

W.C. Handy, in his autobiography, added the following in regard to this specific song as well as to the writing and development of blues songs in general: "The evolution of blues lyrics is no less quaint. Give a Negro any incident, and he will make you a song about it--if he feels bad enough. At the pipe works at Bessemer, for example, back in '92 and '93, the husky duskies had one that went like this:"[9]

Handy went on to provide the verse noted above which he denied having written and which was later repeated by Litwack in his book along with Handy's comments about its alleged source. I have little doubt that this song was actually sung, but its true author and its origins have been lost to time.

Investigation and Deconstruction of the Myth of "Alius Brown"

Extensive research was conducted in an attempt to discover any factual information which might support the tale of "Alius Brown" and his "wonder horse" and to try to determine whether this was a totally apocryphal invention or a story with some factual, albeit exaggerated basis. Surely, if such a folktale was true, it should have received some attention in the news media of that time.

The first glaring issue that arose to shed doubt on the veracity of this purported true event was that there never was anyone by the name of Brown who was the elected or appointed sheriff of Jefferson County dating back to 1819.[10]

In addition, research failed to reveal that there had been any sheriff named "Alius Brown" or of anyone with a name close to it, who had ever served as sheriff of any county in Alabama since the state was admitted to the union in 1819.[11]

Other possibilities for the existence of "Alius Brown" were considered. Although it is known that this individual could not have been the actual "high" or elected sheriff of Jefferson County, perhaps he was a semi-fictional character drawn from one or more individuals who may have actually existed and who may have occupied other law enforcement positions. As it would seem unlikely that the actual sheriff would spend his time personally overseeing prisoners who might try to escape as is noted in the song, that job would probably fall to one of his deputies or, perhaps, to a jailer or warden guarding prisoners working in the fields. In that time period, such oversight would likely have been conducted on horseback. Perhaps the origin of this story may have its basis in another Alabama county or in an adjacent state and maybe it dates back to a much earlier part of the 19th century. Nevertheless, although it might be partially or totally fictional, the story of "Alius Brown" and his mighty horse would have been a psychological force to be feared and reckoned with by prisoners as depicted in this simple song.

So was "Alius Brown" purely a figment of a song writer's imagination or, perhaps, a combination of people? Was the basis of the song drawn from an embellished story knitted together from disparate factual bits of information and pieces of fiction and from the experiences of prisoners over a period of years? Certainly, the part of the song about the remarkable ability of his horse is something which suggests the fantastical. In this regard, blues songs have typically been rewritten, repeated (or covered) with various alterations by numerous musicians over many years. It is often difficult or impossible to trace a particular older song back to its original author. Examples of such popular songs surviving for generations include "Frankie and Johnnie" and "Stagger Lee," both of which were believed by many listeners to have been first written and performed during the 1950s "rock and roll" era, but which actually date back to at least the mid-nineteenth century. Although there may have been numerous changes in the wording of these songs, they followed the same basic themes through their various permutations.

In Search of "Alius Brown"

Since no record of, or reference to, a law enforcement agent with this specific name could be found, this "story" was ready to be relegated to myth status until by chance an actual known individual of interest was discovered who, at least initially, presented indications which suggested that a real person may have been a model for the character "Alius Brown."

This notable man was named Lucien C. Brown and he had served as the Chief Deputy Sheriff during the administration of Sheriff E.L. Higdon from 1907-1911. Brown has already been mentioned in an earlier chapter titled "Work," where it was noted that during the 1908 coal strike, "Chief Deputy Sheriff Lucien Brown, who is also a Major of the guard, is at the camp and running affairs." The person appointed to the position of chief deputy sheriff is typically very powerful. This individual customarily makes decisions about the daily operations of the office and is handpicked and trusted by the Sheriff, who is usually more involved in political issues on a daily basis, rather than responding to the tactical matters and other problems that regularly arise.

Research reveals Brown to have been a prominent person in the political and military circles of that time. Prior to being named chief deputy under Sheriff Higdon, a newspaper article recounted some of his military background. It should also be kept in mind that appointment as an officer in any state militia (or national guard unit as we know it today) was, and often still remains, highly politicized. In these early years actual "elections" to supervisory ranks were made by unit members. In 1898 Lucien Brown was a 1st Lieutenant in the Alabama militia's Company K of the Birmingham Rifles and was later transferred to staff duty in Florida during the Spanish-American war, but remained in the country and was not deployed to Cuba.

CAPT. BROWN NOW COMMANDS RIFLES
Popular and Experienced Military Man
Was Unanimously Elected Last Night
To Succeed Captain Ledbetter

The Birmingham Age-Herald, June 24, 1904

"Capt. Lucien C. Brown was unanimously elected as the commanding officer of the Birmingham Rifles, Company K, Third regiment, Alabama national guard, at a meeting of the company held last night. Captain Brown was Lieutenant in the Birmingham Rifles for about ten years and resigned two years ago to accept a commission as a Captain on the staff of Brig. Gen. Louis V. Clark. During the Spanish-American war Captain Brown was adjutant of the First Alabama regiment, United States volunteers, and he is therefore well equipped in military duties. He will accept the new commission and will assume command immediately."

It is known that Brown eventually reached the rank of Colonel which is remarkable as this was considered to be a particularly high military position held by few soldiers during inter-war years. During his service, Brown served as Staff Judge Advocate in one unit. Brown's business address was listed in the Birmingham city register as being in the Brown-Marx building. These factors strongly suggest that he was an attorney. A later mention of Brown was also found.

DEFENSE TO QUIZ CITY GUN EXPERT
IN SOLDIER TRIAL

The Birmingham Age-Herald, September 6, 1928

"Hamilton, Ala.,---Col. Lucien Brown, of Birmingham, firearms expert, will be the first witness used when the defense opens its evidence in the fourth trial of Sergt. Robert Lancaster, who is being tried for the fourth time on murder charges in connection with the death of Willie Baird, miner, in March of 1921."

Summary

In the final analysis could the mysterious "Alius Brown" have actually been Lucien C. Brown? Although common, the last names are the same. The first names of both individuals are odd, but are similar in sound and "Lucien" could easily have been mispronounced and changed to "Alius" in the song.

Lucien Brown appears to have been a fairly powerful political figure in both the state militia as well as within the sheriff's office. Although a newspaper article from 1904 indicates that Brown may have been a member of the Alabama state militia in 1894 or earlier, it would seem that he would have been too young to have assumed a high ranking position within a law enforcement agency in the early 1890s.

From all of the available evidence, both factual and hearsay, it would appear most likely that the personality of "Alius Brown" referred to in the song could not have been the actual individual named Lucien C. Brown despite his documented association with the Jefferson County sheriff's office and whether or not he possessed a "remarkable white horse."

The author welcomes contact from anyone having additional information regarding this matter or of the final outcomes of any of the other unresolved cases presented in this book at his email address: jmar98@juno.com..

Absent From The Memorial

A fairly concise listing of the names of Jefferson County law enforcement officers who have died in the line of duty since 1889 is included on the memorial wall which is located outside of the entrance to the Jefferson County Criminal Justice Center.

However, as detailed in this and other chapters, the identities of several officers who, for various reasons, were not included on the memorial are listed below. Perhaps at some later date their names will be inscribed on the memorial as well as added to the National Police Officers Memorial in Washington, D.C. and to the Officer Down website.

NAME	DEPARTMENT	DATE OF DEATH
Officer E.L. Bennett	Ensley Police Department	January 20, 1903
Deputy B.H. Young	Jefferson Co. Sheriff's Office	April 30, 1910
Det. J.C. Stoutenborough	Bessemer Police Dept.	Dec. 28, 1911
Officer W.D. Evans	Birmingham Police Dept.	Feb. 15, 1919
Chief Of Police B. Walker	Brighton Police Dept.	August 29, 1919

CHAPTER 10

CAPITAL PUNISHMENT

"For the wages of sin is death..."

---Romans 6:23

The application of capital punishment by the State during the early 20th century was as prolific, if not more so, than it has been in the 21st century. Well into the 20th century, the great majority of states sanctioned the practice and employed it in one form or another. One of the main differences between the use of such punishment then and now was related to the elapsed time between when an individual was convicted and sentenced and the date of his execution. In earlier years, the interval was often measured in a period of weeks or several months at best, as rapid legal appeals were conducted. In contrast, the routinely long process through the various levels of our current judicial system, often continuing for years, if not decades, might be considered by some as "cruel and unusual punishment," both for convicted individuals as well as for family members of the victims.

The other notable difference in the earlier legal system, which extended into the mid 20th century, was the application of capital punishment following convictions for crimes other than murder, such as robbery and rape. Additionally, there were no standard legal exemptions from execution based on a guilty individual being a juvenile as young as 14 years old or having reduced mental competency. Remarkably, it was only in the early 21st century that the abolishment of capital punishment of juveniles and persons who are shown to be mentally impaired was formally outlawed by the U.S. Supreme Court.

As elsewhere in the United States during the early 20th century, blacks in Alabama were much more likely than white individuals to pay the ultimate penalty for committing homicide and other capital crimes. Records indicate that blacks accounted for 57 of the 64 persons executed for murders, rapes and robberies committed in Jefferson County between 1900 and 1940.[1]

WILL GOLSON HUNG IN JAIL YARD YESTERDAY WAS COOL AND COLLECTED
Murderer Of Chief Deputy Sheriff Robert Warnock Met Death With A Smile On His Face

The Birmingham-Age Herald, February 10, 1900

"Will Golson, the slayer of Chief Deputy Sheriff Warnock, was executed yesterday in the Jefferson County jail yard. Among the witnesses to the execution was a young Bob Warnock, the son of the murdered man, who stood near Sheriff O'Brien when he sprung the trap. The body was then cut down and turned over to his wife who had it removed to an undertaker's establishment. The rope was then taken in charge by the friends of the deceased officer and cut up into small pieces which were distributed as souvenirs."

Postscript

On November 27, 1898 Jefferson County Chief Deputy Sheriff Robert W. Warnock was killed in the line of duty by Will Golson, an escaped convict from Autauga County. As officers surrounded his house, Warnock walked up on the porch. Golson opened the door and fired at Deputy Warnock, striking him several times. Golson escaped and was captured after an extensive manhunt.

It is notable, especially during this time period, that Golson was actually brought to trial, convicted, sentenced to death and legally executed particularly in light of the fact that he had killed a law enforcement officer. This was almost the exception, rather than the rule, that justice in this case was served in this fashion. The more common outcome during this era where individuals, whether black or white who were even suspected of committing such a crime, were often forcefully seized from the authorities by an enraged mob of citizens and summarily executed, usually by hanging, shooting, burning or a combination of such methods. Such extrajudicial acts were commonplace, usually went unpunished and were not limited to the South. The usual outcome of coroner or grand jury investigations of these incidents resulted in rulings which condemned such actions as being illegal, but which also typically stated that they were committed by "parties unknown" to the jury which effectively ended further inquiries into the matter.

It was reported that as a result of her husband's death, Mrs. Warnock, in a moment of "mental aberration" twelve months after the execution of Golson, terminated her life with the same pistol with which Mr. Warnock had attempted to defend himself.

In a remarkable set of circumstances, the hanging of Will Golson, Sr., was followed by the legal execution of his son 23 years later for a crime not involving murder.

NEGRO IS HANGED ON GALLOWS THAT CLAIMED FATHER
Golson Pays Death Penalty For Attack On White Woman 23 Years After Execution Of Parent

The Birmingham News June 8, 1923

"Will Golson, negro, followed in the footsteps of his father Friday, paying the death penalty in the Jefferson County Jail on the same gallows that claimed his father, Will Golson the first, 23 years ago. Golson went to his death calmly, betraying no emotions as he mounted the scaffold and never once complaining as the black mask was placed over his face. The trap was sprung at 11:04 o'clock and in 10 1/2 minutes the prisoner was pronounced dead by attending physicians. Golson walked to the gallows and made a short confession of his crime. Chief Deputy Hill placed the rope and black mask over his head and Sheriff J.T. Shirley pulled the lever. Golson fell to his death without a sign of fear.

It was the first execution in the Jefferson County Jail since Will Moton, alias Black Butts, said to have been an Uncle of Golson, and John Whiteside, negro, charged with the murder of a white man, were hanged in July, 1921. A large crowd gathered outside the jail early in the morning, but few were permitted to enter the jail. At 9:45 o'clock Golson's grandfather, J.G. Booth, a preacher, arrived at the jail to see Will for the first time since his father was hanged. "This will be a warning to your brothers," said Booth, "if they follow in your steps they will know what the end is. Willie, you ought to know better than that. This is the second time that I have been in a jail--the last time was to see your father hang."

GOLSON CHIP OFF THE OLD BLOCK, SAYS HIS GRANDFATHER
The Birmingham News, June 8, 1923

"When Sheriff Thomas J. Shirley, of Jefferson County, sprang the trap of the gallows in the yard of the county jail, sending Will Golson, negro, into eternity in the expiation of a crime committed in this Commonwealth several months ago, it recalled a similar instance when the father of the negro, Will Golson the First, paid the death penalty for the taking of the life of Chief Deputy Sheriff Robert Warnock, of this county, a little more than 23 years ago.

Will Golson of this generation made a confession. So did Will Golson the First. Will Golson of this generation went to his death within 10 1/2 minutes and it took his father a few minutes longer. Sheriff Shirley, opposed to the idea of capital punishment, was deeply affected when he sprung the trap Friday of this year. The crows watching the execution this year, mainly of city, county, state and government officers, attorneys, physicians and newspapermen, was smaller than that witnessing the execution of the negro's father. But there was a similarity in the hanging. The grandfather of Will Golson the younger, witnessed the execution of Will Golson the First. From his lips came the words, "Chip of the old Block," but with this qualification added--"not on his maternal side."

The killing of Deputy Sheriff Warnock aroused the entire community. Will Golson was not caught for months. The negro had led a life of profligacy, and like his son, had a vision of meeting his end on the gallows. "Like father, like son. As the twig is bent, is the tree inclined. So runs the story."

SID KING WILL GO TO GALLOWS TODAY
He Had Appetite for Ice Cream Yesterday
Negro In Good Spirits
He Had Been a Mean Man, But Since He Got Religion His Disposition Has Been Happier
The Birmingham Age-Herald, July 31, 1903

"Sid King, the negro who will be hanged in the Jefferson county jail yard today, spent most of yesterday eating ice cream. He said that he seemed to have an appetite only for ice cream. "I don't anymore get it down," he said, "until I feel like I want more." He was treated very considerately in order that his last day on earth might be as pleasant as possible under the circumstances. The condemned man seemed in good humor. "I don't care what they do with my body," he said, "just so I get to heaven. They can put the body in an old box or let the buzzards have it."

King has been a very mean negro during his life, although he is comparatively young. He was under sentence of life imprisonment for murder at the time he committed the crime for which he will pay the penalty this morning. The second murder was committed at Pratt Mines. King was working beside a fellow convict, and with scarcely any provocation struck him in the head with a coal digger's pick, causing death.

Since being confined in the Jefferson county jail he has been in a pleasant mood most of the time. He seems to possess a natural instinct of a negro to take everything as a joke and to be easily amused. He got religion some time ago and was baptized last Sunday by the Rev. Walker, pastor of Shiloh Colored Baptist church. He passes much of his time singing, praying and reading the bible.

The scaffold in the jail yard is all in readiness for the execution. The rope will be adjusted around the condemned man's neck by Deputy Sheriff Love, although the trigger which will cause him to drop to eternity must be pulled by Sheriff A.W. Burgin. In many states another can be deputized to perform this task, but in Alabama a hanging is not legal unless actually done by the sheriff of the county in which it takes place.

The demand for entrance tickets to witness the execution has been very large and many have been refused. Separate tickets were issued for each of the three hangings that were to take place today, but since there will be but one of the tickets specifying between the hours of ten and eleven are the only ones that will be accepted at the gate."

Although major public support of capital punishment in this era can be assumed, the views of those against its employment based on religious or moral objections, as well as due to the possibility of an innocent person being executed or even as a reaction to the occasional difficulties associated with the procedure, were sometimes brought to the public's attention by the news media. Such problems were noted in the following account of a botched execution along with the reproduction of a rather disparaging and direct letter to the governor which was also printed in the newspaper.

FELIX HALL WAS DROPPED TWICE
The First Effort Did Not Produce Death
Maintained Innocence

The Birmingham Age-Herald, October 23, 1903

"The negro, Felix Hall, alias Henry Jackson, was hanged at the jail yard yesterday morning. When the body of the negro had been suspended for fifteen minutes after the drop Hall groaned audibly several times, whereupon the body was again raised, placed on the trap door and the trigger sprung once more, the second drop breaking his neck.

Hall's case is well known in Birmingham and in fact throughout the state. He has claimed all the time that the State was hanging the wrong man and that his real name was Henry Jackson. Even on the scaffold yesterday he repeated the assertion that he was innocent. When he said this some one in the crowd said: "That's right, Henry. I can vouch for it." Deputy Sheriff Love who had charge of the hanging ordered the spectator to keep quiet.

Hall was convicted of the murder of Norwood Clarke, a young white man about three years ago. After his conviction there was some doubt as to his identity and a reprieve was granted by the governor to give the condemned man time to bring forward his proof. Judge Greene was put in charge of the investigation by the governor and after careful examination he is now convinced that Hall is the right man.

Letter to the Governor

Attorney Denegre still believes that the negro was innocent and that the wrong man was hanged. He addressed the following letter to the governor:

Hon. William D. Jelks, Montgomery, Ala.

Dear Sir--According to your instructions Henry Jackson was hanged here today.

Now that the soul of the unfortunate negro has gone to eternity I wish to let you know that your action in the matter surprises me very much to say the least. When a man presumes to hold an exalted position as you occupy, and it is appealed to on a question of life even though it be that of a negro, and the appeal is made by an attorney not paid for his services, it does seem that he would condescend to make an investigation of the case. I may be in error, but it is my humble judgement that the executive power of the state of Alabama is vested in the governor and not the trial judge. The trial judge is my friend and a man of honor, and I know he did what he considered right and just, but it strikes me his connection with the case should have ended when he signed the bill of exceptions.

This letter is from me to you as man to man. I am no longer writing as the attorney for Henry Jackson. If ever again it becomes necessary for me to appeal to the governor of Alabama to intervene in behalf of an unfortunate, friendless and penniless soul, I sincerely hope that the executive chair will be occupied by a man who will not relegate his exalted prerogative to a third party.

Very truly yours,
CHARLES DENEGRE"

ROBT. STONE GOES TO GALLOWS TODAY
Condemned Murderer Says He is Ready to Die
Spends a Restless Night
Jail Resounds With Songs of Other Prisoners
All During the Night
Execution Takes Place Between 10 and 12 O'Clock

The Birmingham Age-Herald, March 25, 1904

"Robert Stone, the negro convicted of shooting guard Thompson at Coalburg mines about two years ago, while attempting to escape, will be hanged this morning in the yard of the county jail. Stone was serving a life sentence for murder when he made his dash for liberty.

Stone passed a wakeful night and slept very little. The jail resounded all during the night with the voices of prisoners singing and praying for the condemned man. The authorities anticipate no trouble on the scaffold today, although it was reported that Stone was getting violent yesterday and had to be heavily manacled. The condemned negro says he is not afraid to meet his death and awaits his fate with stoicism. The warden promised Stone that he should have a nice breakfast this morning, but the prisoner said he did not want anything to eat. He has been provided with a nice suit of clothes and will be bathed and dressed for the scaffold this morning. The prisoner was visited by his sister and brother yesterday. They will probably witness the execution today. Several negro preachers will also be on hand to lead devotional exercises.

The prisoner says he will make a confession and last statement before the trap is sprung. He does not deny his guilt, but says that others are equally as guilty and should be punished. A number of convicts attempted to scale the stockade at Coalburg with Stone and a fusillade of shots were exchanged between the convicts and the guards, among them being Thompson, the man who was killed. It is expected that about a hundred people will be present at the hanging today. The case has attracted general attention in the state and was stubbornly fought. The body will be shipped to Montgomery for interment."

BOB STONE GOES TO DEATH BRAVELY
Did Not Make Expected Confession on the Gallows
His Last Message to the Public Was,
"Goodbye to Everybody. I Am Going to Zion
My Troubles Are Over."

The Birmingham Age-Herald, March 26, 1904

"Robert Stone, a negro twice found guilty of murdering W.H. Thomas, a guard at the Coalburg prison, was hanged yesterday morning at 11 o'clock in the Jefferson county jail yard by Sheriff Andrew Burgin. The execution was witnessed by about two hundred people. The expected statement relative to the shooting of the officer was not made by Stone on the gallows. His neck was broken by the fall, the physicians pronouncing life extinct sixteen minutes after the drop.

Although death was apparently without fear the negro seemed quite nervous on the gallows. Deputy Sheriff Love fixed the rope around the negro's neck and placed the black cap over his head. A minute later the lever was pulled and the body shot into eternity. This was the twenty-fourth execution at which Deputy Sheriff Love has officiated. At the time he killed Guard Thomas, Stone was serving a life term for killing a man in Montgomery county."

WARD AND GRAY TO HANG THIS MORNING
No Grounds For Executive Clemency,
the Governor Is Told

The Birmingham Age-Herald, October 30, 1914

"With the refusal of the governor to interfere, Bennie Ward and Wash Gray, negroes, convicted of robbery and sentenced to death, will be hanged in the yard of the county jail this morning at 10 o'clock. Sheriff McAdory stated that the hanging would be private, only the officials and ministers who have been visiting the condemned negroes being admitted. Both negroes have professed religion and state they are prepared to die. Bennie Ward confessed to his share in the crime several days ago, but Gray maintains his innocence.

The crime for which the negroes are to die was particularly brutal, and it was alleged that they were members of a gang of robbers who terrorized the small storekeepers on the outskirts of the city and committed many robberies and other crimes. The particular crime for which they were convicted was the shooting down in his store of a Hebrew merchant, leaving him for dead and robbing the place. Several other indictments for robbery and murder against the two negroes were retuned by the grand jury."

TWO NEGROES PAY DEATH PENALTY
Bennie Ward and Wash Gray Hanged for Robbery of Merchant

The Birmingham Age-Herald, Octobor 31, 1914

"You shore are killing an innocent nigger," was the statement made by Wash Gray as he stood on the scaffold yesterday morning just before Sheriff McAdory pulled the lever that sent the negro into eternity. Bennie Ward in a lengthy talk from the scaffold confessed his guilt and said he was willing to die for his crimes. He declared that Wash Gray had nothing to do with the crime for which he was to be hanged.

The double hanging took place in the yard of the Jefferson county jail and was witnessed by about 150 persons. A large crowd assembled on the outside of the jail. A few minutes before the hanging the death warrant was read to the men by Deputy Sheriff Fred McDuff. Bennie Ward went to the gallows first, and asking permission of the sheriff, made a 10-minute talk from the gallows. He was pronounced dead by attending physicians 15 minutes after the drop fell. Gray also made a talk and said a long prayer on the scaffold. He was dead in 17 minutes.

The negroes were hanged for the robbery of Andrew Pollock, a Syrian merchant, who was held up in his place of business and after being robbed was shot by his assailants and dangerously wounded. He recovered and identified the two negroes as his assailants.

The statements made by the negroes from the scaffold were in part as follows:

Bennie Ward: "Whisky caused me to be standing on the scaffold. I was not drunk, but I didn't know what I was doing. I did not intend to shoot him, but it was just the devil that caused the bullet to hit him. They convicted an innocent man to die with me. Wash Gray had nothing to do with that trouble. But maybe that was the way God intended for him to die. Wash is innocent. This is the truth and nothing else. Now I am dying for God and I am going to heaven. I want all you people to meet me in heaven. I am willing to die. My soul is willing, but the flesh don't want to. That's always the way--the soul is willing to do something but the flesh is afraid. I never tried dying, but I am going to try it this morning. I don't want to see Wash killed. He didn't do nothing. I didn't kill nobody, but I shot a man."

Wash Gray: "You all are killing an innocent man. I never saw Bennie Ward and I have told them that. They want to kill me and I have to die 'cause the law says so. I am going to heaven. I ain't got nothing in my heart against anybody. I am willing to die, but I just hate to die for something I ain't done. You shore are killing an innocent nigger. My soul is saved. They can't take that. They can take my life, but my soul is the sweetest thing I've got and it will go to heaven. Now, reverend, I'm ready, but I want to pray first."

Just before the trap fell, after the cap had been adjusted, with an airy wave of his hand to the assembled crowd, Gray said his last words: "Well, you all be good." The trap fell."

TWO NEGROES WILL BE HANGED TODAY IN THE YARD OF THE JAIL
Carter Asks For Chicken and Jones for Pork Sausage and Biscuits for Last Breakfast

The Birmingham Age-Herald, June 25, 1915

"Lon Carter and Syd Jones, negroes, will be hanged this morning in the yard of the Jefferson county jail between the hours of 10 and 11 o'clock. Sheriff Batson announces that everything is in readiness to carry out the extreme penalty of the law and both men have stated that they were ready to meet their doom. Yesterday they were baptized by Father Malone, junior assistant of the St. Paul's church, who has been requested by the negroes to administer to them the last spiritual rites.

Lon Carter will be the first to go to the gallows and will be taken to the place of execution about 10 o'clock. An hour afterwards Syd Jones will commence the march to the jail yard where he will take his last look at this world. Both men have shown little fear at their approaching end and it is thought will meet their death without quaking.

Lon Carter was convicted for the murder of his wife, Eliza Carter, at Newcastle. The details of the murder were particularly brutal, as beside other injuries he split her head open with an ax. Syd Jones was convicted for the murder of Will Watson, a fellow convict, by striking him with a miners' pick while at work in the convict mines at Banner. At the time he killed Watson he was serving a sentence of life imprisonment for murder."

NEGROES SUFFER EXTREME PENALTY WITHOUT A TREMOR
Lon Carter and Syd Jones Hanged in Jail Yard-- Latter Claims to Have Killed 13 Men

The Birmingham Age-Herald, June 26, 1915

"Without the slightest hitch on the part of the officials and without the least display of fear or emotion on their part, Lon Carter and Syd Jones, negroes, were executed yesterday in the yard of the jail of Jefferson county. Sheriff Thomas R. Batson took personal charge of the hangings and pulled the triggers that sent the two men to eternity.

Syd Jones died unrepentant, for in a letter addressed to James McAdory he confessed to having committed 13 murders and expressed regret that he had "missed getting Richard Moore," a negro stevedore he stabbed and almost killed in the county jail while awaiting his trial for the crime for which he was sent to the gallows. He claimed to have made peace with his Maker but his general demeanor denied it.

He seemed somewhat proud of the notoriety he had gained and requested that his picture be taken before he ascended the gallows. But little attention is given to his confession other than that part of it that is a matter of record, to-wit: The murder of Bessie Humphrey, a negro woman at Huntsville, a crime for which he was sentenced to life imprisonment in the penitentiary, Sam Watson, a fellow convict, whom he killed while serving his sentence, and the attack on the negro stevedore.

Both men slept well and ate a hearty breakfast, and in reply to questions by newspaper men stated they had nothing to say. The death warrants were read to the prisoners and Lon Carter was the first to be taken to the gallows. Without the slightest hesitation he mounted the steps that lead to the gallows, and in answer to the question as to whether he had anything to say replied, "I have said all I want to say." The noose was quickly adjusted and a moment later the drop fell. In 13 1/2 minutes the physicians pronounced him dead. It was stated by court attendants that this hanging was the quickest and smoothest on record.

Immediately after the body was cut down arrangements were quickly made for the execution of Jones. A new rope was affixed to the gallows. As the procession reached the jail yard the picture of the condemned negro was taken by Deputy Sheriff Jim McAdory, the negro striking a pose with his hat set jauntily on his head. He smiled as he mounted the gallows, and when asked by Sheriff Batson if he had anything to say, replied: "No, sir, except to thank the preacher and the sheriffs for their kindness. I have got no hard feelings against anybody and I hope there are no hard feelings against me." He stood on the trap without a tremor and, as in the case of Carter, the dread preparations were quickly made. At 10:47 the trap was sprung and at 11:01 he was pronounced dead. As no relatives claimed their bodies they were taken in charge by the county authorities and buried in the potter's field.

Father Malone accompanied each man to the gallows and mounted the steps with them. During the preparations he read the prayers of the church for the dying. There was the usual crowd of curiosity seekers, mostly negroes, who long before the hangings took place crowded the vicinity of the jail. Sheriff Batson limited the number of passes, yet a large crowd was present at both hangings. It was a matter of general comment that the execution of the two men was the promptest and smoothest of any that has occurred in late years.

The confession of Jones was addressed to Deputy Sheriff James McAdory with the understanding it was not to be given to the public until after his execution. In it he claims to have killed two white men, a Chinaman, an Indian, a Mexican and eight negroes, four of them convicts. The confession follows:

"Birmingham, June 25, 1915

"Sir-- This is to Mr. Jimmie McAdory:

"Sir-- This is a list of my record: While I was a convict I killed four convicts while being in prison. I will give the names of two, Cleave Waters, 1911, on the 22nd day of May, and another convict, 1907, and another one 1911. I do not care to expose their names, of course. I will for Will Watson be hung June 25. But that's all right. I do not care for that. God will forgive me for all that I have did in this world. But listen, look on the second page, you will see the names of many one. Tomie Thompson and Charles Bennitt and Deputy Sheriff W.S. Murphy of Crawfort, Neb.: Tom Shay, White, Sam Lee, Chinaman, Monterey, Cal., M&O brakeman, Boydwell, Ky.; Bessie Humphrey, Huntsville; Pattie Quirgo, Mexican, at Fort Wingate, N.M.; John Littlejohn, an Indian man at Sheridan, Yoma. Total amount only 13. That's all. I am sorry that I missed getting Richard Moore, September 12, 1912. Just one more would have made the even number. He is the only one that I have missed yet. Yours truly,

"SIDNEY JONES."

ELDERLY MAN AND YOUNG COMPANION SHOT AND KILLED AT HENRY ELLEN
Posse of Deputies and Enraged Citizens Make Search for Perpetrators of crime—
Boy Shot in the Back While Attempting to Escape—
No Clue to Identity of Murderers

The Birmingham Age-Herald, March 24, 1921

"No clue has been found to the identity of the persons who killed J.L. Bourgouise, 75, and Lacy Murphree, 15, who were found dead in the vicinity of Henry Ellen. Eight deputies, headed by Chief Deputy Fred McDuff, and a large number of enraged citizens of Leeds and Henry Ellen spent the entire day searching the densely wooded hills of Henry Ellen yesterday. Mr. Bourgouise and the boy were killed while returning from a fishing trip to the Cahaba river. The man was shot in the breast, the shot being fired at close range, while the boy, whose body was found about 15 feet away, was shot in the back and there were 107 buckshot in his body, according to George C. Moore, Assistant Coroner. Mr. Moore stated the boy had evidently witnessed the murder of the man and had attempted to make his escape by running, as he was shot in the back, and fell face down in a path they were traversing at the time of the double murder. When viewed the boy still held in his hand a small string of fish which he had caught during the day. A watch, ring, Masonic pin and some small change had been taken from Mr.Bourgouise, which leads the coroner to believe the motive of the crime was robbery. However, others in the neighborhood are of the opinion the man and boy ran into an illicit distillery on their homeward journey and was shot by the distillers to keep them from telling of the operation of the moonshine still."

CHAIN OF EVIDENCE LINKS CAPTURED NEGRO WITH THE DOUBLE MURDER NEAR LEEDS
Lynching Feared and Negro Brought to County Jail in Automobile-- Denies Guilt But Refuses to Make Statement

The Birmingham Age-Herald, March 27, 1921

"Ambrey Garrett, negro, alleged murderer of J.L. Bourgeouis, 75-year-old Confederate veteran, and Lacy Murphree, a 15-year-old boy, who were found shot to death in a strip of woods near Henry Ellen was lodged in the county jail last night. The negro was captured at Chattanooga yesterday. When placed behind bars last night, the negro was shaking with fear. All during the ride from Chattanooga, he kept begging the officers not to let the crowd lynch him when they got to Birmingham. When the negro was arrested, a Waltham watch and chain were found on his person. Several neighbors of the murdered man testified before the watch was opened that the dead man's initials were scratched on the back of it. The initials were found when the watch was opened. When confronted with the evidence, the negro, trembling with fear, would only deny he had anything to do with the killing, and asked officers to lock him in a cell so that he would not be lynched. Feeling ran high at Leeds and the surrounding country yesterday and last night. Officers here were afraid that the angered residents might attempt violence.

It was at first thought that the crime had been committed by moonshiners. This clue was dropped later by the officers when word was received that a Masonic ring belonging to the murdered Confederate veteran had been found in a railroad yard on the outskirts of Chattanooga."

NEGRO VOLUNTARILY CONFESSES KILLING BOURGOUIS AND BOY
Solicitor Hears Negro Tell Story—
Says It Adds Little to Evidence Collected By Deputies—
Will Be Tried Week of April 25, Had Police Record

The Birmingham Age-Herald, March 31, 1921

"John Whiteside, alias Ambry Garrett, negro, made a complete confession of the murder of Bourgouis and Murphree yesterday. According to Solicitor Tate, the statement of the man was clear and clean cut as he had ever heard, and tallied exactly with the evidence worked up against him. Whiteside said he was lying in the bushes in the woods through which the aged man and young boy passed and when he saw them he was afraid they would report his whereabouts to officers, so he fired at the old man, killing him instantly. When the boy started to run he then fired on him. He then escaped from the woods and later sold the gun to a farmer in the vicinity for $2 and received a $2 bill for it. This the negro claims to be the cause of his capture, declaring he always did know a two-dollar bill was bad luck.

While the negro did not give any other reason for the double murder, officers are of the opinion his motive was robbery, as he needed money to get away. Following the shooting, several attempts were made by Whiteside to dispose of the ring. This is the clue which led the officers on the trail of the negro and resulted in his being nearly surrounded in the vicinity of Springville from which he escaped by catching a freight train for Chattanooga. Deputy Taylor also boarded a train and kept behind the negro. He found the masonic ring just after he had gotten off the train near a water tank where the negro dropped it. Within a few hours after the arrival of Whiteside, he was apprehended by officers."

TWO PAY PENALTY ON THE GALLOWS, ROBBERY-MURDER
Whiteside and Morton, Negroes, Are Hanged Here Yesterday-- Unusual Crowd Gathers

The Birmingham Age-Herald, August 27, 1921

"One of the largest crowds remembered for such an occasion gathered around the Jefferson county jail yesterday morning to witness the execution of Will Morton and John Whiteside, negroes, who were hanged in the jail yard. The former for highway robbery and the latter for murder. Morton was the first to pay the penalty, the trap being sprung on him at 11:13 o'clock and he was cut down 13 minutes later. The trap on Whiteside was sprung at 12:12, and he was pronounced dead by physicians at 12:24. Rev. James Pearson and other negro ministers accompanied the condemned men to the gallows, where prayers and the singing of hymns preceded the executions.

Long before the time the first hanging was scheduled to take place large crowds gathered and by the time they were admitted to the jail yard they had blocked every entrance to the jail. A number of women witnessed the hangings from the identification room, where seats had been reserved for them. Every available deputy was placed on duty and in addition a number of city detectives were placed in service to handle the crowds which jostled and pushed each other almost to a point of suffocation. The board of pardons denied commutation of sentence several days ago.

Attorneys who defended both condemned negroes were present, as was J.L. Cannon, the dairyman who Morton held up and robbed, as well as a number of people from Leeds, including relatives of J.L. Bourgouis and Lacey Murphree, whom Whiteside confessed to having killed. Morton robbed Mr. Cannon on the Green Springs road last year, when the crime wave was at its height in this district."

Postscript

Some law enforcement officers opposed capital punishment in general for moral and religious reasons. This was particularly the case for those who might be directly responsible for carrying out the executions. In several instances public
commentary, as well as attempted direct action by certain

officials, usually associated with the sheriff's office, were not unknown. In the end, however, when such protests and political activities failed, these agents carried out their duties as required by law.

SHERIFF FINANCES EFFORT TO SAVE ALLEN GERMANY
Last-Minute Plea In Behalf Of Negro Slayer Proves To Be In Vain

The Birmingham Age-Herald, March 6, 1925

The last ray of hope for Allen Germany, negro, went glimmering late Thursday afternoon, following one of the first cases on record where clemency for a condemned negro was sought of a states' chief executive by a sheriff and his staff. Sheriff T.J. Shirley and his deputies raised funds to send Jim Pearson, negro welfare worker, to Montgomery to intercede in behalf of Germany, who is to hang at noon today. Although armed with a strong letter of recommendation from Sheriff Shirley, Pearson's entreaties on behalf of Germany will be in vain, for Governor Brandon, over the telephone late Thursday afternoon told Solicitor Jim Davis that his mind "is made up" and that he would under no circumstances interfere with the execution.

Germany told an Age-Herald reporter who visited him in his cell that he did not fear the morrow, being confident that he would never be executed. Germany was sentenced to death for beheading his wife with a razor several months ago. "I killed her in self-defense. If I hadn't killed her, she would have killed me, but the state's witnesses swore to lies against me and I had no lawyer to protect my interest." Germany was represented at the trial by Roger Bite, appointed by the court.

Explaining his attitude towards Germany, Sheriff Shirley declared he had no special interest in the man, but believed the governor might well grant leniency and commute the negro's sentence to life imprisonment in view of the fact that he confessed to the crime; that he had been a model prisoner; that he was a negro of unusual intellect and apparently had killed his wife, a woman of questionable character, while in a fit of jealous rage.

Preparations for the hanging were completed at the jail Thursday afternoon. Germany will mount the scaffold about noon, after the usual religious routine has been completed, and will be allowed to issue a final statement. Chief Deputy Henry Hill will adjust the black cap and tie Germany's knees and ankles and the trap will be sprung by Sheriff Shirley. Except for courthouse officials, physicians and newspapermen, the hanging will be private. A new hemp rope was hung for a week in the jail yard with a weight attached. Germany has made his own preparations for the end, even in the face of his confident prediction that he never would be hanged."

NEGRO SLAYER PAYS PENALTY UPON GALLOWS
Allen Germany Is Unafraid
In Final Moments Before Death
The Birmingham Age-Herald, March 7, 1925

"Allen Germany, negro wife murderer, dropped to his death shortly before noon Friday, the fifty-seventh victim of the grim steel gallows in the Jefferson county jail, in the shadow of which he had lived for more than a year. Germany lived only eleven minutes after falling through the trap, less time than any of the fifty-six who preceded him. The execution, scheduled for noon, was moved up in an effort to avoid the usual crowds. Several thousand curious persons gained admission to the jail yard, however, and many more were turned away. Many of those remained outside to catch a view of the negro's body as it was removed.

Germany declared he was unafraid to die. Two letters were delivered to Chief Deputy Hill. One of these, to his sister, Josephine Germany, bitterly denounced her for alleged conspiracy against him and declared she had "accomplished her purpose." Germany was removed to the death cell. He walked unsupported and composedly through the long corridor, and unassisted, mounted the scaffold. Germany was asked if he wished to speak. "I do not fear death. I do not believe that I should die on the gallows. I do not believe that any man should. God never intended that man should die that way. I offered to serve out my life in any way that I was fitted, be the years many or few, to make up for my crime, but they would not have it. I could do much with another chance, but I haven't it."

"Just don't choke me to death," Germany responded when asked "is that too tight," by Hill, when he placed the noose close up under the negro's ears. "Are you ready, I am," Germany said, and with the signal Sheriff Shirley sprung the trap which ended Germany's earthly career. Approximately $70, collected from among the spectators by members of Germany's church, will be used to defray the funeral expenses. Jim Pearson who led the collection, promised any surplus would be used to help apprehend negro criminals."

That individuals could face the ultimate penalty for committing crimes other than murder is reflected by the fact that the last person legally executed by hanging in Jefferson County was put to death for the crime of robbery.

Docket Entry:
Date: September 24, 1926
Deceased: Frank Owens, Col.
Address: Welch's Funeral Home
Cause Of Death: By a broken neck, legal hanging

NEGRO HANGED IN COUNTY JAIL FOR HIGHWAY ROBBERY

The Birmingham News, September 26, 1926

"Frank Owens, negro, arrived at the foot of the gallows on the stroke of 11 Friday morning. The trap was sprung by Sheriff T.J. Shirley at 11:12 and he was pronounced dead by attending physicians 14 minutes later. He had paid the extreme penalty demanded by the state for robbery. The body was placed in a pine casket and probably will be turned over to the family following formal release by Coroner J.D. Russum. Owens was hanged for slugging and robbing Richard Warner and L.M. Watkins in the spring of 1924. He had struck them in the head with an ax, or some other instrument, according to the charge. This had followed on the heels of a series of ax murders in Birmingham and the vicinity.

At the close of the farewell service, Owens went about shaking hands with everyone in the cell. Among those clasping his hand was Solicitor Jim Davis, who had fought with such determination for death. Several deputies present were crying. Prior to this he was questioned by a representative of the News. "I sure don't think I'm getting a square deal," he said. "Frank, you don't have to answer this unless you like, but are you guilty or not?" No, I ain't," he responded. "But, even if I was, I don't think I ought to be hung for robbery."

HAD COUNTY WRITTEN FINIS TO 2,000 YEAR OLD CUSTOM OF HANGING?

Precedent Set By Caesar Is About To Be Discarded

The Birmingham News, September 26, 1926

"When Frank Owens, Negro, dropped to his death on the gallows in the county jail yard Friday for assaulting and robbing two white men in 1924, the practice of hanging condemned men—a custom that has survived for more than 2,000 years--was legally ended as far as Jefferson County is concerned. The act which provides for the establishment of an electric chair at Kilby prison in Montgomery becomes effective and those convicted of capital offenses will be electrocuted. The electrocution law provides that all persons condemned in Alabama be executed in Kilby prison. It appears certain that Owens' death was the last official execution to be held in Jefferson County as there are no other condemned men in the local jail.

Every official execution in Jefferson County has been carried out on Friday and in many instances on Friday the 13th. The law does not specify Friday as the official hanging day, but for a number of years virtually all criminals in every state have been executed on that day. Friday is commonly known as "Hangman's Day" largely because of this fact and because of the superstition over the ill luck which has been attached to Fridays for centuries.

Figures and records of the men who have been condemned and executed in Jefferson County are incomplete but the total number here is estimated at from 50 to 75. Walter Jones, a member of the notorious Lewisburg gang convicted in 1912 was the last white man to be hanged in Jefferson County. This execution occurred April 4, 1913. Jones paid the extreme penalty for slaying a Negro, Jim Holland, and is said to be the only case of its kind on record here."

NEGRO WOMAN DIES FOR DEATH IN CAFE
Silena Gilmore Electrocuted For Slaying In Birmingham
The Birmingham Age-Herald, January 24, 1930

"Silena Gilmore, a negro, the first woman to be put to death in the electric chair in Alabama, was electrocuted at Kilby Prison, state penitentiary for the murder of Horace Johnson, Birmingham cafe operator, at 12:05 a.m. and the woman was pronounced dead by the prison physician at 12:14 a.m.

Two shocks were necessary before the woman was pronounced dead. She walked unsupported the few paces from the death cell to the chamber in which the chair was located. The woman blamed liquor for her predicament, and warned those present that the same fate would befall them if they did not leave it alone. The entire proceedings required less than ten minutes."

Postscript

The relatively small group of people, mainly police officers and coroners, who have the job of investigating homicides and who observe the horrific results of man's inhumanity to men, as well as to women and children, are different. They are not the same as those individuals who don't actually get to see, first hand and up close, the obscene results of physical violence in all its permutations. Reading "true crime" books or watching television programs or movies, even those that present graphic depictions of violence, do not provide the same impact. Nor does the unforgettable experience of having to personally notify a victim's survivors. As a result of their continued exposure to all forms of mayhem, these investigators often develop more than just a "hard shell" for their mental self-preservation, but also a harsh sense of justice in regard to the fates of offenders, the epitome of which was evidenced by this letter to the editor of a Birmingham newspaper in the late 1980s:

Increase the voltage?

"For years I have heard and read so many different opinions on the electric chair and the cruel and unjust punishment it causes. As a retired law enforcement officer I would like to voice my own opinion. I joined the Birmingham Police Department in 1946 and retired from the Jefferson County Sheriff's Department in 1985. Many times during those years it was my duty and displeasure to view the broken, crumpled, slashed and shot bodies of murdered men, women and children. Some very gruesome sights.

On June 10, 1950, it was my pleasure to go to Kilby prison and witness the electrocution of three men, one white and two black. It took approximately one hour to complete the executions. I watched their bodies jerk and quiver for a few seconds and their eyeballs burst like light bulbs, but never at any time did I see one Nth the amount of cruel and unjust punishment inflicted on their bodies as was inflicted on the bodies of their victims. I understand in 1950 they were using 2,200 instead of 1,900 volts on the chair. Maybe, if they went back to 2,200 volts it would shorten the so-called cruel and unjust punishment these cold-blooded, merciless killers are exposed to.

Woodie Gamel
5516 Court P"

CHAPTER 11

HONOR

"Led to reexamine white Southerner's own often-repeated explanation of why they killed each other with such frequency and regularity, they, of course, said they did it for honor's sake."[1]

In his book "Vengeance and Justice--Crime and Punishment in the 19th Century American South," Edward L. Ayers provides information which attempts to explain the psychology of violence peculiar to the South. He noted that:

> *"Even after the South's fall in the civil war, one thing remained constant. Self-respect, as the Southerners understand it has always demanded much fighting," a Connecticut native serving in the Freedmen's Bureau explained to fellow Northerners.*
>
> *"A pugnacity which is not merely war paint, but is, so to speak, tattooed into the character, has resulted from this high sentiment of personal value. The meekest man by nature, the man who at the North would not more fight than he would jump out of a second story window, may at the South resent an insult by a blow, or perhaps a stab or pistol shot."*
>
> *"Nor was the pervasive violence confined to the turbulent years of Reconstruction. Even in the 1890s, the bloodshed was still a sign of Southern distinctiveness. The context of Southern violence changed in dramatic ways, but the evidence suggests strong continuities in the archetypal violence of the nineteenth century South: fistfights, shooting affrays, and duels between individual men."*[2]

Ayers also noted that:

> *"Several historians, recognizing the key role of culture in violent behavior, isolate various fatal flaws within Southern culture: a brooding and pervasive sense of grievance and*

> displaced frustration, an undue affection for guns, and a pessimistic evaluation of human nature that automatically assumed violence to be the inevitable--if unfortunate-- recourse in the face of intractable problems. There, according to Charles Sydnor, in the antebellum South "It was considered as brutal and uncivilized to call a man a liar as it was to bruise or cut his body."

> "Honor did not reside only within the South's planter class. All knew that the failure to respond to insult marked them as less than real men, branded them, in the most telling epithets of the time, as "cowards" and "liars." A coward tolerated insult, a liar attacked honor unfairly. To call a Southern man either one was to invite attack. Any man living in the South had trouble if he chose not to respect honor's dictates; he might find it difficult to convince other men his stance was not mere cowardice. To men of all classes, public opinion dictated that they not tolerate affront. Aggression flourished where gambling and drinking flourished. One could hardly fail to be impressed with the prevalence of whiskey-drinking and The frequency of fighting with deadly weapons."[3]

It appears that a number of violent confrontations and deaths during the early years of the 20th century in the Magic City involved members of the legal profession.

LEATHERWOOD MAY NOT RECOVER FROM WOUNDS

The Birmingham Age-Herald, July 17, 1904

"R.L. Leatherwood, the attorney who was struck on the head with a piece of gas pipe by William A. Denson, also an attorney, Tuesday afternoon at the First National bank corner, is lying at the Hillman hospital in a very critical condition, and there are serious doubts as to his recovery. At 2 o'clock this morning it was stated that he was vey low, but resting about as well as could be expected, and that his condition was practically unchanged from what it had been since early yesterday morning.

The blow fractured the skull, and an operation had to be performed by Dr. B.G. Copeland. He removed a portion of the skull behind the left ear and relieved the pressure of the clotted blood, which had accumulated under the skull. While there was a fracture, the bone was not indented and it did not tear on the brain, but the concussion has caused a rupture of some small blood vessels which had coagulated. When the blood was removed the wound was bandaged up again, and the patient has been in a semi-conscious condition ever since. Death may result from the concussion or fever may set in which will have a fatal result.

When Leatherwood was first carried to the hospital and in fact for some time after he arrived there it was not thought that the wound was serious, as there was no distinct evidence of a fracture. But several hours later the serious condition became apparent.

No new facts in regard to the trouble came to light yesterday with the exception that Attorney Denson explained how he happened to have a piece of pipe in his hand. He stated that he was carrying it home to do some repairing about the house and not with the intention of hitting Mr. Leatherwood."

Fame, Misfortune, Justice And Vengeance

Locally, there were no greater factual representations of Ayers' theories regarding violence and honor in the South than those associated with members of the prominent Shugart family.

ANDY BONDHOLZER MORTALLY SHOT BY R.T. SHUGART IN METROPOLITAN BAR
Bartender Says Young Lawyer Threatened to Shoot First Man He Saw
NO WORDS WHATEVER HAD PASSED BETWEEN THE MEN
Friend of Bondholzer, Who Was With Him, Says They Knew Nothing of Shugart's Presence Till the Shot Was Fired.

The Birmingham Age-Herald, January 21, 1904

"Andy Bondholzer, foreman of the Birmingham Machine and Foundry company, was shot and probably fatally wounded last night about 9:45 o'clock by Roland T. Shugart, a young lawyer, in the vestibule of the Metropolitan bar at the corner of Morris avenue and Twentieth street. The wounded man was carried to the Hillman hospital, where an operation was performed to remove the bullet, which lodged in his back. Shugart was arrested and carried to the county jail on a warrant sworn out before Judge Abernathy of the inferior court. The warrant charges assault with intent to murder. Shugart refuses to make any statement whatever.

Probably the clearest account of the shooting is that of J.M. McPherson, bartender in the saloon. He says: "Shugart came into the bar and ordered a drink of whiskey. I poured out some ginger ale to go with it and set it on the counter. Shugart placed his arms on the bar, laid his head down on them and said 'I am going to kill the first --- --- --- that comes into that door.' With that he turned around, pulled his pistol and walked a couple of feet. He saw these two men standing over by the cigar case on the south side of the place and fired two shots. One of them struck Bondholzer. Shugart stumbled backwards and struck a case of whiskey which the negro porter was unpacking in the middle of the floor. He stumbled and then some young man ran in to him. The young man kept slapping at the revolver to keep it away from him and they had a tussle of a few seconds. Shugart then ran out of the side door on Morris avenue. Just as he reached the back door he fired a third shot, which struck over the top of the fixtures."

Arthur Gladhill, a friend of the wounded man, was standing talking with him in the cigar part of the saloon. He made a statement as follows: "Bondholzer had been at my house and we walked down the street together. We went into the bar and got a drink, and then then went into the vestibule where the cigar stand is. The first I knew was when the shot was fired. I turned around and the second shot was fired. I saw Bondholzer fall and I caught him in my arms and laid him on the floor. The man who did the shooting ran out of the back door. As far as I know neither of us had seen Shugart last night and we did not know him. We did not say a word to him and there was no trouble. I have known Bondholzer for a long time and cannot imagine him getting into trouble. He was very quiet and never had any difficulty with any one."

Mr. Levy, proprietor of the saloon, was standing behind the cigar stand on the opposite side of the store from Gladhill and Bondholzer. He had his back turned when the first shot was fired, but saw the second. He said: "The first intimation that there was any trouble was when the first shot was fired. I turned and saw the second one fired. It was toward the ground, and the bullet entered the showcase just in front of where I was standing. I did not hear anything said, and do not know any reason for the shooting." L.C. Contell, a railroad man, had the scuffle with Shugart, and the pistol struck him on the head.

He says he was attempting to keep from being shot when Shugart fell over the case of whiskey.

It is said that Shugart and two other men were walking down Twentieth street together, and that one of them pushed Shugart against a pile of small buckets containing oyster shells which were on the sidewalk. He stumbled and fell on the ground, and got up very angry. It was impossible last night to find these two men who are said to have been with him. After he got up it is said he walked to the saloon and went in and ordered the drink. Roland Shugart is 23 years old and a member of the law firm of Shugart, Bell & Shugart. He is married and lives on Eleventh avenue between Twenty-second and Twenty-third streets, north. He is well known in the city. He did not make any statement at all after he was arrested. Bondholzer lives in East Birmingham. He is a brother-in-law of Alderman John C. Forney. He is unmarried and has no relatives in the city except his sister. Dr. Cunningham Wilson performed the operation at the hospital, but was unable to find the bullet. It was stated at the hospital that Bondholzer could not possible live, although he might linger a day or two."

SHOOTING HAS NOT YET PROVED FATAL
Andy Bondholzer Still Lingers Between Life and Death
SHOT BY ROLAND SHUGART
John T. Shugart, Father of the Man in Jail, Makes a Statement Regarding the Trouble Previous to the Shooting.

The Birmingham Age-Herald, January 22, 1904

"There were practically no new developments yesterday in the facts concerning the shooting of Andy Banholzer by Roland Shugart in the vestibule of the Metropolitan bar. At the Hillman hospital this morning it was stated that Banholzer was resting easily, and that his pulse was slightly stronger. The physicians are still unable to tell whether he will live or die. His condition is still very serious. Attorney John T. Shugart, father of Roland, has given his opinion that Banholzer was an innocent bystander, and that his son shot him by mistake for another man. In speaking of the shooting John T. Shugart said: "I have found out from more than one witness that my son had been attacked on Twentieth street by three rowdy railroad men who were after his money, and that one of them knocked him down with a pair of brass knucks and stamped him in the face. My son was unable to see well and his glasses were knocked from his nose and broken, when the rowdy struck him with the brass knucks. The glasses have been found and identified as those of my son. He walked across the street after he was knocked down and went to this bar to get a drink, and these men followed him. He was unable to see well, and I believe that he mistook Banholzer and Arthur Gladhill for the two men who had attacked him across the street. He shot Banholzer thinking that he was the other man. I have the names of the three men who attacked my son across the street from the bar, but I would rather not give them out, as they might escape, and I want them arrested. These men had seen my son cash a check and knew that he had a roll of bills in his pocket. They were after his money and after he got into the bar room he naturally thought that the two men standing in the vestibule were the two who had knocked him down and followed him. I am not sure yet who will defend my son, although I suppose there will be Mr. Bell and myself as well as M.M. Ullman. Fifty attorneys have been to my office today and offered their services, but I have declined them all."

Policeman Brizendine was on Morris avenue and started after Shugart, ordering him to halt. He refused to do so and the policeman fired his pistol to make him stop. He was finally caught on First avenue and Nineteenth street, where his revolver was taken from his hand."

EVIL OF CARRYING CONCEALED WEAPONS IS FULLY DISCUSSED
Representative Citizens Express Their Views on Lawlessness
PUBLIC SENTIMENT AROUSED
Various Remedies Suggested and a Higher Moral Tone Demanded.
City's Reputation Affected By Homicides

The Birmingham Age-Herald, January 23, 1904

"The unfortunate affair of last Wednesday night when Andrew Bonholzer was shot and seriously wounded by Roland T. Shugart, has again aroused the Birmingham public on the question of carrying concealed weapons. In fact, the law-abiding citizens have become so alarmed over the situation that they are practically unanimous in the opinion that something must be done to stop the practice or the reputation of Birmingham will be seriously impaired, both at home and abroad. They feel that either the practice must be abolished or regulated and that the law should be stringently enforced.

While neither criticizing, defending or condemning Mr. Shugart, until he has been given a fair trial by a jury, the public feels that if he had not carried a pistol Bonholzer would not have been shot and that Shugart would not be in the county jail. The Shugart-Bonholzer affair is not the only shooting that could have been averted had not one or both of the participants been armed. In fact, citizens have been taking an active interest in the matter of carrying concealed weapons and insist that this practice of people going armed is directly responsible for more than 90 per cent of the tragedies which have shocked the people of Birmingham and placed us in a bad light before the outside world.

A traveling man from Dallas, Texas, who is spending a few days in Birmingham, says he heard a very significant remark made concerning Birmingham in front of a hotel in Dallas two weeks ago. A well dressed man overhearing a conversation in which the traveling man said he formerly lived in Birmingham came nearer and said in an ugly tone, "I would not live in that God-forsaken city," and with an oath continued: "A man can't go into that town without getting shot or arrested before he goes two blocks." The traveling man said this is a fair sample of what people think of Birmingham, even in the far west. He says that there is not a town in the entire state of Texas where a man's life is in more danger than in Birmingham. He attributes the trouble to the carrying of concealed weapons and says such an extensive violation of the law in Texas would be considered barbarous. Out there, he says, it is against the law to carry a pistol concealed or unconcealed and that the law is pretty well enforced.

The question naturally arises as to the best method of stopping the pistol toting habit and on this subject citizens have offered a variety of plans. Thoughtful men say that no law can be enforced so long as the public sentiment is against it. Public sentiment is evidently in favor of carrying concealed weapons, so it is claimed, or such a large number of persons would not carry them. Law abiding citizens feel that if the lawless element carry weapons they are of necessity compelled to carry them in self defense.

Others suggest that as long as the practice cannot be abolished it should be regulated. It is proposed to have a law passed allowing citizens to carry pistols who will take out a license and register their names in the office of one of the courts. Several leading men have expressed themselves as favoring a more stringent law, some going so far as to insist that carrying concealed weapons should be penitentiary offense and should not be punishable by fine except in addition to imprisonment.

BONHOLZER SEEMED TO BE BETTER LAST NIGHT
The Birmingham Age-Herald, January 23, 1904

"Andrew Bonholzer, who was shot and badly wounded Tuesday night by Roland T. Shugart in the Metropolitan bar at the coroner of Twentieth street and Morris avenue, was reported this morning as being slightly improved and his pulse became stronger. No date has been set for the trial of Shugart, who is in the county jail, on a charge of assault with intent to murder."

PISTOL CARRYING STILL THE ABSORBING TOPIC
The Age-Herald's Course in Seeking to Quicken Public Sentiment is Endorsed--
Concealed Weapons is a Badge of Cowardice.
The Birmingham Age-Herald, January 24, 1904

"The habit of carrying concealed weapons, which prevails here to a large extent, continues to be the absorbing topic of conversation among the public officials, both city and county, and citizens generally. Many views have been expressed recently as to the best remedy for correcting the existing evil. Several citizens and men engaged in business in Birmingham express the view that the reckless carrying of concealed weapons by irresponsible persons has a tendency to injure the town. A traveling passenger agent of a railroad said last night that it is true people in different sections of the state really fear a Birmingham man unless they know him well."

ANDY BANHOLZER DIES FROM THE EFFECTS OF SHUGART'S BULLET
SHUGART SLEPT AND DID NOT KNOW OF DEATH
The Birmingham Age-Herald, February 1, 1904

"Andy Banholzer died yesterday afternoon at Hillman hospital from the effects of the bullet wound received at the hands of Roland T. Shugart. Banholzer's death was very unexpected. Shugart has not yet been informed of the death of Banholzer. He is in the county jail and he expected to be able to make bond today had the condition of the dead man been as good as it was Friday. The jail authorities said they did not notify him of the death of Banholzer because they did not wish to break his night's sleep. The charges against Shugart will be changed this morning. Shugart is the son of John T. Shugart, one of the most prominent attorneys in the city. Shugart is in the law firm with his father. For several days it was thought that Banholzer would live, but serious complications set in and Dr. Wilson feared that he would not recover. Yesterday morning it was seen that he had no chance to live."

BANHOLZER'S DEATH SURPRISED SHUGART
Man in Jail Had No Intimation Until Monday
BANHOLZER LAID TO REST
The Birmingham Age-Herald, February 2, 1904

"The first intimation that Roland T. Shugart had of the death of Andy Banholzer was when he read it yesterday morning in the Age-Herald. A few minutes afterwards a warrant charging him with murder was served on him by Deputy Sheriff John Burgin. Shugart was very much surprised, as the reports of Banholzer's condition had been favorable, and the prisoner expected to make bond this week. Shugart expressed deep regret that Banholzer was dead, and that he had shot him. He said: "Had it not been for my wife and my family I would rather it should have been me that died in Banholzer's place."

The legal activities associated with both the preliminary hearing and the actual trial of Roland Shugart provided for much excitement and interest, both in Birmingham as well as in Montgomery, the political center of the state. The names of a number of prominent attorneys involved with both the defense and prosecution of this case are still recognized today. The Heflin brothers, Hugh Morrow, Sr., and Roderick Beddow, Sr., were just a few of the attorneys involved in this matter as relatively young adults and whose sons would rise to prominence in political and legal circles in their own generation.

WITNESSES TESTIFY SHUGART WAS ASSAULTED ON 20TH ST.
The Birmingham Age-Herald, February 11, 1904

"Witnesses for the defense testified that Shugart had a difficulty with two men on Twentieth street between Morris avenue previous to the shooting of Banholzer; that he was knocked down by the two men and that they followed him into the bar room, one being armed with a pistol, and the other with a large knife and that after the three reached the interior of the bar room, the difficulty renewed. One witness declared that one of the two men who followed Shugart into the bar room fired the first two shots. This testimony contradicts the testimony offered by the state. The state sought to prove by by its witnesses that the only shooting done in the bar room was by Shugart."

JUDGE GREENE ALLOWS SHUGART $10,000 BAIL
The Birmingham Age-Herald, March 3, 1904

"After forty-two days' confinement in the Jefferson county jail, Roland T. Shugart, the young attorney, was released on a $10,000 bond. He went immediately to his home on Eleventh avenue between Twenty-second and Twenty-third streets, North. Immediately after court adjourned, probably fifty friends, among whom were lawyers, business men and others, rushed to the defendant and grabbed his hand. His face was flushed somewhat and he only replied "Thank you," "thank you," to the congratulations bestowed upon him.

WILLIS BREWER CHARGES H.P. HEFLIN AND J. THOMAS HEFLIN WITH PERJURY
Mr. Heflin Say Warrants Are Sworn Out Purely For Political Effect
RESULT OF INCIDENT IN THE SHUGART TRIAL
The Birmingham Age-Herald, March 31, 1904

"Warrants were sworn out against Secretary of State Thomas Heflin charging him with perjury and subornation of perjury, and against County Solicitor H.P. Heflin charging subornation of perjury. The warrants grew out of the old trouble between Solicitor Heflin and Willis Brewer as a result of the trial of Roland Shugart on a charge of shooting and killing A.J. Banholzer. It will be remembered that at the preliminary hearing, Brewer called Solicitor Heflin a "liar." The lie was given because Solicitor Heflin stated in his speech that he did not believe that Brewer was in Birmingham the night of the killing.

At the trial Brewer testified that he and George Howell, the other defendant in the perjury case, were standing near the entrance of the Metropolitan hotel on the night of the shooting, and that he saw Roland Shugart go into the Metropolitan bar, and that he was immediately followed by two men, one of whom had a long pistol and the other a knife. After several witnesses had sworn that Brewer was in Montgomery on the night of the shooting warrants were sworn out against him as a result of his testimony, charing him with perjury. The state announced not ready and Solicitor Heflin asked that the case be continued. Heflin stated that he was wholly unprepared to go into the trial on account of the absence of witnesses and further stated that he would not nol pross the cases or dismiss them. Judge Benners then dismissed the cases and Solicitor Heflin stated that he would take the matter up before the grand jury when it meets.

Last night Brewer stated hat he intended showing that Secretary of State Heflin was at the theatre in Montgomery at the time that he swore on the stand that he was in Fleming's restaurant. The testimony of the secretary of state was corroborated by Capt. E.W. Booker and Judge Tarver of Montgomery. It wlll be remembered that Secretary of State Heflin swore on the stand that he saw Brewer in Fleming's restaurant in Montgomery between 8 and 9 o'clock on the night of January 20, which was the night that Banholzer was shot in Birmingham. George Taylor is the negro waiter in Fleming's restaurant who testified that he saw Brewer in the restaurant on the night of the shooting in Birmingham. Solicitor Heflin said that he had not been arrested on the warrant, and that he thought the charges were made against him and his brother for political effect purely. "Of course the charges are absurd and ridiculous," said Mr. Heflin, "and I am still of the opinion that Brewer is guilty of perjury and I will bring him to justice as speedily as the law will permit."

The trial of Roland Shugart was an extended version of his preliminary hearing and included much of the same evidence introduced then and at his habeas corpus bond hearing Detailed trial testimony was included in daily editions of The Birmingham Age-Herald and The Birmingham News. There were, however, new surprises regarding some evidence.

BANHOLZER'S BODY WAS DISINTERRED
Bullet Which Caused Death was Found and Extracted
TO BE USED IN EVIDENCE
The Birmingham Age-Herald, June 26, 1904

"The body of A.J. Banholzer, who died from the effects of a bullet wound from the pistol of of Roland T. Shugart, the young attorney, it is alleged, was disinterred from its resting place in Oak Hill cemetery at an early hour yesterday morning under instruction from Solicitor Harrington P. Heflin. After the body was exhumed an autopsy was held by reputable physicians of Birmingham, and a leaden missle was removed. The bullet will be introduced in evidence by the state in the trial of Shugart."

During the trial, witnesses were placed on the stand by the defense to attest to the good character and general peacefulness of the defendant. Included were numerous prominent politicians, judges, attorneys, physicians and businessmen."

DEFENDANT WILL TAKE THE STAND
Jury Eats Blackberries
The Birmingham Age-Herald, June 27, 1904

"Roland T. Shugart, the young attorney who is charged with taking the life of Andrew J. Banholzer, by shooting him in the Metropolitan hotel barroom, will go on the witness stand and testify in his own behalf. The overcoat which the defendant wore on the night of the shooting will also be introduced into evidence by the defense. There has been considerable conflicting testimony with reference to the coat by the witnesses for the state. One declared that the overcoat worn by Mr. Shugart was a short tan coat, while another said it was of a dark material. There has also been some conflicting testimony on the part of the state's witnesses with reference to the moustache worn by the defendant at the time of the shooting. Some witnesses have declared that he wore a long dark moustache at the time, while others say that it was rather short and light."

EVIDENCE IN AND ARGUMENT BEGINS
DEFENDANT ON THE STAND
Said He Was Drunk on the Night of the Shooting of Banholzer and Had No Recollection of What Happened
The Birmingham Age-Herald, June 28, 1904

"The trial of Roland T. Shugart is rapidly reaching its end. Under a ruling of the court only three arguments are to be made by each side, twelve hours time being allotted for the speech making, six hours to the side. The defendant was placed on the stand yesterday and testified in his own behalf. He swore that he had no recollection of what happened on the night of the shooting; that he was drinking heavily at that time. He testified clearly and deliberately. The wife, little daughter and mother of the defendant occupied seats in the court room. On cross-examination Shugart stated: "I am the defendant in this case. Was born and reared in Jefferson county. I am an attorney and have been for about two years. I remember January 20. I got drunk on that afternoon. I left my office on the afternoon of the shooting. First stopped at the Peerless barroom and took a drink. Then went to the Florence barroom and played pool for about an hour. Took several drinks in there, not less than four. Recall having seen the Abbott boys that night at the Stag saloon. Afterwards I went to the Florence barroom again."

At the afternoon session the grewsome story of the exhumation of the body of Banholzer was told. Dr. Cunningham Wilson and Dr. Dowman told of the autopsy held over the corpse and the extraction of the bullet. The bullet was introduced in evidence. It was of a .32 calibro, apparently.

JOHN T. SHUGART PUT UNDER BOND
Charged With Attempt to Bribe a Juror
WAS ARRESTED YESTERDAY
Father of Defendant Roland T. Shugart Arrested at Instance of Solicitor Heflin—- Out on $500 Bond.

The Birmingham Age-Herald, June 29, 1904

"John T. Shugart...was arrested on a warrant charging him with attempting to bribe W.S. Armstrong. Armstrong was summoned to appear in the criminal court to act as a juror when the Shugart jury was selected to try the case. Attorney Shugart was arrested on a warrant sworn out at the instance of Solicitor Harrington P. Heflin. The warrant was served on Mr. Shugart by Sheriff Andrew Burgin during the progress of the trial. Everything passed off so quietly that no one in the court room knew at the time what had transpired. Bail was fixed at $500 which was immediately made by the accused. The solicitor contends that he has information which goes to show that Mr. Shugart offered Armstrong a certain sum provided that he was selected as one of the jurors to try his son, and the trial should end as he desired it to. The indications are now that the jury will take the case into their hands this afternoon."

SHUGART CASE IS IN JURY'S HANDS
The Birmingham Age-Herald, June 30, 1904

"The case of Roland T. Shugart who has been on trial for over a week, charged with taking the life of Andrew J. Banholzer, is now with the jury. Two arguments were made in the case yesterday, one for the defense and the other for the state. The arguments of both of the attorneys were regarded as masterly efforts. They discussed the case in a logical manner and held the close attention of the members of the jury. The crowds at the trial were unusually large. During the argument of Solicitor Heflin he remarked that human life in Jefferson county did not appear to be safe."

ROLAND T. SHUGART NOW A FREE MAN
On Second Ballot Jury Was Unanimous for Acquittal
The Birmingham Age-Herald, July 1, 1904

"Roland T. Shugart, the young attorney charged with taking the life of A.J. Banholzer by shooting him with a pistol in the lobby of the Metropolitan barroom was yesterday morning acquitted by the jury which tried the case. "We, the jury find the defendant, Roland T. Shugart, not guilty as charged in the indictment." For a moment silence reigned. Shortly afterwards, however, a number of attorneys and one or two members of the jury walked over to where the defendant was sitting and shook hands with him. Sam Potter, the foreman, when asked about the case, said: "We simply had no evidence before us upon which to convict the defendant." Other members of the jury refused to discuss the matter."

Public Sentiment at Fault
Editorial
The Birmingham Age-Herald, July 2, 1904

"Denunciation of court, prosecuting officials or jury in the Shugart case are each and all misplaced. The fault is not in any or all of those servants of the people. The fault is in us. "We, the people," are alone to blame for verdicts that render life insecure. No matter what a jury may be theoretically, it is but an expression of public sentiment in fact. It takes the law and the facts and twists and conforms them to popular opinion. If public opinion says no white man who was drunk is to be punished, then no white man who was drunk will be punished. Laws are dead letters unless public sentiment be behind them. In other words, public sentiment is above law, and law can no more rise above public sentiment than water can rise above its source.

Let us then look at home, at ourselves, and not at the Shugart jury. When we do we will find that public sentiment is unsound, even rotten, when a case of killing occurs without malice. Human life is cheaply esteemed. A white man who kills another without special malice is considered guiltless, and the offending jury did but express public sentiment. The remedy is education. There is no other remedy. A change in public sentiment is needed. The laws of Alabama are good enough. They are simple and satisfactory--but public sentiment is lamentably deficient and unsound. Give us better teachers both in and out of school. Teach all to read and to think. There is no other remedy.

This state and condition of things is regrettable. It renders life insecure, keeps away immigrants, and chokes prosperity. It is deplorable, and there is no good in blinking the facts. The real trouble lies in us, and it must be educated out of us if, as Governor Cunningham recently said, we are to attain to modern standards of civilization."

Postscript

Ayers noted that:

> "Even privileged white Southerners began to express concerns about the inefficiency, brutality, and partiality of their criminal justice system. Class played far too large a role, bitterly complained the Greensboro Herald and Journal in 1895: "Nobody but a simpleton believes that ancient fiction that one man's life and liberty are as highly esteemed by the law as another's; and that one man, without reference to the lining of his pockets, has the same chance before the law as his neighbor who may not be able to fee lawyers." While the wealthy could delay cases indefinitely and then escape without punishment, "the poor wretch, white or

black, is promptly forced to trial, ready or n to ready, and as promptly convicted and punished. Such inequalities in the enforcement of our criminal laws have destroyed public confidence in the integrity and impartiality of our courts."4

Following his acquittal for the murder of Banholzer in 1904, public sentiment regarding Roland Shugart was mixed as suggested by the above noted editorial. Shugart apparently decided that it might be best for him leave the Birmingham area. He moved to Denver, Colorado where he practiced law until the next tragic episode in his family occurred.

THOMAS G. HEWLETT KILLED BY HARRY HAYNES IN PEERLESS BAR
John T. Shugart Thought to be Fatally Injured, Three Others Shot
Haynes Declares That He Acted In Self-Defense
Shugart, Lee, Tyus and Poss, the Injured, Were By-Standers---
About Seventeen Shots Fired In Encounter
The Birmingham Age-Herald, May 5, 1906

"Thomas G. Hewlett dead, John T. Shugart perhaps fatally injured, and three others suffering from wounds, narrates briefly the result of a shooting affray between Mr. Hewlett and Harry Haynes in the Peerless saloon. Mr. Haynes is in the county jail on a charge of murder. Mr. Shugart, and the other wounded men did not participate in the shooting. They were merely bystanders. Like in other similar cases opinions differ as to the number of shots fired, but the general belief is there were seventeen in all. At least three pistols were used, two being in the possession of Haynes and the other being held by Hewlett. Mr. Hewlett was the president and controlling spirit in the Alabama Club, one of the oldest organizations of its kind in Birmingham, if not in the state, and the shooting is said to have been the result of ill-feeling engendered by Mr. Haynes and Mr. Hewlett towards one another some weeks ago. The crusade of the police department of Birmingham against gambling is said to have been the original cause of the differences between the two men.

The affray yesterday assumed somewhat the aspect of a duel, and the friends of Haynes declare that although the two men drew their weapons about the same time that Hewlett was the first to open fire. One bullet entered the back of Mr. Hewlett's head and this was the one that proved fatal. Mr. Haynes escaped without a scratch. It is said that Mr. Shugart was talking to Mr. Hewlett when the shooting commenced. Three bullets took effect in the body of Mr. Shugart, one in the side, the other in the groin and the third in the leg. The streets were crowded and there was considerable excitement in the vicinity of the saloon following the tragedy. Two thousand people had gathered around the corner of Nineteenth street and Second avenue, and the yells of the policemen in their effort to keep the streets clear, and the clanging of gongs on the ambulances and dead wagons that were summoned added to the excitement of the scene. Immediately after the shooting the doors of the saloon were closed but this did not keep the hundreds from pushing their way forward and elbowing through the crowd, in an almost fanatic effort to get a glimpse of the inside of the saloon, where three men lay upon the floor. There were perhaps eight persons in the saloon when the shooting first commenced and several of those could be seen fleeing from the place.

    When asked about the trouble which led up to the shooting, Haynes said Mr. Shugart was in no way connected with the shooting. Coroner W.D. Paris viewed the remains of Mr. Hewlett at the undertaking establishment of Lige Loy last night, before the body had scarcely had time to become cold and stiff in death. He was at his home near Green Springs eating his supper when summoned to the city. Detective Bodeker attend that Haynes said "he would not have done it had he not been forced to. He told me that he walked into the saloon to get a drink of absynthe, and that he heard Mr. Hewlett talking about him. He told me further that Mr. Hewlett addressed him, saying, 'Hello Harry,' and that he replied saying 'How are you, Mr. Hewlett.' Mr. Haynes said that Mr. Hewlett asked him if he had his six-shooter with him. He asked 'Why?' so he told me. Mr. Haynes said that Mr. Hewlett then replied, 'If you have got it, we had just as well settle now.' He said that both pulled their guns but that Mr. Hewlett fired twice before he pulled the trigger to the gun he had."

    Haynes is one of the most widely known men in Birmingham. The Peerless saloon has been standing on the corner of Second avenue and Nineteenth street for many years. The place has been the scene of several tragedies during its existence. Mr. Hewlett had been a citizen of Birmingham for eighteen years, and he had a wide acquaintance in Birmingham and throughout the county. For twelve years he served as revenue officer and secret service man for the government. For years Mr. Shugart has been a resident of Birmingham, being a member of the law firm of Shugart & Bell. He has a wife and is the father of Roland T. Shugart, formerly of Birmingham, but now living in Denver. At 2:30 o'clock this morning Mr. Shugart was resting easy at the infirmary. His condition at that hour was extremely critical."

SHUGART SECOND VICTIM OF HEWLETT-HAYNES DUEL

The Birmingham Age-Herald, May 7, 1906

"John T. Shugart, the second victim of the rencontre between Thomas Hewlett and Harry Haynes, died yesterday morning. The deceased was a bystander when the shooting scrape in which Hewlett was killed began, but in trying to stop the tragedy, he received his fatal wounds. He was one of the best known men in Jefferson county. A wife and six children survive. The deceased had hundreds of devoted friends in the Birmingham district who surely lament his untimely end."

Postscript

Following his father's death in 1906, Roland Shugart returned to Birmingham to practice law, but not without being involved in further episodes of reactive violence.

ATTORNEY HANBY FIRES AT SHUGART
Shooting at Third and Twentieth Last Night
BULLET WENT WIDE
Understood Feeling Had Been High Between the Men All Day and That Friends Were Trying to Pacify Them

The Birmingham Age-Herald, August 15, 1912

"James M. Hanby, an attorney, fired a shot at Roland T. Shugart, also an attorney, at the corner of Third avenue and Twentieth street at 8 o'clock last night. The bullet missed Shugart and lodged in the vestibule entry of the Gunn Drug company. Hanby was disarmed and arrested by Officer Perkerson. He was released last night on bond.

A large crowd was on the street at the time of the shooting and it was considered remarkable that no one was injured. The men met on the sidewalk and it is not known just what words passed between them. Hanby suddenly fired and Shugart dashed into the Gunn drugstore.

Officer Perkerson was only a few yards up Third avenue in the direction of the Stag saloon and seeing the group on the corner he ran toward them and reached Hanby just as he fired. He seized Hanby's arms from behind and wrested his pistol from him.

When arrested Hanby insisted that Shugart had met him and told him he was going to kill him. "No man can threaten my life," he kept repeating. "He threatened to kill me on sight." The cause of their trouble is not known definitely, but it is said to have been brewing all day and friends had been trying to make peace between them. The two attorneys occupy adjoining offices on the eighth floor of the Farley building and there is one room between them which they have been using as a joint reception room. It is understood that Shugart objected to some of the visitors Hanby had been having in the offices and had repeatedly remonstrated. This culmination is said to have come yesterday morning when Shugart caused the arrest of one of these visitors whom he considered objectionable. After the shooting last night Shugart told
Patrolman Ivey that he ran because he did not want to kill Hanby, and that he could not afford to have any trouble with him because of Hanby's infirmity."

Roland Shugart's first wife had died in 1909 from tuberculosis. By 1911 Shugart had remarried, however, this union would indirectly lead to a violent final outcome.

In this regard, Ayers noted that:

> "The cleavage between honor and legality widened over time; honor that originally grew in the vacuum of justice soon acquired a force of its own that actively repelled the dictates of the written abstract law. Manhood came to be equated with the extralegal defense of one's honor, a manhood made manifest in control of one's woman and in unquestioning respect from one's peers."[5]

ROLAND T. SHUGART KILLED AND HAYNE MOORE FATALLY SHOT IN FIGHT IN NORTH BIRMINGHAM

Shugart Married Moore's Sister Two Years Ago
and Family Affairs Caused the Trouble
Four Shots Fired By Each In Twinkling Of Eye
Had Not Seen Each Other Until Moore Brothers
Ran From The Store to Catch Car to City
for Which Shugart Was Also Waiting

The Birmingham Age-Herald, April 16, 1913

"After a career in which sensational events were plentiful, the end came abruptly to Roland T Shugart, the well known attorney, who was shot and instantly killed in a pistol fight at the corner of Twenty-ninth avenue and Twenty-seventh street, North Birmingham. Hayne Moore, his slayer, was fatally wounded. A.B. Moore, a brother of Hayne, was arrested by Deputy Sheriffs Cole and McDuff...and released on a $500 bond.

Shugart and Moore were brothers-in-law and the shooting was a result of a family feud of several month's standing. Shugart married Miss Dixie Moore about one and a half years ago against the wishes of her parents, but lately had been separated from his wife. He... was awaiting a car to town. On the opposite corner of the street... I.H. Moore, Jr., and his brother A.B. Moore were also awaiting a car to town. The car came bowling down the street and both of the Moore brothers rushed out to get on the car. It was then, according to eyewitnesses that the Moores noted Shugart standing by a telephone pole. A few hurried spoken worlds followed between Hayne Moore and Roland Shugart and both drew their pistols and commenced firing. Shugart was shot through the heart, causing almost instant death. Moore was struck just below the left shoulder blade, the bullet ranging to the right side. The lungs were pierced. He fell and crawled on the road to hide behind a team of mules. Shugart sank slowly to the ground by the telephone pole firing his pistol as long as his finger had the strength to pull the trigger. He fell to the ground on his face with his pistol outstretched toward his opponent.

The shooting occurred almost in the twinkling of an eye and was over before the amazed spectators could interfere. Both men, it is said, shot with .38 calibre Colt revolvers and were about four feet from each other when the first shots were fired, four from each man. A.B. Moore was seen in the sheriff's office following his arrest on the charge of murder, but refused to make a detailed statement as to the cause that led up to the shooting. He said: "I am all shaken up...it is a most deplorable affair, as to the cause of the shooting it was a family affair and I do not care to discuss that phase of it."

Coroner C.L. Spain said, "I will hold a thorough investigation on this latest killing outrage. Yesterday afternoon I gathered together all of the principal witnesses, and will be ready for the inquest immediately following the death of Hayne Moore, whom I am told will die." The Rev. Curtis Shugart, a Baptist revivalist, and a brother of Roland Shugart, said: "The unfortunate affair was brought about by the fact that my brother brought a suit for divorce against his wife last Saturday, charging misconduct. His wife had warned him that if he brought the divorce suit on that ground that her brothers would kill him. My brother disregarded the warning and started the divorce proceedings and he now lies dead."

Roland Shugart was well known in Birmingham. He was 33 years old and had always lived in Jefferson county. He was an attorney by profession. He was the son of John T. Shugart, the well known criminal lawyer, who was accidentally killed in the Peerless saloon when Harry Haynes and Tim Hewlett engaged in a pistol fight on the night of May 4, 1906. About ten years ago Roland Shugart killed a young man named Bonholzer in the Metropolitan saloon, corner of Twentieth street and Morris avenue. Shugart later removed to Denver, Col., to live. He returned to Birmingham following the death of his father and took up the practice of law. A few months ago he was shot at by John Hanby, his law partner, but escaped unhurt."

VICTIM OF TUESDAY PISTOL DUEL DEAD
I.H. Moore, Jr., Shot by Roland Shugart, Dies Yesterday
The Birmingham Age-Herald, April 17, 1913

"I. Haynes Moore, Jr., who was shot and fatally injured in the pistol fight between Roland Shugart and himself at North Birmingham early Tuesday morning, died yesterday at McAdory's infirmary, where he was taken immediately after the shooting. Hope was never held out for the recovery of Mr. Moore after he was wounded. He sank slowly but steadily and died early yesterday morning."

POULTRY SALESMAN IS SHOT AND KILLED BY ANGRY HUSBAND
Wm. L. Reeves Surrenders After Shooting F.J. Ransom at His Home
Coroner's Jury To Meet Tomorrow
Mrs. Reeves Is Eye Witness to the Tragedy In Home Near Comer Station on the North Bessemer Car Line

The Birmingham Age-Herald, November 25, 1913

"F.J. Ransom, a poultry salesman, was shot and almost instantly killed yesterday morning by William LeRoy Reeves, a floor walker. The shooting and killing of Ransom occurred at Reeves home. Reeves had returned to his home from the city and upon finding Ransom he shot him twice through the head with a .38 caliber Colt pistol. Following the shooting Reeves notified the sheriff's office that he had "killed a man" and that he would await the coming of the officers to surrender.

According to the information of Coroner Charles L. Spain, Reeves was notified in some way yesterday morning that Ransom was at his home, and he at once hurried there. Reeves made the statement that as he entered the room where Ransom was the latter made a quick move towards his hip pocket and Reeves at once drew his pistol and shot Ransom. There was no pistol found on the body of Ransom when he was searched after death.

William LeRoy Reeves is a well-known clothing salesman. He is about 35 years of age and very popular with his employers and all who know him. The dead man, F.J. Ransom, was about 35 years of age and a poultry feed salesman of Newark, N.J. He was married but lived separated from his wife. Coroner Spain stated he would hold an inquest. "This latest killing will be thoroughly investigated and I will allow a jury to decide whether or not Reeves was justified in killing Ransom, whom he found in his home. I have nothing to say further on the matter."

REEVES RELEASED OF MURDER CHARGE BY CORONER'S JURY
"Justifiable Homicide" Is Verdict on Man Who Killed Another in the Presence of Wife

The Birmingham Age-Herald, November 27, 1913

"Justifiable homicide was the verdict rendered by the coroner's jury yesterday afternoon in the inquest on the killing of Fred J. Ransom who was shot to death Monday morning by W. Leroy Reeves. Reeves was given his freedom immediately after the verdict was announced. "I would do it again if it had to be done over," was the concluding statement of Reeves under oath before the coroner's jury. Mr. Reeves was the last of several witnesses examined by the inquisitional body.

Reeves was brought in to testify before the coroner's jury from the county jail where he has been a prisoner. He came into the coroner's office dressed in a neat sack suit, walking briskly. He appeared calm and self-possessed. Reeves himself after being sworn, pulled out a big black cigar and lit it. He testifies in much the same way that he would have dictated a business letter and in that matter of fact way revealed all the innermost secrets of his household. He depicted vividly the domestic tragedy that had been brewing in his home ever since the closing of the State Fair and graphically explained how the shooting had occurred. At no time did Mr. Reeves raise his voice, and throughout the recital he puffed easily on his cigar. At the conclusion of Reeve's testimony, the jury, without a dissenting vote, announced its verdict.

At the morning session of the inquest there were several witnesses examined and it was brought out that Mrs. Reeves was said to have been an old friend of F.J. Ransom before her marriage to Reeves. A few of the letters that passed between the deceased and Mrs. Reeves were offered as evidence as showing her feeling toward Ransom. Much of the testimony was of unpleasant character. The verdict of the jury ends the case unless the father of the deceased swears out a warrant for the arrest of Reeves."

CHIEF OF POLICE SHOT TO DEATH IN CITY HALL OFFICE
Unwritten Law Claimed by Brighton Furnace Man, Who Killed Officer

The Birmingham Age-Herald, August 30, 1919

"Bunch Walker, 30, chief of police of Brighton was shot to death by O. Olive, a furnace man employed by the Woodward Iron company, the shooting occurring in the chief's office in the city hall at Brighton. Domestic troubles are said to have caused the killing,

Olive having stated following the shooting that he would claim the "unwritten law," as his defense.

Walker was seated at his desk, it is said, when the shooting took place. Although there were no eye witnesses to the affair. Citizens of Brighton, hearing the shots ran to the office and were met at the front door by Olive, who handed his smoking revolver to one of the aldermen of Brighton, stating that he had killed the chief of police.

Yesterday afternoon he made the following statement in regard to the affair: "It is just another case of unwritten law. Domestic troubles caused the killing. I work on the night shift at the furnace. Last night my wife told me of visits paid her by Walker and confessed everything that had passed between them. This morning I went to city hall and asked Walker what he meant by his attentions to my wife whereupon he cursed and reached for his revolver. As he did so I fired." Mrs. Olive was formerly Miss Mable Whited of Bessemer.

Chief Walker was formerly connected with the police force at Brighton before enlisting in the army and going to France. He was discharged in January and was made chief of police of Brighton February 1. Brighton is much wrought up over the affair and saddened at the loss of one of their citizens, Walker having been popular where he was known. He was unmarried.

The coroner of Bessemer will make an investigation of the killing today. Many heard the shots as they were fired in rapid succession, all five chambers of the .38 special Smith & Wesson revolver being emptied into the body of Walker. After the excitement of the shooting had subsided Walker's revolver was found between the city hall and another building on the ground. The office in which the shooting took place is on the second floor of the building.

As the crowd began to gather from the excitement, Olive appealed to the mayor for protection. Deputies from Bessemer took him into custody. The first man to reach Waker after he was shot stated that Walker gasped a few times, but never spoke. There was no evidence of a struggle. Olive seemed very calm about the matter, it was said."

"I DO NOT BLAME OLIVE," DECLARES WALKER'S FIANCEE
Mrs. Slaton Avows Love for Slain Policeman--- Mrs. Olive Keeps in Jail With Husband

The Birmingham Age-Herald, September 1, 1919

"I don't blame Mr. Olive for killing Bunch Walker if the deed was committed to protect his wife, although I loved Mr. Walker with all my heart." This was the statement made by Mrs. Carman Slaton, the sweetheart of Bunch Walker, chief of police of Brighton, who was shot to death by Ollie Olive Friday morning.

"However", continued Mrs. Slaton, "I do not believe Mr. Walker would have entered the Olive home without encouragement. There are few men who will take advantage of a woman unless that woman has given them a reason for doing so. On the other hand I do not blame any man for defending his wife, no matter what measures he has to take in order to do it. I have received mysterious notes and telephone calls telling me that I had best break the engagement with Mr. Walker. The notes were not signed nor did the voice over the phone give any names, therefore I do not know who the woman was. Mr. Walker told me that a married woman had tried to get him to break our engagement. He never spoke sarcastic of any woman in my presence. He told me of this other woman, I believe, because he loved me. I do not believe Mr. Walker was entirely responsible for the affair about which he was killed. He was a perfect gentleman throughout the time I knew him and that was for a period of several years and I do not believe he would have taken the advantage of any woman. It stands to reason he was given encouragement. I respected him most highly and shall always honor his memory."

"I have no answer to make to Mrs. Carmen Slaton's alleged statement that I enticed Mr. Walker into my home." Thus replied Mrs. Ollie Olive when asked about the statement of Mrs. Slaton. The statement was made at the county jail where Olive is imprisoned and where Mrs. Olive is almost constantly with him.

Speaking in an assuring manner, Homer Whited, brother of Mrs. Olive, and the first soldier of the A.E.F. to win the croix de guerre, stated that Mrs. Slaton would be required to reiterate her statement at the preliminary hearing. "Until the date set for the hearing," he said, "we will have no more to say in regard to the unfortunate affair." Mrs. Olive said she had known Walker from childhood and always regarded him as a brother until he took the advantage of her.

"My wife made a clean and noble confession regarding her relations with Walker," said Olive, "and I intend to live with her when I have answered to the charge brought against me. I love her and she reciprocates." Mrs. Slaton was a cashier at the Tutwiler Cafe. She abandoned her work when she heard of Mr. Walker's death and last night had not returned to it. "My wife made a clean confession to me of her relations with Walker," said Olive "and it was more than I could stand. I approached him about the matter following the night my wife confessed to me and killed him when he reached for his pistol with which to kill me."

Mrs. Olive visits her husband at the county jail frequently. They declare that the deepest of love exists between them and that they are living with hopes that everything will come out all right."

Postscript

The outcome of any legal proceedings against Olive for the murder of Walker could not be determined. Chief Walker's name is currently not included on the Jefferson County law enforcement officer's memorial.

As an early student of Southern feuds wrote in 1901, "Blood relationship is the greatest bond of social solidarity. An affront to one member of a family is an affront to all his kin. There is no such thing as neutral ground; If not for, you are against."[6]

Ayers noted that in the final analysis:

> "Crime and punishment, as much as anything, measure the continuity of the South with the past: the region still leads the nation in homicide and assault rates, still holds the greatest number of men on death row, and still contains the largest number of handguns. For over a century now, the South has seemed to be disappearing—yet it persists in a thousand subtle and obvious ways. The region always manages to resurrect itself in new guises, for among every new generation walk the ghosts of the old."[7]

CHAPTER 12

SUICIDE

*"I'm gonna lay my head, baby,
down on some railroad iron.
I'm gonna let that L&N train, baby,
satisfy my mind."*
---*Good Tonk Blues*

As noted by Roger Lane, "Suicide as a unique act committed by a particular person may be conceived of as having as many meanings as the number of human beings affected, and the range of psychological possibilities is nearly as wide."[1]

Statistics

During the 15 year period of 1911 through 1930 where deaths by suicidal manner were documented in available Jefferson County coroner's records, there were a total of 402 reported cases for a yearly average of 27 self-inflicted deaths. Based on census records, the average population of Jefferson County during this period was approximately 322,000.

In comparison, during the 16 year period 2000 through 2015 there were a total of 1,294 suicides for a yearly average of 81, during which there was an average yearly population of 659,000. Therefore, suicide rates for these two periods, on a per capita basis, reveals the following results per 100,000 population:

1911--1930: 8.3
2000--2015: 12.3

For comparison purposes, the crude rate of suicide in Philadelphia in 1910 was 12.2. In 1913 the rate for the United States as a whole was 15.8 compared to 13.0 in 2014. These figures indicate a relatively steady per capita rate of suicide over an extended period of over 100 years. In a further comparison of rates for Jefferson County, although the difference between them may appear to be statistically significant, the increased rate in the latter period is believed to be skewed higher mainly due to improved accuracy of the investigation of deaths which have been conducted within the modern medical examiner system. This is opposed to the earlier period where an unknown number of cases of suicide may have gone unrecognized by the lay coroner or, in some cases, intentionally certified as "accident" or "undetermined" by him for various reasons.

Investigation and Certification

In Lane's study of deaths in Philadelphia during the late 19th century, it was noted that:

> "The figures (for suicide) are, of course inaccurate, undercounted, as are all official suicide statistics; no one knows or has ever known how many people deliberately kill themselves in a given year. But such figures indicate something about the social experience and expectations of the society that generates them. The issue is not really one of absolute but of relative accuracy, not the "true" rate, but of the direction of that rate, up or down."[2]

> "There is always the possibility that the official statistics of suicide are so far removed from reality as to be utterly misleading guides to that reality, that massive numbers either escaped diagnosis or were knowingly hidden by physicians and coroners under wholly unrelated labels, such as "apoplexy" or "heart disease." But even if that is the case, the figures are no more unreal than those of the present era; the crude annual rate for the end of the nineteenth century, 12.2 per 100,000 (in Philadelphia) is almost identical to the modern one."

> "In an unbiased world, the coroner himself had no vested finance pal or other interest in concealing suicides, barring some form of bribery by family or friends; indeed, his concern was to patrol the boundaries of his jurisdiction finding warrant whenever possible for "suspicion" in cases of doubt. There were two sorts of possible cover-up: those in which a doctor or other witnesses misrepresented the facts in a suspicious case and those in which the coroner himself knowingly signed a false certificate."[3]

Perhaps to avoid the perceived stigma of a self-inflicted death, it has not been unknown for relatives of a deceased person to rearrange or alter such a scene to make it appear that a death was due to something other than suicide. Such actions could include removal of empty medication containers or other drugs and their paraphernalia, the repositioning of a hanging victim with placement in bed as well as the removal or destruction of "suicide" notes prior to calling authorities. These and other modifications can and have occurred.

In addition, the staging of a scene by the person committing suicide in order to suggest that an accident had occurred, as by placing gun cleaning materials nearby, is not unknown.

Docket Entry:
Date: February 7, 1930
Deceased: A. Sidney Cowan
Cause Of Death: Gun shot wound of left chest.
Remarks: Inflicted while cleaning a gun in his office.
Same being accidental.

The prominence of the victim may have played a role in how the death was officially certified and may have escaped accurate reporting due to an obliging and sympathetic family physician long acquainted with the victim. Perhaps this may also help explain the appreciable difference in the lower crude rate of suicide in Jefferson County in the early part of the 20th century when compared to other cities and the United States as a whole during that time.

As in the following case involving a prominent victim and family, there may exist a silent pressure to avoid labeling a particular death a suicide, even if it is quietly accepted as such. Such actions may occur more often even today in rural counties where the residents and legal authorities live within smaller, closely knit communities and know one another more intimately than in urban areas.

WALKER PERCY DEAD FROM AN ACCIDENTAL DISCHARGE OF GUN
Prominent Attorney Was Preparing For Hunting Trip To Mississippi When Killed By Shotgun at His Home on Highland Avenue

The Birmingham Age-Herald, February 9, 1917

"Walker Percy, lawyer, statesman, sportsman, civic leader, is dead. A leader for 31 years in the growth and development of Birmingham was lost with tragic suddenness yesterday afternoon when, while cleaning his shotgun for a hunt to Mississippi it was accidentally discharged and fired one shell into Mr. Percy's heart and killed him instantly. News that such a figure in the life of Alabama, Birmingham and the south had gone to such an untimely death reverberated throughout the city yesterday afternoon and cast an undertone of sorrow and grief over all.

All circles pay tribute to him--The legal world, where since 1886 he had proved himself a fearless fighter for right--wise and sagacious in council; The civic world, to which he contributed the commission form of government and made possible the abolition of the fee system; the sportsman; identified as a former president of the Country club, a devotee of golf and an admirer of virile athletics and a huntsman of note.

Of all the sports that appealed to him, none was as dear as hunting. Earlier in the afternoon Mr. Percy had engaged in a conversation with his son Leroy Percy, about going to Greenville, Miss., where they would hunt on the estate of his brother, Sen. Leroy Percy. The proposal was accepted and arrangements were being made for leaving Birmingham last night. An hour or so later Mr. Percy went up to his room. Communicating with this is a long narrow room which has served as a store place for his hunting equipment, his golf bags and numerous other adjuncts of sport to make ready for the hunt. It is presumed that Mr. Percy went to clean his guns and get ready for the trip to Mississippi. The position of the body and the 12 gauge shotgun with its one exploded shell would seem to indicate that he had stooped over to pick up the weapon and that it's trigger became entangled in the straps of the hunting case or in the other articles that were on the floor. The force of the shot took effect in his breast and he fell face down to the floor. A call for the family physician was sent out but he could be of no service. It was too late.

The news of Mr. Percy's death was followed by a steady stream of friends who came to the family residence to offer their heart felt sympathy and to offer their services to the family. Hundreds of intimate friends--for it was in that number that he had friends--flocked to the palatial home on Highland Avenue and Beach Street.

Leroy Percy, the first person to reach his father, stated that they "were to have gone to Greenville, Miss., Thursday night. He left me and went upstairs to his room. Shortly after 3 o'clock I heard a muffled noise but did not pay any attention to it. A few minutes later I went upstairs to talk with father concerning our plans and it was then that I discovered his body face down upon the floor in the room where he kept his guns, his golf sticks and hunting togs. From the position of the body and the gun, it seems that he picked up a gun with its muzzle pointing toward him, and that it was accidentally discharged."

On April 17, 1888 he was married to Miss Mary Pratt DeBardeleben. His fortunes as lawyer swelled as time progressed. Mr. Percy was a man who never sought a public office and acclaim. But in working for Jefferson County and Birmingham, Mr. Percy taxed his physical powers and had a nervous breakdown. However, he recovered from this and at the time of his death was in splendid health."

During this period a physician, Dr. C.C. Wiley, was serving as coroner and it was he that investigated and certified the death of Walker Percy. His official opinion as to the manner of death seems hedged, although he appears to grudgingly state the obvious.

Docket Entry:
Date: February 8, 1917
Deceased: Walker Percy, White
Cause Of Death: I was called to 2217 Highland Avenue to investigate the death of Walker Percy (White) and I found deceased came to his death by shooting him self with a #12 bore shot gun pressed against his breast but whether it was suicidal or accidental is unknown to us but probably suicide.
Total Coroner's Fees: $2.25

BIRMINGHAM PAYS FINAL TRIBUTE TO HONORED CITIZEN
Simple But Impressive Ceremony at Funeral of Walker Percy
ATTORNEYS OF CITY ATTEND IN BODY
Representative Citizens From Every Walk of Life Pay Silent Tribute to Man Who Helped Build City
The Birmingham Age-Herald, February 11, 1917

"Under a bank of beautiful flowers, and surrounded by hundreds of sorrowful friends, the remains of the late Walker Percy were committed to their final resting place at Elmwood cemetery. On either side, the ground was studded with immense designs that came from associates, clubs and bodies in Birmingham and the south. As the last words of the services were said, the coffin sank into the depths of the earth.

From every side, there were hundreds of people who witnessed the last rites and then, heavy-hearted, returned to the city, pondering over such a great loss to Birmingham. Men who had built Birmingham; those who, with Mr. Percy, had seen the city grow from a straggling hamlet of 4000 to a metropolis; those who were directing the destinies of the great companies and projects of the city, all seemed to be found among those who viewed the ceremony. There was never a more sorrowful gathering, conscious of a profound loss, than that which paid its final respects to Walker Percy."

Postscript

Walker Percy (b. Birmingham, 1916), a famous poet in his own right and a member of this prominent and troubled Birmingham family, which included a U.S. Senator and a civil war hero, was the grandson and namesake of this well known individual. His father, Leroy Percy, would also commit suicide in 1929 and Percy indicated that his mother's death in a single vehicle collision several years later may also have been self-inflicted. The tragedies suffered by this family, whose members had such fame, respect and fortune, is reminiscent of the poem "Richard Cory" by Edwin Robinson which reads, in part:

> "Whenever Richard Cory went down town,
> We people on the pavement looked at him;
> He was a gentleman from sole to crown,
> Clean favored, and imperially slim.
> And he was rich--yes, richer than a king
> and admirably schooled in every grace;
> In fine, we thought that he was everything
> To make us wish that we were in his place.
> So we worked, and waited for the light,
> and went without the meat, and cursed the bread;
> And Richard Cory, one calm summer night,
> Went home and put a bullet through his head."

Means of Death

It has been noted that there was not much difference in the number of suicides on a per capita basis in most jurisdictions between the early years of the 20th century and those of the early 21st. In addition, a number of the means used to commit suicide, e.g., firearms, hanging and drug overdose can be found in similar ratios in both periods. However, there was a distinct difference found in regard to the methods of self-destruction, especially by women who rarely committed suicide by shooting themselves, then or now, although guns were as readily available then as they are today and where men commonly used firearms to end their lives as often as they currently do.

Docket Entry:
Date: April 3, 1909
Deceased: A.E. Frasher
Address: Birmingham Hotel
Cause Of Death: By drinking Laudanum.
I found deceas of Sueyside.

Docket Entry:
Date: June 25, 1916
Deceased: Jack Montgomery, White
Address: County jail
Cause Of Death: By cutting his throat with a razor while locked up in sell charged with murder.

Docket Entry:
Date: September 27, 1916
Deceased: Joe Norton, White
Address: 1903 3rd Avenue
Cause Of Death: By shooting himself with suicide intent while trying to evade arrest.

Docket Entry:
Date: January 6, 1917
Deceased: Louis Walton
Address: Terminal station
Cause Of Death: By an explosion of nitro-glycerine, dynamite or some other high explosive administered by his own hands with suicidal intent.

Docket Entry:
Date: July 22, 1926
Deceased: Andrew Thomas, Col.
Address: Southern Undertaking funeral home
Cause Of Death: By a broken neck caused by him jumping out of a window on the fourth floor of Hillman Hospital.

Docket Entry:
Date: August 26, 1929
Deceased: W.V. Kirkpatrick, W
Address: 1630 3rd Avenue Bessemer
Cause Of Death: Self-inflicted pistol shot wound of left breast.
Note: Left note on Simpson Coal Company letterhead paper addressed to Coroner Jefferson County, "Just tired of the game."

As women were mainly employed as homemakers in the early years of the 20th century, it appears that they used means which were readily available to them then and which are not typically found in modern times, e.g., natural gas which was commonly used for cooking ovens and space heaters and the employment of which were quite efficient in causing rapid unconsciousness and a painless death. Other methods involved the ingestion of highly toxic substances routinely used in households and medical facilities for cleaning purposes and which were readily available. In addition to the occasional intentional ingestion of products containing lye or strychnine, the employment of substances such as carbolic acid and bichloride of mercury were relatively commonly used methods for committing suicide, not only in Birmingham, but across the country.

Carbolic acid, also known as phenol, has been used in various chemical processes and medical treatments, but also became commonly used as a disinfectant in many homes as early as the late 19th century after its effectiveness as an antiseptic in medical procedures had been shown.

Ingesting carbolic acid is likely one of the worst, most prolonged and painful ways to suffer death. It first destroys the mucous membranes of the mouth, nose, throat, esophagus and stomach. The pain alone is likely unbearable. It then leads to nausea, vomiting, severe headache and other painful and distressing symptoms such as causing shortness of breath as the victim tries to gasp for air. Despite the fact that drinking carbolic acid was beyond painful, by the late 1800's committing suicide by drinking it had become alarmingly popular. Many destitute and despondent persons drank carbolic acid to cause their own horrific death. Consequently, many coroners of the day had their share of carbolic acid suicides.

Another readily available substance of that time was mercury bichloride. In the days before antibiotics, physicians used this substance to treat a variety of diseases, notably syphilis. Highly toxic, odorless and colorless, it was meant to be applied topically to the sores that developed as this disease progressed. Ingestion of this compound would rapidly result in severe abdominal pain, difficulty in breathing and death.

Statistics

In a review of poisoning deaths investigated by the Jefferson County coroner, it was found that mercury bichloride and carbolic acid were employed to commit suicide on a roughly equal basis. In the period ranging from 1911 though 1930, where records were available, there were 41 deaths from carbolic acid ingestion and 45 deaths from mercury compounds.

As with other means of death, there were occasional questionable "rulings" by the coroner, for whatever reasons, as to the manner of a particular death. It is a particular stretch of the imagination to believe that especially where carbolic acid was ingested that it could be anything other than intentional in light of the unmistakeable strong and noxious odor of this substance.

Docket Entry:
Date: August 5, 1911
Deceased: Kate Rosenfeld, White
Address: 1528 So. 15 St, City
Cause Of Death: From carbolic acid poison.
Notes: But we could not determine whether it was taken by mistake or whether it was suicide intent.

Docket Entry:
Date: June 5, 1911
Deceased: Rev. H.R. Schramm, W
Address: Wylam
Cause Of Death: From carbolic acid poison. Same being taken through mistake.

Docket Entry:
Date: October 17, 1917
Deceased: James Whitley, Jr.
Address: 2309 Avenue E
Cause Of Death: By drinking concentrated lye, same being accidental.

Publicity

In Birmingham, as in most larger cities throughout the country, the news media of the late 19th and early 20th centuries would seize on the popularity of the so-called "Yellow Journalism" which was originally practiced with great zest by major competing newspapers in New York City such as between William Randolph Hearst's New York Journal and Joseph Pulitzer's New York World. Whether based on competition for the sale of newspapers or not, this style of sensationalism would find its way even into the regular reporting of those deaths in the community which were deemed by authorities to have been self-inflicted.

Although those cases of suicide by well known persons or those whose acts of self-destruction were conducted in a public setting or in some ostentatious manner would certainly garner attention from the media even today, it was found that such acts performed by the common citizen would routinely be reported in the daily newspapers. Some of these reports would be published with attention getting headlines in large type along with extensive descriptions worded in the "purple prose" commonly employed at that time.

As noted by Lane:

> "Newspapers throughout the period treated suicide as news and an opportunity for the brief expression of moral opinion or sentiment...and shared none of our modern delicacy. "Suicide" and "Apparent Suicide" were frequent headlines...and the brief accounts, most of them cumulatively monotonous in their sameness, always attempted at the end to explain the business in something less than a dozen words."[4]

There was often detected almost a sense of great glee in the opportunity to shock and moralize in the reporting of these events which might better be described by using the German language term "Schadenfreude," meaning the pleasure derived by someone from another person's misfortune. Although condemnation of the act might not be directly forthcoming from a reporter, the inclusion of commentary attributed to others may have served such a subliminal purpose.

ALLEN BLOWS OUT BRAINS AT OPELIKA
Well Known Resident Commits Suicide
at Early Hour Yesterday
The Birmingham Age-Herald, January 16, 1913

"A.O. Allen, a well known and well to do resident of this city, committed suicide here by shooting himself through the right temple. When Edmund Powell, who operates a store in the building directly under Allen's room, opened up this morning he noted blood dripping through the ceiling. Allen was found lying dead, prone upon the floor of his room with a pistol wound and a .38 Smith & Wesson revolver grasped tightly in his right hand.

No cause has been assigned for the rash act, but Allen's friends have noticed recently that at times his mind seemed to be unbalanced."

Although the sensationalism associated with the reporting of these types of deaths would gradually diminish over the years, the routine printing of the factual details of such cases would continue into the middle of the century. By the 1950's this practice by the mainstream media essentially ceased unless some notable factors were involved.

Perhaps the approach to reporting such deaths changed along with society's mores as expressed by a writer on the subject:

"The only thing more morally repugnant than passing judgement on another human being's private struggle and inner world--than choosing self-righteousness over compassionate understanding— Is doing so publicly, especially as a currency of tabloidism."[5]

Law enforcement officials and other death investigators were not exempt from such tragedies affecting their families. These occurrences were, of course, subject to public curiosity and to extensive and detailed coverage by the news media.

DIVORCED COUPLE, CLASPED IN EACH'S ARMS, FOUND DEAD
Thelma Parrish Perkins And Lewis Perkins Shot To Death In Auto
Note Is Left Behind At Scene Of Slayings
Passerby Discovers Bodies On Lonely Road Near Bagley School

The Birmingham News September 18, 1939

"Locked in each other's arms the bodies of a man and a woman were discovered in an automobile parked on a lonely road near Bagley School in the western part of the county shortly after 7 a.m. today. Mrs. Perkins is the daughter of Charles Parrish, former deputy county investigator. Perkins is a brother-in-law of Deputy Sherif Homer Badger and is a special agent for the Louisville & Nashville Railroad.

A note found written on a scrap of paper in the car indicated the shooting took place about 4 a.m. today. County Investigator Gip M. Evans, who was also at the scene, said he would continue his investigation to determine the order in which the couple died and by whom the shots might have been fired. Investigator Evans said Perkins had been sitting in the left of the car and Mrs. Perkins on the right. Mrs. Perkins was shot beneath the left ear while the entrance of the wound which took Perkin's life was below the right ear. Chief Deputy Sheriff Henry Hill said he was informed Perkins and Mrs. Perkins had been divorced only a week ago and that the couple had a baby about 1 month old.

The note found in the car read as follows: "To all those who love us: May God bless you and keep you. Our love was too great to suffer on earth any longer. Goodbye Homer. Goodbye Fannie. Mr. and Mrs. Parrish and all the family. Thanks for all the wonderful things you all did for us. May God rest our souls forever. Lewis & Thelma."

Both the man and the woman had been killed by shots fired from a short-barreled .38 caliber pistol similar to those used by G-men."

Report of Sheriff's Investigation

"After a careful investigation, it was decided by all of the investigation officers that Lewis Perkins shot Thelma Parrish Perkins near the left ear and then shot himself just over the right ear. There was a note which bore out the physical facts with reference to agreement or pact, that the shooting was agreed on and premeditated. Matrimonial differences on record in the Chancery Court seem to have been the cause of their unhappy life."

VERDICT GIVEN IN DEATH OF COUPLE
The Birmingham News, September 19, 1939

"County Investigator Gip M. Evans today returned a verdict of murder and suicide in the fatal shootings of Lewis L. Perkins, 35, and his wife, Mrs. Thelma Parrish Perkins, 31, whose bodies were found in an automobile near a lonely schoolhouse in the western part of Jefferson County. "It is my opinion that Perkins shot his former wife and then turned the gun on himself," Evans said. "I also believe that the two had a pre-arranged death pact of agreement." Meanwhile, separate funeral services were conducted today for Perkins and his wife."

Postscript

The suicide note was remarkable for the consistency of the handwriting which appeared to be the product of one person. The entire note was apparently written in pencil by Lewis Perkins. The first names noted at the end of the note differ in that the "& Thelma" was written with a sharper pencil and the lettering appears consistent with the handwriting of the rest of the note and not written by a second person.

It is unknown what other information investigators possessed that would have indicated to them that Mrs. Perkins voluntarily joined her ex-husband in a suicide pact. It is of interest that a note card was included in the coroner's case file with the brief mysterious inscription: "Case F-542. Note taken for study--1/16/58. C.D. Brooks," which suggests that questions were still being raised 20 years after this incident occurred. The original note was returned to the file. Both individuals were buried at different locations in Elmwood cemetery.

"Each of these suffered the strain of the sickness,
the sadness that lies to the one that has it--
the one that says it will never get better, no safe harbor,
no choice in the matter, no available kindness but to quit.
It is the sickness that makes its victims listless,
hopeless, helpless, lifeless as stones.
Its the grim indifference that I've seen in the eyes..." [6]
---Thomas Lynch

CHAPTER 13

VICE

"The judge he smiled as he picked up his pen,
Ninety-nine years in the federal pen.
Come on, come on and listen to me,
Stay off that whiskey and let that cocaine be.

---Cocaine Blues

As noted by Lane, individuals not involved in legal, mainstream service and industrial work and:

> "ranging from the desperate to the ambitious, presumably continued to flow into the established channels of the hustling subculture, gambling, pimping, whoring, and now selling illegal drugs as well as alcohol. The drug culture, often associated with prostitution, grew especially after the turn of the century. Female users...had long found that morphine, or later heroin, was an anodyne, and males believed that cocaine was an aphrodisiac."[1]

Ayers indicated that:

> "Southern grand juries and newspapers blamed much of the regions' violence on liquor, and there is no reason to doubt them. Southerners apparently drank prodigious amounts of alcohol throughout the nineteenth century. Northerners drank great amounts as well and alcohol fueled many fights there, yet Northern alcohol-related violence was never the problem it was in the South, where alcohol and honor combined to create a volatile mixture."[2]

In regard to the religious and moral dilemmas that faced the citizens of Jefferson County in the early 20th century, Ayers noted that:

> "The social concern of the churches had not changed suddenly to Klan-style bigotry. The nativist sentiment and battle against secularism of the 1920s were continuations of earlier struggles to impose prohibition and "blue laws;" all of these were attempts to dictate

community morality by force. Many churchmen and laymen retained fairly "liberal" social attitudes, but felt that the Klan was working for a common objective--to preserve community moral standards. There is certainly no question that Birmingham's Protestant churches supported the Ku Klux Klan. The Klan's attempts to end bootlegging and its floggings of "moral undesirables" in the community usually elicited either praise or neutrality from the city's pulpits. The local head of the Klan estimated that 51 percent of the white Protestant ministers in the county were members of the Klan and that at least that proportion of the laity favored the organization."[3]

Prohibition

It has been noted that "Alcohol abuse in early 20th century America was far worse than anything we know today. The prohibition movement was a reaction to the widespread abuse of alcohol which had grown rapidly worse with the growth of cities and industry. Many people quite reasonably believed that alcohol abuse was destroying not just the bodies and souls of individuals, but their families and society at large."[4] That reaction may have been extreme, but so was the provocation. As noted by Lane, "Everywhere in the middle and late nineteenth century, the drive to clear the streets of drunkards was part of the demand for higher standards of public order."[5]

If asked when "prohibition" of alcohol began in Jefferson County many, if not most people, will refer to the nationwide implementation in 1919 of the 18th amendment to the Constitution which banned the sale of alcohol for human consumption, other than for prescribed medicinal purposes. In actuality, numerous attempts at the prohibition of intoxicating substances had been tried with varying degrees of success, and were already in place in numerous jurisdictions throughout the country to include Birmingham and Jefferson County. Such statutes would be put in place, rescinded and then reinstated on a sporadic recurring basis during the early 20th century, however, at no time was the availability of alcohol completely suppressed. Bans on alcohol sales would only affect the moneyed interests of the producers and sellers of alcohol such as brewing companies and public saloon owners. They would, in turn, proceed to muster their political resources in order to reverse such laws in continuing back and forth battles between the "wets" and "drys."

During the first world war, "alcohol had been an obvious menace to the fighting efficiency of the nation. The country, already largely dry by state law and local option, had decided to banish the saloon once and for all. The war-time prohibition act was already on the books and due to take effect July 1, 1919. But this was not enough. The eighteenth amendment, which would make prohibition permanent and (so it was thought) effective, had been passed by Congress late in 1917, and many of the states had ratified it before the war ended."[6]

In respect to Birmingham and Jefferson County, early attempts to institute the prohibition of alcohol appeared to have first picked up momentum when anti-saloon organizations realized that although women did not have the vote, they did have influence. "Women and children surrounded polling places in October, 1907 and sang "When the Roll is Called Up Yonder," perhaps as a theological warning to male voters. Jefferson County went dry by 1,800 votes (though the city proper voted wet). Now fully aware of their combined political power, churchmen did not intend to relinquish it. They turned their new-found muscle to Birmingham's unsavory moral climate. Saloons, dance halls, and brothels thrived along with the city's churches and emotional revivals."[7]

In prior years from 1889 through 1911 complex see-saw political battles were fought over alcohol. The Birmingham Board of Aldermen "was dominated by the pro-saloon city Democratic party organization which had strong ties with saloonkeepers, liquor dealers, and the local Philip Schilinger brewery. Until 1907 the pro-saloon faction of aldermen successfully defended the right of the liquor interests to operate unregulated saloons anywhere in the city."[8] But the prohibition law, which went into effect January 1, 1908, "proved too loosely drawn to be enforced, and soon many secret, illegal, "blind-tiger" saloons were operating (along with the required police and political graft system). In August, 1911 Jefferson County held another local option election, called this time by the antiprohibitionists. Birmingham voters cast such a heavy vote against prohibition and for a system of strictly regulated, high-license saloons that they overcame a continuing, but reduced majority for prohibition in the rural portions of the county."[9]

Bodeker Talks of Blind Tigers in Birmingham
The Birmingham Age-Herald, July 30, 1908

"There is much talk going around about Birmingham being practically an open town despite the existence of the prohibition law. The statement is made that the so-called soft drink places are running wide open, and inquiry is made as to Chief Bodeker's attitude toward the "blind tigers."

Chief Bodeker said last night: "It may be true that liquor has been sold in Birmingham in the last few weeks. It will always be that liquor will be sold in Birmingham as in every other prohibition town or in any other town. I want to say, however, that during the past three or four weeks while I have been busy making my campaign for re-election as chief of police, that I have had four men delegated for the special duty of ferreting out "blind tigers." They may have done their duty or they may not have done their full duty. If they neglected their duty it was without my knowledge."

"Now that I have been re-elected I want to say positively and emphatically that I propose to enforce the law to the letter as far as the present police force can do so. I shall now have a corps of good and faithful men on duty at all times to watch for blind tigers and for those who seek to indulge in illicit trade. The present police force cannot do it all. We shall do the best we can, but we shall need the aid of every good citizen in enforcing the law. Every suggestion or report will be welcomed and both myself and the police force will do our duty as best we can."

Docket Entry:
Date: February 20, 1912
Deceased: Horace Curry, Col.
Address: East Thomas
Cause Of Death: Falling off of a porch and breaking his neck, while under the influence of whiskey.

Docket Entry:
Date: December 1, 1935
Deceased: Charlie Gray, C.
Address: Avenue F prison.
Cause Of Death: Alcoholic hemorrhages.
Note: Brought to jail in patrol with four men and two women. Three of the men were paralized drunk and were carried from patrol to cell by key boys. Deceased was removed from transit to hall in an effort to revive him, and he failed to respond.

Enforcement

The implementation and continued enforcement of the 18th Amendment to the Constitution from the time when it took effect on July 1, 1919, until its repeal in 1933, can only be likened to the extended opening of a "Pandora's Box" with far-reaching and unintended, but not completely unforeseen, consequences.

As noted by F.L. Allen:

> "If you had informed the average American citizen that prohibition was destined to furnish the most violently explosive issue of the 1920s, he would probably have told you that you were crazy. If you had been able to sketch for him a picture of conditions as they were actually to be-- rum-ships rolling in the sea and transferring their cargoes of whiskey to fast cabin cruisers, beer-running trucks being hijacked on the interurban boulevards by bandits with Thompson sub-machine guns, illicit stills turning out alcohol by the carload, the fashionable dinner party beginning with contraband cocktails as a matter of course, ladies and gentlemen undergoing scrutiny behind the curtained grill of the speakeasy, and Alphonse Capone, multi-millionaire master of the Chicago bootleggers, driving through the streets in an armor-plated car with bullet-proof windows—the innocent citizen's jaw would have dropped."[10]

Attempts to fulfill the requirements of prohibition laws brought into play personnel from a number of different law enforcement agencies at the Federal, state and local levels. Interactions between these police and revenue agents and the suspected participants in the illegal manufacture, transportation and sale of alcohol would have a wide range of effects and outcomes ranging from officers being commended for their actions in some cases to being accused of overreaction and murder with varying legal outcomes.

GLOVER KILLED IN PISTOL DUEL WITH DEPUTY SHERIFFS
While Searching for Illicit Stills in Sayre District Officers Engage in Duel

The Birmingham Age-Herald, May 27, 1919

"In a pistol duel between Deputies Marshall Smith and J. Jones of the sherif's forces and Wiley Glover, aged 45, of the Sayre district, whom the officers allege was engaged in the manufacture of whiskey, Glover was shot through the stomach and killed early yesterday morning. A shot from the pistol of Officer Jones is thought to have been the cause of death, having been fired, the officers state, after Glover had shot twice at Officer Smith.

Recently the officers were warned not to invade the above district, which is on the Little Warrior river, in their quest for whiskey and illicit stills, but this did not deter Officers Smith, Jones, White and Sam Arnett from making a search. While walking in the woods where they thought stills were located Officers Smith and Jones met Glover, according to their statement. They ordered him to halt, which he refused to do. A few words passed, the officers assert, when Glover pulled a pistol and fired twice. They returned the fire and following the report of Officer Jones' gun, Glover fell upon the ground, fatally wounded. L.E. Felton, a discharged overseas soldier, who was not engaged in the shooting was arrested on a charge of violating the prohibition laws. The officers stated that they found 19 still emplacements in the district before they encountered Glover. They added that they had received warnings that it would be best for them to stay out of the district."

WOUNDS PROVE FATAL
Alleged Bootlegger, Shot By Deputies, Dies After Lingering Illness

The Birmingham News, August 28, 1921

"F.M. Wilkerson, Jr., who was shot several weeks ago on the Montgomery Highway by deputies from the sheriff's office while attempting to escape from the officers with an automobile said to contain 40 gallons of liquor, died from his injuries at the Fraternal Hospital. Wilkerson was accidentally shot in the chase when the bullets fired at the car by Deputies Woodie Sandefer, Virgil Sandefer and Paul Cole in an attempt to puncture the tires and gasoline tank glanced from the banks of the road and struck him. Parents of Wilikerson came to the office of the chief of police seeking the arrest by police officers of the deputies who shot the young man, They were told they would have to take the matter up with the sheriff's office and swear out a warrant."

DEPUTIES HELD ON MURDER CHARGE IN WILKINSON CASE
Death Of Alleged Bootlegger, Shot In Chase, Causes Arrest

The Birmingham News, August 29, 1921

"Deputy Sheriffs Paul Cole, Woodie Sandifer and Virgil Sandifer were in the county jail Monday morning on charges of murder as a result of the death of Marion Wilkinson, alias "Mutt" Wilkinson, who was shot three weeks ago in a liquor chase following the swearing out of warrants by the father of the dead man. The shooting of Wilkinson occurred while the deputies were chasing a big touring car on the highway. Forty gallons of whiskey were found in the car. The deputies, who were held without bail, will be given preliminary hearings."

WILKINSON'S DEATH IS HELD UNLAWFUL
Deputies Must Answer For Slaying Of Occupant Of Alleged Liquor Car

The Birmingham News, September 1, 1921

"Preliminary trial of Deputies Paul Cole, Virgil Sandefer and Woody Sandefer on charges of murder in connection with the alleged killing of Marion Wilkinson by bullets fired by the officers at a car full of liquor, in which Wilkinson and others, it is alleged, were attempting to escape on the Pump House road will be held. A verdict of unlawful homicide in the case was rendered by Coroner J.D. Russum."

DEPUTIES FREED ON CHARGE OF MURDER
Court Holds Testimony In Wilkinson Slaying Insufficient To Prove Guilt

The Birmingham News, September 9, 1921

"Deputies Virgil Sandefer and Paul Cole were acquitted on charges of murder in connection with the shooting of Marion Wilkinson some time ago, when Judge H.B. Abernethy entered an order discharging the two officers following a preliminary trial. The court held that the state had not introduced sufficient evidence to prove that the two officers had shot Wilkinson. Decision in the case of Deputy Woody Sandefer, the third member of the trio charged with the crime, was postponed. Wilkinson was fatally shot several weeks ago when the deputies gave chase to a car in which Wilkinson and his companions are alleged to have been attempting to run liquor into Birmingham."

Postscript

Sandefer's case was sent to the Grand Jury, but there is no evidence that he was indicted for the shooting of Wilkinson. The case was obviously no-billed as Woody Sandefer's involvement in other cases as a deputy sheriff are found in later coroner's records.

Shortly after the constitutional enactment of nationwide prohibition, the process of enforcement of the 18th Amendment by various agencies at the federal, state and local levels rapidly increased. Evidence of this in Jefferson and surrounding counties can be readily found in daily newspaper accounts of that time. In addition, news articles also reflected similar instances of raids on illicit alcohol production facilities throughout the country, many times with fatal outcomes for lawbreakers as well as for enforcement officers.

FARMER KILLED BY FEDERAL OFFICERS IN LIQUOR RAID
In Affray Over Search of Wagon One is Killed and One Lodged in Jail--No Liquor In Evidence

The Birmingham Age-Herald, September 30, 1921

"Kirk Tidmore of Oneonta is dead and Chalmers Huffstutler of Oneonta was placed in the county jail as a result of an affray with federal officers on the Springville road about 20 miles north of Birmingham. According to officers information was received over the long distance telephone that the two men were coming to Birmingham with a load of liquor concealed in a wagon load of vegetables. Drawing up to the side of the wagon, Federal Officer T.C. Dews, who was riding the running board of the car containing the federal agents says he commanded the men in the wagon to stop, saying that the men in the car were revenue officers. The officers stated that a shot was then fired from the wagon, narrowly missing Federal Officer Horton who was driving the car. Following the shot the officers are said to have rushed from the automobile, closing in upon the wagon. Tidmore is said to have fired a shotgun later found in the wagon. A hand-to-hand combat followed the shooting in which Tidmore was shot and that before the men stopped struggling they had to be handcuffed.

Tidmore was taken to Hillman hospital where he died on the operating table. N.L. Pierce stated yesterday that he was unable to state whether the officers found any liquor in the wagon or not. CE. Huffstutler who was with Mr. Tidmore when the shooting occurred made the following statement: "We were driving along and I had slid down in the seat in a comfortable position. There was a sudden command to halt and one of the mules I was driving took fright and as I had the lines in my hand it jerked me down on the double tree. Seeing that the mule was about to run away I was trying to get his head to stop him. It was then the men began to shoot. Tidmore fell to the ground and they had put handcuffs on him before they ever said anything about being prohibition officers. I heard Tidmore ask them what they wanted and then heard him tell them we had no liquor. It all happened so quick ad in the middle of the night that both of us were naturally excited. We had an old single barrel shotgun lying along the back of the seat. It did not have a shell in it and the only shells we had were in my pocket. We never fired a shot. The officers must have fired five or six times. We were bringing a load of vegetables to town to sell. We had no liquor. I myself have always been for prohibition. I voted for it. Tidmore leaves a wife and four children and I have a wife and five children."

OFFICERS FACING MURDER CHARGE IN TIDMORE CASE
Conflicting Testimony Given Coroner By Witnesses at Hearing Yesterday

The Birmingham Age-Herald, October 4, 1921

"Warrants charging T.C. Dewes, W.M. Dewes and W.E. Eubanks, federal prohibition enforcement officers, and J.B. Thompson, Birmingham traffic policeman, with murder in the first degree were sworn out yesterday afternoon by Coroner J.D. Russum, following an inquest into the death of Curtis Tidmore, whom the officers are alleged to have shot and killed several nights ago near Springville as they were attempting to make a search for liquor.

Departing from his usual custom, Coroner Russum made his investigation public and a number of people attended the lengthy session. Ten witnesses were examined. The testimony given by the officers was that they had just returned from a raid in Shelby County and were informed by their chief, Mr. Pierce, that he had a search warrant for a wagon being driven by Kirk Lewis, alias Tidmore, and a man named Huffstutler, who were alleged to be bringing a quantity of liquor into town hidden under a load of vegetables.

They were said to have met the wagon about 16 miles from Birmingham, and T.C. Dewes ordered the two men to halt, telling them that they were federal officers. At this, one of the men opened fire with a shotgun and the other with a pistol. All the officers except Horton admitted that they fired shots at the two men. After a hand-to-hand struggle they succeeded in getting handcuffs on them, and finding that Tidmore was wounded placed him in their car and brought him to a local hospital. They admitted that they found no liquor in the wagon and that they could not find the pistol with which the men are supposed to have been firing, but did find the shotgun.

Huffstutler's testimony contradicted that of the officers. He said the officers came upon his companion and himself and ordered them to hold up their hands. As soon as they did so the mules began to run and the officers began shooting. He said he was not told the men were officers, and did not know what he was charged with until he was placed in the county jail, when he learned that the charge was resisting an officer. He said that neither he nor Tidmore shot. W.J. Huddleston and D.A. Stone testified that they lived within 100 yards of the scene, heard the shots and that they did not hear a shotgun fired. They said they searched the ground the next day and did not find any wads from a shotgun."

PIERCE URGES PUBLIC NOT TO JUDGE HASTILY
Expresses Regret for Tidmore Tragedy and Calls Attention to Other Widows and Orphans Left Among Families of Men Enforcing Prohibition Laws

The Birmingham Age-Herald, October 10, 1921

"N.L. Pierce, chief federal prohibition officer of Alabama issued a statement concerning the killing of Curtis Tidmore several weeks ago by officers of his department. Mr. Pierce expressed his regret for the unfortunate affair, and calls attention to the fact that two of his officers have been killed by alleged moonshiners. He makes a plea that the public refrain from judging the four officers until the case comes up in court."

NO REPORT MADE ON KILLING OF CURTIS TIDMORE
Prohibition Authorities Tell Oliver Alabama Dry Agents Said Nothing of Death--Probe Promised
The Birmingham Age-Herald, October 13, 1921
Washington, October 12 (Special)

"Federal prohibition authorities today demanded of Alabama prohibition officers a full and complete report of the sensational killing of Curtis Tidmore, a Blount county farmer, at the hands of enforcement officers some weeks ago. The delay on the part of the federal authorities was due to the fact that no report, official or otherwise, had reached them. Representative W.B. Oliver of the Sixth Alabama district laid bare the facts today, and authorities were surprised that official information had been withheld. Mr. Oliver was informed that a report would be demanded by wire, and that if acts as he reported were substantiated actions would be taken at once.

The case, Mr. Oliver reported, had caused considerable indignation on the part of the citizens of the state. Resolutions adopted by citizens of Oneonta, in which the tragedy was disclosed, together with the alleged fact that no liquor was found in possession of the victim, were read by federal authorities with surprise and expressions of horror."

OFFICERS INDICTED BY THE GRAND JURY
Federal Officers Charged With Murder In Second Degree In Tidmore Case
The Birmingham Age-Herald, November 2, 1921

"Indictments charging murder in the second degree were returned by the Jefferson county grand jury against T.C. Dews, Jr., and W.E. Eubank, federal prohibition enforcement officers, and James B. Thompson, former police officer, and W.M. Dews. These men are alleged to have shot and killed Curtis Tidmore several weeks ago when they attempted to stop him as he was coming towards Birmingham with a wagon load of vegetables.

TIDMORE TRIAL MAY BE RESUMED
The Birmingham Age-Herald, March 10, 1922

"The trial of the two former federal officers. W.E. Eubanks and W.M. Dews and former Police Officer J.B. Thompson, charged with the murder of Curtis B. Tidmore, Oneonta farmer, who was killed last October by federal officers who attempted to search his wagon about 20 miles out of the city on the Springville road, will probably be resumed this morning.

T.C. Dews, Jr., also a former federal officer, who was charged with the murder, failed to appear in court Wednesday and the case was passed up until a later date. Dews is now serving a six months sentence for defrauding and swindling on a prison farm near Savannah, Ga. A warrant for his arrest has been forwarded to Georgia and will be served upon him as soon as he serves his sentence."

Postscript

As with the Tidmore case, a number of news accounts during the years that nationwide prohibition was in effect suggest that the use of deadly force by law enforcement officers was sometimes perceived by the public as being excessive and overly zealous. This animosity, especially in those cases where apparent innocent persons were killed, occasionally led to increased public pressure on local prosecutors to allow grand juries to investigate these deaths and to recommend whether an officer should be indicted for the homicide of an individual, even though the that person may have thought he was acting under the "color of the law."

Additional research in regard to legal proceedings against those persons considered responsible for the death of Curtis Tidmore failed to reveal any further information. In a 1927 review of related killings by federal agents enforcing prohibition since the Volstead Act was placed on the statute books it was noted that:

> "According to incomplete records kept by the Prohibition Unit at Washington, 113 had been reported killed...but makes no effort to record the killings by local and State officers and agents of other branches of the Federal service. These, it is believed, would bring the total to well over two hundred.
> Of the 113 cases recorded, State authorities brought prosecutions in fifty-seven. Twenty-two of these were taken out of the State's hands by the Federal courts, with the Federal prosecuting attorney acting as counsel for the accused. Of the twenty-two cases, thirteen resulted in acquittals, one in a conviction, one in a plea of guilty, and seven are still pending."

> "A sweeping investigation into the tragedies of the 'shoot first and shoot to kill" enforcement policy of the United States Government to determine how many murderers have escaped punishment because United States attorneys have intervened in Federal courts to protect the killing agents from State court prosecution is almost a certainty. State courts have indicted dozens of the killers, but virtually without exception the slayers have found refuge in the Federal courts under an interpretation of the law which gave them the sole jurisdiction in cases where revenue agents kill in the line of duty. The exact number of citizens killed or of those wounded or permanently disabled is not available even in the Prohibition bureau. It has been charged that Federal judges have been swayed to dismiss murder and manslaughter charges against reckless, swashbuckling killers for fear of destroying the 'morale' of the Prohibition service which has been built up on the assurance that the Government will protect its agents if they can make any sort of a showing that they killed in self-defense."

The report went on to summarize this matter by noting that:

> "It is no doubt possible to make out a legal argument in favor of the agents in every one of these cases. That is to say, it is possible to argue that they were forced to kill in the performance of their duty, just as other police officers are sometimes forced to kill in the performance of their duty; and that their acquittal, under these circumstances, is to be taken for granted. But that argument, while it may dispose of any effort to cast doubt on the workings of justice in individual cases in the past, does not dispose of the situation which now confronts us. That situation is this: we have in the Federal service a Prohibition force which on the word of its 'undercover' officials, is recruited to a large extent from the very class of criminals which it is supposed to hunt down. Yet this highly dangerous class of men is loosed upon us, knowing quite well from the record that it may kill with impunity, since the chance is almost negligible that it will suffer any punishment."[11]

It was possibly just such an outcome that occurred in the Tidmore case following repetitive delays within the legal system. Or perhaps the lack of sufficient proof as to who had fired the fatal shot may have led to dismissal of the charges.

SAM TAYLOR KILLED IN LIQUOR BATTLE
Sheriff's Forces In Running Fight Along Bessemer Road
The Birmingham Age-Herald, March 25, 1924

"Sam Taylor, ex-member of the Birmingham police force, was instantly killed in a running fight between whisky runners and deputies from the sheriff's office at midnight Monday on the road between Birmingham and Bessemer. Taylor jumped from the automobile after being shot and was crushed between the wheels, which is believed to have been the immediate cause of his death. His companions were arrested and placed in the Bessemer jail on charges of violation of the prohibition law. The car contained 12 gallons of whisky and was said to have been specially built for liquor hauling purposes, having especially constructed steel armor plates in the front and rear as protection against bullets."

By the mid 1920s doubt was already surfacing publicly about the efficiency of trying to control the illicit alcohol trade. It also brought into question the reliability and honesty of agents who were appointed to enforce the law.

TWO KILLED IN ALLEGED STILL RAID
Youths Slain While At Work, Claim Deputies;
One Lad In Jail
Shooting Happens Near Mount Pinson
Officers Place Boy In County Prison On Distilling Charge
The Birmingham Age-Herald, March 22, 1928

"Two youths are dead and one is in the county jail under $1,000 bond on a charge of distilling as the result of an alleged raid by deputy sheriffs on a still three miles from Mount Pinson. The dead are Dewey Day, 21, and Troy Day, 18. Raymond Trucks, 18, is in the County jail.

According to information gathered by Assistant Coroner Burge, and reports given Sheriff J.C. Hartsfield by the raiding deputies, the two youths were shot when they refused to surrender to Deputies C.A. Doss and C.H. Thaxton. Trucks surrendered immediately upon seeing the deputies approach. Doss and Thaxton...were searching for a still. Assistant Coroner Burge stated that he had received reports that the Day brothers gestured onwards their pockets when the deputies approached, while Trucks held up his hands. Whether the Days did any shooting, he had not been able to learn, he said. Investigators said they were unable to learn whether Doss or Thaxton did the actual shooting.

Dr. A.S. Hutto, who was called to the scene of the shooting, told an Age-Herald reporter that Dewey Day's body was 100 feet from the still and that Troy's body was 60 feet from the still. Embalmers at Johns said that the older boy had wounds in the lower part of his back and in the region of the lower right ribs and that the younger boy had three wounds, one in the left temple, on the left side and one in the left arm. The two youths are survived by their parents, three other brothers, Jap, Isaac and John, and a sister, all of Mount Pinson. The still was described as of a 30-gallon capacity. They said it was in operation when the shooting took place."

DAVIS TO PROBE KILLING OF DAYS
Deputy Sheriff Held In Killing Of Brothers At Mount Pinson Still

The Birmingham Age-Herald, March 23, 1928

"An investigation into the killing of Dewey Day, 21, and Troy Day, 18, at a still near Mount Pinson, for which Former Deputy Sheriff C.A. Doss is being held without bond in the county jail on a charge of first degree murder, will be started immediately by Solicitor Jim Davis. Mr. Davis said his investigation will be in the form of a preparation for the Grand Jury investigation of the tragedy...and until that time Doss will be held in jail without bond. C.H. Thaxton, the deputy who was with Doss at the time of the shooting, was released after the coroner learned that he had fired two shots into the air as a warning to the two boys. Doss has been suspended as deputy sheriff having turned over his badge and weapons to the sheriff.

In a statement before the coroner, Doss said he shot the Day brothers because they gave indications of making a violent demonstration. He said that after telling the boys that he was "the law" and ordering them to surrender that Dewey Day dodged behind some barrels, making a motion towards his hip, while Troy ran off seeming to thrust his hands in the bosom of his overalls. Doss stated that he repeated his order to the brothers to stop, but that they continued making suspicious motions. He then shot them, he said.

Deputy George Lamb, who was near the scene of the shooting at the time it occurred, told the coroner that the Day brothers showed every sign of making a demonstration at the time they were accosted. However, no weapons were found on either boy, according to testimony brought out by the coroner. Thaxton said he saw a pistol by the side of Troy's body that corresponded to one owned by Doss. The latter deputy said his pistol was in his holster. Doss has been a deputy sheriff for about four months. He said that Wednesday's encounter was the first time he had occasion to use a gun on a human being. The Day brothers were shot with a shotgun loaded with buckshot."

EX-DEPUTY INDICTED IN RAID DEATH
Grand Jury Charges First Degree Murder Against Doss
Former Deputy Is Refused Bond
The Birmingham Age-Herald, April 5, 1928

"An indictment, charging first degree murder was returned by the Grand Jury against C. Arthur Doss, suspended deputy sheriff. Doss has been in the county jail since the shooting of the two boys."

DOSS GOES ON TRIAL IN RAID DEATH
Eyewitness Testifies To Slaying of Youths
In Capture of Still
Defense Contends Boy Armed When Ex-Deputy
Fired Fatal Shot
The Birmingham Age-Herald, May 14, 1929

"The prosecution in the case of C.A. Doss, former deputy sheriff charged with murder in connection with the death of Troy Day, a Mount Pinson youth, expects to complete its testimony Tuesday. Three witnesses were called Monday by the prosecutor, last of whom was Raymond Trucks, 20, reputed eye witness to the slaying. Roderick Beddow, for the defense, had examined Trucks for more than an hour Monday before adjournment. Trucks related purported incidents of the still raid in which Troy Day and his brother, Dewey, were slain.

E.M. Blanton, embalmer for Johns Undertaking Company testified that he embalmed Troy Day and found three wounds caused by buckshot, one in the back of the head, one in the back and another in the back of the left arm. Trucks said he was with the Day boys in the vicinity of the still when they were killed. He said he was there when the officers arrived. Deputies Doss and Thaxton approached the still and cried out to them and the Day brothers got to their feet and ran. Trucks said Doss started shooting from a distance of 25 yards. The boys started running abreast of each other, but separated when Dewey Day was hit, Troy turning to the left and Dewey to the right. Troy fell first. Dewey kept running but his steps began to lag until he fell to the ground. He didn't get up again, but lay with his face in the air.

After the Day brothers had been shot, Doss went to where Troy lay, then came back and said he had found a gun on him. On answer to a question by John Altman, special prosecutor, Trucks said neither of the Day brothers was armed. Roderick Beddow asked Trucks if he had not testified before the coroner that Thaxton was the deputy who said Troy was armed, and the witness answered in the negative."

DEFENSE CLAIMS YOUTH KILLED IN DRY RAID ARMED
Former Deputy Doss To Take Stand In Own Defense Today

The Birmingham Age-Herald, May 15, 1929

"Trial of Doss, which was postponed three times, got underway before Judge H.P. Heflin. Testimony in the trial centered around the question of the presence of a .38 caliber revolver on Troy Day at the time of the killing. Three mysterious strangers entered the case, too, when the defense produced testimony that three men armed with a shotgun walked over the scene of the killing and examined the bodies of the slain youths just before the .38 caliber revolver was said to have disappeared from beneath the body of Troy Day.

The defense seeks to prove, Beddow told the court, that Doss, who was the only deputy present at the time the three men are said to have appeared, and that Doss hid when the men approached, and from hiding watched them stoop over the body of Troy Day, then walk on through the woods and out of sight. Altman objected to the course of the testimony and was told by Beddow that the defense was seeking to prove that Troy Day was armed and that the gun was later stolen.

Deputy Thaxton said Doss shot twice after Dewey appeared to have been attempting to dodge behind some mash barrels and Troy appeared to be drawing a gun. He testified to seeing the gun beneath Troy when the youth fell. Thaxton was asked by Altman if he didn't think that the pistol under Troy Day was Doss' pistol, and the deputy replied that he thought so at first because Doss' shotgun lay nearby. Altman then asked the deputy if he didn't think that it was Doss' gun because "you know it was a frameup to make it appear that the boy was armed." Beddow objected and heated exchange of words followed, but Beddow's objection was overruled. Altman then asked Thaxton what made him think the gun under Day belonged to Doss, and if it was because Doss' gun was missing? Thaxton answered that he remembered Doss had a .38 that looked like the gun under Troy Day."

LAWYERS ARGUE ABOUT REVOLVER IN TRIAL OF DOSS
Three Men And Boy Also Bone of Contention In Pinson Case

The Birmingham Age-Herald, May 16, 1929

"Three men, a boy and a shotgun and their relation to a pistol that is said to have disappeared from the body of a dead man featured in the testimony in the trial of C.A. Doss, former deputy sheriff charged with murder in the death of Troy Day, slain last year in a liquor raid near Mount Pinson. Dewey Day was slain at the same time.

Doss took the stand and related Incidents leading up to the raid on the still. Questioned as to the presence of a weapon on Troy Day, Doss replied that he had seen no gun or other weapon when he went to the boy after the shooting. He said the first he heard of the presence of a pistol on Troy Day was when it was mentioned later by the deputies who accompanied him on the raid. Troy Day was shot, Doss testified, when he half turned while retreating and fumbled in the bosom of his overalls as if seeking a gun.

Beddow, for the defense, sought to impeach the testimony of Raymond Trucks and John Altman, special prosecutor, sought to impeach Doss' testimony. Heated clashes between Beddow and Altman featured taking of testimony and the jury was instructed on several occasions by Judge Heflin, not to consider as testimony questions propounded by the prosecution. Both lawyers were on their feet upon one occasion when Altman was questioning Doss and Beddow charged him with attempting to intimidate the defendant. He objected to Altman's conduct but the objection was overruled."

FATE OF DOSS IN RAID SLAYING IN HANDS OF JURY

The Birmingham Age-Herald, May 18, 1929

"Deliberation began after the jury had returned from lunch, and during the afternoon, while they talked behind closed doors, the court room was half filled in anticipation of an early verdict. Dozens more milled around in the halls outside but as no word came from the jury room the crowd thinned and early in the night only a small percentage of the number remained.

Doss was indicted on a charge of first degree murder after the Day brothers had been killed at the still. The state contended that the Day brothers were unarmed and that the shooting was not justifiable. The defense plead self-defense and contended that Troy Day was armed."

JURY GIVES DOSS TWO-YEAR TERM; ANOTHER INDICTMENT YET PENDING
Tried In Troy Day's Death, Former Deputy Must Face Court For Second Slaying

The Birmingham News, May 19, 1929

"Sentence of two years in the penitentiary will be passed by Judge H.P. Heflin on C.A. Doss, former deputy sheriff, found guilty of first degree manslaughter by a jury. The penalty was fixed in the jury's verdict. Doss was found guilty of the manslaughter charge in connection with the death of Troy Day. He also is under indictment on a murder charge in connection with the death of Dewey Day. The verdict in the death of Troy Day will not affect the disposition of the case against Doss in Dewey Day's death.

Only a few spectators were present when the jury announced ready to return a verdict after 27 hours of deliberation. Many spectators had left earlier in the day when the jury sent out word it was unable to agree on a verdict. The defendant, seated with his wife and other members of his family remained composed as the jury returned its verdict. He was taken to the county jail after a short talk with Beddow."

Postscript

Although Doss was found guilty of manslaughter of Troy Day and was sentenced to two years imprisonment, no further information could be found regarding any additional legal action taken against him in the death of Dewey Day or if Doss actually served any time in prison.

Docket Entry:
Date: October 18, 1935
Deceased: Sammie Lee Decree, C.
Address: Cahaba river near Birmingham.
Cause Of Death: Drowning.
Notes: Was working a still and ran from federal officers during raid. Drowned in river.

Docket Entry:
Date: October 9, 1936
Deceased: Joel Clark, C.
Address: Warrior river, Labuco.
Cause Of Death: Drowned.
Notes: Ran from officers and jumped in river. Officers were raiding still. Negro sank before the officers could reach him in a rowboat. The white men escaped.

Poison

BIRMINGHAM AROUSED OVER DEADLY POISON CONCOCTIONS SOLD AS WHISKEY
Claim Is Made That Several of City's Well-Known Citizens Have Been Killed By Murderous Compounds Bearing Government Stamp

The Birmingham Age-Herald, March 23, 1921

"Birmingham is aroused as it has not been in a long time over the cause of many deaths which have recently occurred. It is claimed that not less than a half dozen citizens of prominence have been killed recently by drinking concocted whiskey which had been brought in by bootleggers. Much of the whiskey has been alleged rye brand with old labels and defaced government stamps on it. The bootleggers have claimed that it has been dropped overboard from foreign ships.

It is also believed that many of the moonshiners in the mountains and hills around Birmingham are causing their mash to ferment quickly by adding Red Devil lye to it, and various forms of washing powders which makes the mash ferment in 24 hours, instead of 30 days, which is the usual time. A very prominent man in Birmingham is said to have died within the month after drinking some $12-a-bottle whiskey. It gave him convulsions in a very short while and when the physicians tried to bleed him his blood looked like black molasses. Several prominent young men have been killed in the same manner in Birmingham in recent months, and everybody knows that two of the most prominent automobile manufacturers in America were killed several months ago by drinking concocted whiskey containing poison.

Many matured men who have been in the habit of taking their toddies for many years, and naturally desire a good whiskey occasionally, have been buying from men who have brought it in from various seaport towns, believing that it was the real stuff. Instead, some of them have bought poison concoctions in apparently honest looking bottles.

A prominent coal operator who has been in the habit of taking a toddy before his dinner for 30 or 35 years, yesterday said: "These men who bring poison whiskey into Birmingham and sell it as real stuff and thereby kill people are just as guilty of murder as the man who goes out with a pistol and commits murder. They should be hung--not merely fined for bringing in this whiskey. I think I know one of the men who has brought in some of the poison stuff, and I propose to see that he is tried for murder if we can lay hands on him. I hear he has left town, but we may get him yet."

"Canned Heat"

"Woke up this morning with the canned heat on my mind. Crying, canned heat, mama, sure, Lord killing me."

---"Canned Heat Blues"

A particularly poisonous ethanol substitute was called "canned heat," or Sterno. It was meant to be used as a fuel source for heating food within a can. Lacking safer intoxicants, Sterno was used as a surrogate alcohol. Since the type of alcohol it contains (methanol) is denatured it is poisonous. Its use became popular during Prohibition and during the Great Depression in hobo camps, or "jungles," where this cheap product in its jellied form would be squeezed through cheesecloth or a sock and the resulting liquid was mixed with fruit juice to make "jungle juice," " sock wine," or "squeeze."

Docket Entry:
Date: January 14, 1926
Deceased: Critz McCormack, W.
Address: Johns Funeral Home
Cause Of Death: From acute alcoholism. Drank canned heat.

WOMAN DECLARED VICTIM OF POISON
The Birmingham Age-Herald, December 17, 1927

"Funeral services for Mrs. Bertha Barbin, 44, who died suddenly at her home, will be announced by Johns upon receipt of word from out-of-town relatives. According to Deputy Coroner William Burge, Mrs. Barbins' death was the result of canned heat poisoning. According to Mr. Burge, more than 80 empty canned heat cans were found in her room."

"Jake Leg"

"Jake leg, jake leg, what in the world you trying to do? Seems like everybody in the city is messed up on account of drinking you."

---Jake Liquor Blues

PARALYSIS OF 300 LAID TO 'LIQUOR'
Poison "Jake" Is Blamed For Strange Malady
In Oklahoma City
Deaths Expected By U.S. Inspector
Physicians Are Unable To Offer Any Relief
To Stricken Victims

The Birmingham Age-Herald, March 8, 1930
Oklahoma City, Okla.,

"Drinks of poison "Jake," popular low-priced intoxicant, had affected more than 300 persons here with a mysterious malady that paralyzed the victims. More than 250 persons were stricken at their homes, where they frantically sought advice from physicians, who could promise them no relief. At least 50 more were in hospitals and clinics, where experts attempted to diagnose the cases and determine whether the malady would be fatal. No deaths had occurred, although physicians reported many victims who had noted only slight muscular twitches early Friday rapidly were becoming paralyzed. All the victims told authorities the illness followed drinking of Jamaica ginger distributed by bootleggers and "blind pig" drug stores.

A federal ban was placed on shipments of Jamaica ginger from Kansas City and St. Louis warehouses. Authorities said the ban would exist until specialists are able to determine the cause of the affliction. Meanwhile, federal and city authorities tested samples of Jamaica ginger from drug stores and liquor taken in raids in a effort to determine the source of the poison.

The condition of victims was pathetic. Most of them were men who live in the south part of the city where the oil field workers and laborers live. They were frightened, as physicians had told some of them they might not recover, and they readily told their stories to authorities describing when they drank the liquor and where it was obtained. The malady affected the feet of the victims first. They complained of muscular twitchings. Then their legs began to ache. Soon the paralysis had spread to their hands. Many could not raise their hands to their faces. Others were on their backs unable to move.

"Jake" is obtained easily here. It is sold in small eight-ounce bottles at some drug stores for 50 cents. Some "joints" sell it for 25 cents a drink over the bar. In the oil field residence section, it is said 20 places disperse "Jake" within one block. One or two bottles will result in intoxication."

The label of a two ounce bottle of Jamaica Ginger indicates that it contains 90% alcohol. This is equal to 180 proof whiskey with absolute or 100% alcohol being the maximum of 200 proof. At this level, the ingestion of two 8 ounce bottles of this substance would certainly result in a high level of intoxication.

As related by Dan Baum in his The New Yorker magazine article "Jake Leg--How the blues diagnosed a medical mystery,"[12] it was noted that:

> "Dr. John Morgan, a professor at the City University of New York Medical School, likes to call himself a pharmaco-ethnomusicologist. Some years back, Morgan was listening to the Allen Brothers' "Jake Walk Blues," released in 1930. In a kazoo-backed Tennessee twang, the brothers sang, "I can't eat, I can't talk, drinking mean jake, Lord, I can't walk." In medical school, in 1961, a professor had mentioned a strange paralysis called

"jake walk" that he had observed during his residency in Cincinnati in the thirties. Morgan has collected a number of songs about the jake leg or the Jake walk. From them we learn that some new kind of paralysis appeared in 1930," he said. "No songs mention it before then. The paralysis was brought on by drinking something called 'jake.' It affected enough souls to instigate an entire subset of folk music. Blacks and whites were affected. It rendered men impotent. And it was no longer inspiring musicians by 1934 which meant it was a cataclysmic but discrete event."

"The outbreak was first detected in Oklahoma City by Ephraim Goldfain, a physician who ran a clinic. On February 27, 1930, a man whose name is lost to history staggered in off the street. The patient's feet dangled like a marionette's, so that walking involved swinging them forward and slapping them onto the floor. Sudden paralysis in those days usually meant polio, but this didn't look like polio. The man's symptoms suggested lead poisoning. He ordered blood and spinal fluid tests. They came back negative. Later that day, another man appeared, exhibiting the same bizarre palsy. And then another. By the end of the day the clinic had admitted five patients with the distinctive paralysis."

"Oklahoma in 1930 was a hard-luck place. Now it was struggling with what looked like a full-blown epidemic. In one frenetic day, Goldfain visited thirty men. The men's feet dangled, their legs hung dead below the knee. Goldfain knew at once that this was no contagion. No children were sick, and hardly any women. The men Goldfain saw all lived in a seedy part of town known for bootlegging. He had only to look at them, and the grimy scratch houses they lived in, to know they were stewbums, boozegobs, hootch histers, drunks. Within a few days, in various locales in the East, the South, and the Midwest, men began folding up. Those who could still walk all had the same rubber-legged gait. The numbers were frightening... the typical victim was an alcoholic man living alone in a cheap rented room, unemployed or holding a menial job. Many were veterans of the Great War."

"The economics of Prohibition, then in its eleventh year, painted a bulls-eye on the urban and small town poor. City swells could buy bonded liquor from Canada; backwoods hillbillies often had access to stills.

> Low-income townsfolk drank what they could get--rubbing alcohol, hair oil, Sterno, doctored antifreeze. What many of them preferred, though, was jake. Jake was Jamaica ginger extract, one of the hundreds of dubious but harmless patent medicines that Americans had been relying on for a century. Because it was as much as eighty-five-percent alcohol it packed the kick of four jiggers of Scotch. And it was legal. Patent medicines had been providing an end run around temperance laws since Maine became the first state to go dry, in 1851. A bottle costing thirty-five cents was available in many pharmacies, groceries, and even dime stores. The Pure Food and Drug Act of 1906 had purified neither. It required only honest labelling. If a patent medicine contained alcohol, morphine, opium, cocaine, heroin, alpha or beta eucaine, chloroform, cannabis indica, chloral hydrate, or acetanilide, the label had to say so. In 1919, the Volstead Act turned every state dry, but it banned only beverage liquor; jake and other alcoholic medicines remained legal. When the mysterious outbreak of paralysis occurred, eleven years later, there was no reason to suspect that Jake had any role."

> "Autopsies of jake-leggers who died from other causes showed damage to the central nervous system, including the spinal cord's anterior horn cells—the same that go bad in cases of polio and amyotrophic lateral sclerosis (A.L.S., or Lou Gehrig's disease). But the spinal column's pyramidal tract cells also suffered from the jake, which gradually led to spasms and rigidity. Higher brain functions weren't affected, a team of University of Oklahoma researchers concluded, although their methodology raises questions. They dosed a chicken with enough jake to make its limbs go limp and noted, "The expression in the eyes seemed to indicate that the mind was not impaired." Once jake was established as the vector, there was no escaping the awkward truth that the victims had brought the affliction upon themselves. Shame was an additional burden on the sufferers; the jake leg's distinctive limp betrayed everybody."

Baum's article goes on to detail how and why "Jake" became toxic during the manufacturing process as well as the not very satisfying outcomes of litigations relating to this sad episode.

Drugs

In addition to problems related to the excesses of alcohol consumption, the late 19th and early 20th centuries saw the rampant use and abuse of narcotic and stimulant drugs. As noted by Litwack, "The cost was minimal. Ten cents, an observer wrote from Atlanta in 1906, will purchase more than enough cocaine "to make a man wholly unresponsible for his acts," and it was often readily available in various forms at a nickel or a dime from a druggist."[13]

The rise in the number of persons addicted to and dying from drugs of abuse in the early 21st century has been reported to be greater than at any time in the past.

However, as noted by D.J. Carroll:

> "rampant opioid addiction rates do have a parallel: here in the United States, especially in the American South, after the civil war. Southern whites during the Gilded Age arguably had the highest addiction rates in the country, and possibly the world. In 1915 Congress passed the Harrison Narcotics Act, which required that anyone who Imported, produced, sold or dispensed narcotics to register, pay a tax and keep detailed records. Addiction rates were not borne equally among Southerners either. White Southerners were far likelier to consume opium or heroin than black Southerners. Why was opium and morphine addiction so rampant in the United States in the Gilded Age? The answer rests with the outcome of the Civil War. Thousands of Civil War soldiers who were wounded during combat were first dosed with opium or morphine in field hospitals during the war. Many came home struggling with addiction to narcotics, first tasted in a hospital. Confederate soldiers returned to a defeated and humiliated South.
> One out of every five southern males of military age were killed in the war. families turned to drugs to cope with the devastating loss of a husband, son, brother or father. Today, much of the opioid epidemic stems from prescription drug abuse...and it fueled the opioid epidemic during the Gilded Age as well.
>
> Opium, heroin and morphine were legal tools for the apothecary or physician during and after the Civil War. The science of addiction had not yet emerged, and doctors prescribed opium and morphine regularly for pain

management and sleeping problems. So large a number of soldiers became addicted as a result of the opiates given them for battle injuries, that post-war morphine addiction prevalent among veterans came to be known as "soldier's disease."[14]

Heroin, an opium derivative, was first produced in 1898. It was widely advertised as being at least ten times as potent a painkiller as morphine with none of the addicting properties. A claim was made that the use of heroin could and would cure opium addiction and physicians made use of heroin in treating varied ailments. In addition to the enactment of federal statutes controlling narcotics, many states and cities also passed laws banning various addictive substances. The so-called "War on Drugs" is certainly not new.

COCAINE HABIT IS CAUSING TROUBLE
The Birmingham Age-Herald, September 8, 1904

"Judge Feagin is having a great deal of trouble with the negro women of the city who are addicted to the habit of eating cocaine and other harmful drugs. Only yesterday there were three of them released from jail on promise to leave the city and never return here again, and in less than an hour one of them appeared in court again and was under the influence of the drug. The woman was immediately sent back to jail but there is nothing to do with this class except. Leave them in jail. There is no employment furnished by the city for negro women and the jail will soon be crowded beyond its capacity.

In speaking of the matter yesterday, Judge Feagin said: "There are hundreds of people in the city who use these deadly drugs to a greater or less degree and there are at least 40 per cent who are in court from time to time. Something should be done to prevent the sale of cocaine. People who do not come to the courts of the city or who never happen around the police headquarters have no idea of the number of people in the city addicted to the cocaine habit, and they would be surprised and shocked if they knew the facts."

NOTORIOUS "DOPE" JOINT IS RAIDED
Police Find Deplorable Conditions In House Where The Inmates Were All Under The Influence Of The Drug
The Birmingham Age-Herald, February 7, 1909

"Early Saturday morning police officers raided the house occupied by Annie Lee, a negro woman, in Alley B between Twenty-fourth and Twenty-fifth streets and found the place to be a veritable "dope joint." The officers found six persons in the house, a white man and five negroes, all of whom were more or less under the influence of cocaine. There were also found in the house several hypodermic syringes used to inject cocaine and quite a quantity of the poisonous drug.

The officers' description of the scene presented upon their entrance is horrible. They state that a majority of the inmates lay sprawling on the floor, dead to the world. The remainder of their description would not look well in print. The search for the drug kept in the house was interesting. All of the persons arrested were thoroughly searched and no cocaine was found, but finally a long phial filled with the drug was found buried in the ashes in a coal scuttle.

The officers quote Judge Feagin to the effect that he intends to break up the cocaine habit if possible. It is understood he has stated his intention of sentencing those arrested to one years' imprisonment at Flat Top, believing that to be the only way of preventing them from getting their "dope."

BIG "HOP JOINT" RAID MADE LAST NIGHT BY POLICE
Seven "Opium Fiends" Arrested in Roden Building in Heart of City
Paraphernalia Taken To Headquarters
Officers Had to Break in Door and Found Seven Devotees
"Hitting the Pipe" and Also "Rolling the Pills"

The Birmingham Age-Herald, December 30, 1910

"One of the largest "hop joint" raids ever carried out successfully in Birmingham was made last night. The "joint" was in the third floor of the Roden building on the corner of Second avenue and Twentieth street. The detectives found all manner of paraphernalia in the room where the den was located. There were opium pipes, cards, chips and all manner of strange things which were confiscated by the officers. The den was located yesterday afternoon and the secret of the raid was well kept. It was a complete surprise to the occupants of the "den" and seven arrests were made. Two of them were women. A charge of "hop smoking" was placed against them. The officers found it necessary to break in the doors to make an entrance to the room. When the panels at last gave way a curious and loathsome scene was disclosed. The inmates of the room were all occupied with opium in some form. Two were making the pills to use in the pipes, two were smoking with every outward evidence of enjoyment, one was playing with the deadly morphine, and a third was fingering the bulk opium lovingly. There was a wild scramble when the door was burst open by the officers, and opium, morphine, pipes and cards were tossed in an indiscriminate heap on the floor. The location of the den in the very center of town was also very surprising.

The raid on the den last night is only the first of a series of raids on the dens of Birmingham. The edict has gone forth that the dens and dives must close and there are special men to back up the order with force if necessary."

TRIES NEW PLAN TO CURE DOPE FIENDS
Ten Victims Taken to City Jail Yesterday
SIGHT WAS PATHETIC
Experiment Is Made by Removing Them to Place Where They Cannot Procure the Deadly Drug so Easily
The Birmingham Age-Herald, August 14, 1912

"A pitiable sight was presented at the city jail yesterday when eight white men and two white women were loaded in the city patrol car and carried to the hospital of the new city jail. They were all confirmed "dope" fiends, principally victims to the cocaine habit. The spectacle was truly deplorable; the wan faces and emaciated bodies of the victims plainly showed the havoc the deadly drug had made and the look of despair in their unnaturally bright eyes betokened the despair deep down in their souls.

They were "rounded up" by Dr. Charles Whelan, the city physician, who knows practically every user of "dope" in the city, and who has been trying to reclaim them by outside treatment. His efforts were unavailing, however, owing to the fact that the users of the drug could buy cocaine at any time. Dr. Whelan decided to try another method. He had a number of the "dopes" arrested and carried them before Judge Douglas of the recorder's court.

Previous to appearing before the judge the doctor had a talk with them and everyone expressed the wish that they could be broken from the use of the drug. He submitted a proposition to them which they all gladly accepted which was to agree to a fine of $90 and a sentence of 180 days with the understanding that they were not to appeal the cases. They were to be taken to the hospital and there to undergo treatment and in the event any of them were broken of the drug habit Dr. Whelan agreed to recommend their release.

Dr. Whelan stated that it was utterly impossible to reclaim any of these unfortunates so long as they can purchase the death dealing drugs, and to that end has started a relentless war on the illegal selling of cocaine and other forbidden drugs. Several druggists have already been arrested for this illegal selling of cocaine.

Among the white men taken to the jail hospital yesterday were several young men connected with some well known families, some of them recent victims to the drug. Others have been using it for years. The city physician says the hardest proposition in dealing with the prevention of the sale of cocaine is the "bootlegger," usually a "dopist" himself, who supplies the dope to the users of the drug."

WORK, WHOLESOME FOOD AND PLENTY OF FRESH AIR IS CURE FOR "DOPE HABIT"
Judge Abernethy's Experiment
With "Dope Fiends" Proves a Success
Seventeen Leave Banner Prison
Both Men and Women Look Like Different Persons
After Serving a Few Months Under Watchful Eyes
Of Prison Guards

The Birmingham Age-Herald, December 26, 1912

"That hard work, wholesome food and cleanliness is a pretty good cure for the habitual use of opiates has been demonstrated in Jefferson county. Seventeen white men and women who had sank to the lowest depths of the "dope" habit…have been arrested and brought before Judge Abernethy on a charge of vagrancy. Many of them had been brought before the judge on a promise to break from the daily habit, but only to be brought back again in a few days or weeks in a more pitiable condition than ever.

The result was that some time ago they were sentenced to hard labor for terms varying from six months to two years, and sent out to

Banner mines to work out their sentence. A more distressing picture could not be imagined than that of these poor unfortunates when taken to the prison. The women were all of the underworld and the ravages of "dope" and dissipation made them truly objects of pity. The men were no better, but even in their utter wretchedness had not reached the depths of degeneration which the women had. All were weak and fearfully emaciated, some of them with large frames would barely weigh 100 pounds, and hopeless misery and despair was depicted on their white and wan countenances. It seemed cruel to send such creatures to the mines, but there being no alternative, to the mines they went. All of this happened over six months ago.

When they got to the stockade they were taken in charge by Dr. R.B. Fore, prison physician. His treatment was heroic as not one gram of the drug that was responsible for their condition was given them. Pure air, food and cleanliness was the medicine they received. It was hard for the "dope fiends" at first and threats of self-destruction were made unless they were given their accustomary drug. The wails and cries of the women were awful, the groans and threats of the men heartrending in the extreme; but this did not last long. When fully assured that neither whines nor wails would get them anything, they began to make the best of the situation and gradually began to eat. Light tasks were provided out in the open air, the men in the garden patch, the women at the washtub. Soon they began to improve and the deathly pallor of their countenance was gradually replaced with a healthy tan. Not one of the 17 "dope fiends" was sick after the first few days.

Paroles were granted and the men and women given their freedom conditioned on their good behavior and abstinence from the use of the deadly drug that had caused their degradation."

Docket Entry:
Date: December 6, 1910
Deceased: Mary Smith, Col.
Address: Avenue I and 23 St. South.
Cause Of Death: The jury found that the deceased came to her death from the habitual use of Laudanum.

Docket Entry:
Date: June 14, 1912
Deceased: E. Russell, W.
Address: 210 1/2 32 St.
Cause Of Death: Heart failure caused from the use of too much cocaine.

Docket Entry:
Date: November 22, 1918
Deceased: Mrs. Lula Carle, White,
Address: 203 1/2 23rd St. North.
Cause Of Death: Found that deceased came to her death by taking paregoric, deceased being dope fiend.

Gambling and Prostitution

*"Well I'm in the racket, yeah you know I'm in the racket.
Well I'm gettin' kind of tired tellin' you, daddy,
your mama's in the racket now."*

---I'm in the racket

In many cities across America, early 20th century society saw the more overt presence of established commercial houses of prostitution than are found today. Despite the outwardly professed greater personal morals of that time, such facilities were accepted by many members of the public as a matter of fact, if not necessity. As with other vices, such activities were allowed to operate openly and were protected through the payment of graft to police officers and politicians until conditions occasionally "got out of hand" and deteriorated to the point where certain elements of society demanded a "crack down" on all illegal activities. Such suppression of vice increased in many jurisdictions as America's involvement in World War I approached. An example was the closing down of the infamous "Storyville" in New Orleans as a response to the fears of parents of soldiers who believed their sons in the nearby Army training camps would be exposed to bad influences and venereal diseases.

In his book "Low Life," Sante noted that:

> "Young women became whores in any number of ways and for any number of reasons. It was one of the few means for women of the lower class to meet men of higher station. So a young woman not actually seduced or sold into the profession might start by freelancing. Opportunities were manifold. There were men on the street, on public conveyances, at places of amusement, who could spare a dollar or two for a rapid sexual fix. Any woman by herself was fair game, and two together might be thought a team. Any woman out after dark would be assumed to be a whore. Too often, however, hazards would intrude. She might very well contract a venereal disease and a poor woman who contracted syphilis or gonorrhea, quite apart from the mortal danger posed by the diseases themselves, would find herself barred from conventional society. A young woman who entered a brothel, where her earnings would be taken by the madam, who would pay her only a meager allowance, and where her movements and activities would be as closely monitored as if she was in a nunnery, could nevertheless count herself fortunate, since the alternatives were so much worse. If she worked on the street, she would find herself progressively devalued, a prey to vultures who would pimp her and rob her and beat her, a prey to the police, who would rob her and demand favors for free and periodically arrest her in any case, a prey to bad liquor, to drugs, disease, malnutrition and the elements. A policeman was quoted in 1909 as referring to "generations" of whores; by a generation he meant two years."[15]

In the crusade to stop lawlessness in Birmingham, "religious leaders sought the elimination of prostitution. The "oldest profession" was practiced openly and thrived on local customers as well as the weekend miners who flooded the city to gamble and drink. City officials ignored the problem until 1905 when they sought to confine it to wards six and seven.

Churchmen rejected this policy of segregating prostitution and continued a decade-long battle to rid the city of the practice altogether."[16] "Although partially defeated on the issue of prostitution, the city's religious forces won the struggle against Sunday amusements. By 1908 they had pressured the city into passing ordinances forbidding such Sabbath pastimes as golf, baseball, tennis, football, hunting, shooting, gaming, card playing, and even dominoes."[17] Despite these laws, these banned activities remained a continuing problem.

MYRTLE MEYERS TAKES CARBOLIC ACID
Dies In House of Ill Repute,
Leaving Note on Dresser In Her Room

The Birmingham Age-Herald, April 16, 1903

"Myrtle Myers, an inmate of a house of ill repute on Avenue A, between Nineteenth and Twentieth streets, committed suicide yesterday by drinking carbolic acid. The woman was discovered in her room soon after she swallowed the poison and a physician was summoned. When he arrived the woman was dead.

Coroner Paris went to the house and investigated the case, reaching a verdict that the deceased committed suicide by swallowing carbolic acid. Mary Houston, a waiting maid, acknowledged that she had been sent by the woman to a drug store to purchase 10 cents' worth of the poison. A note was found on the dresser. The woman had written it on the back of an envelope. It contained directions about sending her body to Chattanooga and good-bye messages to certain of her companions."

TOM SKELTON KILLS WOMAN OF THE TOWN
Ora Dunn Wantonly Shot Down
In House On Twenty-Third Street--
Skelton Escapes--Police On Track

The Birmingham Age-Herald, January 13, 1905

"Ora Dunn, a woman of the town, was shot and killed at 11:45 o'clock last night by a man, supposed to be Tom Skelton, in a house occupied exclusively by women, on Twenty-third street near Second avenue.

According to statements made by persons who were in the house at the time, Skelton, accompanied by another man whose name is known to the police, were admitted to the house at 11:40 o'clock and were shown into a rear room on the first floor. There they were soon joined by two women. Skelton was smoking a pipe. His companion, while dancing with one of the women, bumped into Skelton and knocked the pipe out of his hand. Skelton, it is alleged, picking up his pipe with one hand and drawing a revolver with the other, fired a shot through the heart of the Dunn woman, who was standing silently nearby. The woman screamed, threw up her hands, ran into the hall, fell upon the floor and died almost instantly. Skelton and his companion came out of the room and started up the hall for the front door of the house. In leaving they had to step over the Dunn woman's dead body. Other women of the house who had rushed up to the dead woman's side, caught Skelton by the arm and attempted to detain him and wrest his pistol from him. But with an oath, it is said, he threw them aside and gained the door. Once outside Skelton went south to First alley and ran up the alley.

The woman's body was taken to Lige Loy's undertaking establishment. The coroner will investigate the case today. A horse and a wagon said to belong to Skelton were hitched near Twenty-third street and Second avenue. A saloonkeeper said it belonged to Skelton. Policemen kept watch on the wagon all night but Skelton did not return. It is reported that Skelton lives on a farm about nineteen miles north of Birmingham, and that he is making for his home. The police expect to arrest him within the next few hours.

All reports of the tragedy agree that Skelton's companion was not a friend of Skelton but merely a person who happened to enter the house at the same time Skelton did and that he had no part in the affair. Except as a witness he will not be wanted by the police."

In addition to its concerns regarding the poor state of public health services available to the citizens of Jefferson County, a grand jury report issued in October, 1912 also took issue with a number of matters related to crime and vice in the community:
"Vagrancy: We recommend a more stringent enforcement of the vagrancy law. A large amount of the crime committed in the county is caused by idleness, for which at the present time there is no excuse. Gambling houses and questionable retorts: Gambling houses are being operated in some of the prominent mercantile buildings and hotels owned by some of our well known citizens. The entrant yes to these gambling places are arranged with such ingenuity and cunning as to render it almost I'm possible to gain admission, apprehend and convict this lawless element. Many so-called hotels are nothing more than houses of prostitution where gambling and the illicit sale of whiskey are carried out on almost without interruption and often under the guise of the social club. To these hotels and rooming houses are taken young girls for the purpose of prostitution and in

many cases they are abandoned and become public charges or dependencies upon the charity of the good men and women. Under these conditions we are developing a white slave traffic in our county. We deplore this condition; and if the proceedings of this grand jury were permitted to be published it would make the owners of these buildings hide their faces and blush with shame. The crime is first upon the owners who wink at the occupancy for the sake of the income derived. We ask these questions: Is it right for the owners to rent their property as a market place for the sale of the virtue of innocent girls? Is it right to rent these places to gamblers where the youth and manhood of this community is debauched, disgraced and dishonored? It is a felony to permit one's property to be used for such purposes; we condemn this and recommend that the owners be prosecuted along with the gamblers and the prostitutes who occupy these buildings for the reason that the real beneficiaries of this traffic are the owners. These places have multiplied to such an extent that they are now encroaching upon the residence section of our cities; and unless some move is made to check it the boundaries of the so-called "red light districts" will have to be materially extended. The sheriff's office and the city police department have done some good work; but so far the boast of the princely gambler seems to be true, namely, that the sheriff and his deputies and the city police department are mere toys with which they amuse themselves as a pastime between games on the green cloth and the whiz of the roulette wheel. If the judges will impose hard labor sentences, rather than fines, this will materially eliminate these crimes.

Homicides and Indiscriminate Shooting: The large number of homicides in the county should be the cause of deep thought on the part of every law-abiding citizen. We believe the remedy largely lies in a prompt trial and speedy conviction. It seems that the deputies, constables and policemen are entirely too ready to shoot and frequently do. Not use the proper efforts to make arrests."[18]

"THE LID" IS NOW ON IN BIRMINGHAM
SAYS CHIEF EAGAN
Professional Gamblers and Other Chronic
Law Violators Are "Resting"
"Will Remain So While I Am Chief"

Vagrants and Loiterers in Pool Rooms Are Being Run Out-- Birmingham Is No Longer "Wide Open"

The Birmingham Age-Herald, January 26, 1914

"Acting Police Chief Martin Eagan made another tour of inspection of alleged "raw spots" throughout Birmingham Saturday night and there were a few arrests. This latest trip by Chief Eagan has emphasized the fact that in Birmingham at the present time "the lid" is clamped down hard and fast. All professional gambling houses have closed their doors and their rooms and paraphernalia is covered with dust and cobwebs.

The same condition of affairs now exists with reference to the disorderly houses of Birmingham. These places have been raided so often during the past two weeks and their occupants arrested on various charges that the evil has been broken up and the dive keepers are leaving the city. Another feature of the campaign was the cleaning up of the pool rooms in the downtown district and its youthful occupants were closely questioned. Every young man that could not show that he was employed was arrested as a vagrant. Chief Eagan has caused these young men to seek work and shun pool rooms. The notorious "street corner mashers" were broken up last week by the order to arrest all loiterers.

The negro vagrants and loiterers also felt the heavy hand of Chief Eagan as there were about 200 negroes arrested in the pool rooms and negro dives of Eighteenth street between First and Fourth avenues. "Well, we have the upper hand now," tersely commented Chief Eagan, "and as long as I am head of the police department the gambling houses, the disorderly houses will stay closed. It took two weeks to clean up Birmingham and now every known place of ill repute within the city limits is closed and their owners or managers are in jail or have left town. I can truthfully say that Birmingham is not a "wide open" city anymore and that within another week will be the most law-abiding community in Alabama." Chief Eagan is on the "job."

CHAPTER 14

DISEASE AND MEDICINE

"She's my cockeyed, consumptive Sarah Jane.
She's a puffin' an blowin', Sarah Jane.
She's a puffin' an blowin' an-a-sweatin' an-a-goin'.
She's all pushed out, Sarah Jane.
An' her head pushed out, and her belly pushed in,
She looks very well for the shape she's in,
But she's my darlin' consumptive Sarah Jane."

---Sarah Jane

Jefferson County's available published health data for the early 20th century, to include coroner's records, as a source of accurate statistics regarding true causes of deaths in the community are not trustworthy. Death certificates for the poor were often signed by marginal physicians, attendants in charity wards or by the coroner who, often guessing at the cause of death of an individual, might apply "medical" terminology popular at a particular time, but essentially meaningless in many cases.

During varying periods of record keeping, a particular coroner might repetitively use terms such as "endocarditis" or "acute indigestion" to denote a cause of death. Often he would admit to having no idea of why an individual had died and would state in the record that death was due to "unknown cause and not from violence," the exclusion of which was his main concern.

In regard to public health in many cities across America at that time Litwack noted that:

> "Much of the black population was confined to dilapidated housing in narrow alleyways. Not only did these "cheerless" boxes make for cramped living quarters, but also few of them had running water, forcing the residents to rely on often contaminated well water...and seldom had sewer connections, and the wastes piled up in small, stagnant streams and foul-smelling pools in backyards and streets, becoming natural breeding places for malaria-bearing

mosquitoes. Mortality rates revealed disproportionate numbers of blacks dying from diseases—primarily tuberculosis, pneumonia, typhoid fever, and diarrhea—which gained an easy foothold in weakened and undernourished bodies and which had their roots in filth, ignorance, and poverty."[1]

Tuberculosis

Tuberculosis (TB) is an infectious disease which primarily affects the lungs. It is transmitted via a bacterium as it passes through the air from an infected person who coughs or sneezes to someone near who breathes this air. Also transmitted through impure water supplies, infected food, prolonged contact with other victims in close quarters, unsanitary surroundings and other means, tuberculosis was the world's leading killer at the turn of the 20th century. Triggering vomiting, night sweats and chills it attacked the lungs and so sapped its victim's strength that the terms "consumption," "wasting disease" and "white plague" were common names applied at that time to the condition. The diagnosis of TB meant a slow death sentence.

Until the introduction of effective drug treatments and isolation of TB sufferers, the disease continued to be a predominant cause of deaths around the world into the mid 20th century when it was virtually eradicated in the more advanced western countries. However, TB is now reappearing even in developed countries and its treatment is becoming more difficult due to the emergence of antibiotic resistant strains.

There is evidence that the first tuberculosis infection occurred about 9,000 years ago and spread to humans and animals along trade routes. Signs of the disease have been found in Egyptian mummies as early as 3,000 B.C. After the establishment in the 1880s that the disease was contagious, TB was made a notifiable disease in Britain and there were campaigns to stop spitting in public. The infected poor were pressured to enter sanatoria that resembled prisons; those for the upper classes offered excellent care and medical attention. Whatever the purported benefits of fresh air and labor in the sanatoria, even under the best of conditions, 50% of those who entered were dead within five years. Major progress in the treatment of the disease would not occur until the mid 1940s when Streptomycin became the first effective antibiotic against the bacterium, although the true revolution began in 1952 with the development of isoniazid, the first oral mycobactericidal drug. Improved standards of living to include better hygiene and nutrition are also considered major factors in the decrease in rates of infection.

As with some other subject matter presented in this book, references to tuberculosis can be found within various popular media common to those times. A portion of verse from the blues song titled "Sarah Jane"[2] which introduced this chapter is, upon close examination, more than just a ditty relating to an individual suffering with "consumption." There are specific references to several typical symptoms of the disease exhibited by its victims such as excessive sweating, shortness of breath and the assumption of the so-called "tripod" position of leaning forward with the head tilted down to facilitate breathing. Other popularized references to victims of tuberculosis can be found in stories relating to John "Doc" Holliday, a friend of Wyatt Earp, and who was well known for his participation in the historic "Gunfight at the O.K. Corral." Another famous presentation of a victim of the disease can be found in the 1896 opera "La Boheme," to which the tragic young figure "Mimi" succumbs at its finale.

Statistics

The following statistics regarding assumed deaths from tuberculosis which were investigated by the Jefferson County coroner must be considered as presenting a very conservative picture of the true rate of death from this disease. As the coroner did not officially investigate many obvious natural deaths in the community or those deaths from natural causes that occurred within hospitals, caution must be used in attempting to extrapolate these few numbers to the actual mortality rates which occurred in this county. The true picture of the extent of tuberculosis in Jefferson County must also take into account the number of non-fatal infections (morbidity rates) which may, or may not, have been reported to the health department.

For a period of years where records are available, statistics based on coroner docket entries specifying the cause of death as tuberculosis reveal the following data:

1911---24
1912---16
1917---31
1919---26
1920---23

The average yearly number of these certified deaths during this period is 24 which is believed to be a radical underestimate by at least fivefold of the true number of deaths due directly or indirectly to tuberculosis in Jefferson County during the same period. This belief is based on a review of vital health statistics compiled by other cities across the country, as statistical compilations were unavailable or incomplete for Jefferson County during this time period.

Docket Entry:
Date: December 20, 1916
Deceased: Leslie Smith, Col.
Address: 1608 10th Avenue
Cause Of Death: Pulmonary Tuberculosis.
Remarks: Deceased had not been able to get treatment as she was not able to pay for same.

Public Health

LETTERS TO THE EDITOR
Ensley's Dirty Streets and Alleys
The Birmingham Age-Herald, June 7, 1910

"To the Editor of the Age-Herald.

I am curious to know if there are not many citizens of Greater Birmingham living in Ensley who must notice daily the insanitary and unclean condition of the city of Ensley--both in the business and residence sections. I have lived in Ensley eight or ten years and never before has the town seemed so full of weeds, tin cans, stray papers and trash as now. The whole city has a disease-inviting appearance.

In the low-lying Averytt and Tuxedo district, where certain streets and alleys have never been thoroughly cleaned since they were dedicated flies are swarming, mosquitos are breeding and sickness is brewing. All over the business and residence sections every piece of vacant ground is covered with trash, like old papers, tin cans, etc. The dog fennel is beginning to hide a good deal of this unsightly growth. This only makes the real condition harder to perceive. At no time in Ensley's history have the mosquitoes and flies had such splendid and undisturbed opportunity for breeding and bearing death and disease as now.

While the Tennessee Company and the Ensley Land Company are offering prizes for the best kept premises in Ensley, and while many of the citizens are working hard to keep their individual premises clean, the city in general bears a sadly neglected appearance. The neglect on the part of the civic authorities was evidenced recently when a big dead rat lay on Nineteenth street for several days. Under the old regime the city authorities used to cut the weeds and remove trash from the vacant property every spring. The only work of this kind in evidence now is a rule that everybody-- rich or poor--must buy a garbage can, which the city empties occasionally or whenever it has time to get to it.

I have recently seen negroes in Tuxedo threatened with arrest for not having a garbage can when there was enough filth under the house and around the premises and in the streets and alleys adjoining to fill the garbage wagon. All this talk of a "City Beautiful," a "Fly Crusade," etc., seems absurd in the face of facts as above. What we need is a civic awakening in the importance of a clean and sanitary city.

In conclusion it appears there is a city ordinance restraining cows and hogs from enjoying the liberty of the city. It is nevertheless true that all through Ensley Highlands one must walk the sidewalks circumspectly as a result of the non-enforcement of this ordinance. It certainly can't be that residents of Ensley will be content to live in a city so dirty and neglected as Ensley is now. Ensley citizens worked hard for the passage of the recent bond issue. Can't the city spend a little of it cleaning up and keeping Ensley decent?
Respectfully,
NEILL HUTCHINGS

GRAND JURY SCORES MANY EVILS FOUND IN BANNER COUNTY
Almshouse Pronounced Disgrace to Civilization—Jail Is Condemned

The Birmingham Age-Herald, October 27, 1912

"Severely scoring the owners of buildings used for gambling and immoral purposes and declaring them to be beneficiaries of crime; describing the county poorhouse as a place unfit for human habitation and that the insane ward would be a disgrace to savages; a spirited attack on the fee system, denouncing many of the justices of the peace; condemning the county jail and courthouse, are some of the evils mentioned in the report of the grand jury. In referring to the county jail the grand jury stated that they hesitated to recommend a new and larger jail for fear that under the present fee system it would promptly be filled to overflowing.

Almshouse: We visited the almshouse, and unhesitatingly condemn the place as unfit for human habitation. The buildings are old, insanitary, unclean and unkept--veritable fire traps. The beds and linens are old and dirty and the sheets are too short. The floors are bare and badly worn. The walls should be cleansed, painted and rendered sanitary. The straw mattresses and bedding should be destroyed and replaced with new cotton mattresses and new blankets at once. The buildings are heated with old fashioned stoves which fail to provide uniform heat. The screens in the windows and doors are broken and torn, permitting flies to enter the wards, the kitchen and dining room, thereby transmitting diseases from one inmate to another. The insane ward would be a disgrace to the savages, much less to a civilized community. This is a small building, one story high, dark and dirty and with foul odors--the most reproachful and disgraceful conditions imaginable. When old age and poverty overtakes us and we become the dependencies of a community, we should not be condemned to a fire trap and a cess pool where disease and death hasten the fast approaching end. We find a particular pathetic case of a young boy confined in the insane ward who for several months has been in an apparently hypnotic condition. It would seem to us that he is a fit subject for special hospital treatment, and we recommend that the board of revenue take such action as is necessary to relieve this patient.

The English language fails to supply adequate words to express the conditions that exist at the almshouse; and if any thoughtful person will inspect this institution he cannot but exclaim "God have mercy upon these poor unfortunates." We recommend a new almshouse in a high and dry locality where tubercular patients can be isolated and properly treated. We condemn the board of revenue for the present existing condition, and recommend that they take proper and immediate steps to improve these conditions."

Natural Causes

During the early to mid 20th century and before the introduction of antibiotics, effective medical treatment and improvements in nutrition and public health measures, the average approximate life expectancy in the United States in 1910 was 48 for men and 52 for women, although these figures are markedly skewed by the great number of deaths occurring in infancy and childhood, as well as by fewer individuals who survived past the age of 60. In contrast, by 1998 the average age for men had advanced to 74 and for women to age 80. Therefore, although it is remarkable even today that we find increasing numbers of citizens living past the age of 100, it is understandable that such an achievement was looked upon with a degree of amazement in the early 20th century as noted in some coroner docket entries regarding the deaths of aged individuals.

Docket Entry:
Deceased: Lee Hundley, Col.
Date: July 3, 1909
Address: North Bhm.
Cause Of Death: Heart Failure.
Remarks: I found this old negro was an old time slave negro and was found dead in bed. I called Dr. and he claimed the cause of death was heart failure.

Docket Entry:
Deceased: Mary Hawkins, Col.
Date: April 24, 1910
Address: 241 17 St, Ensley.
Cause Of Death: From Unknown Causes.
Remarks: Deceased was 110 years of age. Was well and hearty and ate a hearty supper. Died 7 o'clock A.M. next morning.

Docket Entry:
Deceased: Juleen Jefferson, Col.
Date: July 4, 1912
Address: 2216 5 Alley N. B'ham.
Cause Of Death: I found deceased came to her death from senility.
Remarks: She was 115 years old.

Docket Entry:
Deceased: Matilda Northington, Col.
Date: January 14, 1917
Address: #9 Mines, Pratt City.
Cause Of Death: Deceased came to her death from old age or senility. Deceased was 104 years of age.

As noted, the application of often nonsensical terminology to denote natural causes of death varied over periods of time and were often based on a guess by the coroner.

Docket Entry:
Deceased: Nora Davis, Col.
Date: July 12, 1909
Address: 45 St and 12 Ave, East Bhm.
Cause Of Death: Cancer secondary to vaxination.
Remarks: I found decease had been ailing for some time from apparantly a vaxination. From the Dr. statement caused a cancer to set up causing deat. Been vaxinated 5 years. Did not take from out side at all but always give deceas great pain. About 4 years something broke out on deceas left shoulder and misery all going to her head causing her death.

Docket Entry:
Deceased: Helen Solman, Col.
Date: August 8, 1910
Address: 2405 10 Alley No.
Cause Of Death: Acute Indigestion.

Docket Entry:
Deceased: Katie Rosa Lee Owens, White.
Date: August 15, 1910
Address: Smithfield
Cause Of Death: Stomach trouble.

Docket Entry:
Deceased: Minnie Koblan, White.
Date: November 7, 1910
Address: 36 St & 10 Ave, City.
Cause Of Death: A congestive chill.

Docket Entry:
Deceased: Virginia Newsom, Col.
Date: February 14, 1911
Address: 1519 2nd Alley, City.
Cause Of Death: Chronic Construction.

Docket Entry:
Deceased: Mary Blunt, Col.
Date: March 30, 1912
Address: 1610 Ave F, City.
Cause Of Death: Tuberculosis and malaria.

Docket Entry:
Deceased: Lillian Goings, Col.
Date: December 25, 1919
Address: Cooper Undertaker.
Cause Of Death: From locked bowels.

Docket Entry:
Deceased: Susan Alice Langred, White.
Date: July 16, 1921
Address: 1223 Steiner Ave.
Cause Of Death: Carseonia of the uterus.

On occasion, a poor understanding of cause and effect from an injury with resultant death from a "natural" process was evidenced as in this docket entry:

Docket Entry:
Deceased: Sanders Nears
Date: December 27, 1909
Address: Gate City.
Cause Of Death: Natural Causes.
Remarks: Evidence showed that the blow on his head, from the B.R. Land P. Co., by a cash register falling on his head, had nothing to do with his death. Cause of death being pneumonia.

Sepsis

As already alluded to, the lack of antibiotics up to the mid 20th century meant that even a minor injury could easily lead to rampant generalized infection, or sepsis. This "blood poisoning"
often overwhelmed an individual's natural defenses and resulted in death.

Docket Entry:
Deceased: Charlie Glispy, Col.
Date: November 7, 1924
Address: Welch Bros. Und. Co.
Defendant: Nannie Lee, Col.
Cause Of Death: By blood poison caused by being cut on the hand.

Tetanus

Tetanus, often called "Lockjaw," because one of the most common signs of this infection is tightening of jaw muscles, is caused by the Clostridium tetani bacterium often found in contaminated soil and animal manure. Until the development and widespread employment of a vaccine and effective treatment for the infection in the 1920s, the outcome was almost always fatal and due to rigidity and convulsive spasms of skeletal muscles with respiratory failure.

SON OF MINISTER DIES IN AGONY FROM LOCKJAW
The Birmingham Age-Herald, July 22, 1903

"Robert Lattimer, the 10-year-old son of the Rev. and Mrs. R.M. Lattimer, died at their residence in East Lake from lockjaw. The little boy suffered great torture for the twenty-four hours just previous to his death and died in agony. Lockjaw was the result of blood poisoning which set in from a bullet wound in the boy's leg.

About a week ago the little fellow was playing with a toy pistol and accidentally shot himself just above the knee. The wound was not considered serious at the time. The wound gave him no trouble until Thursday morning, when the first symptoms of blood poisoning developed. Doctors were unable to do anything for him. Lockjaw developed soon after the blood poisoning was noticed and the boy died in great pain afterwards."

Docket Entry:
Deceased: Paul Earnest Whatlley, White.
Date: April 26, 1917
Address: 3507 Avenue G.
Cause Of Death: From Tetanus.
Remarks: Deceased cut his toes about 9 days before death.

Docket Entry:
Deceased: Mary Lee, Col.
Date: April 24, 1920
Address: Hillman Hospital.
Defendant: Obelia Hampton, Col.
Cause Of Death: From tetanus, caused by licks inflicted...same being a justifiable homicide.

Infectious Diseases

In addition to tuberculosis, there were a number of other communicable diseases which were an ever present and serious danger to relatively large numbers of the populace in the early 20th century. Vast improvements in public health to include more effective medical treatment, safe water and food supplies and vaccinations have, at least across the United States, relegated many of these illnesses to little more than academic interest. However, as has been seen with the recent resurgence of tuberculosis, constant efforts to keep many of these illnesses at bay is a continuing process, especially as it relates to the development of new, effective antibiotics.

Typhoid

Typhoid is an infection due to the Salmonella typhi bacterium. Without treatment the symptoms may last for weeks or months. It is spread by eating or drinking food or water contaminated by the feces of an infected person. It can lead to high fever with confusion. Risk factors include poor sanitation and hygiene. Some people may carry the bacterium without being affected or showing symptoms, however, they are able to spread the disease to others. In the early 1900s "Typhoid Mary" Mallon, a cook in New York City, became infamous when she was identified as a "carrier" of the bacterium and who had caused numerous illnesses and deaths among those for whom she had worked. Her discovery and confinement for the rest of her life was the result of early infectious disease detective work by public health officials.

Docket Entry:
Deceased: Will Osburn, Col.
Date: August 29, 1917
Address: Hillman Hospital.
Cause Of Death: By jumping from 4th story window while in delirious condition, on account of Typhoid Fever, same being accidental.

Influenza

More highly communicable than tuberculosis, this infectious viral disease, also previously referred to as the "Spanish Flu" and "La Grippe," currently remains of high concern to health officials around the world. Its spread and virulence has been greatly reduced due to recurrent yearly immunizations which are routinely accepted by the public at large.

Although yearly outbreaks of the disease, which have been shown to initially spread from certain animals to humans have currently been fairly well controlled, the disease regularly continues to be responsible for millions of deaths. Extensive research which was conducted around the time of World War I discovered that the responsible agent was a virus and this led to the development of a vaccine to prevent its transmission. During the years 1918--1920, the world was enveloped by the worst known outbreak of the disease in modern history. This pandemic led to an estimated worldwide death toll of between 50 and 100 million people. Infections in this country were exacerbated by the raising of a large military force to participate in the war. The close confinement of thousands of soldiers in the barracks of training camps and on ships transporting them to Europe was directly responsible for the illnesses and deaths of numerous military members.

Although not as hard hit as many other cities, Birmingham still saw its share of illness and deaths due to influenza. This disease was different from many other infectious conditions in that its effect was more severe in healthy young adults rather than in small children or the debilitated elderly. This is believed to have been due to the result of an overreactive response of the strong natural immune systems of these individuals which led to severe pulmonary edema and the susceptibility to developing an overlying bacterial pneumonia which was the actual cause of death in many cases.

Docket Entry:
Deceased: Infant of Ivy Prye, Col.
Date: April 16, 1916
Cause Of Death: Deceased came to his death from La Grippe.

Docket Entry:
Deceased: Mary Jane Berry, Col.
Date: November 23, 1917
Address: 1501 Valley St.
Cause Of Death: La Grippe.

Docket Entry:
Deceased: Fannie May Rogers, Col.
Date: October 13, 1918
Address: 721 Smith St., Graymont.
Cause Of Death: From Influenza.

Docket Entry:
Deceased: Mary Hudson, Col.
Date: December 23, 1918
Address: Ishkooda.
Cause Of Death: From Spanish Influenza.

Docket Entry:
Deceased: Lena Woods, Col.
Date: March 5, 1920
Address: Route #6, Box 151.
Cause Of Death: From Influenzal pneumonia.

Meningitis

Prior to the advent of antibiotics in the 1940s, and the later use of vaccines, bacterial meningitis was a common communicable disease and was often fatal. In an attempt to limit the spread of infection to individuals and to the clusters of cases which typically occurred, the primary response by health departments was to put in place mandatory physical quarantines of infected persons, usually within their homes, and with large warning signs placed in front windows or on entry doors to dwellings.

In regard to the death of one Frederick William Faircloth while incarcerated in the Birmingham city jail, a letter to Coroner G.M. Evans from jail superintendent Earl Wilson outlined the circumstances as they were known to him at the time.

"Aug. 16, 1937

This is to advise that on Aug. 15, 1937 One Mr. F.W. Faircloth, white man, Address Nashville, Tenn, was placed in city jail by Officers Joy and Fenland, arresting slip showed this man was charged with Public Drunkenness.

The above party did not seem to sober up as soon as drunk Prisoners usually do. Due to this fact the warden on duty ordered him to be sent to Hillman Hospital for treatment where he was kept under observation for several hours by Hospital Authorities and then dismissed and returned to Jail. About 1 A.M, the following morning while the Warden was making his check, he found this man dead in cell.

Coroner Evans ordered an Autopsy performed...was informed by Dr. Jones that his report will probably show Spinal Meningitis."

Initially, the death of Faircloth in the Birmingham city jail did not appear to garner much attention, however, this situation quickly changed by the next day following inquiries from concerned relatives, one of whom was a former high ranking military officer who would become even more world famous in the years ahead. The sudden radical change in the attitudes of local legal and medical officials, along with their new found concerns regarding this matter, were soon made evident by the news media.

PROBE OPENS IN MENINGITIS DEATH OF CITY JAIL INMATE
RELATIVE OF FORMER ARMY OFFICER DIES
Solicitor Will Confer With Coroner,
Doctor To Determine Action
Frederick Faircloth Dies Six Hours
After Going Back To His Cell

The Birmingham News, August 16, 1937

"Circuit Solicitor George Lewis Bailes said he would confer with the coroner and a doctor who performed an autopsy to learn if a grand jury investigation is advisable in connection with the death of a man who succumbed suddenly of meningitis in City Jail.

Frederick William Faircloth, 38, brother-in-law of Gen. Douglas MacArthur, former chief-of-staff of the U.S. Army, died in City Jail, after being taken to Hillman Hospital where he remained for six hours for a "preliminary examination." An autopsy performed by Dr. Walter C. Jones for Coroner Gip M. Evans disclosed that Mr. Faircloth died of meningitis, probably of the epidemic type which s contagious. An analysis was being made to determine if alcohol had been a contributing factor in his death.

Mr. Faircloth was arrested on a drunkenness charge. He was placed in the "bullpen" with a large number of other men arrested on similar charges. Records at the jail disclosed that 133 persons were arrested during the week-end as drunks.

Dr. J.D. Dowling, director of the Health Department, said he would not order a quarantine of the jail, "because meningitis could be spread as easily by persons on the outside as on the inside of the jail." Records at the Health Department show that 72 persons have died of meningitis in Jefferson County during the first seven months of this year.

Dr. W.A. Hull said three doctors examined Mr. Faircloth when he was admitted. Dr. Hull said there appeared to be nothing seriously wrong with Mr. Faircloth except that he was "slightly irrational." Dr. Hull said, however, that Mr. Faircloth was not given a detailed examination because he merely was admitted with a "drunk record." The doctors concluded that Mr. Faircloth was recovering from a case of alcoholism. Dr. Dowling said a person who died only a few hours after he was examined should have shown symptoms of the disease that was to prove fatal so soon.

Mr. Faircloth had come to Birmingham to work for the Birmingham Flour & Grain Co. Jail records show Mr. Faircloth was taken to Hillman Hospital at 3 p.m. and he was returned at 9 p.m."

Postscript

The missed diagnosis of Mr. Faircloth's actual serious medical condition can likely be attributed to several factors. The first of these was his presumed reported state of alcohol intoxication with symptoms exhibited by him which may actually have been due to the confusion and combativeness which are often seen in the acute stages of meningitis. That something seemed to be "wrong" was first noted by jail guards who realized that Faircloth had not "sobered up" as would be expected after a period of time. His continued symptoms led them to transport him to the hospital for examination. It was at this point that physicians, presented with a history of alleged alcohol intoxication performed a superficial physical examination, egregiously missed the correct diagnosis of meningitis, attributed his symptoms to alcoholism and had him returned to the jail where he was later found dead.

Although a test for alcohol was allegedly conducted on a blood sample taken at autopsy, this would have proven to be negative due to natural metabolism following the extended period of time from his arrest to his death, if it had actually been present to begin with.

Dietary Diseases

Improper food preparation along with dietary and vitamin deficiencies led to certain serious conditions. Occasional references to fatal outcomes from related diseases can be found within the coroner's records.

Parasites

The insufficient preservation and cooking of certain foods, as well as direct contact, were major factors leading to human infestation by a variety of parasites which without effective treatment could lead to death.

Docket Entry:
Deceased: Lucille Mitchell, Col.
Date: August 15, 1912
Address: 3018 1/2 6 Alley, City.
Cause Of Death: I found deceased came to her death from spasms, probably caused from worms.

Docket Entry:
Deceased: Magella Green, Col.
Date: August 16, 1917
Address: 302 13 St. South.
Cause Of Death: From intestinal parasites.

Docket Entry:
Deceased: Mary Clark, Col.
Date: September 28, 1917
Address: #2 Dunston Quarters.
Cause Of Death: From Hook-Worm disease.

Food Poisoning

In addition to medical conditions related to dietary deficiencies and improper food storage and preparation by individuals, there was a general lack of oversight and quality control of food and drug production and preservation.

As noted by Luc Sante:

> "Upton Sinclair's "The Jungle," published in 1906, may have inspired the passing of the Pure Food and Drug Act, but blue milk and bread dough eked out with sawdust and worthless if not outright perilous patent medicines were not yet obsolete in the lives of the poor. People died of tuberculosis and assorted other lung ailments, of complications of child birth, of syphilis, gout, of "chronic indigestion," of "nervous disorders" and in great numbers, from Spanish influenza."[3]

This was true across America to include Jefferson County during the early 20th century. One food related condition, now known to be caused by bacteria, was given the general and now obsolete name "Ptomaine poisoning," with many of these illnesses likely being caused by botulism due to improper canning of food by individuals or industry.

Docket Entry:
Deceased: Grover Julien Keith, White.
Date: January 6, 1910
Address: 2001 5th Ave. North.
Cause Of Death: I found deceas died from Tomain Poison being from Condense Milk. Baby died Jan. 4, 1910.

Docket Entry:
Deceased: Cornelia Kielo, Col.
Date: February 23, 1912
Address: 1007 Jonesboro.
Cause Of Death: From ptomaine poison from eating canned corn.

Docket Entry:
Deceased: W.H. Williams, Col.
Date: June 12, 1915
Cause Of Death: From acute indigestion directly after eating canned fish.

Docket Entry:
Deceased: Mary Young, White.
Date: April 19, 1917
Address: 616 34th Street.
Cause Of Death: From Ptomaine poisoning. Accidental.
Remarks: Child was 7 years old. The entire family except one child poisoned by eating field peas.

Docket Entry:
Deceased: Mary B. Heard, White.
Date: July 23, 1919
Address: 2300 4th Avenue North.
Cause Of Death: It was found deceased came to her death from food poisoning, said to have been caused by drinking Ice cream soda.

Docket Entry:
Deceased: Ida Johnson, Col.
Date: June 21, 1920
Address: #46-B Ensley.
Cause Of Death: From Ptomaine poisoning from eating can peaches.

Docket Entry:
Deceased: Joe Willis Mealer, White.
Date: September 23, 1928
Address: Brown's Und. Co.
Cause Of Death: By eating china berries which caused intestinal poisoning.

Venereal Disease

Syphilis

Although various permutations of venereal disease, including new varieties such as AIDS, continue to be serious public health issues today, the presence of syphilis can be traced back for thousands of years of human history. Before the discovery and employment of antibiotics in the mid-twentieth century, mercury was commonly used with treatments often being worse than the disease itself. Deaths of adults from syphilis were most often associated with the tertiary complications of the disease which could affect the vascular and neurologic systems. In addition, deaths of newborns as the result of congenital syphilis were common.

As noted by Roger Lane:

> *"Perhaps even more than pregnancy, many women endured disease as a kind of occupational risk. There was even less information about treatment of venereal disease than there was about birth control, and syphilis was an important killer still."*[4]

Douglas Blackmon indicated that in the early 1900s:

> *"Even for the most fortunate patients, there was no cure for syphilis. Doctors gave those who could afford it doses of mercury in the belief it fought the progress of the bacteria."*[5]

Docket Entry:
Deceased: Viola Wright, Col.
Date: February 20, 1911
Address: Oxmoor, Ala.
Cause Of Death: I found the deceased came to her death from syphalettic trouble.

Docket Entry:
Deceased: Ira Crawford, Col.
Date: June 19, 1928
Address: 16 St. and 6 Ave. North.
Cause Of Death: Syphilis aortitis.

Advertisement
The Birmingham Age-Herald, September 6, 1904

"DR. Y.E. HOLLOWAY
SPECIALIST
PRIVATE DISEASES

I guarantee you a permanent cure of private troubles and that you may know my guarantee is reliable I refer you with permission to the First National Bank, Alabama National bank, Steiner Brothers, Jefferson County Savings bank and the People's Savings and Trust company, as to the honesty for my contracts. Fully three-fourths of my patients have been treated by some one else before calling on me to be cured. Why not come as soon as afflicted? You will save money, distressing pain and valuable time; besides, there is satisfaction in knowing that the very best treatment is being given you by an honest, competent physician.

I have treated private troubles as a specialty in the city of Birmingham, Ala., since August 3, 1887. I cure syphilis, gonorrhea, gleet, stricture, lost manhood, etc. I cure many patients by mail treatment. Write for prices and terms. I do not use large advertisements and false statements to attract patients which merit has failed to secure. If you fail to be cured by such methods, give me a call and get well.

My offices are the most private and quiet in the city, tenth story of the new First National Bank building, corner of Second avenue and Twentieth street Rooms 1012 and 1014. Take one of the fine elevators to the tenth floor. Office hours: 9:30 a.m. to 5:00 p.m. Sunday, 10 a.m. to 12 p.m."

Postscript
"How could they do that?"

There may be a tendency for every new generation to look back in time to the state of medical knowledge and the treatments for diseases and injury available in the past with some degree of pity for those scientists, doctors and their patients. However, we should realize that not too far in the future we shall be looked upon in a similar fashion. Current and future advances in non-invasive gene therapies for specific diseases will have the next generation of scientists shaking their heads in sadness as they recount the "barbaric" employment of toxic chemicals (chemotherapy), radical surgery (mastectomies) and the burning of tissues with x-radiation in order to "cure" or diminish cancers during the first part of the 21st century. They will likely say in a familiar way: "Those poor souls, they just didn't know any better."

> *"Anyway, the doctor pressed his stethoscope in the usual places and after considerable silence pronounced his diagnosis:*
> *"Eddie, I can't find a thing wrong with you."*
> *Whereupon, Eddie, ever contentious, slumped to the floor, turned purple, and died in an instant, proving for all in attendance, once and for all, the fallibility of modern medicine, and the changeability of life in general."*[6]

---Thomas Lynch

CHAPTER 15

WOMEN

*"You don't know, daddy,
You really don't know my mind.
When you see me laughing, baby,
I'm laughing just to keep from crying."*

—-*Algiers Hoodoo Blues*

Childbirth

For the majority of the female population in the early 20th century most childbirths took place in homes and were assisted by midwives and, occasionally, by physicians. The number of deaths of newborns was high and it was not until the advancement of the "germ theory" by Louis Pasteur, Joseph Lister and other scientists in the late 19th century that the rates of maternal deaths from sepsis, also known as puerperal or "childbed fever," were radically reduced.

The work of these scientists had their basis in the earlier antiseptic procedures put in place by an unsung hero, Ignaz Semmelweis, a Hungarian physician who proposed the practice of hand disinfection in the mid 19th century. This practice, implemented on the midwives' wards reduced mortality rates to below 1%, where the doctor's wards had three times the death rate where it was not used. At that time preceding the recognition of the germ theory, Semmelweis could offer no acceptable scientific explanation for his findings, and some doctors were offended at the suggestion that they should wash their hands, even when going directly from the autopsy room to the delivery room.

Docket Entry:
Deceased: Name not listed.
Date: February 27, 1911
Address: Rock Quarry Quarters, East Thomas.
Cause Of Death: Puerperal sepsis.

Docket Entry:
Deceased: Effie Jackson, Col.
Date: December 7, 1915
Address: Brookside.
Cause Of Death: From blood poisoning which was caused from having child.

Docket Entry:
Deceased: Emma Edwards, Col.
Date: April 14, 1916
Cause Of Death: From after effects of childbirth.

Abuse

Although physical and mental abuse of women continues to be a serious problem in the 21st century, it is an issue that now garners more attention and response by the police, courts, social agencies and the public at large. This is in contrast to the general lack of empathy shown for these victims during the early 20th century when, as with physical child abuse, such behavior on the part of men, while not overtly supported, was certainly deemed more socially acceptable by many than it is today.

As noted by Roger Lane:

> *"...grand juries repeatedly called for the elimination of formal trials and procedures for what they thought were trivial incidents, especially wife-beating, which accounted for about a fifth of all recorded crimes against the person."*[1]

Abortion

The non-availability of legal abortions in the United States prior to the early 1970s, except in rare medically required and sanctioned circumstances, was the main driver for illegal abortions. The degree of competence of the providers and the cleanliness of the surroundings and instruments varied greatly and affected morbidity and mortality rates accordingly.

From a legal standpoint, abortion was one type of homicide which led to especially tangled problems for the criminal justice system in the early 20th century.

As Lane noted:

> "For the individuals involved, the problem of unwanted pregnancy was often desperately acute. Criminal penalties were attached to several of the traditional strategies for avoiding motherhood, and social stigma to the rest. The established response to this cruel dilemma was to ignore its results whenever possible and, in particular, to invoke the official sanctions as rarely and quietly as possible."[2]

Although multiple Jefferson County coroner docket entries were found which were related to maternal deaths resulting from criminal abortions, in most of the earlier cases there were no related newspaper articles located. This may have been due to a lack of desire by public officials to publicize these types of deaths or to name the people involved and not by newspaper reporters and editors who would regularly publish salacious accounts of these deaths when they were made aware of them on a timely basis. Although according to Lane:

> "The circumstances behind most of these cases, and sometimes even their existence, were hidden from the respectable reading public."[3]

In addition, there was often a delay of days to weeks between the time of the performance of an abortion and the death of the individual which typically resulted from sepsis.

Lane also noted that:

> "Some of the abortifacients of the period were dangerously noxious liquids taken by mouth, others were injected directly into the vagina. These chemical methods were supplemented by a variety of suction devices, electric machines and uterine probes, most administered in either ignorance of the problems of contamination and sepsis."[4]

Docket Entry:
Deceased: Helen Harrison
Date: August 25, 1909
Cause Of Death: I found from the Evidence Deceas came to her death by getting poison in some way administered by one C.S. Moore alias C.M. Moore. Evidence shows that an aborsion Was Tryed To Be Performed.

Docket Entry:
Deceased: Mrs. Fannie Swain, white.
Date: March 23, 1911
Address: Green's Und. Est. City.
Cause Of Death: Jury found deceased came to her death by criminal operation, being done at the hands of Mrs. C.A. Trent, being unlawfully done and against the peace and dignity of the state of Alabama.

Docket Entry:
Deceased: Lenora Maclin, Col.
Date: March 2, 1912
Address: 626 Joseph St. Graymont.
Defendants: Dr. W.L. Nourse and Isaac Caswell.
Cause Of Death: Abortion.

Docket Entry:
Deceased: Lula Alma Davis, White.
Date: August 26, 1912
Address: 211 1/2 S. 21 St., City.
Cause Of Death: Septicaemia caused from a criminal abortion at the hands of unknown parties.

Docket Entry:
Deceased: Allie Ellerson, White.
Date: April 1, 1915
Defendants: J.H. Sims, M.D., and W.E. Battle.
Cause Of Death: By performing criminal abortion.

HELD IN CONNECTION WITH DEATH OF GIRL
Serious Charges Against Dr. J.H. Sims and W.E. Battle-- Will Be Given Hearing Monday
The Birmingham Age-Herald, April 3, 1915

"Dr. J.H. Sims, with offices on Fourth avenue and Twentieth street, and W.E. Battle, a flagman in the employ of the Alabama Great Southern railroad, were arrested at the instance of Coroner Spain on the charge of murder and are now confined in the Jefferson county jail without bond. According to a statement made by Coroner Spain they were arrested in connection with the death of Miss Mary Ellison, aged 19 years, who died under mysterious circumstances at the Hillman hospital, the official death certificate attributing her death to pneumonia. A preliminary hearing will be given the defendants before a coroner's jury."

Postscript

Research failed to reveal additional information regarding the legal outcome of this case.

Docket Entry:
Deceased: Infant of Mrs. T.E. Rodgers, White.
Date: November 24, 1915
Defendant: T.B. Stansell
Cause Of Death: By criminal abortion.

Docket Entry:
Deceased: Emmas A. Sanders, White.
Date: January 16, 1920
Address: Hillman Hospital.
Cause Of Death: From general peritonitis following criminal abortion, same being an unlawful act.

Docket Entry:
Deceased: Thelma Kelly, White.
Date: October 27, 1927
Address: Johns Funeral Home.
Defendant: Dr. Robert Puckett, White.
Cause Of Death: By streptococcus hemolytic infection following abortion.

Docket Entry:
Deceased: Miss Mary Francis Harden, White.
Date: May 26, 1928
Address: J.N. Brown Und. Co.
Defendant: Mrs. Mattie Ball, White.
Cause Of Death: Septicemia following a criminal abortion.

WOMAN HELD HERE ON CHARGE OF MURDER
DEATH OF GIRL ENDS IN ARREST
Mrs. Mattie Ball Denies All Knowledge Of Tragedy Here
NURSES AND DOCTORS NAMED WITNESSES
Officials Say Student Died After An Illness Of Three Weeks

The Birmingham Age-Herald, June 20, 1928

"Charged with first degree murder following the death of a 15-year-old schoolgirl, who, authorities charge, died from the effects of an illegal operation, Mrs. Mattie Ball, Central Park, was in the county jail, held without bond. Mrs. Ball was arrested Tuesday on an indictment returned by the Jefferson County Grand Jury.

Officials said the girl died at a hospital after an illness of three weeks and that the illness was induced by the operation. The death certificate gives septic anemia as the cause of death.

Officials who investigated the girl's death said the young woman went to Mrs. Ball's home, where they say the operation was performed. Arresting officers said Mrs. Ball denied all knowledge of the girl's death and expressed surprise when officers called at her home to serve the warrant."

Postscript

As with many similar cases, the legal outcome of this matter is unknown.

Infanticide?

Of all types and categories of deaths investigated by the coroner the accurate determination of cause and manner of a particular newborn or infant's demise could be fraught with difficulty due to a number of factors. The competence of the investigator along with any expert medical advice he might receive from physicians varied greatly. Even today, with modern forensic science laboratory capabilities and examinations performed by highly trained and experienced forensic pathologists, these deaths often present difficulties in the interpretation of whether the cause and manner of death should be certified as natural, accident, homicide or best listed as "undetermined." In cases where there is some degree of decomposition it may be impossible to even determine whether or not a newborn was delivered dead or alive. Physical artifacts caused by animal and insect activity may be misinterpreted by inexperienced investigators as being due to injuries inflicted by some individual.

A number of docket entries were found which indicated that it was impossible to form a definitive opinion as to the manner of death in certain cases. Few competent forensic autopsies were performed in the early 20th century. As noted, due to the presence of postmortem changes in many cases there was little point in conducting these examinations. It is impossible to state precisely how many of these small bodies represented true infanticide. All that can be said is that someone wanted to dispose of the bodies while remaining anonymous. Even though dead from natural causes, congenital abnormalities or difficult childbirth, it may have been considered more expedient for the mother or others in attendance to dispose of the remains rather than to have to deal with the authorities.

Docket Entry:
Deceased: Unknown White Infant
Date: July 17, 1909
Address: Ensley
Cause Of Death: Deceas had been killed or died and was put in a little Attic Room of the residence of Denis Echols and had probably been there at least 2 years before finding deceas. The jury decided the cause of death was unknown to the jury.

Docket Entry:
Deceased: Unknown colored infant.
Date: April 21, 1916
Cause Of Death: Deceased was stillborn baby.
Remarks: Infant was found in old deserted mine. Investigation proved mother of child was Annie Parks.

Docket Entry:
Deceased: Infant of unknown parentage, White.
Date: January 1, 1919
Address: City dump al 10 St & Avo. C.
Cause Of Death: From unknown causes.

Docket Entry:
Deceased: Unknown Infant, Col.
Date: June 23, 1919
Address: 11 Ave. & 21 St. So.
Cause Of Death: Was unable to determine as to how child came to its death. It was found in a sewer pipe.

Overlaying?

Although much less of a problem today largely due to education of the public, deaths of an appreciable number of infants were believed to have been caused by "overlaying" by a parent or others who rolled on top of them in bed while asleep or drunk. As it was a common practice in earlier years for infants to sleep in a bed with adults, reports of such deaths were routinely found in the coroner's records. It appears that the death of any child while in bed with an adult was attributed to "overlaying."

It is unknown how many of these deaths were actually due to the unexplained deaths of infants which is now often referred to as Sudden Infant Death Syndrome or SIDS. In any event, the guilt which was no doubt experienced by the parents of these children was surely great especially when death was attributed to a traumatic cause whether or not that was the actual case.

In these situations the authorities, be they coroners, police, district attorneys, grand or trial juries clearly had little stomach for inflicting further punishment. Often the coroner had neither the desire nor the resources to label apparent stillborn infants where no obvious trauma was present to be due to anything other than natural or otherwise undetermined causes.

Docket Entry:
Deceased: Willie Olis Moore, Col.
Date: September 20, 1909
Address: 21 St. & Alley F, City.
Cause Of Death: A colored infant four months old…by being smothered to death accidentally by negligence on the part of its mother.

Docket Entry:
Deceased: Lillian Gann, Col.
Date: March 5, 1910
Address: Aceola.
Cause Of Death: By being smothered by covering or by being overlay by mother being accidentally done.

Docket Entry:
Deceased: Nathaniel Bunch, Col.
Date: July 8, 1910
Address: 2507 2 Alley.
Cause Of Death: By probably being overlain by its mother, while asleep in bed. Was one month and one day old.

Docket Entry:
Deceased: Howard Wimberly
Date: November 23, 1911
Address: 1309 5th Alley, City.
Cause Of Death: By being overlaid by his mother.

Docket Entry:
Deceased: Johnnie E. Noble, White.
Date: January 11, 1912
Address: #76 Mill Village, Avondale.
Cause Of Death: Accidentally overlaid by parents.

Docket Entry:
Deceased: Wm. Howard Schmidt, White.
Date: January 6, 1919
Address: 104 54 St. Woodlawn.
Cause Of Death: By being smothered to death while in bed with mother, same being accidental.

Postpartum Depression?

While only recently becoming recognized as a real medical condition and being used as a defense or as a mitigating factor during legal proceedings where a mother is accused of killing their child, similar incidents can be found throughout history which only reinforce the proposition that there is "nothing new under the sun."

MRS. A.B. M'MILLAN KILLS HER BABY WITH LARGE DOSE OF CARBOLIC ACID AND SHOOTS HERSELF IN THE BREAST
She Had Been Despondent for Some Time and in Bad Health
Coroner Renders A Verdict Quickly
Says She Killed Son and Herself--
She Was Wife of Policeman A.B. McMillan and a Fine Woman

The Birmingham Age-Herald, April 7, 1903

"Mrs. Susie McMillian gave her 8-months-old baby a large dose of carbolic acid and then committed suicide by shooting herself twice in the breast. She was found lying dead on the floor of her room by her husband when he reached home to get his supper. The doors were locked and he was forced to break one open to gain entrance. The baby was lying dead on the bed with his face terribly burned by the acid.

Mrs. McMillan was burned by powder from the pistol with which she shot herself. Mrs. McMillan's clothing was still burning when she was found. Coroner Paris was summoned and after hearing testimony, he rendered his decision that it was infanticide followed by suicide. Despondency over the loss of her infant daughter, her own poor health and that of her baby boy seems to have been the cause of the deeds.

The family physician also stated to the coroner that the baby had been in bad health for some time, and that Mrs. McMillan was very much disturbed over his condition. Her own health was bad enough, he said, to unbalance her mind. He attributes the deed to temporary insanity. Policeman McMillan is heartbroken, and is hardly able to speak. He was forced to leave the room where the coroner was holding the investigation. He has been unable to give any account of the matter, except that he does not know what caused his wife to commit the double tragedy. She and he have always been most loving, and he was always very attentive to his wife and children. Among the policemen he is known as a rather quiet man, and one who was devoted to his wife and children. It is a peculiar fact that none of the neighbors heard the shots."

MOTHER KILLS SELF 'TO SAVE' UNBORN BABY
The Birmingham Post-Herald
The Birmingham News, October 21, 1937

"An 18-year-old mother, after tucking her one-year-old son carefully into his crib, bent over a shotgun this morning in the bedroom of her Belview Heights home and pulled the trigger. She was killed instantly. The body of Mrs. Riggs was in a semi-reclining position on the bed, a severe wound in her left breast. A shotgun was lying on the floor and the force of the charge had splattered blood on the ceiling and walls. Officers said the woman had evidently bent over the barrel of the shotgun and pulled the trigger with her foot. Her husband, A.O. Riggs, 25, said he believed she took her life because she was expecting the birth of a second child and was despondent because she thought they would not be able to take care of the newcomer properly.

Mr. Riggs, a part-time night worker at the wire plant of the Tennessee Coal, Iron & Railroad Co., found his wife dead when he returned home from his job. He found this note in her handwriting: "Daddy: "When the baby wakes up give him his cereals. All he can eat. "See if the nurse out at Fairfield wants him. Give him to someone who will be good to him. Good-bye, good luck, God bless you both." "Love, "Earnestine."

Mr. and Mrs. Riggs had been married two years. Mr. Riggs said that once before his wife had tried to kill herself in the same fashion, but that he snatched the shotgun away from her. It was shortly before the birth of their first child and she was despondent because she thought they would not be able to give the baby the care that it should have. "She began worrying when she found out that she was going to have another baby," Mr. Riggs said, "I told her that we'd find a way to manage somehow. But she kept worrying about it."

Coroner Gip M. Evans investigated and pronounced the case a suicide."

Homicide

In some cases of infant deaths the presence of overt trauma left no doubt in the minds of investigators that a criminal act had been committed. However, the lack of evidence or the inability to interpret findings from a forensic science standpoint during these early years of the century were often factors leading to the failure to develop further leads in regard to who the mother of the child was or to seek prosecution in a particular case.

Docket Entry:
Deceased: Unknown white infant
Date: June 30, 1911. Found May 19, 1911.
Address: Near AGS Railroad.
Cause Of Death: By having his head crushed at the hands of unknown parties.

Docket Entry:
Deceased: Unknown Baby, Col.
Date: February 6, 1914
Address: Alice Furnace.
Cause Of Death: By having been killed and then thrown into the ash pit at Alice Furnace.
Remarks: The guilty person is unknown to the coroner.

Docket Entry:
Deceased: Thomas Ford, Col.
Date: July 27, 1917
Address: 1001 20th St. No.
Cause Of Death: From broken neck, same being accidental, by falling from bed when only 10 minutes old.

Docket Entry:
Deceased: Unknown white infant.
Date: March 30, 1921
Address: Ave. A & 32 St.
Cause Of Death: From fractured skull.

Docket Entry:
Deceased: Unknown white infant.
Date: March 2, 1922
Address: Buckeye Oil Co. at 10th Ave. & 36th St. No.
Cause Of Death: Deceased was found in cotton seed house and had probably been dead one month, same being an unlawful homicide.

Justice?

Lane adequately summed up the overall situation in the early 20th century as it related to the deaths of newborns and infants which were due to abortion, natural causes or by the intentional infliction of injury when he noted that:

> "No one in that era had any solution for the problems of unwed mothers. The justice system had the grace to let them be when possible. Coroner's juries found ways to excuse or mislabel infanticide when they found it; juries rarely convicted; judges often suspended sentence. The shame and guilt that enveloped these cases were compounded by the fact that only the most luckless or distracted women were ever brought in, the ones whose babies, battered, strangled, or drowned in the communal privy, had been killed without any attempt at concealment. One reason that the men who ran the system were so reluctant to push infanticide is that they knew the official cases were only a small fraction of the number which really occurred. Thousands of babies died...every year, many of mysterious or ill-defined causes, such as "inanition" or "suffocation," perhaps "overlaid" (by others) who had slept with them in bed. One indication of the extent of the guilty deaths is the (great) number of "unknown" infants found dead each year in the city's streets, lots and cesspools."[5]

CHAPTER 16

CHILDREN

*"By the waters of the Llobregat
no one sits down to weep for the children of the world,
by the Ebro, the Tagus, the Guadalquivir,
by the waters of the world no one sits down and weeps."*

---By The Waters Of The Llobregat
Philip Levine

Some issues relating to the deaths of newborns and infants, e.g., abortion, overlaying, infanticide and diseases affecting the population at large have been presented in previous chapters. However, it is relevant to examine more closely some of the other factors surrounding deaths in later childhood as well as the deaths of others at the hands of children.

Disease

Up until the mid-twentieth century, infants and children were very susceptible to various infectious agents just as they are today. However, there is a vast difference between morbidity and mortality rates then and now. Immunizations, as well as improved public health measures and safety systems have been major factors in preventing the great numbers of deaths of children which were an accepted state of affairs during the early 20th century.

The use of now discarded and forgotten medical terminology to describe various diseases, conditions and causes of deaths has been noted. As one example, and as shown in multiple docket entries during the first decades of the 20th century, the Jefferson County coroner continued to regularly assign a peculiar cause of death to numerous infants. The diagnosis of death due to "Bold Hives" and its variants, can be traced back to English coroner's records of the 18th century. It was a folk medical term used for an infant specific illness. It was said that "Newborns entered the world with hives--a mysterious, undefinable entity--inside their bodies. Like measles and chicken pox, hives had to be forced out before it "turned inward," thus into "bold hives". If the hives turned inward, normal body functions were adversely affected. Many people thought that bold hives "wrapped around" or "attacked" the heart and lungs, and that if not properly treated, death was inevitable.[1]

Docket Entry:
Date: July 30, 1910
Deceased: Fannie Pearl Outlaw, Col.
Address: 318 S. 16 St. City.
Cause Of Death: Bold Hives.

Docket Entry:
Date: December 16, 1909
Deceased: Isac Timothy Hall, Col. Infant
Adress: 2413 4 Ave. City.
Cause Of Death: Hooping Cough.

Docket Entry:
Date: July 6, 1917
Deceased: Will Rasberry, Col.
Address: 834 34th St. South.
Cause Of Death: From Mumps.

Accidents

Although deaths during childhood due to accidents continue to plague society, comparison of the means of these types of deaths occurring in the early 20th century as opposed to today reveal obvious differences. For example, the few automobile related fatalities was due to the scarcity of these vehicles then but which currently comprise a large number of child injuries and deaths. This is mainly due to the failure to properly restrain infants and children in automobiles. There is also a contrast in means of deaths associated with the acceptable use of child labor in factories, mills and mines during those earlier years as well as with those deaths associated with trains and farm animals. On the other hand, it appears that accidental firearms related deaths at the hands of other children was a recurring problem then as it is now.

BOY KILLED BY DYNAMITE CAP
Had The Innocent Looking Implement In His Pocket
Body Was Badly Mangled As Result of Explosion
The Birmingham News, February 8, 1909

"As the result of an explosion of a dynamite cap which the little fellow had in his pocket, Herbert Fisher of Sparks Gap, was instantly killed near his home. The little boy was only thirteen years of age. He had the cap in his pocket. It seems that not knowing what he was playing with, he knocked his pocket when it exploded, killing him instantly. The arm and hip of the boy were torn off and he was badly mangled.

The boy was a bright little fellow and his death is a shock to the community in which he lived. Jacobs and Sons prepared the remains for burial. The funeral will take place at Sadler's semetery."

HUNDREDS OFFER SYMPATHETIC AID AT TRAGIC DEATH OF "BILLY" SNYDER
Funeral of Only Son of Widely Known Physician Will Be Held at Residence This Morning

The Birmingham Age-Herald, November 10, 1919

"Hundreds of sympathetic friends called yesterday at the residence of Dr. and Mrs. J. Ross Snyder, 2215 Ridge Park avenue, to express sorrow over the death of their son William Morrow Snyder who was accidentally shot by his playmate, Jack Perkins. "Billy" Snyder was 12 years old and Jack Perkins is 6. Interment will be at Elmwood cemetery.

Few accidents in recent years in Birmingham have caused such widespread regret and sorrow as that of the only son on Dr. and Mrs. Snyder which occurred on the Cahaba river near the Shades mountain reservoir. Dr. Snyder took the boys across Red and Shades mountain for a little outing. They were practicing target shooting with a 22 rifle and Dr. Snyder stepped away for a minute. From the best information the family can gather "Billy" who thoroughly understood the rifle was showing him how to shoot it. He was standing behind Jack with the weapon pointed at the target showing him how to aim. When ready he stepped back a step or two and apparently snapped a twig which caused little Jack to whirl around suddenly and the gun was discharged. The bullet entered Billy's head just above they eye, went through the brain and fractured the skull at the rear. The bullet, however, remained imbedded in the brain.

Dr. Snyder reached him almost instantly and placed him in the automobile and hurried to St. Vincent's and in spite of everything that could be done he died Saturday afternoon. "It was one of those tragic accidents which look like a stroke of fate which couldn't have been avoided," said W.O. Snyder, brother of Dr. Ross Snyder.

Dr. Snyder is one of the most widely known specialists in children's diseases in the south and during the past 20 years has treated thousands of the children of Birmingham. Dr. George A. Hogan, coroner, held an inquest and announced that the death was purely accidental. The death of the Snyder child drew attention to other deaths in recent years from rifles, some of which have had especially tragic circumstances. Comment was withheld, however, because while it was realized that some of the deaths in the past had been the result of careless shooting on the mountain, everyone felt that Saturday's tragedy was so purely an accident that apparently nothing could have been done to prevent it."

Docket Entry:
Date: April 20, 1910
Deceased: Lena Trafficanto, Italian.
Address: Ensley
Cause Of Death: By being run over by a car of the B.R.L & P Co's, same being negligence on the part of the parents as child was only 22 months old and almost 2 blocks away from its home.

Docket Entry:
Date: January 11, 1912
Deceased: Reginald Bertrance Clarke
Address: 611 S 19 St. City.
Cause Of Death: Was accidentally killed by an idiotic mother. Was probably sat upon.

Docket Entry:
Date: May 2, 1914
Deceased: Ollie Dunson
Cause Of Death: By gunshot wounds at the hands of her little child, same being accidental.

Docket Entry:
Date: February 13, 1917
Deceased: Warren Kittrell, Col.
Address: USPI & PG North Birmingham
Cause Of Death: By having a pipe weighing 1,000 pounds falling on him. Same being accidental, through carelessness.
Remarks: This child was only eight years old.

Docket Entry:
Date: October 11, 1917
Deceased: Chas. William Woodward, White.
Address: 919 S. 13 St.
Cause Of Death: Being burnt to death while playing with matches, same being accidental.

Docket Entry:
Date: November 24, 1917
Deceased: Harrison Gaston, Col.
Address: 2202 29th Ave. N.
Cause Of Death: From burns received at the hands of his mother.

Docket Entry:
Date: December 1, 1917
Deceased: Wm. Kerr, White
Address: 201 34 St.
Cause Of Death: From traumatism caused by a large concrete ball falling on his chest while playing, same being accidental.

Docket Entry:
Date: June 25, 1918
Deceased: Wilma Louise Parvers, W.
Address: 4010 2nd Ave. North.
Cause Of Death: From strangulation, by sucking a toy balloon into her throat.

Docket Entry:
Date: January 14, 1919
Deceased: Jerry Lucus, Jr. Col.
Address: 2409 West Fairfield
Cause Of Death: By being burned to death in house, "while mother was away," same being accidental.

Docket Entry:
Date: January 1, 1921
Deceased: Isaac Mays, Col.
Address: Womack Undertaking Co. at Pratt City.
Cause Of Death: Gunshot wound of abdomen, at hands of his little six year old brother, same being accidental.

Docket Entry:
Date: March 17, 1929
Deceased: Quinton, Hill, W.
Address: 417 North 23rd St.
Cause Of Death: Gunshot wound of face.
Remarks: When he and his 11 year old brother were playing "hold up" with their father's pistol and Quinton was shot in the face, same being accidental without criminality.

Docket Entry:
Date: August 22, 1929
Deceased: William Gulley, Col.
Cause Of Death: Fractured Skull.
Remarks: When he was dropped on his head at the juvenile court, by a feeble minded girl. Same being accidental.

Institutions

Publicly supported institutions for children who had been orphaned, were runaways or who were repeat criminal offenders existed throughout this country in the early 20th century. Questions regarding the conditions in these facilities with allegations of sexual, mental and physical abuse and violent deaths of their inmates at the hands of staff members are now being raised and investigated not only in the United States, but in several countries in northern Europe.

In Jefferson County, the Boy's Industrial School was the main facility which held these wards of the state. Although the coroner's records do not include investigations into many of these types of deaths, there were several noted over the years. There was little evidence that such deaths were reported in the local newspapers or to what extent postmortem examinations were performed.

Docket Entry:
Date: July 13, 1912
Deceased: Sam Jones, White.
Address: Boy's Industrial School, East Lake.
Cause Of Death: Hemorrhage of the brain, probably caused from overexcitement and found no blame on the part of the management of the institution.

Docket Entry:
Date: February 17, 1915
Deceased: Leonard Combs, Col.
Cause Of Death: From natural causes.
Remarks: Upon further investigation I find that deceased was brought from Mt. Meigs reform school in a very bad and neglected and filthy condition.

Docket Entry:
Date: September 3, 1919
Deceased: Lawrence J. Thomas, White.
Address: Boy's Industrial School
Cause Of Death: By being scalded by hot water.

LAD, FLEEING FROM SCHOOL, IS KILLED BY FREIGHT TRAIN
The Birmingham News, August 14, 1937

"Billy Todd, 16, will not have to return to the Boy's Industrial School, from which, according to authorities, he fled Thursday. For Billy is dead.

Apparently wishing to put as many miles as possible between himself and the institution from which he had fled, Billy, according to witnesses, was attempting to board a freight train at Magella Station Friday night when someone called to him. He turned around. Another train struck him. He entered the school in August, 1933. Coroner Evans investigated and returned a finding of accidental death. Billy is survived by a brother, Robert, 18, who is still in the Boy's Industrial School."

Homicide

Although infanticide was discussed in a previous chapter, reports of the murder of older children by a parent were occasionally found in the coroner's records. In addition, several deaths of young children at the hands of other children were reported. In one case, the initial attempt to "criminalize" the incident is seen as being questionable from a legal standpoint due to the age of the perpetrator.

SWUNG ON SHOULDERS WHITE BOYS BRING BODY OF NEGRO GIRL 7 MILES
The Birmingham Age-Herald, June 27, 1902

"In a sack swung from a pole which rested on the shoulders of two white boys, the decomposed remains of a negro child 5 years old were brought to Birmingham last night. For $2 paid to each of the boys by the coroner, they brought this corpse seven miles on their shoulders, starting from a small branch near the Cahaba river and near Shades Mountain yesterday.

The body was in advanced state of decomposition and it was almost impossible to remain in the room where it was placed at the undertaking establishment. How the boys endured the stench which came from the body for those long weary miles though the country is a mystery, and it must have taken a bravery almost as great as that shown by the soldiers on the battlefield. The trip with the corpse would have been a long one, but with a dead weight of 50 pounds swung between their shoulders the distance must have seemed ten times magnified to the boys.

The remains are those of a child said to belong to Julia Tannahill, a negro woman living on Shades Mountain. For several weeks this child has been missing and a search has been made through all the surrounding county for it. The negroes have been much wrought up over the matter and it was feared at one time it would result in bodily harm to the mother of the child, who is accused of making way with it.

Coroner Paris has made several trips across the mountain trying to catch the woman and to find evidence enough to convict her. He went over yesterday and it is said he arrested Julia Tannahill. It was then that he promised the boys the money to bring the body to Birmingham. The remains were found in a creek where they must have been lying for nearly three weeks. The body was swollen from lying in the water. The reason alleged for the child's being killed was that it was deformed and would have been a cripple all its life. It is stated that when Julia Tannahill was asked to come and aid the searching party to look for the remains that she refused, and said she was going out to pick blackberries."

Docket Entry:
Date: July 18, 1935
Deceased: Willie Albert Carter, Col.
Address: 35 Ave. & 35 St. North
Defendant: Tom Wiley, Jr. Col.
Cause Of Death: By hitting him with a brick.
Remarks: Wiley, age 6, was sent to juvenile court for causing the death of his playmate. Fighting and throwing bricks at each other. A charge of murder was placed against Wiley.

Patricide

Although no records of homicides of mothers by their children were found, there were a number of cases of the murder of a father by a son, usually as a response to the employment of real or perceived excessive corporal punishment or imminent threats of physical violence at the hands of the parent. The proclivity, and general social and legal acceptance of the routine application of such physical abuse of children up to and during this era, would lead to the occasional inevitable violent response by the victim.

KILLS FATHER FOR WHIPPING HIM AND IS LANDED IN JAIL
Powell Earnest Shoots His Father D.C. Earnest at Jonesboro Home
Says His Father Was whipping Him and Pounding His Head on the Floor

The Birmingham Age-Herald, March 3, 1909

"Another tragic murder was added to Jefferson county's crime record yesterday afternoon when Powell Earnest, 16 years of age, shot and instantly killed his father at his home in Jonesboro. The youth ran after doing the shooting, but was captured after a five mile bloodhound chase lasting nearly three hours, and is now confined in the county jail. There were no eye-witnesses to the tragedy, but the boy alleges that his father was whipping him; that he was pounding his head on the floor, and that he became so mad that he shot him.

He used a Smith & Wesson .32 calibre revolver and fired three shots into his father's body. Death was almost instantaneous, life being extinct when the neighbors, who had rushed to the house on hearing the shots reached him."

FRANKLIN SHOT AND KILLED BY SON NEAR REPUBLIC
Parricide Surrenders to Sheriff and Claims Self-Defense
Father Killed At Dinner Table
The Two Men Had a Quarrel of a Minor Nature Earlier in the Day
Son Expresses Deep Regrets Over the Tragedy

The Birmingham Age-Herald, February 26, 1916

"J.M. Franklin, 50 years old, was shot and killed at Republic, a mining town in the northern part of the county, by his son, S.E. Franklin, aged 23, yesterday afternoon. The young man came to Birmingham and gave himself up to Sheriff T.J. Batson, stating that he had killed his father. He was locked up in the county jail pending an investigation by Coroner C.L. Spain today.

According to Franklin's story, he was seated at the dinner table when a quarrel arose, following which his father advanced upon him with a drawn knife. He said his father was so near on him that he had no chance of escape and the only thing left him to do was to kill him or get killed. He expressed deep regret over the occurrence. The father is said to have been drinking."

YOUNG BOY KILLS FATHER WHILE DEFENDING HIMSELF AND MOTHER FROM ATTACK
J.A. Kirtley Shot and Killed by 11-Year-Old-Son at the Family Residence, Roebuck Springs—
Mother Attempts to Shield Her Boy and Take Responsibility for Tragedy

The Birmingham Age-Herald, March 10, 1919

"J.A. Kirtley, aged 45, chief train dispatcher of the Louisville and Nashville railroad, was shot and instantly killed yesterday morning by his 11-year-old son, Robert Kirtley, at their Roebuck Springs residence. The killing grew out of a family quarrel in which Mr. Kirtley is alleged to have been attacking his wife with a poker when the boy ran to his room, obtained a shotgun, and returning to the scene, shot his father in the head with fatal results.

Mrs. Kirtley immediately phoned the residence of W.T. Sims, next door, and in a few moments news of the killing had spread throughout the neighborhood and friends of the family hurried to the residence, where they found the grief-stricken woman surrounded by her four little children, all apparently dazed by the ghastly sight of their dead father lying in a pool of blood. Mr. Sims was the first to arrive after the shooting and stated he found Mrs. Kirtley and her small children huddled together in the room in which the killing had occurred. "She told me that Mr. Kirtley had attacked her with a poker and threatened to kill her when she grabbed a shotgun and fired upon him."

Another neighbor, Walter Moore, stated, "I summoned Judge Greene as soon as I heard about the shooting," said Mr. Moore. "In spite of Mrs. Kirtley's first statement that she had killed her husband I knew it was someone else as there was blood all over Mrs. Kirtley's clothes, which I knew could not be the case had she fired the shotgun." When Judge Greene arrived he immediately suspected that the boy had done the shooting and was being shielded by his mother, so he called Robert off to one side and the little fellow calmly told him that it was he who had killed his father and not Mrs. Kirtley. After the boy's confession, Mrs. Kirtley admitted that she had not killed her husband, but declared that they boy had done it only to save her life. She stated that Mr. Kirtley had abused her for a long time and had threatened to kill her on several occasions. She declared that on yesterday morning Mr. Kirtley had used vile epithets at the breakfast table before the children and that when she remonstrated with him he choked and otherwise abused her. Robert came in to breakfast after being out since early morning carrying his papers. According to a statement of Mrs. Kirtley, which is corroborated by each of the four children, Mr. Kirtley began to chide Robert as soon as he entered the house. "He used profanity frequently in abusing the boy," Mrs. Kirtley told neighbors, "and when I remonstrated with him about it he grabbed a poker and rushed toward me, saying that he would kill me and the children would be better off without me. He struck me with the poker. I then grabbed hold of his arm to keep him from hitting me again, and as I did so Robert ran back to his room, got his shotgun and returned. As soon as Mr. Kirtley saw him coming he said: "I'll kill you, too," and rushed toward Robert." "I shouted, 'Shoot, Robert; shoot quick,' and he fired."

When found the dead man was lying on his face by a small stove, against which he had evidently fallen after being shot. Robert showed Coroner Rives exactly how the whole affair had occurred, going from one room to another and explaining how his mother was being assaulted, how he hurried back to his own room, got his 16-gauge shotgun, went to the sideboard and loaded it with one shell and returned to the bedroom where he fired at his father not four feet away. After conferring with Judge Greene, officials decided to leave the boy in Judge Greene's custody and to make no arrests. An inquest will be held this morning.

The Kirtleys have lived in Roebuck Springs for more than eight years and were widely known by the large colony of prominent citizens who reside in that vicinity. Rumors of domestic trouble in the family had been heard for sometime by their neighbors, and on two or three occasions, Mrs. Kirtley had complained to friends about the way her husband had beaten her and showed bruises and other body marks brought about by his treatment.

Close friends of the family assert that Mr. Kirtley had always been very hard on the boy and had kept him cowed at times. "Bob is on the honor roll in my Sunday school class, " said Judge Greene, "and he has always appeared to me to be a fine boy. Of course, the whole affair is most regrettable, but it's a clean case of justifiable homicide."

COURT CLEARS BOY OF MURDER CHARGE
Harris, Who Shot His Father, Exonerated---
Was Defending His Mother

The Birmingham Age-Herald, April 5, 1921

"Verdict of justifiable homicide was returned by Coroner J.D. Russum following an investigation into the death of Joe Harris, miner, of Blossburg who was killed, it is alleged, by his 19-year-old son, John Harris, at their home at Churchill last week.

A number of witnesses including many residents of that section who were not even summoned, appeared to testify in the case. According to their testimony, Mr. Harris was very abusive to his family when drinking and on the morning of the day he was killed he beat his wife and ran his daughters and son out of the house. It was necessary to kill the man to save the life of his wife and the other members of the family, witnesses told Coroner Russum, for he had on various occasions, threatened them.

On the day of the killing, the boy stated, he had been out and as he came to the door he saw his father threatening his mother, whom he had thrown across a trunk, with a pistol. He had reloaded the pistol after after firing several bullets into the side of the house and was holding it on Mrs. Harris when young Harris entered the door. He stated that as soon as his father saw him he turned on him and threatened to kill him. At that point the boy said he fired one shot from a revolver he was carrying, the bullet taking effect in the head.

Immediately following the shooting young Harris surrendered. All witnesses testified that the senior Harris was intoxicated at the time of the shooting and several hours prior to that time he had come home and driven the family from the house in their night clothes."

OSCAR BOWERS GOES ON TRIAL FOR MURDER IN CRIMINAL COURT
Boy Will Claim Father Was Responsible For Killing
The Birmingham Age-Herald, March 26, 1923

"When the case of the state against Oscar Bowers is called before Judge William E. Fort, one of the most unusual trials in recent annals of Jefferson county's crime records will be started. Bowers, an 18-year-old Coaldale youth, is charged with killing his father on the night of February 14, 1923. Not only is the case out of the ordinary but the defense outlined by young Bowers is one of the most unique ever presented. He blames his father, W.A. Bowers, for the killing.

Bowers shot his father upon returning from a religious gathering under the influence of liquor. A quarrel resulted between father and son and young Bowers seizing a shot gun, according to witnesses, shot his father. When arrested the following morning he declared he remembered nothing of the affair until told by his mother that he had killed his father.

It was after being confined in the county jail for more than a month that Bowers placed the blame for the shooting on his father. "He taught me to drink," the boy said. "If it had not been for liquor I would not be here." Bowers declared that when he was a small boy his father taught him the love of whisky. "every time he took a drink he gave me one. I have known the taste of liquor since I was nine years old. Pa said it was good for me."

Should Bowers' case be disposed of this week, less than two months will have passed from the commission of the crime and the closing of the record."

BOWERS IS GIVEN TEN YEARS
FOR FATHER'S MURDER

The Birmingham Age-Herald, March 29, 1923

"Oscar Bowers, who was sentenced to 10 years in state prison, will be 28 years old when he faces the world a free man again. He was an emotionless, unlettered 18-year-old country boy when the verdict of the jury trying him for killing his father was read.

Behind the bar his mother, Mrs. Laura Bowers, a gaunt, silent country woman, and her two small daughters heard the verdict that ended the trial of her son. Like son, like mother--she, too, heard the sentence in silence. Mrs. Bowers and her daughters trooped out of the court room, down the stairs and out of the building a quiet, foreboding group. Occasionally the mother, who had fought to save her son, wiped a furtive tear from her eyes. At the corner of the jail she was stopped by a newspaper woman in search of human interest stories."

MAXINE FARMER IS KILED BY SON,
DEFENDING OTHERS
Coroner Russum Renders Verdict Of
"Justifiable Homicide"

The Birmingham Age-Herald, July 6, 1923

"John Glover, 49, farmer, was shot and instantly killed by his son, Dread Glover, 15 years of age, at his home near Maxine. Coroner J.D. Russum declared that the killing was a justifiable homicide.

According to information obtained by the coroner, Glover came home in an intoxicated condition. He asked his 13-year-old daughter, Eva, to fan him. The little girl complied, using his hat as a fan. After a few minutes he cursed her and ordered her away. The little daughter immediately obeyed, but no sooner had she re-entered the house than her father rose and began heaping profanity on her for not fanning him. Her mother interceded but to no avail. Glover announced he was going to kill the whole family.

Mrs. Glover took away from her husband a shotgun and begged him to behave himself. Glover, however, could not be stopped and forced his wife to drop the gun. He picked it up and began to chase over the house and out into the field for his wife and children with the avowed purpose of killing them all. His son then came on the scene and has his father was approaching his mother in front of the house and cursing her he shot him with a rifle. The charge entered Glover's face on the right side and killed him instantly.

At the investigation, Mrs. Glover told Coroner Russum that her husband had threatened to kill her for the past twenty years and quite often he came home and pointed loaded guns at members of the family."

Postscript

The act of patricide, whether found to be legally justified or not, was usually committed by young sons against their fathers. However, there were occasional exceptions to the typical ages of the perpetrator and the victim.

NINETY-YEAR OLD NEGRO KILLED BY SON, AGED SIXTY
Latter Claims His Father Committed Suicide--
Is Arrested by Officer Newby On Charge Of Murder
The Birmingham Age-Herald, September 13, 1914

"In an argument over a hog, Lewis Goins, aged 60 years, a negro, shot and instantly killed his father, Jake Goins, aged 90 years at their home in Acipco last night. The negro stated to the officer when arrested that his father had committed suicide and that he had notified the coroner of his father's act. It appears that the father and son owned a hog and quarreled over the disposition of the porker, whereupon the nonagenarian picked up a small hatchet and attacked his son, who is a negro weighing in the neighborhood of 300 pounds. After an exciting chase around the front and back yards Lewis Goins went inside the house and, procuring a shotgun, informed his father that he would shoot him if he did not cease his attack. The elder negro is alleged to have continued his advance and the son fired with fatal effect.

Following the killing Lewis Goins left for parts unknown but a few hours later called up Coroner C.L. Spain from East Thomas and informed him that his 90 year old father had committed suicide by shooting himself with a shotgun. The coroner listened to the tale and told the negro to wait a few minutes. Coroner Spain, ascertaining from the central office where the negro had called, informed the person who answered the telephone to hold the negro who was lurking in the vicinity, but the negro had escaped. He was later arrested by Officer Newby."

Postscript

Information related to the outcome of the Goins case was found in another article which also provides, in the vocal opinion of the coroner, his view of the judicial system of that time.

CORONER IS AGAIN STIRRED UP BY THE OUTCOME OF TRIALS

The Birmingham Age-Herald, September 24, 1914

"In bitter denunciatory terms Coroner Charles L. Spain stated that indifference in prosecuting persons held by various coroner's juries was responsible for the brutal murder of J.W. Alexander at his store Tuesday night. The coroner stated that "negroes were encouraged to lawlessness by the fact that if arrested they could with a few dollars escape prosecution. Of course, it is rather disheartening for me to gather up sufficient evidence to arrest and hold anyone for trial when the trial itself will resolve into a mere farce as far as active prosecution is concerned. Today in the court several persons were turned loose on the public whom capable coroner's juries had found upon careful investigation to be implicated criminally in killings. They are in a few hours hearing with only a few state witnesses present turned out of jail free to prey on the public at large. These persons cannot be blamed, nor their friends, for fighting hard for their liberty, and let me tell you they fought well. They had their witnesses on hand. They knew what they wanted and got it. The criminal in Jefferson county always fights well. He knows that by continuous fighting and eternal vigilance he will eventually find a loophole which indifferent prosecution always leaves and escapes the punishment of his crime."

"I will cite a case and call names. Today, before Judge Abernathy, Louis Goins, a negro, 60 years of age, who several days ago killed his father, Jake Goins, aged 90 years, by blowing the top of his head off with a shotgun, was acquitted. Self defense was the plea of Louis Goins and he got away with it. Now, at this trial there was no prosecutor present. Judge Abernathy was alone, and had to conduct the prosecution as well as try the case. The negro, Louis Goins, had all his friends and relatives present, and they all appeared as witnesses for him. But I am not satisfied with the result in the Goins case, and I will personally take it up with the grand jury. It will not do very much good, perhaps, but I am going to present all the evidence of recent murders in my possession to the grand jury and let them do what they like about it. I am not going to be a party to encouraging crime. This lack of active prosecution is responsible for the fact that negro desperadoes are patrolling the streets. It is responsible for brutal murders such as the Alexander killing. Think of it, killing a valuable citizen for $17. It makes my blood run cold. Let the citizens think of it."

Abuse

MASKED MOB ALMOST BEATS LIFE OUT OF MAN CHARGED WITH WHIPPING HIS CHILD
Story of Nine-Year-Old Daughter of Jim Wesson Infuriates Mob of Men at Dolomite as She Appears Cut and Bleeding and Tells Details of Horrible Whipping at Hands of Her Father

Mob Overtakes Deputy Sheriffs on Road to Dolomite Take Prisoner After Lively Fight and Leave Him Lying in the Road After Administering Terrible Beating— Wesson Brought to Birmingham and Placed in County Jail—Child in Hospital

The Birmingham Age-Herald, July 25, 1912

"Thirty men, masked and armed, last night attacked Deputy Sheriffs M.F. Parker and J.M. Smithson, who were on their way back from Dolomite with Jim Wesson, took their prisoner away from them and gave him an awful whipping. Wesson is a miner at the Dolomite mines and had been arrested on the charges of beating his little 9-year-old daughter. He was severely cut and bruised from the beating he received at the hands of the mob, and required the attention of a doctor immediately after deputies got their man to Bessemer.

Yesterday afternoon it is said, a little girl walked or rather dragged herself into Dolomite and up to a house. The child was only dressed in underclothing, and those were literally cut to threads and that she was almost covered with her own blood from the cuts and wounds on her little body. She told her story and it was a tale of a pitiful life filled with gruesome, inhuman incidents. The girl said that her father had come home in a raging temper that afternoon and for some trivial offense had taken a club and a rawhide whip and lashed and beat her until she was almost dead. When he let her go, she slipped out of the house and dragged herself, bleeding and bruised, over the three miles to Dolomite, where she told her tale.

Deputy sheriffs at Bessemer were notified at once and a warrant was sworn out for her father, charging him with assault and battery with a weapon. Deputies Parker and Smithson started out in a buggy after Wesson. Meantime, a crowd of men and women had gathered around the child and heard her story. Looking on the little bleeding body their indignation began to rise, and quietly the men began to slip away from the crowd one by one. Later they got together and chose a leader and then started towards the house of the child where the deputies had gone to arrest her father.

Word was carried to the officers by a messenger that a mob had gathered and that they were after the men. The trail that leads beyond Dolomite to the Wesson home is unfit for a buggy and the deputy sheriffs left their buggy in the woods and made the remainder of their journey on foot. When they arrived at the home they received word that the mob was waiting for them at the buggy. A long detour was then made through the woods, and several miles beyond Dolomite they left Wesson in charge of a deputy and went back after the buggy. When they got there the crowd was waiting.

At first it looked as though trouble would start then, but Deputy Sheriff Parker told them that their man had gotten away from them and that they would have to go back to Bessemer after the dogs. The deputy sheriffs then drove off and met their man with the other deputy beyond Dolomite. Less than a mile had been traveled when the mob, 35 strong, masked and armed, overtook them. The deputies put up a good fight, but they were overpowered and the prisoner was taken from them. Parker sustained a broken wrist in the fight when he tried to keep his pistol.

It is said that the screams of the man were heard back on the road to Dolomite as the mob beat him. While the masked men were giving the prisoner the beating that almost resulted in his death the deputies were backed up against the buggy and held at bay by their own pistols in the hands of members of the mob. After about 15 minutes had passed the mob slipped away int the woods, leaving the prisoner lying bleeding and unconscious on the road."

WESSONS ARE FOUND GUILTY AS CHARGED IN THE INDICTMENT
Little Girl Makes Spectators Shudder by Recounting Stories of Cruelty
COUPLE WILL BE SENTENCED TODAY
The Birmingham Age-Herald, November 9, 1912

"We the jury find the defendants guilty as charged in the indictment," was the verdict rendered yesterday in the case of the state against James Wesson and his wife, Nina Wesson, who were jointly indicted on a charge of assault with intent to murder. The defendants were charged with severely whipping their little 12-year-old daughter, Iva Wesson, to such an extent that she was carried to the Hillman hospital, where her life was despaired of for several days.

The defendants were not represented by counsel and Wesson conducted his own case. The principal witness against the defendants was the little girl, who told such a dreadful tale of continued cruelty and brutality that it caused the attendants on the court to shudder. The witness testified that the female defendant would accuse her of misconduct and that her father would beat her until she was unconscious. A number of neighbors of the Wessons corroborated in part the story told by the girl.

The child was cross examined by her father, but her original testimony was not shaken. The man attempted to make the girl acknowledge that she had been guilty of misconduct, but this the child tearfully denied. The defendants both testified that the girl was unmanageable, and that she had been whipped on that account. The case went to the jury and in less than 20 minutes they had agreed on a verdict.

The little girl has found a good home and seems to be well cared for. She was neatly dressed and appears to be very intelligent for a child of her years."

WESSON AND WIFE GIVEN TWO YEARS
Were Convicted of Brutally Whipping 12-Year-Old Daughter
The Birmingham Age-Herald, November 12, 1912

"James Wesson and his wife, Nina Wesson, were sentenced to two years each in the penitentiary by Judge Frank Cahalan. The defendants were tried and convicted of brutally beating the daughter of the man. After receiving the sentence the prisoners were taken back to the jail and will be sent immediately to the stockade."

Delinquency

"Small Change got rained on with his own thirty-eight
And nobody flinched down by the arcade
And the newsman startled to rattle
And the cops are telling jokes about
some whorehouse in Seattle
Someone's hosing down the sidewalk,
and he's only in his teens
'Cause Small Change got rained on with his own thirty-eight."

---Small Change
Tom Waits

YOUTH CAUGHT IN STORE THEFT IS FATALLY SHOT
Boy Not Yet 16 Succumbs To Wound After Policemen Interrupt Burglary
Second Surrenders As His Companion Attempts To Flee From Officers

The Birmingham Age-Herald, August 7, 1937

"Loot amounting to $7.38 and a couple of cold wieners crammed into a couple of equally cold buns, spelled death for one youthful burglar and jail for another. Charles Martin of Gardendale who "would be 16 in November," was the youth killed shortly after midnight by a bullet fired by Officer A.E. Joy in the Catanzano Brothers Grocery, at 1822 Fourth Avenue, North. He was shot one time in the lower part of his body and died two hours later at Hillman Hospital. His companion was Billie Dixon, 16. Young Dixon surrendered to officers, coming from behind a box where he was hiding when he heard the shot fired.

County Investigator Evans said the Dixon youth told him he and the Martin boy entered the grocery and burglarized it after viewing a "crime" picture at a downtown theater. The investigator said the youth told him at the inquest hearing that the film depicted exploits of bank robbers. Evans said the Dixon youth, in a tearful, frightened voice, described how they entered the store, obtained "all the money in the cash register" and then ate some cheese.

Officer Joy, a beat patrolman was walking through Fourth Alley, checking doors, when he saw someone had been tampering with the burglar bars on a back window of the Cantanzano store. As the trio of officers entered the building, the two persons who they "thought were men" began moving about. One of the boys ran up a stairway. He refused to stop when the officers cried, "Halt!" The officer shot-- one time. And Charles crumpled to the floor.

The police chief said the shooting was "justified." He declared that the youth was caught "red-handed in a felony." "While our officers are trained not to shoot too quickly," Chief Hollums said, "they are also trained to shoot when necessary. The officers who entered the building did not know whom they would face--murderers or children. They could see only shadows. When the boy ran, the officer did not know but what he had planned as a way of escape. I think Officer Joy was justified in his action." Investigation of the store showed that the boys, in addition to taking $7.38 from three cash registers, attempted to open the safe and meddled in desks and with the food. An entire rack of cantaloupes and several nearby baskets were cut deeply. Apparently the boys had picked up butcher knives and had slashed right and left as they went through the store.

The grief-stricken father of the Martin boy today was making funeral arrangements to bury his son. Police found no firearms on either boy. Coroner Gip M. Evans after an inquest today returned a verdict of "justifiable homicide."

POLICE ARREST THREE YOUNG BOYS
Charged With Series of Burglaries
IMPROPER READING
Boys Said to Admit That They Went Astray Through Reading of Dime Novels and Cheap Literature

The Birmingham Age-Herald, September 29, 1912

"As a remarkable illustration of the depravity to which boys may drop through ill associations and improper reading, three lads, one in knickerbocker trousers, and apparently about 15 years of age; one in long trousers, 18 years of age, and one little fellow, only 13 years old, were brought to police headquarters by City Detectives Warren and

Daly, charged with being the three lads who have left a trail of crimes and thefts behind them all the way from Chicago to Birmingham.

The three boys were arrested by the officers at the Johnson House, 210 1/2 North Twenty-second street, as the result of information received from certain quarters in this city. They had in their possession two suitcases filled with all kinds of articles, pieces of jewelry, valuable trinkets, a lot of dentist tools and over $75 in cash.

The detectives talked with each one separately, drawing from each a similar story of their life. They had formerly worked as newsboys in several big cities and had read dime novels after working hours. The glamor of he tales and the false ideas and principles which they told of instilled in the minds of the lads a lust for excitement and notoriety.

The boys gave their names as J.P. Hooter, Jack Schmelback and Willie Brust. From their tales it became evident that they had come from a good family and had had in their earlier youth a good rearing. The detectives had expected that the boys would break down and cry and plead when confronted with the evidence of their guilt, but they laughed at the officers and held their heads high.

According to detectives, the set of dentist's tools were stolen from the Union Painless Dentist company in Birmingham, and the money was the remainder of $97.85 which was embezzled from the National Biscuit company at Memphis, Tenn. All three were committed to separate cells in the city jail to await the action of the courts.

Five vividly colored novels were found in the suitcases, full of gay pictures, portraying the exploits of an impossible hero, and setting forth a narration which was laughable in the extremes. The boys themselves credit part of the blame for their present condition to these books."

CHAPTER 17

ELEMENTS

*"I was sitting in my kitchen, lookin' way out cross the sky.
I thought the world was ending, I started in to cry.
The wind was howlin', the buildings beginin' to fall.
I seen that mean old twister comin', just like a cannonball."*

---*St. Louis Cyclone Blues*

Tornadoes

Anticipating and responding to severe weather events in our modern society has greatly evolved with the relatively recent advent of modern technology in the form of improved radars which can almost pinpoint the location, likely paths and the rates of travel of multiple storms and tornadoes in real time. Other advanced warnings from personal emergency weather radios and community sirens, in concert with improvements in fortified shelters, have led to an unknown, but no doubt appreciable number of lives being saved and injuries avoided. However, no matter what preparations may have been taken we can still be affected by the massive forces of nature which are released by these storms. The almost unbelievable destruction wrought by these severe weather events can only truly be appreciated by personal observation of their aftermath.

Presently, as fearsome as the advance notice that a severe storm is approaching us might be, mentally try to place yourself in rural Jefferson County during the early part of the 20th century. If you were lucky, the only warnings that you might have received of impending disaster would have been a sudden gathering of dark clouds on the horizon or the abnormal activities of farm animals or perhaps no warning whatsoever in the middle of a dark night during a severe thunderstorm. The sudden arrival of these tornadoes, cyclones, hurricane force storms or "Acts of God" as they were often termed must surely have been life-altering experiences for those so affected.

Jefferson County coroner's records and local newspaper accounts report only several major tornadoes in this area during the early part of the 20th century which caused large numbers of deaths and injuries, however, numerous smaller storms occurred on an irregular basis and led to smaller numbers of deaths in less densely populated rural communities. It may seem that numerous outbreaks of storms with greater destructiveness have occurred during the latter part of the 20th and early 21st centuries, although any increase in the numbers of deaths, injuries and property damage may actually reflect increased population and infrastructure density.

In the early 20th century, the availability and speed of response of emergency assistance sent to affected rural areas over damaged and poorly maintained roads by the relatively slow forms of transportation such as trains, early motor vehicles and animal drawn wagons was limited. The delay surely affected the morbidity and mortality ratios. Increased numbers of delayed deaths from injuries likely occurred due to inadequate medical treatment including the absence of antibiotics and tetanus vaccines during that time period.

THE TORNADO DEALS DEATH AND DESTRUCTION TWENTY PERSONS KILLED AND HUNDREDS OF HOUSES ARE TORN INTO FRAGMENTS
Terrific Cyclone Sweeps Across
Southern Section of the City
PROMINENT PERSONS DEAD
Dr. G.C. Chapman Was Instantly Killed
by Flying Timbers
and Mrs. Robt. J. Lowe and Babe
Were Crushed to Death

The Age-Herald, March 26, 1901

"A fearful tornado, in all the fury of its pent-up rage, swept down upon the southern section of the city and in its ruthless course up the valley left death and destruction in its wake. The frowning storm king summoned all the wrath at his command and with an awful grinding roar tore hundreds of houses into fragments and claimed twenty human lives, the price of his unwelcome visit.

Twenty persons were crushed and killed by the flying debris and scores of men, women and children were mangled beneath the wreckage, which was strewn from east to west for a distance of more than two miles. Among the dead are Dr. G.C. Chapman, one of the most prominent physicians of the city and the wife and child of Hon. Robert J. Lowe, chairman of the State Democratic Executive Committee.

The fearful catastrophe has cast a heavy gloom over the entire city, but willing hands have set to work to relieve the suffering and distress that sends up its pitiful cry from the pathway of the storm."

NORTHWESTERN PART OF JEFFERSON IS SWEPT BY TORNADO—MANY ARE DEAD
Towns of Sayre and Majestic Are Swept Away
Death Toll of Storms in Other States Heavy
Number of Dead at Sayre is Estimated at 12, and Six Are Thought to Have Lost Lives at Bradford-- Loss at Majestic Not Yet Known.
Nearly One Hundred Are Injured

The Birmingham Age-Herald, May 28, 1917

"About a dozen dead and from 50 to 70 persons injured was the estimate of the results of the tornado at Sayre at a late hour last night. The path of the cyclone was about 100 yards wide and something like 150 houses were leveled to the ground. Immediately following the storm the rain fell in torrents and this probably kept down a disastrous fire. Help from the adjoining mining camps and from Birmingham reached the stricken town and the work of rescue began at once. The rain and darkness hampered the rescue workers. Six are reported killed at Bradford. The washer at the coal mines at Bradford has been blown down as well as a number of other structures.

The little mining village of Majestic has been completely wiped out. Not a building is supposed to have been left standing. The hamlet has a population of about 100 people. Village Springs, a small town on the boundary line of Jefferson and Blount counties has been completely destroyed. Not a structure escaped. The number of killed has not been ascertained."

Docket Entry:
Date: May 28, 1917
Deceased: 17, Col. Deceased. (Names listed in docket entry).
Address: Majestic
Cause Of Death: Result of a storm at Majestic on the night of May 27, 1917, same being accidental or Act of God.

Docket Entry:
Date: May 28, 1917
Deceased: 7, 6 wh., 1 col. (Names listed in docket entry).
Address: Sayre
Cause Of Death: As a result of a cyclone same being an Act of God.

Docket Entry:
Date: May 28, 1917
Deceased: John Wood, S.E. Ford, Hosy Jolly & Mrs. WM. Hermon, all white.
Cause Of Death: From injuries received in cyclone on May 27th and dieing later in various hospitals, same being an Act of God.

Lightning

JOHN T. GLAZE IS KILLED INSTANTLY BY LIGHTNING BOLT
Son-in-law Thomas Waldrop, Standing Beside Him, Badly Burned
MULE IN FIELD ALSO KILLED BY THE STROKE

The Birmingham Age-Herald, June 10, 1910

"John T. Glaze, a resident of Hueytown, was struck by lightning this morning and instantly killed. His son-in-law, Thomas Waldrop, was under the same umbrella, but escaped death and suffered only burns around the neck.

The accident occurred at Rock Creek where Mr. Glaze has a farm. The two men were plowing, and when the shower came up sought shelter under a nearby tree. The lightning struck the tree and ran down the handle of the umbrella, splitting the handle, killing Mr. Glaze, burning Mr. Waldrop and killing a mule that was standing several yards away.

Mr. Glaze had been a resident of Hueytown for some years and is well known there. He was a brother of "Uncle Billy Glaze," president of the Jefferson County Farmer's union, and one of the best known men in the county. He was 58 years of age and is survived by a wife and several children, all grown. His death is keenly lamented by his many friends."

Docket Entry:
Date: July 1, 1910
Deceased: Walter & Addie Fletcher, Col.
Address: Bessemer
Cause Of Death: From being struck by lightning.

Exposure

Docket Entry:
Date: December 14, 1914
Deceased: Rodice Allen, Col.
Cause Of Death: By freezing. Having wandered away during the night in her night clothes. Deceased was insane.

Fire

As with other public health systems, e.g., medical care and early warning systems for approaching dangerous weather conditions, there is truly a world of difference between how the hazards of fire were dealt with in the early 20th century as opposed to our current state of knowledge and technology. The availability of state of the art equipment and the rapid response of highly trained firefighters, not only for fire control, but also for dealing with hazardous material incidents which occur in our modern world is now accepted as a matter of routine.

Until 1915 when the last horse drawn fire apparatus was retired from the Birmingham Fire Department, the antiquated equipment then in use and the fewer fire stations and personnel that were employed along with the lack of reliable pressurized water outlets, were major limiting factors relating to the control of fires. Extinguishing these blazes was more of an afterthought with the main purpose being to keep existing fires from spreading to adjoining structures. Outside of the Birmingham city limits, and in rural Jefferson County, the provision of adequate fire protection was essentially nonexistent.

Other major factors in modern fire control are related to improvements in the construction of homes and businesses, fire code inspections, mandatory installation of sprinkler systems and general improvement in public education regarding fire safety. Today's residences are a far cry from the typical all wood construction of early 20th century dwellings which were often crowded together, especially in the more impoverished parts of the city. This, coupled with completely different systems for the cooking of food and heating of houses than are used today, were major factors which resulted in many thermal injuries and deaths at a time when even a moderate degree of burns could easily be a death sentence due to the lack of adequate medical treatment and subsequent infection.

The source of heat for many dwellings was a stove or other form of space heater which was usually installed in the middle of a house. An additional stove might be used for cooking or heating bath water, however, many of these devices were quite antiquated, not having changed much in hundreds of years and most requiring a wood, coal or oil fuel source as the routine delivery of natural gas for heating purposes would not be provided until the mid 20th century, especially in poorer neighborhoods. The increased use of stoves for heating during the colder winter months led to a not unexpected rise in fire related deaths. The use of dangerous accelerants such as gasoline to start or revive a fading fire source occasionally led to serious conflagrations as did carelessness along with intoxication. The type of billowing, flammable garments commonly worn by many women at that time were, as indicated in coroner's records, often blamed as a factor leading to deaths from burns. Inadequate attention and supervision of the cooking of food and heating of homes by adults also led to fatal burns suffered by children.

Statistics

Although statistics regarding fire related deaths in Jefferson County from approximately 1980 to today are readily available from the medical examiner's computerized data base, similar statistics from the early 20th century in Birmingham, as well as countrywide, cannot be retrieved as the practice in those early years was to include fire deaths into the general category of all "accidental" deaths, therefore precluding meaningful comparisons of death rates due to fire between these periods. However, it is believed that the per capita rates of fire related deaths would have been greater in the early 20th century than currently based on the factors described above.

Docket Entry:
Date: July 22, 1917
Deceased: Georgia Ann Whatley, Col.
Address: 4134 2 Ave, Avondale.
Cause Of Death: From burns received while washing clothes with soap, water and gasoline, same being accidental.

Docket Entry:
Date: October 17, 1917
Deceased: Ellen Lucile Rogers, Col.
Address: Northside Infirmary.
Cause Of Death: From burns caused by catching fire in an open grate, same being accidental.

Docket Entry:
Date: January 22, 1918
Deceased: Johnnie Mae Pugh, Col.
Address: Hillman Hospital
Cause Of Death: From burns of the entire body by catching fire from open grate, same being accidental.

Docket Entry:
Date: February 7, 1918
Deceased: Willie Edwards, Col.
Address: Hillman Hospital
Cause Of Death: By catching fire in a bon-fire, same being accidental.

Docket Entry:
Date: June 12, 1919
Deceased: Wesley Thomas, Col.
Address: 726 23 St.
Cause Of Death: From 2nd degree burn, about two thirds of body, same being accidental.
Remarks: Clothing caught fire while lighting cigarette from charcoal burner.

Docket Entry:
Date: February 27, 1920
Deceased: Rosa Lee K. Gay, White
Address: Ensley Infirmary.
Cause Of Death: By having epileptic fit and falling in fire and burning to death, same being accidental.

Docket Entry:
Date: January 2, 1921
Deceased: Davis Wallace, White
Address: Johns Undertaking Company.
Cause Of Death: From burns of body and extremities by catching fire from an open grate.

Docket Entry:
Date: October 9, 1927
Deceased: Louis Ardello, White
Address: W.C. Vice Funeral Home.
Cause Of Death: By burns of body caused by powder explosion while he was preparing fireworks for negro fair, same being accidental.

Docket Entry:
Date: December 28, 1927
Deceased: Bessie Dawson, Col.
Address: Bradford Funeral Home.
Cause Of Death: By 2nd degree burns of both legs and right hand caused by gasoline catching on fire while she was rubbing her leg with it.

Docket Entry:
Date: March 12, 1929
Deceased: Mozella Finch, Col.
Address: Great Southern Burial Association.
Cause Of Death: 2nd degree burns of the body when her clothing caught fire at her home 1300 Avenue J, Ensley.

Docket Entry:
Date: December 8, 1930
Deceased: A. Colton Chase, White
Address: 3231 North 10 Avenue.
Cause Of Death: Burns of entire body received when he carelessly struck a match while the gas tank of the automobile truck on which he was riding was being filled.

Electricity

As industrialization proceeded rapidly during the early 20th century the applications of electricity within factories and mines also increased exponentially. The ever increasing use of potentially dangerous high voltage and amperage electricity, greatly exceeding the requirements of the typical household, was necessary to power heavy equipment. Its installation and employment by inexperienced workers would lead to numerous accidental deaths during these early years, even for those individuals who supposedly had been trained as electricians.

Docket Entry:
Date: August 22, 1912
Deceased: Luther Quinton, White
Cause Of Death: From coming in contact with live wire in the mines and being electrocuted.

Docket Entry:
Date: August 23, 1912
Deceased: Oscar Green, White
Cause Of Death: From coming in contact with a live wire in the mines and being electrocuted.
Remarks: Oscar Green was the Chief Electrician and went down on the the 23rd to repair the wire where Quinton was killed on the 22nd.

Docket Entry:
Date: July 13, 1927
Deceased: Pink Upshaw, Col.
Address: Southern Undertaking Funeral Home
Cause Of Death: By being electrocuted. Come in contact with live wire while attempting to steal some copper wire.

Docket Entry:
Date: July 19, 1928
Deceased: Mr. David W. Musser, White
Address: Room 603 Redmont Hotel
Cause Of Death: By being electrocuted
Remarks: While administering electric treatment.

Docket Entry:
Date: March 7, 1929
Deceased: Luster Birchfield, Col.
Address: 2943 33rd Avenue North
Cause Of Death: Electrocution when he came in contact with a high tension electric wire while flying a kite with a copper wire on a cinder pile on dump, between the house and the pipe shop.

Postscript

In addition to the appreciable number of deaths which occurred within industrial and mining settings as this new form of potent electrical energy was introduced, and as the "learning curve" for worker's safety progressed, occasional instances of electrical injuries and related deaths would also occur within homes and other settings. As the power of electricity to render a person unconscious and to cause their rapid death became apparent, a number of states would change their method of legal execution from hanging to electrocution. This was first employed in New York in 1890. Alabama would change their method of execution from hanging to electrocution in 1927. Although a number of states have recently changed their primary method of execution to lethal injection, the option for a condemned person to choose electrocution instead remains in effect in Alabama for legal reasons.

Hazing

Although society is still confronted with occasional reports of injuries and deaths from "hazing" activities which usually occur in association with college fraternities, these practices appear to have declined in number due to factors such as increased and widespread publicity, potential criminal penalties and civil lawsuits as well as changes in the perception of the use of these practices by the public and school administrators. Currently, hazing methods are typically associated with various degrees of applying blunt force trauma or forcing the excessive ingestion of alcoholic beverages.

In the early 20th century such initiation practices were more widespread and not limited to colleges and other schools, but were also used by many popular fraternal organizations of that time. Many methods of employing strong, but non-fatal electrical shocks to those persons applying for membership in a particular club were developed and used, much to the amusement of onlookers. However, the noted lack of knowledge of the principles of electricity by those persons applying such "shocks" appears to have led to an increasing number of serious injuries and deaths in scattered locations across the country.

DECLARE KENNY AND GUSTIN DID NOT DIE OF HEART FAILURE
Coroner Is Bitter Against Undertakers for Embalming Bodies

CORONER'S JURY WILL BEGIN PROBE TODAY
Indicated That Supreme Council May Take Action Against Local Lodge
Funeral Arrangements For Two Victims

The Birmingham Age-Herald, July 26, 1913

"The cause of death of Christopher Gustin and Donald A. Kenny during the initiation practices of the Birmingham Lodge of the Loyal Order of Moose was not due to a weak heart or heart failure superinduced by fright during the initiation was the verdict of several reputable physicians. Their verdict after an autopsy was that death was from unknown causes.

Despite the fact that the embalmers of the Johns Undertaking company and of Shaw & Son had embalmed the bodies of Gustin and Kenny without the sanction of Coroner C.L. Spain, the coroner conducted a post mortem examination over both bodies, destroyed the medical certificates that said that heart trouble was the cause of death of Kenny and Gustin and ordered that they should be buried under a burial certificate which said that their death was due to unknown causes.

As yet no arrests have been made, although throughout yesterday rumors flew about town that the coroner had ordered several of the most prominent Moose in the city arrested for maliciousness. Coroner Spain corrected this impression last night when he stated that he had not ordered any arrests, but that today he would empanel a coroner's jury and summon all the eyewitnesses of the tragedy and get their version of the affair.

"This affair will be thoroughly probed to the bottom," said Coroner Spain. "Nothing will be whitewashed and everything that was done in Moose hall will be explained to a coroner's jury. Although the embalmers did their best to block my efforts in finding out the true cause of death of Kenny and Gustin, I held a post mortem investigation over both bodies with reputable physicians in Birmingham and in Ensley and the cause of death in my opinion is due to an overcharge of electricity. All the physicians who looked the bodies over stated that death certainly was not caused by heart trouble. Of course at this time I cannot say that foul play was done in Moose hall during the initiation practices on the so-called tilting board, but something wrong happened up there and it is the intention of the authorities to ascertain what that something was. All the relatives of the dead men came to me yesterday and asked for a thorough investigation. They were not at all satisfied with the hurried arrangements of the embalmers acting under non-authoritative instructions of innocent persons. If the bodies had not been embalmed so hurriedly the ends of justice would have been served much better."

Chief of Police George Bodeker announced last night that his ablest detectives were working on the case in co-operation with the coroner. "This matter must be thoroughly investigated as it is best that the public be informed of the causes that led to the killing of these two men." The deaths of Kenny and Gustin was one of the main topics of conversation in town. Everywhere words of sympathy were heard for the bereaved parents and wives and children of the deceased."

TRAGIC DEATHS TO BRING REFORMS IN LOCAL INITIATIONS
Electricity and Gunpowder Are to be Tabooed in Fraternal Circles

NARROW ESCAPES IN YEARS GONE BY
Generally Believed That Arrests Will Result From Tragedy in Moose Initiation Ceremony on Thursday Night
The Birmingham Age-Herald, July 26, 1913

"It developed yesterday that whereas the Loyal Moose is not the only fraternal organization which employs electricity and electrical devices in its initiation services, that never agin will any secret society attempt in Birmingham so dangerous an experiment. Since the deaths of two neophites the silent order for a general reformation had gone out.

Some time ago, the Elks made use of electrical devices in its initiations but months ago, of its own initiative, abandoned the practice. The Sons of Jove, the members of which are electricians or electrical engineers, naturally resort to electricity in frightening their neophites and producing merriment for the spectators. Innumerable have been the incidents of men knocked down, or rendered hors de combat, in local initiation ceremonies. Since the tragedies of Thursday night, however, it s made plain by fraternity men that not only will electricity be abandoned, but that all other forms of initiation will be limited, abridged, or done away with altogether.

It was generally considered yesterday that the law would be exerted in an effort to ascertain whether or not criminal negligence contributed to the death of the two young men who were killed in the Loyal Moose ceremonies, especially was this considered true in view of the fact that after one death had been produced the ceremonies were continued with another fatality."

CORONER TO BEGIN INQUEST TOMORROW
Will Investigate Deaths of Kenny and Gustin Behind Closed Doors
The Birmingham Age-Herald, July 30, 1913

"Unless there are more homicides and suicides today and tomorrow in Jefferson county it is the intention of Coroner C.L. Spain to begin the inquest into the deaths of Donald Kenny and Christopher Gustin. The coroner reiterated last night that the inquest would not be public and that only the jurors, the Assistant Solicitor and himself would be in the room while the examination of witnesses went on.

"I will begin the inquest Thursday morning at 10 o'clock," said Coroner C.L. Spain last night, "unless somebody else runs wild and kills himself or a few others. Of course as the benevolent board of revenue allows me no assistant unless I pay them myself out of my salary of $100 per month, the public will understand the delay in this case. I have had to investigate in the past three days several murders and suicides throughout the county and had no time for this matter. I believe that Assistant Solicitor Hugh Locke will be designated to assist me in this inquest. All the witnesses will be put under the rule and no attorneys representing any of the parties interested will be allowed to participate in the inquest; they will not even be allowed in the room. The general public will be excluded and I will rule on whether the newspapers will be represented."

Both the Gustin and Kenny families were pleased at the announcement of the coroner that the inquest was at last to be started. They however still insisted that they would demand to be represented by counsel. A warm legal fight is expected when the attorneys representing the families of the dead men seek to be allowed to cross examine the witnesses."

THIRTEEN WITNESSES HEARD IN THE INQUEST INTO DEATHS IN MOOSE HALL
Witnesses Go Into Detail About Initiation Ceremony and Actions of Gustin and Kenny

PHYSICIANS GIVE EXPERT TESTIMONY ON ELECTRIC SHOCK
All Find It Difficult to Understand Just How Deaths Were Caused
Think Bodies Embalmed Too Hastily

The Birmingham Age-Herald, August 1, 1913

"To the best of his belief and knowledge, David U. Williams, secretary of the local lodge of the Loyal Order of Moose, was turning the crank of the electric generator which is alleged to have electrocuted Donald A. Kenny and Christopher C. Gustin during their initiation, according to testimony of Dr. L.C. Neill, lodge physician, before the coroner's jury. Dr. Neill proved a reluctant witness. Attorneys for the Gustin and Kenny families were not admitted, and the inquest was held behind closed doors. At the afternoon session Mr. Spain allowed all the newspaper men in to the proceedings.

The testimony the medical men showed that both Kenny and Gustin were in the best of health and while they would not positively state that electrocution was the cause of death there were many signs which pointed to such a cause. They all agreed with the exception of Dr. Neill that the apparently hasty embalming had rendered impossible finding exactly whether the shock they received at Moose hall had caused death.

Dr. Lupton said that an autopsy was performed. He emphatically denied the possibility that Gustin could have been killed by fear or undue excitement. And further, Dr. Lupton dramatically declared: "That there were two deaths in succession makes me think there was something wrong."

THE CORONER'S JURY IS EXPECTED TO RETURN A VERDICT TODAY IN KENNY AND GUSTIN PROBE NORTHCUTT ADMITS LOCAL MOOSE WERE GROSSLY CARELESS IN THE INITIATIONS

The Birmingham Age-Herald, August 8, 1913

MOOSE OFFICERS HELD GUILTY OF MANSLAUGHTER IN SECOND DEGREE BY CORONER'S JURY
Warrants Sworn Out By Spain for Abbott, Williams, Vanlandingham and Dr. Neill—
Bond Is Fixed at $500 Each--Probe Is Completed
Investigation Consumed Five Days
and Over 50 Witnesses Testified--
Undertakers Are Censured for Embalming
Without Permission of Coroner

The Birmingham Age-Herald, August 9, 1913

"Verdict of the coroner's jury:...we, the jury agree that the deceased came to their death by an electric shock. We further had evidence before us that Gustin was embalmed after instructions by the coroner not to do so until he had seen the body.

In out investigation we have been greatly hampered by the fact that the coroner is so overcrowded with work and so underpaid that he has more than he can possibly do. With the unusual number of deaths by unnatural causes which occur in the county, this handicap should not be placed upon such an important office."

Coroner C.L. Spain last night would not comment for publication on the inquest with the exception of stating: "That it was not the whitewash that some people expected."

Postscript

As noted, the technical issues associated with electricity and its delivery were not well understood by many persons during the early stages of its rapidly increasing employment in their daily lives.

In regard to electricity, the amount of voltage may be significant, but it is a secondary factor as it relates to the power or strength of a shock delivered by or through an instrument. As an example, modern stun guns may deliver anywhere from 50,000 to 8,000,000 volts but the true power of a shock is related to the amperage at which the voltage is delivered, usually in a low range of 20-75 Milliamps (or thousandths of one ampere). At this level such a shock will usually be painful and lead to loss of muscle control and involuntary collapse. In comparison, the voltage required to power a subway train is typically only around 750 volts DC, however, it is delivered at approximately 400 amperes through a "third" power rail. Direct contact with this rail is almost always fatal. Deadly shocks have been received even through the indirect contact of urinating on an electrified rail.

The electrical shock force of stun guns rarely, if ever, directly leads to the death of an individual unless there are other serious preexisting medical conditions present and/or there has been use of illicit drugs. The path that an electric current takes through the body is another notable factor as shocks which traverse the heart or brainstem are often more dangerous than those that do not affect these structures.

The deaths of Kenny and Gustin expedited changes in "hazing" activities by many fraternal organizations not only in Jefferson County, but in their lodges and halls nationwide. That such practices employing electricity could lead to serious injuries and deaths was demonstrated by this incident.

The extent of the great public interest in this matter was driven by the fact that many of the members of the Loyal Order of Moose, as well as of local branches of other well-respected national fraternal organizations, were prominent Jefferson County businessmen and political operatives who were well aware that the publicity associated with these deaths would hardly be beneficial to them and was to be avoided or diminished if at all possible. It was obvious that early attempts to obfuscate any investigation into this incident occurred, to include the embalming of the bodies of the men despite the order of the coroner not to do so, in order to cover up potential evidence. Attempts by the lodge physician to try to explain away the deaths as being due to "fright" were dismissed by other medical experts. Although the death of only one of the men might have successfully been attributed to being due to heart disease or some other preexisting medical condition, the deaths of both men closely in time was a major factor and logically led to the determination of their deaths being due to electrocution.

The fact that several of the men involved were found guilty of manslaughter in the second degree by the coroner's jury would not, in itself, allow for any punishment as the coroner and his juries were precluded from penalizing anyone. This verdict, however, would open the legal path for presentation of the findings to a grand jury and potential criminal prosecution at the circuit court level. It is unknown whether any further action occurred regarding this matter. Most likely, those men who were initially charged by the coroner pled guilty to a lesser charge at a later date with imposition of probation and a fine. As is often the case, a public record regarding the outcome could not be found.

The remaining issue relates to the possibility of civil litigation against those charged and, more importantly, of the involved organization. It is most likely that the families of both of these young and otherwise healthy men agreed to an out of court settlement and received monetary compensation for their unnecessary losses with little or no public acknowledgement of responsibility or disclosure of the amount of any settlement made by the fraternal organization. As with many cases of this nature, both then and now, a defendant with appreciable assets does not usually wish to take the chance of being punished with a large monetary award to a plaintiff by a jury whose members might be greatly offended by the egregious circumstances of a particular incident.

CHAPTER 18

VEHICLES

*Doing my best to get back to you,
Ain't nothing I'd rather do,
Look for me Sunday,
Hope I'll be there honey
With something special just for you.*

---B Movie Boxcar Blues
Delbert McClinton

Following the civil war the industrial revolution began to expand exponentially with the improvement of existing technologies and the employment of different forms of energy. The invention and development of new machinery and techniques, especially as they related to improving the timely transportation of people and goods, were major factors in the westward expansion of this nation and which also led to rapid changes which turned small towns into large cities almost overnight.

It should be realized that certain things that we readily accept regarding transportation could hardly be conceived of by the majority of the population in the early part of the 20th century. Roadways were mainly unpaved, limited in extent and in a generally poor state of repair. This was especially so in rural areas and prior to the explosion of automobile usage which forced the development of roadway systems to accommodate the increased traffic. Few gas stations reduced the distances which could be travelled. At first, the cost of automobiles limited them to those who were wealthy enough to afford them.

There were no established interstate highways as we know them today with the initiation of this system taking place during the economic boom years associated with the Eisenhower administration. As young men returned from World War II, married and started families there was a requirement not only for suburban housing and highways, but also for commuter train transportation to and from city work centers. Interestingly, the local Bessemer

Superhighway was designed in the 1930s to be the nation's first freeway. It fell short of that goal due to the depression and lack of funding, although it was still considered a marvel for that time.

In regard to the transportation of goods, there were no tractor trailer trucks for delivery over long distances. A dearth of refrigerated containers limited the movement of fruit and vegetables to short distances and these products, therefore, had to be grown and distributed locally. In addition, until after World War II there were few commercial aircraft available to transport large numbers of people and goods over long distances. Not too long ago the availability and rapid delivery of food items from around the world that we currently take for granted could not have even been dreamed of.

Trains

"All the machinery was on the outside, and when they came pounding along the rails, drive wheels turning, drive rods stroking, pistons exploding with sound and fury and sending a swirling cloud of bituminous coal smoke overhead, the ground shook. The sounds of their coming and going were unmistakeable and unforgettable. The wail of a steam locomotive whistle, heard at night through an open window, was like no other."[1]

"It has been noted that in 1929, there were 47 trains out of Birmingham each day. Now there is one."[2]

The extent, expansion and later reduction of the railroad system in the United States can best be appreciated by comparing maps of railroad track existing at the commence- ment of the Civil War in 1861 to that of the 1940s and then to current maps depicting active passenger lines.

By 1870, approximately 53,000 miles of railroad track extended across the country. This expanded to 200,000 miles in 1890 and up to 230,000 miles by 1930. Railroads transported cattle to midwest processing centers, grains to bakers and cereal producers, as well as large quantities of coal and oil to auto manufacturers and other heavy industries.

Currently, other than daily heavy commuter usage mainly along the northeast corridor or serving other large cities and their suburbs, longer distance passenger travel on trains is currently viewed as a means of sightseeing or of taking a sentimental outing on the means of travel which was routinely used by our ancestors. The transportation of millions of individuals for any appreciable distance during the early 20th century, and through the World War II years, was heavily reliant on passenger railway systems. In comparison, although the movement of large quantities of certain commodities such as grain, coal and chemicals is still a staple of the freight rail system, the number of trains criss-crossing the country has been greatly reduced along with a comparable reduction of employees required to operate and maintain them.

The extensive railroad system which developed during the late 19th and early 20th centuries would, naturally, lead to various legal issues and disputes peculiar to this industry. The litigation which resulted would necessarily produce attorneys specializing in "railroad law." Many related textbooks, extensive case law rulings and court opinions resulted from the trial and settlement of these matters.

Accidents

Railway related accidents in England and the United States were a recurring problem especially during the development and expansion of this form of transportation in the 19th and early 20th centuries. Alabama was no exception with a number of accidents sporadically occurring throughout the state during this period. However, few accidents with multiple fatalities occurred within Jefferson County. Initially, the lack of major accidents here would seem to be contradictory based on the great number of passenger, industrial and freight trains from various railroads and companies moving through the major hub of Birmingham. However, the fact that these trains had to travel at reduced speed when nearing or in the city, the increased presence of switchmen and dispatchers, as well as the employment of safety procedures, likely contributed to fewer incidents.

There were two major accidents just prior to and after the main period of time reviewed in this book and which occurred just outside of Jefferson County. Both incidents involved trains which had left or were proceeding to Birmingham. The first of these took place on

December 27, 1896, when a L&N Railroad train which had earlier left Birmingham crashed into the Cahaba river in Bibb County. The cause of the wreck was believed to have been due to sabotage and led to the deaths of between 22 and 30 persons. The second accident occurred on November 25, 1951, when the diesel powered Southern Railway's southbound Crescent and the northbound Southerner collided head-on near the tiny hamlet of Woodstock, not far from the Jefferson County line. As a result, there were 17 fatalities among passengers and crewmen with another 68 people injured. A detailed description of this incident and its causes was provided in a story written by Lyle Key.[3]

One of the few other documented railroad accidents with multiple fatalities which occurred in Jefferson County took place in 1920.

TRAINMEN DYING AS RESULT A.G.S. WRECK LAST NIGHT NEAR TRUSSVILLE
Birmingham Men Among Missing and Fatally Injured in Head-On Collision Between Freight Trains
The Birmingham Age-Herald, February 16, 1920

"One engineer is dying, another engineer and two firemen are missing, and a brakeman badly scalded as a result of a head-on collision of two freight trains of the Alabama Southern railroad just north of Trussville last night. No official report of the cause of the collision could be ascertained, but it was stated that both trains were running at a fair rate of speed when they came together. The death toll of the wreck, which tore up the track for some distance, smashed between twenty and twenty-five freight cars, and tore down telegraph wires for some distance, has reached five. C.A. Riley, engineer, the first to be brought back to Birmingham, died at St. Vincent's hospital. The other engineer, P.A. Edwards and three negroes, two firemen and one brakeman, are believed to have been killed almost instantly when the two trains came together."

Statistics

Nationwide mortality statistics have been compiled on a yearly basis by federal authorities. The recorded numbers of deaths during the early 20th century associated specifically with railroad related accidents are difficult to find. This is because, as with fire related fatalities, these incidents were often included in the general "accident" category of means of deaths. However, we are able to tabulate the specific annual numbers of local fatal railroad related incidents from a review of Jefferson County coroner docket book entries. Although providing the figures for the total numbers of these deaths on a yearly basis, the individual records often do not detail the circumstances of the accident or specify the types of victims and include railroad workers, pedestrians and those persons in motor vehicles struck by trains.

Most likely, the available statistics obtained from the Jefferson County records do not appreciably deviate from other similar sized jurisdictions across the nation during this period. The absence of several docket books from the period of the Great Depression of the 1930s precludes a review of the numbers of similar deaths during that time period which may have exceeded prior years due to the greater number of individuals "riding the rails" as well as the increase in motor vehicle traffic.

Annual Railroad Related Fatalities

1910: 43	1922: 20
1911: 28	1923: 35
1912: 42	1924: 26
1916: 20	1925: 31
1917: 25	1926: 33
1918: 46	1927: 48
1919: 33	1928: 19
1920: 32	1929: 25
1921: 29	1930: 25

Total: 560 deaths over a period of 18 years results in an average of 31 railroad related fatalities per year during this time period.

In contrast, an analysis of more recent statistics compiled by the Jefferson County Coroner/Medical Examiner's Office provides a wealth of data that allows for a comparison between this period and the noted statistics from the early 20th century.

During the period from 1981 through 2015 only several documented cases of deaths of railroad employees were found. Yearly statistics for all categories of railway related deaths during this period are as follows:

1981: 7	1993: 6	2005: 2
1982: 2	1994: 5	2006: 3
1983: 4	1995: 4	2007: 1
1984: 3	1996: 3	2008: 2
1985: 3	1997: 4	2009: 1

1986: 7	1998: 2	2010: 1
1987: 4	1999: 4	2011: 5
1988: 9	2000: 2	2012: 2
1989: 3	2001: 5	2013: 3
1990: 3	2002: 1	2014: 3
1991: 9	2003: 5	2015: 5
1992: 3	2004: 1	

Total: 127 deaths over a period of 35 years results in an approximate average of 4 railroad related fatalities per year during this time period.

In comparing the statistics from these two time periods there is an obvious statistically significant difference between the numbers of railroad related deaths with a decrease in the pure number of fatalities likely due to decreased railway traffic and improved safety practices which included the employment of many more automatic crossing gates. The statistics related to railroad related deaths on a per capita basis, similar to those figures noted in the previous chapters regarding mines and homicide, have also shown a radical reduction.

The coroner's records also provide more detailed descriptions of the circumstances surrounding deaths in the modern period. From 1981 through 2015 the following figures depict the means of deaths with data heavily skewed towards pedestrians and vehicles being struck by trains along with the noted major decrease of deaths of railroad workers.

Train and Motor Vehicle: 47
Train and Pedestrian: 80
Total: 127

Workers

"Born the son of a railroad man
Who rode 'em until he died
I'd like to live like my daddy did
But there's no more trains to ride."

---No More Trains To Ride
Merle Haggard

Docket Entry: Date: December 13, 1910
Name: L.A. Caudle, White
Address: Ensley
Cause Of Death: Being crushed between two cars on the B.S.R.R. in trying to make a coupling.
Remarks: We the jury hold no one responsible for the accident.

Docket Entry:
Date: November 21, 1914
Deceased: George C. Pierce, White
Cause Of Death: By being crushed between engine and cut of cars on main line, which is known as Mickle yard and was the proximate cause of his death and this the negligence of W.M. Meehan, Engine Foreman and Matt Smith, colored switchman.

Docket Entry:
Date: March 22, 1918
Deceased: Oscar J. Meeks, White
Address: L&N yards
Cause Of Death: From fractured pelvis caused by being caught between cars.

Docket Entry:
Date: March 30, 1919
Deceased: Theodore Jones, White
Address: 27 St. L&N RR
Cause Of Death: From traumatism by being crushed between locomotive tank and a train of flat cars.
Remarks: Same being due to wanton negligence. Parties as yet undetermined by the court.

CONDUCTOR KILLED BY FREIGHT TRAIN
Trainman Falls From Car and is Badly Mangled
Inquest Today

The Birmingham Age-Herald, October 18, 1919

"Harry F. Crawford, age 55, was instantly killed yesterday afternoon when he fell from the rear end of a string of freight cars which he was placing on a siding at Twenty-third avenue, between Twenty-sixth and Twenty-seventh streets, to allow a passenger train to pass. It is believed that he lost his footing while he was swinging on the rear car, after he had thrown the switch. He fell under the car, the wheels cutting off both legs and mangling the body severely.

Mr. Crawford was one of the old employees of the Frisco railway, and was a member of the Order of Railway Conductors, the Tribe of

Ben Hur and the Knights of Pythias. He lived in West End and is survived by his widow and several children."

Docket Entry:
Date: March 6, 1920
Deceased: James L. Ford, White
Address: St. Vincent's Hospital
Cause Of Death: By explosion of boiler on switch engine, same being accidental.

Docket Entry:
Date: April 1, 1921
Deceased: Curtis C. Ayers, White
Address: Southern Railroad yards
Cause Of Death: By body being cut in two by being run over by Southern Railroad train.

SWITCHMAN KILLED IN RAILROAD YARDS
Howard Russell Caught Between Freight Cars and Instantly Killed

The Birmingham Age-Herald, November 5, 1922

"Howard Russell, 20, switchman for the Louisville and Nashville railroad, was instantly killed at midnight last night when caught in between two box cars that were being coupled together in the yards of the road at Railroad avenue and Twenty-seventh street. The body of young Russell was badly mangled from the accident.

Police information was that confused switching signals were possibly the cause of young Russell's death. Their information was that he had stepped in between the cars to adjust the coupler in making up a train, and while there the train moved in on him, his body being caught between the two couplers and crushed."

FLAGMAN BURNED TO DEATH IN CAB AS OTHERS LEAP
Engine Strikes Freight Car In Dark Tunnel Near Cardiff, Ala.
Fellow Workers Hear Cries of Pain as Crushed Caboose Roars in Flame

The Birmingham News, February 4, 1937

"One man died in a roaring inferno in a rear-end collision involving two Southern Railway freight trains in a tunnel 14 miles from

Birmingham. The dead man was Edgar Faulkner, of Avondale, flagman on an extra coal train which was coming from Littleton, Ala. Southern Railway freight train No. 58, also going east, crashed into the rear of the coal train when the latter was about halfway through the tunnel which is 300 feet long.

Faulkner and Jim Caldwell were riding in the caboose of the coal train when the heavy locomotive of the other train ploughed into it in the darkness of the tunnel. Caldwell managed to jump to safety. Faulkner, however, was caught in the caboose when it was telescoped against the walls and roof of the tunnel. The remains of the caboose and coal car immediately in front caught fire. Railway men and bystanders heard Faulkner's piteous cries for help as, trapped in the growing holocaust, he tried frantically to get free. They were unable to get to him. Caldwell said, "Another minute and I would have suffered the same fate as Falkner. There was nothing anyone could do after that crash. It would have been suicide to even attempt to get near that raging inferno in which Mr. Falkner was trapped." Faulkner's body was burned to ashes when it was found. Mr. Falkner was a railroad man more than 30 years."

Pedestrians and Vehicles

Docket Entry:
Date: November 24, 1910
Deceased: Mrs. Nancy Bass, White
Address: Alton Crossing near Trussville, Ala.
Cause Of Death: By being negligently struck by a locomotive on the Alabama Great Southern railroad, deceased having no warning whatsoever of her impending danger.

Docket Entry:
Date: December 10, 1910
Deceased: Sam Accardi, Italian
Address: Ensley
Cause Of Death: Being run over by an engine operated by the T.C.I. R.R. Co., and we the jury hold the engineer responsible for the death and recommend that the engineer be held to the action of the grand jury.

UNKNOWN MAN IS KILLED BY TRAIN
Body, Badly Mangled is at Shaw's Parlors To Be Identified

The Birmingham Age-Herald, May 14, 1912

The body of an unknown man lies at the undertaking parlors of E.T. Shaw & Son, waiting to be identified by someone, if identification can be established. The man was run over and killed last night at Ninth avenue and Thirteenth street by Frisco train No. 104. The body was so badly mangled that it was difficult last night to tell whether he was white or black. There was nothing on his body with which he could be identified. The undertakers think he is an Italian.

Policeman Brent was sent to where the body was found by police headquarters and he notified Coroner Brasher. The coroner ordered the body turned over to the undertakers."

CARPENTER'S BODY GROUND TO PIECES
Found Strewn Along Louisville and Nashville Track Yesterday Morning

The Birmingham Age-Herald, December 7, 1912

"The body of Mason Willis, a bridge carpenter, was found along the tracks near the Woodward furnace yesterday morning early. The body was horribly mangled, being almost torn to pieces, the theory being that Willis was run over by a Louisville and Nashville train. The body was cut in two pieces, being strewn along the track for some distance.

The accident happened a short distance from the camp of the gang Willis was working with. It was stated that after getting off from work Willis went to Bessemer and it is supposed that he was struck by a train while on the way back to camp."

Docket Entry:
Date: March 14, 1917
Deceased: Ed Pippen, Col.
Address: 25 Ave Between 24 & 25 St. N.
Cause Of Death: By being run over by train of Sloss Sheffield S&J Co, while trespassing.
Remarks: This negro was one legged and was a pauper. Has a wife (alleged) at Marion, Ala. Her name is Lucy Pippin. Route 2, Box 30, Bessemer, Ala or Marion, Ala. Remains turned over to county.

Docket Entry:
Date: November 15, 1917
Deceased: Mildred Littlejohn & John D.C. Scott, White
Address: Palos
Cause Of Death: From being crushed by a train, while on trussel.

FOUR KILLED WHEN TRAIN CRASHES INTO FORD AUTOMOBILE AT JASPER CROSSING
Entire Family of Mr. and Mrs. Beavers
Killed in Accident--
Mother May Die and Father Hurt
BODIES OF VICTIMS HORRIBLY MANGLED
Bold Employees of Stock Yard
Render First Aid to Injured--
Coroner Rives to Investigate Accident

The Birmingham Age-Herald, May 28, 1918

"Four persons are dead this morning as a result of an accident yesterday afternoon, when the Illinois Central Seminole limited crashed into the Ford limousine owned and driven by Newton J. Beavers of Sayre at Jasper crossing, Sixteenth street and Twenty-first avenue. The entire family of Mr. & Mrs Beavers, consisting of three children, were killed and parents badly injured.

The body of Cora Mae Beavers, aged 34, was completely severed at the waist, the two halves of the body being thrown over 50 feet on either side of the track. The other three victims died from crushed skulls. The car was a total wreck. Beavers was driving the car at the time of the accident and the view of the track upon which the train was approaching was partly obscured by the body of the car. The auto was smashed to pieces by the heavy engine, which struck it squarely in the center. The engineer tried in every possible manner to avert the catastrophe, stopping his train in less than half its length.

The victims were rendered first aid by employees of the stock yard before the arrival of the ambulances, but were in great agony, the little boy Newton, Jr., being badly scalded by escaping steam from the engine. The body of Cora May Beavers, the 14-year-old girl, whose body was ground apart at the waist by the wheels of the locomotive, presented a horrible sight, the blood gushing from the open wound and a portion of the body missing. The body was found in two parts, each over 100 feet from the other. It was one of the most horrible accidents that has happened in the city in many months."

Docket Entry:
Date: March 15, 1923
Deceased: Dr. Lewis Whaley
Address: Lardona Station, Boyles
Cause Of Death: By automobile being struck by a passenger train, same being accidental.

Docket Entry:
Date: September 17, 1923
Deceased: Estelle Hall, Col.
Address: Peoples Undertaking Co., Bessemer
Cause Of Death: By being struck by a passenger train while attempting to run across the track.

Docket Entry:
Date: November 5, 1923
Deceased: Charlie Brown Wiggins, White
Address: Johns Undertaking Co.
Cause Of Death: By traumatic fracture of both legs. Hit by train while sitting on railroad track drunk, same being accidental.

Docket Entry:
Date: December 1, 1926
Deceased: Viola Smith, Col.
Address: Southern Undertaking funeral home.
Cause Of Death: By crushed body and broken right leg when she was run over by a box car while picking up coal on railroad track, same being accidental.

Docket Entry:
Date: May 22, 1927
Deceased: R.K. Baxter, White
Address: Ridout's Funeral Home
Cause Of Death: By a broken left arm, face cut up and brains knocked out when he was hit by an AGS train.

Hoboes

*"Well I broke down in East St. Louis
On the Kansas City line.
And I drank up all my money
that I borrowed every time.*

*You know I up and left with
just the clothes I had on my back.
Now I'm sorry for what I've done
and I'm out here on my own.*

*Well it was a train that took me away from here
but a train can't bring me home."*

---Train Song
Tom Waits

James R. Chiles wrote a story about the depression era "hobo,"[4] which included an overview of the history of these homeless individuals who were also called by various other derogatory names such as bums, drifters, vagrants, tramps and yeggs.

The beginnings of the rail-borne transient can be dated to economic depressions of the post civil war period and which was made possible by the growth of the railroads which led veterans to take to the rails looking for work out west. A new and more serious economic depression would greatly increase the numbers of these transients. As noted by Chiles:

> "This was the spring of 1933 and all across the country, desperate young men were reaching for the grab irons of boxcars. For a time during the Great Depression, more than a million men entered the world of the American hobo. There were thousands of boys, and some girls and women too. They flipped freights, rode the rods, decked rattlers and ditched bulls. Far from dissolute and deprived, these hoboes relied on courage and unimaginable fortitude to face danger, hardship and humiliation. Most were just trying to get along and get by in the grim backdrop of a depressed economy. Their numbers kept growing. Little towns could be overrun when freight trains pulled in. Beatings, chain gangs and often death awaited the hobo who strayed into the wrong

small town. By early 1933 the nation was in deep economic trouble, with one out of five able-bodied workers jobless. In the years 1929 to 1931, the Missouri Pacific's hobo count rose from 13,000 per year to 200,000. A survey of transients during the Great Depression suggested that perhaps 8,000 women were on the road as hoboes. Perhaps 200,000 children were loose on American railroads and highways at the peak of the national misery. Young people who travelled alone were in real danger from sexual predators. Particularly in a boxcar cut off from escape or help, hoboes and other transients lived in a strip of land as lawless as the wild frontier."[5]

The role of the railroad "special agent" was presented in the chapter relating to police. Their main job was to keep transients off any railroad property. In describing the required survival skills of a hobo, Chiles noted that:

"Most important was learning the finer points of how to "flip" a train—boarding a train, riding it safely and staying on by avoiding bulls."[6] "That left hoboes to jog alongside a train as it pulled out, then swing aboard while trying not to slip under the wheels. Of the 216 trespassers who died on the Missouri Pacific's Property in 1931-32, most were men who met with accidents getting off and on the trains. At the peak of the depression, 6,500 illegal railroad riders were killed or injured in a single year. Statistics show that for thousands of men it was the way to a dusty death and a nameless grave at trackside."[7]

Reaction by local civilian law enforcement agents, as well as by railroad police and some train workers became more severe as the number of hoboes increased. Chiles indicated that:

"Railroads often did have legitimate gripes against hoboes...who were known to build fires inside boxcars during the winter and occasionally the blazes got loose and burned up the cars. Even so, the accidents caused by hoboes didn't seem to warrant the violence unleashed upon them by many bulls...who learned to flush out hoboes riding the rods by lowering a piece of iron tied to a rope between two cars. The bull would pay out the rope and let the iron whip about underneath the car, killing any hobo unlucky enough to be riding below. And thus another nostalgic image tumbles, that of the noble life of the road.

If you spent long enough on the road, you were sure to experience the duality of humankind: some rail workers were brutal, but most were willing to give hoboes a break of some kind. Rail workers aiding and abetting of hoboes was a quirk of humanity that drove railroad executives wild. Though policemen kept up the old brutal ways through the Depression, no amount of clubbing and shooting could have kept all the hoboes off the trains. By 1930 most railroads had given up even trying to pinch them explaining that hoboes laughed when threatened with arrest: jail would give them a warm place to rest up."[8]

My father, who was a brakeman and a freight train conductor with the Pennsylvania Railroad during the 1930s, told me that he had "never kicked a hobo off" any of his trains, although he said that there were some railroad workers who were "obvious sadists who took great delight in kicking them off moving trains," seriously injuring or killing them. He added, "Who were they going to complain to?"[9]

Chiles summed up his essay by noting that:

"By the start of World War II, the hobo era was fading fast. Where once detectives on the Santa Fe might find 500 transients on a freight train, by the early 1950s a thorough search would turn up fewer than 10. And the 1950s saw railroads shift from steam to diesel, which hit hobo lifestyles hard. The simpler operation of diesels cost them the outbuildings they used to shelter in, the friendly railroad families who provided handouts, and lumps of coal that fueled jungle fires. There were fewer trains and they took longer runs with fewer stops where a hobo could get himself aboard."[10]

Docket Entry:
Date: August 11, 1912
Deceased: Rick Washington, Col.
Address: Boyles
Cause Of Death: From a railroad accident on the L&N railroad. Said death was probably due to hoboing.

Docket Entry:
Date: August 22, 1917
Deceased: Augusust Seahorn, Col.
Address: Coaling
Cause Of Death: By traumatism by falling through car. Drop doors on coal car accidentally dumped while train was running.

Docket Entry:
Date: October 28, 1917
Deceased: Maria E. McQuire, White
Address: New Castle
Cause Of Death: She came to her death from bruises caused while falling off of moving train, same being accidental.

Docket Entry:
Date: November 15, 1923
Deceased: Willie Fluellen, Col.
Address: 36 St & 10 Ave.
Cause Of Death: By body badly mangled by being run over by a freight train while attempting to unlawfully catch said train.

Docket Entry:
Date: February 26, 1928
Deceased: Neil Wright, Col.
Address: Spaulding
Cause Of Death: By his toes being cut off his right foot, left leg cut off when he was run over by an L&N train while attempting to catch said train.

Docket Entry:
Date: March 7, 1931
Deceased: Unknown white man
Address: L&N yards at Boyles
Cause Of Death: Traumatic fractures of head and body received when he fell under a train while attempting to catch a freight train.

Although several specific incidents in the Jefferson County area which were associated with "Special Agents" of the various railroads have been noted in the chapter on police, the following case presents a detailed look at a fatal interaction between law enforcement agents and violent transients during the height of the Great Depression.

QUARTET ATTACKS OFFICER IN L&N YARD, HE STATES
One of Victims in Hospital, Two Others Taken To Southside Jail
NUMEROUS ROBBERIES ARE LAID TO HOBOES
Deputy Arnett Was Probing Train Yard Thefts At Time Of Shooting
The Birmingham Age-Herald, January 12, 1936

"One man was killed and three others seriously wounded in the Boyles yards of the Louisville & Nashville Railroad by Sam Arnett, deputy sheriff, after they were said by the deputy to have attacked him. The men are:

Robert Grant, 40, Columbia, Tenn, who was shot through the heart, and died almost instantly.

Vincent Phillips, 20, New York, shot in the left arm and hip.

Jack Mangrum, 22, Columbia, Tenn., shot in the hip.

W.R. Summer, 35, Dement, Ill., shot in the neck.

Deputy Arnett told County Investigator Evans he went to the scene of the shooting after numerous complaints had been received from officials of the railway that hoboes had established a "hobo jungle" in the yards and during the last several weeks had been responsible for numerous robberies and attacks on the trainmen as well as residents of that section. Arnett said he and Deputy H.C. Peveler dressed in overalls to resemble "hoboes." Within a few minutes after their arrival, the four men approached them from the other side of the tracks and asked him if he was waiting to catch a freight train. When he replied in the affirmative, the men invited him to come over and join them. Just as he approached the four men, Arnett said, Grant and Summer grabbed him and demanded to know what he had in a bindle he was carrying under his arm. After a brief tussle with the men, Arnett said he struggled free, and when the men started for him again he drew his pistol and fired into the group. Grant, struck in the heart by the first bullet ran almost a block and then fell. The other three men, also struck by the remaining four bullets fired by the deputy, ran in different directions.

All three men denied they had attempted to rob Deputy Arnett and disclaimed any knowledge of recent holdups in the railway yards. Deputy Peveler's version of the shooting given to Investigator Evans was virtually the same as Arnett's."

> *"Will there be any freight trains in heaven?*
> *Any boxcars in which we might hide?*
> *Will there be any tough cops and brakemen?*
> *Will they tell us we cannot ride?"*
>
> ---Hoboes Meditation
> Jimmie Rodgers

Homicides And Coverups

The ubiquity of trains during the early 20th century, and the massive disfiguring trauma that these machines could inflict upon anyone unlucky enough to be struck by one, could often be a complicating factor in the identification of a particular victim. In the days prior to the modern routine use of fingerprints, dental comparisons and DNA analysis, the process of positive identification was heavily dependent on personal effects found on a body or the ability to locate someone who could view the remains and affirm the identity of the deceased. In the case of victims struck by trains, the physical trauma could preclude such personal identification.

Conversely, the expected physical disfigurement could intentionally be used to the benefit of individuals who might try to cover up preexisting trauma due to gunshot, knife or blunt force wounds which would, hopefully, be expected by them to be obliterated or to be confused with injuries sustained by the force of the train's impact.

A number of docket entries indicate that the coroner strongly believed that an individual had been murdered and then had his body placed on a railroad track. It is, of course, unknown how many other individuals were found on tracks over the years after being hit by trains with the true circumstances of their deaths not discovered due to the deplorable state of the forensic sciences, to include the relatively few autopsies which were performed by competent examiners at that time. Reporting of the details regarding the deaths of several black individuals identified in coroner docket entries as being victims of homicide and whose bodies were then placed on railroad tracks were not found within local newspapers.

Docket Entry:
Date: September 13, 1911
Deceased: Joe Hill, Col.
Address: Lige Loy Undertaking Co. Killed near Elyton.
Cause Of Death: From being murdered and put on the track of the Alabama Great Southern Railroad.

Docket Entry:
Date: June 30, 1915
Deceased: Jake Crockland, Col.
Cause Of Death: That deceased had been run over by a railroad train.
Remarks: From conditions I judged the deceased had previously been killed and placed on the tracks.

Railroad Foreman Thrown Under Train by Negro and is Literally Cut to Pieces
Following Quarrel Negro Mounts Running Board of Switch Engine and Hurls Foreman Under Moving Wheels to Instant Death--
Negro Refused to Make Statement About the Crime

The Birmingham Age-Herald, January 26, 1919

"Julian Hendricks, night foreman for the L&N railroad at the Eighteenth street yards, met instant death at 12:15 yesterday morning when he was thrown off the front running board of a moving switch engine by Will Jordan, a negro working under him. Hendricks' body was severed in three places and mangled almost beyond recognition. The killing occurred at the Twenty-seventh street crossing near the Sloss furnaces, after an alleged dispute between the two men.

A flagman at the crossing stated that Hendricks and the negro had a quarrel over some work, and the negro boarded the engine at the crossing. Hendricks shouted some order about the work to him and he is alleged to have answered, "I can tend to my own business." The flagman asserts that he saw the negro strike Hendricks over the head and then throw him under the wheels of the engine where he met his death. The negro was immediately arrested by L&N detectives.

Hendricks' home was in Atlanta. He was 24 years old. The negro charged with his death is about 33 years old and lives at 2518 1/4 Second alley. He refused to make any statement concerning the awful crime."

Docket Entry:
Date: February 22, 1920
Deceased: Joe Early, Col.
Address: Frisco RR track near ACIPCO.
Cause Of Death: By being hit n the head by a lump of coal that was thrown off a coal car crushing skull, at the hands of Zannie Crum and Jim Harris, Col., same being an unlawful homicide.

Docket Entry:
Date: May 29, 1927
Deceased: Irvin Haynes, Col.
Address: Southern Undertaking funeral home.
Defendant: Unknown
Cause Of Death: By his head and body being crushed, run over by a switch engine.
Remarks: After making a thorough verbal preliminary investigation into this man's death, I am of the opinion that this man was killed and put on the tracks.

TRAIN KILLS 3; FOUL PLAY HINTED
YOUTHS ARE FOUND DEAD NEAR HERE
Enginemen Say Trio Seen Too Late
To Prevent Running Over Them
INQUIRY BEGUN BY KIN OF ONE VICTIM
Pal Says Lads Held By Railroad Agents
When He Left Them

The Birmingham Age-Herald, September 29, 1930

"While the bodies of three youths killed Sunday morning by a Frisco Railroad train near Adamsville lay in a morgue here, police and county officials in two states began an investigation of the circumstances under which the boys met their demise. W.H. Henry, father-in-law of Joe E. Fuchs, had retained an attorney and was proceeding with the investigation on the theory that the boys may have met with foul play. The other two men killed were identified as Frank and Grady Kelly, of Haleyville, Ala.

Enginemen reported to authorities that the boys apparently were asleep on the track and that the engine passed over them as it rounded a sharp curve before the train could be stopped. Coroner Russum said there were no marks on the bodies which would indicate that the boys had been shot or beaten prior to being run over by the train."

Docket Entry:
Date: October 1, 1930
Deceased: J.E. Fuchs, Frank Kelly and Grady Kelly, White.
Address: Mile Post #723-37
Cause Of Death: Traumatic injuries to body.
Remarks: When they were struck by Frisco passenger train, same being accidental.

> *I got the railroad blues, baby,*
> *freight train on my mind.*
> *Well she blows in Memphis, baby,*
> *she blows way down in New Orleans.*
> *If that train keeps ablowin',*
> *I hope to find that man of mine.*
>
> —-*Freight Train Moanin' Blues*
> Billie and De De Pierce

Trolleys

From late 19th century mule and horse drawn wooden carts to an extensively tracked electrical trolley system which reached from Bessemer to East Lake by the end of World War II, the citizens of Jefferson County could rely on this inexpensive system for their local daily transportation needs. The technical simplicity of its operation and maintenance allowed for the relatively easy and inexpensive extension of additional lines into the expanding suburbs.

The use of electrically powered trolleys, and later buses, by overhead powered lines continued until April 19, 1953 when all streetcar service in Birmingham ended. This was followed by the use of gasoline powered buses. However, this system was continually diminished as ridership decreased, in part, due to personal motor vehicle ownership becoming more affordable. This was related to the increased production of vehicles for civilian use following the end of World War II.

Accidents

As with trains and other potentially dangerous machines including the ever increasing presence of automobiles, trolleys were associated with numerous injuries and deaths of those pedestrians who often interacted with them on city streets and, especially, while attempting to get on or off moving vehicles.

Docket Entry:
Dare: March 1, 1911
Deceased: Oscar Anderson, White
Address: Ensley
Cause Of Death: By being run over by a street car belonging to the B.R.L.&P. Co,
Remarks: The jury recommends that the motorman be held to the grand jury of Jefferson County for reckless running of said street car.

Docket Entry:
Date: April 22, 1911
Deceased: Ruth B. Threatt, Col.
Address: 10 St & 3 Ave, City
Cause Of Death: Being run over by a car owned and operated by the Birmingham Railway Light and Power Company.
Remarks: The jury recommends that the B.R.L.&P. Co. reprimand the conductor in charge.

JNO. MANLEY'S HEAD IS CUT OFF BEFORE EYES OF HIS WIFE
Brick Mason Instantly killed by a North Bessemer Street Car

The Birmingham Age-Herald, December 1, 1912

"His head being cut off as his wife looked on, John Manley, a brick mason, aged about 55 years, was Instantly killed when he was struck by a North Bessemer car. His body was horribly mutilated, the head being completely severed and the lower limbs mashed almost to pieces. From Fairview station he walked down the North Bessemer car tracks. The North Bessemer car from Birmingham came up behind him and he either did not get entirely off the tracks or the suction drew him back under the wheels. His wife was standing on the front porch of the house, a few yards distant, waiting for her husband to arrive, and was a witness to the accident.

Mrs. Manley, a frail little woman, told a pitiful story of the accident and saw the car strike her husband. "There are no relatives except a sister in Philadelphia. Mr. Manley was born in Ireland but came to this country when but a youth. He lived in Johnstown, Pa., and his father, mother and seven brothers and sisters were drowned in the big Johnstown flood, leaving him all alone. He served later on in the English army and saw service in the English war in Africa. He was a gunner in the English artillery, receiving a medal from Queen Victoria for bravery. He was with Lord Roberts when he went to relieve

Gordon, and after his many narrow escapes, it is an awful thing for him to die like this." The funeral services will be conducted by the Order of Moose, of which Mr. Manly was a member, interment to take place in Elmwood cemetery."

Racism and Homicide

Modern memory suggests that individual and group protests against racial segregation on public transportation was a phenomenon beginning in the mid 20th century and which occurred only in the south. However, historical accounts reveal that the occurrence of such incidents could be found on an irregular basis in cities at least as far north as Philadelphia during the early 20th century. Individual altercations could occasionally lead to extreme physical violence. Such encounters also demonstrated the widespread availability and routine carrying of concealed weapons by many members of the public at that time, as well as their willingness to use them.

As noted by Litwack in regard to public forms of transportation:

"Some municipalities prescribed separate cars; most settled on partitions that separated the races on the same car, with blacks relegated to the rear seats. With some exceptions, that became the standard arrangement. In Birmingham, blacks sat in the front section, and attempts to reverse the order clashed with custom. "After all," one white resident noted, "it is not important which end of the car is given to the nigger. The main point is that he must sit where he is told."[11]

DISPATCHER KILLS UNKNOWN NEGRO
Was After Street Car Conductor With Knife on North Ensley Line
Conductor Barcliff Had Been Cut on Hand by Negro Before Dispatcher Jennings Fired

The Birmingham Age-Herald, August 15, 1912

"W.B. Jennings, a dispatcher for the Birmingham Railway, Light and Power company shot and killed an unknown negro man who was a passenger on the trailer. Immediately after the shooting

Jennings gave himself up. After ascertaining the negro was dead, Coroner Brasher was notified. Jennings was released after being told to report to the coroner's office this morning. The case will be brought before the coroner's jury.

The shooting occurred on the North Ensley car at East Thomas station. The negro man, whose name is unknown, boarded the car at Pratt City. That he was under the influence of liquor was testified by several. He chased the conductor through the entire length of the trailer toward the front platform. The dispatcher, Jennings, was standing here, and as they came up he pulled a revolver from his hip pocket and shot the negro twice in the breast, and once in the side as he fell. The man died almost instantly before anyone could find out his name or where he lived.

Dispatcher Jennings made the following statement: "I was standing on the platform when the conductor went to the back to quiet the negro. A few minutes later, startled by the cries of the colored passengers, I turned to see the conductor coming down the aisle at a terrific clip, and the negro man behind him with a long bladed knife in his hand. I could not shoot then, because the conductor was between us, but when he reached the platform, I pulled him aside and shot three times. I think that all the bullets took effect. If I had not shot him that negro would have seriously wounded Barcliff with his knife, and when I pulled him aside it was a case of shooting him or letting him drive that knife into my heart."

Litwack wrote that:

> "The courts, along with the police, played a critical role as the enforcers of Jim Crow. Once previous customs became lodged in the statute books, it was important that any breaches be swiftly punished as examples to others of how the new order would be implemented. That included upholding the authority of conductors in public transportation to mete out their own brand of justice to passengers who didn't know their "place."[12]

NEGRO KILLED BY PASSENGERS AS HE CREATES A PANIC
John Wynn Shoots at Conductor When Asked to Move From White Section
Many Shots Fired On A Tuxedo Car

The Birmingham Age-Herald, June 15, 1917

"John Wynn, a negro, was shot and killed on an Owenton-Ensley car yesterday morning near Tuxedo Junction after he had caused a panic among passengers by shooting several times at W.D. Peoples, the conductor. A number of shots were fired at the negro by passengers on the car. The conductor was shot in the hand by the negro, who is said to have become

angry when asked to move from the white section of the car.

Detectives said late yesterday that they had not obtained the names of the participants in the affair. There are no clues the detectives can work upon, all persons on the street car at the time of the shooting having left it either before reaching the city or before officers began their investigation. The shooting on the crowded street car caused intense excitement among the women and children. Men in front and the rear, crowding toward the negro, who cooly stood firing at Mr. Peoples, cut off the exit and the women were forced to take seats.

Wynn's insistence that he be allowed to sit in the white section of the street car is said by officers to have resulted in the shooting of the conductor. The negro got on the car, inbound, at Tuxedo Junction. For a short time he stood on the platform and when he had paid his fare he is said to have gone beyond the negro section to the white section. Conductor Peoples in his report to the police, said he asked the negro to move back to the section provided for negroes. At this request the negro is said to have abused the conductor, telling him that negroes were imposed upon down south. The conductor again asked the negro to move. Becoming angry, the negro whipped out a revolver and fired at the conductor. Peoples, unarmed, held his position in the aisle while the negro fired several times. One bullet struck the conductor's hand, severing one finger.

An unidentified white man, a passenger on the car, handed Peoples a revolver. The safety spring had not been reversed and Peoples made a futile effort to fire at the negro. Realizing it was impossible for the conductor to use the revolver, several passengers on the car joined in the shooting. The number of shots fired possibly will never be known, but it is believed that three, possibly four or five, joined in the shooting with several standing nearby with drawn revolvers. The shot that ended the negro's life was fired from over the shoulder of Peoples, who during all the excitement had not moved from the aisle. Investigators showed that the negro was shot three times with different calibre pistols. Each wound would have caused death the officers state. During the intense excitement several negroes left the street car through the windows."

The coroner impanelled a jury to investigate this case and despite the fact that none of the people who shot Wynn were identified, the docket entry indicates, "The jury after hearing the evidence in this case came to the decision the deceased came to his death from gun shot wounds at the hands of parties or party unknown, same being justifiable."

CONDUCTOR SHOT ON ENSLEY CAR BY NEGRO PASSENGER
Passengers Panic Stricken When Shooting Occurs and Negro Makes Good His Escape
The Birmingham Age-Herald, January 29, 1919

"J.W. Perkins, a conductor on the Owenton-Ensley car line was shot through the lung and probably fatally injured by an unknown negro last night. The shooting occurred while the car was traveling between Sixth and Seventh avenues on Seventeenth street and caused much excitement in the neighborhood.

The shooting followed a dispute between the conductor and a negro passenger, who was accompanied by a woman, as to whether the woman had given him a nickel or a dime for car fare. The conductor insisted that only a nickel for the two passengers had been paid. Without warning the negro stood up, pulled a pistol, and as the conductor turned, shot him in the back. Pushing through the excited and crowded passengers, he forced open the doors of the car and leaped out and made his escape. During the intense excitement which followed his woman companion disappeared. They both succeeded in getting away completely before the startled passengers realized what had happened and no pursuit was made.

When the car was brought to a stop people residing in the neighborhood gathered quickly and for a time much excitement prevailed as the conductor lay wounded and bleeding on the floor of the car. When Shaw's ambulance arrived Perkins exclaimed to the motorman: "It's no use, I am dying." He was rushed to St. Vincent's hospital, where it was found that the bullet had entered his back and passed through his left lung.

The police authorities were quickly on the scene, but the negro and his companion had entirely disappeared. They secured, however, a fairly good description of the negroes and their arrest is expected."

CONDUCTOR SHOOTS TWO NEGROES ON PRATT-ENSLEY CAR
Trouble Narrowly Averted Following Killing of Negro and Wounding of Another

The Birmingham Age-Herald, June 16, 1919

"Serious trouble was narrowly averted last night when Johnnie Green, negro, was shot three times through the head and instantly killed, and Bernard Green, his brother, was shot through the leg and seriously wounded by Conductor L.D. Summerlin, of an outboard Pratt-Ensley car. The shooting took place at Thrash station following a quarrel between the conductor and the negro about car fare. A call came to police headquarters to the effect that a race riot was threatened at Thrash station. A large crowd of negroes crowded around the car and making threats against the conductor. Officers pushed their way through the crowd and found the body of one negro lying on the car, and the other nearby badly wounded. The conductor had left the scene.

Succeeding in dispersing the crowd, the officers summoned the coroner, who ordered the body of the dead negro turned over to Echols & Strong, negro undertakers. The officers went to the car barn to arrest Summerlin but he had disappeared and as yet remains at large."

KILLING OF GREEN UNLAWFUL VERDICT OF CORONER RIVES
Conductor Summerlin Held on Murder Charge Following Investigation by Coroner

The Birmingham Age-Herald, June 18, 1919

"After hearing the testimony of a large number of witnesses, Assistant Coroner John R.T. Rives yesterday returned a verdict of unlawful homicide in the case of Conductor L.D. Summerlin, who shot and killed Johnnie Green, negro, on a Pratt-Ensley car Sunday night. On the completion of the inquest a warrant charging murder was sworn out for Summerlin before Judge H.B. Abernethy by a kinsman of the deceased negro, and the white man was committed to the county jail without bond. Conductor Summerlin also shot and severely wounded Bernard Green during the quarrel.

The testimony was to the effect that Green, touched the conductor on the back after he had asked him several times for change, when Summerlin turned around and fired on the negro three times, killing him instantly. One of the bullets took effect in the leg of Bernard Green, who was standing near. Only one witness out of quite a number heard, testified that Green was advancing on the conductor when he fired the first shot."

Postscript

This was a rare case where the coroner initially and quickly ruled that the death of Johnnie Green was an "unlawful homicide" when perpetrated by a white man of "authority" against a black individual. It is believed that this occurred because of the egregious circumstances surrounding the incident as noted by many witness statements and the fact that the conductor fled the scene after the shooting. He most likely did so to avoid being assaulted by the gathering irate crowd.

Although the coroner returned a verdict against the conductor and the case likely made its way into the regular court system, this was another case where research failed to locate information relating to a final judicial outcome.

An example of spur of the moment "vigilante" type activity that was not pursued further by the police is seen with another incident which occurred on a public transportation vehicle.

NEGRO KILLED ON THE BESSEMER CAR LINE
Following Dispute Over Fare,
Shot Is Fired by Unknown Party
The Birmingham Age-Herald, October 11, 1919

"George Peoples, a negro, of North Birmingham, was shot and instantly killed by an unknown party last night on the North Bessemer car line. Peoples, who was riding in the negro section of the car, got into an argument with the conductor, W.A. Murphyee, over the amount of fare to be paid. It is alleged that the negro refused to pay the conductor the full fare, amounting to 18 cents, claiming that only

16 cents was due, and after refusing to the pay the 2 cents difference due, got into a heated argument with Murphyee. It is alleged that Peoples threw the conductor down and then drew a large knife out of his pocket and slightly cut the conductor on the hand. In the meantime, the motorman and several other white men rushed to the conductor's aid and succeeded in separating the two men.

A moment later the negro dropped with a bullet through his heart. He was shot from behind and died immediately. The pistols of Bennett and Murphyee were examined, but the chambers were found to be filled. The shooting created a lot of excitement among the passengers."

Automobiles

"We had motor trouble, it turned into a struggle,
Half way 'cross Alabam'.
And that hound broke down and left us all stranded
in downtown Birmingham."

---Promised Land
Chuck Berry

Although gasoline powered motor vehicles had been introduced on a rapidly increasing scale during the early years of the 20th century, it was not until after the end of World War I that their numbers exponentially increased, especially within the smaller developing cities of the south. As noted by F.L. Allen, "In 1919 there had been 6,771,000 passenger cars in service in the United States; by 1929 there were no less than 23,121,000."[13]

In these early years, the rapidly increasing presence of numerous motorized vehicles coincided with an appreciable increase in the number of related injuries and deaths of drivers, passengers and pedestrians, mainly due to the lack of experience in the operation of these oftentimes difficult to control cars and trucks. This, combined with their ever increasing capability of speed and the inattention of both drivers and those persons crossing streets, as well as the lack of traffic management by signals and police officers, were major factors associated with the increased injury and death rates. This was true not only in Birmingham, but across the nation where motorized vehicles quickly replaced slower means of transportation by animals.

The modern investigation of vehicular collisions relies on advanced scientific methods and tools to include complex mathematical equations and computer technology in attempts to reconstruct in detail the series of events that led to, and resulted from, a particular collision. These incidents may often involve multiple vehicles and often have far-reaching effects in regard to future legal proceedings.

In earlier years, the process of accident investigation appeared to be a basic and rather simple matter as shown in this example of a report from 1923:

Sheriff's Office
Jefferson County.
BESSEMER DIVISION

Bessemer Ala., Dec the 9th 1923

John. McClendon Killed by Automombeil Neare E.B.Canoles on the Loveless Bridge Road the best infermation is that the Car became uncontrogble it seams that he had A foot Excellater and it got hung up and the car ran away and he being an enexperience driver he lostcontrle of it and the Car turned over and caught his head under the running board and crushed his scull N.W.Williams City and C.S.Carter andA.B.Dugger Brighton picked him up and started to the Hospittle with him but he died before reaching the Hospitle and the body was turned over to Jacobs

Witnesses E.B.Canoles Bessemer R.F.D.#3

N.C.Williams City

L.C.Davis Mine forman Readers

C.S.Carter and A.B.Dugger Brighton

J.N. Smithson D.N

J. J. CROWE, Deputy Coroner Bessemer

Docket Entry:
Date: October 14, 1911
Deceased: Ed N. Schuster, White
Address: Green Undertaking Co., City.
Cause Of Death: From an automobile accident. Same being unavoidable.

Docket Entry:
Date: August 5, 1915
Deceased: Mike Salivar, White
Cause Of Death: From fractured skull.
Remarks: Deceased was standing on running board of an automobile and fell off.

Docket Entry:
Date: November 23, 1917
Deceased: Fred Schilling, White
Address: South Highlands Infirmary.
Cause Of Death: From internal injuries received when he was run over by ice wagon, same being accidental.

Docket Entry:
Date: September 10, 1919
Deceased: Jack Harris, Col.
Address: 4704 9th Ave. Wylam.
Cause Of Death: By being run over by ice wagon, same being accidental.

Docket Entry:
Date: January 2, 1922
Deceased: T.L. Brawley, White
Adress: Jacobs Undertaking Co.
Cause Of Death: From fractured skull and crushed chest caused by automobile accident on race track at fairgrounds.

Docket Entry:
Date: April 24, 1929
Deceased: William Hinton, Col.
Cause Of Death: Traumatic injuries to body.
Remarks: Received when he fell from an ice wagon that he was stealing a ride on, directly in front of another ice wagon that ran over him.

FIRE TRUCK OVERTURNS, KILLS 2
3 OTHER FIREMEN INJURED
Crash Is Described As Following Swerve to Avoid Collision
BURNING OVERALLS CAUSE FOR ALARM

The Birmingham Age-Herald, June 19, 1937

"Two city firemen were killed and three others were injured, one seriously, when a fire truck overturned at the intersection of Twenty-Fourth Street and Fourth Avenue, South.

Police investigators said they were told the truck on which the victims were riding overturned when it swerved upon approaching an automobile in which Assistant Chief William Hanlin was riding. Firemen and the assistant chief were responding to a box alarm where a set of overalls were burning in a rubbish heap. The two firemen fatally injured in the accident were dead upon arrival at hospitals. Both the dead were married and are survived by families.

Officers said they were told by witnesses they saw the truck swerve sharply, apparently in an effort to avoid colliding with the assistant chief's automobile, and then overturn on the pavement after clearing the sidewalk curb. Walter Fair, one of the death victims, was at the wheel of the truck. Surviving Fair are the widow and two children."

Poison Claims Life of Mrs. Fair, Fireman's Widow

The Birmingham News, November 1, 1937

"It would have been their twelfth wedding anniversary, yesterday, had not Fireman Walter Fair been killed when a fire truck overturned last June and had not his widow taken poison yesterday at her home in Pinson. Mrs. Fair, despondent over her husband's death, carried out threats made off and on throughout the Summer, that she was going to kill herself. She died at Norwood Hospital five hours after she swallowed poison.

Fair was killed along with four of his mates when a fire truck from Station 4 overturned. County Investigator Gip M. Evans returned a verdict of suicide from the effects of poisoning."

> *"...and when they pulled her from the wreck you know,*
> *she still had on her shades.*
> *They say that dreams are growing wild,*
> *just this side of*
> *Burma Shave."*
>
> ---Burma Shave
> Tom Waits

Aircraft

As the popularity of aviation increased dramatically following its introduction in Europe and America during the early years of the 20th century, so did the rates of fatalities associated with their use. The main reasons for these accidents can be attributed to several factors to include the questionable airworthiness of some early models of aircraft, the inexperience of pilots and the "learning curve" for safely operating these oftentimes difficult to control vehicles.

Numerous fatal aircraft accidents occurred during the increase of flying activities prior to and during World War I, in both training and combat operations. However, the war also provided greater numbers of experienced pilots. It also gave inspiration for the design and production of more advanced and safer aircraft and for the development of pilot skills, albeit with many growing pains. An example of this can be found during the 1920s with the appreciable number of fatalities associated with the transportation of mail by aircraft to include flying at night and in bad weather conditions. As noted by David Doochin, "Being an airmail carrier was one of the most dangerous jobs in America. From 1918 to 1926, there were 35 pilots who died trying to deliver the mail, and there were 15 deaths alone in 1920."[14]

The expansion of flying activity also led to "barnstorming" at local fairs, stunt flying and other "reckless" practices. Birmingham was an active hub for developing aviation during those early years and has hosted military aviation units, a major aircraft repair facility and the Southern Museum of Flight. The original 106th Aero Squadron was formed here in 1917.

AVIATOR STEPHENSON FATALY INJURED AT THE FAIR GROUNDS

When Up About 40 Feet He Apparently Tried To Jump and Plunged To Ground In Presence of Thousands of Spectators—Fell Clear of Machine, But Skull Was Fractured and Broken Ribs Punctured His Lungs

The Birmingham Age-Herald, October 8, 1912

"After being in the air scarcely two minutes in his first flight at the State Fair grounds, Aviator Joseph Stephenson fell to the ground yesterday afternoon at 4:30 o'clock and received injuries that will probably result in his death.

Stephenson, in his biplane, had made all preparations for his flight yesterday, skidding along the ground in starting, he arose to a height of about 30 or 40 feet. After flying a short distance he was seen to turn the machine and attempt to alight. A second later he apparently tried to jump, but fell to the ground with the nearby machine. However, he did not fall under the airplane, but escaped clear clear of the wreckage. Johns ambulance rushed the injured man to the Robinson infirmary, where it was stated last night that he had very little chance for recovery. In the fall his skull was fractured. Some of his ribs were broken and his lungs punctured and his body badly bruised. His face had been severely cut by the wires on the machine.

Mrs. Stephenson was on the ground and saw her husband fall. She was among the first at the scene of the wreckage and accompanied the injured man to the hospital where she is constantly at his bedside. A few moments before the flight Mrs. Stephenson was in the best of spirits and posed for a picture. Before going up in the machine, however, Stephenson had remarked that he did not feel right and thought something might happen.

The biplane used by Stevenson is one of his own inventions. In the fall yesterday the machine was not so badly wrecked, only the wings being somewhat damaged and the runners bent. The low altitude doubtless kept the machine from being a complete wreck.

Half an hour later another of the intrepid men of the air shot upwards to a beautiful flight, and despite the horrible affair of a moment previous, remained poised, tempting death, for an indefinite period."

Docket Entry:
Date: June 3, 1921
Deceased: Vermon Oral Hodges, White
Address: Johns Undertaking Co.
Cause Of Death: By body and head being crushed, caused by accidental falling of air plane.

Docket Entry:
Date: September 21, 1926
Deceased: Orville Morrow, White
Address: J.N. Brown's Funeral Home
Cause Of Death: By fractured base of skull and traumatic shock. Plane fell with him, same being accidental.

Docket Entry:
Date: February 5, 1927
Deceased: Alonzo C. Turner, White
Address: Echols & Angwins Funeral Home
Cause Of Death: By a fracture of shoulder and head caused by an airplane falling with him, same being accidental.

MESSER'S AIRSHIP IS IN MISHAP
C. Pat Murphy and J.G. Ramsey
In Critical Condition At Hospital

CRAFT DIVES FROM 150 FEET HEIGHT
Ambulance Attendants Say Pair
Badly Crushed From Accident

The Birmingham Age-Herald, June 12, 1928

"Crashing 200 feet in a commercial plane at Roberts Field, C. Pat Murphy and J.G. Ramsey were seriously injured and taken to South Highlands Infirmary where Ramsey's condition was said to be critical. Both men were said to have possible fractures of the skull.

Attaches of Roberts Field said the plane had circled over their field several times and landed there once. Shortly after it took off, it was said to have suddenly dived to the field. Glen Messer, owner of the plane, professed belief that the controls of the ship had "froze" causing the pilot to lose control. Murphy is believed to have been piloting the the plane and he had been a pilot for 13 years.

Officers at Roberts Field said they had called the police before the crash to take the men in charge after they had performed their daring stunts over the government fielded and had landed in violation of the rules of the field."

PROBE PUSHED IN FATAL AIR CRASH
Funerals To Be Monday
For Two Victims Of Woodlawn Wreck

The Birmingham Age-Herald, January 11, 1937

"George A. Wiggs, Nashville, Tenn., aeronautical inspector of the Bureau of Air Commerce, will continue his investigation into the Woodlawn fatal airplane crash Monday while funeral services for the two youthful aviation enthusiasts, John E. McCarty, who was piloting the plane...and for Edwin C. Grounds will be held.

The plane, a small monoplane, owned by Glenn Messer, crashed in a muddy field at Forty-Eighth Street and Second Avenue, South, only half an hour after a takeoff at MunicipalAirport. Mr. Messer said that before the youths took off, he checked the plane and found it t be in perfect condition.

Witnesses said the plane executed several "wingovers" at a very low altitude. Mr. Messer said that the pilot attempted a vertical bank and the plane slipped out of it and since there was no altitude left for the pilot to get it under control again, crashed. County Investigator Gip Evans returns a finding of accidental death in the crash."

Elevators

Although not typically thought of as a "vehicle," the widespread employment of this early modernized conveyance used to move people and goods up and down, rather than "outwards," affected many people on a daily basis as industrialization rapidly progressed. As cities and their populations saw rapid growth, an obvious outcome of this expansion led to the requirement for utilizing limited area which led to building business and living spaces upwards. Although these changes in construction were first seen in larger cities in the late 19th century, the early 20th century would see the rapid construction of high rise buildings spread to expanding smaller towns across the country. In Birmingham, according to Wikipedia, "The Heaviest Corner on Earth" was a promotional name given to the corner of 20th Street and 1st Avenue North in the early 20th century. The name reflected the nearly simultaneous appearance of four of the tallest buildings in the South, the 10-story Woodward Building (1902), the 16-story Brown Marx Building (1906), 16-story Empire Building (1909), and the 21-story American Trust and Savings Bank Building (1912)." All of these structures would require elevators with human operators. Many of these conveyances would not be fully automated until the mid part of the century. Locally, up until the remaining women operators became eligible for retirement in the mid 1970s, several elevators at the Jefferson County courthouse would continue to be manually controlled.

In addition to office buildings, various types of electrically powered elevators would also find common use in industrial and manufacturing settings such as mines, warehouses, factories and department stores. Despite advances in safety features, elevators could still be dangerous with associated injuries and deaths resulting from their extensive use. These accidents could usually be attributed to either inattention on the part of passengers or by errors committed by their operators, rather than from mechanical failure.

Statistics

In a review of available Jefferson County docket book entries to include a 28 year period from 1909 through 1937, no less than 32 direct elevator related fatalities, to include falls down elevator shafts, were recorded.

The number of these deaths during this period, averaging slightly more than 1 per year, may not seem excessive on a numerical or per capita basis. However, as with other means of traumatic deaths it would not be unusual to find that the unknown number of non-fatal injuries sustained in association with elevators could conservatively by expected to outnumber fatalities by at least a 3:1 ratio.

Boy's Head Completely Cut Off By Elevator
The Birmingham Age-Herald, January 20, 1909

"To have his head mashed completely off of his shoulders was the fate encountered by Charlie Hull, a 14-year-old boy employed at the warehouse of the Wimberly-Thomas Hardware Company on Eighteenth St. and Avenue A.

The accident occurred yesterday afternoon shortly after 2 o'clock. There was no one to witness the accident, which occurred in the elevator shaft at the warehouse, but the theory of the boy's death, outlined by Coroner B.L. Brasher, is considered a plausible one.

The boy's body was found at the bottom of the elevator shaft, the head being under the counterweight. It was young Hull's business to carry orders and messages to the various floors of the building, and it is supposed by the coroner that he got down into the elevator pit to take out a crosscut saw handle which was found there after his body was taken out. It is believed that while the boy was in the pit the counterweight descended and he was caught under it. His head was literally mashed from his shoulders and his death is believed to have been instantaneous. The remains of the deceased boy are being held in the morgue of Lige Loy, pending funeral arrangements."

ELEVATOR KILLS WITNESS BROOKS AT COURTHOUSE
TERRIBLE ACCIDENT OCCURRED YESTERDAY MORNING ABOUT 11 O'CLOCK
Evidently Thought The Car Was Falling

The Birmingham Age-Herald, December 3, 1912

"Jay Brooks, a miner aged about 48 years, living near the Crocker mines, was crushed to death yesterday morning by an elevator at the County Courthouse, being caught between the elevator and the sill of the fourth floor. The corridors of the courthouse were crowded at the time of the accident and scores of people were witnesses of the horrible accident.

According to witnesses the elevator had ascended to the fourth floor, the boy operating the elevator running it a little above the floor. In attempting to bring the car down even with the fourth floor, the machinery became clogged or jammed and refused to work. Burton, the negro operator, then got out of the car and went to the basement of the building to repair the machinery, the other people remaining in the car. While working at the machinery in the basement, the elevator four floors above began to descend with the passengers still in it and the operator below. In passing the fourth floor Brooks, evidently thinking that the elevator was falling, grasped the steel grating of the door and held on tightly, his feet leaving the floor of the elevator and the top of the car crushing his head against the sill of the floor. The car continued downward, the top passing on down over Brooks' chest, crushing practically every bone in it. His neck was broken.

Miss Micker fainted while the cries of the occupants of the car and the screaming of other witnesses brought a large crowd to the scene. Brooks had been a witness in a case in Judge Fort's court. His son, Jim Brooks, was also a witness and was on the fourth floor when his father was killed. Coroner Brasher will investigate the accident within the next few days."

DANIEL IS KILLED BY FALL THROUGH ELEVATOR SHAFT
Accident Happens at Young & Vann's Supply House Funeral Will Be Held Today

The Birmingham Age-Herald, March, 1913

"Freeman B. Daniel, a well known brick manufacturer, was almost instantly killed by falling down an elevator shaft in Young & Vann's supply house, Eighteenth street and First Avenue. The fatally injured manufacturer was picked up and carried by Johns' ambulance to St. Vincent's hospital where he died without recovering consciousness.

The accident happened after Mr. Daniel had purchased some goods and was waiting for the elevator to take him down to the next floor. The door of the elevator shaft was open and in some way Mr. Daniel lost his footing and fell down the shaft, a distance of 12 feet, landing on his head. At the hospital it was found that Mr. Daniels' skull was crushed and there was no hope for his recovery.

Freeman R. Daniel was 56 years of age and was well known throughout the Birmingham district. He first came to Birmingham in the early eighties from Selma. He was Avondale's first mayor and the last mayor, as under his administration Avondale became a suburb of Birmingham."

Docket Entry:
Date: November 22, 1910
Deceased: James Malone Honnall, White
Address: American Bakery & Candy Company.
Cause Of Death: Falling through an elevator shaft of the American Bakery and Candy Company.
Remarks: Same being due to his own negligence and we the jury recommend that same company place a regular elevator boy or man on said elevator, also place lights and bells on same.

Docket Entry:
Date: February 9, 1914
Deceased: Mr. Frank P. Jarvis, White
Address: American Trust Building.
Cause Of Death: By his head being crushed by an elevator of the American Trust Bank building.
Remarks: Said elevator was operated who started the elevator up before the door was properly closed, thereby negligently causing his death but without malice intentions.

Docket Entry:
Date: August 15, 1918
Deceased: Martis Rushton Goodwin, White
Address: Tutwiler Hotel
Cause Of Death: From traumatism, caused by being crushed between the floor and elevator, same being accidental.

Docket Entry:
Date: April 22, 1920
Deceased: Mamie Davis, Col.
Address: Nunnally's 20 St. store.
Cause Of Death: By being crushed in an elevator, same being accidental.

Docket Entry:
Date: April 17, 1925
Deceased: Arthur L. Tanton, White
Address: Lige Loy Funeral Home
Cause Of Death: By his head being cut off by an elevator, same being accidental.

Docket Entry:
Date: September 3, 1925
Deceased: R.E. Ashley, White
Address: Ridout's Funeral Home
Cause Of Death: By a crushed chest and broken neck when he was caught in the elevator shaft of the Alabama Power Company's building, same being accidental.

Docket Entry:
Date: December 28, 1925
Deceased: Joseph S. Vogt, White
Address: Johns Funeral Home
Cause Of Death: By traumatic fractures of skull and body same being caused when he fell down elevator shaft at Tutwiler Hotel, same being accidental.

Docket Entry:
Date: August 29, 1929
Deceased: Robert Bullock AKA Robert Legg
Address: Between 24 & 25 Street on 3rd Avenue North.
Cause Of Death: When he was caught between elevator and wall when he was trespassing in a vacant building.

Docket Entry:
Date: December 5, 1937
Deceased: Lelton Jackson, White
Address: Hillman Hospital
Cause Of Death: Crushed by elevator while attempting to catch it.
Remarks: Coroner Evans agreed that the negro elevator operator was only partly to blame for the accident, pointing out that the Jackson youth was partly blind.

CHAPTER 19

ANIMALS

"Lets face it: our lives are miserable, laborious, and short."

---Animal Farm
George Orwell

Although industrialization proceeded at a rapid pace in the Birmingham-Jefferson County area during the early 20th century, changes in the local means of transportation of goods and of farming would only gradually take place. One did not have to travel far outside the Birmingham city limits (or in some areas within it) to enter rural areas where farm animals played a major role in the existence of those persons living "out in the country."

One of the more rapid and extensive changes seen during this period was the replacement of animals as a form of locomotion by the gasoline powered motor vehicle. In a short period of time such businesses as blacksmithing and buggy manufacturing were radically reduced or completely gone and automotive repair skills were in sudden demand in urban areas. However, the changeover to these more "modern" devices came much more slowly in rural areas. It would be many years before the widespread employment of motorized tractors would replace the horse and mule as the means for plowing and other farming requirements. In addition, the availability of pork, beef and poultry products would continue to be dependent on their local production and distribution.

As the populations of cities across the country rapidly increased, problems relating to public health would continue to arise. Their causation could, in many instances, be traced back to animal waste products which were contaminating water sources within cities with poorly developed or the complete lack of adequate sewer systems. In addition, the presence of farm type animals within the increasingly crowded urban areas was becoming a public nuisance. The reaction of local governments was to implement ordinances which prohibited the keeping of these types of animals within city limits. Such laws can currently be found in place in essentially all incorporated cities and towns across the country.

With certain restrictions, many cities in Alabama, including Birmingham, currently allow for chickens to be kept at private residences. Although it is unknown when Birmingham first legally excluded farm and large animals from the city limits, the current ordinance states, in part, "No horse, cow, calf, swine, sheep, goat, chickens, geese or ducks shall be kept in any dwelling or part thereof. Nor shall any such animal be kept on the same lot or premises with a dwelling. This offense is punishable by up to 90 days in jail and/or $500.00 fine."

Large Animals

Deaths directly associated with larger farm animals of varying and rapidly changing temperament, such as bulls, horses and mules, can be found within the Jefferson County coroner's records. Such injuries and deaths were obviously more prevalent within the rural communities of Alabama during this time period. Larger animals could suddenly become violent and inflict fatal injuries even to those persons accustomed to working with them on a daily basis. It is certain that non-fatal injuries far outnumbered those which led to reported deaths.

BOY GORED TO DEATH BY A MADDENED YOUNG BULL
George Hughley Meets Horrible Death Near Graves Trying To Ride Animal
Beast Smelled Blood On Ground and Began Wild Charge Through the Woods— Turned and Gored His Helpless Victim

The Birmingham Age-Herald, October 17, 1904

"While attempting a daring ride yesterday, George Hughley, a bright young boy of 14 years, was gored to death by a maddened young bull, near his home at Graves mines, while his playmates looked on, unable to lend assistance to their unfortunate companion.

Young Hughley and several of his playmates had caught a young bull and had tied a rope around the horns of the animal. In a spirit of fun, Hughley, who was the leader of the crowd had the boys tie him on the bull in order that he might "break" him to ride. Astride the new mount, everything went well for the first few yards of the ride, while the young boys running by Hughley's side made the woods fairly ring with their joyous shouts.

The procession had advanced some distance into the heart of the woods when the bull suddenly stopped, pawing the dirt high over his head and rending the air with unearthly bellows. He then started off in a mad chase through the woods. For a time the boy held his seat firmly, manifesting extraordinary coolness. By some means the rope slipped, throwing the rider to the ground, and the bull instead of halting, appeared to be more ferocious. When the boy fell helpless to the ground the bull, after dragging him for some distance, turned on the unhappy youth and began plunging his horns into the youth's body.

The animal's sudden fury was the result of scenting some fresh blood that had been spilled in the woods on the day before by the slaughtering of some cattle. When young Hughley fell several of his companions had hurried away in search of help. Three or four men responded, bringing their guns with which to kill the bull, but before they reached the scene young Hughley had breathed his last.

Trampling the life out of his helpless victim did not seem to appease the anger of the brute. The rescuing party rushing up fired on the bull, shooting him several times before he fell. After being literally plugged with bullets the wild beast fell to the ground and died without a single kick or groan. The men then rushed quickly forward in hope that the brave young boy might yet be alive, but he had breathed his last. His bloody and mangled form was picked up and carried to the home of his father. In addition to being badly bruised externally and internally both of his arms and his neck were broken."

Docket Entry:
Date: July 7, 1909
Deceased: Lester Thiesman
Address: 2 Ave and 16 St.
Cause Of Death: Deceased was run over by a Runaway Horse and killed and said horse was owned by the American Londery Co. of Birmingham, Ala.

Docket Entry:
Date: May 22, 1914
Deceased: W.A. Russell, White
Cause Of Death: From being thrown out of buggy while turning a corner at high rate of speed.

Docket Entry:
Date: September 4, 1918
Deceased: Wm. Rufus Owen, White
Address: Sayreton
Cause Of Death: From hemorrhage due to puncture of left femoral artery by being gored by bull, same being accidental.

Docket Entry:
Date: September 6, 1919
Deceased: J.R. Bookout, White
Address: Birmingham Infirmary
Cause Of Death: By being killed by runaway horse, caused by collision of an automobile and buggy.

Docket Entry:
Date: December 17, 1919
Deceased: Frank Miller, Col.
Address: Mackey's Morgue
Cause Of Death: I found that deceased party came to his death in the year 1907, March 7th, by being kicked by a mule, same being accidental.
Remarks: Deceased party has been kept at Mackey's morgue twelve years waiting to be claimed by his relatives who never claimed him and said party was buried by the city at Ketona.

Docket Entry:
Date: October 31, 1921
Deceased: Tommy Worthington, Col.
Address: Bell Undertaking Co.
Cause Of Death: From fractured skull by being kicked by a mule.

Docket Entry:
Date: November 29, 1921
Deceased: Edward Sanders, Col.
Address: Shortridge Undertaking Co.
Cause Of Death: From crushed chest by being kicked by a horse, same being accidental.

Docket Entry:
Date: November 1, 1924
Deceased: Marvin Jackson, Col.
Address: Jordan Undertaking Co.
Cause Of Death: Gunshot wounds of abdomen. Was trying to steal a cow.

Docket Entry:
Date: November 14, 1924
Deceased: Mrs. Ollie Bailey, White
Address: W.C. Vice Undertaking Co.
Cause Of Death: By an injured spine when team ran away with her, same being accidental.

Docket Entry:
Date: November 13, 1926
Deceased: Lee Marsh, White
Address: Johns Funeral Home
Cause Of Death: By blood poison caused by being bitten by a hog.

Docket Entry:
Date: May 15, 1930
Deceased: Will Williams, Col.
Address: Gardendale
Cause Of Death: Traumatic injuries to chest received when the automobile truck in which he was riding overturned after striking a mule then a telephone pole.

Domestic Animals

There were various issues associated with smaller farm and domestic type animals in urban areas prior to implementation of enhanced animal control procedures and public health regulations.

BOWERY TOM CAT MEETS SAD DEATH
While Lounging In Saloon Well-Known Yellow Striped Feline Goes Mad During Political Argument—Is Shot
The Birmingham Age-Herald, November 14, 1903

"Thomas, of the Bowery, one of the best known cats in Birmingham, met an untimely end in the saloon of Pete Goss last night when, during an epileptic fit he was mortally wounded with a 38-calibre ball from a revolver in the hands of Mr. Goss.

Thomas had wandered across the alley into the rear of the Goss establishment, and while the glasses clinked merrily at the bar he languished near a one-cent weighing machine which had long since been discarded and placed in a far away corner as an ornament. As a conversation touching municipal politics began to wax warm it reached the delicate ear of Thomas and in a moment his yellow strriped coat began to extend a la Monsieur le Porcupine.

The argument grew animated as the minutes sped by and Thomas became very much excited. His nerves withstood the strain as long as possible but when someone offered to bet that either Melville Drennen or L.B. Musgrove would be the next governor it seemed as if forty thousand needles shot through his frame and poor Thomas was crazy. After a series of very queer antics the debaters became frightened at the gentleman from the Bowery and Pete was compelled to pull his "gun." Seeing that all hope for the visitor was gone, Mr. Goss, in a humane spirit, took a plug at the writhing yellow cat. The bullet struck Thomas amidships and he leaped four feet in the air only to give an unearthly shriek and disappear into the mysterious labyrinths of the alley. In a few moments he had breathed his last.

Looking for a murder a crowd rushed into the saloon from all directions only to find that a poor cat had been laid to rest. It is an ill wind that blows nobody good and Pete's act of mercy served as a great advertisement. Every man who fell a victim to the joke felt inclined to buy a drink and the bar flourished."

FIRST MAD DOG OF SEASON SHOT DOWN
Big Crowd Gathers At Mouth Of Alley To See Policeman Shoot At Canine Which Foamed At Mouth
The Birmingham Age-Herald, March 20, 1904

"Big crowds gathered around the mouth of Third alley at Eighteenth and Nineteenth streets to see two policemen kill a mad dog, the first of the season. The policemen fired four shots at the dog, three of them taking effect.

About 5 o'clock a small dog was seen running down Eighteenth street with foam at his mouth. Some one started a cry of mad dog and a big crowd gathered at a safe distance to throw rocks, sticks and anything else they could at the dog. Policemen McDonald and Hawkins were attracted by the crowd. Policeman Hawkins fired once and missed, and Policeman McDonald shot the dog through the body. The dog fell, but jumped up at once and started running. A second shot was fired by Policeman Hawkins, striking the dog in the head. It fell again, but a second time it staggered to its feet and attempted to continue. A fourth shot, this from the gun of Policeman McDonald reached a fatal spot and the dog died immediately.

In its run down Eighteenth street the dog snapped at several people, and once buried its teeth in the trousers leg of a negro man, but that was the nearest it came to causing any trouble."

Although organized dog fighting was made illegal in all states by the 1960s, enforcement was lax and penalties were light. Although greatly decreased in extent from earlier times, the practice continues to this day. However, prior to its prohibition in Alabama, the reporting of the outcome of recent fights could be found in the daily newspapers.

BIG DOG FIGHT HELD THURSDAY
Several Thousand Dollars Said
To Have Changed Hands
When Montgomery Fighter Defeated Birmingham Dog

The Birmingham Age-Herald, April 30, 1910

"After an hour and 15 minutes of fierce fighting, "Naylor," a Montgomery bulldog, won a decision on a foul over "Pure Gold Pete," a Birmingham member of the bulldog family.

The fight was held at Vanderbilt Thursday afternoon and was witnessed by nearly 200 lovers of the sport. Several thousand dollars, it is understood, exchanged hands as the result of the fight and the Birminghamers are blue over the result. Practically every man witnessing the fight is said to have had a bet placed on the fight. It was a game fight for every bit of the 75 minutes which it lasted."

Docket Entry:
Date: June 18, 1915
Deceased: Sidney Williams, Col.
Cause Of Death: Came to his death while deceased and Genivive Williams were trying to kill a snake and being done with a gun being accidental.

Docket Entry:
Date: June 6, 1925
Deceased: Mark England, White
Address: W.J. Bell Funeral Home
Cause Of Death: By being overcome by black dane, same being accidental.

Chickens

"I don't mind telling this whole wide world
Someone's doin' me wrong.
I don't be able to catch on yet
But they gonna get catched for long.
Take a little tip from me,
Stay away from my chicken house, boys
If you figure your life's worthwhile."

---Stay Away From My Chicken House
Ca. 1920s

    The extent and complexity of the social issues and legal implications associated specifically with chickens warrants a separate review. Even within city limits their presence was ubiquitous. Many households maintained their own varying sized contingent of these animals for a number of reasons and uses. These included immediate availability of the animal or its eggs for personal consumption or their sale for income. In the early 20th century when the availability of cash was reduced, the barter of these animals and their products were for some people a matter of survival and of much worth to them. Such value can be difficult for us to understand when we are currently able to pick up a previously processed and cooked chicken at the supermarket for $4.99. Such a dinner during these earlier years could only become available following the killing, plucking, gutting, singeing and cooking of the animal by the owner or, possibly, by someone who had come into possession of it through theft. Under the latter circumstances this could become a dangerous, and sometimes deadly, proposition.

    As our law enforcement and judicial systems evolved, summary execution of violators by vigilantes for property theft of horses and cattle in the developing western part of the country was discouraged and, eventually, legally prohibited. However, it is notable that in Jefferson County the murders of individuals caught by a homeowner while stealing his chickens was typically sanctioned by the "system," through the coroner, as being a "justifiable" act as late as the 1930s. There did not appear to be any outcry against this use of deadly force from the public, newspaper editors or the legal authorities. The race of the deceased perpetrator did not seem to make any difference, nor did the facts that the thief was typically not armed, did not directly threaten the owner and was usually shot, often in the back, and from an appreciable distance as he fled.

This routinely demonstrated mindset of officials, as well as the public, speaks to the valuation placed on this simple animal over and above the life of a human being, as well as to the perceived rights of the owners to inflict deadly force in the case of property crimes such as theft and burglary. This subject will be further explored in the chapter relating to weapons.

Newspaper accounts relating to the theft of chickens often presented humorous descriptions with racist overtones. An appreciable number of these cases found within the coroner's docket books were not reported in the newspapers, especially when they took place in the more rural parts of the county.

SAD FATE OF THE YELLOW LEGGED HEN
Ebony Hued Old Sleuth Has Made The Chickens Cheap in Birmingham by Methode de Snatche

The Birmingham Age-Herald, June 15, 1903

"The lives of chickens in Birmingham are not worth as much now as they were a month or two ago. Not for the reason that the prices have dropped, for these are chickens on the roost, but because the negroes are just getting next to the roost snatching business, and every night some fowls disappear never to be seen again by their owners. About this time of the year the ebony colored individual who hailed from far off Africa many years ago gets industrious in his still hunt for the feathered tribe, and more necks are wrung than at any other time while the sun is making its 365 daily trips.

The spring chicken has just ripened into a well know hen, and fattened on the early worm. He looks good to the negro, who proceeds to plan a raid and get some yellow legged fowl. The following morning there is consternation in the house of the owner of the aforesaid chicken, and the telephone at police headquarters is the instrument through which the tale of woe is poured into the ear of the accommodating desk sergeant.

Quod errata demonstrandum--a brace of fine looking blue coats is sent to scout and an ebony is caught in the act. He has a nom de plume of Louis White and against that on the register of the city hotel appears the words, "burglary and grand larceny," through which the negro is identified the following morning in the court of "Jedge" Feagin. The chicks are identified by M. Hurst of Fourteenth street and Fifth avenue, in whose hen house they were formerly wont to sleep securely every p.m."

CHICKEN THIEVES BEHIND THE BARS
Organized Gang Broken Up By Ensley Officers
The Birmingham Age-Herald, January 19, 1907

"Officers John Wren and Cochran have succeeded in landing behind the bars of the city jail six negroes who are said to be parties of a regular organized band of chicken thieves. For some time past the residents of the town have suffered at the hands of the chicken thief, and so many complaints have been made to the police that Mr. John Wren, an officer in plain clothes, went to work to capture the guilty parties.

Several clues were followed up and sufficient evidence was found to cause the arrest of one Penny Underwood, who after having passed through a rigorous examination, gave the names of other parties implicated with him. It is said that the band was well organized and used a vacant house in which to store the chickens when stolen and when a sufficient number was collected a drayman, who was also arrested, would go to this place and take a coop of the chickens to a restaurant run by a negro woman, and she would keep an account of the number delivered to her and when she had fed them to the unsuspecting public, the amount realized was supposed to have been divided equally among the number interested in the deal. Some of the chickens recovered have been identified and the officers say they have conclusive evidence of the guilt of those arrested."

NEGRO IS KILLED STEALING CHICKENS
Shot By George Butler Near Lipscombe
The Birmingham Age-Herald, September 5, 1909

"Will Blevins, a negro deacon of the church, was shot and instantly killed this morning about 4 o'clock by George Butler, a resident of Lipscombe. It seems that Butler heard a noise in the chicken house and going out with his shot gun to investigate saw a man break and run. Butler called to him and upon his refusal to halt fired one barrel after him. The negro ran a few steps and fell dead. The entire load took effect in his right groin tearing a large hole in the flesh. No arrests have been made in connection with the shooting."

Postscript

No further information regarding the outcome of this case was found in the newspapers. The following docket entry was made by Coroner B.L. Brasher the day following the incident: "I found deceased came to his death by gun shot wound…while stealing chickens. I found that said shot was a justifiable homicide."

150 CHICKENS ARE STOLEN IN A WEEK
The Birmingham Age-Herald, March 7, 1911

"For the past five days the police have been greatly troubled by chicken thieves operating in the neighborhood of Avenue F from fourteenth to thirtieth streets and in North Birmingham, North Highlands and other parts of the city.

Numerous thefts of chickens have been reported to the police department during the month of March and attention has been called to the numerous depredations by constant complaints. The scouts at the central station and those at the outside precincts have been instructed to be on the lookout for chicken thieves and it is hoped results will be had.

Attention is called to the fact that most citizens keep their fowls in a flimsy outhouse and do not lock them at night. This makes it an easy matter for the thieves to get the chickens. The only charge that can be made against them upon capture is petit larceny. All citizens who have chickens or other birds are requested to build a substantial fowl house and put a lock on it. To steal the chickens the thief would have to break the lock, which constitutes burglary, which is a more serious crime than petit larceny."

Docket Entry:
Date: November 26, 1913
Deceased: Alex Cleveland, Col.
Address: Bessemer
Cause Of Death: From gun shot wounds at the hands of Geo. Houser, same being a justifiable homicide.
Remarks: Deceased was shot while stealing chickens.

UNKNOWN WHITE MAN IS KILLED
Shot by Hawkins While in His Chicken House— Not Yet Identified

The Birmingham Age-Herald, December 24, 1913

"The remains of an unknown white man who was shot and almost instantly killed at 3 o'clock yesterday morning by Will D. Hawkins at 713 Wellesly avenue, East Lake, are being held at the morgue of the Woodfin Undertaking Company at Woodlawn awaiting identification. There have been no arrests in the affair. Coroner Charles L. Span will conduct a preliminary inquiry in a few days.

Mr. Hawkins gave (police) the following account of the shooting: "Mr. Hawkins told me that he heard a lot of squawking in his henhouse, and that he got his gun and opening the window, called out to the men in his chicken house to stay there and not come out or he would fire." "Mr. Hawkins stated that the men disregarded his warning and came out, and that he fired twice. One man fell and the other made his escape. He then called police headquarters. We found the unknown man nearly dead. I tried to get him to speak but he died without uttering a single word. He was a man about 35 years of age, of small build, weighing about 140 pounds. He was dressed shabbily and had a growth of beard about 10 days old. There were no papers or anything about his person that would lead to his identification. At the chicken house we found six hens with their heads freshly twisted off. All the signs bore out the statement of Mr. Hawkins and after notifying the coroner we left the case in his hands."

CHICKEN THIEF IS SHOT AND KILLED BY GRAYMONT CITIZEN

The Birmingham Age-Herald, September 1, 1916

"An unidentified negro man was shot and fatally wounded at 2 o'clock yesterday morning by Glover Moore, 301 Emma avenue, Graymont. Mr. Moore was awakened by a noise in his chicken house and emptied a shotgun loaded with buckshot at the noise. After he had shot, he notified police headquarters that he had shot at a thief in his chicken house, but did not know whether he had struck his mark or not.

    Officer Lee Sorrel was sent to the scene to investigate. Officer Sorrell, Mr. Moore and several persons started to search for the negro. He was found a few yards from the residence of Mr. Moore with a load of buckshot in his head. A negro ambulance was called, but the negro died before it arrived. Two baskets of Mr. Moore's chickens were found by the side of the dying negro."

Docket Entry:
Date: August 31, 1916
Deceased: Sam Baker, Col.
Address: 301 Emma Ave., Graymont.
Cause Of Death: It was found deceased came to his death at the hands of Glover Moore by shooting him; the same being a justifiable homicide.
Remarks: Sam Baker was stealing Mr. Moore's chickens.

Docket Entry:
Date: February 18, 1917
Deceased: Robert Wilson, Col.
Address: 2616 Alley E
Cause Of Death: Gun shot wounds at the hands of P.B. Sheppard, Col., the same being justifiable.
Remarks: Deceased was shot on February 18th and died February 20th. This man was supposed to be a chicken thief.

Docket Entry:
Date: May 15, 1917
Deceased: Mose Kendrick, Col.
Address: 3300 Avenue D Ensley
Cause Of Death: From buck shot wounds at the hands of O.B. Phillips, white, same being a justifiable homicide.
Remarks: Deceased was stealing chickens at time he was shot.

Docket Entry:
Date: October 14, 1925
Deceased: Mrs. J.M. Honeycutt, White
Address: Johns Funeral Home
Cause Of Death: By 2nd degree burns of face, chest, hands and abdomen. Caught fire while singeing a chicken, same being accidental.

1 PERSON KILLED, 3 ARE INJURED
Week-End Toll In Birmingham Mounts As Accidents Grow
The Birmingham Age-Herald, February 6, 1928

"Traffic accidents, knives and guns took a toll of one dead and three injured seriously in accidents, shootings and cutting affrays during the week-end.
The dead: Frank Clemmons, negro, of 1919 Third Avenue, South, shot by H.G. Norman, 815 Tuscaloosa Avenue, who was attracted to the back yard by the ringing of a burglar alarm in the chicken coop. He arrived at the coop just in time to see the negro emerging. He fired several times, he told police, one shot taking effect in the negro's back."

CLEMMON'S KILLING HELD JUSTIFIABLE
Negro Shot While In West End Dies

"Justifiable homicide was the verdict of Coroner J.D. Russum in the death of Frank Clemmons, negro, who died of gunshot wounds received when he stepped from a chicken coop at the home of W.W. Wilson, 1815 Tuscaloosa Avenue. The shooting occurred Saturday night.

H.G. Norman admitted that he fired at the negro after a burglar alarm had warned him that some one was in the chicken coop. The negro was taken to Hillman Hospital where he died Monday morning."

NEGRO PROWLER SHOT TO DEATH
Woman Watches Him Leave Henhouse; Husband Opens Fire
The Birmingham Post, May 13, 1939

"A Negro described as a chicken thief was killed early today when an Ensley resident of a neighborhood aroused over recent petty thievery emptied his gun at a prowler in his poultry lot. The body of the Negro, unidentified, was found three hours later in an alley 100 yards away from the scene of the shooting.

Aroused by a squawking in the rear of her house, Mrs. J.D. Stewart, 3112 Avenue J, Ensley, looked out a window to see a Negro leave the chicken house with a burlap bag. She continued to watch and wait and within a few minutes he returned. Then Mrs. Stewart awakened her husband, an employee of Birmingham Slag Co., and he shot at the prowler as he appeared in the chicken house doorway. The first shot felled him, and Mr. Stewart continued to shoot as he crawled from the yard. Police searched the neighborhood but were unable to find the injured Negro. They theorize that he hid in high weeds in a vacant lot and dragged himself into the alleyway after they had left. He was shot once through the chest.

Several weeks ago the Stewarts had two tires and wheels stripped from their car by thieves who have been operating in Ensley. Several other garage break-ins and chicken thefts have been reported in the immediate neighborhood. Police theorize that the thief took two hens from the Stewart's coop, hid them in the alley, then returned to get the remaining two hens and a rooster when he was shot."

SLAIN THIEF HAD POLICE RECORD
Industrial Press, May 18, 1939

"Wright Hill, Negro chicken thief, who was shot and killed last Friday night, while invading the Stewart chicken-house, served a 60-day sentence at Fairfield for chicken-stealing less than six months ago, it was revealed today. Fairfield police said Hill was "an old head" at the pilfering of chickens."

Docket Entry:
Re: Wright Hill (c) who came to his death May 13, 1939, in the rear of 3112 Avenue J, Ensley, Ala., from pistol shot wound at the hands of J.D. Stewart (w) same being a justifiable homicide.

CHAPTER 20

WAR

--"Gas! Gas!
...In all my dreams, before my helpless sight,
He plunges at me, guttering, choking, drowning.
If in some smothering dreams you too could pace
Behind the wagon that we flung him in,
And watch his white eyes writhing in his face,
His hanging face, like a devil's sick of sin;
If you could hear, at every jolt, the blood
come gargling from the froth-corrupted lungs,
Obscene as cancer, bitter as the cud.
Of vile, incurable sores on innocent tongues,
My friend, you would not tell with such high zest
To children ardent for some desperate glory,
The old Lie; Dulce et Decorum est
Pro Patria mori."

---Dulce et Decorum Est
Wilfred Owen [1]

In association with the Spanish-American war at the turn of the 20th century, there was a newfound jingoism associated with the continuing political expansion of the power and empire of the United States into Cuba, the Philippines and other south pacific countries formerly governed by Spain. This was coupled with the exercise of control over a number of Central and South American countries for the direct benefit of businesses such as the United Fruit Company. Therefore, the political and military involvement of our government in relation to the on-going "war to end wars" in Europe should not have come as a surprise.

The truths of the horrors of our Civil War, as told by the grandfathers and fathers to the sons of a generation born into this new age, had faded with time and, as usual, only memories of "glory" remained. On April 2, 1917, President Woodrow Wilson would ask Congress for a Declaration of War against Germany in order that the world would "be made safe for democracy" and once again, as in wars past, young men readily marched off to battle with the general support of the public while giving little thought to the horrific consequences.

Local Issues

Large military training bases in central Alabama were mainly located in Montgomery and at Camp McClellan in Anniston. As no large military camps were present in the Jefferson County area, the records of the coroner's office contain few investigations into the deaths of military personnel during this period.

Docket Entry:
Date: May 29, 1917
Deceased: Roy J. Webb, White, Private, U.S.A.
Address: Johns Undertaking
Cause Of Death: Pistol shot wound at hands of Eugene Sherrings, white, same being accidental while examining pistol.

Docket Entry:
Date: September 17, 1917
Deceased: Private Dennis Bonnett, U.S.A.
Address: Woodstock
Cause Of Death: By being run over by a train, same being accidental.

Statistics
Morbidity and Mortality

The American involvement in World War I over a period of one and a half years would lead to 53,400 battle deaths and more than 63,000 other non-combat deaths in service, mainly due to disease. Of these non-combat deaths, the majority were related to the Influenza epidemic of 1917-18. The overcrowded conditions within large training camps, as well as on troopships headed to Europe, became perfect breeding grounds which allowed for the rapid spread of the virus and other respiratory infections and which would quickly reach epidemic proportions.

Similar ratios of combat related deaths and those due to disease could be found between the army population in general and that of the Alabama centered 167th Infantry Regiment of the "Rainbow Division." The 167th would distinguish itself in many hard fought battles leading to the reported statement of General Edward H. Plummer who, "impressed by their ferocity and esprit de corps,but exasperated by their rambunctiousness (said): "in time of war, send me all the Alabamians you can get, but in time of peace, for Lord's sake, send them to somebody else!"[2]

"The ferocity of the Alabamians, so apt to get them in trouble at home, proved invaluable in the field. At the climactic Battle of Croix Rouge, the hot-blooded 167th exhibited unflinching valor and, in the face of machine guns, artillery shells, and poison gas, sustained casualty rates over 50 percent to dislodge and repel the deeply entrenched and heavily armed enemy."[3] 162 officers and men from the 167th died in this battle.

There were also a number of local men who were members of the 167th Infantry who died in the war. Originally dedicated in 1919, and with new panels installed in 2012, the 21st Street viaduct in downtown Birmingham is the site of two memorial plaques to some of that unit's soldiers. The names of forty-four men are listed on one of the tablets which notes that they were "killed in action or died of wounds in the World War,"[4] although several of the men listed died from accidents, disease and suicide. The majority of these men had been residents of Birmingham or were from small towns within or near Jefferson County. However, the inscription does not include all of the names of those soldiers from the Birmingham area who died in the war, but were not members of the 167th Infantry.

In this regard, the memorial is misleading. It should be noted that in addition to those persons listed on the plaque, 219 soldiers who were from the Birmingham-Jefferson County area, and who were assigned to other units, died in the war with the following breakdown by type:

Killed In Action---43
Died From Wounds---18
Died From Disease---137
Other (accident, suicide, other causes, unknown)---21

A compilation of all types of deaths of soldiers from Alabama who died during the war totaled 2,427 which includes the 44 men listed on the 167th Infantry memorial plaque. Although the ratios of deaths due directly to combat activities and those due to disease are similar, a review of the recorded means of deaths due to disease reveals the exceptional role played by the influenza pandemic. These deaths occurred in war zones, on troop transport ships and at training bases within the United States. Out of those Alabama soldiers who died from disease the majority were associated with influenza or subsequent pneumonia with the following breakdown:

1917---132

1918---1,103

Other infectious diseases such as mumps and measles, as well as dysentery, played a lesser role.

Although the average monthly death toll from disease for the year 1918 was approximately 91, this figure does not reveal the sudden, devastating situation which commenced in October of that year. In that one month alone 566 Alabama soldiers died mainly as the result of respiratory diseases. The rate of deaths rapidly tapered off after October, however, November and December of that year would show an additional 164 disease related deaths.[5]

The effects of the influenza pandemic can be appreciated by noting the greater percentage of associated deaths due to disease which exceeded twice the number of direct combat related deaths. In all instances, however, the main reason for the large number of deaths of soldiers due to respiratory diseases can be traced to their rapid spread in the close living conditions which they endured. The morbidity rate of soldiers who contracted influenza but who survived is unknown. The prominent role played by communicable disease in regard to the morbidity and mortality rates of soldiers has been an important constant factor during most major wars of the past. The American Civil War and Napoleon's attempted conquest of Russia are prime examples.

Although the number of direct combat related deaths of American military personnel over a period of less than two years is striking, it is important to note the massive approximate so-called "butcher's bill" for the active combatants of other involved countries.

Killed and missing in action:

German Empire:	1,800,000
Russia:	1,700,000
France:	1,150,000
Austria-Hungary:	1,016,000
British Empire:	953,000

TOTAL: 6,619,000

The statistics listed above are considered to be conservative estimates. They do not include soldiers wounded in action who survived or the millions of civilian deaths due to injuries, disease and starvation. An example of the mind-numbing intensity of this war can be found in the fact that: "The first day of the Battle of the Somme, in northern France, was the bloodiest day in the history of the British Army and one of the most infamous days of World War One. On 1 July 1916, the British forces suffered 57,470 casualties, including 19,240 fatalities. They gained just three square miles of territory."6

The death of Birmingham native Captain Mortimer H. Jordan was the most locally publicized combat related fatality of the war.

CAPT. MORTIMER H. JORDAN, DIES IN FRANCE FROM WOUNDS RECEIVED FIGHTING FOR COUNTRY'S HONOR
One of Most Popular Young Men Ever Reared
in Birmingham Makes Supreme Sacrifice
DIED FROM WOUNDS RECEIVED IN ACTION IS BRIEF MESSAGE
News Spread Over City With Greatest Rapidity
When It Reached City Yesterday Afternoon

The Birmingham Age-Herald, August 12, 1918

"In defense of the liberty of the world, Mort Jordan has died. Yesterday afternoon came the message to Mrs. Jordan: "I regret to inform you that Capt. Mortimer H. Jordan, Birmingham Ala., died July 31, from wounds received in action. "H.P. McCAIN, Adgt. Gen."

That was the laconic message. There was no doubt, however, that when the time came, Mort Jordan, at the head of his men, threw himself into the hell of shrieking shell and received the hurt as he would have received it, bravely, nobly, in defense of flag and country. For he was the knightliest soul who ever died so young. Captain Jordan is survived by Mrs. Jordan, a son who bears his name, and a daughter, his mother, and other relatives. Maj. William Jordan, a brother is at the front.

The terrible news, as horrible news is wont to do, buried itself with remarkable celerity into the homes of Birmingham. Grief was universal, and as deep as love. No man or child withheld the the tribute of a tear. For Mort Jordan was known of everybody, and everybody included him among his personal assets, staked in the battle against the German dream of world dominion.

A curious development was the fact that the death was not unexpected. So many friends knew--but dared not whisper--that he was to die. It is Mort Jordan's type that dies. It is the man who, imbued with love of a noble cause, filled with determination that that cause shall not perish from the earth--the chivalrous man who holds his life, when placed by honor, as nothing more than a whispering wind or a vagrant cloud, pays the cost of victory, and lives a thousand years. It is such glory as this that does not stale or grow dim in the lapse of time.

Mort Jordan was born in Birmingham nearly 37 years ago. He was a rollicking but manly and courteous school boy. At the University of Alabama he was an intelligent student, but more a fellow of laughter and song and noble speech, artful, mischievous, devilish. Following his college days, he equipped himself for the medical profession. Subsequently, he practiced and was married. But he declined to settle down into a grewsome grind for business honors and profits. There was no surprise, therefore, that when the call came to ams, he was among the first to respond. When the world knew that nothing in honor could prevent the entrance of the United States into the European war, Mort Jordan prepared with seriousness, with a fiendish perseverance, with a terrible determination to do his share in sustaining and enhancing the honor and glory of his country, and his people.

He received his wound--his wounds, McCain said--in action. On came the German tide, man after man, column after column--came running and swearing in the grim business of war and death. Out of their trench leaped the Alabamians. Across No Man's Land they ran to meet the horrid hun. Their cheer rang out as German artillery hurried its shells among them. Mort Jordan fell--and as he fell, his arm, automatically, perhaps, described a circle, and his finger pointed: "Onward."

He is buried somewhere in France. There grows above him the French lily and the English rose. Over all, in silken folds, Old Glory waves."

CAPT. MORTIMER JORDAN TO SLEEP WITH AMERICAN WAR HEROES IN HISTORIC ARLINGTON, VA.

The Birmingham Age-Herald, June 21, 1921

"Reverent memories of a loved citizen will sway the hearts of Birmingham people this week, revived by the return of the body of Capt. Mortimer H. Jordan, who gave his life for freedom on the plains of Picardy, for burial in that last resting place for American heroes, Arlington cemetery, Va.

Funeral services will be held Thursday, attended by close relatives of the dead hero. His mother and widow, his brother and wife, Dr. and Mrs. William Jordan and Dr. Cecil Gaston have gone to Washington for the ceremonies. Side by side with two other Birmingham officers, his personal friends and comrades, who made the supreme sacrifice in the cause of liberty, Captain Bryan Tomlinson and Lieut. Meredith Roberts, Captain Jordan will sleep the last long sleep. His body will be laid next to that of these two men, already interred under Arlington's sod. Leading his men on the fields of France, Captain Mort Jordan fell mortally wounded before machine gun fire of the Huns under Ludendorff, during the late days of July, 1918, saw its last sun, the soul of Mort Jordan fled skyward.

Nearly forty years ago, Mort Jordan was born in Birmingham--on the present site of the Tutwiler hotel. He was a rollicking but courteous lad, an intelligent student at the University of Alabama. Following his college days, he equipped himself for the medical profession. When the call to arms came in 1916, he was one of the first to take the trail toward Mexico. When the war was declared on Germany, he went across with the famous Alabama unit later to be known as the Rainbow Division.

Nearly three years have passed since Captain Mortimer H. Jordan "went west," but the memory of his lovable character is still as freshly verdant in the mind of Birmingham as in brighter days before the great conflict on the Marne. All Birmingham still mourns the death of this citizen and warrior."

In his short essay, "Myths Are More Durable Than Facts," Bill Bonner noted that "There is nothing unusual about Rhinebeck, New York. A statue in bronze depicts a muscular soldier with his rifle. And at the base of the statue is a plaque that reads: "He died so that we may live."

Over the decades, the townspeople and visitors must have read this inscription many thousands of times. Had anybody noticed that it was not true? Probably not. In World War I, never was there any risk that the Huns were going to invade New York State and put the citizens of Rhinebeck to the sword. Then, as now, anyone would have laughed at the idea.

But the plaque remains. It is part of the mythology of modern life. Soldiers are meant to believe that they are protecting the homeland. And we are supposed to believe that out boys in uniform are doing us an important service.

There are myths. And there is reality. The reality of World War I is that it was an adventure organized by the Wilson administration that had nothing to do with protecting American lives. Instead, it did the exact opposite. It endangered them. The war got 53,513 Americans killed. Had the U.S. stayed out of the war, in all probability, they would have lived. The plaque lies."

"We passed their graves:
The dead men there,
Winners or losers,
Did not care.

In the dark
They could not see
Who had gained
The victory"

---Peace
Langston Hughes

CHAPTER 21

WEAPONS

"Mr. Saturday night special
Got a barrel thats blue and cold
Ain't good for nothin'
But put a man six feet in a hole."

---Saturday Night Special
Lynyrd Skynyrd

Roger Lane noted that:

"As the handguns introduced in the 1850s grew steadily more available and cheaper—by the 1880s the price of a revolver had dropped to about two dollars, or two day's pay—with equally inevitable consequences for the murder rate. Other things being equal, the presence of knives and razors increases the odds that a given quarrel will turn fatal, and a firearm increases them further still, making murder a matter of an instant's flash of anger, a few pounds of pull on the trigger. It is true that the two dollar pistols of the 19th and early 20th centuries were by no means a routinely deadly weapon, and an astonishing number of people were up and around shortly after being shot. The under powered bullets of that day were often deflected by ribs, brow and cheekbones. But however weak by modern standards, these handguns were more dangerous than knives, and as more men carried them, the effect was to increase the number of truly reckless and thoughtless killings. The climbing rate of homicide was thus explained, not simply by the spread of the gun culture but even more simply by the spread of the guns themselves. Both contributed to the problem."[1]

Lane's deductions regarding the availability and use of firearms during the early 20th century in Philadelphia could also be applied to Jefferson County as a whole and, in particular, to the growing urban areas of Birmingham and Bessemer during the same time period. The ready availability of firearms then and now has been, and continues to be, a pressing social issue although the access to modern weapons has added another higher level to the potential for the infliction of serious injuries and to the number of deaths.

Statistics

In an earlier chapter the mechanisms of homicidal deaths in Jefferson County were presented with a comparison between the years 1911 and 1997. In a remarkable coincidence there were exactly the same number of homicides both by firearms and sharp instruments in both of the years which were compared. Deaths caused by blunt force trauma were also closely aligned. The only major difference occurred between the number of reported homicides by poisoning with four documented cases in 1911 and none in 1997. However, it is strongly believed that the true number of homicides by poisoning during the earlier era as reflected by these statistics is extremely conservative due to both the poor state of the science of toxicology analysis as well as by the surreptitious nature of such acts and the widespread availability of toxic substances, such as arsenic.

As was also shown, the total numbers of homicidal deaths by all mechanisms in each of the years compared varied by only one death. This, once again, supports the statistical findings which demonstrate an appreciably greater per capita rate of violent deaths during the early 20th century in comparison to more recent years.

Trap Guns

Trap guns, also known as spring guns, were often shotguns which had been rigged to fire when a string or other triggering device was tripped by contact of sufficient force to "spring" the trigger so that anyone stumbling over or treading on it would discharge the gun. Spring guns had been used as booby traps against poachers and trespassers. In 1827, due to the changing morals of society, the use of indiscriminate force for the protection of property was proscribed by statute in the British Commonwealth. Although much European common law had been transferred into the legal system of the United States, many years would elapse before widespread changes banning the use of such unattended weapons would become law in most jurisdictions. These statutes would come to be implemented on an irregular basis during the early 20th century and were based on the principle that although it is not necessary to make a property safe for trespassers, it is not legal to make property more dangerous through the intentional placement of booby traps.

The current Alabama statute, as well as legal case law, indicate that if a person sets up a trap to protect his property, he could be both criminally and civilly liable for any injury or death, even of an unwanted intruder such as a burglar.2 The basis for such laws rests on the principle that the infliction of injury or death is not appropriate as a response to property crime and, even more importantly, to avoid reckless harm to innocent persons such as children, paramedics, firefighters or police officers entering a dwelling or business for whatever reason and who might accidentally set such a device off.

The outcome of civil lawsuits in cases where injury and death had occurred would vary greatly by jurisdiction, as would the pursuit of criminal charges and convictions against those persons who had set the traps. In some cases, even when prosecutions were pursued by local authorities based on existing statutory law, the process of "jury nullification" would often occur based on the mores of the local populace and the particular "jury of the peers" of the accused individual. As noted in Wikipedia, "Jury nullification is a concept where members of a trial jury can vote a defendant not guilty if they do not support a government's law, do not believe it is constitutional or humane, or do not support a possible punishment for breaking a government's law."

In Jefferson County, as in other jurisdictions, records and newspaper accounts indicate that "nullification" by juries in these types of cases occurred on a regular basis well into the first half of the 20th century. That such actions by jurors were accepted was a reflection of local society and its existing mores. This was in a fashion similar to the previously noted public approval of the "justifiable" homicides of fleeing chicken thieves where, in many instances, the legal review did not extend past the coroner's quasi-judicial ruling.

There is evidence that an Alabama state statute prohibiting the use of trap guns was in existence in the early 20th century and that, on occasion, it was initially followed by the Jefferson County coroner. However, newspaper accounts would provide evidence of different final outcomes within the legal system.

Docket Entry:
Date: February 6, 1918
Deceased: William Bottrell, White
Address: 2200 Avenue F
Defendant: Dr. S.P. Burge, White
Remarks: I, Geo. A. Hogan, Coroner, certify that I held a preliminary investigation inquest with the following result: It was found that he came to his death from gun shot wound by being shot in a trap, at the hands of Dr. S.P. Burge, same being unlawfully done and against the peace and dignity of the State of Alabama.

BURGE'S SHOTGUN TRAP WORKS; VICTIM IS WM. BOTTRELL
Avenue F Druggist to Be Given Hearing on February 15 for Alleged Burglar's Death
The Birmingham Age-Herald, February 7, 1918

"William Bottrell was almost instantly killed yesterday morning at Burge's drug store, 2200 Avenue F, when Bottrell and two companions, it is alleged, were robbing the store. A shotgun "trap" discharged, striking Bottrell in the left leg about the knee and severed the main artery. He bled to death before medical aid could be summoned. Bottrell was about 29 years of age and is survived by his wife and mother.

S.P. Burge, owner of the store, who set the trap was released on bond until his preliminary hearing. Burge told of how he had set the trap. He placed the shotgun on a chair, facing the cash register, about 10 feet away. Strings were attached to the gun and cash register so as to cause the gun to fire when the cash register was opened. The shell was loaded with fine birdshot.

That the store was being robbed was without question. The side door had been prized open, and a quantity of medical supplies, cigars, candy and alcohol was on the soda fountain counter, ready for removal. According to police authorities, they have a good clue to Bottrell's companions who deserted him after he had been shot. Two men were seen running from the scene."

BURGE PHARMACY TRAP GUN CLAIMS ITS THIRD VICTIM
A 17-Year-Old Boy Loses Hand as Result of Attempted Robbery of Drug Store
The Birmingham Age-Herald, January 23, 1919

"A trap gun in the Burge pharmacy, 1200 Avenue F, claimed its third victim yesterday morning when Eugene Gurthie, a 17 year-old boy, discharged the gun after entering the store through a rear window, and his hand was severed above the wrist by the charge.

The store was entered about 4 o'clock in the morning and it is believed that there were at least nine other youths implicated. This is the third time in the past 12 months that the trap gun has taken toll on marauders. Will Bottrell was killed last February and Joe Hagan, a negro, was wounded in July. Eugene Gurthie appeared at the Hillman hospital with his arm torn to shreds. Police investigating the scene of the tragedy found the floor and cigar counter covered with blood and pieces of flesh.

F.R. Burge, proprietor of the pharmacy, appeared at police headquarters yesterday morning, but no action was taken against him. On the two former occasions he was exonerated by the courts."

GUN TRAP CLAIMS AUTHOR VICTIM
Merchant Meets Fate
He Had Planned To Befall Burglars

The Birmingham Age-Herald, June 25, 1923

"Walking into a shotgun trap he had set in his store for a burglar, A.C. Sikes, 53, well known merchant of Madison Station, received a double load of buckshot into his chest late Saturday night, dying almost instantly. Mr. Sikes was alone at the time. His fiends think he had returned after closing the store, as all doors and windows were locked except the side entrance, and the lights had been put out. Hearing the report of the gun, neighbors found the merchant lying dead several feet from the spot where he must have received the wound.

Mr. Sikes' store had been entered several weeks before, thieves obtaining a large quantity of merchandise and a sum of money. The shotgun trap was placed so that it pointed directly at the only opening between the counters so that anyone passing through would spring the trigger."

Docket Entry:
Date: June 22, 1925
Deceased: George Williams, Col.
Address: Brookside
Cause Of Death: Gunshot wounds of abdomen. Shot with trap gun.

COMMISSION MAY FORBID TRAPGUNS
Snares For Burglars Are Proving Dangerous
The Birmingham Age-Herald, February 6, 1928

"An ordinance forbidding the setting of trapguns will be presented in the City Commission at its meeting Tuesday. The question of regulating the use of trapguns, which have become common in small stores as a defense against burglars has been under consideration for some time. During the last few years several burglaries have been frustrated by means of the trapgun.

Fire Chief Akin complained of the practice a few weeks ago, when firemen entering as store at night to extinguish a fire, stumbled over wires leading to a gun. The gun was not loaded. Chief Akin takes the position that trapguns create an unnecessary hazard in fire fighting."

Sharp Force

"...a wretched, spiteful, straight-razor totin' woman."

---Polk Salad Annie
Tony Joe White

The numbers of homicides caused by all types of sharp instruments were the same at seventeen in 1911 and in 1997. The majority of these types of deaths in both periods were caused by knives. Only several cases were found in the early 20th century where death was caused by the use of a straight razor.

Docket Entry:
Date: September 30, 1925
Deceased: Jerome Harris, Col.
Defendant: John Simpson, Col.
Address: Southern Undertaking Company
Cause Of Death: By his throat being cut with a razor.

Docket Entry:
Date: November 29, 1928
Deceased: Ora D. Chester, Col.
Address: Welch Brothers Undertaking Company
Cause Of Death: By her throat being cut with a razor.

At first, the few deaths caused by straight razors seems at odds with both the availability of this type of instrument as it was then commonly used for shaving. In addition, there were numerous references to its use as a weapon in the popular media of that time. However, the rarity of documented fatalities is likely explained by the slicing, superficial injuries commonly caused by these instruments, rather than the more typical deeply penetrating wounds which resulted from stabbing with a knife. Most likely, non-fatal injuries inflicted with razors vastly exceeded the number of fatalities.

Docket Entry:
Date: April 10, 1929
Deceased: Mary Pierce, Col.
Address: Joe Young Undertaking Company
Cause Of Death: By knife stab wound of left chest after Mary Pierce had struck Nellie Yancy over the head with a baseball bat. Same being justifiable homicide.

Similarly, only rare docket entries were found where the weapon listed was an icepick. This tool, common to the era before electric refrigeration, apparently led to more non-fatal traumatic injuries than to deaths.

Docket Entry:
Date: August 15, 1926
Deceased: Bertha Harp, Col.
Address: Joe Young's Funeral Home
Cause Of Death: By stab wounds of the neck inflicted with an ice pick.

Firearms

TOY PISTOLS AND FIREARMS RESPONSIBLE FOR INJURIES
Three Persons On One Block Victims Yesterday Morning--
Brasher's Son Is Injured In The Hand

The Birmingham Age-Herald, December 26, 1917

"The residence of W.W. Shelnutt at 1007 North Forty-sixth street was converted into a temporary hospital yesterday morning when three small children living on the block were injured by toy pistols.

The first victim was Teddy Shelnutt, aged 8, who was shot through the left hand by the explosion of a blank pistol. A doctor was called and was in the act of dressing the wound when Earl Crews, aged 12, was brought into the house with a painful wound in the left hand. While the doctor was waiting on the second victim, Willie Perryman, a little girl six years old, was brought in with a bad wound in her nose, caused by being shot with an air gun in the hands of a playmate. The bullet missed the little girl's eye by a narrow margin, and although the wound was very painful, it is not serious. Neither of the boys received dangerous wounds, but they are suffering quite a great deal from burns. W.W. Shelnutt is a policeman working in Woodlawn, on the morning shift.

The toy pistol also was in evidence yesterday afternoon when Cecil, the little 11 year old son of Coroner R.L. Brasher, shot himself in the hand with one of the "toys" and sustained two badly lacerated fingers on the right hand. The little fellow was playing "Indian" when this accident happened. The accident, while painful, is not serious, and after having his hand dressed the boy was able to enjoy the Christmas festivities."

THOS. MOLTON, JR., MYSTERIOUSLY KILLED WHILE LEAVING THE JEFFERSON THEATER
Bullet Apparently Entered His Head From Some Unknown Source
NO SHOT WAS HEARD BY THOSE NEARBY
Top of Skull Was Fractured But the Efforts to Locate the Bullet By Probe Last Night Were Unsuccessful

The Birmingham Age-Herald, December 26, 1917

"Thomas H. Molton, Jr., the 12-year-old son of Mr. and Mrs. T.H. Molton, residing in Highland park, adjoining Idlewild, died last night from injuries so mysterious that they have completely baffled the police force and well known physicians of Birmingham. Young Molton was injured yesterday afternoon in front of the Jefferson theatre on Second avenue. He was leaving the matinee performance in company with his aunt, when the top of his head was pierced by what is thought to have been a rifle bullet fired from a great distance.

Mrs. Molton is almost prostrated by the death of her son and physicians are in constant attendance at her bedside today. The shock of the incident was more than her frail constitution could bear."

THOMAS MOLTON IS LAID TO REST
Body of Boy Mysteriously Killed Is Interred in Oak Hill Cemetery

The Birmingham Age-Herald, December 28, 1917

"One of the saddest aftermaths of the Christmas celebration occurred yesterday morning with the funeral of Thomas H. Molton, the 12-year-old son of one of the oldest, and most prominent families of this city. The untoward circumstances under which the lad met death and the mystery of the accident has shocked the entire community. The family home was thronged with the extensive family connection and scores of friends of the bereaved parents. The array of floral designs bore mute tributes of love and affection to the youth who only a short time previous had been well and happy.

Thomas H. Molton, Jr., was the only son of Mr. & Mrs. Thomas Molton, Sr., and is also survived by two sisters. The condition of Mrs. Molton, who was seriously ill following the fatal occurrence, was noticeably improved."

BULLET WAS FIRED FROM NORTHSIDE
Explanation of Death of Molton Boy
Rifle Bullet Lodged About Three-Quarters of an Inch to Rear of Center of Base of Skull

The Birmingham Age-Herald, December 28, 1917

"In view of the widespread interest in the subject, the details concerning the death of the 12-year-old son of Mr. & Mrs. T.H. Molton, were furnished by his attending physician upon request by The Age-Herald, as follows.

"Tom reached the sidewalk in front of the Jefferson theatre just as the crowd which attended the performance was coming out of the playhouse. He was standing, as soon as he arrived, on the outer curbing of the sidewalk, facing north, bareheaded, looking upward into the theatre entrance. As he held the hand of his aunt, he sank to the ground. It was discovered that he was desperately wounded and medical attention was sought. He subsequently died, as is known, without having regained consciousness.

The bullet entered the top of the head about one-eighth of an inch to the left and front of the center of the skull, passed through the brain and lodged one-half inch to the left and three-quarters of an inch to the rear of the center of the base of the skull. We know that the bullet was fired from a .41 calibre rifle. There is no doubt concerning the calibre of the barrel from which the bullet came, and as the bullet was plainly 'rifled' every indication points to a rifle as the weapon used. The shot was fired from the north side, it is in all respects probable. The boy was facing north and had the shot come from the south side it would have struck to the rear of the center of the skull and would have ranged to the front and not to the rear of the head.

There is no doubt but that the shot was fired without the man firing it having any idea where the bullet would fall. When the rifle was fired it was pointed almost straight into the air. There is no way of estimating from what a height the bullet descended. Had the boy been wearing his cap at the time of the accident the result would have been the same."

Docket Entry:
Date: December 19, 1914
Deceased: Paulino Salamone, White
Defendant: Carmilla Salamone, White
Cause Of Death: Gun shot wounds at the hands of his wife. Same being accidentally done while firing off pistol to give a fire alarm.

Docket Entry:
Date: September 20, 1920
Deceased: William M. Cosby, White
Address: Shaw Undertaking Company
Cause Of Death: By the accidental discharge of a pistol in his pocket which was discharged by striking the fender of an automobile in which he was riding.

Docket Entry:
Date: January 7, 1924
Deceased: Sanders Savage, White
Address: Womack Undertaking Company Pratt
Cause Of Death: Gun shot wounds with a toy pistol, same being accidental without criminality.

Docket Entry:
Date: January 2, 1925
Deceased: George Lykes, Col.
Address: Joe Young Funeral Home
Cause Of Death: Gun shot wounds of right thigh while playing with a toy pistol, same being accidental.

Docket Entry:
Date: September 25, 1925
Deceased: C. Rose Alias Corrado Rosano, White
Address: W.C. Vice Funeral Home
Cause Of Death: Gun shot wounds of head, side and mouth. Self inflicted. Same being suicide.

Docket Entry:
Date: February 5, 1930
Deceased: Wiliam Dawson, Col.
Address: 229 North 27th Court
Cause Of Death: Gun shot wound of abdomen received when he was attempting to prize out some cartridges from an old pistol with an ice pick.

Docket Entry:
Date: June 26, 1937
Mrs. Mary Zwald, White
Address: 1321 Huntsville Avenue
Defendant: John Zwald, White
Cause Of Death: Joh Zwald age 61 shot and killed his mother age 85 with a shotgun. Thought his mother was a burglar.

Miscellaneous

In contrast to other means and mechanisms of deaths presented so far there were occasional fatalities caused by various atypical objects and weapons which did not fit the more common categories or which occurred under odd circumstances.

Docket Entry:
Date: October 20, 1910
Deceased: Henry Laster, Col.
Defendant: Maggie Laster Alias Maggie Avery, Col.
Address: 10th Avenue & 22nd Street North.
Cause Of Death: Being struck in the head with an axe.

Docket Entry:
Date: January 21, 1911
Deceased: Ollias Sadler, Col.
Defendant: Claude, Alias Dyke Sanders, Col.
Address: Gaudin's Undertaking Company
Cause Of Death: Struck in head by billiard cue.

Docket Entry:
Date: March 28, 1914
Deceased: Jesse Roberson, Col.
Defendant: Bob Battles
Cause Of Death: By fracture of skull inflicted by street broom.

Docket Entry:
Date: April 25, 1927
Deceased: Tollie Carrington Metcalf, White
Defendant: W.W. Phillips, White
Address: Lige Loy Funeral Home
Cause Of Death: By fractured skull caused by being hit with a slop jar. Remarks: Defendant was indicted for 1st degree murder.

Docket Entry:
Date: September 16, 1927
Deceased: John Henry Hoskins, White
Defendant: Grtrude Hoskins, White
Address: Echols & Angwin Funeral Home
Cause Of Death: By being struck with an iron at the hands of his wife. Remarks: Wife in insane asylum at Tuscaloosa.

Docket Entry:
Date: May 30, 1928
Deceased: Lu Jenla Logan, Col.
Defendant: Earnest Johnson, Col.
Address: Southern Undertaking Company
Cause Of Death: By being hit with a burning kerosene lamp thrown at her.

CHAPTER 22

FORENSICS

*"Let Conversation Cease. Let Laughter Flee.
For This Is The Place Where Death Delights
To Help The Living."*

---Inscription at the entrance to the
New York City Medical Examiner's Office

As the population began to increase exponentially in the early 20th century, advances in the forensic sciences, especially in relation to the investigation of suspicious and violent deaths, gradually began to improve. The introduction of advanced scientific techniques first appeared in the larger cities of the Northeast where trained physicians replaced the inefficient and sometimes corrupt coroner systems. For the most part these physicians, referred to as medical examiners, were given the legal power to authorize and conduct postmortem examinations, to include autopsies, for the good of the general public and the legal system whenever required in order to determine the cause and manner of certain deaths. Similar changes were slow to occur in smaller cities, towns and counties across America. This lack of appropriate forensic services continues to this day and affects a large proportion of citizens living in smaller suburban and rural communities where adequate investigative resources are unavailable outside of the few statewide medical examiner systems. Jurisdictions within the deep South states were especially affected by the dearth of expert forensic assistance due to the minimal funding which was available for such services. The course of changes in Jefferson County in relation to death investigation has been explored in an earlier chapter.

New approaches and technologies related to the forensic sciences also brought various "experts" to the fore. Those who could provide convincing interpretations of physical findings and technical matters to juries, whether correct or not, or having any basis in science, were suddenly in demand by both prosecution and defense attorneys. An early example of this was related to the relatively new science of firearms examination and bullet comparison which began to become popular in the 1920s. A major trial which drew worldwide interest took place in Massachusetts in 1921 when two admitted Italian anarchists, known as Sacco and Vanzetti, were tried for the murder of a guard during a robbery. Forensic science played a major role in this case where "expert" witnesses would testify as to how firearms evidence had been collected, marked, preserved, stored and then compared to a suspect weapon. During the trial, allegations of the possible substitution of projectiles as well as questions as to the reliability of the purported "expert" skills of examiners, were rife.

Despite a vigorous defense both men were found guilty and executed in 1927, however, the forensic science issues associated with this case continued to be discussed for many years. This eventually led to a major review of the original findings and physical evidence in 1986 by a board of renown forensic scientists with inconclusive results which are still debated today.[1]

> *"Among competing hypotheses,*
> *the one with the fewest assumptions should be selected."*
>
> ---Occam's razor

A case which involved various investigators who attempted to sort out and interpret confusing information to include true and false statements made by "eyewitnesses" and examinations by wound ballistics and firearms "experts" can be found in a review of the Rochell-Vaughn matter.

The investigation of this highly publicized incident included many false trails, "red herrings" and dead ends and revealed the problems associated with the refusal of some investigators to keep an open mind when new evidence strongly suggested that they should change their initial opinions. Although much excitement was generated by the news media during the course of the investigation, correct interpretations of the physical findings were eventually made which led to the appropriate outcome of this matter.

DOUBLE SHOOTING MYSTERY THICKENS ROCHELL-VAUGHN TRAGEDY BECOMES DEEPER INVOLVED
Truck Driver Relates Story of Revolver Duel
With Third Automobile
Former Policeman Is In Serious Condition
The Birmingham News, October 14, 1928

"Throughout Saturday authorities looked in vain to pierce the veil of mystery attaching to the double shooting early in the day of Mrs. Nancy Rochell and Clyde A. Vaughn. Mrs. Rochell, wife of Ramon R. Rochell, wealthy soft drink manufacturer, was found dead by the side of Vaughn in a Hudson sedan on the Cahaba Road, near the entrance to Mountain Brook Estates, fashionable residential section. Vaughn, a former policeman, was slumped over the wheel of the car, mumbling in a semi-conscious condition. He has a bare chance of recovery. The bullet did not pass through the most vital portion of the brain. The man made no mention of the shooting. Every bit of evidence obtained by investigators served only to make the case more involved. One theory studied concerned reports of a running gun battle with another car. Coroner Russum, however, was not impressed by this theory, he said.

It was reported that two persons had been found who saw another car drive up beside the machine in which Vaughn and Mrs. Rochell were riding and then heard shots. A bullet hole in the windshield was believed to lend credence to these reports. Mrs. Rochell, 26 years old and mother of four children, had been missing from her home since she departed ostensibly on a shopping tour Friday. When she failed to return to her husband and children early Friday evening, police were asked to join in a search which resulted in her Lincoln car being found on First Avenue. Nothing was heard from the woman until the tragedy was reported.

The first passerby to reach the car said he found the body of Mrs. Rochell slumped over beside Vaughn on the front seat. Vaughn, in a semi-conscious condition was attempting to start the car. The first officer to reach the scene found the passerby holding a pistol with three empty chambers which he sad was found in Vaughn's hand. Two bullets had entered Mrs. Rochell's head while one shot had entered Vaughn's right temple, passing out through the forehead.

The story of another car firing on the couple was related by a negro truck driver who said he was an eyewitness to a pistol duel. While driving toward Birmingham, and as he approached the Vaughn car, the negro said a small coupe passed him and slowed up as it neared the death car. Several shots were fired from the coupe, the negro said, and Vaughn answered the first penetrating the windshield. The Vaughn car evidently had travelled some distance after the shooting, traces of the tragedy having been found along a 100 yard stretch of highway.

Both Mrs. Rochell and Vaughn were widely known in Birmingham. Mrs. Rochell was a very attractive woman of the brunette type. Vaughn, who is married, was suspended from the police force and later discharged as a result of a recent altercation among policemen at the State Fair Grounds. He first became a member of the department in 1919, leaving the service in 1922. He again became a member in July, 1923, remaining on the force until last month when he was suspended."

CORONER REFUSES TO LET REPORTERS READ AUTOPSY IN SHOOTING
Dr. Graham Tells of Finding Bullet In Woman's Body
Declines, However, To Discuss Case
Rochell Slaying Mystery Deepens
As Number Of Shots Is Probed

The Birmingham Age-Herald, October 15, 1928

"The coroner refused to let newspapermen read the autopsy report in connection with the fatal shooting of Mrs. Nancy Rochell. Dr. G.S. Graham said he had recovered a bullet, or part of a bullet, from Mrs. Rochell's head during the autopsy. The coroner had previously said that the bullet had entered the woman's cheek to the right of the nose, and that it apparently had split, leaving two wounds on the exit side of the head at or near the left ear. The refusals came after the question arose that if only one shot entered the woman's head did the bullet split into three pieces?

Following the autopsy report, Coroner Russum said that the gun found in the death car had been fired only two times. Previous reports were that the gun had been fired three times and that the woman had been shot twice. Presence of the bullet-shattered windshield in the automobile added to the mystery of the shooting.

Investigating officers reported that a hair, apparently from Vaughn's head, was found on the windshield near the point where the bullet had shattered the glass. The bullet hole was near the left side of the windshield. Two of the first passersby to reach the scene of the shooting was reported to have said that he noticed only two fired shells in the gun found in the car. This was affirmed by at least one investigating officer. None of these, however, reported taking the shells or bullets out of the gun, basing their opinion on hammer marks and the absence of hammer marks on the shells. Other investigating officers said that, in their opinion, the gun found in the car had been fired three times.

Developments indicated that Vaughn and a woman had left Birmingham late Friday night, the night preceding the killing. C.E. Dudley, who operates a barbecue stand on the Cahaba Beach Road, told officials that Vaughn and a woman whom he did not know stopped at his place of business about 11:30 p.m. Friday and bought drinks and that they then headed away from Birmingham."

STORY OF DEATH CAR SHOT IS BARED
ACCOUNT OF FIRING TOLD BY VENDOR
He Declares He Saw Two "Scrimmage" In Motor Then Heard Pistol
Blood On Woman Viewed Dry Then

The Birmingham Age-Herald, October 16, 1928

"An entirely new version in the killing of Mrs. Nancy Rochell and the wounding of Clyde Vaughn, former policeman, which tends to explode virtually all theories previously advanced, has been revealed. The latest story came from Oscar Gothard, charcoal vendor, who claims to have been looking into the automobile occupied by Mrs. Rochell and Vaughn when the last shot was fired. Gothard said he saw a "scrimmage" between two people on the front seat of the car; " heard a pistol shot; saw smoke coming from the automobile and went with several other men to the machine and found the woman crouched on the floor, apparently dead, and Vaughn in a sitting position on the front seat, blood stemming from a wound in the head. Gothard was uncertain as to whether one or two shots were fired. Gothard contradicts the theory that Mrs. Rochell was slayed at the same time and on the scene where Vaughn was wounded, with the empathic declaration that blood on the woman's hands when she was found was dry, indicating, he said, she had been shot awhile previously. Gothard said the pistol was not clutched in Vaughn's hand, as had previously been reported.

The question of how many shots were fired became the central theme in the investigation of the fatal shooting. An autopsy report made public by the coroner says that Mrs. Rochell was shot twice. Vaughn was shot once. Examination of a gun discovered in the car revealed three empty shells. The coroner expressed the belief that two of the shells had been fired Saturday and the third shell either a day or two days preceding the tragedy. The opinion was expressed by some investigators that three separate shots have been accounted for the morning of the shooting, two inflicting wounds in Mrs. Rochell's head and the third inflicting a wound in Vaughn's head. Other investigators expressed the opinion that the bullet which struck Vaughn might possibly have passed through the former officer's head and then hit Mrs. Rochell, inflicting a wound approximately one inch deep on the left side of the woman's head. In addition to the wounds received by Vaughn and Mrs. Rochell, at least one bullet passed through the windshield after hitting either Mrs. Rochell or Vaughn, and whom it was fired by, officials have not yet been able to determine.

Developments Monday tended further to complicate the case. Early reports had said that at least one person had been an eyewitness to a purported running gun battle between occupants of the death car and an occupant or occupants of a coupe. An authoritative report that there were no powder burns on Vaughn's head where the bullet entered also indicated that the shot was fired from a distance, it is said. The autopsy performed on the body of Mrs. Rochell revealed indications of powder burns around the wound on her cheek, just to the right of the nose. This bullet made its exit through the left ear. The second bullet to enter Mrs. Rochell's head entered slightly above and to the right of the left ear. This bullet was said to have been recovered. There was no apparent discoloration of the skin about this wound. Meanwhile, Vaughn is still in serious condition but that he has a chance to recover. Vaughn has not yet made any statement concerning the shooting."

VAUGHN LOW AS MYSTERY GROWS
INQUIRIES CHECK TALE OF VENDORS
Ex-Policeman Is Reported Victim of Meningitis
From Head Wound
Little Hope Held For His Recovery
Probers Fear Death May Prevent Statement
In Rochell Shooting

The Birmingham Age-Herald, October 17, 1928

"With Clyde Vaughn, former policeman, reported as being in a "critical condition," investigators into the mysterious fatal shooting of Mrs. Nancy Rochell and the wounding of Vaughn continued to set forth conflicting theories in the case. Survival of Vaughn was considered doubtful.

Investigators devoted their time to the further checking of Oscar and W.C. Gothard, charcoal vendors, who gave an entirely new version of the tragedy. The Gothards were emphatic that only one shot was fired in the car on the spot where the tragedy was discovered. Their stories deepened the mystery from several standpoints. The question was immediately raised as to where Mrs. Rochell was wounded. The officer who took charge of a pistol found on the front seat of the death car, continued to maintain that only two shots had been fired from the weapon. Other investigators insisted, on the other hand, that there were two wounds in Mrs. Rochell's head and that Vaughn had been shot once. Although it was generally conceded by all sides that the shooting of Mrs. Rochell occurred at some point other than where the tragedy was discovered, investigators also found it impossible to fathom this angle. They followed a trail of blood along the paved highway for a distance of a few yards south of the spot where the car was parked, and this was as far as they were able to go."

FRESH CLUES SPUR ROCHELL PROBE
STARTLING NEW LEADS FOLLOWED
Two Distinct Stories Are Told Investigators
Working On Case
Vaughn Is Still In Same Condition
Grand Jury May Investigate Case At Session Next Week

The Birmingham Age-Herald, October 23, 1928

"Startling new developments are believed to have been revealed in the investigation into the mysterious fatal shooting of Mrs. Nancy Rochell and the serious wounding of Clyde Vaughn, former policeman. Investigators have been told two distinct stories. They say that, if each is true, there were two phases of the tragedy; that if the two phases are borne out that at least one of the victims was shot from outside the car in which they were seated. Taken together the new developments present an entirely new complexion to the case. Summarized, these developments are:

1. Certain investigators are working on a theory that one of the occupants of the death car was shot some distance from where the car was later found and at an appreciable interval of time.
2. That some moments later and further down the Cahaba Beach Road toward Birmingham from the point where the first shot was fired, one or more shots were fired from outside the car.
3. That persons who were near the scene of the tragedy, some between the death car and Birmingham and the others between the death car and the reservoir, reported having seen a car pass along the Cahaba Beach Road, at a high rate of speed and going away from Birmingham.
4. That the persons between the death car and Birmingham reported that this purported second car passed their car and that when they reached the point where the death car was found that the tragedy had already occurred.
5. That the persons back of the death car heard shots and a moment later saw a car speed by them headed away from Birmingham.

The persons in front of the death car indicated that the car which passed them would have passed the death car at about the time that the shooting was believed to have occurred. The persons back of the death car indicated that the car which later sped by them passed the death car at about the same moment that two shots were heard. These persons told investigators that it was their impression that there were two men in the car which passed them.

In line with these new developments, however, the question of how many shots were fired continues to be the key point. Other witnesses have said that when they examined the gun a few moments after the shooting that hammer marks were visible on only two shells, one witness saying that he counted lead in four bullets."

VAUGHN DID NOT SHOOT SELF, OFFICER BELIEVES

The Birmingham Age-Herald, October 25, 1928

"That Clyde Vaughn probably did not shoot himself and that Mrs. Nancy Rochell probably was shot from a distance, rather than from within the death car, were the beliefs expressed by W.J. Courtney, ballistics expert in the Attorney General's office when given details of the mystery. Courtney also gives as his opinion the bullet which was taken from the body of Mrs. Rochell can be identified even though it does not correspond in weight with any known rifle or pistol bullet. The fact that it was badly mutilated does not necessarily bar its identification either, he asserted.

The states' expert is not in Birmingham to probe the Vaughn case, but gave his views and his reasons for them when urged to do so by persons interested in the mystery. The fact that a bullet passed completely through the head of each is cited in support of his theory which he upholds with scientific experiments conducted by the U.S. Army, as well as in laboratories, have proved that the velocity of a bullet increases for some distance after it leaves the barrel before it starts to diminish. Had Vaughn fired the pistol at himself, Mr. Courtney believes, it is more likely the ball would have lodged somewhere in his head and the same reasoning he applies to the one which passed through the head of Mrs. Rochell. He declared that, where a person commits suicide by shooting, the bullet does not always pass through the body or head where any great bone resistance is offered.

As to the identification of the bullet fired, through its weight, Mr. Courtney declared bullets lose weight when they plow through any surface depending upon the distance from which they are fired and the solidity of the object which they hit. In experiments, more lead was lost in firing fro short distances, than from long. An expert rifleman was quoted, in a report to Coroner Russum, as saying that the bullet given him, as that taken from the body of Mrs. Rochell weighed 132 grains and that there was no bullet of that weight which corresponds with any "known pistol bullet as loaded into a .32 short or long Smith & Wesson or Colt, .38 short or long nor .38 Smith & Wesson special." Mr. Courtney pointed out that the bullet which weighed 132 grains after being removed from the body could have

been any of the three following, depending upon the distance from which it was fired: A .38 S&W weighing 145 grains, A .38 special S&W and Colt weighing 158 grains or a
.38 Colt long weighing 150 grains. If it were determined which of these had been fired, then of course, he pointed out, the approximate distance from which it was fired could be determined."

FORMER MOTOR SCOUT IS ORDERED ARRESTED
Wounded Policeman Indicted
As Probe Of Rochell Death Draws To Close

The Birmingham News, November 5, 1928

"Clyde A. Vaughn was indicted by the Jefferson County Grand Jury in connection with the death of Mrs. Nancy Rochell. This was the first definite development in the case since the young matron was shot to death on the Cahaba Road and was the first public intimation as to who was responsible for the two bullet wounds in her head. Vaughn, a former policeman, had not been placed under arrest at noon. It was understood that officers would confer with medical authorities to ascertain if Vaughn's condition would permit his removal to jail. Vaughn's physical condition is said to be gradually improving with his mental condition unchanged. Reports regarding his condition have varied widely since the shooting and for awhile it was believed that recovery was doubtful.

Mrs. Rochell, mother of four young children and wife of a wealthy soft drink manufacturer, was killed as she rode toward Birmingham with Vaughn after she had been missing from her home since the preceding afternoon. She had been shot in both sides of the head, one bullet having passed through while the other was found buried in the back of her head, near the base of the skull. Vaughn had been shot through the frontal brain, the bullet having entered his head from the right side. One bullet had pierced the windshield of the car. The report of the Grand Jury followed hearing of 30 witnesses.

Both physical facts and testimony offered by witnesses have made all those difficult to follow and served to point out the case as one of the most mysterious in Jefferson County's crime history. She had told her husband that she was going on a shopping tour. When she did not return police were asked to aid in a search and her car was found parked on a downtown street. It developed later that she was with Vaughn late in the afternoon; that the couple had stopped at a filling station and later bought soft drinks at a barbecue stand at New Merkle.

No one has been found who saw them after that during the night. The operator of the stand told investigators that he sold them drinks again the following morning as they were returning toward Birmingham. He said they were in an amiable mood as evidenced by their conversation. Raymond Rochell, the woman's husband received his first information regarding her whereabouts in the report to him of her death by The Birmingham News."

CLYDE VAUGHN WILL BE BURIED FROM HIS HOME
Last Rites Are Planned Wednesday; Death Seals Mystery

The Birmingham Age-Herald, November 28, 1928

"Funeral services for Clyde Vaughn, former police officer, who died Tuesday at Hillman Hospital following wounds received in the mysterious Cahaba Road shooting in which Mrs. Nancy Rochell, Birmingham matron was killed, will be held Wednesday in the residence, 1437 North Forty-Second street. Burial will be at Elmwood cemetery.

Vaughn was under indictment on a charge of first-degree murder in connection with the death of Mrs. Rochell, whose lifeless body was found beside him in a parked automobile. Vaughn was never conscious long enough to relate his version of the shooting.

The death of Vaughn appeared to have sealed definitely the mystery attached to the shooting. County Solicitor George Lewis Bailes announced that the case is a closed issue as far as his office is concerned."

Postscript

As with many complex death investigations initial appearances and potential physical evidence, as well as information provided by alleged "eyewitnesses" can be helpful or, in some instances be incorrect or intentionally false. This was also demonstrated by the often overwrought newspaper accounts related to this case.

Although various errors occurred in the investigation due to misinterpretations of the initial physical findings at the death scene, none would be more misleading and damaging than those related to the incorrect opinions expressed regarding the gunshot wounds sustained by Rochell, and later, of the injuries to Vaughn. These errors, coupled with questionable opinions regarding firearms and ballistics examinations, would be the main reasons for the delay in the proper reconstruction of this case. The final determination was that this was a matter of a homicide committed by Vaughn and that his delayed death was due to an intentionally self-inflicted wound with no involvement of any purported "outsiders."

The erroneous interpretations of Rochell's wounds by a well meaning but forensically inexperienced hospital pathologist would only further the confusion of investigators. The initial opinion that Rochell had been shot twice in the head, along with Vaughn's single gunshot wound, didn't fit with the fact that only two fired shell casings were in the gun. There is only one brief mention in a newspaper article indicating that the projectile recovered from Rochell had been disrupted. It is evident that a piece of this bullet had then exited adjacent to the right side of her nose and with another portion exiting her right ear with the defect of the nose being incorrectly interpreted as being a second wound of entry. This damage to the bullet would also account for the reduced weight of the recovered portion of the projectile which "experts" stated did not fit the weight of any known bullets. This opinion, coupled with statements regarding the ability to determine the distance to a target from which a projectile was fired based on its weight, can be dismissed as "junk" science.

The misinterpretations of both Rochell's and Vaughn's gunshot wounds can likely be attributed to a lack of knowledge and experience regarding certain basic principles associated with firearms and so-called "wound ballistics." Factors which must be taken into consideration by an examiner include the caliber and type of weapon, length of the barrel and bullet and gunpowder composition. Knowledge of such factors may allow for an estimate of the range of fire, or distance from the muzzle of the gun to the target when the weapon was fired. Such interpretations may be complicated by the presence of intervening physical factors such as the presence of dense hair over a wound of entry or, in the case of Vaughn, the probability that any products of combustion were forced into the depths of his wound of entry. This is often found with self-inflicted contact gunshot wounds of the head. It does not appear that an autopsy of Vaughn was conducted which would have led to such a finding.

Finally, it is interesting to consider what a trial of Vaughn might have been like had he survived and recovered. It is believed that the conflicting "eyewitness" statements, autopsy and firearms findings coupled with the confusion of investigators would have allowed for a vigorous defense of Vaughn, especially by a prominent attorney of that time such as Roderick Beddow, Sr.

Forensic science continues to evolve today with advanced technology such as DNA comparisons and the employment of complex analytical equipment. However, certain tests and examinations which had been accepted within the scientific and judicial communities for some time such as bite mark, hair and partial fingerprint comparisons are currently being revisited and, in some cases, discarded as not being truly based on scientific principles.

Positive Scientific Identification

Well, who are you?
I really wanna know.
Tell me, who are you?
'Cause I really wanna know.

---Who are you
The Who

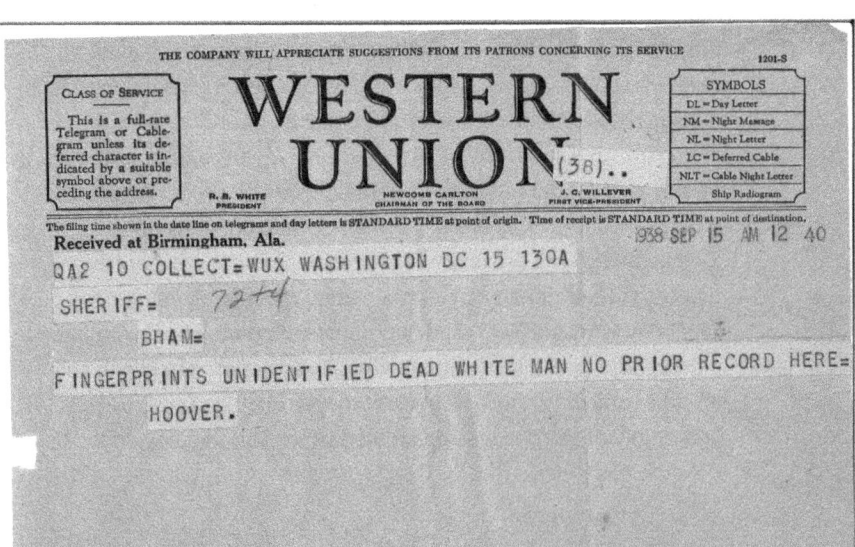

One of the basic principles of modern medical-legal death investigation relates to the ability to establish the positive identification of a deceased individual. Preferably, this should be accomplished by utilizing some type of scientific method rather than depending on an identification by someone who knew the individual in life based only on their facial features. Many misidentifications have been made under such circumstances, especially when severe trauma is present. In the case of many homicides, the positive identification of a victim becomes the starting point in an investigation.

Currently, forensic scientists can draw on a number of techniques in order to insure the positive identification of the majority of human remains which are brought to them for examination. Many individuals have established the means for their own identification during their lifetimes in the form of fingerprints and dental records which can be compared to postmortem findings. In addition, the use of DNA comparisons between deceased individuals and their relatives has become an increasingly important tool in identifying remains which exhibit advanced decomposition or which have become skeletonized. There will no longer be remains of "unknown" soldiers recovered due to the current universal collection and storage of DNA samples from all military service members.

In contrast to the present scientific state of the art in the identification of human remains, the typical coroner of the early 20th century was limited in the available techniques he could draw on for this purpose. Fingerprint and dental records during this time period were almost nonexistent and would not start to become available until police departments routinely took and stored fingerprints from those who were arrested and the military started to document prints and dental records during World War I. Therefore, direct visual identification by relatives or friends was used whenever possible, as were personal effects found on the individual or through laundry marks present on clothing.

The following case highlights issues involved with the positive identification of human remains. In addition, the extremely poor state of the forensic sciences during the early 20th century also included the lack of training and experience of coroners which would often lead to the failure to recognize or to properly interpret injuries. This case is also a classic example of the uncorrected misinterpretation of the cause and manner of death in a railroad related incident in the face of unappreciated contrary physical evidence and eyewitness statements.

BELIEVED MAN FOUND ON TRACKS WAS MURDERED
Great Mystery Surrounds Man Run Over By Train
BULLET IS FOUND IN HIS FOREHEAD
Engineer of Train Thought He Had Killed Man Until Undertaker Discovered Bullet-- Coroner Brasher's View

The Birmingham Age-Herald, December 25, 1911

"One of the greatest mysteries in its history is now facing the police force of Birmingham. Last night, the eve of the happiest holiday of the whole year, faint clews were found which point to the murder of a prosperous looking, well dressed man. Yet, even his name is not known and the shrouds of mystery surround the case so closely that it seems doubtful if the dead man's name will ever be known.

Not knowing in what manner death had occurred, workmen employed by the Louisville and Nashville railroad brought the body of an unidentified stranger to the undertaking establishment of Shaw & Son yesterday. They claimed that the man had been sitting on the track and that he had been struck by the local passenger train.

The engineer of the train was positive that the man was killed by the train, but when the body was examined at the morgue a large bullet was found embedded in the middle of his forehead. The bullet was about three-quarters of an inch long and was very thin, evidently not coming from a rifle. The skull had been fractured by the shot and Coroner Brasher stated that death must have been caused by the bullet.

The engine of the train had mangled the lower part of the body. Whether the man had been struck in the forehead by a stray bullet from a revolver, stunned by the blow and then fell on the track, or whether he was murdered and the body placed on the rails, is still a mystery. The engineer of the train said that the man was sitting up when the train struck him, and if this is the case, the body must have ben propped up if the man had been murdered before hand.

The dead man appeared to be about 35 years of age and was very well dressed and his hands showed no signs of hard labor. He also had a number of gold teeth. The idea that the man was murdered and robbed is refuted by the fact that a 15 jewel Waltham watch was found in his pocket. There was a pocketbook with about 50 cents change in it. No papers that would identify the man could be found, and one of the mysterious features of the case is that all of the laundry marks on the collar, shirt and underclothing had been cut away. The place where his name had evidently been marked in his hat was also scratched out.

Coroner Brasher said last night: "there is no doubt in my mind but what the man was murdered and the body placed on the track by the murderer. The bullet in the skull would have caused instant death, and there was no weapon of any description found near the scene, suicide would have been impossible. The man was murdered and the body placed on the track in an effort to hide the deed, and the perpetrator of the deed was a mighty clever fellow, for I believe it was he who destroyed the laundry marks and other means of identification." These clews are what make the police and the coroner believe that the man was murdered and the guilty ones are trying to hide the identity of both themselves and their victim."

IDENTITY OF MAN FOUND ON TRACK IS ESTABLISHED
The Man Was Run Over By a Train
But a Bullet Hole Was Afterward Found In His Forehead

The Birmingham Age-Herald, December 26, 1911

"Henry E. Robinson, Chicago, Ill.," was the address written upon a suit case which, it is believed, belonged to the man who was run over by a train, and whom the police believe was murdered. It will be remembered that undertakers discovered a bullet imbedded in the man's skull directly in the center of the forehead.

The discovery of the possible identity of the mysterious stranger was made when Coroner Brasher found in the dead man's clothing a railroad check for a suit case. When the suit case was opened identifying documents were found. The coroner went to the scene of the accident yesterday, but said he had as yet made no official investigation. Mr. Brasher stated that there was no doubt in his mind but what the man had been shot by a second party, either for revenge or with the intention of robbery."

VERIFIES IDENTITY OF H.E. ROBINSON
The Birmingham Age-Herald, December 27, 1911

"O. Williams of Gadsden removed all doubt as to the identity of the man who was struck by the train Christmas eve, and who is believed to have been murdered and the body placed on the track to hide the deed. Williams could give no cause for a possible murder and was at a loss to explain the death.

The fact that a fine gold watch was found on the person of the dead man refuted the robbery theory. It is believed that Robinson was shot, either purposely or accidentally, while on the railroad track. The theory that he was murdered and the body placed on the track is given a setback by the fact that both of the dead man's legs were broken above the ankles, evidently being struck by the cow catcher of the engine. In this case he would have had to have been standing up when the train struck him. If so it is thought that he was struck by a stray bullet and dazed, or else that he was left on the track as dead. The manner of his death is still a mystery and no clue to a possible murderer can be found.

Mr. Shaw of the Shaw & Son Undertaking establishment, stated that the engineer of the train that ran over Robinson said that Robinson was walking down the track and looked around when the engine whistle blew but made no effort to get off the track. Was Robinson shot and left for dead by the side of the road but was only dazed and made his way to the railroad track where he was struck by the train?"

Postscript

A review of the investigation into the circumstances surrounding the death of Henry Robinson by the coroner and police, with their initial proposition that Robinson was "undoubtedly" murdered, is instructive for various reasons and provides insight into the state of the forensic sciences and death investigation in Jefferson County, as well as in many other jurisdictions, during the early 20th century. This case provides a good example of "tunnel vision" with the refusal of the investigators to assess all of the evidence and to keep an open mind about other possibilities of how the victim may have come to his death.

It should always be a staple of the initial approach to any death investigation to first consider that the death is due to murder at the hands of another person until proven otherwise. However, as an investigation proceeds and additional and new information is collected in the form of witness statements, physical evidence and the application of forensic science techniques by competent examiners, it is often necessary to change one's original theories about a particular case.

In the matter of Robinson, the initial conclusion drawn by the undertakers and accepted by the coroner, that the piece of metal found embedded, apparently superficially in his forehead, was a "bullet" led to an unshakeable mindset on the part of the coroner that the victim must have been shot either with intent, or possibly accidentally, by a "stray" projectile. It became difficult for the coroner to deviate from this belief which had now become "embedded" in his own mind as the only possibility and especially after he had publicly expressed the certainty of his conclusion. It is likely that this piece of metal, which didn't actually look like a bullet, was an artifact. That such a piece of metal debris littering the railroad track which became associated with the violent trauma which had been sustained by Robinson when being struck by the train, does not appear to have been entertained as a possibility for its origin. It is not surprising that an autopsy was not performed as such a procedure was rarely conducted during this time period. Had one been done it would have likely put the "bullet theory" to rest early in the investigation when the head wound would have been shown to be superficial and without vital response.

Other attempts at the theoretical reconstruction of this incident were also fraught with inconsistencies. The belief that the already deceased victim was placed in a sitting position on the rail is a physical impossibility unless he had been dead for an extended period of time and rigor mortis had become fully formed while he was in a sitting position. The location of certain injuries supports the eyewitness statement of the engineer that he saw the man upright and walking just prior to being struck. The supposition that his killer cut out the laundry tags in his clothing to hide his identity stretches the imagination. It more likely suggests that such was the act of the deceased individual himself prior to his committing "suicide by train," and who did not want his identity to be discovered.

Due to either his stolid belief that Robinson was murdered, or his refusal to admit that he was wrong in the face of the evidence, it is notable that Coroner Brasher apparently would not change his mind regarding this matter as on December 31, 1911, he entered the following confusing official docket entry: "I, B.L. Brasher, Coroner of Jefferson County certify that I held a preliminary investigation on the body of H.E. Robinson, white, with the following result: I find from the evidence that the immediate cause of death was due to a railroad accident. I found that after he had been killed by a bullet wound in the center of his forehead, and a fracture from the wound, about one inch and a half which in my judgement would have produced death in the course of time. In my judgement deceased was in an unconscious condition at the time he was struck by the train."

It appears that this now became another case of an unsolved "murder" that never actually occurred. Although not directly stated, one can readily "read between the lines" in newspaper articles that seem to suggest that the reporters believed investigators, particularly the coroner, were incorrect in their assumptions about the manner of this death. It appears that the reporters did a better job of reconstructing this matter than was done by the officials but did not want to further embarrass, antagonize or alienate persons that they had to routinely obtain information from by taking them to task publicly.

Poisons and Toxicology

Along with advances in the forensic sciences in general, the early 20th century would see major improvements in the techniques and instrumentation associated with the science of toxicology.

The detection of toxic substances in the form of various poisons and drugs had been of prime interest to law enforcement agents for many years. Although tests became available to determine the presence of a number of substances such as narcotics and heavy metals, there were no consistent methods available for determining the amounts of these drugs and poisons in human remains. Therefore, it was difficult to differentiate their origins as being from naturally occurring elements such as within food and water or whether there were extremely high levels which might suggest that a poison was self-inflicted or may have been administered surreptitiously by another person.

Homicide by poisoning is typically a "household" crime. There is usually some degree of intimacy with emotional ties between the victim and the perpetrator, who likely share the same home which allows for proximity and privacy. By definition, murder by poisoning is always a premeditated act.

Successful prosecutions of persons suspected of the intentional poisoning of individuals in order to cause their deaths for whatever reason can be difficult. The following conditions and factors must be taken into consideration and proven beyond a reasonable doubt.:

1. Proof that the accused had access to the poison responsible for the death.
2. Proof that the accused had access to the victim.
3. Proof that the death was caused by poison and that death due to natural causes had been ruled out.
4. Proof that death was homicidal as opposed to accidental or suicidal.

As with any trial for first degree murder, proof of intent, which is the purpose or aim behind an act, is required. Although proving a motive, or the instigating force responsible for doing a deed is not legally required, the presentation of such by the prosecution may carry persuasive weight in a jury's consideration of whether the guilt of the accused has been proven beyond a reasonable doubt.

The naturally occurring heavy metal element Arsenic is present in trace amounts in our soil and water and, therefore, in body tissue. It can be found on analysis of body fluids and tissues as well as in stomach contents when it has been recently ingested. In the early 20th century Arsenic was routinely included in various compounds used for the control of mice, rats and insects. This particular highly toxic substance was easily obtained during that time period with no questions asked. When a death occurred which raised the suspicions of authorities as to whether an individual had been intentionally poisoned with with Arsenic, a repetitive problem presented itself in regard to the difficulty in quantifying the amount of that element which was present and, therefore, the ability to properly interpret the findings. This was related to the fact that the chemical properties of Arsenic, a heavy metal, made it an ideal tissue preservative and had been regularly included in embalming fluid since the Civil War. If a body had been embalmed before tissue samples had been taken for testing, it would preclude analysis and the formation of an opinion as to its origin. As an aside, the preservative power of Arsenic has led to forensic scientists drawing seriously erroneous conclusions as to how long a person had been dead following the exhumation of remains which had been embalmed many years earlier with compounds containing this element. One case involved a disparity of 112 years in the estimate of time of death of a civil war soldier whose remains were initially believed to be those of an individual who had recently died.2

Those persons responsible for investigating deaths realized that in addition to developing tests for determining the quantity of Arsenic present, they would also have to have that ingredient permanently removed from embalming fluids used by morticians. This would occur with the passage of the Pure Food and Drug and the Harrison Narcotics Acts of 1914, which although mainly concerned with limiting uncontrolled access to narcotics and for safety measures for the processing of food, also included a provision which banned the use of Arsenic in embalming fluids. Although its presence in rat and insect poisons would continue for many years, the advances in quantitative toxicological analyses would allow for a determination of how much of the substance was present in tissue and stomach content samples. The presence of large doses of this and other metallic poisons in a deceased person's body would become a major factor in the pursuit and conviction of criminals who used what they believed were "silent weapons" as a means of murder.

Even with the current advanced state of toxicology, there are procedural requirements for handling human remains which have been exhumed and are being tested for the presence of Arsenic and other heavy metals. These would include the collection of soil and water samples in and around a gravesite and their testing for the presence and amount of the substance. Likely, trace amounts of Arsenic will be found but not at the levels found in the remains of a poisoned individual. This will preclude any argument that the poison had "leached" into the body from its surroundings after burial. Analysis of hair and nails can also be helpful in the timing of multiple poisoning episodes.

The importance of the routine practice of conducting such tests has been learned the "hard way" by examiners over the years as doubts regarding the validity of interpretations of toxicological evidence have been presented to juries by defense attorneys when such baseline analyses had not been conducted.

TESTING TWO STOMACHS FOR PRESENCE OF POISON
The Birmingham Age-Herald, January 16, 1909

"Within a few days Coroner B.L. Brasher will be able to give out interesting information for which the public has been waiting for some time. The coroner is just now a very busy man, but he stated that several cases upon which he has been working will come to a head in a few days.

Despite the fact that the body of J.I. Taylor, who died at East Lake about eight months ago, was disinterred from the grave at Mt. Pinson more than a month ago, the first information relative to the exhuming of the remains seems to have been given out yesterday. After having been interred for seven months the body of Taylor was removed from its grave nearly a month ago. The stomach was removed and placed in the hands of Chemist Rinaldo Williams for a chemical analysis. It will be recalled that the charge was made that Taylor came to his death by poisoning. Hence the investigation.

Mr. Williams also informed the coroner that he would be ready within a few days to submit a report of his analysis of the stomach of the late Coroner W.D. Paris, who died late in December. It was suspected by some that Coroner Paris had been poisoned and Solicitor Heflin ordered a chemical analysis of the stomach."

ASSASSIN TAKES LIVES OF TWO PROMINENT MEN WITH POISON
Guy R. Coleman and Stephen H. Strickland Meet Horrible Death At Dinner
HAD TASTED WHISKEY WHICH WAS SENT HIM
Officers Are Entirely at Sea as to Who Caused Double Tragedy Which Has Shocked the Whole Community
The Birmingham Age-Herald, December 21, 1910

"Within fifteen minutes after having taken what he supposed was a drink of whiskey with his friend, Stephen H. Strickland, Guy R. Coleman, a prominent fraternity man, connected with the Dunn-Lallande Contracting Company, died in agony yesterday afternoon at

3:30 o'clock at his boarding place, 2122 Fourth avenue, north, and Mr. Strickland died about twenty minutes later at the infirmary. It was later found that the liquor was poisoned and the belief is expressed by physicians and the coroner--that it contained strychnine.

Mr. Coleman, in company with Mr. Strickland, had just seated themselves at the dinner table when they were both seized with convulsions resulting from the drink. The drink had taken effect in the short time it required the two men to walk from one house to the other. Almost immediately Mr. Coleman was attacked with convulsions and at the same time Mr. Strickland showed signs of the same sickness. To those who were assisting him Mr. Coleman said, "We only took a little drink, hardly enough for one. It was a small sample bottle that was given me." He was shaken with convulsion, and could say no more for several seconds. His next speech was, "That stuff was doped, it was poisoned."

According to L.E. Anderson who was present, Mr. Coleman realized his own condition sooner than anyone else, and acted in a way which indicated that he knew more than he would tell. "He was sufficiently conscious to leave some instructions in regard to some private matters, but he avoided any question as to how he got the sample bottle of whiskey. He only said it was 'sent him.' Shortly before he expired he said, "My God, its hard to die like a dog." Mr. Coleman was district deputy grand chancellor of the Knights of Pythias of Alabama. He was also a thirty-second degree Scottish Rite Mason and a Shriner.

Immediately after the death of Guy R. Coleman the police department was notified and Detectives Ray, Tully, Williams and Cates hurried to the scene. They questioned everyone in the house, but did not succeed in eliciting any important information. The theory is advanced that the bottle contained bead oil which is used to adulterate whisky and which is deadly poison. It is thought that the two men procured a bottle of the chemical and drank it thinking it was whisky. The bottle contained enough oil to have killed 20 men.

Coroner Brasher held a preliminary autopsy over the bodies last night in the parlors of the Lige Loy Undertaking company. The stomachs and kidneys were removed and found to be in a horrible condition, being irritated greatly by the chemical. Dr. Wilder, at the conclusion of the autopsy, said: "While I can give no official verdict as to the exact cause of the deaths, from the convulsions of the two men I am sure that it was strychnine." Coroner Brasher advances a different theory from the police. He believes it to be a case of deliberate murder and expressed the following opinion immediately after the autopsy: "My opinion of the case is that the deaths of Mr. Coleman and Mr. Strickland were the result of a deliberate plot to murder Coleman. He has an enemy somewhere in Birmingham who prepared the bottle which may have contained some whisky and sent it to him. I have been considerably annoyed today by the claims of some two or three men who stated that they had been deputized by me to investigate the death of the two men. I have deputized no one and would only like to find out who it was that went to the residence and told them that he was deputy coroner. A man went to Loy's parlors and told the same story. He wanted a bunch of keys belonging to Coleman and secured them. The coroner has no deputies."

STRYCHNINE FOUND IN THE STOMACHS OF POISONED MEN
Chemist Says Small Bottle if Full Contained About 8 Grains of Poison

The Birmingham Age-Herald, December 31, 1910

"Chemist J.C. Long made his official report on the result of the analysis of he contents of the stomachs of Guy R. Coleman and Stephen H. Strickland to Judge S.E. Greene. The report shows that the poison used was strychnine and 2.79 grains were recovered from the body of Coleman and 0.83 grains from that of Strickland.

An analysis of the small bottle of whisky from which the two men are supposed to have drunk were also made and of the large bottle of whisky and some soup which the two men ate for dinner. No poison was found in the large bottle of whiskey or the soup, but the remainder of the contents of the small bottle contained 0.138 grains of strychnine. The bottle holds 50 cubic centimeters of solution, and taking this as a basis the whisky in the bottle contained 8 grains of strychnine. This was enough poison to kill 20 men."

PRETTY YOUNG GIRL HELD FOR COMPLICITY IN DOUBLE MURDER
Miss Ola Gunters Arrested in Jacksonville, Fla., Brought to Birmingham Yesterday By Two Deputy Sheriffs-- Denies Any Knowledge of Killing of Two Well Known Young Men

The Birmingham Age-Herald, July 14, 1912

"Miss Ola Gunters of Jacksonville, Fla., 19 years old and pretty, a former resident of this city has been placed under arrest on account of her alleged connection with the murder of Guy R. Coleman and Steve Strickland which occurred on the 20th of December, 1910, at Coleman's boarding house near the corner of Fourth avenue and Twenty-first street.

When Miss Gunters reached the city yesterday, accompanied by the two deputy sheriffs, her attorney and a matronly traveling companion, she was taken at once to the county jail. Owing to the fact, however, that Dr. Oates, the state prison inspector, had forbidden the sheriff to confine white women in the county jail, "because it is an unfit place," Miss Gunters was later put under the custody of a special deputy whose services she will pay and taken to the Hotel Hillman, where she will be held pending further developments in the case.

The girl talked freely and frankly about herself and her whereabouts for several months prior to the crime and up to the present time. She answered each question intelligently and without the slightest hesitation and while showing distress at the unpleasant situation in which she is placed expresses the greatest confidence that as soon as the facts in the case are known so far as she is concerned she will be released.

Miss Gunters gives an impression of good breeding and is refined both in appearance and manner. To a reporter she gave the following statement: "In the early part of October, 1910, I went to New Orleans. I lived in Louisiana until November 29, 1910. I returned to Birmingham and remained in the city several months. On April 1, 1911, I went to Jacksonville, Fla., where I have lived up to the present time. I never knew either Mr. Coleman or Mr. Strickland and certainly had nothing to do with the tragedy that led to their death. I was ignorant as to the charge against me when I was first arrested and don't know on what grounds they connect me with that awful crime. I have nothing to hide; I can prove my whereabouts for the past two years. I was not in the city when the crime was committed and cannot imagine how I was even suspected of having anything to do with the crime. I hope to be released as soon as these facts are known."

Her attorney, Mr. Hartridge, stated they made no efforts to resist coming to Birmingham. Mr. Hartridge expressed his confidence that the girl would be released. While the officers were extremely reticent in discussing the case, it is understood that Miss Gunters will be charged only with being an accessory to the crime. In fact, it was stated that the publication of her arrest yesterday caused three persons suddenly to leave the city, whom it was expected to connect with the crime.

The warrant for Miss Gunters' arrest was sworn out by Coroner B.L. Brasher on information received from the sheriff's office. The coroner declines to state what is the evidence which led to the swearing out of the warrant. Miss Gunters was a resident of Birmingham for several months, lived for five weeks at the corner of Twenty-first street and Fifth avenue, near the house where the murder was consummated."

MRS. IDA SCHMIDT IS ARRESTED IN POISONING CASE
Ola Gunters Is Given Her Freedom by Solicitor Heflin
MRS. SCHMIDT HAD LEFT CITY LATELY
Second Prisoner in Noted Case Refuses to Talk-- Gunters Woman Happy When Told of Her Release

The Birmingham Age-Herald, July 16, 1912

"Ida Schmidt of Birmingham is under arrest with the same crime for which Ola Gunters was arrested, complicity in the murder of Guy R. Coleman and Steve Strickland in December of 1910. Mrs. Schmidt was arrested in Atlanta yesterday. Mrs. Schmidt said that she "positively would make no statement." When met at the terminal by a reporter she said she had "no use for newspaper men" and that she would not talk to them. Mrs. Schmidt seemed not at all concerned over her arrest and talked and laughed as though she were taking an automobile ride over the city.

Deputy Irving Steele said that he did not expect that they could hold his prisoner very long, unless developments in the case turned up early today. He said: "The release of Ola Gunters has hindered us again. Ola Gunters at one time lived with Mrs. Schmidt. We will land this case yet, however, and when we do, things will stir."

At the instance of Solicitor H.P. Heflin the case against Ola Gunters was nolle prossed. Solicitor Heflin stated that he had investigated the charge against the young woman and that he did not consider the evidence submitted to him sufficient to hold her on the charge."

MRS. IDA SCHMIDT TURNED LOOSE BY JUDGE BENNERS
Heflin Causes Something of Sensation by Statement to the Court
Mrs. Sallie C. Wheeler Testifies That the Schmidt Woman Had Confessed Crime to Her

The Birmingham Age-Herald, July 25, 1912

"The evidence is not sufficient to hold the defendant and she is discharged," said Judge I.H. Benners at the conclusion of the preliminary hearing of the case of Ida Schmidt. She was charged with the murder of Guy Coleman and Steve Strickland, two prominent business men of the city whose death by poison in December, 1910, caused a big sensation.

The star witness for the state were Mrs. Sallie C. Wheeler, who claimed to be employed by the Pinkerton Detective agency, and who testified that she had extracted a confession from the Schmidt woman by posing as a fortune teller, and A.C. Hellwig of New Orleans, formerly in charge of a local detective agency, who also testified to hearing certain admissions of guilt by the defendant.

The sensation of the trial was when the name of Emil Lesser, one of the best known men in the district was brought into the case. Mrs. Wheeler testified that the defendant had told her that she had received $800 as the first installment for her part in the poisoning of the two men, and that the money was paid by a prominent business man of the city, but when asked if the money had been paid by Emil Lesser, the defendant declined to say. There was nothing brought out in the testimony to connect Mr. Lesser with the crime in any particular except the statement of Mrs. Wheeler which was not corroborated.

In reference to Dial, the drug clerk arrested in connection with the case, Mrs. Wheeler testified that on one occasion Ida Schmidt heated a poker and made Dial go on his knees and swear he would not reveal his knowledge of the poisoning of the two men. She also testified that the Schmidt woman was paying Ola Gunters $50 a month to stay away from Birmingham. A.C. Helwig corroborated the testimony of Mrs. Wheeler in many particulars, and asserted that the Schmidt woman had repeatedly confessed knowledge of the crime. At no point did the witnesses contradict themselves, and they answered all questions clearly and promptly.

At the conclusion of the evidence the state offered to submit the case without argument, but to this the defendant's counsel objected. Mr. Burr briefly stated the state's case. He was followed by the attorneys for the defense, who made strong arguments for the release of the defendant and vigorously denounced the evidence submitted by Mrs. Wheeler as being unreasonable and far fetched.

At the conclusion, Solicitor Heflin addressed the court and said: "Your honor, it is the duty of the state to protect the innocent as well as to punish the guilty. You have heard the evidence in this case and it is for you to decide. I don't know how the evidence against this defendant has impressed you but I am free to confess it has not impressed me. I say hold the defendant if you think her guilty; If not discharge her." This statement of Mr. Heflin caused a mild sensation, and at the conclusion Judge Benners stated the state had failed to make out a case and discharged the defendant.

A.C. Helwig made the following statement in reference to the case: "I feel that the evidence submitted to the court was sufficient to hold the defendant. I have been in the private detective business for eight years and I have never seen a case turned down before with such evidence as was produced at the trial today. My regret is that we could not have had a change of venue to another county. I believe Ida Schmidt guilty and that she should have been held on the charge."

Postscript

With the criminal charges dropped against all three persons arrested in association with this case it is assumed that no further action was taken and the murders remained unsolved. No additional news articles regarding the matter were found. From an investigative standpoint, this case represents a classic example of although "knowing" that individuals are likely guilty of a crime, but being unable to meet the level of legally required proof "beyond a reasonable doubt" at a trial before a jury. In this case, the opinion of the preliminary hearing judge was that there was not even enough evidence to send the matter to a grand jury for consideration of an indictment, no less a petit jury trial.

Guilty Until Proven Innocent?

STATE OF ALABAMA
JEFFERSON COUNTY

"I, B.L. Brasher, Coroner of Jefferson County, certify that on May 23, 28 and Jun 4, 1912, 12 Avenue and 20 Street, City I held a preliminary investigation inquest on the body of Mrs. Mittie Fulton Albright, White, with the following result: Jury found deceased came to her death from being poisoned at the hands of Jesse Albright. Same being unlawfully done and against the peace and dignity of the State of Alabama. Remarks: Died May 16, 1912. Warrants were for Jesse & Martha Albright."

EXPECT SENSATION IN THE ALLBRIGHT INQUEST
The Birmingham Age-Herald, May 24, 1912

"The first day's session of the inquest over the death of Mrs. Mittie Allbright was held yesterday. Although nothing was given out as to the nature of the evidence disclosed at the hearing. Coroner Brasher stated that something sensational would develop.

The proceedings have attracted no little attention. Coroner Brasher stated last night: "The husband of the deceased did not desire the inquest. He insisted that it not be held, as he did not want his wife's body exhumed and when we do I firmly believe that we will find more strychnine in the stomach than anything else."

SAYS ALLBRIGHT GOT STRYCHNINE
Was Three Days Before His Wife Died
HUSBAND ARRESTED
Coroner Brasher States Body of Dead Woman Will Be Exhumed Today and Stomach Examined by Chemist
The Birmingham Age-Herald, May 25, 1912

"Jesse Allbright, husband of Mittie Allbright, concerning the death of whom Coroner B.L. Brasher is holding an inquest, was arrested yesterday on the charge of murder. Coroner Brasher stated last night that the body of Mrs. Allbright would be exhumed this morning and the contents of the stomach of the dead woman analyzed.

Coroner Brasher said: "The evidence shows that Dr. Whaley is absolutely blameless in the death of Mrs. Allbright, as is the druggist, Mr. Milner. Dr. Whaley stated that the prescription he had written was harmless and was intended as a sleeping potion. The druggist testified before the jury that he had sold Jesse Allbright, the husband, five grains of strychnine three days before Mrs. Allbright died. He proved this by showing his poison sale record as is required by law."

It was rumored that inasmuch as the body of Mrs. Allbright had been embalmed that it would be impossible to analyze the contents of the stomach as the formaldehyde used in embalming would destroy all traces of any other substance, but Coroner Brasher stated that the embalming fluid might be analyzed and the percentage of other substances ascertained. Mr. Allbright has refused to make any statement of the affair whatever."

MRS. ALLBRIGHT'S BODY IS EXHUMED
"Examination Will Require 8 or 10 Days," Says Coroner Brasher
The Birmingham Age-Herald, May 26, 1912

"Coroner B.L. Brasher, accompanied by a physician and Rinaldo Williams, chemist, returned last night from Dora, Ala., where they went to exhume the body of Mrs. Minnie Fulton Allbright, who died under suspicious circumstances May 18. Her husband, Jesse Allbright, has been subsequently placed in jail, charged with murder.

Coroner Brasher stated last night: "We exhumed the body of Mrs. Allbright and extracted the stomach, liver and kidneys, which we brought back with us. The analysis will be begun immediately, but it will be 8 or 10 days before it is completed. In the meantime everything connected with the case is quiet."

CORONER'S JURY CHARGES ALBRIGHT WITH MURDER
Verdict Charges Husband With Poisoning Of His Wife, Mrs. Mittie Fulton Albright
The Birmingham Age-Herald, June 5, 1912

"The coroner's jury investigating the death of Mrs. Mittie Fulton Albright, who died under suspicious circumstances on May 16, yesterday brought in a verdict holding that the woman had been poisoned and charged Jesse Albright, her husband, with the poisoning. A large number of witnesses were examined at yesterday morning's trial.

The body of Mrs. Albright had been exhumed and the contents of the stomach examined by chemist Rinaldo Williams. The report of the chemist was that he had recovered from the stomach and its contents one-sixth grain of strychnine alkaloid."

Postscript

A review of microfilmed newspaper records following the reported referral of the Albright matter to the Grand Jury for its consideration revealed a detailed final report issued in September, 1912 to include the names of all persons indicted for murder. There is no mention of an indictment being issued against Jesse Albright or, for that matter, a "no bill" naming him.

No further mention of the Albright case could be found during the following several months. It is possible that despite the "evidence" presented at the coroner's inquest where murder warrants were issued for Jesse and Martha Albright it was later decided by authorities not to pursue the matter. This may have been due to the equivocal toxicology findings. Additionally, although there was much innuendo directed towards Jesse Albright early in the investigation the lack of a confession or of any eyewitnesses to the actual act of the alleged homicidal poisoning of Mittie Albright may also have been factors related to the outcome of this case.

Another case of an alleged homicidal poisoning took place two years later when accusations were made against an individual for the murder of his wife.

Docket Entry:
I, C.L. Spain, Coroner of Jefferson County, certify that on September 4th, 1914, I held a preliminary investigation inquest on the body of Mrs. Nancy Fields, White, with the following result: Jury came to the decision that deceased came to her death by Strychnine poisoning at the hands of her husband, Issac W. Fields, same being unlawfully done and against the peace and dignity of the State of Alabama.

CHEMIST FINDS NO TRACE OF POISON
Coroner Will Have Mrs. Fields Body Exhumed for Further Examination

The Birmingham Age-Herald, September 14, 1914

"Coroner Charles L. Spain has received a partial report from the chemist who has been analyzing the contents of the stomach of the late Mrs. Isaac Fields, who, it is alleged, was poisoned by her husband some weeks ago at Brookside. In the report, the chemist states that he could find nothing that would warrant the belief that Mrs. Fields had been poisoned.

However, Coroner Spain stated last night that he understood that Mrs. Fields had not eaten anything for several hours prior to her sudden death and therefore as the chemist stated there was nothing in the stomach to analyze. It is now the coroner's intentions to exhume the body and make a further examination for signs of strychnine poisoning.

Isaac Fields, who is a well known farmer of Brookside, is at present prisoner in the county jail. At the coroner's inquest held at Brookside a few days ago the jury brought in a verdict to the effect that Mrs. Fields had come to her death by poisoning at the hands of her husband."

Postscript

Although Coroner Spain insisted that he would exhume the remains of Mrs. Fields for further testing, there is no indication that this was done. If the body had been embalmed the chemist likely informed the coroner that since strychnine is an alkaloid and not a heavy metal, that its presence in tissue samples would not be detectable using the analytical methods available at that time.

Both the Albright and Fields cases serve as indictments of the coroner system and its procedures during this period in that even though his "jury" returned a quasi-judicial "ruling' of supposed guilt, the proceedings and outcomes were generally directed by the coroner. The presentation of evidence by selected witnesses fell far below that required in a higher court of law where any testimony would be subject to the rules of evidence and to cross-examination by defense attorneys.

In actuality, both of these cases failed to reach trial before a petit jury either because a grand jury refused to indict an individual based on the evidence presented or the district attorney refused to proceed further due to his belief that a guilty verdict could not be obtained based on the lack of supporting evidence.

These and other cases suggest that an early "rush to judgement" on the part of the coroners and their juries existed and that this was one factor which would lead to the dissolution of the coroner jury system in Jefferson County by the late 1920s. It would then gradually disappear from use in all of the other counties of the state by the mid twentieth century.

Docket Entry:
Docket Date: April 30, 1910. Died April 19, 1910
Deceased: Wiley Alexander, Col.
Address: Jonesboro
Defendants: Joe Kelley, Henry Wyatt and Palsey Alexander
Cause Of Death: From poison being put in his food.

Docket Entry:
Docket Dates: June 17 & 20, 1911
Dates Of Death: May 6 and May 29, 1911
Deceased: Pearlie & Edwin Williams, Col.
Address: East Birmingham
Cause Of Death: Poisoning by arsenic.
Remarks: Jury found deceased came to their deaths by being poisoned at the hands of Bill Williams and Mary Williams, colored. Dr. Strickland took out the stomach of Edwin Williams and Pearlie Williams was taken out by Dr. Johnson. In Pearlie's stomach was found .46 grains of arsenic and 1.09 in Edwin's.

Docket Entry:
Date: September 2, 1911
Deceased: Mary Emerson, White
Address: 217 62 Street, Woodlawn
Cause Of Death: By drinking milk which contained carbolic acid. Said carbolic was said to have been put in the milk by unknown parties.

CHAPTER 23

UNKNOWN

"Show me the manner in which a nation or a community cares for its dead and I will measure with mathematical exactness the tender sympathies of its people, their respect for the laws of the land and their loyalty to high ideals."

---W.E. Gladstone
(attributed)

    As in other communities across the nation, the duties of the coroner, in addition to the investigation of suspicious deaths, included the responsibility for the disposition of unidentified and unclaimed human remains found within his jurisdiction. In the early 20th century the capabilities for the scientific positive identification of deceased individuals were quite limited. The collection of fingerprints from those persons arrested for committing crimes was in its infancy and they could only be retained locally as no national database would be established until 1924. Other procedures such as the comparison of dental work and x-rays would not come into use until much later.

    During these early years the identification of skeletonized remains as well as those of transients, which were often found in proximity to railroad lines, was almost impossible. Unless a deceased person had resided in the area where their body was found and could be visually identified by relatives or neighbors, it was unlikely that they would be. The disposition of these unidentified remains, as well as those of persons whose relatives were financially unable to provide for burial, became the responsibility of of the local government and taxpayers. Simple burials in designated county cemeteries would be provided. One of these so-called "Potter's Fields" was located on land adjacent to the current Birmingham zoo. Later burials would take place in Ketona and currently take place in Morris in north Jefferson County.

"Drive your cart and your plow over the bones of the dead."

---Proverbs of Hell
William Blake

CORONER UPSET BY HUMAN BONES
Finds That Regular Traffic In Them Is Conducted at Some of The Boneyards of the City

The Birmingham Age-Herald, June 30, 1909

"Coroner B.L. Brasher is greatly perplexed with a discovery which would indicate that human skeletons are being sold at the junk yards in and around Birmingham as old bones. If clews can be picked up and followed out to a solution of the mystery it is not improbable that a sensation, or several of them, may develop.

A short time ago a man reported to the coroner that there were quite a number of human bones to be found in a great heap of bones in a junk yard situated on Tenth avenue and Thirteenth street, north. The coroner went to the junk yard to investigate the matter and the report was verified when he found the bones of human arms and legs. He collected the pieces of the skeleton and has removed them to his office for future reference in the investigation which he proposes to make.

The coroner states that he was informed by the keeper of the junk yard that during the past three months he might have collected "a flour barrel full of human bones" at the one junk yard, and it is stated by the coroner that "they bring the same price per pound as horse and cow bones, or any other kind, for that matter."

Coroner Brasher was informed that the bones which he now has in his possession were carried to the boneyard from the city's dumping ground on avenue F among a great lot of other bones. It is understood that the negro who has charge of burying the dead animals at the dumping ground is granted the privilege of digging up the bones six months after burial and that he sells them for whatever price he can get.

The coroner is of the opinion that the finding of the bones at the junk yard is an indication of foul play, believing that murdered persons have been thrown in the trenches along beside dead animals and buried unceremoniously. Coroner Brasher stated that he would urge the city and health authorities to co-operate with him in an investigation which he intends to make as thorough as possible."

Docket Entry:
Date: July 15, 1910
Deceased: An Unknown Negro Man
Address: Coalburg
Cause Of Death: From gun shot wound while robbing a box car. Same being a justifiable homicide.

Docket Entry:
Date: September 6, 1911
Deceased: Unknown White Man
Cause Of Death: By being run over by a train owned and operated by the AGSRR Company. Negligence on the part of the deceased.

Docket Entry:
Date: September 14, 1911
Deceased: Unknown Negro Infant
Address: Old Potter's Field, across Red Mountain
Cause Of Death: Unknown Causes.

Docket Entry:
Date: April 5, 1914
Deceased: Unknown Colored Man
Cause Of Death: Gunshot wounds at the hands of party or parties unknown.
Remarks: Body had been lying in woods about one mile south east of Parkwood, Ala for six weeks or two months.

Docket Entry:
Date: November 21, 1914
Deceased: Unknown Negro Woman
Cause Of Death: From blow on head crushing the skull, and badly burnt body.
Defendant: Party or parties unknown.

Docket Entry:
Date: January 31, 1917
Deceased: Unknown Negro Man
Address: Terminal yards
Cause Of Death: Being run over by switch engine Southern railroad #1658 while trespassing.

Docket Entry:
Date: November 10, 1917
Deceased: Unknown White Man
Address: Bessie Junction
Cause Of Death: From traumatism, by being run over by train same being accidental.

Docket Entry:
Date: April 3, 1918
Deceased: Bo, Otherwise Unknown, Col.
Address: Hillman Hospital
Cause Of Death: From starvation.

Docket Entry:
Date: April 26, 1921
Deceased: Unknown Negro Man
Address: Gas plant
Cause Of Death: Gunshot wound of head
Defendant: H.E. Robinson, White.

Docket Entry:
Date: March 17, 1923
Deceased: Unknown Negro Man
Address: Five Mile Creek a quarter of a mile below Upper Coalburg.
Cause Of Death: Gunshot wounds of body.
Defendant: Party or parties unknown.

Docket Entry:
Date: December 26, 1923
Deceased: Unknown White Man
Address: Johns Undertaking Company
Cause Of Death: By traumatic fracture of head and body, hit by train while walking on track.

CHAPTER 24

ATLAS OBSCURA

*"What has been will be again,
what has been done will be done again,
there is nothing new under the sun."*

---Ecclesiastes 1:9

Although there may be "nothing new under the sun," odd and rare permutations of various causes, means, and manners of deaths do occasionally occur. These become remarkable by the absence of similar cases within the memories of contemporary investigators and other observers who are naturally confined to a particular limited time period. The circumstances surrounding these deaths may confound their classification and placement within any one of the general categories presented so far in this book. In addition, certain peculiar matters which seemed to be important to society during this particular time period are briefly reviewed.

Falls

Deaths due to falls from varying heights and under differing circumstances were relatively common occurrences as documented in the coroner's records.

Docket Entry:
Date: October 20, 1909
Deceased: A.H. Umphres, White
Address: 300 1/2 South 20th St.
Cause Of Death: By falling from window or being thrown out.
Remarks: The jury decided that cause of death was unknown to the jury, but evidence showed that he was thrown out or fell from window on third floor. Deceased had not been in his right mind for about ten years after having been sun struck. He has been quite insane for the past year.

Docket Entry:
Date: October 17, 1916
Deceased: Mark Coleman, Col.
Address: Sherman Heights, Ensley
Cause Of Death: By accidentally falling from a plank on top of a high porch while asleep and accidentally breaking his neck due to his own fault.

Docket Entry:
Date: February 23, 1918
Deceased: Ben Walters, Col.
Address: 908 Nelson St.
Cause Of Death: From Drowning. Same being an unavoidable accident by falling in the well.
Remarks: Deceased was found after being in well for two weeks.

Docket Entry:
Date: February 24, 1919
Deceased: Dorothy G. Dunson, White
Address: 2407 Avenue C
Cause Of Death: From concussion of brain caused by falling out of bed, same being accidental.

Docket Entry:
Date: March 2, 1920
Deceased: James Robert Cook, White
Address: Birmingham Infirmary
Cause Of Death: From fractured skull by falling backwards while flying a kite, same being accidental.

Docket Entry:
Date: May 7, 1920
Deceased: Sam Smith, Col.
Address: Hillman Hospital
Cause Of Death: From fractured skull from falling off the top of Age Herald Building, same being accidental.

Docket Entry:
Date: June 26, 1924
Deceased: Jeff Davis, Col.
Address: Hillman Hospital
Cause of Death: By traumatic fracture of leg by jumping from porch while running from police, same being accidental.

Docket Entry:
Date: September 2, 1924
Deceased: Alford Marrel, Col.
Address: Hillman Hospital
Cause Of Death: By a fractured skull when he jumped out of an automobile en route to alms house, same being accidental. Alford Marrel being insane.

Docket Entry:
Date: January 15, 1930
Deceased: Willard Davis, Col.
Address: Booker Heights, Ensley
Cause Of Death: Shock-peritonitis following a stab wound of the rectum.
Remarks: Received when he fell on a pick used as a gate weight.

Docket Entry:
Date: July 17, 1937
Deceased: Samuel A. Ford, White
Address: 3rd Alley & 18th St. North.
Cause Of Death: Fractured skull received when he fell from a window. Mr. Ford was attending a dance at the Ben Hur Hall and was sitting in a window in the rear of the building, from which he fell into Third Alley, apparently being overcome by heat.

Miscellaneous

DYNAMITE EXPLOSION KILLS THREE MEN
Negro Was Thawing Frozen Explosive
BUILDING IS WRECKED

The Birmingham Age-Herald, December 31, 1910

"A disastrous explosion occurred yesterday at Camp Branch, where the Central Water company is constructing a tunnel in connection with the impounding reservoir of the Steel corporation, in which two white men named Joe Otwell and Will Freman and a negro named Tom Sturkey were killed, and Will Sampson, a negro was fatally injured.

The accident occurred in the engine house at the portal of the tunnel. The negro Sturkey was drying out a box of dynamite which was frozen and placed the box near a boiler. The other men were in close proximity. From some unknown cause the dynamite exploded, literally blowing Sturkey to pieces and instantly killing the two white men and another negro was so badly burned and bruised that he can hardly recover.

The explosion was a terrific one, wrecking the building and mangling the bodies of the unfortunate victims. The remains of the negro Sturkey were gathered together and placed in a box and brought to Ensley, as were the bodies of the two white men, and taken in charge by Echols & Angwin, where they were prepared for interment. Coroner Brasher will hold an inquest tomorrow and investigate the cause of the explosion."

Docket Entry:
Date: March 19, 1911
Deceased: Sam Harper, Col.
Address: Palos, Ala.
Cause Of Death: I was called to Palos, Ala., to investigate the death of Sam Harper, Col. After making the investigation I found Deceased not dead. I was notified by Deputy Sheriff Kenneybrook that Will Staggs had killed a negro and that deceased had fallen in creek.
Remarks: Charged only for mileage for making the 40 mile trip ($2.00).

Docket Entry:
Date: August 2, 1911
Deceased: Jas. H. Montgomery
Address: Courthouse
Cause Of Death: Heart failure
Remarks: Mr. Montgomery was in the second division of the criminal court at a meeting of the Republican party and fell out of his chair dead.

Docket Entry:
Date: November 23, 1923
Address: Cooper's Undertaking Company
Cause of Death: By internal injuries around right kidney region while playing football.

Docket Entry:
Date: April 21, 1925
Deceased: Lenie Betts, Col.
Address: Shortridge Funeral Home
Cause Of Death: By a broken back bone, same being caused while being initiated into a lodge, same being accidental.

Docket Entry:
Date: July 22, 1925
Deceased: Wm. Jackson Columbus McCombs, White
Address: Mt. Pinson
Cause Of Death: By a fracture of right side of skull, barn fell on him, same being accidental.

Docket Entry:
Date: May 15, 1930
Deceased: Richard Cooper, White
Address: 516 South 6th Avenue
Cause Of Death: Burns of the upper part of body.
Remarks: Received when his clothing caught fire from a torch he was using and a negro man threw a bucket of gasoline on him instead of water at the city blacksmith shop. Same being accidental without criminality,

The Assassination of Father James Edwin Coyle and its Aftermath

*"Some people come back to haunt you
no matter how deep you bury them."*

—-Unknown

Docket Entry:
I, Coroner J.D. Russum, Jefferson County, certify that on August 12th, 1921, I held a preliminary investigation on the body of Father James Edwin Coyle, (W) with the following result; I was called to 2120-3rd Ave. north, to investigate the death of Father James Edwin Coyle, and it was found that deceased came to his death by gun shot wound of head, at the hands of Edwin R. Stephenson, (W) same being an unlawful homicide, being done against the peace and dignity of the State of Alabama.
For issuing 8 subpoenas $2.00
For serving 8 subpoenas $4.00

Total: $6.00

Much has been written regarding the assassination of the Catholic priest Father James Coyle, and the consequences of that act, both intended and unintended.

In an article in the Alabama Review it was noted that:

> "Perhaps the single most spectacular incident of religious intolerance during the 1920s occurred on the evening of August 11, 1921. Father James E. Coyle, pastor of St. Paul's Catholic church and a focus of Catholic-Protestant conflict, was shot to death by Rev. E.R. Stephenson, a Methodist minister and Klansman, who performed marriages at the local courthouse. Stephenson's daughter had married a Catholic in a ceremony performed by Father Coyle. The enraged father admitted the shooting and was charged with second-degree murder, but the Birmingham community sympathized with Stephenson. His defense council, Hugo Black, a local attorney and active Sunday School teacher at First Baptist Church, won acquittal from a sympathetic jury. National opinion blamed the bigotry on the city's churches and the acquiescence of the press, while denouncing Birmingham as the "American hotbed of Anti-Catholic fanaticism, " where the "murder of a priest had been added to the achievements of bigotry."[1]

Hugo Black went on to serve as a Senator from Alabama and In 1937, Black's appointment to the U.S. Supreme Court came under fire from critics who accused him of being a former member of the Ku Klux Klan. In this regard, W. R. Snell wrote that:

> "Politically as in other areas the invisible Empire was firmly entrenched in the Birmingham area by 1924 and claimed 18,000 members and 15,000 of the city's 32,000 registered voters. Many of the county and city officials were members or sympathized with the Klan. With so many registered voters as members, additional Klansmen were elected to office. Sheriff T.J. Shirley was well-known as a Klansman, and at least two judges and more than a score of county and city officials were claimed by the organization."[2]

KLAN MEMBERSHIP, LATER RESIGNATION RELATED BY BLACK
Justice Asks Country To Judge Fitness On Senate Record
Religious Hatred Campaign Charged
Devotion To Freedom Of Worship Stressed In Reply To Critics

The Birmingham News, October 2, 1937

"Justice Hugo L. Black said he once joined but later resigned from the Ku Klux Klan. He asked the nation to judge his fitness for Supreme Court service by his 10-year Senate record. That record "refutes every implication of racial or religious intolerance," he asserted in a radio reply to those who have contended that Klan membership made him unworthy to serve upon the nation's highest court. He indicated plainly that he had no intention of resigning from the justiceship to which he had been appointed by President Roosevelt.

"The insinuations of racial and religious intolerance made concerning me are based on the fact that I joined the Ku Klux Klan about 15 years ago," he said. "I did join the Klan. I later resigned. I never rejoined. What appeared then, and what appears now, in the records of the organization, I do not know. I never have considered and do not now consider the unsolicited card given to me shortly after my nomination to the Senate as a membership of any kind in the Ku Klux Klan. I never used it. I did not even keep it." His reference at this point apparently was to charges that he had received a life membership in the Klan. Thousands of folks arranged their evening plans to listen in. A tremendous audience was assured because the Klan charges against Black had stirred up a national storm of controversy. It was charged that Black had been elected to the Senate in 1926 with the active and welcome support of the Ku Klux Klan, then at its peak in Alabama. There were demands for an investigation of the Alabaman's fitness for the bench."

Around the time of the start of the public and media attention to the issue of Hugo Black's prior membership in the Ku Klux Klan, an event regarding the suspicious, violent death of a former Birmingham klansman added to the volatility of the matter.

Docket Entry:
Date: September 19, 1937
Deceased: Roy Pearl Day, White
Cause Of Death: From injuries received when he was run over by an L&N R.R. train near Vanderbuilt Crossing, Birmingham, Ala., same being accidental.

MYSTERY SURROUNDS DEATH OF MAN WHO MADE KU KLUX - BLACK AFFIDAVIT
Coroner, However, Asserts That Day's Case Is Closed Now

The Birmingham Post, September 18, 1937

"A bricklayer, Roy P. Day, a member of the Ku Klux Klan, a few weeks ago allegedly signed an affidavit along with about 15 others purporting to reveal that Justice Hugo Black was a member of the hooded order. He was a close friend of another bricklayer, Winston Williams, who during the last week has openly announced that he was present the night Justice Black, then Senator Black, was made a life member of the Klan.

On the night of September 8, the mangled body of Mr. Day was dragged from below the wheels of an L&N freight train. At the time of his death the coroner, Gip M. Evans, after investigating, returned a verdict of accidental death. Since then the Black-Klan issue has been raised throughout the nation. Coincident with the Black-Klan issue, conflicting stories relating to the untimely death of Mr. Day began to circulate. Today his death has become entangled in a mesh of contradictory statements, leaving the impression that Mr Day died under strange, unexplained circumstances. Substantiation of the belief that Mr. Day met with some kind of foul play that led to his death is revealed in the report made by the crew of the train that struck Mr. Day. The report read in substance that the engineer saw a figure lying on the tracks, but that he was too close when he noticed it to stop the train. The report also said it was believed the man apparently was dead before the train struck him.

Coroner Evans took the testimony as to how the accident happened from the engineer...who said that the body was lying across the tracks with the feet up over the rail and the head near the rail opposite in a diagonal position. The coroner rendered a verdict of accidental death, with the notation that Mr. Day was known to be a man who drank heavily and he believed he had been drinking the night he met his death. He said he believed he stumbled down the railroad tracks and fell into the position on the tracks he was in when struck by the train. "As far as I am concerned," Coroner Evans said, "my investigation is closed."

Mr. Evans ordered the dead man's stomach sent to the City Laboratory for examination, but embalming fluid already had been injected into the body when the order was made and it was impossible to ascertain afterward because of the nature of the fluid whether Mr. Day had been drinking heavily or at all at the time. When the body was recovered $1.59 in change and a pawn ticket for $3.65 were found in Mr. Day's pockets. He had pawned some of his clothes that morning. That only $1.59 of the original $3.65 was in his pockets led to the belief that Mr. Day had purchased liquor with the difference.

Mr. Day spent the last three or four hours before his death at the Bricklayer's Union Hall. Roscoe McDuffie said he had talked to Mr. Day as late as 5:10 p.m. He said he had not been drinking nor did he appear drunk when he talked to him. George Griffith, bailiff in Circuit Court probably was the last man at the union hall to see and talk to Mr. Day at about 7:45 p.m. as he left, but he could not be positive at the time, and that it might have been an hour earlier. Mr. Day was struck by the train at 8:20 p.m. "He was drinking, all right," Mr. Griffith said. "he fell over a step as he came around the side of the building."

The family of Mr. Day is in a quandary. Mrs. Day, now a widow, the mother of four children, said she could not explain the death of her husband. "He had no enemies that I know of," she said. But she is puzzled about the fact that her husband was found so far off the route that he would take home ordinarily. "I can't believe that he met with foul play. Perhaps he took the wrong street car and then tried to take a short cut home." The Day home is about three miles from the union hall. At the point where he would have caught one that would have taken him off his regular route. If he did this he might have realized it about the time he reached the railroad crossing and gotten off and then proceeded to take a short cut home. Mrs. Day said her husband had been a member of the Klan. "He was a member of the Klan back in 1925-26 and later, but he dropped out. I was a member myself," she said. "We both quit because we couldn't afford to pay the dues."

The engineer, Mr. Craig, said he "feels positive" Mr. Day was lying across the railroad track before the engine struck him. "I'm positive I would have seen him if he had been walking along the track, I believe he was either dead before the train hit him, or else drunk." Mr. Craig said he was not aware his engine had passed over anything until a brakeman told him, "I believe we've run over somebody." "I stopped the train right away and we ran back to where the body was, about 10 car-lengths back. His body was perfectly still when I got there and I didn't see any blood. It looks like there would have been some blood if he had first been killed by a train."

DAY DEATH CASE CLOSED---EVANS
County Investigator Sticks To Finding Of Accident; Scoffs At Rumors
The Birmingham News & Age-Herald, September 19, 1937

"A charge that "New York politics" was responsible for contradictory statements about the death of Roy P. Day, 54, Woodlawn brick mason and reputed former member of the Ku Klux Klan, was made by County Investigator Gip M. Evans. Evans, who returned a finding of accidental death after Day was killed by an L&N freight train, said he was convinced his finding in the case was correct and he would not reopen the case for investigation.

The investigator said his investigation showed that Day frequently drank intoxicating liquors and that he had been drinking the day before the train ran over him, crushing the man's chest and severing the legs. "All this appears to have resulted from the Black-Klan issue…in an attempt to smear Justice Black." Reports are that not only was Day a member of the Klan, but that he was a friend of Winston Williams, who was reported to have been present in a Klan hall when Black was made a life member of the hooded order."

Names

"Well, now, they often call me Speedo,
But my real name is Mr. Earl.
Well, now, some may call me Joe,
Some may call me Moe,
Just Remember Speedo,
He don't never take it slow.

---*Speedo*
The Cadillacs
and Esther Navarro

    According to Wikipedia, a nickname is "a substitute for the proper name of a familiar person, place, or thing, for affection or ridicule." In general, the attribution of a single short and distinct name for a particular person also allows for instant recognition within a limited population or neighborhood. A particular nickname is usually reserved for one specific individual within a community. It may have been either invented by that person for himself, although it is more likely that it had been attributed to him or her by others based on some habit or physical characteristic.
    Aliases, or different proper names, are typically used by an individual to confuse the actual identity of that person, often from law enforcement agents. In early 20th century America, nicknames and aliases abounded and multiple names were often utilized for various reasons. However, the effectiveness of a previously arrested individual changing one's name for nefarious reasons has been greatly diminished in today's society due to the current ability to rapidly check computerized fingerprint records.

Docket Entry:
Date: July 11, 1910
Deceased: Leonard Johnson, Col.
Address: Roper
Cause Of Death: Gun shot wound.
Defendant: "Big Boy" and "Tennessee"

Docket Entry:
Date: November 12, 1910
Deceased: W.L. Wallace, White
Address: 13 St. & Ave. I.
Cause Of Death: Gun shot wounds
Defendants: Will Brown Alias Walter Brown Alias Jim Jones Alias Joe Green Alias Jim Love, Col. and Walter Manderson, White, Otherwise unknown.

Docket Entry:
Date: May 1, 1911
Deceased: Henry Jones, Col. alias "Ding Dong"
Cause Of Death: Gun shot wounds
Defendant: Unknown parties.

Docket Entry:
Date: January 12, 1914
Deceased: Elisha Surecting, Col.
Address: 1205 Ave. D, South
Remarks: By being burned to death at the hands of two negro boys known to the public as "Daddy" and "Buddy" same being murder in the first degree.

Docket Entry:
Date: April 13, 1917
Deceased: "Kid Easy"
Address: Alley C between 23 & 24th Street.
Cause Of Death: By having his throat cut.
Defendant: Layden A. Powell, Col.
Remarks: Deceased was removed to Hillman hospital in Davenport & Harris and dead a few minutes later.

Docket Entry:
Date: April 9, 1919
Deceased: Gun shot wounds of face and neck.
Address: Hillman hospital
Remarks: Witnesses: Mary Williams alias "String Bean" Van Sellers, alias "Guarantee." Victoria Walker, alias "Vick". Johnnie Ward, alias "Slim."

Docket Entry:
Date: June 19, 1920
Deceased: Annie Rice, Col.
Address: 104 French Town, Pratt City.
Cause Of Death: From stab wound of left shoulder.
Defendants: Nancy Lee, Sr. and Nancy Lee, Jr.
Witnesses: Annie Walker, No. 1 and Annie Walker No. 2.

Docket Entry:
Date: November 12, 1921
Deceased: John Nallbach, White
Address: Avenue F & 12 Street.
Cause Of Death: By being run over by an automobile.
Defendant: Eugene Smith, alias "Speed."

Docket Entry:
Date: November 28, 1925
Deceased: Beatrice Brown, Col.
Address: Echols & Strong Funeral Home
Cause Of Death: By being kicked in the stomach.
Defendant: Ed Jones aka Ed Warter alias "King Buzzard," Col.

Docket Entry:
Date: March 26, 1928
Deceased: Allen Moore, Col.
Address: Davenport & Harris Funeral Home
Cause Of Death: Broken back and fractures of body when struck and run over by an automobile alleged to have been driven by J.H. Jackson alias "Cowboy."

During the course of conducting research for this book many additional odd and notable nicknames for deceased individuals and perpetrators were found within the coroner's records. Although the basis for some of these names seem to be evident or easily imagined, others are not as clear and their origins have been lost to time.

Baby Speed	Dedi Boom	One Eyed Neal
Bad Eye Jesse	Dollar Bill	Pig Iron
Big Eight	Fat Head	Popcorn
Big Nine	Few Clothes	Promiscous Praytory
Black Boy	Geechie	Railroad
Black Annie	Goo Goo	Scophus
Black Dick	Hammer Mouth	Shorty
Blind Pete	Jabbo	Skinney
Blue Negro	Jimbo	Snowball
Boll Weevil	Kiddie Boo	Son
Bubber	Little Sister	Sport Boy
Bully	Long Boy	Waterworks
Choke	Mississippi	

Superstition

*"I don't want my rooster crowin' after the sun go down.
Don't bring peanuts in my house,
it will make a good man turn around.*

*I don't want nobody to put their bare hands on my head.
I don't eat everyone's cooking, I am suspicious
of my corn bread.*

*Don't touch me with your broom, don't let my lamp get low.
Don't let the dogs start to howling 'cause somebody
have got to go.*

*Take your hat off of my bed and hang it on a nail.
If I set down on your trunk I am bound to go to jail.*

*I don't want my brother to put his bare feets in my shoes.
Somebody stole my rabbits' foot and I've got
the suspicious blues."*

---*The Blues What Am*
Jazz Gillum

  Before religion there was superstition which is embedded deeply within us. It connects us to an ancient layer of our identity. It is a belief that there is more to the world than what we see. Superstition is a human constant which has often been turned to in an attempt to explain the unexplainable. Its expression can be found in prehistoric cave drawings and in modern man's hesitation to walk under a ladder. Its physical presentations have varied from human sacrifice to Tarot card readings with various permutations between these extremes. Current interest in such matters can be found in our popular literature, zombie movies and video games.
  Although the styles, details and names of the various, often quasi-religious practices may vary, almost all employ certain procedures which relate to the warding off of "evil spirits," placing hexes on enemies or bringing financial or romantic benefits to an individual. However, only those persons in a community who were generally accepted to possess the "power" to effectively deploy these methods

would be relied upon to do so. Practices employed by these various "dark" religions vary from group to group. The use of animal sacrifices can be found in "Santeria" as practiced in a number of Caribbean countries. The hexes and spells of "Voodoo," as imported from Haiti to southern Louisiana is another example.

In the early 20th century a version of superstitious beliefs which were mainly confined to the mid deep South states, e.g., Alabama, Mississippi and Georgia came to be popularly termed "Hoodoo." These practices had their origin with enslaved persons from Africa and included many of the trappings of voodoo such as the employment of incantations to allegedly ward off evil spirits or to place or remove hexes placed on an individual by another person.

During this time period physical objects designed to be carried on the person in order to protect them from various threats were often employed. One of these items was known as the "mojo bag." This small cloth sack was tightly closed so that it could not be easily or casually opened. It was often carried around the person's neck or in a clothing item such as a brassiere. Anyone who would purposely or accidentally open the bag would likely never do so again. The extremely disagreeable odor of certain contents, such as the herb Asefetida, or the presence of parts of dried animals would discourage anyone from opening it. It was also believed that to disturb it would bring the person doing so bad luck.

Research into the reporting of matters relating to the issue of superstition in early 20th century Birmingham would, once again, lead to the discovery of newspaper articles which regaled contemporary white readers with amusing, but racially demeaning accounts and anecdotes common to that time.

NEGRO SLAIN MUST BE BURIED FACE DOWNWARD
The Birmingham Age-Herald, August 31, 1903

"The negroes have many superstitions in regard to the burial of persons of their race who have been slain. On Saturday in the burial of a negro woman who had been murdered at Sayreton one of the most peculiar of these beliefs cropped out. The negroes would not allow the undertaker to lay the body in the coffin as is ordinarily done with the face upwards. They insisted that the corpse should be laid on its face, and until it was so placed they all refused to have anything to do with the funeral.

The reason they gave for insisting that the face be turned downward instead of upward was that it would certainly make the murderer return to the place and give himself up. They claim most positively that when the face is turned downwards that the murderer cannot possibly stand against the gnawings of his conscience, and that the thought of the crime will haunt him day and night until he is, forced, even against his will, to return to the place and "give up" to the police.

Another peculiar circumstance came to light in this burial. Although the killing was done Tuesday, the negroes refused to call in an undertaker until Saturday morning. In this hot weather decomposition sets in early, and when the undertaker did arrive the body was in terrible condition. They had to let the body lie until the spirit could haunt the negro man who had killed the woman. The undertaker states that it was one of the worst funerals he ever had to attend.

Yesterday a rather intelligent negro was asked about these superstitions and he said: "That's right, captain. That man can't escape. The ghosts will haunt him until he comes back and gives himself up. If they had buried that woman with her face upwards he would have been all right, and would not have had to return, but now he can't escape."

EPILOGUE

> "But the sad and well known fact of the matter is that
> most of us will stay in our caskets and be dead a long time,
> and that our urns and graves will never make a sound.
> Our reason and our requiems, our headstones and high
> masses, will neither get us in nor keep us out of heaven.
> The meaning of our lives, and the memories of them,
> belong to the living, just as our funerals do.
> Whatever being the dead have now,
> they have by the living's faith alone."[1]

---Thomas Lynch

So now we have come full circle and might ask what may be the purposes of this book? Perhaps it is to present examples of poorly performed death investigations during the early 20th century, the system of which was greatly hindered by a lack of resources, trained law enforcement and medical personnel. Maybe it is also a means to once again expose the dehumanizing, but accepted radical political and racial overtones of a "different" people in this earlier time period, but with the same frailties, prejudices and predilections for man's inhumanity to man--as it was in ancient times and as it remains today. Although we may have made major advances from a society which was steeped in awful racism and hate to our current state-- greatly improved, but seemingly always to remain a work in progress.

In trying to understand our human desires to remember and to be remembered, we might consider the perspective of the theory of the "Ocean of Time," as noted by F. Gonzalez-Crussi who described it as:

> "*an overpowering tide (which) shall engulf us all and by its repeated washings erase our traces until there is absolutely no mark of our existence—monumental memorials notwithstanding. Make no mistake about that. Modern medicine has granted us a short reprieve and might well increase our longevity. But it has not granted us immortality and never will. Overt or implicit claims of the P.R. department notwithstanding.*[2]

Or perhaps as more simply expressed by a song verse:

> "The moon is shining, and thats a good sign.
> Cling to me closer and say you'll be mine.
> Remember, darling, we won't see it shine,
> A hundred years from today."

—A Hundred Years From Today

> "Well, I suppose nothing is meant to last forever.
> We all have to make room for other people.
> Its a wheel.
> You get on, You have to go to the end.
> And then somebody else has the same opportunity,
> to go to the end and so on."

---Vivian Maier

NOTES

PREFACE
1. Joe Gould's Secret. Up In the Old Hotel and Other Stories. Joseph Mitchell. 1992.
2. Weld. Earned Versus Deserved. Mark Kelly. March 23-30, 2017. pg. 4.
3. Washington Post. David Nicholson. From a review of an unnamed book regarding Blues music. Unknown date.

PROLOGUE
1. The Undertaking. Life Studies From the Dismal Trade. Thomas Lynch. 1997. pg. 117.
2. Evidence. Luc Sante. 1992. pg. ix.
3. The Birmingham News. Virgil Pierson. August 7, 1946.
4. Evidence. Luc Sante. 1992.

CHAPTER 1
THE CORONER
1. The Office of Coroner in Alabama. C.B. Ransone, Jr. 1957. pg. 8.
2. Autopsy. Milton Helpern. 1977. pg.5.
3. Ibid. pg.6.
4. The Office of Coroner in Alabama. C.B. Ransone, Jr. 1957. pg. 11.

CHAPTER 2
STATISTICS
1. The Visual Display of Quantitative Information. Edward R. Tufte. 1983. pgs. 40-41.
2. The Alabama Review. April, 1977. pg.118.
3. Ibid.
4. The Birmingham Weekly. November 19, 1998. pg. 8.
5. Ibid.
6. Vengeance and Justice. Crime and Punishment in the 19th-Century American South. Edward L. Ayers. 1984. Pg. 12. By permission of Oxford University Press, USA.
7. U.S. Census Bureau. Statistics for 1880-1940.
8. Ibid. Statistics for 1950-2010.
9. Low Life--Lures and Snares of Old New York. Luc Sante. 1991. pg. 362.

10. Violent Death in the City. Suicide, Accident and Murder in 19th Century Philadelphia. Roger Lane. 1979. pg. 78.
11. Ibid. pg.90.

CHAPTER 3
PASSION

1. Webster's New World. Roget's A-Z Thesaurus. 1999.
2. County Commission Agent's Investigation into Death of L.K. Horton. Reports of Suspect and Witness Interrogations. August 3-5, 1931. Jefferson County courthouse, Bessemer, AL. pas. 1-121. Entries abridged.

CHAPTER 4
RACE

1. Trouble In Mind. Black Southerners in the Age of Jim Crow. Leon F. Litwack. Pgs. vii-xviii.

CHAPTER 6
PRISON

1. From Alabama's Past, Capitalism and Racism In a Cruel Partnership. Douglas A. Blackmon. The Wall Street Journal. July 16, 2001. pgs. A1 & A10.
2. Reforms in Government. Control of Negroes in Birmingham, Alabama, 1890–1920. C.V. Harris. The Journal of Southern History. Nov. 1172 #4. pg. 586.
3. From Alabama's Past, Capitalism and Racism In a Cruel Partnership. Douglas A. Blackmon. The Wall Street Journal. July 16, 2001. pg. A10.
4. Reforms in Government. Control of Negroes in Birmingham, Alabama, 1890–1920. C.V. Harris. The Journal of Southern History. Nov. 1172 #4. pg. 585
5. Biennial Report of The Alabama Penitentiary. J.B. Anderson, Chaplain. 1880-82. pg. 29.
6. Vengeance and Justice. Crime and Punishment in the 19th Century American South. Edward L. Ayers. 1984. pg. 196
7. From Alabama's Past, Capitalism and Racism In a Cruel Partnership. Douglas A. Blackmon. The Wall Street Journal. July 16, 2001. pg. A10.
8. Vengeance and Justice. Crime and Punishment in the 19th Century American South. Edward L. Ayers. pg. 196.
9. Reforms in Government. Control of Negroes in Birmingham, Alabama, 1880–1920. C.V. Harris. The Journal of Southern History. 585. Nov. 1172 #4 pg. 585.

10. Banner Mine Tragedy of 1911. Encyclopedia of Alabama. www.encyclopediaofalabama.org. Updated Jan. 21, 2010.
11. Ibid.
12. Reforms in Government Control of Negroes in Birmingham, Alabama. 1880—1920. C.V. Harris. The Journal of Southern. History. Nov. 1172 #4. pg. 582.
13. Ibid. pgs. 582-584.
14. Ibid. pg. 587.
15. Slavery by Another Name. Douglas A. Blackmon. 2008. pgs. 2-3 and pg. 310.
16. Ibid. pgs. 95-97.
17. Ibid. pg. 313.
18. Ibid. pg. 315.
19. Ibid. pgs. 2-5.

CHAPTER 7
WORK

1. Various written sources. Ca. 1910-1939.
2. The Birmingham View. Through The Years In Photographs. Unknown date. pg. 57.
3. Only Yesterday. An Informal History of the 1920s. Frederick Lewis Allen. 1931. pgs. 17, 45-46.
4. Personal communication. Fannie Landarsky Goldstein. Ca. 1963.
5. Slavery by Another Name. Douglas A. Blackmon. 2008. pgs. 289-91, 308.
6. Ibid. pgs. 314, 320-21.
7. Race, Class And Power In Alabama Coalfields, 1908-21. Brian Kelly. 2001. pgs. 14-15, 18-19.
8. Ibid. pgs. 9-10.
9. Ibid. pg. 20.
10. Ibid. pgs. 23-24.
11. Antiradical Violence in Birmingham During the 1930s. R.P. Ingalls. The Journal of Southern History. vol. 47, #4. Nov. 198.
pg. 524.
12. Ibid. pgs. 522-23.

CHAPTER 8
HOMICIDE
1. Evidence. Luc Sante. 1992. pg. 59.
2. Violent Death in the City. Suicide, Accident and Murder in 19th Century Philadelphia. Roger Lane. 1979. pgs. 59-60.
3. Ibid. pg. 53.
4. Ibid. pg.83.
5. Roots Of Violence In Black Philadelphia 1860-1900. Roger Lane. pg. 89.
6. Ibid. pg. 108.
7. The Infamous Birmingham Axe Murders. Prohibition Gangsters & Vigilante Justice. Jeremy W. Gray. 2018.

CHAPTER 9
POLICE
1. Organized Crime In The United States. Section 11. pg. 70
2. Trouble In Mind. Black Southerners in the Age of Jim Crow. Leon F. Litwack. pgs. 263-65.
3. Ibid. pg. 265.
4. Ibid. pg. 15.
5. Encyclopedia of Alabama. Great Depression in Alabama. Matthew L. Downs. University of Mobile. Updated April 21, 2015.
6. Jefferson County Coroner/Medical Examiner Office statistics. 1981--2017.
7. Officer Down Memorial Page. www.admp.org/search/browse/Alabama.
8. Trouble In Mind. Black Southerners in the Age of Jim Crow. Leon F. Litwack. pg. 478.
9. Father Of The Blues--An Autobiography. W.C. Handy. pg. 141.
10. Website www.jeffcosheriff.org/pastsheriifs.html.
11. Alabama Sheriffs Association. Montgomery, AL. Personal communication. 2015.

CHAPTER 10
CAPITAL PUNISHMENT
1. http://geneaologytrails.com/ala/jefferson/jeffalexecutions.html .

CHAPTER 11
HONOR
1. Vengeance And Justice--Crime and Punishment in the 19th Century American South. Edward L. Ayers. pg. 12.
2. Ibid. pg. 10.
3. Ibid. pgs. 12-14.
4. Ibid. pg. 227.
5. Ibid. pgs. 234-35.
6. Kentucky Mountaineers and Their Feuds. S.S. MacClintock. American Journal of Sociology 7. July, 1901. pgs. 172-73
7. Vengeance And Justice--Crime and Punishment in the 19th Century American South. Edward L. Ayers. 1984. pg. 276.

CAPTER 12
SUICIDE
1. Violent Death in the City. Roger Lane. 1979. pg. 13.
2. Ibid. pg. 14.
3. Ibid. pgs. 15-16.
4. Ibid. pg. 30.
5 Brain Pickings. Maria Popova. April, 2014.
6. The Undertaking. Life Studies From The Dismal Trade. 1997. Thomas Lynch. pg. 166.

CHAPTER 13
VICE
1. Roots Of Violence In Black Philadelphia 1860-1900. Roger Lane. pg. 165.
2. Vengeance And Justice--Crime and Punishment in the 19th Century American South. Edward L. Ayers. 1984. pg. 14.
3. The Alabama Review. April, 1977. pg. 128.
4. The Birmingham View. Through The Years In Photographs. pg. 14.
5. Roots Of Violence In Black Philadelphia 1860-1900. Roger Lane. Pg. 85.
6. Only Yesterday--An Informal History of the 1920s. Frederick Lewis Allen. 1931. pg. 17.
7. The Alabama Review. April, 1977. pg. 118.
8. The Journal of Southern History. November 1172 #4. pg. 573.
9. Ibid. pg. 577.

10. Only Yesterday--An Informal History of the 1920s. Frederick Lewis Allen. pg. 204.
11. Prohibition Killings. Results of Federal Enforcement. 1927.
12. Annals of Epidemiology. Jake Leg--How the blues diagnosed a medical mystery. Dan Baum. The New Yorker. Sept. 15, 2003. pgs. 50-57.
13. Trouble In Mind. Black Southerners in the Age of Jim Crow. Leon F. Litwack. pg. 435.
14. Muster. Civil War Veterans and Opiate Addiction in the Gilded Age. Dillon J. Carroll. journalofthecivilwar.org. November 22, 2016.
15. Low Life. Lures and Snares of Old New York. Luc Sante. pgs. 178-79.
16. The Alabama Baptist. October 12, 1904.
17. Ibid. February 27, 1907; June 19, 1912; June 18, 1913.
18. Report of the Jefferson County, Alabama Grand Jury. October, 1912.

CHAPTER 14
DISEASE AND MEDICINE

1. Trouble In Mind. Black Southerners in the Age of Jim Crow. Leon F. Litwack. 1998. pg. 337.
2. Sarah Jane. William M. "Jazz" Gillum. Recorded April 4, 1936. Chicago, IL.
3. Evidence. Luc Sante. 1992. pg. 86.
4. Roots Of Violence In Black Philadelphia 1860-1900. Roger Lane. pg. 130.
5. Slavery by Another Name. Douglas A. Blackmon. 2008. pg. 322.
6. The Undertaking. Life Studies From The Dismal Trade. Thomas Lynch. 1997. pg. 140.

CHAPTER 15
WOMEN

1. Roots Of Violence In Black Philadelphia 1860-1900. Roger Lane. pg. 86.
2. Violent Death in the City. Suicide, Accident and Murder in 19th Century Philadelphia. Roger Lane. 1979. pg. 90.
3. Ibid. pg. 93.
4. Ibid. pg. 92.
5. Roots Of Violence In Black Philadelphia 1860-1900. Roger Lane. pgs. 129-30.

CHAPTER 16
CHILDREN
1. Folk Medicine in Southern Appalachia. Anthony Cavender. The University of North Carolina Press. 2003. pg. 135.

CHAPTER 18
VEHICLES
1. A Memory of Trains. The Boll Weevil and Others. Louis D. Rubin, Jr. The University of South Carolina Press. 2000. pgs. 1-2.
2. The Birmingham News. Beth Thames. May 1, 2016. pg. C8.
3. Birmingham Rails. The Last Golden Era. From World War II to Amtrak. The Thanksgiving Day Wreck at Woodstock. Lyle Key. Red Mountain Press. 2007. pgs. 165-68.
4. "Hallelujah, I'm a Bum." James R. Chiles. Smithsonian magazine. July 31, 1998. pg. 68.
5. Ibid. pgs. 67-76.
6. Ibid. pgs. 67-69, 76.
7. Ibid. pg. 71.
8. Ibid. pgs. 71-72, 76.
9. Irving D. Glass. Personal communication. Ca. 1965.
10. "Hallelujah, I'm a Bum." James R. Chiles. Smithsonian magazine. July 31, 1998. pg. 74.
11. Trouble In Mind. Black Southerners in the Age of Jim Crow. Leon F. Litwack. pg. 232.
12. Ibid. pg. 256.
13. Only Yesterday: An Informal History of the 1920s. Frederick Lewis Allen. Harper and Row. 1931. pg. 136.
14. The Pilots Who Risked Their Lives to Deliver the Mail. David Doochin. Atlas Obscura. June 16, 2016.

CHAPTER 20
WAR
1. Dulce et Decorum Est. Wilfred Owen. Abridged from his poem thought to have been written between 8 October 1917 and March, 1918. Note: Owen was killed in combat on 4 November 1918, seven days prior to the Armistice ending World War I. "Requiescat In Pace."
2. The University of Alabama Press. Review of "Send the Alabamians." Nimrod Thompson Frazer. 2014.

3. Ibid.
4. Soldiers Of The Great War. Vol. 1. Soldiers Record Publishing Association. 1920.
5. Alabama WWI Casualties. www.angelfire.com.
6. World War One. BBC iwonder-WWI. Presented by Dan Snow. bbc.co.uk.

CHAPTER 21
WEAPONS
1. Roots Of Violence In Black Philadelphia 1860-1900. Roger Lane. pg. 139.
2. Alabama Code Title 13A. Criminal Code 13A-1-2 (1) Booby Traps.

CHAPTER 22
FORENSICS
1. Once More Into The Breech: The Firearms Evidence in the Sacco and Vanzetti Case Revisited: Part 1. Journal of Forensic
Sciences. April, 1986. pg. 63 and Part 2. July, 1986. pg. 1050.
2. Conversations with Pathologists. Bill Bass. University of Tennessee. 29-30 Nov, 2007. www.pathsoc.org/converssations.

CHAPTER 24
ATLAS OBSCURA
1. The Alabama Review. April, 1977. pg. 129.
2. The Ku Klux Klan in Jefferson County, Alabama, 1916-1930. William Robert Snell. Dissertation M.A. Samford University. 1967.

EPILOGUE
1. The Undertaking. Life Studies From The Dismal Trade. 1997. Thomas Lynch. pg. 13.
2. The Day of the Dead And Other Mortal Reflections. F. Gonzalez-Crussi. Harcourt Brace & Company. 1993. pg. 140.

COPYRIGHT ACKNOWLEDGEMENTS

---Excerpts from "Trouble In Mind: Black Southerners In The Age Of Jim Crow" by Leon F. Litwack, copyright 1998 by Leon F. Litwack. Used by permission of Alfred A. Knopf, an imprint of the Knopf Doubleday Publishing Group, a division of Penguin
House LLC. All rights reserved.

---Selections licensed from "Roots Of Violence In Black Philadelphia 1860-1900" by Roger Lane, Cambridge, Mass.; Harvard University Press, copyright 1986 by the President and
Fellows of Harvard College.

---Excerpts as specified in Notes from "Vengeance & Justice, Crime and Punishment in the 19th Century American South." By permission of the Oxford University Press, USA.

---Excerpts as specified in Notes from "Slavery by Another Name." Copyright 2008. Douglas A. Blackmon. By permission.

---Excerpts as specified in Notes from "Hallelujah, I'm a Bum." Copyright James R. Chiles. Smithsonian magazine. July 31, 1998. By permission.

---Permission for use of excerpts from "Jake Leg--How the blues diagnosed a medical mystery." Dan Baum. New Yorker magazine. Sept. 15, 2003.

---Permission for use of excerpts as specified in Notes from the books "Evidence" and "Low Life—Lures and Snares of Old New York." Copyrights by Luc Sante. 1992 and 1991.

---Permission for use of excerpt in Preface from Weld article "Earned Versus Deserved." Copyright Mark Kelly. 2017.

---Permission for use of excerpts as specified in Notes from the book "The Undertaking. Life Studies From The Dismal Trade." Thomas Lynch. W.W. Norton & Company. Copyright 1997.

ABOUT THE AUTHOR

Jay Glass served as Chief Deputy Coroner for Jefferson County and was involved with civil and military death investigations for over 40 years. During this time, Glass also served as a Reserve Special Agent with the Air Force Office Of Special Investigations and was an adjunct instructor at UAB where he taught a course in death investigation for many years. As a certified Pathologists' Assistant he has performed thousands of medical-legal autopsies and has testified as an expert witness in hundreds of court proceedings.

He is currently working on a second book detailing his experiences with a number of high profile death investigations in Jefferson County during his tenure with the Coroner/Medical Examiners office and as a military investigator.